SENSATION & PERCEPTION

THIRD EDITION

SENSATION & PERCEPTION

THIRD EDITION

Stanley Coren
University of British Columbia

Lawrence M. Ward
University of British Columbia

Based on previous editions
that included contributions by

Clare Porac
University of Victoria

Harcourt Brace Jovanovich College Publishers
Fort Worth   Philadelphia   San Diego
New York   Orlando   Austin   San Antonio
Toronto   Montreal   London   Sydney   Tokyo

ISBN: 0-15-579647-X
Library of Congress Catalog Card Number: 88-81033
Printed in the United States of America

We wish to thank the following for permission to reprint photos:
For *Chapter 1 opener:* New Jersey State Museum Collection, Trenton, Purchase FA 1968.73; *Chapter 2:* © George Hall/Woodfin Camp; *Chapter 3:* Courtesy of Deric Bownds, Stan Carlson, University of Wisconsin; *Chapter 4:* Christian Delbert Photography/Picture Cube; *Chapter 5:* © Larry Lorusso/ Picture Cube; *Chapter 6:* © Henry Groskinsky; *Chapter 7:* © Roberta J. Shefke; *Chapter 8:* © Margerin Studios/FPG; *Chapter 9:* Photograph by L. L. Brown courtesy of The Institute of Psycho-Structural Balancing, San Diego, CA; *Chapter 10:* The Soloman R. Guggenheim Museum; *Chapter 11:* © 1988 M. C. Escher c/o Cordon Art-Baarn-Holland; *Chapter 12:* The San Diego Opera; *Chapter 13:* Ed Carlin/Picture Cube; *Chapter 14:* E. Nagle/FPG; *Chapter 15:* Aronson Photographers/Stock Boston; *Chapter 16:* Elizabeth Crews/Stock Boston; *Chapter 17:* © Norman Snyder; *Chapter 18:* United Nations Photo 36252. For *Figure 10-1:* © Margaret K. Porter; *Figure 13-5:* © Paulette M. Russo; *Figure 15-5:* © Paulette M. Russo.

Preface

Take away the sensations of softness, moisture, redness, tartness, and you take away the cherry. Since it is not a being distinct from these sensations; a cherry, I say, is nothing but a congeries of sensible impressions or ideas perceived by various senses; which ideas are united into one thing.

GEORGE BERKELEY, 1713

Virtually everything we know about the world has entered our minds through our senses. We all realize that without even one of our senses our experiences would be incredibly limited. Consider the impossible problem of explaining the difference between the color blue and the color green to a person who has been blind since birth. And how would you explain to a person who has no taste buds how the taste of chocolate and vanilla differ from each other? Such aspects of the world will never exist for these individuals. For the blind person, salt and pepper differ only in taste; for the person with no ability to taste, salt and pepper differ only in color. For those of us who have the senses of sight, hearing, taste, touch, and smell, our daily experience is a continuous flow of changing percepts, with each new sensation carrying information about the world.

Sensation and Perception, Third Edition, provides an introduction to the study of our senses and how we perceive through them. It has been revised substantially since the Second Edition, and contains over 45 percent new material. These changes reflect many of the recent findings that have emerged, or coalesced into meaningful patterns, since the completion of the previous edition. We

have rewritten six of the chapters ''from the ground up'' and reorganized or amalgamated materials from other chapters. Every chapter has been updated to reflect the most recent literature. However, we have retained all those features that instructors felt made the Second Edition such a useful book. For instance, concrete examples are used throughout the text in order to make the subject matter ''come alive'' for students. Whenever possible, common or natural instances of perceptual phenomena are described during the discussion of the concepts underlying them. Each chapter is preceded by an outline that serves as a preview to its contents; the outlines also provide a structure to guide students as they review the chapters.

Although terms are defined when they are introduced, a glossary is provided at the end of each chapter as well. Any item printed in **boldface** in the text is also listed in the chapter glossary. Students will find that these glossaries serve as a succinct review and chapter summary, and can be used for self-testing and study purposes.

One special feature of our book is the inclusion of 106 Demonstration Boxes. Each box describes a simple demonstration designed to allow the students to actually experience many of the perceptual phenomena described in the text. Most require only the stimuli in the box itself, or commonplace items that can be found in most homes or dormitory rooms. The majority of these demonstrations require only a few moments of preparation, which we feel is time well spent in improving the understanding of the concepts under discussion and in maintaining student interest. Some instructors have reported that having students perform the demonstrations in class has been very useful. In such cases, the demonstrations may also serve as the focal point for a lecture or for classroom discussion.

The book is designed to survey the broad range of topics generally included under the heading of *sensation and perception*. The reader will notice that no single theory of perception is championed. In general, we have attempted to be as eclectic as we could, describing the various viewpoints in areas of controversy and attempting to present a balanced overview so that instructors of different opinions might be comfortable using the book.

The topics in this book were selected on the basis of our experience in teaching our own courses; therefore, much of the material has already been class tested. We have included three chapters—"Attention," "Speech and Music," and "Individual Differences"—that are not often seen in sensation and perception textbooks. These areas have attracted a good deal of experimental work in recent years, and they are sufficiently relevant to many issues in perception that we felt students should study them.

In order to keep the book to a manageable size, we have occasionally been selective in our coverage. Our first priority was to cover the central concepts of each topic in enough detail to make the material clear and coherent. To have included all the topics ever classified as part of the field of sensation and perception, we would have had to present a "grocery list" of concepts and terms, each treated superficially. Such an alternative was unacceptable to us.

Each of the chapters has been written so that it is relatively self-contained and independent of the other chapters, although this is not always completely possible. Therefore, when material from other places in the book is used in a discussion, the location of that information is always cited. This has been done to provide users with maximum flexibility as far as the sequence of chapter presentation is concerned, thus permitting the instructor to impress his or her orientation upon the material. A brief appendix on some basic aspects of neurophysiology has also been provided for the first time in this edition.

The chapter sequence in this Third Edition is quite different from that used in the previous editions. At the request of many individuals who have taught from the earlier versions, we have now organized the book by sensory systems, with the first half of the book covering the basic physiology and sensory responses and the second half covering those topics involving more complex and cognitive interactions. Chapters 1 and 2 provide an introduction to the problems of sensation and perception along with methodological and theoretical aspects of psychophysical measurement; Chapters 3, 4, and 5 cover the physiology and basic sensory qualities of vision; Chapters 6 and 7 do the same for audition; and Chapters 8 and 9 cover the chemical and mechanical senses. These first nine chapters thus cover the major topics usually grouped together under the heading of *sensation*. Chapters 10 through 15 cover the perception of space, form, speech and music, and time and motion, the perceptual constancies, and the perceptual aspects of attention; and Chapters 16, 17, and 18 discuss how individual variables such as age, experience, learning, gender, culture, drugs, and personality may affect the perceptual response. These last nine chapters thus cover the topics most frequently grouped together as *perception*.

Those of you who have encountered earlier versions of this book should know that Clare Porac has retired from this project in order to pursue her research and other writing projects. Clare's contributions were always organized, intelligent, and of the highest professional quality. Although she did not directly participate in this revision, we have striven to retain the clarity in writing and well-structured discussions that have characterized her contributions to the first two editions.

In our attempts to collect and interpret the information for this book, we have been assisted at various stages by our colleagues. Some have read preliminary versions of chapters and made useful suggestions. We would like to specifically thank Ray Corteen, Jim Enns, Ronnie Lakowski, Richard Tees, and Janet Werker, all of the Psychology Department of the University of British Columbia. We would also like to thank the personnel of the Human Perception and Psychophysics Laboratories, and especially Wayne Wong and Odie Geiger for assisting with library work and all of the small but necessary chores that eat up innumerable hours of a textbook writer's time.

In addition, we would like to thank Barry Anton, of the University of Puget Sound, Robert Frank, of the University of Cincinnati, Robert Levy, of Indiana State University, and Lyn Mowafy, of Vanderbilt University, for their helpful comments and suggestions after reviewing the previous edition.

Finally, the reader might notice that there is no dedication page. This is not to say that we do not wish to dedicate the book to anyone. It reflects the fact that there are too many people who have been important in our personal and professional lives to list on any single page (no matter how small the print). Perhaps it is best to simply dedicate this book to all of those researchers who have provided the knowledge that we have attempted to organize and review between these covers, and to all of those researchers who will provide further insights into sensation and perception for future authors to collate, review, digest, wonder at, and learn from.

S.C.
L.M.W.

Contents

CHAPTER

1

Sensation and Perception

ASPECTS OF THE PERCEPTUAL PROCESS
THEORIES OF PERCEPTION
THE PLAN OF THE BOOK

Can you answer the following questions? What color is the sky? Which is warmer, fire or ice? Which tastes sweeter, sugar or vinegar? Which has a stronger smell, burning wood or burning rubber? Which sounds louder, a chirping bird or the crack of a rifle? Such questions probably seem quite trivial, and the answers obvious. Perhaps we should phrase the questions differently. How do you know what color the sky is? How do you know how hot fire is relative to ice? How do you know that sugar is sweet? Again, you might feel that the answers are obvious. You see the color of the sky, you feel the temperatures of a flame and an ice cube, and you taste the sweetness of sugar—in other words, the answers come through your senses.

Let us push our questioning one step further. How do you know anything about your world? You might say that you learn from books, television, radio, films, lectures, or the actual exploration of places. But how do you obtain the information from these sources? Again, the answer is through your senses. In fact, without your senses of vision, hearing, touch, taste, and smell, your brain, the organ that is responsible for your conscious experience, would be an eternal prisoner in the solitary confinement of your skull. You would live in total silence and darkness. All would be a tasteless, colorless, feelingless, floating void. Without your senses, the world would simply not exist for you. The philosopher Thomas Hobbes recognized this fact in 1651 when he wrote, "There is no conception in man's mind which hath not at first, totally or by parts, been begotten upon the organs of sense." The Greek philosopher Protagoras stated the same position around 450 B.C. when he said, "Man is nothing but a bundle of sensations."

You may protest that this is a rather extreme viewpoint. Certainly, much of what we know about the world does not arrive through our eyes, ears, nose, and other sense organs. We have complex scientific instruments, such as telescopes, that tell us about the size and the shape of the universe by analyzing images too faint for the human eye to see. We have sonar to trace out the shape of the sea bottom, which may be hidden from our eyes by hundreds of feet of water. We have spectrographs to tell us about the exact chemical composition of many substances, as compared to the crude chemical sensitivity of our noses and tongues.

Although such pieces of apparatus exist, and measure phenomena not directly available to our senses, this does not alter the fact that it is the *perception of the scientist* that constitutes the subject matter of every science. The eye of the scientist presses against the telescope or examines the photograph of the distant star. The ear of the scientist listens to the sound of sonar tracing out the size and distance of objects, or his eyes read the sonograph. Although the tongue of the scientist does not taste the chemical composition of some unknown substance, his eye, aided by the spectrograph, provides the data for analysis. Really, the only data that reach the mind of the scientist come not from instruments but from the scientist's senses. The instrument he or she is looking at can be perfectly accurate, yet if the scientist misreads a digital readout, or does not notice a critical shift in the operation of a measurement device, the obtained information is wrong and the resulting picture of the world is in error. The minds of the scientist, the nonscientist, our pet dog sniffing about the world, or a fish swimming about in a bowl, in fact, the minds of all living, thinking organisms, are prisoners that must rely on information smuggled in to them by the senses. Your world is what your senses tell you. The limitations of your senses set the boundaries of your conscious existence.

Because our knowledge of the world is dependent on our senses, it is important to know how our senses function. It is also important to know how well the world created by our senses corresponds to external reality (i.e., the reality measured by scientific instruments). At this point, you are probably smiling to yourself and thinking, "Here comes another academic discourse that will attempt to make something that is quite obvious appear to be complex." You might be saying to yourself, "I see my desk in front of me because it is there. I feel my chair pressing against my back because it is there. I hear my telephone ringing because it contains a bell that makes sounds. What could be more obvious?'' Such faith in your senses is a vital part of existence. It causes you to jump out of the way of an apparently oncoming car, thus preserving your life. It provides the basic data that cause you to step back from a deep hole, thus avoiding a fall and serious bodily harm.

Such faith in our senses is woven into the very fabric of our lives. As the old saying goes, ''Seeing is believing.'' Long before the birth of Christ, Lucretius stated this article of faith when he asked, ''What can give us surer knowledge than our senses? With what else can we distinguish the true form from the false?'' Perhaps the most striking example of this faith is found in our courts of law, where people's lives and fortunes often rest solely on the testimony of the eyes and ears of witnesses. A lawyer might argue that a witness is corrupt or lying, or even that his memory has failed, but no lawyer would have the audacity to suggest that her client should be set free because the only evidence available was what the witnesses saw or heard. Certainly no sane person would charge the eye or ear with perjury!

The philosophical position that perception is an immediate, almost godlike knowledge of external reality has been championed not only by popular sentiment but also by philosophers of the stature of Immanuel Kant (1724–1804). Unfortunately, it is wrong. Look at the drawings shown in Figure 1-1. Clearly, they are all composed of outlined forms on various backgrounds. Despite what your senses tell you, A, B, and C are all perfect squares. Despite the evidence of your senses, D is a perfect circle, the lines in E are both straight, and the lines marked x and y in F are both the same length.

The ease with which we use our senses— seeing, apparently through the simple act of opening our eyes, or touching, apparently by merely pressing our skin against an object—masks the fact that perception is an extremely sophisticated activity of the brain. Perception calls on stores of mem-

ory data. It requires subtle classifications and comparisons, and myriad decisions before any of the data in our senses becomes our conscious awareness of what is ''out there.'' Contrary to what you may think, the eyes do not see. There are many individuals who have perfectly functioning eyes yet have no sensory impressions. They cannot perceive because they have injuries in those parts of the brain that receive and interpret messages from the eyes. Epicharmus knew this in 450 B.C. when he said, ''The mind sees and the mind hears. The rest is blind and deaf.''

''So what?'' you mutter to yourself. ''So sometimes we make errors in our perceptions, the real point is that the senses simply carry a picture of the outside world to the brain. The picture in the brain represents our percept. Of course if we mess up the brain we will distort or destroy perception.'' Again, this answer is too simple. If we look outside and see a car, are we to believe that there is a picture of a car somewhere in our brains? If we notice that a traffic light is green, are we to believe that some part of the brain has turned green? And suppose that there were such images in the brain, carried without distortion from the senses, would this help us to see? Certainly, images in the brain would only be of value if there were some other eyes in the head, which would look at these pictures and interpret them. If this were the case, we would be left with the question of how these internal eyes see. Thus, we would eventually be forced to set up an endless chain of pictures and eyes and pictures and eyes, because the question of who is perceiving the percept, and how, still remains.

If we are to understand perception we must consider it in its natural context. Sensation and perception are some of the many complex processes that occur in the continuing flow of individual behavior. There is no clear line between perception and many other behavioral activities. No perception gives direct knowledge of the outside world, rather such knowledge of the outside world is the end product of many processes. The wet-looking black spot on the edge of a desk could be the place where

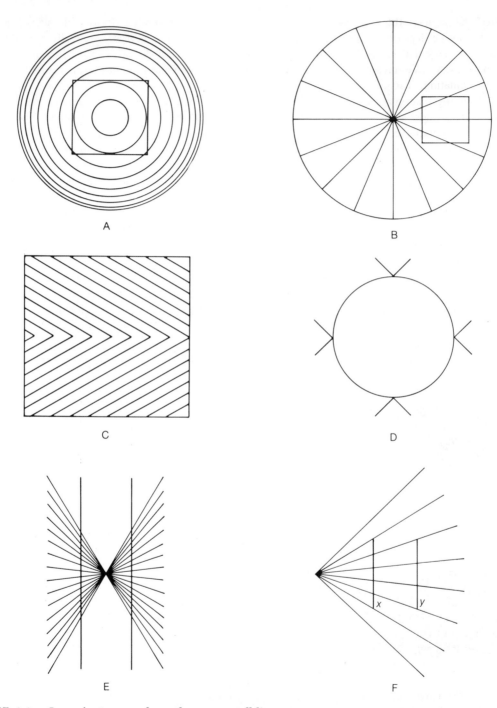

FIGURE 1-1   Some instances where the senses tell lies.

ink was spilled. Of course, this percept could be wrong. The ink may be dry, or the spot might not be there at all. The desk that is seen and touched, might not really exist. We might be dreaming, drugged, or hallucinating. Too extreme, you say? Consider the following example that actually happened to one of the authors. One night he walked across the floor of his darkened home. In the dim gloominess of the night, he saw his dog resting on the floor, clearly asleep. When he bent to touch the dog, he found that it was a footstool. He stepped back, somewhat startled at his stupidity, only to bump against the cold corner of a marble-topped coffee table. When he reached back to steady himself, he found that the corner of the table was, in fact, his dog's cold nose. Each of these perceptions, dog, stool, table, and dog again, seemed, when first received in consciousness, to be accurate representations of reality. Yet, sensory data are not always reliable. Sometimes they can be degraded or not completely available. There seems to be no clear distinction between perceiving or sensing an object and guessing the identity of an object. In some respects, we can say that all perception of objects requires some guessing. Sensory stimulation provides the data for our hypotheses about the nature of the external world, and these hypotheses form our perceptions of the world.

Many human behaviors have been affected by the fallible and often erroneous nature of our percepts. For example, the most elegant of the classic Greek buildings, the Parthenon, is bent. The straight clean lines, which bring a sense of simple elegant grandeur, are actually an illusion. If we schematically represent the east wall of the building as it appears, it is square (as shown in Figure 1-2A).

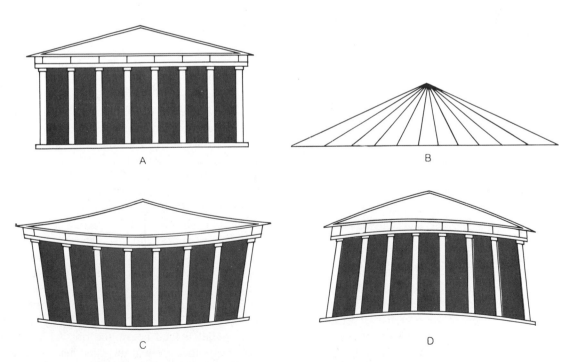

FIGURE 1-2   (A) The Parthenon as it appears; (B) an illusion that should cause the Parthenon to appear as C; (D) the way the Parthenon is built to offset the illusion.

Actually, the Parthenon was built in a distorted fashion in order to offset a series of optical illusions. There is a common visual distortion in which we find that placing angles above a line (much as the roof is placed over the architrave) causes the line to appear slightly bowed. One form of this illusion is shown as Figure 1-2B where the ends of the horizontal line appear slightly higher than the center. If the Parthenon were built physically square, it would appear to sag as a result of this visual distortion. This is shown in an exaggerated manner in Figure 1-2C. But the sagging does not appear because the building has been altered to compensate for the distortion. Figure 1-2D illustrates what an undistorted view of the Parthenon would look like. The upward curvature is more than 6 centimeters on the east and west walls and almost 11 cm on the longer north and south sides.

The vertical features of the Parthenon (such as the columns) were inclined inwards in order to correct for a second optical illusion in which the features of rising objects appear to fall outward at the top. Thus, if we projected all of the columns of the Parthenon upward, they would meet at a point somewhat less than 2 kilometers above the building. Furthermore, the corner columns were made thicker since it was found that when these columns were seen against the sky, they appeared to be thinner than those seen against the darker background formed by the interior wall.

These were conscious corrections made by the Greek architects. To quote one of them, Vitruvius, writing around 30 B.C.: "For the sight follows gracious contours, and unless we flatter its pleasure by proportionate alterations of these parts (so that by adjustment we offset the amount to which it suffers illusions) an uncouth and ungracious aspect will be presented to the spectators." In other words, the Parthenon appears to be square, with elegant straight lines, because it has been consciously distorted to offset perceptual distortions. If it were geometrically square, it would not be perceptually square.

It is amazing to discover the degree to which our conscious experience of the world can differ from the physical (scientific) reality. Although some perceptual distortions are only slight deviations from physical reality, some can be quite complex and surprising, such as that shown in Demonstration Box 1-1.

Such distortions, in the form of disagreements between percept and reality, are quite common. We call them **illusions** and they occur in predictable circumstances for normal observers. The term *illusion* is drawn from the Latin root *illudere,* meaning "to mock," and in a sense they do mock us for our unthinking reliance on the validity of our sensory impressions. Every sensory modality is subject to distortions, illusions, and systematic errors that misrepresent the outside environment to our consciousness. There are illusions of touch, taste, and hearing, as well as visual illusions. Virtually any aspect of perception you might think of can be subject to these kinds of errors. For instance, such basic and apparently simple qualities as the brightness of an object or its color may be perceptually misrepresented, as shown in Demonstration Box 1-2.

Many perceptual errors are merely amusing, such as that in Demonstration Box 1-1, or thought-provoking, as in Demonstration Box 1-2. Others may lead to some embarrassment or annoyance, such as might have been felt by the artisan who created the picture frame shown as Figure 1-3A. Although his workmanship is faultless, he has been undone because the grain of the wood is too prominent. Despite the fact that the picture is perfectly rectangular, it appears to be distorted. Unfortunately, some perceptual errors or illusions are quite serious. In Figure 1-3B, we have shown a surgeon probing for a bullet. She is using a fluoroscope, which presents the outline of the patient's ribs, and her probe is positioned so that it is exactly on line with the bullet lodged below the rib. As you can see, it appears that she will miss and her probe will pass above the bullet despite the fact that the probe

DEMONSTRATION BOX 1-1. Gears and Circles

The pattern shown in this box should be viewed in motion. Move the book around so the motion resembles that which you would make if you were swirling coffee around in a cup without using a spoon. Notice that the six sets of concentric circles seem to show radial regions of light and dark that appear to move in the direction you are swirling. They look as though they were covered by a liquid surface tending to swirl with the stimulus movement.

A second effect has to do with the center circle that seems to have gearlike teeth. As you swirl the array, the center gear seems to rotate, but in a direction *opposite* to that of the movement of the outer circles. Some observers see it moving in a jerky, steplike manner from one rotary position to another and other observers see a smooth rotation. Of course, there is no *physical* movement within the circles, and the geared center circle is also unchanging, despite your conscious impression to the contrary.

DEMONSTRATION BOX 1-2. A Subjective Color Grid

The figure in this box consists of a series of thinly spaced diagonal black lines alternating with white spaces. Study this figure for a couple of seconds, and you will begin to see faint, almost pastel streaks of orange-red and other streaks of blue-green. For many observers, these streaks tend to run vertically up and down the figure crossing both white and black lines; for others, they seem to form a random, almost fishnetlike pattern over the grid. These colors are not present in the stimulus; hence they are *subjective,* or *illusory,* colors.

is angled perfectly. Figure 1-3C shows an even more disastrous occurrence of an illusion. It represents a radar screen with various flight regions marked across its face. The two oblique streaks represent jet aircraft approaching the control region, both flying at about 950 kilometers per hour. The information displayed is similar to that which an air traffic controller might use. From it he might conclude that if these two aircraft continue in the same direction they will pass each other with a safe distance between them. At the moment represented here, however, these aircraft are traveling toward each other on the same line. If they are flying at the same altitude it is very likely that they will collide.

These examples illustrate how important discrepancies between perception and reality can be. Therefore it becomes important for us to know how our perceptions arise, how much we can rely on them, under what circumstances they are most fallible, and under what conditions our perceptions most accurately represent the world. An exploration of these questions is the purpose of this book.

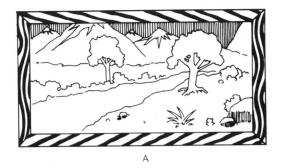

A

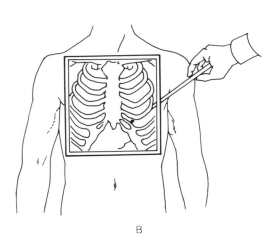

B

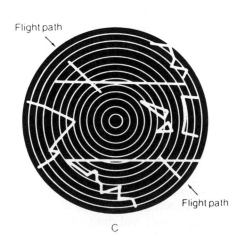

Flight path

Flight path

C

FIGURE 1-3   **Some perceptual distortions in common situations.**

ASPECTS OF THE PERCEPTUAL PROCESS

The study of perception is diverse. Partly this is the result of the length of time that perceptual problems have been studied. The Greek philosophers, the pre-Renaissance thinkers, the Arabic scholars, the Latin scholastics, the early British empiricists, and the German physicists and physicians who founded both physiology and psychology considered issues in sensation and perception to be basic questions. When Alexander Bain wrote the first English textbook on psychology in 1855 it was entitled *The Senses and the Intellect,* with the most extensive coverage reserved for sensory and perceptual functions. The major portion of both the theorizing and the empirical work produced by Wilhelm Wundt, who is generally credited with the founding of experimental psychology, was oriented toward sensation and perception. In addition to the diversity caused by a long and varied history, perception has been affected by many "schools" of thought. Each has its own major theoretical viewpoint and its own particular set of methodological techniques. Thus, we encounter psychophysicists, gestaltists, functionalists, analytic introspectionists, transactionalists, sensory physiologists, sensory-tonic theorists, "new look" psychologists, efferent theorists, artificial intelligence experts, and computational psychologists, to name but a few. There are even theorists (such as some behaviorists) who deny the existence of, or at least deny our ability to study, the conscious event we call perception. Despite this chorus of diverse voices and viewpoints, there seems to be a consensus about the important aspects of perceptual study.

Before we look at the major areas of emphasis in the study of the perceptual process let us first offer a disclaimer. We recognize that it is difficult, perhaps impossible, and most certainly unwise to attempt to draw sharp lines separating one field of inquiry from another. However, there are certain problem areas, or orientations, that characterize certain groups of investigators, and these seem to be definable. The study of **sensation,** or sensory processes, is concerned with the first contact between the organism and the environment. Thus, someone studying sensation might look at the way in which electromagnetic radiation (light) is registered by the eye. This investigator would look at the physical structure of the sense organ and would attempt to establish how sensory experiences are related to physical stimulation and physiological functioning. These types of studies tend to focus on less complex (although not less complicated) aspects of our conscious experience. For instance, these investigators might study how we perceive brightness, loudness, or color; however, the nature of the object having a given brightness, sound, or color would not make much difference to them.

Someone who is interested in the study of **perception** is interested in our conscious experience of objects and object relationships. For instance, the sensory question would be "How bright does the target appear to be?" whereas the perceptual questions would be "Can you identify that object?" "Where is it?" "How far away is it?" and "How large is it?" In a more global sense, those who study perception are interested in how we form a conscious representation of the outside environment, and in the accuracy of that representation. For those of you who have difficulty in drawing a hard-and-fast line between the concepts of perception and sensation, rest easy. Since Thomas Reid introduced the distinction in 1785, some investigators have championed its use and others have totally ignored the difference, choosing to treat sensation and perception as a unitary problem.

Cognition is a term used to define a very active field of inquiry in contemporary psychology. The word itself is quite old, probably first introduced by St. Thomas Aquinas (1225–1274). He divided the study of behavior into two broad divisions, *cognition,* meaning how we know the world, and *affect,* which was meant to encompass feelings and emotions. Today's definition of cognition is equally as broad as that of Aquinas. Although many investigators use the term to refer to memory, association, concept formation, language, and problem solving (all of which simply take the act of perception for granted), other investigators include the processes of attention and the conscious representation and interpretation of stimuli as part of the cognitive process. In other words, cognition tends to be somewhere between the areas that were traditionally called *perception* and *learning;* and it incorporates elements of both. The similarity between many of the problems studied by cognitive psychologists and those studied by perceptual psychologists is best seen by the fact that both often publish in the same journals and on similar topics.

Information processing is a relatively new term. This approach emphasizes how information about the external world is operated on (processed) to produce our conscious percepts and guide our actions. Information processing is typically assumed to include a *registration* or sensory phase, an *interpretation* or perceptual phase, and a *memoric* or cognitive phase. Thus, rather than being a separate subdiscipline, the information processing approach attempts to integrate sensation, perception, and cognition within a common framework. It relies on a **levels-of-processing analysis** in which each stage of processing, from the first registration of the stimulus on the receptor to the final conscious representation entered into memory, is systematically analyzed.

None of these labels should be taken as representing inflexible, or completely separate, areas of study. At a recent professional meeting one well-known psychologist lamented, ''When I first started doing research, people said I studied perception. After a while, they said I studied cognition. Now they say I'm studying human information processing. I don't know what's going on—I've been studying the same set of problems for the last ten years!''

THEORIES OF PERCEPTION

In the same way that there are many aspects of perception, there are also many theoretical approaches to perceptual problems. One important approach may be called **biological reductionism.** It is based on the presumption that for any given aspect of the observer's sensation there is a corresponding physiological event. According to this approach, the main goal of the perceptual researcher is to isolate these underlying physiological mechanisms. The search for specific neural units whose activity corresponds to specific sensory experiences, characterized by researchers such as David Hubel and Torston Wiesel (1979), is common to such theories.

Other theoretical approaches are often less bound to a specific class of mechanism. For example, **direct perception** involves a set of theories that begins with the premise that all the information needed to form the conscious percept is available in the stimuli that reach our receptors, or in relationships among these stimuli that are invariant predictors of what is ''out there'' in the environment. This theoretical position is characterized by the work of J. J. Gibson (e.g., 1979), who argued that certain aspects of the environment are immediately impressed on the observer and need no further computation or additional information based on inferences or experience.

Recently, a number of perceptual theorists, whose thinking has been influenced by developments in artificial intelligence systems, have adopted an alternative approach that contains some of the same flavor of direct perception. Such theories are usually presented in the form of computer programs or computational systems that might allow machines to directly interpret sensory information in the same manner that a human observer might. Typical of such theorists is David Marr (1982), who began with the general presumption made in direct perception that all the information needed is in the stimulus inputs, but added the suggestion that this interpretation might require the detection of fairly subtle dimensions in the stimulus and might also require a number of computations and several stages of analysis. This added feature has resulted in the label **computational approach** being applied to such theories.

A much older (but still active) theoretical approach begins with the recognition that our perceptual representation of the world is much richer and more accurate than might be expected on the basis of the information contained in the stimuli available at any one moment in time. Theories to explain this fact often begin with the suggestion that perception is much like other logical processes. In addition to the information available to our sense organs at the moment, we can also use information based on our previous experience, our expectations, and so forth. This means, for example, that a visual percept may involve other sources of information, some nonvisual in nature, some arising from our past history and cognitive processing strategies. The similarity of many of these mechanisms to reasoning leads us to refer to this type of theory as **intelligent perception.** This approach probably originated with Helmholtz in 1867, and survives today in the work of researchers such as Irving Rock (1983) who have a more cognitive orientation. These theories are also called **constructive theories** of perception, since our final conscious impression may involve combining a number of different factors to "construct" the final percept.

It is quite likely that each of these approaches is useful in describing some aspects of the perceptual process (see Coren & Girgus, 1978; Uttal, 1981); however, different orientations tend to lead researchers in different directions, searching for different types of mechanism. Each approach is likely to be valid for some parts of the problem and irrelevant to others. This is a common occurrence in many areas of endeavor. For instance, a metallurgist might look at a bridge and consider its material components, whereas a civil engineer might look at the load-bearing capacity of the entire struc-

ture, and a city planner might look at the same bridge in terms of traffic flow. At first glance there may seem to be very little overlap between the various views, since the city planner does not care about the specific shape of the bridge structure, and the engineer cares only about the structural aspects of the beams, not their specific alloy constituents. Yet each level of analysis is valid for some specific set of questions. This book addresses the problem of how people build a conscious picture of their environment through the use of information reaching their senses. We follow the lead of many contemporary theorists and try to use data from all levels of the perceptual process, and discussions in terms of several different theoretical positions, in order to give an integrated picture of the process of perception. After all, the label we apply to our approach is of considerably less importance than the answer itself.

THE PLAN OF THE BOOK

The orientation of this book is implicit rather than explicit. Although theories are introduced and discussed in the various chapters, no all-encompassing theoretical position has been adopted. We have chosen to be "militantly eclectic" in our orientation. Thus, this text is mostly concerned with perceptual and sensory *processes*. In general, the presentation of the material follows a levels-of-processing approach, in that the first half of the book is concerned with the more basic sensory processes and is organized around specific sensory systems, such as vision or audition, and the second half of the book is concerned with the more clearly perceptual processes that have strong cognitive influences, and are often not bound to any single sensory modality.

We have tried to make the individual chapters relatively self-contained. We begin by explaining how sensations and perceptions are measured (Chapter 2). We then proceed with the physiological structures and the basic sensory capacities associated with vision (Chapters 3 through 5), audition (Chapters 6 and 7), and the chemical and mechanical senses (Chapters 8 and 9). For those who feel a bit "rusty" about some of the very basic physiological facts, we have also included a "Primer of Neurophysiology" as an appendix. Chapters 10 to 15 deal with those problems that have traditionally been treated as part of classical perception, our perceptual representation of space, time, motion, form, and size. The more cognitive aspects of perception are also introduced here in those chapters that deal with the issues of music, speech perception, and attention. The last three chapters (16 to 18) deal with perceptual diversity, which incudes many of the factors that make the perceptual experience of one individual different from that of another. These factors include the changes that occur in the developing individual because of the normal aging process, life history, experience, learning, and personality factors, to name a few.

You will notice that each chapter includes a series of Demonstration Boxes. These are experimental demonstrations that you can perform for yourself using materials that are easily found around a house or other living quarters. They illustrate many aspects of the perceptual process. Quite often they demonstrate concepts that are very difficult to put into words, but which, when experienced, are immediately understandable. You are encouraged to try these demonstrations since they are an integral part of the book. In the same way that perception involves interaction with the world, these demonstrations allow you to interact with your senses in a controlled manner and to gain insight into yourself.

We hope this book will provide you with some understanding of the abilities and the limits of your senses. This knowledge should expand your comprehension of many behavioral phenomena that depend on perception as a first step. Perception seems to be the final judge of the truth or the falsity of everything we encounter as part of our human experience. How often have you heard the phrase "Seeing is believing" or "I didn't believe it until I saw it with my own two eyes"? Yet you have already seen in this chapter that such faith in the truthfulness of our conscious percepts is often misplaced. In 500 B.C., Parmenides considered how perception can deceive us, summarizing his feelings in these words: "The eyes and ears are bad witnesses when they are at the service of minds that do not understand their language." In this book, we will try to teach you their language.

GLOSSARY

The following definitions are specific to this book.

Biological reductionism   The theoretical premise that each sensory experience is associated with particular physiological events.

Cognition   The process of knowing, incorporating both perception and learning.

Computational approach   Involves the presumption that certain perceived qualities require computation and that these computations can be precisely described mathematically.

Constructive theories   These maintain that perception may involve the integration of several sources of information, and may be affected by cognitive factors and experience.

Direct perception   The theoretical position that all the information needed for the final conscious percept is in the stimulus array.

Illusions   Distortions or incongruencies between percept and reality.

Information processing   The processes by which stimuli are registered in the receptors, identified, and stored in memory.

Intelligent perception   The theoretical presumption that cognitive processes and experience can affect perception.

Levels-of-processing analysis   Analysis of the contribution of each stage of processing to the final percept, beginning with the receptor and continuing through cognitive mechanisms.

Perception   The conscious experience of objects and object relationships.

Sensation   Simple conscious experience associated with a stimulus.

Psychophysics

The ocean liner glides slowly through the thick stormy night. Somewhere in the distance is New York harbor. With the visibility near zero the captain is forced to rely solely on the ship's radar system for information about the position of obstacles impeding the passage of his ship. The ship is in a heavily traveled trade route, and the crew must continually be alert for possible collisions with other ships. The radar operator is watching her screen intently, searching for a radar echo caused by the presence of another ship nearby. Actually, she is also wrestling with a basic sensory-perceptual problem, that of **detection.** She is trying to answer the question "Is there anything there?"

She is sure she sees an echo. Now the question becomes "What is it?" Is it an echo from another ship or just a "ghost," a false echo often encountered in stormy weather? The radar operator is facing a second basic problem, **identification.** We normally solve the detection and identification problems quickly and automatically, since we generally encounter stimuli that are so strong, and provide so much information, that they pose little problem for us. The complex nature of detection and identification only emerges in the context of a difficult or degraded stimulus situation.

The echo turns out to be just a "ghost" and the order is given to maintain the previous heading (compass direction). The helmsman has been given the bearing and now holds the ship's direction so that the compass needle always points to the correct place on the dial. At this moment, he is asking himself, "Has the needle drifted slightly toward the north?" If so, he must compensate by turning the wheel so that the needle moves back to the desired compass point. He is continuously concerned with the problem of whether the compass needle is centered on the desired heading. This task also evokes an important perceptual process, called **discrimination.** "Is this stimulus different from that one?" is the general discrimination question.

Finally, through the clearing weather the entrance to New York harbor appears. The ship is taken in tow by a tugboat and maneuvered toward its berth at the dock. The captain of the tugboat peers from his bridge, carefully judging the distance between the ship and the concrete wall of the pier. He must continually ask himself, "How far does the ship appear to be from the pier?" Such questions are part of another sensory problem, "How much of X is there?" This is the problem of **scaling.**

These four problems, *detection, identification, discrimination,* and *scaling,* are the central concerns of the area of perceptual psychology called *psychophysics.* Psychophysics owes its name and origin to Gustav Theodor Fechner (1801–1887), a physicist and philosopher who set out to determine the relationship between the magnitude of a sensation registered in the mind and the magnitude of the physical stimulus that gave rise to it. Hence, the name *psychophysics* (from the Greek roots *psyche,* or "mind," and *physike,* which refers to naturally occurring phenomena). Fechner not only established the philosophical rationale for studying the relationship between sensations and physical stimuli but also developed many of the experimental methods still in use today. These methods of collecting and analyzing data are employed in every aspect of the study of sensation and perception (see, e.g., Laming, 1986) and of many other areas of psychology, including even social, personality, and clinical psychology (Baird & Noma, 1978; Grossberg & Grant, 1978; Wegener, 1982).

DETECTION

The basic task for any sensory system is to detect the presence of energy changes in the environment. Energy changes may take the form of electromagnetic (light), mechanical (sound, touch, movement, muscle tension), chemical (tastes, smells), or thermal stimulation. The problem of detection is centered around the problem of how much of such a stimulus (relative to a zero energy level) is necessary for an individual to say that the stimulus is heard, tasted, smelled, or felt. Classically, this minimal amount of energy has been called the **absolute threshold.** In 1860, Fechner defined a threshold stimulus as one that "lifted the sensation or sensory difference over the threshold of consciousness." The idea is that below some critical value of a stimulus a person would not be expected to detect that stimulus. As soon as this threshold value is exceeded, however, we would expect the observer to always detect its presence.

We can represent this relationship by a graph on which we plot the percentage of time an observer would be expected to detect the presence of a stimulus (values along the *ordinate,* or vertical axis) against stimulus magnitude (values along the *abscissa,* or horizontal axis). This has been done in Figure 2-1 using arbitrary values for stimulus intensity. Notice that the percentage of time that the stimulus is detected takes a sudden step up from 0 to 100 percent when the stimulus reaches a value of 3.5. The absolute threshold is thus 3.5.

Method of Limits

How do we measure absolute thresholds? Let us conduct a relatively simple but typical experiment to measure the threshold of hearing. In this experiment an observer sits in a soundproof room wearing headphones. The experimenter presents a very faint, undetectable tone of a particular and constant frequency and increases its intensity in small steps until the observer reports, "I hear it." On alternate trials the experimenter starts with a tone that can easily be heard and decreases the intensity until the observer reports, "I no longer hear it." This method of determining a threshold is called the **method of limits.** Kraepelin gave it that name in 1891, because a stimulus series always ends when the observer reaches a limit or a point of change in his judgments. The two modes of presenting the stimulus (increasing or decreasing) are usually called *ascending* or *descending stimulus series.* A sample of the kind of data such an experiment might generate is shown in Table 2-1.

The first thing we notice about the data in Ta-

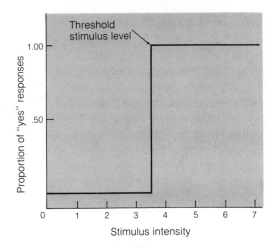

FIGURE 2–1   Absolute threshold.

ble 2-1 is that the absolute threshold for hearing is not a fixed value as we first proposed, but appears to vary from trial to trial. For instance, in Trial 6 the observer could no longer detect the stimulus when we presented a tone with an intensity of 8; in Trial 4, a stimulus intensity of only 5 was detected. Such data indicate that the absolute threshold is anything but absolute. It seems that the threshold varies from measurement to measurement, or moment to moment. As early as 1888, Joseph Jastrow speculated on the reason for this variability in the threshold over time. He theorized that lapses of attention, slight fatigue, and other psychological changes could cause the obtained fluctuations. Demonstration Box 2-1 shows how you can experience this threshold variability for yourself.

We can compute an estimate of the average absolute threshold from the tabled data simply by taking the average stimulus intensity at which a response shifted either from an "I hear it" to an "I don't hear it," or from an "I don't hear it" to an "I hear it." This gives us a threshold value of 6.65 intensity units. These computations are shown at the bottom of the table. Table 2-1 also shows that there is a slight difference in the threshold value depending on whether it was computed from an as-

Table 2-1.   Determination of the Absolute Threshold of Hearing by the Method of Limits

Sound intensity (scale units)	Trials					
	↑ 1	↓ 2	↑ 3	↓ 4	↑ 5	↓ 6
16						+
15						+
14		+				+
13		+				+
12		+		+		+
11		+		+		+
10		+		+		+
9		+		+		+
8		+	+	+	+	−
7		−	−	+	+	
6	+[a]	−	−	+	−	
5	−[b]		−	+	−	
4	−		−	−	−	
3	−		−	−	−	
2	−		−	−		
1	−		−			
Threshold for series computations	5.5	7.5	7.5	4.5	6.5	8.5

$$\text{Mean descending threshold} = \frac{7.5 + 4.5 + 8.5}{3} = 6.8$$

$$\text{Mean ascending threshold} = \frac{5.5 + 7.5 + 6.5}{3} = 6.5$$

Mean absolute threshold   = 6.65 sound units

a. "I hear it."
b. "I don't hear it."

cending or a descending series of stimuli. Such differences may arise from observers continuing to report yes in a descending series and no in an ascending series, a tendency called the **error of perseveration.** It is also possible to have an **error of anticipation.** Here an observer feels that she has said yes too often and decides that it is time to say no even though she still faintly hears the tone. To balance out such possible constant errors we use alternating ascending and descending stimulus se-

ries, and we begin each series of the same kind at different stimulus intensities.

The method of limits has been modified to produce a different method for measuring absolute thresholds called the **staircase method.** Here the experimenter attempts to capture the absolute threshold by changing the direction of the steps whenever the observer changes her response. Thus, we might increase the intensity of a tone, step by step, until the observer reports that she hears it, and

---

DEMONSTRATION BOX 2-1.   The Variability of the Threshold

For this demonstration you will need a wristwatch or an alarm clock that ticks. Place the clock on a table and move across the room so that you can no longer hear the ticking. If the tick is faint, you may accomplish this merely by moving your head away some distance. Now gradually move toward the clock. Note that by doing this, you are actually performing a method of limits experiment since the sound level steadily increases as you approach the watch. At some

distance from the watch you will just begin to hear the source of the sound. This is your momentary threshold. Now hold this position for a few moments and you will notice that occasionally the sound will fade and you may have to step forward to reach threshold, whereas at other times it may be noticeably louder and you may be able to step back farther and still hear it. These changes are a result of your changing threshold sensitivity.

---

then start to decrease it, one step at a time, from that level until it is no longer heard, and then again start to increase it by steps. Notice that in this way the value of the test stimulus flips back and forth around the threshold value. The advantage of this procedure is that it allows the experimenter to "track" the threshold, even if sensitivity is continually changing, such as after administration of some drugs, or during adaptation to different background stimuli (Bekesy, 1947; Jesteadt, 1980).

Why does the threshold seem to vary from moment to moment? First we must recognize that we have been assuming that the only stimulus present is the stimulus we are asking our observer to detect. This is quite false. A constantly present and ever-changing background of stimulation exists for any signal we present. If you place both your hands over your ears to block out the room noises, you will hear a sound one observer poetically called "the sound of waves from a distant sea" and another, somewhat less poetically, "the faint hissing of radio static." Similarly, if you sit in a completely lightproof room in absolute darkness, you do not see complete blackness. Your visual field appears to be filled with a grayish mist (which has been termed "cortical gray") and occasionally you can even see momentary bright pinpoint flashes here and there. Any stimulus we ask an observer to detect must force itself through this spontaneously

generated fluctuating background. It is as if every stimulus to be detected is superimposed on a background of noise generated within the observer.

As this *endogenous,* or internal, noise level changes, so does our measured threshold, in the same way that a person standing in the midst of a noisy crowd must talk louder in order to be heard. Some experimenters have resorted to the introduction of experimentally controlled background noise in order to achieve more constant conditions than would be possible if they relied on the constancy of internally generated noise. Under these circumstances, the experimenter has a better idea of the noise level with which the stimulus is competing. Many of the experiments we will discuss have employed such a controlled background noise level. By *noise* we mean any background stimulus other than the one to be detected. Of course, if we define *noise* in this way we may have visual, chemical, mechanical, and thermal, as well as auditory noise.

Method of Constant Stimuli

Discussion of another method will allow us to see more clearly the nature of the absolute threshold. This method is preferred when the threshold must be measured precisely, but it is much more time-consuming to use because it requires so many stimulus presentations and responses. Suppose we take a set of stimuli ranging from clearly imperceptible to clearly perceptible and present them, one at a time, to our observer. We present each stimulus many times in a prearranged irregular order. The observer is simply required to respond yes when she detects the stimulus and no when she does not. This procedure is called the **method of constant stimuli,** a name derived from the fact that a fixed or constant set of stimuli is chosen beforehand and presented a fixed or constant number of times to each observer. Some typical data obtained with this method are presented graphically in Figure 2-2.

We see in the figure that as the stimulus energy increases, the relative number of times the observer says yes (meaning the stimulus was perceived) gradually increases. It is not the single jump we might have predicted from the definition of absolute threshold illustrated in Figure 2-1. These S-shaped curves, called *ogives,* are obtained commonly with the method of constant stimuli in all sensory systems.

What does the proportion of yes responses indicate in such experiments? One basic assumption made by psychophysicists is that any type of behavior, such as saying "Yes, I see it," has some

strength. The strengths of various behaviors can be represented by numbers, which indicate their relative magnitudes. The measure that has found most favor among contemporary workers in the field is a numerical estimate of the likelihood that the particular response in question will occur. We call this likelihood the *response probability*. We can estimate the response probability for detecting the stimulus, or more exactly for saying "Yes, I see it," by using the formula

$$p(\text{Yes}) = \frac{\text{Number of ``Yes'' Responses}}{\text{Number ``Yes'' + Number ``No''}}$$

The data in Figure 2-2 make it clear that the probability that an observer will detect a stimulus is not an "all or none" affair (as in Figure 2-1), but rather changes gradually as the stimulus intensity increases. Then where is the absolute threshold? Here, as in many places, we must make a somewhat arbitrary decision. The point usually taken as the absolute threshold is that value where the probability of saying yes is the same as the probability of saying no. This is simply the stimulus intensity that the subject claims she detected 50 percent of the time. In Figure 2-2 we have indicated this threshold value by dotted lines. The threshold is about 3.5 energy units for this observer.

Here are some examples of approximate threshold values as measured by these methods. The visual system is so sensitive that a candle flame can be seen from a distance of more than 48 kilometers on a dark clear night. In the auditory system, we can detect the ticking of a wristwatch in a quiet room at a distance of 6 meters—sensitivity beyond this point would allow us to hear the sound of air molecules colliding. As for our other senses, we can taste 1 teaspoon of sugar dissolved in 7½ liters of water and smell 1 drop of perfume diffused through the volume of an average three-room apartment (Galanter, 1962).

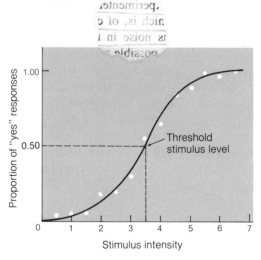

FIGURE 2–2   **Typical data from method of constant stimuli in detection.**

Signal Detection Theory

Some of you may have been bothered by one aspect of the psychophysical measurement techniques we have been discussing. We are supposedly studying an observer's sensory capacities, yet we have not been talking about the probability that an observer *detects* a stimulus, but rather the probability that he says "Yes, I hear (or see, or whatever) it." We can imagine that if an observer feels that this is a "test" of some sort, where it would be good for him to appear to be quite sensitive, he might say yes on almost every trial. What is to prevent this from happening? Although we might argue that people are basically honest, and would not lie about whether or not they heard a stimulus, this is not the sort of guarantee on which scientists would like to rest their conclusions. We are not criticizing the reliability of observers in psychophysical experiments, for most are quite sincere and honest. Rather, we are pointing out that at the very low stimulus energies used in most detection experiments an observer may be unsure about whether a sensation has been experienced. This may result in being unsure as to whether or not to respond yes on any particular trial. Thus, on some trials a "guess" response is made. Therefore, in order to assess sensory capacities accurately, we must take into account the observer's decision-making behavior.

Experimenters became aware of this problem early in the history of psychophysics. They first attempted to cope with it by inserting **catch trials,** which were trials in which no stimulus was presented. They reasoned that if observers were honest in reporting what was detected, they would respond no on these catch trials. If the yes response came too frequently, the observer was warned by the experimenter. Alternatively, an attempt was made to adjust the calculated threshold to account for the guesses, or the data were simply discarded. Over many experiments, however, it became clear that the observers were not trying to fool anyone. Somehow their behavior was reasonable, although it was not clear what they were doing.

If we now change our classical absolute threshold experiment so that we can study not only the observer's ability to detect a stimulus when it is there but also his guessing behavior as reflected in a yes response when no signal is present, we have entered the domain of **signal detection theory** (see Baird & Noma, 1978; Egan, 1975; Green & Swets, 1966). It is a mathematical, theoretical system, which recognizes that the observer is not merely a passive receiver of stimuli but is also engaged in the process of deciding whether or not he is confident enough that the stimulus was present to say "Yes, I detected it."

For the purposes of the following discussion we shall list all the possible behaviors in a new type of detection experiment and give them names. Table 2-2 is a schematic representation of the standard signal detection experiment. There are two types of "stimulus" presentations (at the left of the table). A *signal absent* presentation is like a classical catch trial in which no stimulus is presented and the observer sees or hears only the noise generated by the sensory system. *Signal present* is a trial in which the experimenter actually presents the target stimulus (of course, superimposed on the endogenous noise of the sensory system). There are also two possible responses in the experiment (at the top of the table). *Yes* indicates that the observer thinks a stimulus was presented on a particular trial (that is, signal present), and *no* in-

Table 2-2. Outcomes of a Signal Detection Experiment

Signal	Response	
	Yes	No
Present	Hit	Miss
Absent	False alarm	Correct negative

dicates that the observer thinks the signal was absent. The combination of two possible stimulus presentations and two possible responses leads to four possible outcomes on a given trial (the four cells of the table). When the signal is present and the response is yes the observer makes a **hit.** But if the observer responds yes when the signal is absent, then a **false alarm** is made. The other cells are called **misses** and **correct negatives.** The relationships among these responses depend not only on the nature of the signal but also on the decision processes occurring within the observer.

Consider a typical experiment as an example. Suppose we want to measure an observer's ability to detect a tone. The tone for a given experiment will be constant in intensity and frequency. After a ready signal, the observer is required to respond by pushing one button to indicate "Yes, the signal tone was present" and a different button to signify "No, it was not." Let us also consider some different experimental conditions that might be introduced. The first is one in which the signal was presented in 50 percent of the trials, and no signal was presented for the remaining 50 percent. A typical set of data for one observer, expressing the proportions of trials on which the four possible outcomes occurred (the **outcome matrix**), is shown in Table 2-3.

Notice that on 25 percent of the trials when the signal was absent the observer responded "Yes, the signal was present." Why should the observer report that a signal was present when it was not? First, clearly he is not always sure that whatever he heard was actually the signal. Because of this many

nonsensory aspects of the situation might influence his pattern of responding. Consider the effect of his expectations. If the observer knows that the signal is present on almost every trial he might find himself responding yes to even the faintest or most ambiguous of sensations (perhaps even generated by endogenous noise in his own nervous system). This is sensible behavior if the stimulus occurs most of the time, because on these "doubtful" trials he will quite often be correct. However, if the signal rarely occurs, he would be less tempted by ambiguous, faint sensations and might want to wait until he experienced a stronger sensation before saying yes.

If our description of what the observer is doing is correct, then we should be able to change his response pattern by changing his expectations, even though his sensitivity remains the same. Typical results from the same observer are presented in Table 2-4. In one case the signal was present in 90 percent of the trials and in the other only 10 percent of the trials. Notice that when the signal is occurring frequently the observer says yes often. This gives him many hits, but also many false alarms. When he expects the signal only occasionally he

Table 2-3.   Outcome Matrix When Stimulus Is Present 50 Percent of the Time

Signal	Response	
	Yes	No
Present	0.75	0.25
Absent	0.25	0.75

Table 2-4.   Outcome Matrices for Two Different Conditions

Stimulus present 90 percent of the time

Signal	Response	
	Yes	No
Present	0.95	0.05
Absent	0.63	0.37

Stimulus present 10 percent of the time

Signal	Response	
	Yes	No
Present	0.35	0.65
Absent	0.04	0.96

says no more often, thus reducing the number of false alarms, but also reducing the number of hits. How, then, do we measure the observer's sensitivity? By our former definition of threshold (the point at which a signal is detected 50 percent of the time), the tone is clearly above threshold in the first instance, whereas in the second it is clearly below threshold. This does not make sense, since neither the tone's strength nor the observer's sensitivity has changed. We need some way of separating the observer's sensitivity from his decision strategy.

We can approach such a method of analysis by exploring how the observer's responses change for a particular signal strength if we vary only his expectations by varying the relative frequency with which the signal occurs. We will obtain proportions of hits and false alarms for each different signal probability, as we discussed above. If these proportions of hits and false alarms are plotted against each other as in Figure 2-3, we obtain a **receiver operating characteristic curve** (frequently abbreviated **ROC curve**), which displays the relationship between proportions of hits and false alarms as the likelihood of the signal changes. The terminology was inherited from the communications engineers who first developed signal detection theory. A more descriptive term for those interested in perception would be *isosensitivity curve,* since the curve represents the range of possible outcome matrices for one level of sensitivity. As in the previous example, Figure 2-3 shows that when the signal is rare, the observer frequently says no even when the signal is presented. At the high end of the curve, where the signal occurs frequently, the observer says yes quite often even when the signal is not there.

An ROC curve (in any modality) reflects an observer's response pattern for one signal strength. If we increase the strength of the signal, we find that the curve has a more pronounced bow, as shown by the curved black line in Figure 2-3. If we decrease the signal strength, the curve becomes flatter and approaches the 45-degree line, which represents chance responding. Thus, the amount of

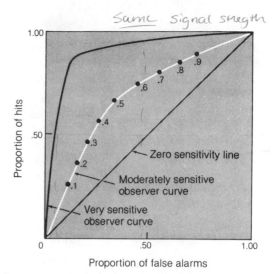

FIGURE 2–3   ROC curves. Notice how the shape of the curve changes for different levels of sensitivity. The black dots on the white curve represent results with indicated probability of signal presentation.

bow in the curve can serve as a measure of the perceived signal strength. An alternative way to interpret an ROC curve is in terms of variations in the sensitivity of an observer to a signal of a particular strength. Thus, the two curves in Figure 2-3 could also be interpreted as reflecting two different sensitivities of a single observer (the more bowed the curve the more sensitive) or the curves of two different observers with different sensitivities to the same signal strength.

We may also vary the observer's response pattern, while holding the signal intensity constant, by varying the importance or the payoff for a given response. For instance, if we pay 10 cents for every correct detection of the stimulus and do not penalize the observer for false alarms, the optimal strategy is to guess yes on every trial. This will maximize the amount of money that can be earned in the test situation. Contrast this to a situation where we deduct 10 cents for each false alarm and do not reward for correct detections. Here a reasonable observer would minimize the losses by saying no on every trial. Actually, most situations fall somewhere between these two extremes. For instance, we might pay our observer 10 cents for every correct response and deduct 5 cents for every wrong response. This situation may be represented in a matrix of numbers as shown in Table 2-5. Such a set of rewards and penalties is called the **payoff matrix.** Changing the payoff matrix causes changes in an observer's response pattern in much the same way that varying an observer's expectations concerning stimulus frequency would, so an observer's *motives* as well as *expectations* affect responses during the detection experiment. Thus, by systematically varying the payoff matrix of an experiment, we can vary an observer's numbers of hits and false alarms and produce an ROC curve similar to that generated by varying the relative frequency of signals. Note that it is the observer's *response pattern* (e.g., the overall number of yes responses) that varies as the ROC curve is produced, *not the sensitivity to the stimulus.* Because the manipulation of motivation in this case is done by varying the payoff matrix, and thus the amount of money paid to an observer, this type of experiment has been given the snide name "sweatshop psychophysics."

Perhaps the theoretical and methodological bases for signal detection will become clearer if we look at the detection problem from a different conceptual angle. We have said that even when no stimulus is present an observer's sensory systems are still active, generating sensory noise. The amount of noise probably varies from moment to moment. This fluctuation in noise level is probably

caused by the operation of physiological, attentional, and other variables on the sensory and perceptual systems of the observer. Signal detection theorists represent these fluctuations in the form of a **probability distribution,** which is graphed in Figure 2-4 as the "signal absent" curve. The abscissa is the amount of sensory activity (or sensation level), and the ordinate can be thought of as the likelihood of occurrence of any particular level of sensation over a great many trials. This means that even in the absence of any external signal, the observer experiences some level of sensation that is represented by a particular location along the abscissa. This level is experienced with a relative frequency represented by the height of the curve at that point.

When a signal is actually presented it occurs against this background of sensory noise. Of course, the signal produces some sensory response of its own, which then adds to whatever amount is already present. The effect of this is the creation of a new distribution of sensory activity, the "signal present" curve. On average, the level of activity elicited by the signal added to the sensory noise is more intense than that of the noise alone. This is shown by the fact that the mean of the signal present curve is shifted toward higher values of the sensory activity axis in Figure 2-4. When the signal is weak, however, it will not add enough sensory activity to make the two distributions (signal absent vs. signal present) completely distinct. The two distributions in Figure 2-4 would overlap if drawn on the same set of axes. You can see from Figure 2-4 that some levels of sensation could result either from presentations of a signal or simply from noise alone.

Imagine you are an observer sitting inside the head trying to decide if a signal has been presented. The only information you have is the intensity of the sensation. Remember, however, that sometimes the noise produces a sensation that is just as intense as that produced by the signal, as shown in Figure 2-4. As a rational observer, you would probably solve this problem by setting a **criterion,** or cutoff

Table 2-5.   A Typical Payoff Matrix for a Psychophysical Experiment

Signal	Response	
	Yes	No
Present	10¢	−5¢
Absent	−5¢	10¢

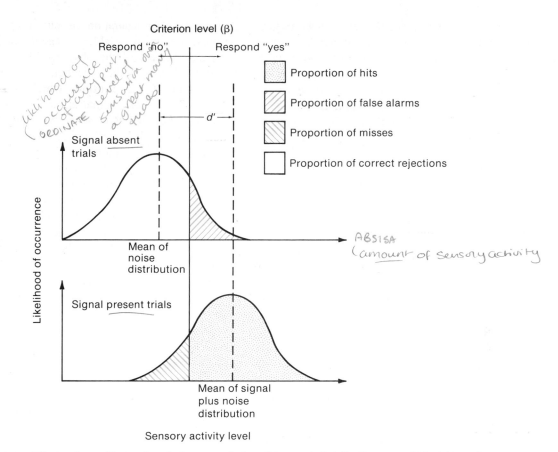

FIGURE 2–4 Illustration of how signal absent and signal present distributions result in hits, misses, false alarms, and correct negatives for a particular criterion setting. Notice that the two curves are actually plotted on the same axes—they are separated for clarity. The curves would overlap if plotted together.

point, for sensation level. This is the value you are willing to accept as probably indicating that a signal is present. If a sensation level is below the criterion (to the left in Figure 2-4), you respond no; if it is above the criterion, you respond yes. This simplifies the problem greatly, since you must only decide, based on your motives and expectations, where to put the criterion. From that point on, the experienced level of sensation more or less automatically determines the response. The criterion value is usually symbolized by the Greek letter **β (beta)**.

If this is what the observer is doing, then we can specify the proportions of hits and false alarms we might expect, depending on where he places his criterion. According to signal detection theory, the proportions of the various outcomes observed in an experiment (see Table 2–2) may be represented as that proportion of the *area* under the appropriate probability distribution curve to the right or left of the criterion location. Thus, if Figure 2–4 represents an actual situation, the proportion of signal present trials on which a yes response would be given (the proportion of hits) is represented by the area under the signal present curve to the right of the criterion, since the observer would say yes whenever the sensation level was above, or to the right of, the criterion. Similarly, the proportion of false alarms is represented by the area under the signal absent curve to the right of the criterion, since that is the proportion of trials on which the sensation level generated by the sensory system in the absence of a signal exceeded the criterion level set for the yes response. The other two possible outcomes are also represented in Figure 2–4.

The motivation and expectation effects on an observer's response pattern in a detection experiment are now interpretable. Essentially, these variables affect the placement of the criterion and, hence, the proportion of hits and false alarms. For instance, suppose that the observer is a radiologist looking for a light spot as evidence of cancer in a set of chest X rays (see e.g., Swensson, 1980). If the radiologist thinks she has found such a spot, she calls the patient back for additional tests. The penalty for a false alarm (additional tests when no cancer is present) only involves some added time and money on the part of the patient, whereas the penalty for a miss (not catching an instance of real cancer) might be the patient's death. Thus, the radiologist may set a criterion value that is quite low (lax), not wanting to miss any danger signals. This means she will have many hits and few misses, but also many false alarms, a situation shown in Figure 2–5A. Conversely, if the observer is a radar operator looking for blips on a screen signifying enemy missiles, he might be much more conservative. Here the penalty for a false alarm could be war, whereas the penalty for a miss might be only a few seconds lost in sounding the alarm. He would set a high (strict) criterion in order to avoid false alarms, but at the penalty of reducing the number of hits. This would be equivalent to the situation shown in Figure 2–5B. In this same manner, each point on any given ROC curve simply represents a different criterion setting.

Although we indicated that the location of the criterion alters the pattern of response, we did not mention the effect of criterion location on the sen-

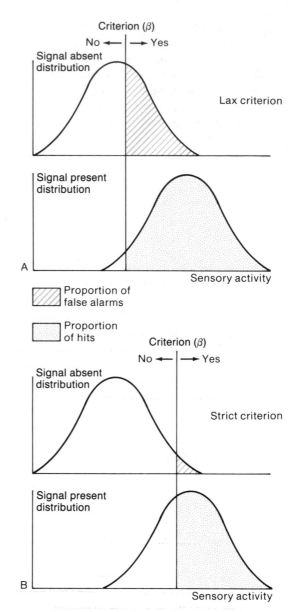

FIGURE 2–5   The effect of motives or expectations on criterion placement and proportion of hits and false alarms.

sitivity of the observer. That is because there is no such effect. In signal detection theory, sensitivity refers to the average amount of sensory activity generated by a given signal as compared with the average amount of noise-generated activity. This is similar to the everyday use of the word *sensitivity*. Thus, a radio receiver that produces a large electrical response that allows a weak signal to be heard above the background static is more sensitive than one that produces only a small electrical response to that signal, which may then be obscured by static and noise.

Within our present framework, the perceptual analog of sensitivity is the distance between the centers (means) of the signal absent and the signal present distributions. This is merely a measure of the difference in average sensation levels as a function of the presence or absence of a signal. We call this distance measure of sensitivity d' (see Figure 2–4). When the distributions are far apart, and overlap very little, as in Figure 2–6B, d' is large and the ROC curve is far from the diagonal and sharply curved. When the distributions are close together, and overlap to a great extent, d' is relatively small, as in Figure 2–6A. The corresponding ROC curve is close to the diagonal, which you may remember represents zero sensitivity. Signal detection theory attempts to measure an observer's sensitivity to a signal independently of his decision strategy, while acknowledging that both might affect the actual responses made in the experimental setting. Instructions for calculating d' and β using proportions of hits and false alarms obtained from any typical signal detection experiment (e.g., Tables 2–3 and 2–4) can be found in Computation Box 2–1.

This must seem like an unusually elaborate procedure for investigating a seemingly simple problem, namely, the determination of the minimal amount of energy necessary for stimulus detection. However, an observer is a living organism whose expectations and motives affect his or her perceptual behaviors and judgments nearly as much as stimulus reception itself does. These nonperceptual effects must be removed if we are to look at the pure sensory responses. Our original notion of an absolute threshold has proved to be too primitive. The detection threshold is simply a convenient statistically defined point. As an alternative we may

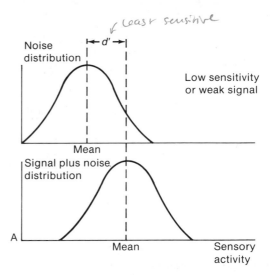

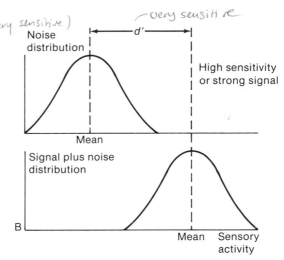

FIGURE 2–6   The effect of sensitivity and signal strength on d'.

use the d' measure, which provides an index of the observer's sensitivity to stimuli, instead of the traditional detection threshold measures.

IDENTIFICATION

The doctor listened very carefully, paused for a moment to adjust the stethoscope to a more comfortable position, and listened again to the sounds

COMPUTATION BOX 2-1   Calculating d' and β

To calculate d' and β, first obtain the outcome matrix from a signal detection experiment. Then find the false alarm rate from the outcome matrix in the HIT/FA column of the accompanying table. Read across the table to the Z column (Z is the usual label of the abscissa of the graph of the standard bell curve). Call the value tabled there Z(FA) and write it down. Repeat these operations for the hit rate, calling the tabled value Z(HIT) and writing it down. Be careful to record the sign of the tabled Z values—Z(HIT) will often be negative. Then to obtain d', plug Z(FA) and Z(HIT) into the following equation:

$$d' = Z(FA) - Z(HIT)$$

Remember that subtracting a negative number, if Z(HIT) happens to be negative, is equivalent to adding a positive number, i.e., $2 - (-3) = 5$. The value of β can be obtained similarly, except that you should use the ORD column (for *ordinate*, the height of the bell curve) to obtain the values of ORD(HIT) and ORD(FA), and then plug those numbers into the following equation:

$$\beta = ORD(HIT)/ORD(FA)$$

If the exact values of the hit or false alarm rate do not appear in the table, interpolate between the nearest surrounding values that do appear, or simply round the hit and false alarm rates to the closest number that does appear. Your answer shouldn't be too far from the exact value of d' or β

HIT/FA	Z	ORD	HIT/FA	Z	ORD
.01	2.33	0.03	.50	0.00	0.40
.02	2.05	0.05	.55	−0.12	0.40
.03	1.88	0.07	.60	−0.25	0.39
.04	1.75	0.09	.65	−0.38	0.37
.05	1.64	0.10	.70	−0.52	0.35
.08	1.40	0.15	.75	−0.67	0.32
.10	1.28	0.18	.80	−0.84	0.28
.13	1.13	0.21	.82	−0.92	0.26
.15	1.04	0.23	.85	−1.04	0.23
.18	0.92	0.26	.88	−1.18	0.20
.20	0.84	0.28	.90	−1.28	0.18
.25	0.67	0.32	.92	−1.40	0.15
.30	0.52	0.35	.95	−1.64	0.10
.35	0.38	0.37	.96	−1.75	0.09
.40	0.25	0.39	.97	−1.88	0.07
.45	0.12	0.40	.98	−2.05	0.05
.50	0.00	0.40	.99	−2.33	0.03

emanating from the patient's chest. The sounds were quite clear and distinct. The problem was simply to decide whether they indicated a normal or a pathological heartbeat. This doctor is wrestling with a problem that does not involve stimulus detection, for the sounds are clearly above the detection threshold. However, it does involve identifying one of a number of possible alternative stimuli. To identify a stimulus is one of the major tasks the perceptual system is asked to perform.

The difficulty of any identification task depends, in part, on the number of possible stimulus alternatives an observer is asked to distinguish among. Consider an observer who claims she can identify her favorite brand of cola. Suppose we gave her two unmarked glasses of cola and asked her to sample them and try to select her own favorite brand. If she did select the correct brand we would not be very surprised, since she would be expected to do so 50 percent of the time by chance alone, even if her taste buds were nonfunctional. If our "expert" selected her own brand out of 25 brands presented to her we would be much more likely to take her claim seriously, since the probability that she would by chance alone find her brand out of 25 alternatives is only 1/25. Measures of the difficulty of the identification task must therefore take into account the number of stimulus alternatives. STATS.

Information Theory

To solve the problem of specifying the difficulty of an identification task, psychologists in the early 1950s turned to ideas arising from the efforts of engineers to assess the performance of radio and telephone communications systems. Books by Shannon and Weaver (1949) and by Wiener (1961) made it clear that the problems faced by the psychophysicist and by the communications engineer were quite similar. The engineer deals with a message that is transmitted through a communication channel and decoded by someone or something at the receiver end. The degree to which the final decoded message reflects the original message depends, in part, on the ability of the system to transmit information without distortion (this is what is meant by the *fidelity* of a system), and on the complexity of the input. The psychophysicist has an analogous problem. Stimulus information is transmitted to an observer through a sensory system, and it is then decoded in the central nervous system. The degree to which the observer's identi-

fication of the stimulus corresponds to the actual stimulus input will be affected both by the ability of the sensory system to handle the stimulus input without distortion and by the complexity of the input.

The quantitative system for specifying the characteristics of the input message is known as **information theory.** Information theory is *not* really a theory at all, but rather a system of measurement. The amount of information in a given stimulus display is defined so that the nature of the object being measured is irrelevant. What, then, do we mean by *information?* We mean what the everyday use of the word implies. If you tell us that this week will contain a Sunday morning, you have conveyed very little information, since we know that every week contains a Sunday morning. If you tell us that this Sunday morning there will be a parade in honour of Jiffy the Kangaroo, you have conveyed a great deal of information because you have specified which one out of a large number of possible alternative events was about to occur.

One way to quantify information is to define it in terms of the questions a person must ask to discover which member of a stimulus set has occurred. Suppose we had only two possible alternatives, A or B, and you were to search for the target among them. You need only ask "Is it A?" to determine unambiguously which alternative had been selected as the target. If you receive an answer of "No" you know immediately that B is correct. Similarly, if you had to determine which of four stimuli, A, B, C, or D, had been chosen as the target, you could determine it with two questions. The answer to the question "Is it A or B?" reduces your number of possible alternatives to two, since a "No" answer reveals that it is either C or D, whereas a "Yes" indicates that it is A or B. We already know that only one more question is necessary in order to identify the correct item. Each necessary question, structured to eliminate exactly *half* of the alternatives, defines a **bit** of information. *Bit* is a contraction of the words *binary digit* (which can be either a 0 or a 1, that is, there are *two* possible digits).

Table 2-6. Log₂n for Selected Numbers

Number of stimulus alternatives (n)	Number of bits (log₂n)
2	1
4	2
8	3
16	4
32	5
64	6
128	7
256	8

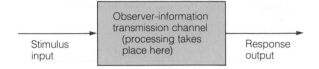

FIGURE 2–7   A human information channel.

The number of bits of information needed to determine exactly one stimulus alternative is the logarithm to the base 2 of the total number of possible stimulus alternatives. The logarithm of a number n to the base 2, which is written $\log_2 n$, is merely the power to which the number 2 must be raised to equal n. Thus, if we have four alternatives we must raise 2 to the second power (i.e., $2^2 = 2 \times 2 = 4$) and $\log_2 4 = 2$. Similarly, Table 2–6 gives the corresponding number of bits for n alternatives (a more detailed table can be found in Garner, 1962). Each time the number of stimulus alternatives is doubled the amount of information rises by 1 bit. Of course, for intermediate values the number of bits will not be a whole number (for example, seven alternatives gives 2.81 bits).

Channel Capacity

It is important at this point to define the concept of **information transmission.** Let us consider an observer as a channel, in the way communications engineers do. Our observer may be represented as in Figure 2–7. A stimulus is presented to the observer, who is asked to try to identify it. By identification we mean giving a response that is the correct, agreed-upon label for the particular stimulus presented. We can say that information is transmitted by the observer to the extent that the responses given match the actual labels of the stimuli presented. That is, if the observer correctly identifies a stimulus, and gives the correct label as a response, information (the correct label) has been transmitted from one end to the other, through the channel represented by the observer. If the response matches the stimulus perfectly for all stimuli, then the observer is a perfect information transmitter.

Consider an example in which we are calling out alphabetic letters from a set containing eight items: A, B, C, D, F, G, H, X. If the observer correctly identifies (response) the letter we have called out (stimulus) then she has transmitted 3 bits of information ($\log_2 8$). Suppose identification is not perfect. This means that only some of the stimulus information is being transmitted. Thus, if the observer hears a faint "eee" sound, with the first part of the letter cut off, she does not know exactly which letter was called out. However, she can eliminate A, F, H, and X, which have no "eee" sound; hence, she has reduced the number of stimulus alternatives by half, and we would say that 1 bit of information has been transmitted. In general, the greater the probability that the observer will identify the stimulus—that is, the more she "picks up" from the presentations—the more information she is capable of transmitting.

Consider a hypothetical experiment in which each of four stimuli are presented 12 times and observers are asked to identify which stimulus was presented. In Table 2–7, Observer A shows perfect information transmission because every time Stimulus 1 is presented our observer correctly identifies it, and every time 2 is presented it is named correctly. Observer B shows poorer information transmission. Notice here that when Stimulus 2 is

Table 2-7. **Stimulus-Response Matrices for Three Observers**

Observer A: Perfect information transmission

	Response			
Stimulus	1	2	3	4
1	12			
2		12		
3			12	
4				12

Observer B: Some information transmission

	Response			
Stimulus	1	2	3	4
1	8	4		
2	2	8	2	
3		2	8	2
4			4	8

Observer C: No information transmission

	Response			
Stimulus	1	2	3	4
1	3	3	3	3
2	3	3	3	3
3	3	3	3	3
4	3	3	3	3

presented, the observer calls it Stimulus 2 most of the time; but sometimes he calls it Stimulus 1 and sometimes he calls it Stimulus 3. When he does say that it is Stimulus 2, however, there is a fair likelihood that it is Stimulus 2. He is much better than Observer C, who seems to be responding without reference to the stimulus presented. Observer C is transmitting none of the available stimulus information. Formulas for computing the amount of in-

formation transmitted in such experiments may be found in Garner and Hake (1951).

How many bits of stimulus information can an observer transmit perfectly? Let us first look at a group of stimuli selected from a one-dimensional physical continuum, such as sound or light intensity. The number of stimuli from one continuum that a subject can identify perfectly has been found to be surprisingly small. For the judgment of the pitch of a tone, Pollack (1952) found it to be about 5 different pitches, which is equivalent to about 2.3 bits of stimulus information. Garner (1953) found much the same result for loudness, around 2.1 bits. Eriksen and Hake (1955) measured several visual continua and found information transmission to be limited to 2.34 bits for brightness, 2.84 bits for size, and 3.08 bits for hue. Overall, the number of stimuli that may be perfectly identified on any single continuum turns out to be approximately seven plus or minus two (7 ± 2), depending on the particular stimulus continuum being tested (see Miller, 1956).

This limit is called (again using communications theory terminology) the observer's **channel capacity,** and typical measurement of channel capacity is shown in Figure 2–8. Notice that even though we increase the amount of information available in the display, our subject has reached his limit of recognition (about 2.5 bits) and can transmit no more information.

Several theories have been proposed to explain this general finding. In the most popular of these, the limit reflects cognitive or response processes (e.g., Durlach & Braida, 1969; Gravetter & Lockhead, 1973; Luce, Green & Weber, 1976; Marley & Cook, 1984). A less popular view is that the limit is set by the response characteristics of sensory neurons, and is thus an absolute limit for a single sensory continuum (Norwich, 1981).

Seven seems to be a very small number of stimuli to be able to identify. Each of us knows that singers, for example, seem able to identify (indeed sing) hundreds of different songs. Every one of us can certainly identify dozens of faces and thou-

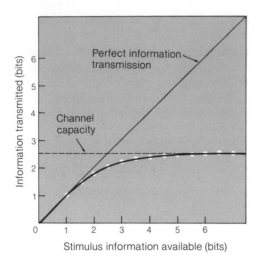

Information transmitted (bits) (y-axis)

Perfect information transmission

Channel capacity

Stimulus information available (bits) (x-axis)

FIGURE 2–8   Channel capacity. The straight diagonal represents perfect information transmission. The curve represents typical performance. The dotted horizontal line is channel capacity.

sands of words. How can this be, in light of our inability to transmit more than about 3 bits of information per stimulus dimension?

You might think that if the stimuli were more widely spaced and discriminable, channel capacity would be higher. The discriminability of stimuli, however, has very little effect on identification performance (Pollack, 1952). Another possible explanation is that our everyday performance is explained by practice or repetition. Except in extreme cases, where a person might have years of intensive practice on a single dimension, the practice effect is also not large enough to explain our everyday performance. For instance, you hear a new word today and now you can identify that word with ease, even though you have only encountered it once. You can also recognize that this word is different from every other word in your vocabulary. We are not at all surprised at such a performance, yet this type of identification may involve the transmission of some 16 bits of information (or more, depending on the total number of words in your vocabulary). Given that our channel

capacity is so limited for any single stimulus dimension, how can this occur? The answer involves the *number of dimensions* along which the stimulus varies.

For example, Pollack (1953) found that if he varied only pitch information transmission averaged about 1.8 bits, whereas if he varied only loudness information transmission was about 1.7 bits. When both dimensions were varied simultaneously, however, information transmission was 3.1 bits. This is more than was obtained for either dimension separately, although not the 3.5 bits expected if the information transmission on the separate dimensions were simply summed. Nonetheless, the more dimensions the stimulus varies along, the better recognition performance is. Certain ways of combining dimensions seem to produce better performance, by making stimuli "stand out" more clearly, or capitalizing on the small gains obtainable by familiarity (Lockhead, 1970; Monahan & Lockhead, 1977). Thus, by proper selection of stimulus dimensions, Anderson and Fitts (1958) were able to obtain information transmission levels of 17 bits on a single flashed stimulus. This means that their observers could perfectly identify 1 stimulus out of more than 131,000 alternative stimuli!

The importance of stimulus dimensions and how they are combined has led modern investigators to place less emphasis on the *quantity* of information available and more emphasis on the *quality,* or kind, of information and the characteristics of the information processor (see Cutting, 1987; Garner, 1974; Neisser, 1967). The basic ideas of information theory, especially those associated with the number of stimulus alternatives, have been important in calling attention to critical issues in identification. They have taken their place as foundation concepts, almost assumptions, and modern researchers build on them rather than study them for their own sake (although see Norwich, 1981, 1984, 1987). Chapter 11 considers some of these modern extensions of and alternatives to information theory in the study of object identification.

DISCRIMINATION

The artist glances at his model's hair and then back down at the paint on his palette. He mutters to himself, "Still not the same." He daubs a bit more black, mixes the color through, and glances up again. "That is a perfect match," he grunts. This artist is engaging in an act of discrimination. He is determining whether two colors are the same or different. He does not care what the color actually is, it can be burnt sienna or just plain brown, he cares only whether or not the paint matches his model's hair color. Discrimination problems ask the question, "Is this stimulus different from that one?"

The study of discrimination has focused on the question, "By how much must two stimuli differ in order to be discriminated as not the same?" Suppose the melody "Oh! Susanna" were played on a piano once in the key of C and once in the key of G. Are these two musical stimuli the same or different? The answer to this question depends on the stimulus dimension being judged. If we are judging whether the melodies are the same or not we would answer differently than if we were judging the key in which the melodies are played.

To avoid such confusions, the standard discrimination experiment involves variation of stimuli along only one dimension. Thus, in a study of the discrimination of weights we might hold the size and shape of our stimuli constant and vary only the weight. In the earlier studies, observers were presented with pairs of stimuli and asked to make the response "heavier," "lighter," or "same," or some similar set of judgments appropriate to the stimulus dimension being judged. One of these stimuli was designated the **standard.** This is a stimulus that appears on every trial and is compared to a graded set of similar stimuli differing along the dimension being studied. These graded stimuli make up the set of **comparison stimuli.** This is simply a variant of the method of constant stimuli (which, you may remember, is used to determine the absolute threshold) to which we add the standard. We are also measuring a threshold here, only this is a threshold for the perception of a difference between the standard and the other stimuli. It is called a **difference threshold.**

As psychophysicists worked with the measurement of difference thresholds for various stimulus dimensions, it became clear that the "same" response category was being used by observers whenever they were unsure or unwilling to state that there was a perceptible difference. Experimenters soon resorted to using only two response alternatives instead of three. For example, in a weight judgment experiment, the observer would only be permitted to respond that the comparison stimulus is either "heavier" or "lighter." If he feels that the comparison and the standard are the same, he is still forced to indicate (by guessing) in which direction they appear to differ. The advantage of this procedure was demonstrated by the painstaking work of Brown (1910). He showed that in a weight judgment experiment, stimulus differences as small as 0.2 gram (which is about 0.008 ounce) produced more correct than incorrect judgments, even when the observer felt that the stimuli were the same and that he was merely guessing.

The results from such an experiment are easy to display. In the weight judgment experiment, for instance, the standard was presented with each comparison stimulus many times. We can plot the proportion of the presentations on which any given stimulus was judged heavier than the standard. Such a plot is illustrated in Figure 2–9. This plot is similar to results from the classic experiment on weight judgment by Brown (1910). He used a 100-g standard and a set of comparison weights ranging from 82 to 118 g in 1-g steps. Each comparison stimulus was judged 700 times against the standard stimulus. Notice that the shift from reports of "lighter" to reports of "heavier" is not very abrupt, as it would be if the threshold were always a single, unique value. Rather, we find a gradual change in the probability of a "heavier" response as the stimulus changes from much lighter than the standard to much heavier. Since the change is grad-

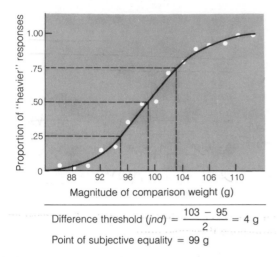

Difference threshold (*jnd*) = $\dfrac{103 - 95}{2}$ = 4 g

Point of subjective equality = 99 g

FIGURE 2–9   Typical data from the method of constant stimuli in discrimination with calculations of difference threshold *(jnd)* and point of subjective equality.

ual, we again must make some decision regarding how we will define the difference threshold.

Clearly, the point where *p* (heavier) is equal to 0.5—that is, where the stimulus was called "lighter" 50 percent of the time and "heavier" 50 percent of the time—is not appropriate. This 50-percent point probably represents the stimulus that appeared most like the standard, since the choices are evenly divided on either side of it. Therefore, it has been called the **point of subjective equality.** The lightest stimulus for which *p* (heavier) is equal to 1.0 represents perfect discrimination (because here a physically heavier stimulus is judged heavier 100 percent of the time). The stimulus where *p* (heavier) is equal to 0.5 represents no perception of difference. Therefore, the point where *p* (heavier) is equal to 0.75 (halfway between these values) represents a value where the *difference* is noted 50 percent of the time. Following similar reasoning, *p* (heavier) equal to 0.25 is the point at which a stimulus difference in the lighter direction is noted 50 percent of the time. By convention, we take the interval from the 0.25 point to the 0.75 point, called the **interval of uncertainty,** and divide it by

2 to give us a value that we call the **just noticeable difference,** or ***jnd***. The *jnd* computed for the data in Figure 2–9 is about 4 g. This means that when a pair of stimuli are separated by 4 g, the subject will be able to detect the difference between them about half the time. You can probably see that the *jnd* is simply the average of the threshold for "greater than" and the threshold for "less than." In other words, it represents the threshold for "different" averaged across the direction of the differences.

If discrimination were good, we would expect very small differences between stimuli to be noticed. This corresponds to a small *jnd*. In Figure 2–10 the black line shows a good discriminator with a *jnd* of 0.5 units, whereas the white line shows a poor discriminator with a *jnd* of 2 units. As the *jnd* increases in size and discrimination ability decreases, the curve begins to flatten. The extreme of no discrimination at all would be represented by a horizontal line parallel to the abscissa at *p* (heavier) equal to 0.5.

You may have noticed an interesting aspect of the data pictured in Figure 2–9. The point of subjective equality is not equal to the standard in these data. The stimulus that *appears* to be equal to the standard of 100 g is actually 1 g lighter. This is a

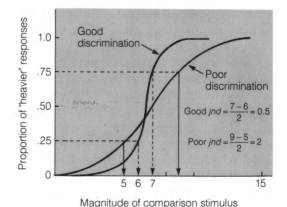

FIGURE 2–10   Difference thresholds *(jnds)* for observers of different sensitivity.

typical result in many psychophysical experiments involving the presentation of stimuli that are separated in time. The stimulus presented first (generally the standard) is judged to be less intense than the later stimulus. This effect has been named the **negative time error.** It is negative because the standard is judged as less intense than it should be. Fechner (1860/1966) and Wolfgang Kohler (1923) thought this error was caused by the fading of the image or the memory trace of the sensation of the standard with the passage of time. However, work done with auditory stimuli has shown that with proper selection of a time interval the error can be positive rather than negative (Kohler, 1923). Such errors are probably the result of particular cognitive or judgmental factors closely related to the adaptation level (see later), which, as we have seen before, tend to influence even the most apparently simple perceptual tasks (Hellstrom, 1979, 1985).

Weber's Law

Is the *jnd* a fixed value for any given sense modality, or does it vary as a function of the nature of the stimulus input or the state of the observer? Following the lead of Ernst Heinrich Weber (1834), Fechner (1860/1966) conducted an experiment in which he measured the *jnd*s for lifted weights using standard weights of different magnitudes. We may plot the size of the *jnd*, that is, the amount by which we must increase the stimulus so that it is discriminable as different from the standard 50 percent of the time, against the magnitude of the standard. This has been done for some illustrative data in Figure 2–11. First, notice that the *jnd* is not a constant value. It appears to increase in a linear fashion with the size of the standard. In other words, as the stimulus magnitude increases so does the size of the change needed for discrimination to occur. The intuitive force of this relationship is well illustrated in an example proposed by Galanter (1962): "If in a room with ten candles you had to add one more in order to detect an increase in illumination, then if the room contained one hundred

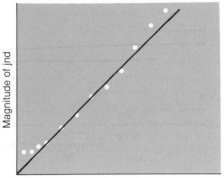

FIGURE 2–11   Effect of intensity of standard on difference threshold *(jnd)*.

it would be necessary to add ten candles in order to detect the same apparent increase in illumination" (p. 133). This relation between the size of the *jnd* and the size of the standard intensity is called **Weber's law** after its discoverer.

Weber's law is simply written as

$$\Delta I = KI$$

where ΔI is the size of the *jnd*, I is the intensity of the standard stimulus, and K is a constant. The constant K is always a fraction and is equal to $\Delta I / I$. It indicates the proportion by which the standard stimulus must be increased in order to detect a change. This fractional value is called the **Weber fraction.** Thus, if the Weber fraction is 0.02, it means that we must increase the intensity of a stimulus by 2 percent for a difference between it and the original stimulus to be detected. This proportion (the Weber fraction) is the same regardless of the intensity of the standard stimulus. In a weight judgment experiment, for example, to discriminate a stimulus as different from a 2-g standard the weight must be increased by only 0.04 g (2 × 0.02 = 0.04). To discriminate a stimulus as different from a 200-g standard, it must be increased by 4 g (200 × 0.02 = 4). A simple demonstration of Weber's law is given in Demonstration Box 2–2.

DEMONSTRATION BOX 2-2.   Weber's Law

It is easy to demonstrate Weber's law for the perception of heaviness. You will need three quarters, two envelopes, and your shoes. Take one quarter and put it in an envelope and put the remaining two quarters in the other. If you now lift each envelope gently and put it down (use the same hand), it is quite easy to distinguish the heavier envelope. Now insert one envelope into one of your shoes and the other envelope into your second shoe, and lift them one at a time.

The weight difference should be almost imperceptible. In the first instance the targets differed by the weight of the quarter and the difference was discriminated easily. In the second instance, although the weight differential was the same (one quarter), the overall stimulus intensity was greater because shoes weigh much more than the envelopes and the quarters alone.

Conceptually, consider the Weber fraction to be a measure of the overall sensitivity of a sensory system to differences along a stimulus continuum. The larger the Weber fraction, the larger will be the *jnd*s for any stimulus dimension, hence the larger the change needed for discrimination. Note that K has no units (such as grams), so that it does not depend on the physical units used to measure I and ΔI. Thus, we can compare Weber fractions across different stimulus dimensions without having to worry about how the stimulus values were measured. The Weber fraction simply represents the average ratio of *jnd* size to the size of the standard level at which the *jnd* was measured, over an entire range of standard values. Table 2–8 presents typical Weber fractions for a variety of continua. As you can see, some of the Ks are relatively large (for example, those for brightness and loudness), and some are quite small (for example, electric shock).

How well does Weber's law fit the data? For many years there was considerable argument about this issue. Measurements were taken in many sense modalities to check the relation. The clearest picture of the results is given by plotting the value of the Weber fraction, $\Delta I/I$, against the standard stimulus intensity. If the Weber fraction is actually constant, we should see a horizontal line, parallel to the abscissa. Figure 2–12 shows a composite of

Table 2-8.   Typical Weber Fractions ($\Delta I/I$) (Based on Teghtsoonian, 1971)

Continuum	Weber fraction
Brightness	0.079
Loudness	0.048
Finger span	0.022
Heaviness	0.020
Line length	0.029
Taste (salt)	0.083
Electric shock	0.013
Vibration (fingertip)	
60 Hz	0.036
125 Hz	0.046
250 Hz	0.046

data from loudness discrimination experiments by Miller (1947) and Riesz (1928), and we see a considerable deviation from the expected constancy at both extremes. Although these deviations at the extremes look very large, this is only because we have plotted the stimuli in logarithmic units. The flat part of the curve actually exceeds 99 percent of the total range of intensities used. Thus, Weber's law is a useful summary in spite of the deviation of the data from a perfect fit. Moreover, even the deviations are beginning to be understood (see Green 1976; Norwich, 1987).

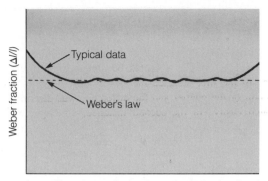

Weber fraction (ΔI/I)

Typical data

Weber's law

Logarithm of magnitude of standard stimulus (log *I*)

FIGURE 2–12   **Typical data for test of Weber's law. The dotted line is predicted by Weber's law:** $\Delta I / I = K.$

Signal Detection Theory in Discrimination

Although signal detection theory was presented (and first developed) in the context of the detection problem, it can be extended to the discrimination situation. Certainly there are decisional components that influence whether or not an observer discriminates a difference between two stimuli. To use the signal detection procedure to assess discrimination, we must redesign the method of constant stimuli experiment so that the observer is asked to say which of two very similar stimuli was actually presented on a given trial. This is like an identification experiment with only two stimuli.

The signal detection analysis of this experiment is quite similar to that used for detection. Instead of trying to ascertain whether the sensation experienced on a given trial came from the signal present or the signal absent distribution, the observer must decide whether it is from the Signal 1 or the Signal 2 distribution. If the stimuli were very similar the sensory response curves would overlap when plotted on the same set of axes, and an observer would be faced with a situation very similar to that faced by the observer in the absolute detection situation. Look back at Figure 2–4 and men-

tally relabel the two distributions *Signal 1* and *Signal 2*. Two stimuli can give rise to a variety of different sensation levels, with different probabilities. Since the curves cover the same general area of the sensation axis, there is no way to be certain which stimulus elicited a given sensation level on any one trial. The best the ideal observer can do is to place a criterion somewhere on the sensation axis, and simply determine whether the sensation level experienced is above or below that criterion. If above, the appropriate response would be that the presented stimulus was a 2; if below, a 1. Just as in the absolute detection situation, where the observer places the criterion will greatly affect the proportions of different responses he gives. In turn, criterion placement will be affected by the observer's expectations as to the relative frequency of presentation of the two stimuli, and the observer's present motivational biases.

As in the detection experiment, different criterion placements will define an isosensitivity curve when we plot the proportion of hits against the proportion of false alarms. The measure of sensitivity to the difference between the two stimuli is still called d' and is still unaffected by changes in the criterion. Actually, d' is determined by the physical difference between the two stimuli and the sensitivity of the observer's sensory system; both are factors that determine the difference between the average levels of sensation evoked by the stimuli. Thus, d' represents a measure of just how discriminable two very similar stimuli are. As such, it is closely related to the difference threshold and to the Weber fraction (Treisman, 1976; Treisman & Watts, 1966).

Reaction Time

We have been looking at stimuli that are difficult to discriminate correctly. Even when we are working with stimuli well above the difference threshold, we may feel that some discriminations are easier to make than others. Red is more easily differentiated from green than from orange. When we are working with sets of stimuli that exceed the difference threshold, the frequency methods we have used up to this point are too crude to measure interstimulus differences in detectability or discriminability. To provide a more sensitive measure we must turn to one of the oldest techniques in sensory psychology: **reaction time.** Reaction time is defined as the time between the onset of a stimulus and the beginning of an overt response. It was first introduced in 1850 by one of the early giants in perception and physiology, Hermann von Helmholtz, who used it as a crude measure of the speed of neural conduction in a limb.

There are two varieties of reaction time. **Simple reaction time** involves pressing or releasing a telegraph key (or making some other simple stereotyped response) immediately on detecting a stimulus. **Choice reaction time** involves making one of several responses depending on the stimulus presented (for example, press the right-hand key for a red stimulus and the left-hand for a green). Simple reaction times are generally used in detection paradigms. We have known for a long time that the more intense a stimulus, the faster the reaction time. Figure 2–13 shows typical median reaction times to the onset of a tone plotted against the stimulus intensity (Chocolle, 1940). When the stimulus intensity is low and near the detection threshold (although it is still quite detectable), the reaction times are longer. Thus, when the stimulus is more difficult to apprehend, reaction time is longer. Similar results have been obtained for visual stimuli (Cattell, 1886; Grice, Nullmeyer & Schnizlein, 1979). Simple reaction time has also been used to measure discrimination. Here, however, observers had to detect a change in stimulus intensity. Here we find that the larger the change in the stimulus intensity (either an increase or a decrease), the shorter the reaction time (Welford, 1980).

Choice reaction time has been used in studies of discrimination and identification. These reaction times tend to be somewhat longer than simple re-

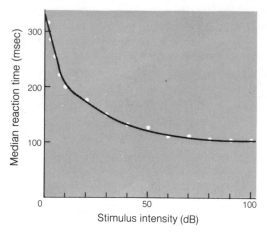

FIGURE 2–13 Effect of stimulus intensity on simple reaction time. (Based on Chocolle, 1940)

action times (Posner, 1978). The classic discrimination experiment utilizing reaction time was done by Henmon (1906). In this experiment the observer had two response keys—one for each hand. In one instance, the observer was presented with pairs of lines differing only in length and told to depress the key corresponding to the side on which the line was longer. Henmon found that the greater the difference between the line lengths the shorter the reaction time. He reported similar results for colors and tones.

A striking example of the relationship between choice reaction time and the discriminability of stimuli utilized a slightly different technique. In an experiment by Shallice and Vickers (1964), observers were required to sort decks of cards into piles according to which of two lines on the cards appeared longer. The time it took to sort the cards was the measure of reaction time. This measure is, of course, the sum of a number of reaction times, where we consider the sorting of each card as a single response. The standard stimulus in this experiment was a 4.5-cm line. In the data shown in Table 2–9, we see that the more difficult the dis-

Table 2-9. Differences in Reaction Time as a Function of Differences in Line Lengths Measured via Card Sorts (Based on Shallice & Vickers, 1964)

Difference in length (cm)	Sorting time (sec)
1.1	39.4
0.9	40.0
0.7	40.1
0.5	41.0
0.4	42.0
0.3	42.9
0.2	46.5
0.1	52.4

Table 2-10. Reaction Time as a Function of Number of Stimulus Alternatives (Based on Merkel, 1885)

Number of alternatives	Reaction time (msec)
1	187
2	316
3	364
4	434
5	487
6	534
7	570
8	603
9	619
10	632

crimination, the longer the sorting time. A simple demonstration of this effect is given in Demonstration Box 2–3.

Crossman (1953) has shown that these reaction time differences are related both to the discriminability of the stimuli and to the amount of information they contain. We are referring to information in the technical sense discussed in the section on identification. If this is the case, then we would expect choice reaction times to increase as

we increase the number of response alternatives, and indeed, this result has been known for many years. Merkel (1885) showed with number stimuli that the reaction time increased as the number of response alternatives increased. The data in Table 2–10 show this clearly.

Hick (1952) attempted to explain these results by postulating that the observer extracts information from the stimulus display at a constant rate (cf.

DEMONSTRATION BOX 2-3.   Reaction Time and Stimulus Discriminability

Take a deck of common playing cards and select out of it 10 of the picture cards (Kings, Queens, and Jacks) and 10 numbered cards from the red suits (hearts and diamonds) to make a new deck of 20 cards. Compose another deck of 20 by using the numbered cards (include the Aces) of the black suits (clubs and spades). Shuffle each deck separately and place it in front of you, face down. Next you need a clock or a watch with a sweep second hand. Wait until the second hand reaches the 12, pick up one of

the decks and begin to sort it into two piles. The first deck gets sorted into number and picture cards; the second gets sorted into spades and clubs. Note the time it takes to sort each deck. You may want to repeat the task a couple of times so that you are sorting smoothly. Notice that the sorting time for the spades and clubs (a more difficult task since it involves making small form discriminations on similarly colored cards) is longer than the easier discrimination task of sorting picture and number cards.

DEMONSTRATION BOX 2-4.   Number of Stimulus Alternatives and Reaction Time

Take a deck of playing cards and separate 16 cards using only the low numbers Ace, 2, 3, and 4. Next, make up another deck of 16 cards using 2 each of the 5, 6, 7, 8, 9, 10, Jack, and Queen. Now shuffle each deck. Measure the time it takes to sort each deck into piles by number (4 piles for the first and 8 for the second deck) using a watch or clock with a sweep second hand as you did in Demonstration Box 2-3. Notice that the reaction time becomes longer (measured by sorting time) as the number of alternative stimuli that must be recognized and responded to becomes greater. Thus, sorting the 4-stimulus deck is more rapid than sorting the 8-stimulus deck.

Norwich, 1981), so the more information that must be obtained from the display, the longer the reaction time. In an experimental situation where a display of lights served as stimuli and finger pressings of telegraph keys served as responses, he found a linear function relating reaction time and the logarithm of the number of stimulus alternatives. This relation, called **Hick's law,** states that choice reaction time is a linear function of the amount of information in the stimulus. You may demonstrate effects of the number of stimulus alternatives on reaction time by consulting Demonstration Box 2–4.

SCALING

The dog trainer glanced at her new St. Bernard pupil and estimated his shoulder height to be 75 cm and his weight to be 80 kg. In so doing she was actually engaged in the perceptual act called *scaling*. Scaling attempts to answer the question, "How much of *X* is there?" *X* can be a stimulus magnitude, a sensation magnitude, or the magnitude of such other complex psychological variables as similarity or even pleasantness.

To begin with, a *scale* is a rule by which we assign numbers to objects or events. The scale attempts to represent numerically some property of objects or events (see Michell, 1986). A variety of different types of representations may be established, and each has its own characteristics (see Luce & Narens, 1987; Narens & Luce, 1986; Stevens, 1946). The most primitive and unrestricted type of scale is a **nominal scale.** Its etymology specifies its nature, since *nomin* is derived from the Latin word for "name." When numbers are assigned in a nominal scale, they serve only as identity codes or surrogate names. The numbers imply nothing more about the quantity of some property than do the numbers on football jerseys.

Whenever we are dealing with something for which it is possible to say that an object or event contains more or less of the property than some other object or event, we can create an **ordinal scale** of that property. An ordinal scale simply ranks items on the basis of some quantity. An example might be the "Best-Seller" or "Top Fifty" lists that order books or records on the basis of how many have been sold. It is clear that although this scale may prove to be more useful for measurement than a nominal scale, we are still very restricted in what we can do with the numbers.

The third type of scale is the **interval scale.** It not only answers the questions implied by the labels *more* or *less* but also tells *by how much*. It employs not only the sequential properties of numbers but also their spacing, or the *intervals* between them. A good example of an interval scale is the scale of temperature represented by the common household thermometer. Here the size of the difference between 10 deg and 20 deg C (50 deg and 68 deg F) is exactly the same as between 40 deg and 50 deg C (104 deg and 122 deg F). Such scales are very useful, since most statistical techniques can be meaningfully applied to interval scale values. Interval scales suffer from one major drawback, however. They do not have a *true* zero point; rather, convenience or convention usually dictates where the zero will be. Thus, in the centigrade scale of temperature, the zero point is the freezing point of pure water.

The most numerically powerful scale in general use is the **ratio scale.** Creation of this type of scale is possible only when equality, rank order, equality of intervals and of ratios, and a true zero point can be experimentally determined. Unfortunately, ratio scales are more often found in the physical than in the behavioral sciences. Such things as mass, density, and length can be measured on ratio scales since the zero points are not arbitrary. For example, 0 g represents the complete absence of mass, and we can meaningfully say that 10 g is twice as massive as 5 g. Negative values of mass exist only in the fantasies of dieters.

All sensory qualities cannot be scaled in the same way. Some perceptual experiences have an underlying aspect of intensity (for instance, brightness), whereas others do not (such as hue). When we are dealing with a stimulus or an experience in which it makes sense to ask "How much?" or "How intense?" we have a **prothetic continuum** (Stevens & Galanter, 1957). On prothetic continua changes from one level of sensation to another come about by adding or subtracting from what is present. Thus, when we increase the weight of a stimulus, the corresponding psychological sensation of 'heaviness" increases. Such prothetic continua can be meaningfully measured on scales of any of the types we have discussed (with the possible exception of a ratio scale—this is still controversial). In the other type of sensory continuum, changes in the physical stimulus result in a change in the apparent quality rather than the apparent quantity of a stimulus. When we have a stimulus or experience in which the only question it makes sense to ask is "What kind?" we are dealing with a **metathetic continuum.** Thus, a change in the wavelength of a light may cause its appearance to change from red to green. There seems to be no quantitative difference between these two hues, they just appear to be different. Occasionally both types of continua will be present in the same sense impressions. For instance, in touch, the amount of pressure applied is a prothetic continuum, but the location of the touch is a metathetic continuum. Metathetic continua can be dealt with using nominal scales, but scales that imply order have generally not been successfully applied to such sensory qualities (but see Schneider & Bissett, 1981).

Indirect Scaling: Fechner's Law

When the perceptual investigator wishes to establish a sensory scale for which numbers will be assigned to the intensity of sensations, there are two alternative approaches. The first is a **direct scaling** procedure in which individuals are asked to assess directly some aspect of the strength of the sensation. Although this might be the easiest procedure, it is often difficult for the untrained observer. In addition, many early psychologists distrusted the accuracy of such direct reports because there seemed to be no easy way to convert them to numerical values. For this reason **indirect scaling** methods, based on discrimination ability, formed the basis for the first psychological scales. It must not be thought that using an indirect procedure is necessarily bad. After all, we measure temperature indirectly, using the height of a column of mercury as our indicator.

The first person to attempt to describe the relationship between stimulus intensity and sensation intensity was Gustav Theodor Fechner. To do this, he had to invent a way to measure the quantity of the sensory experience. As his starting point, he assumed that Weber's law was correct; as we have seen, it does hold over a wide range of stimuli. His next assumption engendered a good deal of controversy and experimental testing. Fechner assumed that the subjective impression of the difference between two stimuli separated by one *just noticeable difference* was the same regardless of the absolute magnitude of the two stimuli. Thus, if we take two dim lights that are separated by 1 *jnd* and we take two lights that are 30 or 40 times brighter, but again separated from each other by 1 *jnd,* we should perceive the two pairs of stimuli as differing by equal sensory steps. Finally, Fechner assumed that sensation differences could be represented by adding or subtracting *jnds.*

If we accept Fechner's postulate that Weber's law is true and that the subjective sizes of all *jnd*s are the same, then only a *small physical* change is necessary to achieve a 1-*jnd* change for a weak stimulus, whereas a *large* change is needed for a 1-*jnd* change when the physical stimulus is intense. Perceptually, this means that the intensity of the sensation grows rapidly for weak physical stimuli and more slowly as the physical stimulus is made more intense. The relationship between the intensity of the sensation and the intensity of the physical stimulus is shown in Figure 2–14. This curve is described by the equation,

jnd's above threshold

$$S = W \log I$$

where *S* is the magnitude of sensation a stimulus elicits, *I* is the physical magnitude of the stimulus (units above the absolute threshold stimulus magnitude), and *W* is a constant that depends on the value of the Weber fraction ($\Delta I/I$). This equation is called **Fechner's law.** The actual mathematical procedures by which Fechner derived this relationship are discussed by Falmagne (1974, 1985) and Baird and Noma (1978), among others. We are using the number of *jnd*s above the absolute threshold as a measure of the strength of the sensation generated by a given stimulus (*S*), and we are saying that the equation above relates this number to the

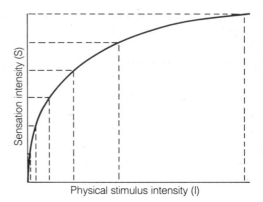

FIGURE 2–14   Fechner's law. It takes larger and larger differences between stimuli (*I*s) as stimulus intensity increases to give rise to the same size differences between sensations (*S*s).

physical intensity of the stimulus (*I*). The constant *W* is different for different sensory continua, since it depends on the value of the Weber fraction for the continuum scaled. Remember that this is an indirect scale since the strength of the sensation is never directly measured. To create this scale the only thing that must be measured is the size of the *jnd*. Once that has been determined, the rest is easy, and requires only counting *jnd*s. Fechner's technique was to use this aspect of the discriminability of stimuli (the *jnd*) as the unit of measurement of the intensity of an observer's sensory impression.

Direct Scaling

Since Fechner's time, many psychophysicists have insisted that indirect scaling is neither necessary nor preferable. Because we are interested in the *apparent* intensity of a stimulus to an observer, why not simply require judgments based on how intense a stimulus *seems* to be? The observer's responses could then be used directly to establish a scale of measurement. The first attempt to do this was in 1872 by one of Fechner's contemporaries, a Belgian investigator named Plateau. To test Fechner's law he had eight artists mix a gray that was half-way between a particular black and a white. Notice that this requires direct relative judgments of three stimuli, black, white, and gray. Fechner's law predicts that this psychological midpoint should correspond to the average of the logarithm of the physical intensity of the black stimulus and that of the white stimulus. Unfortunately, the results, although somewhat similar to the prediction, did not fully support Fechner's law. Rather, the grays mixed by Plateau's artists seemed to fall halfway between the cube roots (1/3 power) of the intensities of the black and the white stimuli. This numerical discrepancy suggests that Fechner's law may only be an approximation to the relationship between physical and sensory intensity. We care about such mathematical deviations because a major purpose of scaling is to make possible a precise description of the relationship between the strength of the physical stimulus and the strength of sensations.

Category Judgment

Sanford was among the early investigators who attempted to measure sensation directly. As early as 1898, he had worked out a technique that involved having observers judge a number of envelopes, each of which contained different weights. The subjects were instructed to sort the weights into five categories. Category 1 was to be used for the lightest weights and Category 5 for the heaviest, with the remaining weights distributed in the other categories in such a way that the intervals between the category boundaries would be subjectively equal. Thus, the difference in sensation between the upper and the lower boundaries of Category 1 should be the same as that for Category 2. In other words, all categories should be the same size. This method has been called **category scaling** or **equal–interval scaling.** There is a similarity between this method and an identification task, except that in category scaling we usually have fewer categories than stim-

uli. Also, of course, there is no such thing as a correct or an incorrect answer, since the very nature of the experiment implies that we cannot know in advance what a correct category assignment might be.

If our observer has spaced the category boundaries equally in terms of the magnitudes of the sensory differences between them, we can, without making any other assumptions, mark off equal category intervals (to represent the midpoints of the categories) along the ordinate of a graph and label them with the category names. On this graph we can plot the average category label assigned to each stimulus intensity over several trials. The curve obtained for typical data (Figure 2–15) is concave downward and closely approximates the curve predicted by Fechner's law (Figure 2–14). The fact that we can predict the shape of the category scale from simple discrimination data is quite an impressive feat. To Sanford it seemed to provide support for the contention that a logarithmic relationship exists between physical stimulus intensity and perceived magnitude.

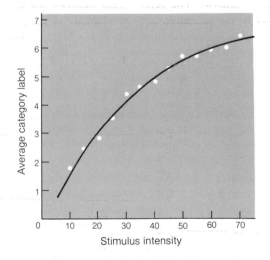

FIGURE 2–15   Some typical data from a category judgment experiment. The dots represent average category judgments of the various stimulus intensities.

Since Sanford's work, category scaling has been studied in great detail. Category scales have been found to be relatively stable over several different manipulations, including the labels applied to the categories (numbers versus words) and the number of categories used (Stevens & Galanter, 1957). Other variations in procedure, however, dramatically affect the form of the scale. For example, how the stimuli presented are spaced along the physical intensity dimension (Carter & Hirsch, 1955) and how often the various stimuli are presented (Parducci, 1965) both affect the relation of the category scale to the stimulus values on physical scales. Also, the range of stimulus intensities presented is important (Parducci, 1965), and the category judgments themselves are affected by the memories of previous stimuli and responses (Ward, 1972, 1987). Several theories have been presented that describe in detail the various factors that affect where subjects locate their category boundaries (for example, Kornbrot, 1984; Treisman & Williams, 1984) and how this affects the resulting scales. These biases indicate that we should use caution in interpreting scales of measurement formed from category judgments, although some authors argue that they are nonetheless the best type of scales to use (e.g., Anderson, 1970).

Magnitude Estimation: Stevens's Law

Although in category judgments observers are directly responding to variations in stimulus magnitude, there is still some "indirectness" involved. Stimuli that are similar but still discriminably different from one another may be grouped into the same category. Also, responses are limited to a few category labels. S. S. Stevens popularized a procedure called **magnitude estimation** that avoids these problems. The method is so simple and direct that one wonders why it had to be "invented" at all. In this procedure, observers are simply asked to assign numbers to stimuli on the basis of how intense they appear to be. Stimuli are usually judged one at a time and the only restriction on responses is that only numbers larger than zero can be used.

In a typical magnitude estimation experiment, in which we wish to scale the apparent length of lines, we would start by showing a *standard stimulus*. We might then say: "This stimulus has a value of 10. You will be presented with several stimuli that differ in length. Your task is to assign numbers to these other stimuli in relation to the one with a value of 10. Thus, if you see a line that appears to be twice as long as that one, you should assign to it the number 20. If you see a line one-fifth as long, you should assign to it the number 2. You may use any numbers you choose as long as they are larger than zero." In this task the number assigned to the standard stimulus is called the **modulus.** It serves to keep the numerical estimates of different observers within the same general range of values. As you can see, this is a very direct way to attempt to measure sensation. The very nature of the task (where a stimulus judged to be *m* times larger than the standard is given a number *m* times as large) implies that the resultant scale might be a ratio scale. There is, however, continuing debate on this point.

Stevens fully expected the results of such experiments to confirm Fechner's law. When he plotted the data from an experiment in the magnitude estimation of loudness (Stevens, 1956), however, he found that the graph differed from what Fechner's law had led him to expect. The equation he found that best described the relationship of the median magnitude estimates to the stimulus intensities was

$$L = aI^{0.6}$$

where L is the subjective loudness obtained through the observer's magnitude estimates, a is a constant, I is the physical intensity of the sound, and 0.6 is a power to which I is raised. In succeeding years, Stevens and a host of others produced magnitude

Table 2-11.   Representative Exponents of the Power Functions Relating Sensation Magnitude to Stimulus Magnitude (Based on Stevens, 1961)

Continuum	Exponent	Stimulus conditions
Loudness	0.6	Both ears
Brightness	0.33	5° target—dark
Brightness	0.5	Point source—dark
Lightness	1.2	Gray papers
Smell	0.55	Coffee odor
Taste	0.8	Saccharine
Taste	1.3	Sucrose
Taste	1.3	Salt
Temperature	1.0	Cold—on arm
Temperature	1.6	Warmth—on arm
Vibration	0.95	60 Hz—on finger
Duration	1.1	White noise stimulus
Finger span	1.3	Thickness of wood blocks
Pressure on palm	1.1	Static force on skin
Heaviness	1.45	Lifted weights
Force of handgrip	1.7	Precision hand dynamometer
Electric shock	3.5	60 Hz—through fingers

estimation scales for a multitude of sensory continua. All these scales seemed to be related to the physical stimulus intensities by the general relationship

$$S = aI^n$$

where S is the sensory intensity and n is a characteristic exponent that differs for different sensory continua. Since this relation states that the magnitude of the sensation is simply the intensity of the physical stimulus raised to some power, this relationship is often called the **power law** or, after its popularizer, **Stevens's law.**

In the power law the magnitude of the sensation change, given a change in stimulus intensity, depends on the size of the exponent. In general, the exponent for any one continuum is quite stable. As long as the experimental situation is kept reasonably standard, and the same measures of physical stimulus intensity are used (Myers, 1982), the average exponents produced by different groups of observers for the same continuum are quite similar. Some of them are small fractions (0.3 for brightness), some are close to 1 (for line length), and others are quite large (3.5 for electric shock). Some typical exponents are given in Table 2–11.

If we plot some of the relationships between judged sensory intensity and physical stimulus intensity, we find that the curves for power functions with different exponents (n) have dramatically different shapes. This can be seen in Figure 2–16. With exponents of less than 1 (for example, brightness), the curves are concave downward, meaning that as the stimulus becomes more intense, greater stimulus changes are needed to produce the same degree of sensory change. When exponents are greater than 1 (for example, shock), the curves are

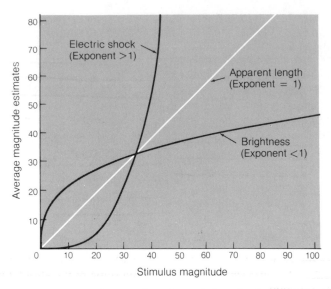

FIGURE 2–16   Power functions for brightness, length, and electric shock. Notice how the shape of the curve changes as the exponent changes.

concave upward, meaning that as stimuli become more intense, the same physical stimulus change produces an even larger sensory change than at lower stimulus intensities. Since each sensory continuum might give a different curve describing the relationship between sensory and physical intensity, it is fortunate that a simple procedure exists that allows us to estimate the power function from any set of data. If we plot the logarithm of the average magnitude estimates (the average numbers observers assign to their sensations) against the logarithms of the stimulus intensities, any curve of the general form $S = aI^n$ will appear as a straight line. In Figure 2–17 the curves in Figure 2–16 have been replotted in this way. We can now estimate n from the curve by measuring the distances marked Δy and Δx in the figures and computing $\Delta y/\Delta x$. The constant a is the point at which the line crosses the ordinate. More sophisticated methods of estimating the parameters in Stevens's law and those in Fechner's law are described by

Thomas (1983). Demonstration Box 2–5 (p. 48) allows you to perform a magnitude estimation experiment for yourself.

We mentioned earlier that category judgments are subject to several sources of bias, and thus category scales should be constructed and used with caution. Unfortunately, although magnitude estimations have proved to be quite useful, and average magnitude estimations behave quite lawfully, they nonetheless are also subject to a variety of biases. The particular stimulus used as the standard, the modulus used, the range of stimuli presented, the clarity of the stimuli, how people use numbers, and previous stimuli and responses can all affect observers' magnitude estimations (see e.g., Baird, Lewis & Romer, 1970; Poulton, 1979; Ward, 1973, 1979). Relatively bias-free scales may be produced by carefully choosing stimuli and procedures (Poulton, Edwards & Fowler, 1980), but as we have noted before, it is impossible to eliminate completely the observers' judgmental inclina-

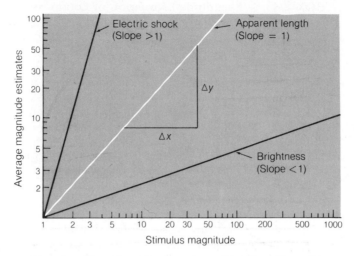

FIGURE 2–17   The same power functions as in Figure 2–16 plotted on logarithmic axes. In such "log-log" plots, all power functions become straight lines, with the slope of the straight line determined by the exponent (n) of the power function.

tions, habits, or strategies from any such perceptual task. Because of this difficulty, some (e.g., Schneider & Parker, 1987) have argued that we should consider abandoning numerical estimation techniques. However, few are willing to give up the simplicity and direct appeal of these techniques, so the debate continues.

You might wonder why category judgments seem to give a logarithmic relationship that supports Fechner's law, whereas magnitude estimates are related to stimulus magnitude by a power law. Actually, Stevens and Galanter (1957) found that category judgments only approximately fit a logarithmic relationship. Since then several investigators (Gibson & Tomko, 1972; Marks, 1968, 1974; Ward, 1971, 1972, 1974) have shown that category judgments also fit the power law, but with exponents (n) that are about half the size of those produced by magnitude estimation. Marks (1974) and Torgerson (1961) have suggested that these different results reflect different but equally valid ways of judging the same sensory experience. For ex-

ample, if my 10-kg dog and my 100-kg brother both gain 1 kilogram in weight, we may ask, "Have they both gained the same amount?" If we are making an equal interval judgment (analogous to that required for category scaling) the answer is yes, since both have increased by 1 kilogram. If we are making an equal ratio judgment (magnitude estimate), my dog has increased his body weight by 10 percent and my brother by only 1 percent. Thus, the weight gain is far from the same. Both judgments require estimates of the magnitude of a single event, and both are useful, but the scales (and resultant stimulus-sensation curves) are different (see also Marks, 1979b; Popper, Parker & Galanter, 1986).

Cross-Modality Matching

If the size of the exponent varies with the nature of the response, you might wonder whether these scales tell us more about how humans use numbers than they do about how sensation varies with

DEMONSTRATION BOX 2-5. Magnitude Estimation of Loudness

To produce a graded set of sound intensities for this demonstration you will need a long ruler, a coin (we've designed the demonstration for a quarter), an empty tin can or water glass, a soft towel, and a friend. Place the can on the folded towel and have your friend drop the coin from the designated height so that the coin hits the can on its edge only once and then falls onto the towel (silently, we hope). You should sit with your back to the apparatus.

At the start, your friend should drop the coin from a 70-cm height. Try to remember how loud that sounds, and assign it a value of 10. If you feel that a test sound is twice as loud as the first sound, call it 20, if it's half as loud call it 5, and so on. You may use any numbers you feel are appropriate as long as they are greater than 0. Your friend should then drop the coin from heights of 1, 10, 70, 100, and 200 cm, in some mixed order, while you call out the number corresponding to its apparent loudness and your friend records your judgment for each stimulus (height).

Do this for two or three runs through the stimuli, and then average your magnitude estimates for each height.

To determine if these judgments follow a power law, plot them on the log-log coordinates provided in the accompanying graph. The vertical axis is the logarithm of the magnitude estimate and the horizontal axis is the logarithm of the sound intensity, based on the height of the coin drop. Draw the straight line that best fits the data points. Usually, the data points fall close to such a line and do not curve significantly. You can compute directly the exponent (n in the power law $S = aI^n$) by computing the slope of your straight line. Simply pick two points on the line and measure Δx and Δy for these points with a ruler, as pictured in Figure 2-17. Now divide Δy by Δx and you should get a value somewhere around 0.3. This exponent means that the sensation of loudness increases less rapidly than does the actual sound intensity.

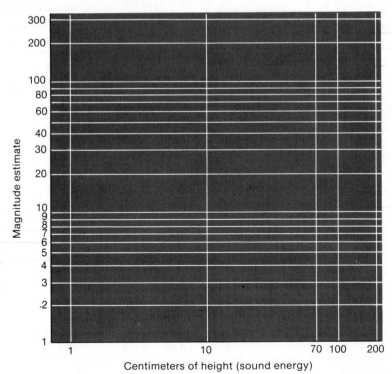

stimulus intensity (see Baird, 1975; Baird, Lewis & Romer, 1970). In order to counter such criticism, Stevens invented a scaling procedure that does not use numbers at all. In this technique, an observer adjusts the intensity of a stimulus until it appears to be as intense as another stimulus from a different sensory continuum. Thus, you might be asked to squeeze a handgrip until the pressure felt as strong as a particular light was bright. This procedure is called **cross-modality matching,** since the observer is asked to match sensory magnitudes across sensory modalities. Actually, magnitude estimation can also be viewed as a form of cross-matching in which the number continuum is matched to a stimulus continuum (Oyama, 1968; Stevens, 1975). When we plot the data from cross-

modality matching experiments on log-log axes (as we did for magnitude estimation experiments), we find that the average matches fall onto a straight line. Despite the fact that we no longer use numerical estimates from the observers, the data still obey the power law for sensory intensities. Figure 2–18 shows this for a number of modalities matched with handgrip pressure.

Cross-modality matching is often more difficult to use than direct magnitude estimation because the subject must adjust one of the sensory continua in order to give a response, rather than simply reporting a number or category label. Furthermore, in spite of Stevens's hopes, cross-modality matches too are affected by a variety of biases (see e.g., Baird, Green & Luce, 1980; Ward,

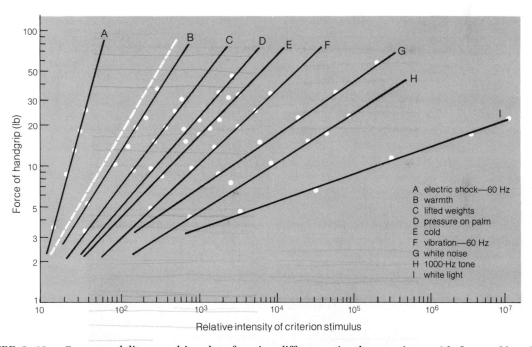

A electric shock—60 Hz
B warmth
C lifted weights
D pressure on palm
E cold
F vibration—60 Hz
G white noise
H 1000-Hz tone
I white light

FIGURE 2–18   Cross-modality matching data for nine different stimulus continua with force of handgrip as the response continuum. Because the values on both axes are logarithmically spaced, all the straight lines indicate power function relationships between stimulus and response magnitude. The dashed white line has an exponent of 1.0. (From S. S. Stevens, 1961, in W. A. Rosenblith, ed., *Sensory Communication,* Cambridge, MA: MIT Press. Copyright 1961 by the MIT Press.)

1975, 1979), and depend in important ways on the context within which they are made (Marks, Szczesiul & Ohlott, 1986; Ward, 1987).

Because psychophysicists want to obtain as accurate an estimate of the exponent as is possible in order to describe the relationship between the physical stimulus and its perceived magnitude with maximum precision, new refinements of the classical scaling procedures are always being introduced. For instance, a recent modification of the cross-modality matching technique makes the task somewhat easier for the observer, and seems to give somewhat more reliable results. This procedure is called **mixed-modality scaling** (Ward 1982a). In mixed–modality scaling, observers don't actually match sensory magnitudes. Instead, they judge two different sets of sensory stimuli (for instance, lights and sounds), both of which are intermixed in the same experiment. Observers try to use the same scale as the stimuli alternate between the modalities. The experimenter later uses some sophisticated mathematical techniques to determine the relationship between the two sets of judgments, and also to estimate the exponents of the power functions for the two sensory modalities. The first example of mixed-modality scaling, called **magnitude matching** because observers made *magnitude estimates* of stimuli from two sensory continua, was introduced by J. C. Stevens and Marks (1980). In other variants, observers make category judgments (Ward, 1982a) or they make cross-modality matches of each of the two sensory continua to a third, more convenient, continuum (such as duration—see Ward, 1986).

The theoretical importance of such techniques rests in the exponents derived from them for the power law, in this case particularly the cross-modality matching functions. Remarkably, the exponents usually agree regardless of the technique used to estimate them (Ward, 1986). In addition, they generally agree with the values obtained from traditional magnitude estimation techniques (Stevens, 1975; Teghtsoonian, 1975). Given all the evidence

(and all the dissenting views), the power law still seems to be a reasonable first approximation to the description of how sensory intensity is related to stimulus intensity.

Adaptation Level Theory

Part of the circus strongman's job was to carry various members of the animal cast onto the circus train. One visitor watched in amazement as one after another he lifted the dancing ponies and placed them in their railroad car. "Aren't they heavy?" asked the visitor. "Not if you've just carried three elephants," came the reply. The essence of this apocryphal tale is that no stimulus can be appreciated in isolation. Stimuli are always seen in the context of the stimuli that precede and surround them. Thus, sportscasters of average height look like midgets when interviewing professional basketball players, but like giants when interviewing professional jockeys. They have, of course, not changed size, but their apparent size has changed as a result of the frame of reference provided by the heights of those around them. Contextual effects have long been known to influence judgments of sensory magnitude in many psychophysical tasks, even when the context is in another modality than the one being judged (see e.g., Marks, Szczesiul & Ohlott, 1986; Ward, 1987). You can experience this kind of context effect by using Demonstration Box 2–6.

Helson (1964) attempted to explain how the magnitude of one stimulus can affect our judgments of the magnitude of other stimuli. His theory has both quantitative and qualitative aspects. In Helson's theory, the organism is thought to accommodate itself to the changing environment around it. This accommodation involves establishing a *reference level* against which all other stimuli are judged. Stimuli below this reference, or **adaptation level,** are judged in one way (to be weak) and stimuli above it in another way (to be intense). Stimuli at or near the adaptation level are judged to

---

DEMONSTRATION BOX 2-6.   The Effect of Visual Context on Judged Weight

You will need two envelopes for this demonstration. One should be rather small (about 7 by 13 cm or so) and one should be large (approximately 20 by 28 cm). Put 15 nickels in each envelope. With the same hand, lift the large envelope and next lift the small. Which appears to be heavier? You will probably feel that the small envelope was considerably heavier although the weights were physically equal. This is an example of how a visual context (the envelope size) can alter our perception of heaviness. The same weight in the context of a smaller container seems heavier than when judged in the context of a larger container.

---

be medium or neutral. This implies that all judgments are relative. A stimulus is not simply weak or intense, it is weak or intense compared to the subjective adaptation level.

For Helson, adaptation levels are established by pooling the effects of three classes of stimuli. The first class is called **focal stimuli.** These stimuli are the center of an observer's attention and are usually the ones being judged. Clearly, the magnitude of these stimuli will in some way determine the observer's judgments, which is the basic assumption of all scaling procedures. The second class of stimuli is called **background stimuli.** These are other stimuli that occur closely in space and/or time to the focal stimulus, providing the immediate background against which a focal stimulus is judged. The final set of stimuli is called **residual stimuli.** These are stimuli that are not current for the observer, but are the residue of stimuli the observer has experienced in the past. To be more concrete, consider the example in which we judged the height of a sportscaster surrounded by basketball players or jockeys. The physical height of a sportscaster is the focal stimulus. The background stimuli are the heights of the surrounding athletes. The residual stimuli are the heights of all persons previously encountered, including those of athletes seen in the past. All these stimuli combine to form the adaptation level.

Helson (1964) defined the adaptation level quantitatively as a weighted product of all three classes of stimuli: focal, which we will designate F, background, B, and residual, R. The formula for the adaptation level (AL) is

$$AL = F^{W1} B^{W2} R^{W3}$$

where $W1$, $W2$, and $W3$ are weighting coefficients that reflect the importance of any one class of stimuli in the determination of the overall adaptation level. Helson (1959) generally wrote this formula as

$$\log AL = W1 \log F + W2 \log B + W3 \log R$$

which shows clearly that we are dealing with a type of weighted average.

This formulation is not arbitrary. It is based on category judgment data similar to those used to test Fechner's law and it provides a surprisingly good approximation for a large class of judgmental data. Although there have been some interesting extensions of adaptation level theory (e.g., Restle, 1971, 1978), there are also a number of other quantitative formulations that make slightly different assumptions about how stimulus magnitudes affect each other. These formulations result in different mathematical expressions (e.g., Anderson, 1970, 1975). All these alternatives, however, still acknowledge the fact that surrounding stimuli,

stimuli experienced in the past, and patterns of attention, as well as the actual stimulus judged, can affect our judgments of stimulus intensity.

Such effects in our judgment of stimulus magnitude may be observed in many different tasks. For instance, consider a simple experiment by Engen and Tulunary (1956) in which subjects were required to find a weight that appeared to be exactly half the weight of a standard. They found that the mean weight judged to be one-half as heavy as the standard was consistently lighter for an ascending series of comparison weights (starting with the light weights and moving gradually to heavier) than for a descending series. The weight judged half as heavy as a 300-g weight was 179 g for a descending series (with the heavier weights of the series forming the context) but only 140 g for an ascending series (with judgments made in the context of lighter weights).

Similar shifts caused by context can also produce visual illusions (Coren & Girgus, 1978). For instance, consider Figure 2–19. The two black circles are physically the same size, although they appear to be different. It is easy to understand this illusory effect if you recognize that when you are looking at circle A, the adaptation level is shifted toward the smaller size of the surrounding elements, whereas when you are looking at circle B, the adaptation level is shifted toward the larger size of the elements in that region. Because of this, circle A is above the adaptation level established for its immediate vicinity, and hence appears larger, and circle B is below the adaptation level in its region, and hence appears smaller.

Adaptation level influences not only judgments of magnitude but also discrimination between stimuli. It is significantly more difficult to discriminate stimuli that are both on the same side of the adaptation level than to discriminate stimuli, equally close together, that appear on different sides of the adaptation level (Streitfeld & Wilson, 1986). The adaptation level forms a reference point both for sensory magnitude and for discrimination.

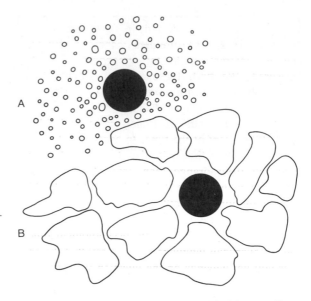

FIGURE 2–19   The circle surrounded by smaller elements appears larger than the circle surrounded by larger elements, although both are the same size. (Based on Coren & Girgus, 1978)

There may be no simple relationship between stimulus magnitude and sensory magnitude. What we perceive is not simply a photographic reproduction of the stimuli in the environment but is affected by all the myriad forces that have impinged on us in the past and that provide the context for the perceptual situation in which we presently find ourselves. We will find that these conditions hold for all the sensory modalities we shall study in the following chapters. Perception is an active process, and processes within the observer can sometimes be more important in determining the sensory experience than are factors in the external environment.

The psychophysical measurement techniques introduced in this chapter will appear in many disguises throughout the rest of the book. We will not usually stop and identify these techniques, or the rationale for using them. The methods by which perceptual data are collected, however, are important because the measurement technique will frequently interact with the phenomena to be measured. We find, for example, that when we look at raw identification scores in one experiment, red and green are equally discriminable from orange because the individual hues are correctly identified 100 percent of the time. In contrast, when we measure reaction times, it takes longer to discriminate red from orange than green from orange, indicating a difference in discriminability. Is this a contradiction of fact? Not necessarily. Every method of measurement is tuned to a different task, and often measures a different psychological function. In everyday language you can say that the answer you get depends on the question you ask.

GLOSSARY

The following definitions are specific to this book.

Absolute threshold   The minimal amount of energy required to detect a stimulus.

Adaptation level   A subjective reference point against which stimuli are both quantitatively and qualitatively judged.

Background stimuli   Adaptation level theory term for stimuli that form a context for a focal stimulus but are not judged by an observer.

β (beta)   In signal detection theory, the criterion for sensation level that separates a "yes" response from a "no" response.

Bit   The amount of information in a stimulus measured by the logarithm to the base 2 of the number of stimulus alternatives.

Category scaling   A psychophysical scaling method in which stimuli are grouped in a predetermined number of categories on the basis of their perceived intensity. Also called equal-interval scaling.

Catch trials   Trials in which no stimulus is presented. Used in threshold measuring experiments.

Channel capacity   The limit to the number of bits of information an observer can transmit on a single sensory dimension.

Choice reaction time   Reaction time to make different responses to different stimuli.

Comparison stimuli   A graded set of stimuli differing along a specific dimension that are to be judged relative to a standard stimulus.

Correct negative   Signal detection theory term for a signal-absent trial to which the observer's response is "No."

Criterion   In signal detection theory, a sensation level that differentiates "yes" from "no" responses. *See* β.

Cross-modality matching   A scaling procedure in which the observer adjusts the intensity of a stimulus until it appears to be as intense as another stimulus from a different sensory continuum.

d′   In signal detection theory, the distance between the means of the signal-absent and the signal-present distributions.

Detection   Psychophysical problem involving being aware that a stimulus is present.

Difference threshold   The minimum amount of stimulus change needed for two stimuli to be perceived as different.

Direct scaling   A procedure in which individuals are asked to assess directly the intensity of a sensation.

Discrimination   Psychophysical problem involving noticing a difference between stimuli.

Equal-interval scaling   *See* Category scaling.

Error of anticipation   In the method of limits, a change in response before the percept actually changes.

Error of perseveration   In the method of limits, continuing to give the same response although the percept has changed.

False alarm   Signal detection theory term for a signal-absent trial to which the observer's response is "Yes."

Fechner's law   The logarithmic relationship, proposed by Fechner, between the intensity of sensation and the intensity of physical stimulus, $S = W \log I$.

Focal stimuli   Adaptation level theory term for stimuli at the center of an observer's attention, usually those being judged.

Hick's law   A law stating that choice reaction time is a linear function of the amount of information in the stimuli to be differentiated.

Hit   Signal detection theory term for a signal-present trial to which the response is "Yes."

Identification   Psychophysical problem involving naming stimuli.

Indirect scaling   Any method, often based on discrimination ability, by which sensation intensity is measured indirectly.

Information theory   A quantitative system for measuring the difficulty of an identification task in terms of the number of stimulus alternatives that must be distinguished.

Information transmission   The degree to which the output of an information channel (for example, an observer in an identification experiment) reflects the information input to it.

Interval of uncertainty   In a discrimination experiment, the difference between the stimulus intensity judged greater than the standard 25 percent of the time and that judged greater 75 percent of the time.

Interval scale   A scale in which differences between adjacent values are meaningful but that has no absolute zero point.

Just noticeable difference (*jnd*)   The stimulus difference noticed 50 percent of the time, computed as the interval of uncertainty divided by 2.

Magnitude estimation   A psychophysical scaling procedure requiring the observer to assign numbers to stimuli on the basis of the intensity of the sensations they arouse.

Magnitude matching   A technique whereby observers make magnitude estimates of stimuli from two different sensory continua intermixed in the same experiment.

Metathetic continuum   A stimulus continuum involving the quality of sensations, such as color or pitch.

Method of constant stimuli   A method for determining thresholds in which each of a number of stimuli above and below the suspected threshold is presented and judged repeatedly.

Method of limits   A method for determining thresholds in which stimulus intensity is systematically increased or decreased until a change in response occurs.

Miss   Signal detection theory term for a signal-present trial to which the observer's response is ''No.''

Mixed-modality scaling   A psychophysical scaling procedure in which observers make judgments (including magnitude estimations, category judgments, or cross-modality matches) of stimuli from two different sensory continua on the same scale.

Modulus   In magnitude estimation, the standard numerical value assigned to one of the stimuli at the beginning of the judgment procedure; it determines the range of numbers to be used by the observer in the procedure.

Negative time error   In discrimination experiments, when the point of subjective equality is less than the value of the standard stimulus.

Nominal scale   A scale in which the values can be used only as names of objects or events, thus reflecting only identity.

Ordinal scale   A scale involving the ranking of items on the basis of more or less of some quantity.

Outcome matrix   In signal detection theory, a matrix containing the proportions of trials on which the four possible outcomes occurred.

Payoff matrix   In signal detection theory, a matrix describing the set of rewards and penalties given an observer based on his performance in a psychophysical experiment.

Point of subjective equality   The comparison stimulus intensity that appears most like the standard in a discrimination experiment.

Power law   The relation stating that the magnitude of sensation varies as the intensity of the physical stimulus raised to some power. Also known as Stevens's law, $S = aI^n$.

Probability distribution   A graphic representation of the likelihood that a given event will occur.

Prothetic continuum   A psychological continuum that involves quantitative aspects (how much) of stimulation, such as loudness or brightness.

Ratio scale   A measurement scale in which the rank order, spacing, and ratios of the numbers assigned to events have meaning; it also has an absolute zero point.

Reaction time   The interval between the onset of a stimulus and the beginning of an overt response.

Receiver operating characteristic (ROC) curve   In signal detection theory, the graph of probabilities of hits (ordinate) versus false alarms (abscissa) generated by criterion changes.

Residual stimuli   Adaptation level theory term for stimuli that are no longer present but affect the current adaptation level.

ROC curve   *See* Receiver operating characteristic curve.

Scaling   Psychophysical problem involving the measurement of how much of something is present.

Signal detection theory   A mathematical, theoretical system that formally deals with both decisional and sensory components in detection and discrimination tasks.

Simple reaction time   Reaction time for simply detecting the onset of a stimulus.

Staircase method   A method for measuring absolute thresholds in which the experimenter alters the direction of changes in stimulus intensity each time the observer changes his or her response.

Standard   A stimulus against which the comparison stimuli are judged in a discrimination experiment.

Stevens's Law   *See* Power law.

Weber fraction   The proportion by which the standard stimulus must be increased in order to detect change, $K = \Delta I / I$.

Weber's law   The relation stating that the size of the just noticeable difference (*jnd*) increases linearly with the size of the standard, $\Delta I = K I$.

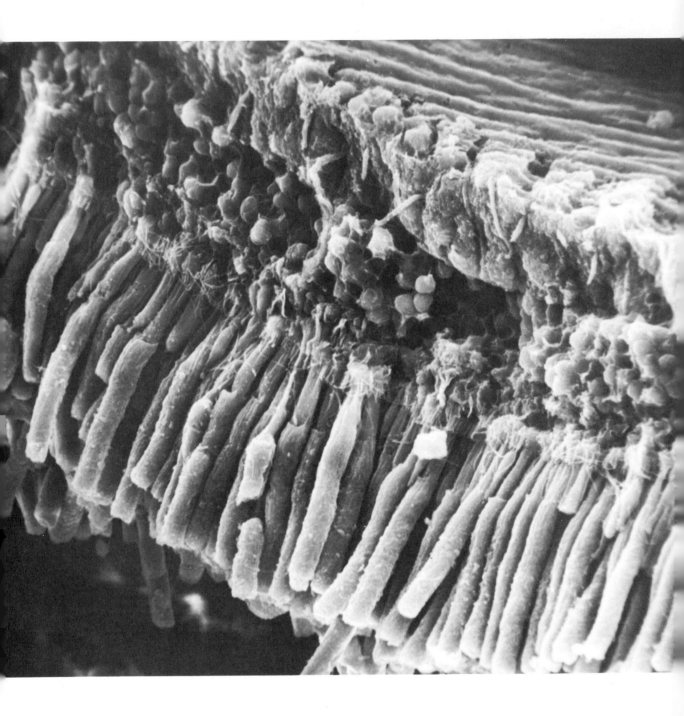

CHAPTER 3

The Visual System

Although perception occurs within the brain, your only real contact with the external environment is through your sense organs. Recalling the old saying, ''The eyes are the windows to the world,'' it is clear that the physical properties of this ''window'' will affect the nature of your perception in the same manner that the physical properties of a glass window will affect your view. If the window is colored, your perception of the world will be tinted. If the window is dark, or dirty, your ability to discern objects will be reduced. If the window is curved, so as to magnify the images, your perception of the size of objects viewed through the glass may also be distorted. Thus, it is important for you to know the nature of the ''window'' through which you look at the world, or, more simply, to understand the physiological makeup of the visual system.

LIGHT

Each of the sensory systems is maximally responsive to a different form of physical stimulation. Taste and smell respond to chemical stimuli, touch to mechanical pressure, and hearing to the vibration of air molecules. The physical stimulus for sight is electromagnetic radiation. We call the particular form of electromagnetic radiation that produces a visual response *light*.

In 1704, Sir Isaac Newton advanced the theory that any form of electromagnetic radiation, including light, acts as if it were a stream of particles traveling in a straight line. Each particle is called a **quantum,** and a quantum of light is called a *photon*. The intensity of light is then given by the number of photons. Although this conception of light is extremely useful in physics, it is only important to the understanding of vision when we deal with stimuli that are relatively dim. At low levels of light intensities are often described as the number of photons reaching the visual receptors. The smallest amount of light possible is one photon.

Light often acts as if it were a stream of particles, but at other times it acts as if it were made up of waves. James Clerk Maxwell (1873) showed that light travels not only in a straight line but also as an oscillating wave. He suggested that if we consider the change in the electromagnetic field surrounding the train of photons, we can treat light as purely a wave phenomenon, with the wavelength defined as the physical distance between the peaks of the photon waves.

Electromagnetic energy can have wavelengths over a broad range, varying from trillionths of a centimeter to many kilometers in length. Very short wavelengths are not visible, nor are very long wavelengths. As you can see in Figure 3-1, very short wavelengths include gamma rays, X-rays, and ultraviolet rays. Longer wavelengths vary from those we call electricity through the broadcasting wavelengths associated with TV and radio (which may be more than 100 meters in length). The section of the electromagnetic spectrum that we see as visible light is really quite small, extending from 380 to about 760 nanometers. A **nanometer** is a billionth of a meter and is usually abbreviated *nm*. The older method of specifying wavelength was **millimicrons,** which was abbreviated *mμ*. Perceptually, variations in wavelengths correspond roughly to the hue or color of light. In normal eyes, wavelengths of about 400 nm are seen as violet, 500 nm are seen as blue-green, 600 nm are seen as yellow-orange, and 700 nm are seen as red. However, the perception of color depends on much more than wavelength alone, as you will find out in Chapter 5.

THE STRUCTURE OF THE EYE

Most vertebrate eyes, from those of fish to those of mammals, have a similar basic structure. A schematic diagram of the human eye is shown in Figure 3-2. The eyes may be found lying in protective bony sockets within the skull and are spherical structures about 20–25 mm in diameter. The outer covering,

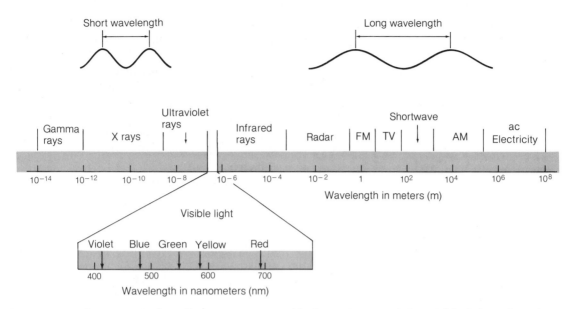

FIGURE 3-1   Electromagnetic radiation spectrum, with the region containing visible light enlarged.

which is seen as the "white" of the eye, is a strong elastic membrane called the **sclera.** Because the eye is not made of rigid materials, it maintains its shape by means of fluid pressure from within.

The front of the eye contains a region where the sclera bulges forward to form a clear, domelike window, about 13 mm in diameter, called the **cornea** (Martin & Holden, 1982). The cornea is the first optically active element in the eye. It serves as a simple fixed lens that gathers and focuses light. Because the cornea is extended forward, it actually allows reception of light from a region slightly behind the observer, as is shown in Demonstration Box 3-1.

Behind the cornea is a small chamber filled with a watery fluid called the **aqueous humor.** This fluid is similar in nature to the cerebrospinal fluid that bathes the inner cavities of the brain. This is not surprising since embryological evidence has shown that the neural components of the eye actually develop from the same structures that eventually form the brain.

When you look at a human eye your attention is usually captured by a ring of color. This colored membrane, surrounding a central hole, is called the **iris.** When you say that a person has brown eyes, you really are saying that he has brown irises. The actual color, which may vary from blue through black, appears to be genetically determined. The function of the iris seems to be to control the amount of light entering the eye. It may be of some interest to note that although blue eyes seem to have been viewed as more appealing by some poets, dark irises, such as brown or black, more effectively shield the eye from light. The light enters through the hole in the iris, which is called the **pupil.** The size of the pupil appears to be controlled by a light reflex. When the light is bright the pupil may contract to as little as 2 mm in diameter, whereas in dim light it may dilate to more than 8 mm. That is about a sixteenfold change in the area of the aperture. Demonstration Box 3-2 shows how you may observe the effect of light on pupil size.

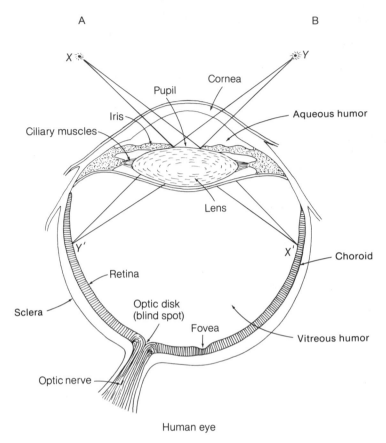

FIGURE 3-2   **Structure of the human eye, with a demonstration of the image formation of two targets (*X* and *Y*).**

The constriction of the pupil serves an important function. Despite the fact that the eye needs light to function there are some advantages to viewing the world with a small pupil. Although the amount of light entering the eye is reduced, imperfections in the lens produce fewer distortions with a small pupil, and the depth of focus (which is the range of distances over which objects are simultaneously in focus) is vastly increased. We might say that the eye takes advantage of better light by improving its optical response. In dim light, the ability of the eye to resolve or discriminate details (called **acuity**) is less important than the increased

sensitivity obtained by increasing the amount of light entering the eye; thus the pupil increases in size to let in more light. The pupil size also changes as a function of emotional and attentional variables. Under conditions of high interest the eye tries to gather more light and the pupil tends to be large, a cue often used by smart traders as an index of a customer's interest in an item. Clever customers often negate the usefulness of this cue in bargaining situations by wearing dark glasses. Similarly, the dimness of candlelight dilates the pupils and makes lovers appear to be more attentive and interested.

DEMONSTRATION BOX 3-1.   Vision "Behind" the Eye

It is easy to demonstrate that the visual field actually extends to a region somewhat behind the eye. In order to do this, simply choose a point that is some distance in front of your head and stare at it. Now raise your hand to the side of your head as shown in the figure, with your index finger extended upward. Your hand should be out of view when you stare at the distant point. Now, wiggle your finger slightly, and bring your hand slowly forward until the wiggling finger is just barely visible in your peripheral vision. At this point stop and, with your head as still as possible, move your finger directly in toward your head. You will notice that your hand will touch a point on your temple somewhat behind the location of the eye, indicating that you were actually seeing somewhat ''behind yourself.''

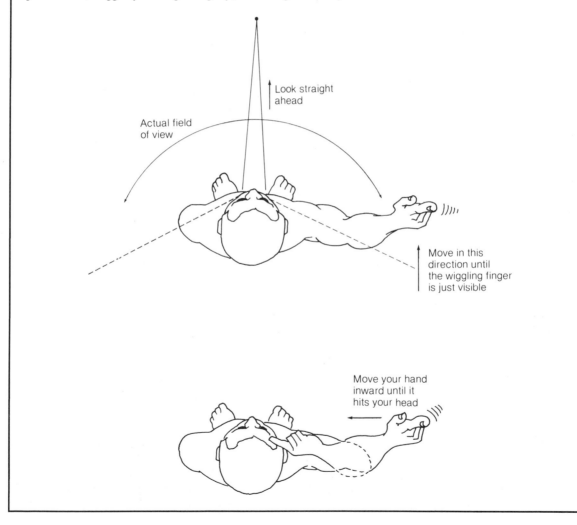

DEMONSTRATION BOX 3-2.   The Pupillary Light Reflex

For this demonstration you need a friend. Dim the light in the room, but leave enough light so that you can still see the size of the pupil. Notice how large your friend's pupil appears to be under these conditions. Now turn on an overhead light or shine the beam of a flashlight into your friend's eye and note how the pupil constricts. Removal of the light will cause the pupil to dilate again. The light reflex of the pupil was the first reflex ever studied by Whytt (1751), who is credited with the discovery of reflex action. It is still sometimes called *Whytt's reflex*.

The Crystalline Lens

Most vertebrate eyes contain a **lens,** located directly behind the pupillary aperture. Since the curvature of the lens determines the amount by which the light is bent, it is critical in bringing an image into focus at the rear of the eye. The process by which the lens varies its focus is called **accommodation.** The lens changes focus by changing its shape (Dalziel & Egan, 1982). The natural shape of the human lens tends to be spherical, but when the ciliary muscles that control it relax, the pressure of the fluid in the eyeball and the tension of the zonal fibers connecting the lens to the inside wall of the eye cause it to flatten. Under these conditions, distant objects should be in focus. Contraction of the ciliary muscles, from which the lens is suspended, takes some of the tension from the lens and it regresses to a more spherical shape. When it is rounder, near objects are in focus. The effect of lens shape on point of focus is shown in Figure 3-3.

An individual's age is important in determining the focusing ability of the lens. It is interesting to note that the ability to accommodate is not pres-

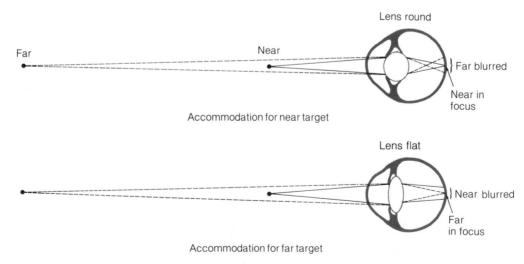

FIGURE 3-3   Accommodation (focusing) of an image by changing the shape of the crystalline lens of the eye.

ent at birth. For a newborn infant, until about the age of 1 month, only images of objects that are approximately 19 cm away are in focus (Dobson & Teller, 1978; Teller & Movshon, 1986). Images of targets closer or farther away than 19 cm are proportionally blurred. However, during the second month of infancy, the accommodative system begins to respond more adaptively (see Chapter 16).

The ability of the lens to change focus decreases with age after about age 16. This is because the inner layers of the lens die and lose some of their elasticity (Weale, 1986), and it thus becomes more difficult for the ciliary muscles to change the lens's curvature to accommodate to a near object. This results in a form of **refractive error** (light-bending or focusing error) called **presbyopia,** which simply translates to "old-sighted." Functionally, this condition increases the **near point distance.** The near point refers to how close an object may be brought to the eye before it can no longer be held in focus and becomes blurry. Thus, older persons without corrective lenses often may be seen holding reading material abnormally far from their faces in order to bring the print into proper focus.

Another feature of the lens, which warrants mention, is the fact that it is not perfectly transparent. The lens is tinted somewhat yellow, and the density of this yellow tint increases with age (Coren & Girgus, 1972a). The yellow pigment serves to screen out some of the ultraviolet light entering the eye. Animals with clear lenses (such as many birds and insects) can see ultraviolet light, as can people who have had their lenses surgically removed (e.g., Emmerton, 1983; Hardie & Kirschfeld, 1983). The yellow pigment in the lens also screens out some of the blue light, and thus alters your perception of color somewhat. For example, you may have heard individuals arguing over whether a particular color was blue or green. If they are different ages, the source of the argument may lie in the fact that because the lens yellows with age, each is viewing the world through a different yellow filter.

As we noted above, the major purpose of the lens is to focus the image in the eye. An eye having normal accommodative (focusing) ability is called **emmetropic.** Sometimes there is too much or too little curvature in the cornea or, alternatively, the shape of the eye is too short or too long, so that the accommodative capacity of the lens is not sufficient to bring targets into focus. If the eye is too short, or if the light rays are not bent sharply enough by the cornea, distant objects are seen quite clearly, but it is difficult to bring near objects into focus. The common term for this is *farsightedness,* and the technical term is **hypermetropia.** If the eye is too long, or if the light rays are bent too sharply by the cornea, near objects are sharply in focus but distant objects are blurred. This condition is called *nearsightedness* or **myopia.** The optical situations that result from these difficulties are shown in Figure 3-4.

The Retina

The large chamber of the eye is filled with a jelly-like substance called the **vitreous humor.** This substance is generally clear, although shreds of debris can often be seen floating in it. Try steadily viewing a clear blue sky and note the shadows that move across it; these shadows are from floating debris in the vitreous humor.

The image formed by the optical system of the eye is focused on a screen of neural elements at the back of the eye called the **retina.** The term *retina* derives from the Latin word meaning *"net,"* because when an eye is opened up surgically (or its interior viewed with an optical device such as an ophthalmoscope) the most salient feature is the network of blood vessels lining the inner cavity. Demonstration Box 3-3 shows how you can observe these blood vessels in your own eyes.

The sheet of neural elements that makes up the retina extends over most of the interior of the eye. In diurnal or daylight-active animals, the retina is backed by a light-absorbing dark layer called the **pigment epithelium.** This dark pigment layer

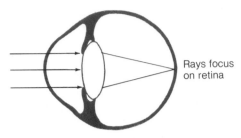

Emmetropic eye (normal)

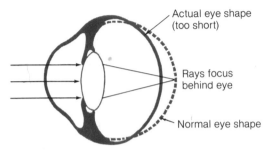

Hypermetropic eye (farsighted)

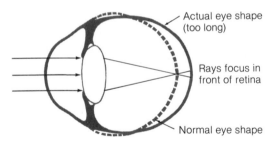

Myopic eye (nearsighted)

FIGURE 3-4   **Three common refractive conditions of the eye.**

serves the same purpose as the black inner coating in a photographic camera, reducing the amount of reflected and scattered light that could blur or fog the image. In nocturnal or night-active animals, where the detection of light is more important than image clarity, the light that penetrates the retina is reflected back through the retina by a shiny surface known as the **reflecting tapetum.** This permits the light to pass through the retina twice (once as it

enters and once as it is reflected out), effectively doubling its intensity. Although the result is a sizable increase in sensitivity, it is obtained at the expense of a considerable degrading of the image through fogging and blur, especially at higher illumination levels. The existence of this reflecting surface explains why cats' eyes seem to glow in the dark when a flashlight is pointed toward them.

The retina consists of three major layers of neural tissue and is about the thickness of a sheet of paper (see Figure 3-5). It is here that the light is changed or *transduced* into a neural response. The outermost layer of the retina, closest to the scleral wall, contains the **photoreceptors.** There are two types of photoreceptors that are distinguishable on the basis of their shapes—long, thin, cylindrical cells called **rods,** and shorter, thicker, somewhat more tapered cells called **cones.** The outer segments of these cells contain pigments that absorb the light and start the visual response. The next level of the retina consists of **bipolar cells,** which are neurons with two, long, extended processes. One end makes synapses with the photoreceptors; the other end makes synapses with the large retinal **ganglion cells** in the third layer of the retina.

In addition to photoreceptors, bipolars, and ganglion cells, there are also two types of cells that have lateral connections. Closest to the receptor layer are the **horizontal cells.** These cells typically have short dendrites and a long horizontal process that extends some distance across the retina. The second set of cells that are lateral interconnecters are called **amacrine cells.** These large cells are found between the ganglion and bipolar cells, and seem to interact with spatially adjacent units. Actually, over 30 types of amacrine cells, differing in size and chemical properties, have been isolated (Masland, 1986). Both the horizontal and amacrine cells serve to modify the visual signal, and allow adjacent cells in the retina to communicate and interact with one another (Kolb, Nelson & Mariani, 1981; Naka, 1982; Tomita, 1986).

Light reception occurs within the rod and cone cells. Contrary to what we might expect, the ori-

DEMONSTRATION BOX **3-3.**   Mapping the Retinal Blood Vessels

For this demonstration you will need a pocket pen-light and a white paper or light-colored wall. Hold the penlight near the outside canthus (corner) of your eye. Now, shaking the bulb up and down you will see a netlike pattern on the light surface. This pattern is generated by the movements of the shadows of your retinal blood vessels across your retina. By steadily shaking the bulb with one hand and tracing the shadows with the other, you can produce a map of your own retinal blood vessels.

entation of rods and cones is inverted, with the pigment-bearing end pointing toward the rear of the eye rather than toward the lens. Thus, the retina may be viewed as if it were a transparent carpet lying upside down on the floor of the room, with the pile of the carpet corresponding to the rods and cones. The incoming light must therefore pass through the carpet (the retina) before reaching the photoreceptors. Although this arrangement might appear to be somewhat counterproductive, it actually makes good sense. The photoreceptors need a rich oxygen supply, and to meet this need there are many blood vessels in the epithelial layer at the rear of the eye. If the retina were "right-side up," so many blood vessels would be needed that the light input would be partially blocked. Therefore, the "upside-down" organization is more functional.

The Fovea

Not all areas of the retina are of equal importance in the perceptual process. The most important section of the human retina is located in the region

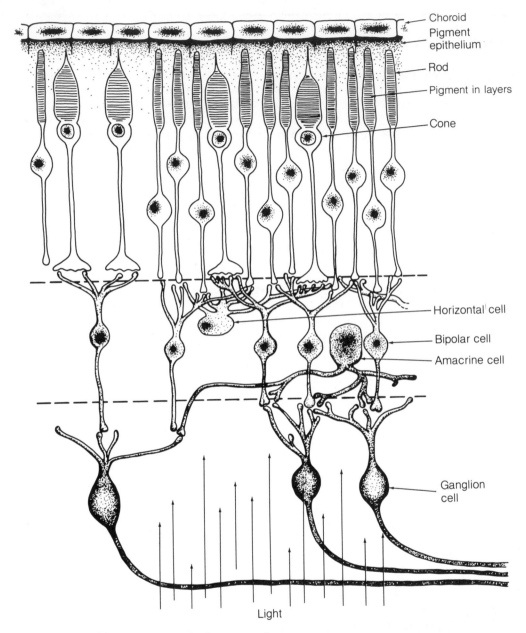

Choroid
Pigment epithelium
Rod
Pigment in layers
Cone
Horizontal cell
Bipolar cell
Amacrine cell
Ganglion cell
Light

FIGURE 3-5   Schematic diagram of the human retina.

around the origin of the **optic axis,** an imaginary line from the center of the fovea that passes through the center of the pupil (see Figure 3-7). If we view a human retina through an ophthalmo-scope we note a yellow patch of pigment located in the region of the origin of the optic axis. This area is called the **macula lutea** (or just *macula*), which simply translates to "yellow spot." Demonstration

---

DEMONSTRATION BOX 3-4.   The Macular Spot

Under appropriate conditions it is possible to see the macular spot in your own eye. In order to do this you will need a dark blue or purple piece of cellophane. Brightly illuminate a piece of white paper with a desk lamp. Now, while looking at the paper with one eye, quickly bring the piece of cellophane between your eye and the paper. Now as you look at the paper you see what appears to be a faint circular shadow in the center of it. The sight of the shadow may only last for a couple of seconds. Sometimes its visibility can

be improved by moving the cellophane in front of and away from your eye, so that you have a flickering colored field. Some individuals can see the spot when staring at a uniform blue field, such as a clear summer sky. This percept is caused by the fact that the yellow pigment in the macula absorbs the blue light and does not let it pass. This causes a circular shadow, which can be briefly seen. It is often called *Maxwell's spot,* after James Clerk Maxwell, who noticed its presence during some color-matching experiments.

Box 3-4 describes a procedure in which you can see your own macula. In the center of the macula is a small depression that looks much like the imprint of a pinpoint about 1/3 mm in diameter. This small circular depression is called the **fovea centralis,** or translated, the "central pit." The fovea is critical in visual perception. Whenever you "look" directly at a target, it means that your eyes are rotated so that the image of the target falls on the foveal region.

The fovea is quite unique in its structure, and is schematically depicted in Figure 3-6. In the cen-

ter of the foveal depression, the upper layers of cells are apparently pushed away so that the light passes through a much thinner cellular layer before reaching the photoreceptors. The photoreceptors themselves are very densely packed in this region. This section of the retina contains only cones; there are no rods at all. Foveal cones have a different shape than the more peripheral cones depicted in Figure 3-5. They are much longer and thinner (often only 0.001 mm in diameter), so that they somewhat resemble rods.

In a laborious study, Osterberg (1935) exam-

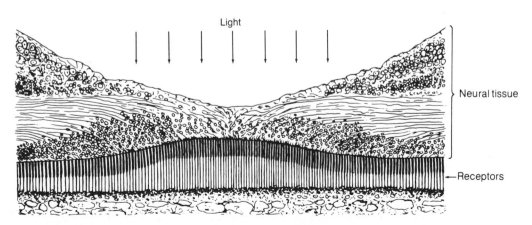

FIGURE 3-6   Sketch of a cross section through the fovea. Light comes from the direction of the top of the page.

ined the retina of a human eye that had been re-moved as the result of an accident. By fixing the fresh retina in a suitable fluid it is possible to pre-serve it indefinitely. He counted the number of rods and cones in this human retina, demonstrating that there are no rods in the center of the fovea at all. Outside of the fovea the number of cones rapidly decreases. The number of rods, however, rapidly increases beyond the foveal region, reaching a peak concentration at about 20 degrees of visual angle from the fovea and then decreasing again. This general distribution (which is shown in Figure 3-7) has been verified in recent computer mappings of the retina (Curcio, Sloan, Packer, Hendrickson & Kalina, 1987).

Rods and Cones

The presence of two types of retinal photoreceptors suggests the existence of two types of visual func-tion. In the early 1860s the retinal anatomist Max Schultze found that nocturnal animals, such as owls, have retinas that contain only rods. Animals that are diurnal, or only active during the day, such as the chipmunk and pigeon, have retinas that are all cones. Animals that are active in the twilight, or during both day and night, such as rats, mon-keys, and humans, have retinas comprised of both rods and cones. On the basis of these observations Schultze offered what has been called the **duplex retina theory** of vision. He maintained that there are two separate visual systems. One is for vision under dim light conditions and is dependent on the rods; the other is for vision under daylight or bright conditions and is dependent on the cones. Vision under bright light is called **photopic** (which trans-lates to "light vision"), and vision under dim light is called **scotopic** ("dark vision").

Early clinical studies (Kries, 1895) provided some behavioral data that supports the idea that the eye contains two different visual systems. For in-stance, individuals whose retinas contain no rods, or only nonfunctioning rods, seem to have normal vision under daylight conditions. However, as soon as the light dims beyond a certain point (into what you might call a twilight level of intensity) they lose all sense of sight and become functionally blind. These individuals suffer from **night blind-ness.** The implication is that in the absence of rods scotopic vision is lost. A quite different pattern is found for individuals lacking in functioning cones. These people find normal levels of daylight quite painful, totally lack color vision, and have very poor visual acuity. Under dim levels of illumina-tion, however, they function normally. Such indi-viduals suffer from **day-blindness** and provide

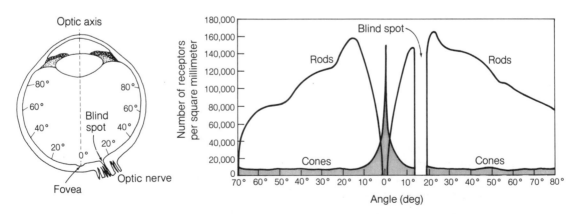

FIGURE 3-7   The distribution of rods and cones in the human retina. The left figure gives the locations on the retina of the "angle" relative to the optic axis on the right figure. (Modified from Lindsay & Norman, 1977)

evidence that a functioning cone system is necessary for normal photopic vision and also for the perception of color. The specifics of the perception of brightness and color are discussed in Chapters 4 and 5.

Before a rod or a cone can signal the presence of light, it must first interact with the light in some way. Chemically, such interaction involves absorbing, or capturing, one or more photons. Any substance that absorbs light is called a *pigment*. A substance that absorbs a lot of light would appear to be darkly pigmented, since most of the photons hitting it would be absorbed and very few would be reflected back to the eye of the viewer. As we noted earlier, the outer segments of both the rods and the cones contain visual pigments. If you refer back to Figure 3-5, you will see the pigments arranged in layers in the outer segments of the photoreceptors. For rods, the photosensitive pigment is arranged in a stack of around 2,000 tiny disks, like coins inside a tube; for cones, the pigment is part of a single large elaborately folded membrane that forms the layers of photosensitive material.

Rods and cones do not contain the same pigment. The first successful isolation of the pigment in rods was made in 1876 when Franz Boll isolated a brilliant red pigment from the frog retina (which contains predominantly rods). He noted that this pigment bleached, or lost its apparent coloration, when exposed to light. This reaction indicated that the substance was photosensitive. He further noted that the pigment regenerated itself in the dark. Thus, it fulfilled the elementary requirements of a visual pigment in that it responded by changing chemically in the presence of light, yet it still remained capable of resynthesizing itself. Kuhne took up the study of this pigment in 1877 and, in one extraordinary year, laid the groundwork for our understanding of its action. This pigment has been named **rhodopsin** (which means "visual red" rather than "visual purple" as it is sometimes called). In the century since the work by Boll and Kuhne, we have been able to work out much of the photochemical reaction in rhodopsin.

Basically, rhodopsin is a compound that is made up of two parts: **retinal,** a complex organic molecule derived from vitamin A, and **opsin,** a protein that has the capacity to act as an enzyme. As is the case for many organic compounds, the retinal component can exist in several different shapes called *isomers*. When a molecule of rhodopsin absorbs a photon of light it isomerizes, or changes shape, then splits into its two component parts. A complex sequence of events, outlined in Figure 3-8, then begins. This involves the activation of several enzymes, resulting in the breakdown of the molecule that normally keeps the cell membrane open to allow the flow of sodium ions (Stryer, 1987). (In order to understand what happens next you should know a little about how information is transmitted to and by neurons and receptors. If you are a bit unsure in this area you should stop and read the "Primer of Neurophysiology" we've included as an appendix at the back of the book.) Once the flow of positively charged sodium ions into the rod stops, the rod cell **hyperpolarizes**—that is to say that the normally negative charge of -40 millivolts across the cell membrane becomes even more negative, perhaps -70 to -80 mv. This hyperpolarization indicates that the rod has been stimulated by light (Hubbell & Bownds, 1979; Schnapf & Baylor, 1987).

To be ready for another response this process must be reversed. The rhodopsin regenerates in the dark from the retinal and opsin with the help of vitamin A and other enzymes. There is some evidence indicating that light actually provides the energy to resynthesize rhodopsin, although this process is somewhat too complex to discuss here (Blazynski & Ostroy, 1981; Rodieck, 1973). Notice that vitamin A is vital to the resynthesis and in the absence of vitamin A rhodopsin cannot be formed. In isolated communities where fish products or appropriate vegetables are not available, the absence of vitamin A in the diet shows up in "epidemics" of night blindness, as the rods become nonfunctional (Wald, 1968).

The identification and analysis of cone pigments has proved to be more difficult and elusive than that of rhodopsin. However, we have learned

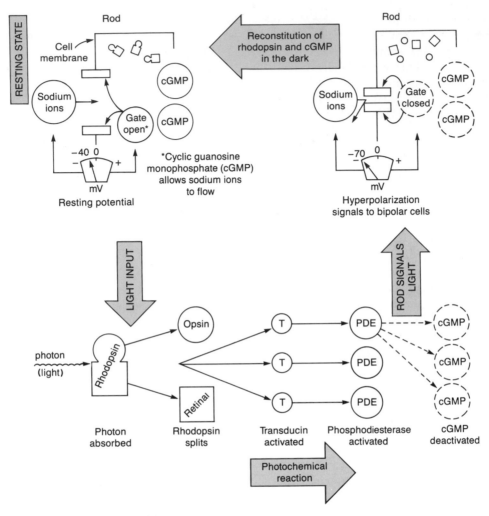

FIGURE 3-8   The rod response cycle that transforms the capture of a photon into hyperpolarization, which signals that light has been received.

that a purple-colored pigment **iodopsin** ("visual purple") is present in the cone cells of some birds. On exposure to light, iodopsin breaks down into retinal and another form of opsin. The opsin found in cones is often called **photopsin** to distinguish it from that in rods, which is called **scotopsin.** Opsins are large complex protein molecules, and the opsin protein in cones is slightly different from that found in rods. The retinal, however, appears to be

the same in rods and cones. Research indicates that all photopigments, regardless of the animal species studied, are composed of the same retinal and a specific protein or opsin that is characteristic of each pigment (Dartnall, 1957; Metzler & Harris, 1978). The biochemical events that lead to hyperpolarization in the presence of light, as we outlined above, are believed to be similar for rods and cones (Bridges, 1986; Schnapf & Baylor, 1987). This hyperpolarization serves to stimulate the bipolar cells. The bioplar cells in turn stimulate the ganglion cells. At the same time, complex interactions occur between neighboring bipolar and ganglion cells via the horizontal and amacrine cells that connect to them. The axons of the ganglion cells then carry the resulting neural signals out of the eye toward the brain.

NEURAL RESPONSES TO LIGHT

In order to get the information about the retinal image out of the eye and up to the brain, the axons of the retinal ganglion cells extend in a transverse fashion across the retina and gather together to exit from the eye by means of a hole through the retina and the scleral wall. The resulting bundle of axons forms the **optic nerve.** Through the center of the optic nerve come the blood vessels that sustain the metabolic needs of the eye. Since the bundle of axons must exit through the retina, there are no photoreceptors in this region. Because of this there can be no visual response to light striking this portion of the retina and it is appropriately called the **blind spot.** The circular pattern of neural axons as

they form the nerve to exit the eye has led anatomists to refer to the blind spot as the **optic disk.** You may easily demonstrate the absence of vision in this region of the retina by referring to Demonstration Box 3-5.

The output of the retina is transmitted to the brain via the optic nerves. The nerve impulses transmitted via the ganglion cell axons that make up the optic nerve are not ''raw'' sense data, but are the result of a large amount of neural processing that has already taken place in the retina itself. In order to understand how much processing has occurred, one might consider that there are some 120 million rods and another 5 million cones in each human eye. There are only about 1 million axons in each optic nerve. Clearly, then, each receptor cell does not have its own private pipeline to the brain, but rather the responses of a very large number of photoreceptors may be represented in one optic nerve fiber. This comes about when the combined activity of the 125 million rods and cones, plus the output of several million more intervening bipolar, horizontal, and amacrine cells, converge on the much smaller number of ganglion cells. We will soon see how the information is modified as it is collected.

DEMONSTRATION BOX 3-5. The Blind Spot

The region of the retina where the optic nerve leaves the eye contains no photoreceptors and thus is blind. You may demonstrate this for yourself by using the figure here. Close your left eye and with your right eye look at the X in the figure. Keeping your eye on the X, move the page toward you. At some point the little open square will seem to disappear. At this point its image is falling on your blind spot. Notice that when you have the page at the correct distance, not only does the square seem to disappear, but also the line appears to run continuously through the area where the square should be. This indicates that we automatically ''fill in'' missing information. We fill it in with material that is similar to nearby visible material. This accounts for why you are not normally aware of the blind spot. You are simply supplying the missing information to fill in this ''hole'' in the visual field.

Since the information carried to the brain by a single ganglion cell can represent the combined activity of a large number of rods and cones, a single ganglion cell may respond to light from a sizeable region of the retina. Such a region, or area of the retina, in which light alters the firing rate of a cell, is called that cell's **receptive field.** Thus, a single ganglion cell serves as a clearing house for information coming from a substantial zone of receptor cells in the retina. In order to understand how visual information is processed, we would want to know how specific ganglion cells respond to various forms of light stimuli. Before attempting to do this, however, it is important for you to understand the nature of neural responses in general, and how they are measured experimentally. If you have not already done so, this might be a good time to read the "Primer of Neurophysiology" that we've included as an appendix to the book.

Retinal Responses and Receptive Fields

Most contemporary studies of the response of retinal ganglion cells to light have followed the lead of Hartline (1940) and Kuffler (1953), who inserted an electrode through the eye of an anesthetized cat and recorded from single ganglion cells in the retina. Generally, when a single small spot of light is displayed on a screen, thereby stimulating the retina of the animal observing it, three different types of responses from a cell may be elicited, depending on the location of the spot in the field. The first type of response is the one most typically expected when a neuron is excited, a burst of neural impulses immediately following the onset of a stimulus. This response has been dubbed an **on response.** Alternatively, the cell can give a burst of impulses coincident with the termination of a stimulus. Such a response is termed an **off response.** Some responses are hybrids because both the presentation and the removal of a stimulus causes a burst of neural impulses. These are designated **on-off responses.** Typical examples of these responses are shown in Figure 3-9.

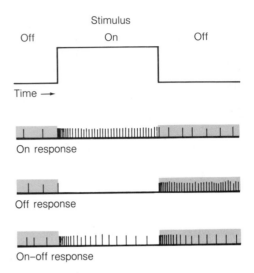

FIGURE 3-9   On, off, and on-off neural responses in the retinal ganglion cells.

When investigators use very small stimulus lights (about 0.2 mm in diameter) the nature of the retinal ganglion cell response tends to vary from on, through on-off, to off, depending on the location of the stimulus. A map of the shape of the overall receptive field of the retinal ganglion cell (the region of retinal stimulation to which the cell responds) shows that the responses are distributed circularly with two distinct zones within each receptive field. Typically, the receptive field has a relatively circular center that gives on responses when stimulated. That is, the ganglion cell responds with an on response to the onset of a light stimulus. The outer portion of the receptive field gives the opposite result. That is, the onset of a light does not produce a response, but its offset does. Between these two regions, roughly at the boundary between the on and off regions, is a narrow region where on-off responses occur. Typical receptive fields are shown in Figure 3-10, where on response regions are marked by + and off by − (remember, on-off responses occur at the border between these regions).

As Figure 3-10 indicates, some receptive fields have the opposite organization, with the cen-

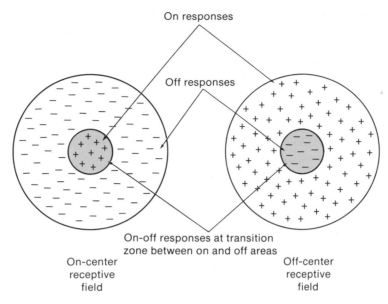

FIGURE 3-10   Circular center-surround retinal receptive fields of two types.

tral region giving off responses and the surrounding region showing on responses. There are approximately equal numbers of off-center cells and on-center cells in the retina. The ganglion cells that show the on and off center responses are visibly different. Apparently, the off-center cells make contact with their respective bipolar and amacrine cells at a more peripheral level in the retina (closer to the photoreceptors) than do the on-center cells (Kaneko, Nishimura, Tachibana, Tauchi & Shimai, 1981; Nelson, Kolb, Robinson & Mariani, 1981). Furthermore, there is evidence suggesting that specific amacrine cells, with different neurotransmitters, may shape particular receptive field properties in ganglion cells (Dacey, 1988; Masland, 1986).

X, Y, and W Cells

We now know that there are several different types of ganglion cell responses, which differ along a number of important characteristics. Three specific classes of cell, which have been given the completely atheoretical names of **W, X,** and **Y cells,** have attracted the most research (Lennie, 1980;

Rodieck, 1979; Tomita, 1986). To begin with, these retinal ganglion cells differ in the speed with which neural impulses travel along their axons. Overall, the Y cells are the fastest, with neural conduction speeds of about 40 meters per second, whereas the X cells respond with conduction speeds of one-half that of the Y cells. The most sluggish are the W cells, which are physically very tiny and conduct very slowly (10 m/sec). W cells may have complex receptive field responses of unique types that differ from those we showed in Figure 3-10, with some responding only to stimuli moving in a particular way and others having on-off centers (Schiller, 1986). The sluggish manner in which W cells respond, however, has led most people to assume that the basic analysis of the visual scene is mostly done by the X and Y cells (e.g., Sherman, 1985).

X and Y cells differ along a number of important dimensions. Both have the center-surround, on-off arrangement we have described. However, X cells are physically smaller than Y cells and have smaller center-surround receptive fields. Proportionally, there are many more X than Y cells, and they differ in terms of their distribution across the retina. Virtually no Y cells are found in the foveal region, and the number of Y cells increases as we move outward into the peripheral retina. The characteristic neural response pattern of X and Y cells also differs. X cells, when stimulated, respond in a rather sustained manner, continuing their neural activity as long as the stimulus remains or for some time after it ends. Y cells, however, have a much more transient response. They tend to give only a brief burst of activity when the stimulus comes on or goes off, falling silent quickly thereafter.

Another difference between X and Y cells is illustrated in Figure 3-11. Part A shows a schematic drawing of the receptive field of a retinal ganglion cell in which half the field is evenly illuminated with light and the other half is dark. Suppose that we now switched the illumination to the pattern shown as B or C. If we were stimulating an X cell it would continue to respond exactly as it had been responding. In other words, as long as the same amount of illumination is present in the center and surround, the X cell does not distinguish between the different locations of illumination. However, any switch in the pattern of illumination will provoke a vigorous response in a Y cell. Since such changes in the distribution of illumination across the receptive field are usually caused by movement of an object, the usual interpretation of this fact is that Y cells may be specialized for movement detection and X cells specialized for the analysis of

stationary patterns (Kruger, 1981). However, several other lines of data suggest that the attributes to which each type of cell responds may be more complex (e.g., Sherman, 1985).

THE VISUAL PATHWAYS

As we noted in an earlier section, the axons of the retinal ganglion cells gather together and exit from the eye at the blind spot. This bundle of axons, which forms the optic nerve, is the beginning of the pipeline of information that eventually ends in the brain. However, there are two distinct anatomical routes that lead to the common end point, and each carries somewhat different information.

The primary visual pathway is the **geniculostriate system;** the secondary pathway is the **tectopulvinar system.** Both begin in the same fashion, with the information traveling out of the eyes along the optic nerves. As can be seen in Figure 3-12, the first significant event occurs where the two optic nerves come together at a point that looks like an X. This point is called the **optic chiasm** (from the Greek letter χ, which is called *chi*). In lower animals, the optic nerve from the right eye crosses completely to the left side of the head and vice versa. In many mammalian species, particularly those who seem to use combined input from the two eyes to obtain better depth perception (this is discussed more fully in Chapter 10), some of the fibers do not cross. In primates, such as man, approximately one-half of the optic nerve fibers cross to the opposite side of the head. These are the fibers that represent the two inside or *nasal* retinas. Those from the outside or *temporal* halves of each retina do not cross but continue on the same side. Such an arrangement implies that the two halves of the visual field will be projected to the opposite sides of the brain. You should also remember what is happening optically in order to keep the situation straight. Since the crystalline lens in the eye reverses the image up-down and right-left, the right visual field is projected onto the

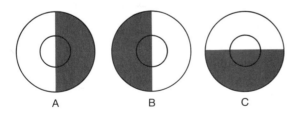

A   B   C

FIGURE 3-11   If the illumination pattern on a center-surround receptive field was half light and half dark as shown in A, and then was shifted to a new orientation (either B or C), an X cell would not respond to the change but a Y cell would.

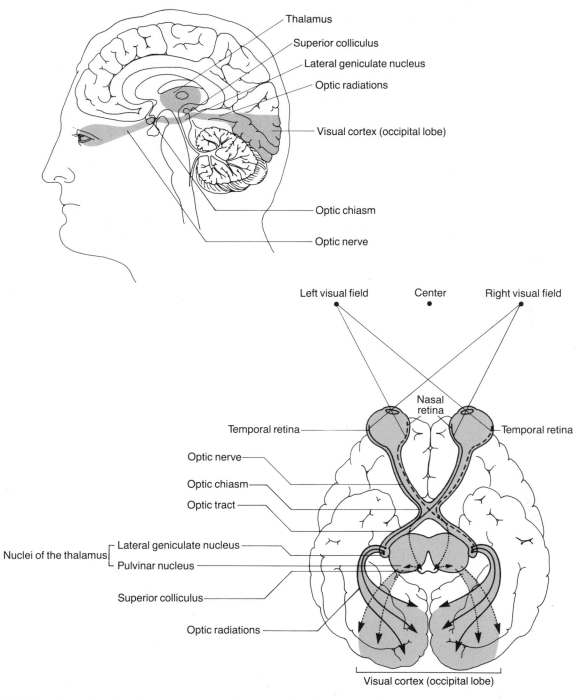

FIGURE 3-12   The visual pathways from the eye to the visual cortex.

nasal half of the retina of the right eye and the temporal half of the retina of the left eye. The axons from the left half of each retina (or left *hemiretinas*) terminate in the left side of the brain. Thus, information from the right side of your field of view ends in the left side of your brain, and vice versa as shown in Figure 3-12.

As we begin to trace out the visual pathways we will need a few maps to help us. A general map is given in Figure 3-12. We'll provide you with a few additional ones as we progress.

The Geniculostriate System

Beyond the optic chiasm the pathway is no longer called the optic nerve, but rather the **optic tract.** The central relay center for most of the sensory information reaching the brain is a large body in the midbrain known as the **thalamus.** For most primates the major termination for the optic tracts is reached when the fibers synapse in the **lateral geniculate nucleus** of the thalamus. The lateral geniculate is arranged in six layers, each of which seems to receive input from only one eye, although there is some interaction between the layers. Different layers may process different types of visual information (Livingston and Hubel, 1988). Each layer contains a map of the visual field, in that there is a point in each layer that corresponds to a point in the visual field, or a point in the retina. Later on we will find that there are many maps of the visual field in the brain (Orban, 1984).

Electrophysiological studies of the lateral geniculate nucleus have shown that its neurons are spontaneously active. This means that these cells are always producing some number of neural impulses, even in the dark. Although this may seem a bit surprising, spontaneity is a characteristic of brain cells. We do not fully understand why this activity maintains itself. It may simply be because the neurons are alive and announce this by occasional random responses. This continuing train of responses does augment the information coding capacity of the cells, however, since signals may now be either excitatory (cause an increase in the firing rate over the baseline activity level) or inhibitory (cause a decrease in activity relative to the resting response rate).

As is the case with the retinal ganglion cells, lateral geniculate cells do not respond to visual stimuli unless the stimulation occurs within their receptive fields. Thus, the activity of a particular lateral geniculate neuron provides information about the location of an object in space because it responds only to those objects projected onto the patch of retinal receptors that define its receptive field. These receptors, in turn, respond only to objects in a particular region of the visual field. Generally, the receptive fields of the lateral geniculate cells are similar to those of the retina. If we map a lateral geniculate cell by projecting points of light onto a screen in the visual field in front of an animal, we find that the cell response appears similar to that of a retinal ganglion cell. For instance, most such cells have an on center and an off surround, or the reverse. One interesting finding is that the X and the Y cells go to different regions of the lateral geniculate, hence acting much like parallel and independent pathways (Schiller, 1986). In addition, lateral geniculate cells, which receive X and Y inputs from the retina, show X-like and Y-like responses to moving and stationary stimuli (Lehmkuhle, Kratz, Mangel & Sherman, 1980; Lennie, 1980; So & Shapley, 1981).

There is one feature that makes the lateral geniculate responses extremely interesting. Much evidence suggests that some cells respond differentially not only to the location of a light but also to its color (DeValois & Jacobs, 1984; Hurvich, 1981). For instance DeValois and DeValois (1975) reported that one type of cell in the lateral geniculate of monkeys responds with an increase in firing rate when the center of the receptive field is stimulated by a red spot of light, whereas it shows an off response (a decrease in activity relative to the spontaneous firing rate) when the center is stimulated by a green light. This finding suggests the possibility of encoding both color and location information in the same cells, a concept we will encounter again in Chapter 5.

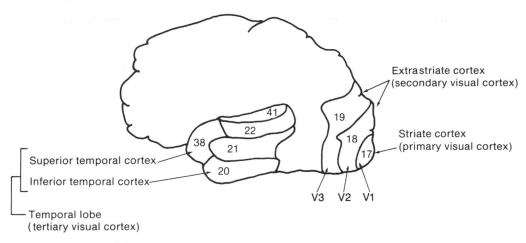

FIGURE 3-13   The principal visually responsive regions of the cortex, and associated regions, with Brodmann's numbering of the areas and several alternate labeling systems.

When the axons of the lateral geniculate neurons leave the geniculate, they spray out and form a large fan of fibers called the **optic radiations.** These fibers eventually synapse with cells in the cortex in the rear (or posterior) portion of the brain, known as the **occipital lobe.** Several alternate labels have been used to refer to this region of the brain. The most popular system for locating parts of the cortex is the numbering system devised by Brodmann (1914) based on the appearance of cells. In Brodmann's numbering system this primary area of visual function, that is, the place where the fibers from the lateral geniculate terminate, is designated **Area 17.**

Since when sliced vertically there is a banded appearance to the cortex, this region is also called the **striate** ("striped") **cortex.** An alternate, but informative, label used for this area is the **primary visual cortex.** Some of the geniculate fibers also project to an area adjacent to Area 17, which is Area 18. It is one of the regions known as the **extrastriate cortex** (*extra* has the meaning here of "beyond"), which is usually regarded as part of the **secondary visual cortex.** Actually, Areas 17, 18, and 19 each contain a separate representation of the visual field, with each point of the field represented by a region in the cortex. There are over

20 such separate maps in the primate cortex (e.g., Essen, 1984). Recently researchers have begun to name these maps separately. Thus, Areas 17, 18, and 19 are referred to as V1, V2, and V3, designating the first 3 visual maps in the cortex. Figure 3-13 shows these areas, and some others we will discuss shortly.

The Tectopulvinar System

There is a second pathway to the visual cortex, which is also indicated in Figure 3-12. This begins when a number of fibers from the optic tract branch off to go toward the brain stem. Most pictures of the brain do not show the brain stem or midbrain structures because they are hidden by the cortex. In Figure 3-14 we have shown schematically where these structures are located, and we have marked off some of the areas that are of concern to us. The region of the brain stem of interest is, in an evolutionary sense, a much older, more primitive visual center known as the **tectum.** In some lower animals most visual processing occurs here. The part of the tectum that receives most of the incoming fibers is the upper pair of what appear to be four bumps on the back (or dorsal) surface of the brain

stem; these are known as the **superior colliculi.**
Not all of the retinal ganglion cell types project to
the superior colliculi, however. Only Y- and W-
type inputs come here. X inputs seem only to be
part of the geniculostriate system, whereas Y and
W cells seem to be part of both (Orban, 1984).

From the superior colliculi the pathway continues on to the thalamus. However, rather than
projecting to the lateral geniculate nucleus, the
pathways go the **pulvinar** and the **lateral posterior
nuclei,** which are located nearby, as you can see
from Figure 3-14. From here, the fibers project to
the cortex. None are destined for the primary visual
cortex (Area 17), but rather they extend to the secondary visual areas (Areas 18 and 19).

Do the two different visual pathways serve
different perceptual functions? Basically, the geniculostriate system seems to be involved in the fine-
grained perception of patterns, and perhaps colors,
whereas the tectopulvinar system seems to coordinate the localization of objects in space, the guidance of eye movements, and gross pattern
perception (Essen, 1984; Ungerleider & Mishkin,
1982). Perhaps the most dramatic demonstrations
of these separate functions come from studies of
lower vertebrates. In one study, Schneider (1969)
showed that removal of the lateral geniculate of the

golden hamster left the animal with an inability to
recognize patterns, whereas removal of the superior
colliculi left it with the ability to identify patterns
but an inability to localize them well enough to approach them. Deficits in spatial localization and
depth perception have also been shown for cats
when the tectopulvinar system is blocked (Ogasawara, McHaftie & Stein, 1984). This type of result
seems consistent with the speculation that the two
anatomical visual pathways serve the different
functions of localization and identification, although some overlap in function seems likely.

THE VISUAL CORTEX

There are over 100 million neurons in the visual
cortex. Only the smallest fraction of these have
been thoroughly studied in attempts to discover
their response characteristics. What we do know of
these cells is based largely on research done with
microelectrodes, employing techniques similar to
those used in the mapping of the receptive fields
for the retinal ganglion and lateral geniculate cells.
Much of the pioneering work was done by David
Hubel and Torstein Wiesel, who received the Nobel prize in 1981 for this research effort.

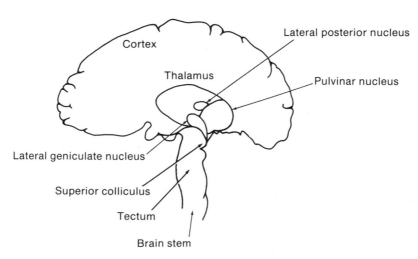

FIGURE 3-14   **The visually responsive areas of the thalamus and optic tectum.**

We have already mentioned that there are several places in the cortex where there is a rather direct topological (point-for-point) mapping of the external visual world, with specific points in the environment corresponding to specific points in the cortex. This was initially established for Area 17 based ôn clinical data from cases of accident or war injury, where penetrating missile wounds have injured specific parts of the cortex. When a piece of the occipital cortex is so damaged, the patient is blind in part of the visual field. Such a damaged area is technically called a *lesion,* and the blind patch in the visual field is called a **scotoma** (meaning "dark spot"). Through the use of such lesions, the correspondence between sections of cortex and parts of the visual field can be mapped, although the cortical map does not correspond exactly with the external scene in all of its dimensions. For instance, the fovea is represented by an inordinately large quantity of cortex relative to its actual size on the retina. This is in accord with its disproportionate importance relative to other retinal regions. When we say that points on the cortex correspond to points in the visual field, we do not mean to imply that if you are looking at a house there is a house-shaped pattern of electrical excitation in the cortex. Rather, it indicates that much of the analysis of features of visual input occurs within individual cortical neurons and patches of adjacent cortex.

Receptive Fields in the Visual Cortex

Following the methodological procedures of Hubel and Wiesel (1962, 1979), many investigators have mapped receptive fields of cortical cells in animals. For instance, recording electrodes have been placed (or implanted) in cortical cells in Area 17 and the cell's electrical responses to stimuli projected onto a screen in front of the animal measured, as we illustrate in the Appendix, Figure A-5 (DeValois, Yund & Helper, 1982; Heggelund, 1981a, 1981b). When cortical cells are mapped in this way, the familiar circular on and off regions of ganglion and lateral geniculate cells are still found. However, the majority of the measured receptive fields have elongated central regions.

A map of some such cells is shown in Figure 3-15. This type of cell, which Hubel and Wiesel labeled a **simple cell,** generally has no spontaneous activity at all and never seems to respond to diffuse illumination covering the whole screen. Sometimes such cells respond, although grudgingly, to small spots of light. However, because of the elongation of the central region of the receptive field, the best stimulus for such a cell is a dark or light bar or line flashed in the appropriate location in the receptive field. Figure 3-15 shows the receptive fields that might be mapped from several simple cells. Beneath each of them you will see the stimulus that produces the maximal response for each of these receptive fields. Notice that in every case the edge between the light and the dark must be at a particular orientation in a particular location. If the edge of the line is flashed on the receptive field at a different angle, a greatly reduced response may be obtained or perhaps no response at all. For this reason such cortical cells are said to have **orientation specificity,** which the simple circular center–surround cells do not have.

There are other kinds of neurons in the visual cortex that seem to be tuned to even more complicated pattern properties of a stimulus. These more elaborate feature-analyzing neurons have been labeled **complex cells.** They have larger receptive fields than do simple cells, although their size may vary tremendously. Like simple cells, complex cells respond maximally to stimuli when they are in a particular orientation. However, they rarely respond to any flashing patterns. What they prefer is a bar or edge moving somewhere within the receptive field, and its location does not appear to be particularly important. In other words, the complex cells seem to generalize their response over a wider area of the visual field. Figure 3-16 shows the responses of a complex cell to two different moving light slits, one in the optimal and the other in a nonoptimal orientation. Notice that both direction of movement and orientation are important factors in determining the response.

Receptive field shape

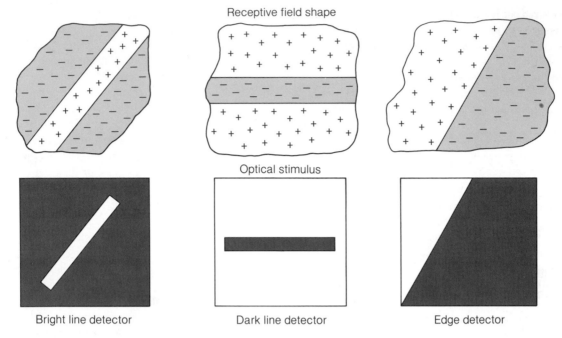

Optical stimulus

Bright line detector   Dark line detector   Edge detector

FIGURE 3-15   **Receptive fields of simple cortical cells:** + **indicates a region in the receptive field that gives an on response, and** − **indicates an off response.**

These complex cells do not exhaust the types of cells recorded in the cortex. At a slightly more sophisticated level are certain special complex cells that are often called **hypercomplex cells.** These respond not only to the orientation and to the direction of movement of the stimulus, but also to the length, the width, or other features of shapes, such as the presence of corners. Figure 3-17 shows an example of some hypercomplex cell responses.

Organization of the Primary Visual Cortex

Simple, complex, and hypercomplex cells are not randomly intermixed in the visual cortex. Instead, particular cell types are organized spatially into an incredibly detailed structure. The cortex in Area 17 is arranged in six layers, numbered 1 to 6, beginning with the outermost (surface) layer. The only layer receiving direct inputs from the lateral genic-

ulate body is Layer 4. In this layer we find the largest number of simple cortical cells, and we also find cells with the simple circular center-surround receptive field found at lower levels of the visual system. Above this level, in Layers 2 and 3, we find that nearly 90 percent of the cells have strong orientation sensitivity. Layers 5 and 6 contain certain special complex cells, with the receptive fields of cells in Layer 5 being quite large and particularly sensitive to the direction of stimulus movement and those in Layer 6 being rather long, narrow, and directionally sensitive. This arrangement is depicted in Figure 3-18.

Cells sensitive to various orientations are not randomly distributed either. Instead, cells with a particular orientation sensitivity tend to be aligned in a column, as diagrammed in Figure 3-19. As we move across the cortex, the orientation specificity shifts by about 10 deg per column. Moving in the other direction, we encounter columns of cells that

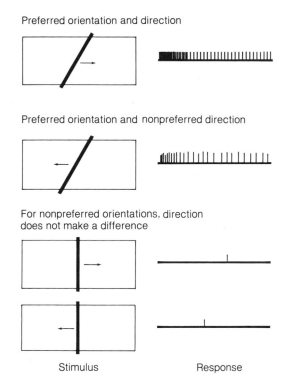

Preferred orientation and direction

Preferred orientation and nonpreferred direction

For nonpreferred orientations, direction does not make a difference

Stimulus   Response

FIGURE 3-16   **Some typical complex cortical cell responses.**

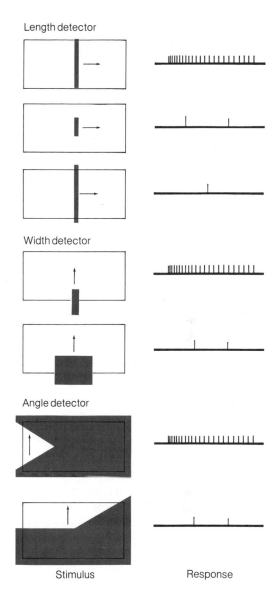

Length detector

Width detector

Angle detector

Stimulus   Response

FIGURE 3-17   **Some typical hypercomplex cortical cell responses.**

have the same orientational sensitivity, however each column looks at a slightly different part of the visual field, thus forming a sort of "slab" of cells with a specific orientational tuning.

One final aspect of the organization of the cortex must be mentioned. Each cortical cell tends to be more responsive to one particular eye than to the other, hence showing a relative **eye dominance.** These inputs are also spatially separated, with a slab of cells responding to one eye located next to one driven by the other eye. These are systematically arranged in alternating stripes across the cortex. A region of cortex containing all 360 deg of orientational specificity, and including a region responsive to both the left eye and right eye, forms a larger unit sometimes called a **hypercolumn.** Such a piece of cortex might be between 0.5 and 1 mm

square, and 2 mm deep, and is diagramed in Figure 3-19. Our catalog of cell types and arrangements does not exhaust all the forms of special receptive field properties that may be perceptually important. We shall mention others when we talk about

Layers of cortex

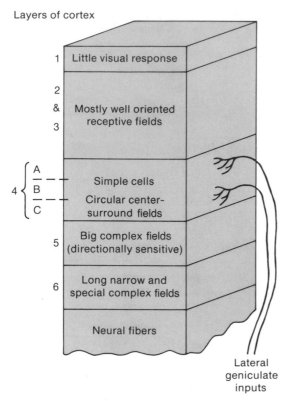

FIGURE 3-18   Location of various visually responsive cells in the layers of the striate cortex (Area 17).

tainly, many pattern-recognition machines have been built using this principle. For instance, the machine that reads the numbers on your bank check is tuned to respond to certain, highly stylized, numerical stimuli by matching the patterns on paper to internally represented codes. Unfortunately, in mammalian species the significance of such feature-extraction cells for the perceptual process has not yet been determined. There also is evidence that removal of large areas of the primary visual cortex (and hence most of these orientation-specific cells), although greatly reducing visual acuity, actually does not have the massively disruptive effects that might be expected if higher-level perception were directly dependent on extraction of simple features by these receptive cells (e.g., Lehmkuhle, Kratz & Sherman, 1982). Furthermore, it is now known that if we alter an animal's visual experience from birth, we can alter the distribution of orientations and features to which cortical cells are responsive. The significance of such changes will be discussed later when we deal with the effects of experience in Chapter 17. As Barlow (1985) has pointed out, it is very difficult to go directly from single-cell responses to higher-level perceptual phenomena. It is often much more useful to go the other way, from the perceptual phenomena to the search for a physiological unit that might support it.

The Temporal Lobes

Both the geniculostriate system and the tectopulvinar system have inputs to the secondary visual areas 18 and 19. From here the information seems to travel onward to the temporal lobes of the brain, which roughly correspond to the regions of the brain directly behind the temples of your skull (Rockland & Pandya, 1981). Here, recent evidence suggests, there are additional maps of the visual field and some very complex visual processing takes place. In order to localize these tertiary visual areas you might look back at Figure 3-13.

The first part of this region to be studied was

brightness, spatial frequencies, color, and depth perception in later chapters. For the moment, however, these give a general idea of the types of visual analysis that may be monitored at the single-cell level in the primary and secondary visual cortices.

Such a detailed architecture, spatial arrangement, and specificity at the cellular level is bound to elicit certain forms of theoretical speculation. Thus, the existence of orientation-specific or feature-specific cells in the cortex suggests that pattern perception may take place by decomposing visual stimuli into component features or contours. These would then be resynthesized at a later point according to some plan or template (Frisby, 1980). Cer-

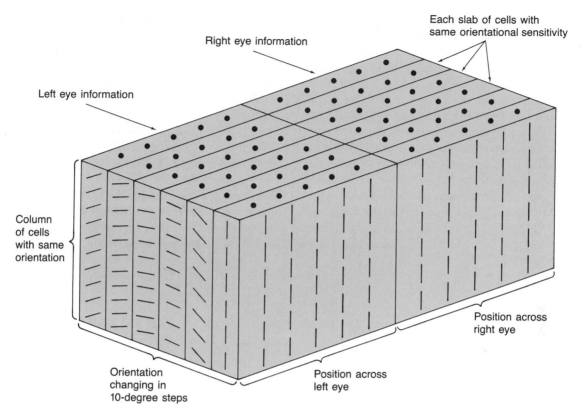

Right eye information

Left eye information

Each slab of cells with same orientational sensitivity

Column of cells with same orientation

Orientation changing in 10-degree steps

Position across left eye

Position across right eye

FIGURE 3-19   Diagram of a hypercolumn, which is a small region of visual cortex containing inputs from both eyes and all visual orientations, separated spatially, as shown.

the lower portion, called the **inferotemporal cortex.** The visual significance of this section of cortex was accidentally discovered by Kluver and Bucy in 1937 while observing monkeys who had undergone surgery that removed most of both temporal lobes. They called the syndrome **psychic blindness.** The animals could reach for, and accurately pick up, small objects; hence, they were clearly not blind. However, they did appear to have lost the ability to identify objects by sight. An example of this is shown in what was named the **concentration test.** Here, a piece of food or a metal object is presented to the monkey approximately every 30 sec. Generally, a normal monkey will eat the food, and discard the nail or steel nut after examination by

mouth. Within a few trials, a normal monkey will let the metal objects pass by and select only the food. For animals with inferotemporal lobe loss, however, both the food and the inedible object were picked up on virtually every trial. The animal seemed to show no evidence of learning to discriminate between the targets. Wilson (1957) found that such monkeys could discriminate between an inverted and an upright *L* by touch, yet with inferotemporal lesions they could not make the same discrimination visually.

This syndrome is similar to a human defect called **visual agnosia** (Kolb & Whishaw, 1985). Such patients can see all parts of the visual field, but the objects they see mean nothing to them.

Patients with lesions of the right temporal lobe also show deficits on a variety of visual tests. For instance, they have difficulty in placing pictures in a sequence that relates a meaningful story or pattern. They also have difficulty in learning to recognize new faces. Furthermore, such patients make poor visual estimates of the number of dots in an array, have difficulty recognizing overlapping figures, have poor memory for nonsense forms, and generally have poor picture memory. We'll have more to say about such agnosias when we consider some pathologies of perception in Chapter 18.

Needless to say, some investigators have begun to map single neurons in the inferotemporal cortex. Some microelectrode measurements in the monkey brain have produced startling results, suggesting that neurons found in this part of the brain have amazing response specificities. Although this research area is quite new, neurons sensitive to size, shape, color, orientation, and direction of movement have already been discovered in this region of the brain (Desimone, Albright, Gross & Bruce, 1980). There is even a report that one neuron produced its best response when the stimulus was the outline of a monkey's paw. Gross, Rocha-Miranda, and Bender (1972) report that one day they discovered a cell that seemed unresponsive to any light stimulus. When they waved a hand in front of the stimulus screen, however, they elicited a very vigorous response from the previously unresponsive neuron. They then spent the next 12 hours testing various paper cutouts in an attempt to find out what feature triggered this specific unit. When the entire set of stimuli was ranked according to the strength of the responses they produced, they could not find any simple physical dimension that correlated with this rank order. However, the rank order of stimuli, in terms of their ability to drive the cell, did correlate with their apparent similarity (at least for the experimenters) to the shadow of a monkey's hand. The relative adequacy of a few of these stimuli in producing a neural response is shown in Figure 3-20. Interestingly enough, fingers pointing downward elicited very little response when compared to fingers pointing upward or to the

side. An animal looking at his own hand would most likely see a hand with fingers pointing upward. Such complex response specificity has been observed a number of times in this region of the cortex (Desimone & Gross, 1979).

Even more startling degrees of stimulus analysis seem to be emerging from a region of the temporal lobe called the **superior temporal cortex.** Here Bruce, Desimone, and Gross (1981) found cells in monkeys that responded selectively to drawings of faces. The more realistic, and monkeylike, the face, the stronger the response. Distorting the stimulus, by removing the eyes, scrambling the features, or presenting a cartoon caricature, resulted in weaker responses. Kendrick and Baldwin (1987) have found similar cells in sheep that respond preferentially to sheep faces and, interestingly, to human faces as well. Thus, it seems possible that in your temporal cortex there might be a template for the perception of your grandmother, your car, or many other familiar stimulus shapes.

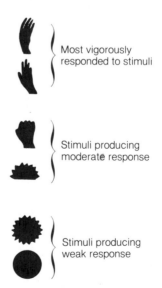

FIGURE 3-20   The stimuli in the figure were used to excite a neuron in the inferotemporal cortex of a monkey. Notice that the more handlike a stimulus is, the more vigorous the response.

Alternate Visual Maps

We mentioned earlier that there were many alternate maps of the visual field in the cortex. More than 20 have been described for primates, with over a dozen of these in the temporal cortex, at least 3 in the occipital region, and others dotted around the brain (Essen, 1984). The pattern of innervations, in the forms of X, Y, and W cells, and the specific pathways to the cortex activated can take on quite a complex pattern, as can be seen in the summary presented in Figure 3-21.

Why are there so many different maps of the visual field? To begin with, you must remember that the function of the visual system is not to recreate an image of the outside world in the brain, since there is nobody in there to look at such an image even if it were there. The function of the visual system is to identify objects and locate them in space. A number of investigators (e.g., Cowey, 1981; Livingston and Hubel, 1988; Phillips, Zeki & Barlow, 1984) have suggested that each map of the visual field is set up to extract some subset of properties from the visual image. Thus, one map might be relatively specialized for color, another for orientation or movement, yet another for distance or texture, and so forth. The reason for the topographic mapping may be to isolate ''an object'' with ''a property'' with ''a specific location in space.'' We will encounter this concept again when we talk about object and form perception in Chapter 11 (see also Treisman, 1986). This means that the destruction of any one of these cortical maps may produce very subtle disruptions of visual processing, rather than massive global effects, such as the total loss of the ability to read type on paper.

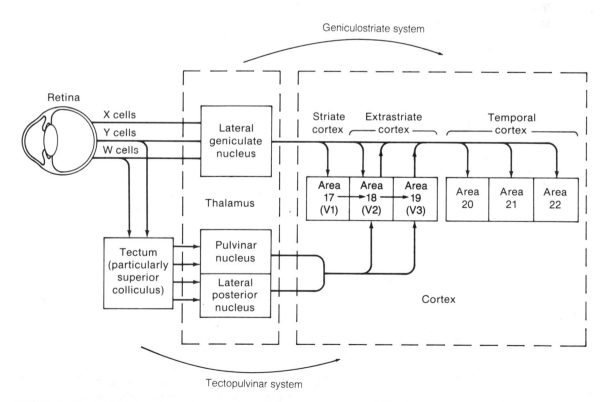

FIGURE 3-21   A highly schematic overview of the visual system, indicating the two visual pathways and their connections with the major subcortical and cortical centers.

GLOSSARY

The following definitions are specific to this book.

Accommodation   The process by which the lens of the eye varies its focus.

Acuity   The ability of the eye to resolve or discriminate details.

Amacrine cells   Large, laterally interconnecting neurons found in the retina near the ganglion cell layer.

Aqueous humor   The fluid occupying the small chamber between the cornea and the lens of the eye.

Area 17   According to Brodmann's numbering system, another name for the primary visual cortex, which is one part of the occipital lobe of the brain receiving inputs from the geniculostriate system.

Areas 18 and 19   Secondary visual cortex receiving inputs from both the geniculostriate and tectopulvinar systems.

Bipolar cells   Neural cells in the retina between the photoreceptor and ganglion cell layers.

Blind spot   Portion of retina through which optic nerve passes and therefore an area without photoreceptors. This region shows no response to light.

Complex cells   Cells in the visual cortex that respond to features such as line orientation and direction of movement.

Concentration test   Method for determining ability to discriminate objects visually following inferotemporal lobe loss.

Cones   Short, thick, tapering cells in the photoreceptive layer of the retina, used in bright-light and color vision.

Cornea   The transparent, domelike part of the eye formed by the bulged sclera.

Day blindness   Visual difficulty under bright-light conditions, caused by an absence or nonfunctioning of cones.

Duplex retina theory   The concept of two separate visual systems, rod-dependent for dim-light vision and cone-dependent for bright-light vision.

Emmetropic   Referring to an eye with normal accommodative ability.

Extrastriate cortex   Areas 18 and 19 in the occipital lobe of the cortex, the secondary visual cortex.

Eye dominance   Refers to the fact that most cortical receptive cells can be driven better by one eye than the other.

Fovea centralis   A small depression in the retina that contains mostly cones and where acuity is best.

Ganglion cells   Third layer of the retina through which neural signals travel after the photoreceptor and bipolar cells.

Geniculostriate system   The primary visual pathway passing through the lateral geniculate nucleus to the striate cortex.

Horizontal cells   Retinal cells with short dendrites and an axonal process that extends horizontally.

Hypercolumn   A small piece of visual cortex, sensitive to input from both eyes and to a full range of orientation specificity.

Hypercomplex cells   Cortical cells that respond to complex stimulus features regardless of where they occur in the receptive field.

Hypermetropia   Farsightedness.

Hyperpolarization   The change of the electrical potential of a cell toward increasing negativity.

Inferotemporal cortex   A cortical region located in the temporal lobes of the brain, which may be associated with recognition abilities and, pathologically, with visual agnosia.

Iodopsin   The cone pigment present in some birds.

Iris   The opaque, colored membrane controlling the amount of light entering the eye by changing the size of the pupil.

Lateral geniculate nucleus   The first major relay center in the geniculostriate system for optic nerve fibers leaving the retina. It is in the thalamus in primates.

Lateral posterior nucleus   A visual center in the thalamus, part of the tectopulvinar system.

Lens   A transparent body in the eye. It can change shape, thus altering the focus of the retinal image.

Macula lutea   A yellow pigmented area of the retina centered over the fovea.

Millimicron (mμ)   A thousandth of a micron, or a millionth of a millimeter. Now usually called a *nanometer*.

Myopia   Nearsightedness.

Nanometer (nm)   A billionth of a meter (a millionth of a millimeter).

Near point distance   The nearest point to which an object may be brought to an eye and still remain in focus on the retina.

Night blindness   The inability to see under low-light (twilight) conditions, caused by an absence of functioning rods.

Occipital lobe   The rear portion of the brain, which serves as the primary visual processing center.

Off response   A neural response commencing with the termination of a stimulus.

On response   A neural response commencing with the onset of a stimulus.

On-off response   A burst of neural responses given both at the onset and at the termination of a stimulus.

Opsin   Protein part of the rhodopsin pigment.

Optic axis   Hypothetical line from the center of the pupil to the fovea, used as a reference point for distances across the retina.

Optic chiasm   The point at which the two optic nerves meet and the nasal fibers cross to the contralateral side.

Optic disk   The region of the retina where the optic nerve leaves the eye. *See* Blind spot.

Optic nerve   The collection of axons from retinal ganglion cells as they exit the eye.

Optic radiations   The large fans of neural fibers spreading out from the lateral geniculate nucleus to the occipital cortex.

Optic tract   The path of the optic nerve once it is past the optic chiasm.

Orientation specificity   A property whereby cortical cells respond selectively to visually presented lines at a particular orientation.

Photon   A quantum of light energy.

Photopic   Referring to vision under bright-light conditions.

Photopsin   The protein segments of the photochemical in cones.

Photoreceptors   Photosensitive cells in the retina (rods and cones).

Pigment epithelium   The light-absorbing dark layer backing the retina in diurnal animals.

Presbyopia   Farsightedness found in older individuals.

Primary visual cortex   Primary area of visual function in the occipital lobe (Area 17).

Psychic blindness   The condition in which animals are able to locate objects yet are unable to identify them.

Pulvinar nucleus   A visual center in the thalamus.

Pupil   The opening in the iris of the eye through which light enters.

Quantum   The smallest amount possible of any form of electromagnetic radiation. *See* Photon.

Receptive fields   For any particular cell, the region of the visual field in which a stimulus can produce a response.

Reflecting tapetum   The shiny surface backing the retina in some nocturnal animals.

Refractive error   Light-bending or focusing error.

Retina   The rear portion of the eye containing photoreceptors and several types of sensory neurons.

Retinal   Part of the rhodopsin pigment, similar to vitamin A.

Rhodopsin   The photopigment found in rods.

Rods   Long, thin, cylindrical photoreceptors in the retina, used in low-light vision.

Sclera   Strong, elastic outer covering, seen as the "white" of the eye.

Scotopic   Referring to vision under low-light conditions.

Scotoma   A localized blind spot.

Scotopsin   The protein portion of rhodopsin—a type of opsin.

Secondary visual cortex   Brodmann's Areas 18 and 19 in the occipital lobe.

Simple cell   A cortical cell that responds to lines of particular orientation and location.

Striate cortex   Area 17 in the occipital lobe.

Superior colliculi   The termination points of optic nerve fibers in the brain stem.

Superior temporal cortex   An area of the temporal lobe whose cells show a high degree of response specificity to visual stimuli.

Tectopulvinar system   A secondary pathway to the visual cortex that includes nuclei in the brain stem and the thalamus.

Tectum   A primitive visual center in the brain stem.

Thalamus   A large mass of neural tissue located at the base of the cerebrum, which serves as a major "switching center" for sensory information.

V1   Area 17 in primates.

V2   Area 18 in primates.

V3   Area 19 in primates.

Visual agnosia   Syndrome in which all parts of a visual field are seen, but the objects seen are without meaning.

Vitreous humor   The jellylike substance filling the large chamber of the eye.

W cells   Slow-conducting retinal ganglion cells whose function is not yet fully established.

X cells   Moderate-conduction-speed retinal ganglion cells that may be important in detailed pattern vision.

Y cells   Fast-conducting retinal ganglion cells that may be important in motion perception.

CHAPTER
4

Brightness and Spatial Frequency

The following scene must have played countless times on cinema screens in Grade B horror movies.

It is night, and in the darkness two old ragged beachcombers can barely be seen moving along the water's edge. Suddenly, one stops.

"Hey, Charlie, I think there's something out there."

"W-What is it?"

"I can't make it out. It's some sort of glow. It's too dim to make out what it is."

This scene illustrates the most basic property of vision, namely, that it depends on the presence of light. The most primitive visual percepts are simply reactions to the intensity of the incoming energy. These responses are represented in consciousness as a brightness or glow. We often sense the presence of light before sufficient energy exists for us to apprehend shape or form. Thus, the next line in the scenario above usually goes, "It's getting brighter," and then as the energy becomes sufficient to apprehend the object itself, "Oh my God! It's some sort of creature!" As we shall see, the perception of brightness is much more complex and surprising than the script of this particular film.

PHOTOMETRIC UNITS

Electromagnetic energy, or light, can vary along three dimensions: intensity, wavelength, and duration (see Chapter 3). All dimensions are important in the perception of brightness, although brightness varies most directly with intensity. Of course, to make sense of the perceptual effects, we must first be able to specify the physical intensity of the stimulus. This is not as simple as it seems.

Light measurement is based on the visual effects produced by visible radiation and is called **photometry.** Photometric units are used to describe the stimulus and these units are, by convention, expressed in terms of energy. Unfortunately, over the years a confusing array of photometric units has been developed, most of them designed for some

specific purpose by some technical or academic subdiscipline. The result was chaos. Even among the most scholarly, few can tell you how many *nits* there are in an *apostilb* or a *blondel,* or how any of these units are related to a *candle* or a *lambert.* In 1960, the International Conference on Weights and Measures established the *Système International d'Unités,* which is a uniform system of measurement (known commonly as the **SI System**). Throughout this book we use these **standard units.** Should your reading bring you into contact with some of the older forms of photometric measurement, we can only refer you to some more advanced texts such as Wyszecki and Stiles (1967) to try to make sense of the quantities involved.

Basically, there are two ways light can reach the eye: *(a)* directly from a radiating source, such as a light bulb, fluorescent tube, firefly, or the sun; or *(b)* by reflection from surfaces that have radiant energy falling on them, such as walls and paper. Different types of measures are used for these different types of light input. All photometric units, however, are ultimately based on the amount of light emitted from a single candle. The nature of this *standard candle,* its photic energy, and the specific measures derived from it have been fixed (albeit somewhat arbitrarily) by an international body called the *Commission Internationale de l'Eclairage,* usually known as the **CIE.**

Each different aspect of light is designated by its own name and requires a different measurement unit. The amount of energy coming from a light source is called its **radiance.** The unit of radiance is the standard candle, which produces an energy of slightly more than 0.001 watt at a wavelength of 555 nanometers. This quantity of luminous energy is called a **lumen.** The amount of light falling on a surface is another photometric quantity called **illuminance.** The amount of light reflected from a surface is called its **luminance,** and the *percentage* of light falling on a surface that is reflected is called its **reflectance.** The amount of light reaching the retina is called the **retinal illuminance.** Finally, the phenomenal impression of the light intensity of a stimulus is called its **brightness.** Thus, if we have a slide projector shining on a screen, the amount of light energy leaving the bulb determines its *radiance,* the amount of light falling on the screen is its *illuminance,* the amount of light reflected from the screen is its *luminance,* and our perceptual or phenomenal impression is the *brightness* of the screen. Table 4-1 summarizes the most common photometric quantities, how they are measured, the units used, and some of their specific properties.

Before becoming too involved with measurement, however, it is important to remember that, perceptually, brightness is not explained simply by the amount of light reaching the eye. As we noted in Chapter 2, when we plot the magnitude of the brightness sensation against the physical stimulus intensity we get a nonlinear relationship. The ap-

parent brightness measured by a direct scaling technique (such as magnitude estimation) grows approximately as the cube root of the physical intensity (to be precise, the phenomenal sensation grows at a rate equivalent to the light intensity raised to the 0.33 power). This means that if you had a theater stage illuminated by 8 lights and you wished to increase the perceived brightness of the area, doubling the number of lights to 16 would not double the perceived brightness but would only increase it by one-third. If you wanted to double the phenomenal brightness, you would have to increase the number of lights to 64!

Figure 4-1 shows the general shape of this relationship graphically. Notice that the curve in Figure 4-1 greatly resembles the logarithmic curve of Fechner's law (remember Chapter 2, and particularly Figure 2-14). Although this would not be the

Table 4-1   Photometric Units

Photometric term	What is measured	Unit	How measured	Comments
Radiance or luminous flux	Radiant energy from a light source	Lumen	A candela is the light of a 1-lumen source at a distance of 1 m shone on a square meter	Defined in terms of a standard candle (candela)
Illuminance	Light falling on a surface	Lux	1 lumen/m^2	As the source moves farther away illuminance decreases
Luminance	Light reflected from a surface	Candelas per square meter	Lumens reflected from a surface	Independent of distance of eye from surface
Reflectance (albedo)	Proportion of light reflected from surface	Percentage reflectance	$\dfrac{\text{Luminance}}{\text{Illuminance}} \times 100$	Really ratio of reflected to incident light
Retinal illuminance	Amount of light incident on the retina	Trolands	1 candela/m^2 seen through pupil of 1 mm^2 area	Roughly 0.0036 lumens/m^2 through a 1-mm^2 pupil
Brightness	Phenomenal impression of light intensity	Not yet agreed on, but bril is best contender	Relative matching and scaling techniques	Psychological rather than physical quantity

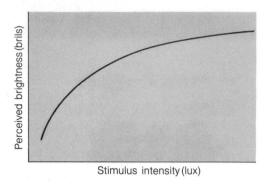

FIGURE 4-1   **The nonlinear relationship between stimulus intensity and brightness.**

case for power functions with larger exponents (e.g., electric shock), the resemblance of the power and log laws for brightness means that the old custom of measuring brightness in terms of logarithms of photometric values still provides a relatively accurate representation of the relationship between the intensity of the physical stimulus and the sensation. For this reason various photometric values, such as the brightness scales used in television studios, are frequently presented in logarithmic units, especially when designed for visual purposes. This serves to equalize the sizes of sensory changes as a function of changes in physical intensity. The unit of brightness in the graph in Figure 4-1 is the **bril,** which was suggested by S. S. Stevens. Each bril represents about one-tenth of a log unit above threshold, in much the same way that a decibel (see Chapter 6) represents one-tenth of a log unit above threshold in audition.

FACTORS IN BRIGHTNESS PERCEPTION

Adaptation

The perception of brightness depends on the current state of sensitivity of your eye, in much the same way that the brightness of the final photographic

image depends on the sensitivity of the film. An amount of light that would produce a faint image on insensitive film may produce an overly bright image on very sensitive film. You are probably aware of the effects of your eyes' changing sensitivity when you walk from a darkened room into the bright sunlight, only to find that everything appears to be so bright and "washed out" that a few moments must pass before objects are clearly visible. The opposite occurs when you walk from a bright outside into a darkened room. Now everything appears to be very dark, and objects are difficult to resolve in the gloom. After a while you can discern objects, although adaptation to darkness takes somewhat longer than adaptation to a brighter environment. We call the process of adaptation to a darker environment **dark adaptation** and that to a brighter environment **light adaptation.** Although we cannot slip off our daylight retina and put on the twilight one in the way that we change film in a camera to deal with changes in lighting conditions, the sensitivity of our eyes changes through these two adaptation processes.

We can monitor directly the changes in sensitivity associated with dark adaptation. First we adapt an observer to bright light by putting him in a brightly lit room for a few minutes, then we turn off the lights. Now we test to find the observer's *absolute threshold* for the detection of light. This is done at fixed time intervals after the onset of darkness, using one of the standard psychophysical methods outlined in Chapter 2. Such an experiment usually reveals that the observer at first needs relatively strong stimuli to reach threshold. However, the eye rapidly becomes more sensitive over the first minute or two, at which point it begins to stabilize at a level that is about 100 times more sensitive (2 log units) than when we initially turned off the lights. After about 10 min of darkness, the sensitivity begins to rapidly increase again. During this second period, the threshold drops quickly for 5 or 10 min, then again stabilizes, reaching a relatively constant level after about 1/2 hour. When we graph the change in threshold for a typical ob-

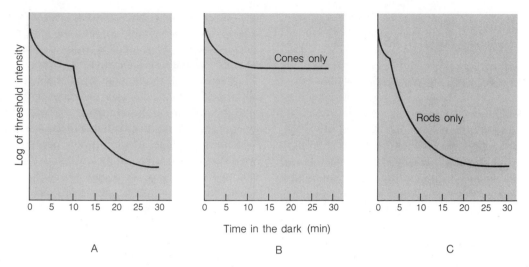

FIGURE 4-2   (A) The normal time course of dark adaptation, (B) dark adaptation in the cones (or central fovea), and (C) dark adaptation in the rods (or periphery).

server, as we have done in Figure 4-2A, we can see a break, or *kink,* in the sensitivity curve. The kink indicates a change in the rate of dark adaptation.

Whenever a sudden transition or break is found in a curve, it often suggests that a second mechanism or process has come into operation. This is confirmed in the present case by the fact that a marked change occurs in conscious perception near this sharp break in the curve. For instance, if we used a greenish light (or nearly any color, for that matter) to measure the threshold, the observer would be able to identify the color throughout the first 10 min or so of the test session. At about the point at which the sensitivity suddenly begins to increase again, the test stimulus would seem to lose its color and become grayish. An old proverb is based on this loss of color vision under dim levels of illumination: "At night, all cats are gray."

In Chapter 3 we talked about the differences between rods and cones. At that time, we reviewed some evidence indicating that rods are found predominantly in animals active during the twilight hours (or in conditions of dim illumination), whereas cones are found predominantly in the retinas of animals that are active during daylight. It was suggested that cones provide **photopic** or daylight vision (including the perception of color) and rods provide **scotopic** or twilight vision. Humans have rods *and* cones; hence, it seems possible that the two segments of the dark adaptation curve represent separate rod and cone contributions. The cones seem rapidly to reach their level of maximal sensitivity. The rods take longer to adapt. When they do, the threshold begins to drop, but at the expense of a loss in color vision. The point at which the adaptation of the rods catches up to that of the cones is the break in the dark-adaptation curve shown in Figure 4-2A.

We can verify this experimentally. Suppose we return to the experimental situation we used to track the course of dark adaptation, but now change the stimulus so that a tiny pencil of light is focused only on the fovea when taking threshold measurements. Since the fovea contains only cones (Chapter 3), this method will allow us to track dark adaptation in cones. Such an experiment gives us the data shown in Figure 4-2B. Notice that this looks just like the first segment of the curve in Figure 4-2A. No second increase in sensitivity occurs, no matter how long we continue in darkness. To demonstrate the lower or rod portion of the curve we repeat the experiment, only now we focus our pencil of light about 20 degrees from the center of the fovea, where the retina contains predominantly rods. When we do this, we get the curve shown in Figure 4-2C, in which the first rapid change (attributable to cone action) is almost completely absent.

An even more spectacular way to show the separate rod and cone origin for the two portions of the dark adaptation curve was provided by Hecht and Mandelbaum (1938). They placed a normal observer on a vitamin-A-deficient diet for 57 days. Since this vitamin is critical for the synthesis of rhodopsin, the pigment in rods, the diet effectively eliminated the action of these receptors. After 57 days, the observer had a dark adaptation curve similar to that in Figure 4-2B. Not only was the rod portion of the curve almost totally absent, but the individual was almost completely night-blind and unable to see dimly illuminated targets. By the way, the observer completely recovered when he went back to his normal diet. Perhaps similar naturally occurring instances have given carrots, a vegetable high in vitamin A, their reputation for being ''good for the eyes.''

Overall, these experiments indicate that two separate physiological mechanisms are involved in the perception of brightness: the cone system for brighter illumination and the rod system for dimmer illumination. There is even some evidence suggesting that when bright light is present, and the cones are active, they actually inhibit or ''turn off'' the action of the rods (Drum, 1981).

There is still much to be learned about the nature of the adaptation process. Clearly, any incoming light will bleach the available photopigments in the rods and cones, and time will be needed for them to regenerate. As more pigment becomes available, the sensitivity of the eye should increase. Although such a process does seem to play a role (MacLeod, 1978), dark adaptation actually involves changes in the sensitivity and responsiveness of neural processes as well (Green & Powers, 1982; Shapley & Enroth-Cugell, 1984). Later in this chapter we shall see that even higher-level cognitive responses may influence our perception of brightness. Demonstration Box 4-1 allows you to see the effects of dark adaptation for yourself.

Retinal Locus

As we saw in Figure 3-7, rods and cones are unevenly distributed across the retina. The fovea contains only cones, which are less sensitive to weak stimuli, and the more sensitive rods are more plentiful in the periphery. Suppose the apparent brightness of a light depended directly on the sensitivity of the stimulated receptors, as well as on the intensity of the light. If that were the case, then moving a constant light stimulus across the retina, stimulating less sensitive cones near the fovea and more sensitive rods in the periphery, should change the

---

DEMONSTRATION BOX 4-1.   Dark Adaptation

To show the dramatic increase in sensitivity associated with dark adaptation you should first carefully blindfold one eye. Use a couple of cotton balls and some tape to do this. After about 30 minutes darken the room, or step into a reasonably dark closet. Remove the blindfold and compare the sensitivity of your two eyes by alternately opening one eye at a time. The dark-adapted eye should see quite well in the dim illumination, but the other eye will be virtually blind.

apparent brightness of the light. This has been verified experimentally (Drum, 1980; Osaka, 1981). Peripheral targets appear brighter. This finding is also embodied in a bit of folk wisdom. At some time in antiquity people noted that looking directly at a dim object, such as a star, could cause it to disappear from view. For this reason, early astronomers would often look at a point off to the side of a star in order to let its image fall on the more sensitive peripheral retina (containing mostly rods). This technique allows such a dim target to be perceived more clearly. If you ever try this yourself, look at a point about 20 deg of visual angle from the star you wish to see. This would allow the star's image to fall on the part of the retina where the density of rods is greatest and would give you maximum sensitivity.

Wavelength

The wavelength of the light stimulating the eye will also affect our perception of its brightness. For instance, yellow light (medium wavelengths) almost always appears to be brighter than blue light (short wavelengths). The usual procedure for assessing the relative brightness of lights of different colors is to use a *bipartite target*. This is simply a circular target that has been divided in half. One half contains the *standard color* that is to be matched in brightness, the other half is the *comparison color* that is adjustable. Systematically pairing various colors and then matching their apparent brightness provides a set of measures of the relative amounts of energy needed to produce equal sensations of brightness for various wavelengths of light. For convenience, the wavelength requiring the least energy to equal the brightness of the standard is set at a value of 1.0. All other wavelengths, being less effective, are assigned values less than 1, depending on their relative brightnesses.

Once this conversion has been made, a curve can be plotted as in Figure 4-3. Such a curve is called a **luminosity curve.** Notice that we actually have two curves in this figure. The first is labeled

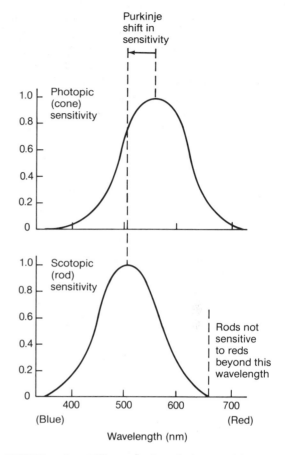

FIGURE 4-3   Differences in relative sensitivity to various wavelengths under photopic and scotopic illumination conditions.

photopic and represents the results we would obtain from the matching experiment if we were working at daylight levels of light intensity. It shows a peak sensitivity for wavelengths around 555 nm and the apparent brightness falls off rapidly for shorter (toward the blue) or longer (toward the red) wavelengths. If we repeat this matching experiment under conditions of dim illumination, in which only rod vision is operating, the observer will not be aware of the color of the stimuli, and both halves of the field will appear gray regardless of their wavelength. Nonetheless, some wavelengths will still look brighter than others. Thus, we can map out the luminosity curve that is marked *scotopic* in Figure 4-3. Under these conditions the curve is somewhat different, with a peak around 505 nm. This curve is shifted toward the short wavelengths, suggesting that we may be more sensitive to blue light under dim viewing conditions.

The change in the apparent brightness of light of different wavelengths as the intensity is changed was first described by the Czechoslovak phenomenologist Johannes E. Purkinje, and in his honor this phenomenon is referred to as the **Purkinje shift.** He first noticed the change while looking at his garden as twilight was falling. As the light dimmed, the apparent brightnesses of the various colors began to change. Reds that had been bright relative to blues and greens began to look darker, while the bluer tones appeared relatively brighter. Because scotopic vision lacks the sensation of color, daylight greens or blues change to moonlight grays, while daylight reds change to moonlight blacks. Demonstration Box 4-2 allows you to experience this shift in sensitivity for yourself.

There is an interesting application of the Purkinje shift. You may remember from watching war movies that the briefing rooms next to airstrips or the control rooms of ships and submarines are often depicted as illuminated by red light. This red is not used solely for dramatic effect in the film but is actually used in such settings. Rods are relatively insensitive to the red end of the spectrum, hence red light is virtually equivalent to no light at all for the rods. However, the cones still function at these longer wavelengths if there is sufficient stimulus intensity, so the cones may be used while the rods are beginning to dark adapt. The dashed line at the upper end of the scotopic curve in Figure 4-3 shows a wavelength where this is true. Thus, pilots about to fly night missions or sailors about to stand the night watch can be briefed or can check their

---

DEMONSTRATION BOX 4-2.   The Purkinje Shift

For this demonstration you will need a dark room and some way of providing a light whose intensity you can vary without altering its color. A good method is to use a television set as a light source. This may be done by tuning the set to an unused channel and turning the contrast control to a minimum. This reduces the visibility of the random dots that normally appear on the screen. Now, if you darken the room so that the television is the only source of illumination, the brightness control on the set will be a means of controlling the room light. An alternate procedure in the absence of a television is to turn on a light in a room and enter a closet, shutting the door after you. The amount of light entering the closet can be controlled by opening the door by differing amounts. Turning your back to the door allows for a diffusion of the light to any target that you wish to be illuminated. Unfortunately, if the outside room is well lit, opening the door by a few centimeters will provide a good deal of light; hence, control of illumination may be improved by dimming the light in the outside room.

Now, look at Color Plate 1. Here we have two colored spots, one blue and one red. When viewed in moderate or bright light (the brightness control on the television is set to high, or the closet door is more widely ajar), the blue and the red spot appear to be approximately equal in brightness. Now, make the light very dim (close the door almost completely, or turn down the brightness control on the television). In the bright light, you were viewing the spots with cone vision. Now, if you dim the lights sufficiently, only rod vision will be activated. After 5–10 min, as your eye dark adapts, the blue spot will appear to be significantly brighter than the red spot. In fact, the red spot may actually disappear. The effect may be accentuated by staring at the white spot. This shifts the images away from the fovea to an area of the retina containing a greater number of rods.

instruments under red illumination, and then go directly into the dark without waiting the many minutes necessary to complete dark adaptation.

Time and Area

In addition to the intensity, wavelength, and retinal location of the stimulus, our ability to detect a spot of light depends on other stimulus properties. For instance, a photographer knows that when she is taking a picture under dim illumination she may have to lengthen the exposure time in order to collect enough light to adequately register the image on the film. In bright sunlight a short exposure will usually do. Actually the same amount of physical energy is necessary to expose the film properly in each case; it just takes longer to collect the requisite amount under dim illumination. In physics this relationship is known as the **Bunsen-Roscoe law.** This law describes the photochemical reaction of any light-sensitive substance, whether it be film or visual pigment. There is a similar trade-off between stimulus duration and stimulus intensity in vision when we are dealing with the problem of the absolute threshold for the detection of light. We can express this relationship using simple algebra. If we define C as the critical amount of light energy necessary to reach threshold, I as the stimulus intensity, and T as the stimulus duration, the relationship is

$$T \times I = C$$

When applied to vision, this is known as **Bloch's law.** Thus, we must increase the length of time a dim stimulus is presented in order for it to be detected, whereas a more intense stimulus can be presented for a shorter duration and still be detected. This time-versus-intensity trade-off only works over stimulus durations less than about one-tenth of a second. This limiting value may vary a bit, being somewhat longer if you are completely dark-adapted and somewhat shorter if you are very light-adapted (Montellese, Sharpe & Brown, 1979). This

means that if the duration is greater than one-tenth of a second, the probability that you will detect a stimulus is no longer affected by stimulus duration but depends only on stimulus intensity. Bloch's law, like many other things in vision, only holds under certain circumstances. For instance, it holds better in the periphery (where there are many rods) than in the fovea (Gottlieb, Kietzman & Bernhaus, 1985) and may also depend on the wavelength of the stimuli used (Schwartz & Loop, 1984).

The size of a stimulus is also important in determining its detectability. In Chapter 3, we noted that there is a good deal of convergence in the visual system. A number of rods or cones may synapse with the same bipolar cell, and several bipolar cells may synapse with the same retinal ganglion cell. Consider a hypothetical example. Suppose four units of neurotransmitter per second are sufficient to activate a bipolar cell, and that bipolar cell has four receptors making synapses with it. If we provide a tiny spot of light, which is only strong enough to elicit one unit of neurotransmitter per second from the retinal receptor, and the light is only wide enough to stimulate two receptors, clearly the bipolar cell will not respond. If we double the size of the stimulus so that all four receptors are illuminated, however, the bipolar cell will receive a total of four units of neurotransmitter per second and it will become activated. Thus, as the area of a stimulus increases, even if its intensity does not change, the likelihood increases that we will recruit enough photoreceptors to begin a chain of neural activity. An alternative way of conceptualizing this is in terms of retinal receptive fields, such as those illustrated in Figure 3-10. Increasing the stimulus size might be thought of as simply "filling in" the center of the receptive field with light, thus adding more on responses to the overall activity.

For relatively small areas, covering visual angles of 10 minutes of arc or less (about 1 mm viewed at arm's length), there is a direct relationship between area and intensity. If A signifies the area stimulated, and I and C are stimulus intensity and critical amount of light energy, respectively, as before, we can describe the relationship as

$$A \times I = C$$

This is known as **Ricco's law.** Thus, if we increase the intensity of a stimulus we can decrease its size and still be able to detect it, and vice versa for a decrease in stimulus intensity.

For stimulus sizes greater than 10 min in visual angle, increasing the area has a reduced effect. The effect of area on detection for larger stimuli is described by

$$\sqrt{A} \times I = C$$

In other words, for larger stimuli a greater increase in area is needed to achieve the same compensation for a decrease in stimulus intensity. This second area-intensity relationship is known as **Piper's law.** Beyond 24 deg of visual angle no further benefit is gained by increasing the size of the stimulus, and the likelihood of detection depends solely on the intensity.

Because these effects are supposedly a result of the summation of neural responses converging on a single retinal ganglion cell, a few additional relationships might be expected. For instance, the degree of summation (or convergence) varies as we move across the retina, with more convergence on a single ganglion cell found in the periphery. Receptive fields are smaller in the foveal region (Randsom-Hogg & Spillman, 1980), which suggests that increasing stimulus area might have a different effect at different positions across the retina, with the area increases facilitating detection more for stimuli in the periphery, and this seems to be the case (Lie, 1980).

Maximum Sensitivity

After this discussion, you may be wondering just what the ultimate limit of sensitivity might be if the stimulus were adjusted to the optimal wavelength, size, duration, and retinal position, and the observer were fully dark-adapted. The classic experiment to answer this question was conducted by Hecht, Schlaer, and Pirenne (1942). They found that the threshold for the perception of a brightness sensation occurred when only six quanta of light (photons) were stimulating the retina. Further computations showed that at this ultimate threshold it was probable that each of six different rods was responding to a different one of the six photons. This is, of course, the maximum sensitivity that is possible theoretically. Even at higher levels of illumination, however, it is possible to show that fluctuations of only a few photons may affect our perception of brightness, thus showing the exquisite sensitivity of the eye as a light detector (Krauskopf & Reeves, 1980; Zuidema, Gresnight, Bouman & Koenderink, 1978).

BRIGHTNESS CONTRAST

Strange as it may seem, our perception of the brightness of targets often depends more on the luminance of adjacent objects than on the luminance of the target itself. Figure 4-4 demonstrates this. Here we have four small squares, each of which is surrounded by a larger square. The central squares are actually all printed in the same gray; thus, the amount of light that reaches your eye from each is the same. Notice, however, that the apparent brightnesses of these small squares are not equal. Their brightnesses vary depending on their background, with the grays printed on dark backgrounds appearing lighter than the grays printed on light backgrounds. This effect is called **simultaneous brightness contrast.**

Everyday experience tells us that your conscious experience of brightness will increase as the amount of light reaching your eye increases. Unfortunately, our perceptual experiences often defy such "common sense." Despite increases in the amount of light reaching your eye, the apparent brightness of a surface may actually *decrease* de-

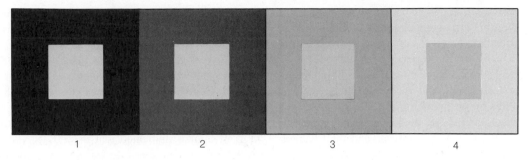

FIGURE 4-4   Simultaneous brightness contrast, showing how the background can alter the perception of the central gray regions.

pending on the brightness of the background on which it rests. This helps to explain why the color black on a television screen appears darker than the apparent darkness of the screen when the set is turned off and no light is being emitted from it at all! This surprising brightness paradox is more clearly shown in Demonstration Box 4-3.

The fact that surfaces vary in brightness as a function of the intensity of their background suggests that there is some form of spatial interaction present, perhaps between adjacent retinal regions that are illuminated by the light reflected from the surfaces. Notice that surfaces on a light background, such as Square 4 in Figure 4-4, appear

darker. The response from the part of the retina exposed to Square 4 has been reduced. This suggests some sort of inhibition of the response as a function of activity in surrounding retinal areas.

Actually, physiological evidence indicates that such inhibitory spatial interaction does take place in the eye. Most of this evidence has been collected from *Limulus* (the horseshoe crab), an animal commonly found on the eastern shores of the United States. *Limulus* has several sets of eyes, but the ones that are most important for research purposes are the lateral eyes, which are faceted (as in the eye of a fly). In such a compound eye, a separate optical system exists for each facet, and each has its

---

DEMONSTRATION BOX 4-3.   The Interaction of Luminance and Background

For this experiment you will need your variable light source again (either the closet or the television). Hold up Figure 4-4 and look at the central squares, with your light source providing a low (but not dim) level of illumination. As you increase the level of illumination from its lowest value, the center target in Square 1 should grow brighter. Now repeat the procedure while looking at the center target in Square 4. Notice that as the luminance level increases, this target square actually gets darker. Since all the center squares are identical in reflectance, the differences in

their apparent brightness depend solely on their backgrounds. This may seem strange because we tend to associate black with the absence of light. Since you are already in a room or a place that potentially can be darkened, turn off all the light sources and close your eyes (to eliminate any stray illumination). Notice that what you are seeing is not black, but rather a misty gray (often called *cortical gray*). Thus, the absence of light is gray, not black. Only in fields that contain some areas of bright illumination can real black be seen.

own primitive retina. Since each eyelet has its own optic nerve, this arrangement spreads out the neural fibers somewhat.

With skill (and a dissecting microscope) it is possible to separate out a single nerve fiber, drape it over an electrode, and record its electrical activity. Much of the work on the visual system of *Limulus* was carried out in the laboratories of the Nobel-prizewinner H. K. Hartline and his frequent collaborator Floyd Ratliff. They were able to dem-

onstrate the inhibitory neural interactions between nearby receptors using a very simple but elegant experiment (Hartline & Ratliff, 1957).

First, they monitored the responses from the cell in *Limulus* that is functionally equivalent to a ganglion cell, called the *eccentric cell,* while the receptor attached to it was stimulated. The fact that the onset of the light increased the activity of the cell, of course, indicated that its activity was controlled by stimulation of the particular receptor they

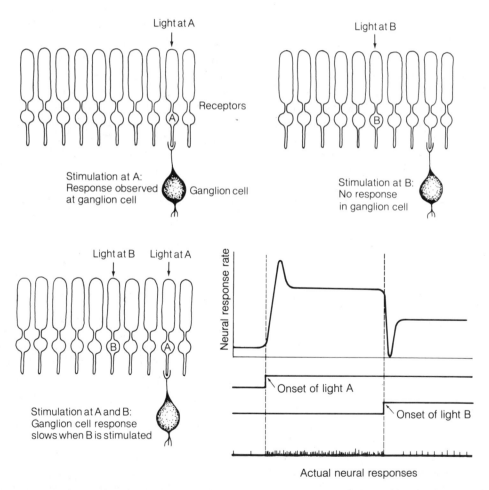

FIGURE 4-5   Lateral inhibition: Stimulating *A* produces a response in the ganglion cell, whereas stimulating *B* does not. Stimulating *B* while *A* is active depresses its response because of lateral inhibition. (From Lindsay & Norman, 1977)

had illuminated. Let us call this ganglionlike cell and its receptor *A*. Next, Hartline and Ratliff illuminated a receptor located a short distance away (call this one *B*). There was no increase in the activity of *A*, indicating that there were no excitatory connections between *A* and *B*. Now the researchers again stimulated *A* and, while the light remained on at *A*, they turned on a light at *B*. Now they observed that the stimulation of *B* actually *decreased* the response of cell *A*. This experiment is shown diagrammatically in Figure 4-5. The importance of these results is that they demonstrate that visual cells may be inhibited by the activity of adjacent visual units. This process is called **lateral inhibition** because the inhibition acts laterally (sideways) on adjacent cells. The amount of inhibition any given cell applies to its neighbors depends on how strongly it is responding and how close the cells are to each other. The more a cell is stimulated, and the closer it is to another cell, the more intensely it will inhibit the other.

It is now easy to understand why the surface in Square 1 is seen to be brighter than the surface in Square 4 in Figure 4-4. In the part of the retina exposed to the bright surround (Square 4) many cells are active and, as a consequence of this activity, they are actively inhibiting their neighbors. This inhibition from the bright surround should reduce the neural response rate in the central square, making it appear dimmer. The part of the retina exposed to the surface with the dark background does not receive as much inhibition from its less strongly stimulated neighbors. Since the amount of stimulation from the central squares is the same, but the cells exposed to Square 1 are undergoing a lesser amount of inhibition, Square 1 appears to be brighter. Thus, lateral inhibition provides a basis for explaining brightness contrast effects.

Lateral inhibition can also explain more complex effects observed in other stimulus configurations. Ever since the 1860s, when Ernst Mach studied patterns with an intensity distribution like that shown in Figure 4-6B, investigators have been intrigued by a particular brightness phenomenon

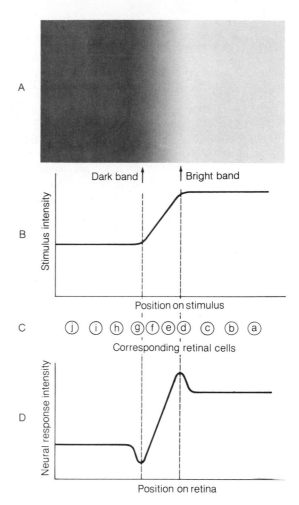

FIGURE 4-6 (A) A Mach band pattern, (B) the actual distribution of stimulus intensity, (C) corresponding retinal cells (see the text), and (D) neural response intensity distribution. (A and B based on Cornsweet, 1970)

such a distribution generates (Weale, 1979). In this figure, we have a uniform dark and a uniform light area, with an intermediate zone that gradually changes from dark to light. However, when we look at the actual stimulus depicted in Figure 4-6A, we do not see a uniform change in brightness flanked by two uniform areas. Instead, two bands

DEMONSTRATION BOX 4-4.   Mach Band Patterns

Mach band patterns do not reproduce well in print. This is probably because the range of luminances possible from ink on paper is not very large. It is actually quite easy to produce your own Mach band pattern using a distribution of light. All you need is a card or a book that is opaque and has a straight edge, and a large light source. If you are in a room that has fluorescent or large frosted light fixtures in the ceiling, these produce a fine uniform source of illumination.

When you hold the card near a surface, you cast a shadow. As shown in the accompanying diagram, there is a full shadow under the surface and full light on the other side. In between there is a graded shadow, the *penumbra,* which gradually moves from light to dark. Hold the card still and look at the brightness pattern—you will easily see the dark and light Mach bands. You may increase the visibility of the bands by moving the card closer to the surface. This reduces the size of the penumbra and makes the area of gradual change in intensity steeper, as shown in the diagram. Since this puts the bright and dim areas nearer one another, it enhances the effect of the inhibitory process.

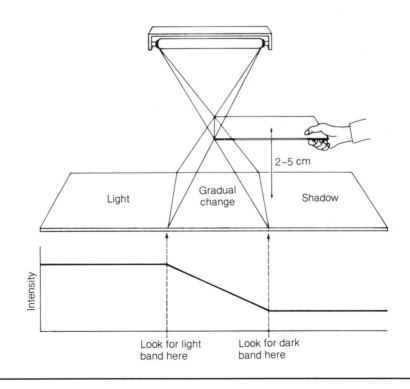

or blurry lines are visible at the points marked by the arrows in the figure. One is darker than any other part of the figure and the other is brighter. They are called **Mach bands,** in honor of their discoverer Ernst Mach. Their presence can be explained by lateral inhibition.

We have indicated the location of some retinal cells illuminated by the Mach-band-producing pattern in Figure 4-6C. Cell *b* is stimulated by bright incoming light, but it is also strongly inhibited by the activity of the adjacent cells *a* and *c*. Cell *d* is stimulated to the same extent as cell *b*. But on one side it is strongly inhibited by *c* while on the other side it is somewhat more weakly inhibited by *e,* which is not receiving as much light. The important thing to derive from this discussion is the fact that cells *b* and *d* have the same degree of stimulation, but *d* is less strongly inhibited. In this case, we might expect that its corresponding response would be more vigorous than that in cells like *b*. This should cause the region around *d* to appear relatively brighter. Next consider cell *i*. It is not stimulated very much, but neither are the nearby cells *h* and *j*. This means that *i* is not being strongly inhibited by surrounding units. Cell *g* is receiving the same small amount of stimulation as *i*. However, while *g* is weakly inhibited on one side by *h,* it is more strongly inhibited on the other side by *f,* which is responding more vigorously because of the higher intensity of light falling on it. Thus, although *g* and *i* receive the same amount of stimulation, *g* is more strongly inhibited than *i*. This means that its response will be decreased, causing an apparently darker region to appear there. The relationship between the input and the neural (and perceptual) response is diagramed in Figure 4-6D. It is quite easy to produce a Mach band pattern for yourself, as shown in Demonstration Box 4-4. It seems likely that a very wide array of brightness perception phenomena can be explained by theories that assume particular patterns of inhibitory and excitatory interactions between sensory neurons (see e.g., Cornsweet, 1985; Grossberg, 1987).

COGNITIVE FACTORS IN BRIGHTNESS PERCEPTION

The relatively simple manner in which changes in brightness can be explained by spatial interactions between retinal cells is quite exciting, especially given the apparent precision suggested by some relatively sophisticated mathematical descriptions of these interactions (e.g., Arend & Goldstein, 1987; Ratliff, 1965). Unfortunately, brightness perception is much more complex, and there are instances where predictions made from lateral inhibitory or excitatory considerations can be wrong. As an example, consider Figure 4-7. The gray under the white stripes is identical to that under the black stripes. Notice, however, that the gray under the white appears to be lighter than the gray under the black. This is the opposite of the prediction we would make based on the action of lateral inhibition, that the white stripes should *darken* the gray rather than *lighten* it. The phenomenal impression, then, is the reverse of brightness contrast, and it is called **brightness assimilation** (Shapley & Reid, 1985). This effect seems to depend on a *cognitive* factor. The term *cognition* is used to cover all mental processes by which we come to know the world. Thus, processes such as learning, reasoning, intuition, or attention are all cognitive factors, as we noted in Chapter 1.

Attention seems to be a relevant variable for the appearance of brightness assimilation. The part of the visual field you are attending to shows greater brightness contrast (Brussell & Festinger, 1973; Coren, 1969), whereas regions you are not attending to show brightness assimilation (Festinger, Coren & Rivers, 1970). Observers usually describe the pattern shown in Figure 4-7A as a gray field with *white lines on* it and Figure 4-7B as a *set of black lines on* a gray background. Festinger et al. reasoned that the lines have a ''figurelike'' quality that captures the attention (this aspect of perception is discussed more fully in Chapter 11). Since the gray is then a nonfigural background to

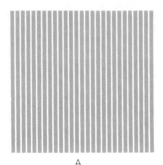

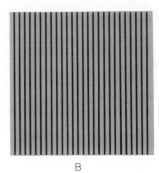

A   B

FIGURE 4-7   Brightness assimilation, where the gray under the white stripes appears lighter than the gray under the black.

which we pay little attention, it shows assimilation. If this is the case then voluntary shifts in attention, so that it is focused on the gray regions, should alter the brightness effect from one of assimilation to one of contrast: the gray under the white stripes should now appear to be the darker member of the pair. This is exactly what happens (Festinger, Coren & Rivers, 1970). You can demonstrate this for yourself by focusing your attention on the gray for a few moments, and soon the grays will appear to differ in a contrast direction, rather than showing brightness assimilation.

Another attentional mechanism may account for the fact that we fail to notice recurrent periods of total "blackout" in the visual system. These periods occur when we blink, which we do about 10 to 15 times a minute. Each blink causes a total blackout for 100 to 150 msec, yet it usually goes unnoticed. When the observer consciously attends to the presence of blinks, some darkening can be seen, but direct measurements show that observers underestimate the duration of the blackout by 90 percent and also underestimate the amount of actual darkening by about 75 percent (Manning, Riggs & Komenda, 1983; Volkman, Riggs, Aimee & Moore, 1982). This suppression is probably a cognitive adjustment to maintain continuity in the conscious flow of perception.

Some brightness effects depend on other cog-

nitive factors, namely, the assumptions the observer makes about the nature of the world, or even the way in which regions of the visual field *appear* to be arranged (Flock & Nusinowitz, 1984; Gilchrist, Delman & Jacobsen, 1983). We have more to say about this in Chapter 14 where we discuss the issue of *brightness constancy*.

VISUAL ACUITY

Visual acuity refers to the ability of the eye to resolve details. There are different types of visual acuity, each dependent on the specific task or specific detail to be resolved. The type of visual acuity most commonly measured is **recognition acuity,** which was introduced by Herman Snellen (1862). This task uses the familiar *eye chart* found in most ophthalmologists' or optometrists' offices, composed of rows of letters of progressively smaller size. The observer is asked simply to identify the letters on the chart and the size of the smallest identifiable letters determines acuity. Acuity is usually measured relative to the performance of a normal observer. Thus, an acuity of 6/6 indicates that an observer is able to identify letters at a distance of 6 meters that a normal observer can also read at that distance (you may be more familiar with the designation 20/20; 6 m is equivalent to 20 ft). In other words, the measured acuity is normal. An acuity of 6/9 (or 20/30) would mean that an observer is able to read letters at 6 m that are large enough for a normal observer to read at a distance of 9 m. Here, the visual acuity is less than normal.

A more general means of specifying the limits of acuity is to use the minimum **visual angle** of a detail that can be resolved. The visual angle is a measure of the size of the retinal image. Figure 4-8 shows what is meant by visual angle and demonstrates a simple computation based on the size and the distance of the object. Generally speaking, a normal observer can resolve details of 1 minute of arc (about the size of a quarter seen at a distance of 81 m, which is nearly the length of a football field), although different tasks often produce different limits of acuity (Beck & Schwartz, 1979).

The identification of letters on a Snellen chart is not the best way to measure acuity, since letters differ in their degree of identifiability. For instance, O and Q, or P and F, are letter pairs that are easily confused, where as L and W or O and I are quite easy to discriminate. Because these differences might affect acuity measurements, Hans Landolt (1889) introduced a different task that used circles with a gap in them as targets (see Figure 4-9). The gap can be oriented either up, down, to the right, or to the left, and the observer's task is to indicate the position of the gap. The circles differ in size and the smallest detectable gap is the measure of acuity.

A variety of other tasks is used to measure visual acuity. The most primitive measure is simply the specification of the smallest target of any type that can be detected. The relationship between brightness perception and acuity is most apparent for this task, where the target is a light line or spot against a dark background, or a dark line or spot against a light background. **Vernier** or **directional acuity** requires an observer to distinguish a broken line from an unbroken line. **Resolution** or **grating acuity** is measured by an observer's ability to detect a gap between two bars, or the orientation of a grid of lines. This particular form of acuity task has certain theoretical implications, which we discuss in the next section. Figure 4-9 shows examples of the above-mentioned acuity targets with arrows pointing to the crucial detail. Notice that each detail is merely a region of the field where there is a change in luminance.

It is reasonable to expect that the minimum resolvable detail size would be determined by the size of the retinal receptors or the size of the retinal receptive fields. Thus, in order to determine whether one or two spots of light are present, we might assume that it would be necessary to have at least one unstimulated retinal receptor (or receptive field) between two light-stimulated retinal receptors (or receptive fields). Surprisingly, for tasks such as vernier acuity, people can resolve much finer details than we would predict on the basis of these considerations. Acuities of 5 seconds (a second of arc is 1/3600 of a degree) or less are possible, despite the fact that the smallest receptive fields are

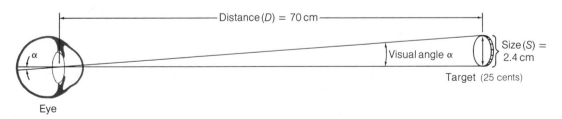

FIGURE 4-8   Computation of the size of the visual angle of the image of a quarter viewed at a distance of 70 cm (approximately arm's length), where the observer's line of sight is perpendicular to the lower edge of the coin. Tangent of visual angle = size/distance, therefore tan α = S/D = 2.4/70 = 0.034. Thus, α is approximately 2 deg.

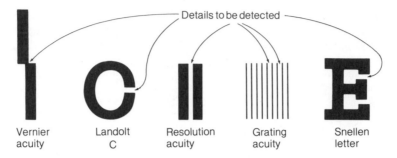

FIGURE 4-9   **Some typical acuity targets and the details to be discriminated.**

around 25 times larger than this (Klein & Levi, 1985; Westheimer, 1979). In fact this is about one-sixth the diameter of the smallest retinal cones. Resolution of details less than about 10 sec is often referred to as **hyperacuity** and suggests that some fairly complex neural circuitry, and pooling of neural responses, may be involved in acuity tasks (Carlson, 1983; Wilson, 1986).

Because acuity tasks are closely related to brightness discrimination, it is not surprising to find that acuity varies as a function of the many factors shown to be important in the perception of brightness. For instance, the adaptive state of the eye determines the minimum details that can be discriminated under particular viewing conditions (Lie, 1980). Thus, if you step out of the bright sunlight into a dim room, you may find it impossible to read even the large type of the headlines of a newspaper for a few moments. As your eyes adapt to the dim surroundings, however, you can soon easily read even fine print. Even a brief flash of light, bright enough to alter an observer's state of adaptation, markedly reduces an observer's ability to detect and identify acuity targets (Miller, 1965).

The detection of details in acuity targets also shows an interaction between time and stimulus intensity, very much like that described by Bloch's law for light detection. This means that you can increase the likelihood that a detail will be detected by either increasing the difference between the intensity of the target and that of its background, or by increasing the amount of time the observer views the stimulus. Although Bloch's law only holds for times less than 100 msec for simple light detection, the trade-off between time and intensity holds for up to 300 msec in acuity tasks in which observers are trying to detect pattern details (Kahneman, 1966; Kahneman, Norman & Kubovy, 1967).

Retinal position is also as important for acuity as it is for brightness perception (Jennings & Charman, 1981). The figure in Demonstration Box 4-5 allows you to experience the drastic reductions in visual acuity for targets that are imaged some distance from the fovea. When we measure relative acuity for various locations on the retina, we find that it varies as shown in Figure 4-10. Notice that acuity is best in the central fovea and drops off rapidly as we move into the periphery. This curve looks remarkably like the distribution of cones across the retina diagramed in Figure 3-7. It also looks much like the distribution of X cells in the retina (Peichl & Wassle, 1979). Direct physiological measurements of the responsiveness of X and Y cells shows that X cells have smaller receptive fields and seem to respond better to small stimuli. This has led a number of researchers to suggest that the limits of visual acuity are set by the prevalence of X cells, which are best designed for detection and analysis of small details in stationary visual arrays (Andrews & Pollen, 1979; Robson, 1980).

Because the part of the retina that is highest in

DEMONSTRATION BOX 4-5.   Visual Acuity as a Function of Retinal Location

Visual acuity is best in the fovea. The range of clear vision extends less than 10 deg away from the foveal center. Lay this book flat on the table and view the accompanying diagram from a distance of approximately 12 cm. Cover your left eye with your left hand and look directly at the point marked 0°. Without

moving your right eye, you will note that the letter over the 0° mark is relatively clear, and that the letter at 5° is also legible. However, the letters at 10° and beyond begin to appear fuzzy, and the letters at 40° and 50° are virtually unreadable.

K	B	X	M	P	A	S
+	+	+	+	+	+	+
50°	40°	30°	20°	10°	5°	0°

---

visual acuity contains mostly cones, which then send their signals to X-type ganglion cells, we can predict some further interactions between brightness and acuity. Since cones are only operative at higher levels of illumination we would expect better acuity at higher illumination levels. When we measure the relationship between acuity and illumination directly we obtain the curve shown in Figure 4-11. Notice that when the illumination is

low, in the scotopic (rod) range, acuity is poor, and it improves only slightly as the light intensity is increased. However, as we begin to shift into the photopic (cone) range, acuity improves rapidly. Of course, at too high a light level the acuity is reduced again because of the effects of glare (not shown). Demonstration Box 4-6 provides a stimulus figure and instructions for demonstrating the relationship between acuity and illumination.

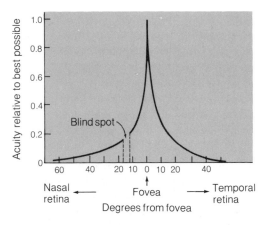

FIGURE 4-10   The distribution of visual acuity across the retina.

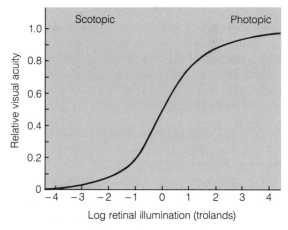

FIGURE 4-11   The effect of illumination on visual acuity.

DEMONSTRATION BOX 4-6.   Acuity and Intensity

You will need your variable intensity light source again (either television or closet). Under very dim illumination, view the bundle of converging lines shown in the diagram. Notice that at some point, where the lines are relatively close together, you can no longer resolve individual lines and the bundle appears to be gray. This is the limit of your grating acuity under these conditions. Place your finger or the point of a pencil at the point where the individual lines are no longer resolvable. Now gradually increase the intensity of the light source and notice that you can now begin to resolve lines at a higher point in the bundle. In fact, under normal room illumination, the lines in the area where acuity began to fail under lower illumination may now be discriminable. Notice also that the apparent blackness of the lines and whiteness of the paper (in other words the psychological contrast) also improves under higher light conditions.

One aspect of the relationship between acuity and illumination has important implications for some common situations. In 1789 Lord Maskelyne, Director of the Royal Greenwich Observatory, noticed that he became noticeably nearsighted at night. This common tendency to accommodate the eye inappropriately near, even when the object of interest is far away, is called *night myopia* (Leibowitz, Post, Brandt & Dichgans, 1982). Practically, it degrades the sharpness of the retinal image, interfering with the ability to see details under twilight and nighttime observation conditions. This reduction of acuity may be an important component in many nighttime driving accidents (Leibowitz & Owens, 1977).

SPATIAL FREQUENCY ANALYSIS

Spatial Fourier Analysis

A complete description of the relationship between brightness perception and acuity must take into account a great deal of information. Imagine any test pattern of light. Next, realize that when this pattern stimulates the eye there are 125 million or more retinal receptors per eye, each receiving an amount of light ranging from zero up to many millions of units. Pity the poor perceptual researcher who must now find a method of describing all of this activity (not to mention the poor brain that must interpret it). If we had to catalog every point of light and its intensity before we could understand the major phenomena associated with brightness and acuity, our information about these topics would be limited indeed. Many researchers realized this and began to look for some reasonably small set of relationships among the variables that affect brightness perception that could be used to describe visual arrays, hoping that such a simplified description might yield deeper insight into these phenomena.

In some ways, the most successful attempt to summarize brightness and acuity data to date has involved the use of a mathematical technique based on **Fourier's theorem.** This theorem states that it is possible to analyze any periodic pattern into a series of sine waves. In Chapter 6 we apply this theorem to complex sound waves, in which sound pressure level at some point in space varies over time in an irregular but repeated pattern. For our current problem we are concerned with how light intensity varies across space, namely across the retinal image. According to Fourier's theorem we can analyze *any* such complex pattern of light intensity across space into a series of simpler sine wave patterns, each of which would be seen as a regularly varying pattern of light and dark, if seen alone.

You might recall from trigonometry that a sine wave is simply a regular, smooth, periodically repeating function that can be precisely specified mathematically. Figure 4-12A shows a graph of a sine wave, and beside it a distribution of light that varies in the same way, growing more intense where the function rises and less intense where it falls. The pattern in 4-12A is called a **sine wave grating,** because the intensity of reflected light from the page varies sinusoidally as we move horizontally across the figure and the whole pattern forms a sort of blurry grating or grid. As applied to light distributions, Fourier's theorem states that by adding together (synthesizing) a number of such gratings we can produce *any* specified light distribution. Moreover, although individual sine wave patterns have only gradual changes in intensity, by adding many of them together we can even produce light distributions that contain sharp corners, such as that shown in Figure 4-12B. This pattern is called a **square wave grating,** since the light changes are sharp and give a boxlike intensity pattern. Successive addition of the appropriate frequencies of sine waves (or more accurately, the sine wave gratings they represent) gradually gives a better and better approximation of the sharp corners of the square wave grating. Figure 4-13 shows this graphically.

If we take this approach to describing the patterns of light that act as stimuli to our visual

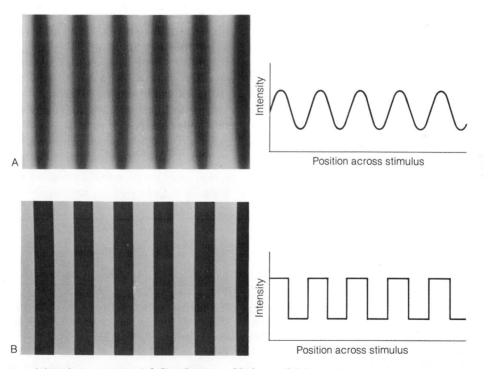

FIGURE 4-12   (A) A sine wave spatial distribution of light, and (B) a square wave spatial distribution of light. (Based on Cornsweet, 1970).

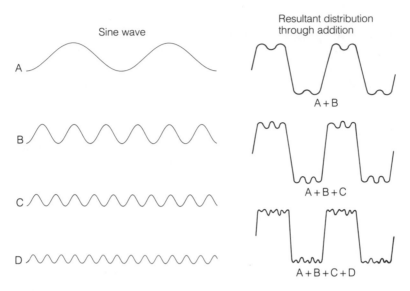

FIGURE 4-13   Gradually adding higher-frequency sine waves to the distribution leads to better approximations of a square wave through the process of Fourier synthesis.

systems, we no longer have to catalog the intensity of every point in the pattern. Now we can describe a light pattern precisely with a relatively compact mathematical expression indicating the particular sine wave gratings to be added together to reproduce it. Even if the mathematics sometimes become complex, the resulting description is still far simpler than a catalog of the light hitting 125 million or more individual retinal receptors. (See Levine & Shefner, 1981, or Weisstein, 1980, for a more complete introduction to Fourier analysis.)

Modulation Transfer Function

Fourier analysis (breaking up a pattern into its component sine waves) and *Fourier synthesis* (adding together a set of sine wave variations to create a more complex pattern) provide more than a simple shorthand for the description of light patterns. They serve as powerful tools for analyzing how the visual system responds to stimuli. Consider for a moment how we might test the fidelity of a photographic system. The simplest way of doing this is

to use a series of gratings, such as those shown in Figure 4-12. Some of the gratings will have very broad bars and spaces. In such gratings the light intensity rises and falls slowly as we move across the spatial extent of a surface, hence they are said to have *low spatial frequencies* (the frequency of changes in light intensity across space is low). Other gratings will have narrow bars and spaces. In these gratings the light intensity changes rapidly (at a high rate) as we move across space, hence they are said to have *high spatial frequencies*. Now we photograph each grating to see how well it is reproduced. At some point, when the bars and spaces become quite narrow, the system will reach its limit. The lens will no longer be able to resolve the individual bars, and all of the bars and spaces will merge into a gray blur. This is exactly the same type of task we would use to measure the *resolution acuity* or *grating acuity* of human observers, except that here we are looking at the resolution acuity of an optical system.

When photographic engineers do this type of analysis for an optical system, they measure its resolution in terms of the maximum number of lines per inch that can be resolved. Since very finely packed arrays of lines, corresponding to high spatial frequencies, cannot be resolved and are simply blurred, we say that optical systems *attenuate* the high-frequency components of the pattern. A graphic or mathematical description of the way certain spatial frequencies are lost because the system can not resolve them, whereas others are retained because they are within the system's resolution capacity, is called the **spatial modulation transfer function.** It measures the system's ability to "transfer" to the final image the spatial modulation (or intensity change over space) present in the target stimulus.

To assess the human visual system's limitations in resolving changes in light intensity over space, *contrast matching* is used to measure the modulation transfer function. Consider gratings A and B in Figure 4-14. Although both are square wave gratings, they differ in terms of their physical *contrast,* the ratio of the reflectances of the light and the dark areas; grating A has a lower contrast than grating B. Now consider the difference between B and C. Both are square wave gratings but B has a lower spatial frequency than C. Despite the fact that the physical contrast is the same (both are the same black ink with the same white inter-

spaces), the perceived contrast (the apparent difference between light and dark regions) is much less for the higher frequency with the black looking a bit lighter and the white a bit darker in C than in B. You can increase this difference by propping the book up and stepping back a foot or two. In a contrast matching task, observers would be asked to match the apparent contrast of such targets (or more usually sine wave gratings) by adjusting the intensities of the light and the dark regions until the two patterns matched. In this way, we could map the differences in visibility of various spatial frequencies.

An alternative method of measuring sensitivity to various spatial frequencies involves measuring the contrast threshold. This is the amount of contrast needed for you to detect that there is a grating present, rather than a uniform gray. Either of these techniques will give us a representation of how sensitivity changes as we change the spatial frequency of the stimuli, which is the modulation transfer function where the stimulus modulations (or intensity changes in the environment) are being transferred to (detected in) the observer's conscious experience of the pattern.

When we measure a typical modulation transfer function for a human observer, it looks like the solid line shown in Figure 4-15. As the graph

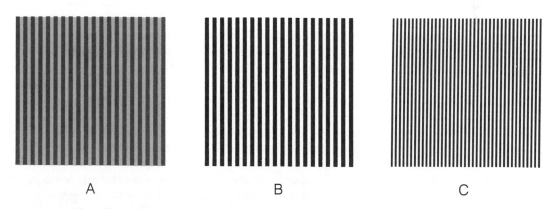

A	B	C

FIGURE 4-14   The effect of spatial frequency on the apparent brightness and contrast of patterns. Notice that the higher frequency pattern has less apparent contrast.

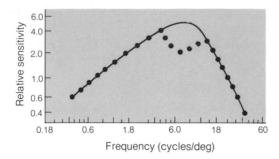

FIGURE 4-15   The modulation transfer function, which shows the relative visibility of targets of various spatial frequencies. The solid line represents the normal transfer function; the dotted line represents the transfer function after selective adaptation to a 6 cycle/deg stimulus.

shows, human observers are quite sensitive to spatial frequencies around 6 cycles per degree (6 cycles of the sine wave over each degree of visual angle). Sensitivity decreases rapidly the higher the spatial frequency. This loss at higher frequencies is probably a result of the fact that the eye is an optical system, containing a lens, and any such system has a high-frequency cutoff. Notice also that there is some loss of resolution in the lower spatial frequencies (less than 6 cycles/deg). This loss results from the fact that as the bars and spaces become wider, the lateral inhibitory interactions that sharpen the contours and increase apparent brightness differences between adjacent regions become less effective. In much the same way, Demonstration Box 4-4 showed that Mach bands were accentuated when the intensity changes were near one another. Thus, intensity changes are most effective in producing the phenomenal impression of a brightness difference when these changes occur at intermediate spatial frequencies (as determined by the Fourier analysis). When intensity changes occur too frequently within the visual image they are difficult to resolve. Similarly, when the physical changes are too infrequent, there is no perception of brightness differences.

The modulation transfer function provides a convenient basis for predicting apparent brightnesses in many types of stimulus configurations and the spatial frequencies we can detect serve as a measure of our visual acuity. Thus, the modulation transfer function serves as a sort of a summary of our visual resolution ability and responsiveness to light. For example, there are changes in the modulation transfer function as we grow older, with a general reduction in sensitivity to frequencies higher than 4 cycles/deg. These changes can accurately predict reductions in visual acuity and certain aspects of our depth perception (stereopsis) measured by other techniques (Greene & Madden, 1987).

Neural Spatial Frequency Channels

Imagine an extremely self-assured scientist sitting at his personal computer, complete with all the programs necessary to do Fourier analyses of any light patterns that might happen to be of importance or interest, muttering to himself, "If I find Fourier analysis so useful in analyzing patterns of light, maybe the visual system does too. Perhaps the visual system is set up to conduct some sort of spatial frequency analysis for any given pattern of light. Certainly, if it did, it would benefit from the same sort of concise description of the incoming light pattern that I obtain, and could thus also avoid having to deal individually with the millions of responses of millions of photoreceptors."

Actually, this suggestion is not as strange as it might seem. At a general level, the first stage of spatial frequency analysis can be accomplished by mechanisms that we know exist and have already discussed—the circularly organized retinal receptive fields described in Chapter 3. Recall that each of these has an excitatory, or *on,* region that when stimulated by light causes an increase in neural response rate, and an inhibitory, or *off,* region that causes a decrease in the neural response rate when stimulated by light (and a burst of responses on the light's termination). Before we discuss how such an arrangement can do a spatial frequency analysis, we must first introduce a bit of terminology. Every cycle of a sine wave grating has both a dark and a light phase, as we saw in Figure 4-12. This means that the dark stripe (or the light stripe) is one-half of the sine wave cycle. Now, every circular receptive field is "tuned" to a sine wave frequency whose *half cycle* is equal to the size of its central excitatory or inhibitory region. To visualize this type of structure, consider Figure 4-16.

Suppose we have an on-center receptive field of the size illustrated in the figure. If the spatial frequency is too low, that is to say the stripes are too wide, the stripes of illumination will fall on both the center and the surround. Even though the central on region of the field is stimulated, there is an equal degree of stimulation of the inhibitory surrounding off region of the receptive field. Because of lateral inhibitory interactions the two types of

responses tend to cancel each other out. Thus, the total response of the ganglion cell with this receptive field is low. Now consider the other extreme, where the spatial frequency is very high, and there are many stripes falling across the field. The on and off regions of the field are each stimulated by about equal proportions of light and dark, again producing little or no net response. Finally, consider a spatial frequency in which the half cycle width is approximately the same as the central region of the receptive field. If the bright stripe now covers the central region of the on center cell, there will be a vigorous on response. There will be little inhibition from the surrounding off region, which lies mostly in darkness from the dark half of the cycle. Thus, the net response to this grating would be relatively stronger than to any other size grating. Notice that the same sort of analysis of spatial frequency can

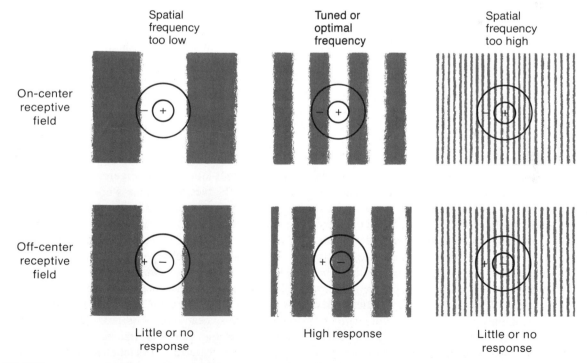

FIGURE 4-16   A demonstration of how a circular receptive field organization of a particular size can perform a crude spatial frequency analysis.

occur in the off-center cell, only here the optimal response is obtained when the dark half of the cycle is over the central region of the receptive field. Each receptive field is maximally responsive to a specific spatial frequency of light intensity changes.

This crude analysis of spatial frequencies could serve as the first step of a Fourier analysis of an incoming stimulus pattern if a few additional requirements were met. For example, there must be a broad range of receptive field sizes so that "tuning" would be fine enough to approximately determine sufficiently many of the spatial frequencies that make up the pattern. This requirement seems to be easily fulfilled since, as we noted in Chapter 3, X and Y cells differ quite a bit in the speed and nature of their responses. They also differ in their ranges of receptive field size, with X cells tuned for higher spatial frequencies than Y cells. Thus, there may be a number of different channels in the visual system, each tuned to a different range of spatial frequencies and each composed of cells with a different receptive field size. There is some evidence that the Y-like lower spatial frequency channels interact with, and can inhibit, the X-like higher spatial frequency channels (Hughes, 1986; Olzak, 1986). Moreover, a model assuming only six such channels (or receptive field sizes) can explain some of the remarkable feats of acuity people are capable of, namely the hyperacuity we discussed above, which shows resolution abilities better than would be predicted on the basis of the physical size of the retinal receptors (Bradley & Skottun, 1987; Wilson, 1986).

Of course, for such Fourier analysis to be of value perceptually there must be higher-level cells, perhaps in the visual cortex, that preserve the spatial frequency information extracted by the tuned receptive fields of the retinal ganglion cells. There is evidence that such cells exist in the cortex. These cells have not only preferred edge orientations to which they respond maximally but also preferred ranges of spatial frequency (Derrington & Fuchs, 1981; DeValois, Albrecht & Thorell, 1982; DeValois & DeValois, 1987). Although the existence of such cells does not prove that Fourier analysis

occurs in the visual system, it at least suggests that the equipment to perform such an analysis does exist.

Selective Adaptation

Many of the findings supporting the idea of spatial frequency channels in the visual system arise from **selective adaptation** studies. (The use of the word *adaptation* here involves the concept of *neural satiation,* or fatigue, which makes it quite different from the dark or light adaptation discussed earlier in the chapter.) In such a study, an observer is exposed to a specific spatial frequency for a moderately long time (perhaps several minutes). If there is a specific group of neurons tuned to that particular frequency, they will, of course, immediately start responding when their optimal stimulus appears. If the stimulus remains in view for a long period of time, these neurons will continue to respond but at an ever-decreasing rate, until eventually they respond only weakly. Since this weak response might last for a minute or two after exposure to the *adapting stimulus,* we have then temporarily disabled a particular group of spatial frequency channels and this should have detectable perceptual effects.

As an example of how this technique works, suppose we begin by measuring the modulation transfer function of an observer, just as we did to produce the solid line in Figure 4-15. Then, we have an observer stare for a while at a grating of about 6 cycles/deg (the adapting stimulus), in order to adapt the spatial frequency channels associated with this middle range of frequencies. When we next measure the observer's transfer function we now get the results shown as the dotted line in Figure 4-15. Notice that there is a depression in sensitivity around the adapted spatial frequency. Put simply, this means that it is now harder to detect gratings in this range of spatial frequencies, and larger amounts of physical contrast are needed to produce the same perceptual effects. This is what we would expect if the channels tuned to the adapting stimulus frequency have been fatigued, and hence no longer are responding as effectively. Of course, if we used a different adapting stimulus, the region of reduced sensitivity would be different, depending on its spatial frequency (Graham, 1980; Harris, 1980).

There is one particularly interesting perceptual effect that can be produced using this technique. Remember that spatial frequency roughly corresponds to the size of elements in a pattern. Thus, low spatial frequencies correspond to large elements, or in our gratings to wide stripes, and high frequencies correspond to small elements. Suppose we had somehow disabled all of the low spatial fre-

quency channels. With only the high frequency channels operating, they would be the major determinant of our responses to any stimuli, since the other channels are responding only weakly. Since the action of these higher-frequency channels usually signals the presence of higher spatial frequencies, we might expect that the pattern would appear to be dominated by high-frequency (smaller) elements compared with a situation where all channels were operating normally. Demonstration Box 4-7 allows you to demonstrate this effect for yourself.

Although spatial frequency analysis seems to provide a useful approach to the problems of

---

DEMONSTRATION BOX 4-7.   Selective Adaptation of Spatial Frequency Channels

If you look at the figure, you will see that one of the squares on the left has broad bars (low spatial frequency) and the other has narrow bars (high spatial frequency). The pattern on the right contains two gratings, both of which have the same spatial frequencies, but they are neither as high nor as low as the ones on the left. Hold the illustration about 80 cm away from you. Now look at the horizontal bar between the upper and lower patterns on the left for about 20 to 30 sec. Move your gaze from one portion of the bar to another, but keep your eyes on the bar. As you look steadily at the bar, the channels tuned to low spatial frequencies from the upper part of your visual field and these tuned to the high spatial fre-

quencies from the lower part of your visual field are fatiguing, or adapting. Now if you transfer your gaze quickly to the dot between the identical gratings on the right, you will notice that they no longer seem to be the same. The top part of the grating now appears to be spaced more finely, with thinner stripes than those on the bottom. The low frequency channels have been disabled in the upper region of the visual field. With more high spatial frequency channels active, the percept is shifted toward higher frequencies; hence, the stripes are seen as smaller and more dense. The opposite effect is occurring in the lower region of the field.

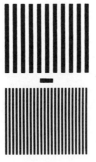

A

B

brightness and acuity, it does not provide us with complete answers, any more than does lateral inhibition. The final perceptual response that emerges in consciousness, what we perceive as a particular brightness, size, or detail, involves the operation of all levels of the perceptual system. In later chapters (e.g., Chapter 11) we shall see how spatial frequency analysis is useful in understanding some aspects of form perception, and how cognitive factors interact with the basic sensory mechanisms we have discussed so far to determine our perception of complex stimuli in our environment.

GLOSSARY

The following definitions are specific to this book.

Bloch's law   The trade-off relationship between stimulus duration and stimulus intensity in their effect on absolute threshold: $T \times I = C$.

Brightness   The phenomenal impression of the intensity of a light stimulus.

Brightness assimilation   The reverse of simultaneous brightness contrast. Here, added light elements lighten a stimulus and added dark elements darken it.

Bril   A unit for measuring the apparent brightness of stimuli.

Bunsen-Roscoe law   The physical law describing the photochemical reaction of any light-sensitive substance as a function of the intensity and duration of light exposure.

CIE   The Commission Internationale de l'Eclairage, an international organization responsible for light measurement.

Dark adaptation   The progressive increase in visual sensitivity after a change from a higher to a lower level of illumination.

Directional acuity   *See* Vernier acuity.

Fourier's theorem   States that any periodic wave can be mathematically analyzed into a series of simple sine or cosine waves.

Grating acuity   *See* Resolution acuity.

Hyperacuity   Resolution of details that are smaller than the diameter of one retinal receptor; usually, any acuity less than 10 sec of visual angle.

Illuminance   The amount of light falling on a surface.

Lateral inhibition   The process of adjacent neurons inhibiting one another.

Light adaptation   The progressive decrease in visual sensitivity after a change from a lower to a higher level of illumination.

Lumen   The unit of radiance equal to the light emanating from a standard candle, which is slightly more than 0.001 watt at a wavelength of 555 nm.

Luminance   The amount of light reflected from a surface.

Luminosity curve   A plot of the relative brightnesses of light of different wavelengths.

Mach bands   The perception of dark and light lines at regions near abrupt changes in an intensity gradient.

Neural satiation   A process in which specific groups of neurons fatigue in response to optimal and continuous stimulation. The presumed cause of selective adaptation.

Photometry   The measurement of light.

Photopic   A term for high-light (daylight) visibility conditions and vision under these conditions.

Piper's law   The trade-off relationship between area and intensity in the detection of stimuli between 10 min and 24 deg of visual angle in size: $\sqrt{A} \times I = C$.

Purkinje shift   The change in the apparent brightnesses of light of different wavelengths as an observer goes from a light-adapted to a dark-adapted state.

Radiance   The amount of energy emitted by a light source.

Recognition acuity   A type of visual acuity commonly measured by means of letter identification and scaled relative to a norm of identification at 6 m distance from the observer (6/6).

Reflectance   The proportion of incident light that a surface reflects.

Resolution acuity   The observer's ability to detect a gap between two lines, or the orientation of a grid of lines.

Retinal illuminance   The amount of light reaching the retina.

Ricco's law   The trade-off relationship between area and intensity in the detection of stimuli smaller than 10 min of visual angle in size: $A \times I = C$.

Scotopic   A term for low-light (night) visibility conditions and vision under these conditions.

Selective adaptation   Weakening the response of particular spatial frequency channels by exposing the observer to those spatial frequencies for several minutes. *See* Neural satiation.

Simultaneous brightness contrast   Perceptual phenomenon in which a target area of a given luminance appears brighter when surrounded by a darker background than when surrounded by a lighter background.

SI system   The Système International d'Unités, a uniform system of measurement.

Sine wave grating   A pattern of light intensity that varies from light to dark following sinusoidal gradations.

Spatial modulation transfer function   A graphical description of the way an optical system's ability to resolve spatial modulations (intensity changes across space) varies with spatial frequency.

Square wave grating   Sharply alternating light and dark stripes.

Standard units   Internationally agreed-on measures of photic energy.

Vernier acuity   The measure of an individual's ability to distinguish a broken line from an unbroken line.

Visual acuity   The ability of the eye to resolve details.

Visual angle   A measure of the size of the retinal image.

CHAPTER
5

Color

"My dad was color-blind, but didn't find out until he was nearly fifty. He was always doing strange things. He couldn't be trusted to pick tomatoes from the garden because he was always mixing up the ripe and the green ones. We finally suspected that something was wrong when he commented that he really admired cherry pickers for their ability to recognize shapes. 'After all,' he said, 'the only thing that tells 'em it's a cherry is the fact that it's round and the leaves aren't. I just don't see how they find 'em in those trees!'''

Like this student, you may be surprised to find out how important a factor color is in determining your ability to acquire information about the world. For instance, consider Figure 5-1. Although the figure appears to be a random collection of gray shapes, there is a word hidden in it. Each letter is spelled out by a series of similar shapes. If you study the figure for a moment, you will begin to see how difficult it is to pick out the word (if you can do it at all), despite the fact that the shape and brightness information are there. In this task you are much like the color-blind person trying to pick out bunches of cherries, among the leaves, by shape alone. Now flip to Color Plate 2, where we have added the dimension of color to the figure. Notice that in this color plate the hidden word

"leaps out." Thus, color provides an important stimulus dimension that aids in the localization and identification of objects, which explains why some occupations, such as air traffic control, require normal color vision (Kuyk, Veres, Lahey & Clark, 1986). For some species, color vision is a matter of life and death. For instance, if bees lacked color vision, their task of locating the nectar-bearing flowers hidden among shrubs, grasses, or leaves would be almost impossible. The survival of this species may well depend on the ability to spot a glint of color that indicates the presence of blossoms.

COLOR STIMULUS

The human eye registers as light wavelengths between 360 and 760 nanometers. Sir Isaac Newton was able to show that stimuli of different wavelengths within this range produce different color sensations. Newton's experiment was quite simple. He took a glass prism and allowed some sunlight to pass through it from a slit in a window shade. When he held a sheet of white on the other side of the prism, the light no longer appeared to be white; rather, it took the form of a colored spectrum,

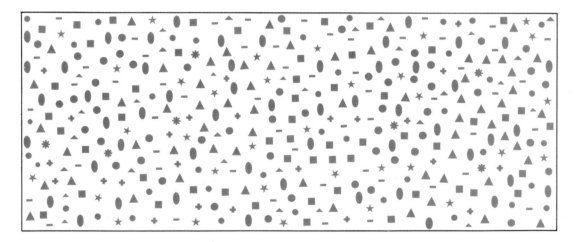

FIGURE 5-1   Can you find the hidden word? If not turn to Color Plate 2.

looking much like the arrangement of light in a rainbow (see Figure 5-2A). Newton knew that light bends when passing through a prism, and that the amount of bending (called *refraction*) depends on wavelength. There is less refraction of the longer wavelengths (600–700 nm) and more bending of the shorter (400–500 nm). Thus, a prism takes the various wavelengths of light that make up sunlight and separates them according to wavelength. The fact that we see this spread of light as varying in hue shows that color perception depends on the wavelength of the light. Table 5-1 shows some typical color names associated with some selected wavelengths of light.

Newton also inserted another prism (in the opposite orientation) so that the light was now refracted in the direction opposite to the effect of the original prism. This, of course, recombined all of these wavelengths into a single beam. Now when he placed a piece of paper into this beam it again ap-

Table 5-1.   Wavelengths of Light and Associated Color Sensations

Color Name	Wavelength (nm)
Violet	450
Blue	470
Cyan	495
Green	510
Yellow- Green	560
Yellow	575
Orange	600
Red	660
Purple	Not a spectral color but a mixture of ''red'' and ''blue''

peared to be white, with no hint of the original colors that went into the combination. This indicates that the sensation of white results from a mixture of many different wavelengths (see Figure 5-2B).

An important technical distinction should be made here, Figure 5-2 does not describe how white light is broken up into ''colored light.'' Colored light does not exist; rather, what does exist is visible radiation of different wavelengths. If there were no observer there would be no color. Newton pointed this out when he said, ''For the rays, to speak properly, are not coloured. In them is nothing else than a certain *Power* and *Disposition* to stir up a sensation of this or that Colour.'' When we talk about the color stimulus, we should actually speak of radiation of different wavelengths, since the sensations of red, green, blue, or any other color reside in the observer. Having made this technical distinction, we must admit that it is extremely convenient to talk about red light or green light, and for the sake of brevity we will not hesitate to do so in some of our later descriptions. Remember, however, that when we refer to a ''blue light'' we are referring to those wavelengths of light that elicit the sensation of blue, namely, the shorter wavelengths in the visible spectrum.

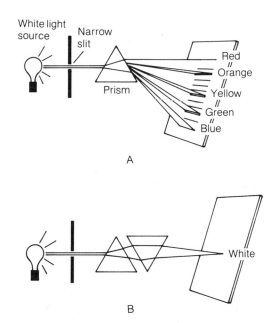

FIGURE 5-2   Newton's experiments: (A) separation of white light into its various wavelengths gives the color spectrum; (B) recombination of spectral lights gives white light.

Objects appear to be colored because they reflect to our eyes only selected wavelengths of light. Consider a common object, such as an apple with white light falling on it. It appears to be red. We have already seen that white light, such as sunlight, is a combination of all wavelengths. Since the light stimulus that reaches your eyes produces the sensation of red, all of the wavelengths except the longer (red-appearing) ones must have been absorbed by the surface of the apple. Colored objects or surfaces contain pigments that selectively absorb some wavelengths of light while the rest are reflected and thus reach your eye. It is this selective "subtraction" of some wavelengths from the incoming light that gives an object its color. If a surface does not absorb any of the wavelengths reaching it but reflects them all uniformly, it appears white rather than colored. Colored filters work in much the same way, that is, by absorbing some wavelengths of light. For instance, if a white light is projected through a green filter, the resulting beam is green. This means that the filter has absorbed most of the long and short wavelengths, allowing only the medium-range, or green-appearing, wavelengths to reach the eye.

You should be alerted to the fact that simply specifying the wavelength, or wavelengths, in a stimulus does not seem to fully describe the way the color appears to an observer. For instance, a stimulus with a dominant wavelength of 570 nm may appear yellow while another with the same wavelength composition might appear brown. For this reason, additional factors other than wavelength are used to classify colors.

Color Appearance Systems

Suppose you were marooned on a desert island that had a beach covered with many colored pebbles. Lacking anything else to do, you set about the task of classifying the colors of all the pebbles in some meaningful way. The first classification scheme that might come to mind would involve grouping stones together on the basis of their hues. Thus, you would end up with a pile of red stones, another of green stones, and so forth. Once you have your piles of stones, you would next have to look for some meaningful arrangement for the piles. For instance, you might notice that orange seems to fall, in terms of appearance, somewhere between red and yellow. The yellow-greens, of course, seem to fall between yellow and green. Once you reach the blue end of your line of stones, however, you might find yourself running into a bit of a problem. The purple stones seem to fall somewhere between the blues and the reds. This means that a straight line arrangement is not adequate. Instead, you might arrange the pebbles as shown in Figure 5-3.

This crude color arrangement scheme is circular in form. You have probably seen it before in books on art, decorating, or design, where it is usually called the **color circle** or **color wheel.** In this arrangement, you have separated the colors according to **hue,** which is the psychological dimension that most clearly corresponds to variations in wavelength. Very often when we use the word *color*, in everyday life and in this chapter, we are actually referring to *hue*. Let us consider the effect of wavelength on sensation by looking at the effects produced by pure or **monochromatic stimuli.** A monochromatic stimulus contains only one

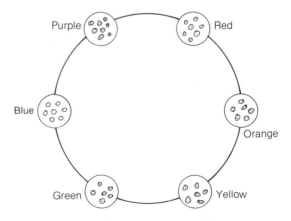

FIGURE 5-3   A primitive color circle for encoding the colors of pebbles.

wavelength (from the Greek *mono* meaning "one" and *chroma* meaning "color"). These stimuli are similar to those found in the spectrum generated by Newton's prismatic separation of light and therefore are often called **spectral colors.** Such monochromatic stimuli do not produce all the hues found in the color wheel. For instance, we find that there is no single wavelength that produces the sensation of purple. This sensation requires a mixture of blue and red wavelengths. Similarly, there is no place in the spectrum where we can find a red that doesn't appear to have a tinge of yellow. In order to achieve such a hue, we must add a bit of blue (short-wavelength) light.

Meanwhile, back on the beach, it has become clear that our color wheel classification scheme based only on the psychological attribute of hue seems incomplete. A close look at the piles of pebbles reveals marked color differences. For instance, among the red pebbles you might find that some are deep red color and others are pink; another group may be almost pure white with only a hint of red coloration. This observation corresponds to the physical dimension of **purity.** Clearly the purest color you could get would correspond to a monochromatic or spectral hue, and as you add other wavelengths, or white light, the color would appear to become "washed out." This psychological attribute of color appearance is called **saturation.** It is quite easy to integrate saturation into the color circle by simply placing white in the center. Now imagine that the various degrees of saturation correspond to positions along the spokes or radii emanating from the center of the wheel. The center represents white (or gray) and the perimeter represents the purest or most saturated color possible. Figure 5-4 shows the color wheel now modified to include saturation. Notice that the point corresponding to pink (a moderately desaturated red) is plotted near the center along the line connecting red and white, whereas a crimson is plotted further away from the center along the same line.

To the average observer, hue and saturation do not completely describe all the visible nuances of

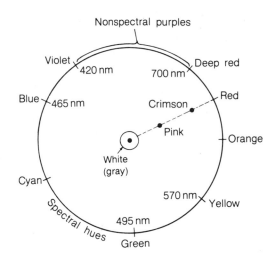

FIGURE 5-4   **The color circle modified to allow the encoding of both hue and saturation. Spectral colors are on the outer rim, white is in the center.**

color. It is quite possible to have two colors match in both of these attributes but still appear to be different. For instance, a blue spot of light projected onto a screen would not appear to be the same as another spot identical in all respects except that it has been dimmed by putting a light-reducing filter in front of it. Thus, the sensory quality of **brightness** (which we discussed in Chapter 4) must be worked into our system of describing colors. Since we have already used the two dimensions capable of being reproduced on a flat piece of paper, it is clear that the addition of a third color dimension (brightness) forces us to use a solid instead of a flat representation.

The shape of the three-dimensional color "space" can be derived from common observation if we recognize that at high brightness levels colors appear to be "washed out," whereas at low brightness levels colors seem "weak" or "muddy," meaning that they are of low saturation. Thus, the hue circle must shrink at these extremes, since saturation seems to vary over a confined range, and very high degrees of saturation are never observed at very high or low levels of brightness.

If we combine the three psychological attributes of hue, saturation, and brightness, we get something that looks like Figure 5-5. It appears to be a pair of cones placed base to base. This is usually called the **color spindle** or the **color solid.** The central core as we move up or down represents brightness and is comprised of all the grays running from white (at the top) to black (at the bottom). We can imagine that at each brightness level, if we sliced through the color solid in the direction shown in the diagram, we would get a color circle in which the hue would be represented along the perimeter. Totally desaturated colors (the grays) are at the central core, as we've already noted; hence, saturation is represented by moving from the center outward. This is the basic representation used in many color appearance systems. Probably the most popular in use among psychologists is the one developed by Munsell (1915) and modified by Newhall, Nickerson, and Judd (1943) to agree with the way typical observers arrange color stimuli. To actually classify colors you can use a **color atlas,** in which each page represents a horizontal or a vertical slice through the color solid. Color samples illustrating colors found in varying locations in the color solid are given in such atlases, allowing the observer to identify and label any given test color.

Color Mixture

Pure colors of a single wavelength usually are produced only under precise laboratory conditions. Most of the light reaching your eye is composed of a mixture of many different wavelengths. Generally, the **dominant wavelength** will determine what hue you see, although this is not always the case. When we combine two or more wavelengths of light a new color, with a different psychological hue and saturation, is often seen. Once the colors are mixed, the eye can no longer discriminate the individual wavelengths that make up the mixture. Thus, you can have a pure yellow made up of 570-nm light and another yellow that matches it, composed of a mixture of a 500-nm green and a 650-nm red. You will not be able to distinguish between these hues, nor will you be able to isolate the red and the green that went into the mixture. Colors that appear to be the same but are made up of different wavelengths of light are called **metameric colors.**

There are two types of color mixtures. The first, and the simplest to describe, is called **additive color mixture.** Additive mixtures occur when we mix light. For instance, if we project a red circle on a screen, the light reaching the eye from the projected circle is red. If we project a blue circle on the screen so that it partially overlaps with the red circle, the light reaching the eye from the region where the circles overlap contains both blue and red light. Thus, each new wavelength projected onto the same region of the screen *adds* to the mixture of wavelengths reaching the eye. Figure 5-6A shows a situation that might occur if we used three projectors with the first projecting a red beam, the

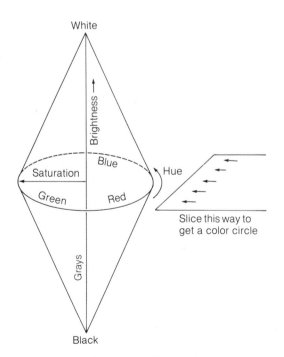

FIGURE 5-5   **The color solid.**

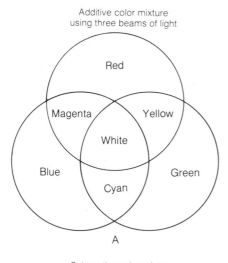

Additive color mixture
using three beams of light

A

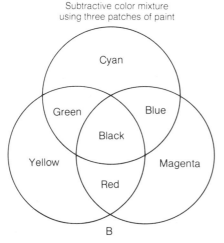

Subtractive color mixture
using three patches of paint

B

FIGURE 5-6 **Color-mixture systems: (A) additive; (B) subtractive.**

happens where the red and green overlap—we get the sensation of yellow. Where all three beams overlap we get the sensation of white. Demonstration Box 5-1 shows another way to get additive color mixtures.

These results cannot be duplicated using paints. If you tried mixing all your paints together to get white, you would get a shade of gray or black instead. This is because pigments do not work in the same way as lights. Something that appears red, such as a tomato, will have a surface pigment that absorbs most of the short and medium wavelengths, reflecting to your eyes only the long (red) wavelengths. A pigment that gives you a color similar to grass green might absorb most of the long wavelengths and the short wavelengths, reflecting to your eye mainly middle wavelengths. Thus, when you mix the red and the green paints together, you end up with a mixture in which only the middle wavelengths are reflected by the green, yet these are absorbed by the red pigment. Hence you are essentially subtracting all the wavelengths, leaving only a muddy gray.

Since pigments work by subtracting or absorbing wavelengths of light, a mixture of pigments is called a **subtractive color mixture.** Such pigment mixtures produce colors that are considerably less predictable than mixtures of lights because the wavelength-absorbing property of pigments is complex. For example, Figure 5-7 shows the wavelengths reflected by some typical pigments. Notice how irregularly they reflect the light and imagine the problems in predicting what the resultant mixes might reflect and absorb.

Suppose, however, that we are dealing with relatively simple pigments, where the yellow reflects only middle and long wavelengths, the cyan only long and middle wavelengths, and the magenta only long and short wavelengths. If we now painted circles of these pigments so that they overlapped, we would get a crude representation of what would generally be expected in subtractive color mixtures. Since the yellow pigment works by absorbing all the short wavelengths, and the

second a green beam, and the third a deep blue (almost violet) beam. If the circles of light were arranged so that they partially overlapped with one another, we would get a series of additive mixtures. Where red and the deep blue overlap we get a reddish-purple generally called *magenta.* Where the deep blue and the green overlap we get a lighter hue that is greenish blue, usually called *cyan.* Something that some people find quite surprising

DEMONSTRATION BOX 5-1.   Color Mixture

There is a simple way to obtain additive color mixtures without using projected beams of light. Consider Color Plate 4A, in which you see a checkerboard of tiny red and green squares. In Color Plate 4B you see a yellow disk. Prop up the book so that you can see the color plates when you move across the room. Now, standing at a distance, look back at the figures. What formerly appeared to be red and green now appears to be yellow and should match the yellow disk. At a distance, the optics of the eye can no longer resolve the individual squares. The light from each of them smears, or blurs, across the retina giving rise to the color mixture effect.

This technique is similar to the technique used in your color television set. If you take a magnifying glass and hold it up to the screen, you will see that each region is made up of a series of tiny dots. When you sit at normal viewing distance, you can no longer resolve the individual dots. They have combined within the eye to give you an additive color mixture. A similar technique was used by the French painter Georges Seurat, who replaced the traditional irregular brush stroke used in painting with meticulously placed dots of color. Thus, instead of mixing paints on his palette, he allowed the mixture to be accomplished optically within the eye of the onlooker viewing the painting from an appropriate distance.

cyan pigment absorbs all the long wavelengths, their mixture absorbs both the short and the long wavelengths, leaving us only with the middle or green-appearing portion of the spectrum. When we combine yellow with magenta, we find that the yellow subtracts the short wavelengths and the magenta subtracts the middle wavelengths, hence only the long or red-appearing wavelengths remain. In a similar fashion, overlapping cyan and magenta leaves us with only the blue wavelengths, because all others are subtracted, and the mixture produces blue. Clearly, when all three pigments overlap everything is absorbed and we get black, as shown in Figure 5-6B. In general, it is more convenient to deal with additive color mixtures since they are easier to conceptualize.

The color circle, which we have already discussed, provides a convenient means of predicting the appearance of additive color mixtures. But note that the color circle describes, rather than explains, how colors interact. For instance, the spacing around its circumference corresponds to the way the various hues appear to an average observer rather than to a regular spacing according to wavelength. To use the color circle to predict a color mixture is actually quite simple. Suppose we mix a spectral red (about 650 nm) with a spectral yellow (about 570 nm). We can depict this as in Figure 5-8, where the resultant mixture is represented by the line connecting these two colors. If we combine the yellow and the red in equal proportions we will

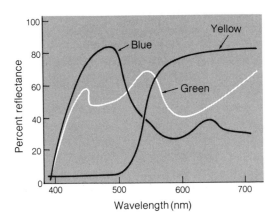

FIGURE 5-7   The relative wavelength composition of a blue, a yellow, and a green pigment.

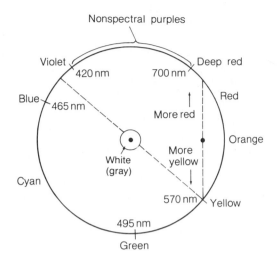

FIGURE 5-8 **Using the color circle to predict color mixtures.**

get a color that corresponds to the dot in the center of the line. We can determine what this color will look like by simply drawing a line from the center of the color circle through the dot to the perimeter. When this is done, we find that we get an orange corresponding to about a 600-nm spectral stimulus. Increasing the amount of yellow shifts the point along the line in the direction closer to the yellow hue. Adding more red shifts the point along the line in the other direction. You will notice that we started out with two spectral, or pure, hues (marked on the perimeter), however, the resultant mixed color is no longer on the perimeter but is closer to the center of the color circle. The purest colors possible (the spectral colors) are placed on the perimeter of the color circle; more desaturated colors are found closer to the center (nearer white or gray). From this we can conclude that any color mixture is less saturated than either of the two component colors that went into it. No mixture of colors can ever be quite as saturated as a monochromatic or spectral color.

Mixing more than two hues (or hues containing more than a single wavelength) is a little more complex. If we mix three colors, the resultant color

sensation is given by the center of a triangle produced by connecting the three colors. If the amount of each hue differs, the center point of the triangle shifts toward the dominant hue.

CIE Color Space

An interesting effect occurs when we mix two colors that are exactly opposite to each other on the color circle. For example, mixing a violet with a yellow along the line shown in Figure 5-8 results in a colorless gray. This is because, when the proportions are correct, this mixture lies in the center of the circle. Colors whose mixture produces such an achromatic gray are known as **complementary colors.**

One of the most important facts about color mixtures emerged in the 1850s. The German physicist and physiologist Hermann von Helmholtz (1821–1894) and the Scottish physicist James Clerk Maxwell (1831–1879) carried out a set of color matching experiments. They reported that by combining an appropriate set of three monochromatic light sources in appropriate amounts, they could match any other hue. These three wavelengths were to be known as **primaries.** Actually, the choice of primaries is rather arbitrary. Primary colors need only be reasonably far apart, with the requirement that the mixture of any two of them alone will not match the third.

Wright (1929) made a set of measurements in which observers matched the hue of the various spectral sensations. He selected as his primary colors a red of 650 nm, a green of 530 nm, and a blue of 460 nm. The observers matched the color of two patches of light, where the first was the test color and the second could contain any combination of the three primaries. Wright's results are shown in Figure 5-9, which indicates the relative amount of each of the three primaries needed to match any given wavelength. You might notice that some of the values are negative. This indicates that some of the particular primary had to be added to the test sample in order to reduce its saturation to the point

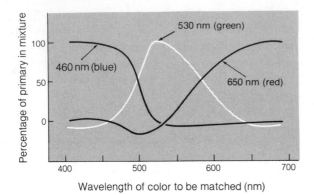

FIGURE 5-9   The proportion of each primary (a 460-nm blue, a 530-nm green, and a 650-nm red) needed to match any spectral color.

where it could be matched by a mixture of the two remaining primaries. In other words, some matches could be made only if one of the three primaries was not included in the mixture but was added to the test sample.

The fact that any selected color can be matched by a mixture of three appropriately se-

lected primary colors suggests an alternate way of specifying the hue of a stimulus, namely, in terms of the proportion (sometimes "negative") of the three primaries needed to reach this match. Geometrically this suggests a triangular space with a primary color at each corner. Color mixtures may then be represented in the same way as they are on the color circle. Thus yellow, which is a mixture of red and green, is represented by a point on the line between red and green. If we add more red the point moves toward the red primary, and if we add more green it moves toward the green. As in the color circle, white is represented by a point in the middle, and is comprised of an equal proportion of the three primaries. Also, as in the color circle, a red of lower saturation (the whitish red or pink) would be represented by a point moved inward toward the center. Such a diagram is shown in Figure 5-10.

In 1931, a special body of the Commission Internationale de l'Eclairage (CIE) standardized the procedure for specifying the color of a stimulus. They decided to use a color space created by the

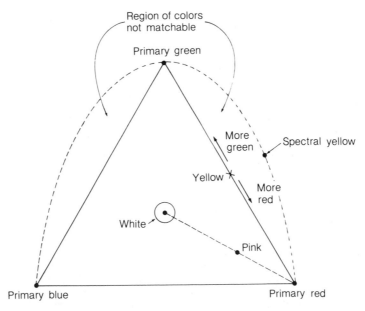

FIGURE 5-10   Specifying colors using a color triangle.

mixing of three primaries as described above. Unfortunately, if we select any three *spectral* primary colors, a number of perceptual and mathematical problems result. The major perceptual problem is the fact that there are other spectral colors that cannot be represented within the triangle. For instance, a pure spectral yellow cannot be represented (unless it is one of the primaries, which creates other problems), since any color mixture can never be as saturated as the pure spectral color itself. To solve this perceptual problem, the CIE selected three *imaginary* primary colors. They arranged the imaginary primaries at the corners of the triangle shown in Figure 5-11. These imaginary primary colors are more saturated than any real colors can be. (Remember, this is done so that all colors can be represented *within* the space.) Notice that we have labeled the horizontal and vertical axes of the triangle with the labels x and y.

We can now represent *any* color as a point in the color space. The reason that we can plot a mixture of three colors by using a point that has only two spatial coordinates is because the **CIE chromaticity space** has been arranged so that y represents the proportion of green in the mixture and x represents the proportion of red in the mixture.

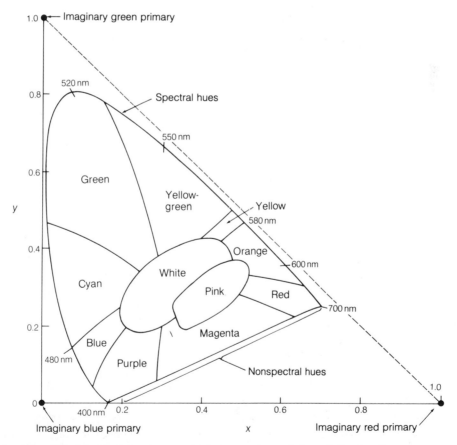

FIGURE 5-11   The CIE chromaticity space, which is a variant of the color triangle system using three imaginary "super" primaries.

Clearly the proportions of red and green and blue in any mixture must sum to a total of 1.0 (you can think of these as representing percentages, where all the items must sum to 100 percent of the light). If we know the proportions of green and red in the mixture, we need only subtract these from 1.0 to find the proportion of blue. The actual colors that can be perceived do not fill the full triangle (remember the primaries we are using are imaginary "super" colors). Instead, they fill a horseshoe-shaped area with the spectral colors forming the outside boundary. We have labeled this area on the figure so that you can see the regions filled by various colors. Thus, if we have a color at .2x and .6y, we would know that it is comprised of 20 percent red, 60 percent green, and (subtracting from a total of 100 percent) 20 percent blue. Looking at the figure you can find the point described by these x and y coordinates and see that this color would look green.

Notice that brightness is not represented anywhere on this diagram. As in the color space we discussed earlier, brightness requires a third dimension. The color space in the figure can be thought of as a single slice through a three-dimensional color space, just as we demonstrated in Figure 5-5. This third dimension would be called z. Using the CIE color system we can specify any color stimulus by its **tristimulus values,** which are simply the x and y coordinates for the hue of the stimulus, and a z coordinate for the brightness of the stimulus.

THE PHYSIOLOGY OF COLOR VISION

To this point, we have dealt with the physical color stimulus, some methods of specifying the appearance of a color, and some aspects of combining various wavelengths of light. None of the foregoing descriptions specify how a particular color sensation arises. In order to understand this, we must deal with both physiological and psychological fac-

tors. Let us consider these in light of the two major theoretical positions that have emerged during the last 150 years.

Trichromatic Color Theory

Much research has gone into the search for the physiological basis of color vision. One of the earliest findings was discussed in Chapter 4, where it was reported that under scotopic levels of illumination, when only the rods are active, no color vision is found. On the basis of these observations, it was concluded that cones are the retinal receptors that provide the first stage of the color response. Therefore, how the cones provide information about the wavelength of the incoming light becomes the first question to be answered.

Most normal people can discriminate among thousands of colors under a myriad of conditions; however, holding brightness and saturation constant the average human observer can discriminate about 200 different hues. Suppose that we wished to create an artificial eye with this same ability. The simplest procedure might seem to require a separate cone that responds to each of the discriminable hues. Unfortunately, such a scheme is not practical. For any given colored stimulus we would only have 1/200 of the cones active, which means that our visual acuity would be much poorer than research has shown it to be. In addition, such a system would mean that our acuity measured under white illumination would be many times better than our acuity measured under monochromatic stimulation. This also is not found.

An alternate scheme would be to have only one type of retinal cone with 200 different code signals by which it could indicate the discriminable hues. This could be done via a sort of neural Morse code. Although it may be the case that such a neural Morse code can play a part in some aspects of color vision (see "Models of Color-Coding" section), the evidence for such a mechanism is still controversial. Research suggests that each cone contains only one pigment. If so, how would the cone itself "recognize" the wavelength of the light? The only thing that the cone "knows" is the amount of pigment that has been bleached. Although different wavelengths of light may bleach more or less pigment, simply increasing or decreasing the intensity of the stimulus could also cause the same variations in degree of bleaching. It thus seems unlikely that a single cone would be able to discriminate 200 hues.

An explanation was suggested almost 200 years ago by Thomas Young (1773–1829). Young suggested that only a few different retinal receptors, operating with different wavelength sensitivities, would be necessary to allow humans to perceive the number of colors they do. He further suggested that perhaps as few as three would do. His theoretical notion was revived in the 1850s by Helmholtz, as we have already noted, when he and Maxwell were able to show that normal observers need only three primaries to match any color stimulus. These data were taken as evidence for the presence of three different receptors in the retina. Since the usual color matching primaries consisted of a red, a green, and a blue, it was presumed that there were three types of receptors, one responsive to red, one to green, and one to blue. Since these receptors are cones, and cones operate by the bleaching of pigment, we may suggest three hypothetical pigments. The first we would call **erythrolabe** (translated from the Greek this means "red-catching"), another **chlorolabe** (meaning "green-catching"), and the third **cyanolabe** (meaning "blue-catching"). This **trichromatic theory** (from the Greek *tri* meaning "three" and *chroma* meaning "color") finds some very convincing support in the study of defective color vision.

Color Vision Defects

Virtually all individuals differ from what is usually called "normal" color vision in one way or another. However, some show drastic deficiencies in their ability to discriminate colored stimuli and, in popular speech, are said to suffer from **color blind-ness.** This term is much too strong, since only a very small percentage of individuals are totally incapable of discriminating colors. According to a trichromatic theory of color vision, we can predict five different varieties of color abnormality. The first, and most drastic, would be found in those who have no functioning cones. Since all their seeing would be done only with the rod system, they would be expected to have no color discrimination ability. In addition, they should find photopic, or daylight, levels of illumination to be quite uncomfortable. A slightly less drastic malady is one in which only one variety of cone is functioning in addition to the rods. With this problem, vision should be possible under both photopic and scotopic conditions but there would still be a lack of any color discrimination ability. Any wavelength of light hitting one of the functioning rods (or the single-cone system) would produce some bleaching of the pigment. Even though different wavelengths might bleach different amounts, this is not enough to allow color discrimination since the response produced by any one wavelength of light can be matched by merely adjusting the intensity of any other. In other words, the individual with no functioning cones, or the one with only one functioning cone type, responds to light in much the way that a sheet of black and white film does. All colors are recorded simply as gradations in intensity of the response. Such individuals are called **monochromats.**

We might also suppose that some individuals, rather than lacking two or three sets of cones as does the monochromat, might only have one malfunctioning cone system. Given two functioning cone systems, they should have some color perception, though it would differ from that of a normal observer. In effect, they should be able to match all other colors with a mixture of only two primaries (rather than the three required by color-normal observers). Such individuals are usually called **dichromats** (from the Greek *di* meaning "two" and *chroma* meaning "color"). The existence of such individuals has been known since the 1700s. The

English chemist John Dalton (1766–1844) was such a dichromat, a fact he learned rather late in his life. Supposedly, it first came to his attention when he wore a scarlet robe to receive his Ph.D. degree. Since he was a Quaker, a sect that shuns bright colors, this caused quite a stir, until it became clear that woolen yarn dyed crimson or yarn dyed dark blue-green appeared to be the same color to him.

There are three predictable forms of dichromacy, depending on whether it is the red-, green-, or blue-responding cones that are inoperative. The specific confusions are predictable from the color-matching curves of normal observers shown in Figure 5-9. Dalton's type of color defect is usually referred to as **protanopia** (the Greek prefix *proto* means "first," and red light is generally designated as the first primary). A protanope is insensitive to long wavelengths normally perceived as red light. If a red light is made very much brighter than a green light, a protanope could easily confuse them, whereas, a color-normal observer would perceive both that the red light was brighter than the green and that they differ in hue. Dalton described his subjective experiences when viewing a spectrum such as that produced by Newton's prism. Most individuals perceive six different colors, blending one into another. Dalton reported: "To me it is quite otherwise. I see only two, or at most three distinctions. These I should call yellow and blue, or yellow, blue, and purple. My yellow comprehends the red, orange, yellow, and green of others and my blue and purple coincide with theirs."

The most common form of dichromacy is called **deuteranopia** (the Greek prefix *deuteros* means "second," and green light is by convention the second primary). Individuals with deuteranopia presumably have a malfunction in the green cone system. With deuteranopia, they are still able to respond to green light; however, they cannot distinguish green from certain combinations of red and blue.

Trichromatic theory also predicts that there is a third form of dichromacy caused by the absence or malfunction of the blue cone system. Although a name existed for this phenomenon, **tritanopia** (from the Greek *tritan,* for the "third" primary), there was no confirmed report of this difficulty until about 1950, when a magazine article containing a color-vision test plate appeared as part of an intensive search throughout England. This national search resulted in the discovery of 17 tritanopes (Wright, 1952). These individuals, instead of seeing the spectrum as composed of blue and yellow as do other dichromats, see the longer wavelengths as red and the shorter ones as bluish green. The discovery of this last class of individuals provides strong support for a trichromatic theory of color vision.

Color defects are a fairly common problem. Some instances of it are relatively mild and result in what is called **anomalous trichromatism.** Color matches of individuals with this problem require more red (**protanomaly**) or more green (**deuteranomaly**) than do color matches of normal observers. If we count all individuals with any form of color deficiency, we find that just over 8 percent of all males show color weaknesses, whereas slightly less than .05 percent of all females show similar deficits. Color defects are genetically transmitted and recent studies have conclusively mapped the pattern of this transmission (Nathans, Piantanida, Eddy, Shows & Hogness, 1986).

What colors does a dichromat actually see? It is really not possible to know how the colors of a dichromat compare with those seen by a color-normal observer. However, a glimpse into the visual world of the color-defective has been provided by a rare person who was deuteranope in her left eye but color-normal in her right eye. Graham and Hsia (1958) had this observer adjust the color seen by her normal eye so that it appeared to be the same hue as the color seen by her defective eye. The results of her matches are shown in Figure 5-12. As can be seen from this figure, the colors over the entire range of red to green (from about 750 to 502 nm) all appeared to have the same yellow hue (about 570 nm), and all the colors from green to

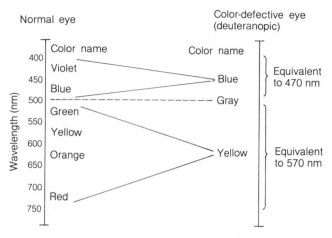

FIGURE 5-12   Color matches of a normal eye to a "color-blind" eye (deuteranopic) in the same observer. (Based on Graham & Hsia, 1958)

violet appeared to be blue (matching a 470-nm stimulus). The region that appears to be blue-green to the normal observer (around 502 nm) was perceived as being a neutral gray in the defective eye. Knowledge of the nature of the color confusions among dichromats allowed Coren and Hakstian (1987, 1988) to develop a simple questionnaire that assesses whether individuals are likely to be colorblind. You can test yourself with this questionnaire using Demonstration Box 5-2.

Physiological Basis of Trichromatic Theory

Although the data from color mixing and color defects seem to support a trichromatic theory of color vision, direct physiological evidence for the three cone pigments did not appear until the 1960s. The measurement procedure involved is conceptually simple but technically quite difficult (Bowmaker & Dartnall, 1980; Brown & Wald, 1964; Marks, Dobelle & MacNichol, 1964). It involves a device called a **microspectrophotometer.** With this device a narrow beam of monochromatic light is focused on the pigment-bearing outer segment of a cone. As tiny amounts of light of various wave-

lengths are passed through the cone the amount of light absorbed at each wavelength is measured. The more light of a given wavelength that is absorbed by the cone pigment, the more sensitive is the cone to light of that particular wavelength. Such measurements were taken using cones from the retinas of goldfish, monkeys, and finally from humans.

Although researchers are still refining the detailed description of the cone pigments (e.g., MacNichol, 1986), the general pattern of the results is unambiguous. There are three major groups of cones. A typical set of measurements, taken from a human eye that had to be surgically removed (Bowmaker & Dartnall, 1980), shows maximum absorptions in the ranges of 420, 534, and 564 nm, respectively (rods have a maximum absorption of 498 nm measured on this same eye, using the same technique). Figure 5-13 shows the relative absorption of these three pigments (where 1.0 is the maximum amount absorbed by the pigment). Clearly, on the basis of their sensitivity peaks, we should call the short-wavelength-absorbing pigment "violet," the middle "yellow-green," and the long "orange" if we wish to be more precise than the blue, green, and red labels we have been using.

DEMONSTRATION BOX 5-2.   Color Vision Screening Inventory

To see if you may have a color-vision deficit simply take this test, which is the *Color Vision Screening Inventory** developed by Coren and Hakstian (1987, 1988). For each question you should select the response that best describes you and your behaviors. You can select from among the following response alternatives: *Never* (or almost never), *Seldom, Occasionally, Frequently, Always* (or almost always). Simply circle the letter corresponding to the first letter of your choice.

1. Do you have difficulty discriminating between yellow and orange?   N S O F A

2. Do you have difficulty discriminating between yellow and green?   N S O F A

3. Do you have difficulty discriminating between gray and blue-green?   N S O F A

4. Do you have difficulty discriminating between red and brown?   N S O F A

5. Do you have difficulty discriminating between green and brown?   N S O F A

6. Do you have difficulty discriminating between pale green and pale red?

7. Do you have difficulty discriminating between blue and purple?   N S O F A

8. Do the color names that you use disagree with those that other people use?   N S O F A

9. Are the colors of traffic lights difficult to distinguish?   N S O F A

10. Do you tend to confuse colors?   N S O F A

Scoring Instructions: Responses are scored 1 for *Never*, 2 for *Seldom*, 3 for *Occasionally*, 4 for *Frequently*, and 5 for *Always*. Simply add together your scores for the 10 questions. If your score is 17 or higher, you have an 81 percent likelihood of failing a standard screening test for color vision. If your score is in this range you might want to get your color vision tested by your doctor or in a perception laboratory.

*The *Color Vision Screening Inventory* is copyrighted by SC Psychological Enterprises Ltd., and is reprinted here with permission.

Rushton (1962, 1965) introduced a similar technique for measuring the photopigments in living human observers that does not require a microspectrophotometer. First, he sent a beam of light into the eye and then took measurements on the amount of light reflected back out of the eye. By taking the difference between the amount of light sent and the amount reflected, an estimate was obtained of the amount of light at each wavelength absorbed by the photopigments in the intact human eye. Next, he flooded the eye with light of a particular distribution. Thus, red light might be expected to activate the long-wavelength-catching pigment most strongly, hence it would, with continued exposure, be "bleached out." When he remeasured the amount of light absorbed at each wavelength, the difference between light reflected back by the "bleached" and "unbleached" retinas gave absorption curves similar to those shown in Figure 5-13 for pigments marked "red" and "green" in the fovea. Rushton reasoned further that protanopes and deuteranopes, according to trichromatic theory, should be missing one or the other of the two longer wavelength pigments. When he used his procedure with color-defective observers, he found that they were missing the appropriate pigments.

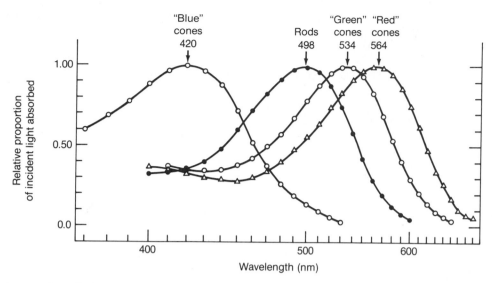

FIGURE 5-13   The relative absorption of various wavelengths of light by the three different cone types and the rods of a human. (Based on Bowmaker & Dartnall, 1980)

Rushton could not find evidence for cones containing blue-matching pigment in the fovea, which suggests that all observers are dichromats, specifically tritanopes, for targets seen in central vision. This conclusion has been verified using psychophysical techniques as well (Bornstein & Monroe, 1978; Williams, MacLeod & Hayhoe, 1981). Recent evidence based on destruction of blue cones in the monkey retina by prolonged exposure to short-wavelength light has confirmed the fact that there are no blue cones in a circular region 25 minutes in diameter in the central fovea (e.g., Sperling, 1986). The relative rarity of blue cones probably also explains why blue contributes less than red or green to many aspects of the visual process (e.g., Kaiser & Boynton, 1985).

Because the cones are differentially distributed across the retina (e.g., Sperling, 1986), your color response is different over different portions of the eye. The central foveal region is relatively blue-blind, and sensitivity to blue light first increases then decreases with increasing distance from the fovea. Sensitivity to green light diminishes with in-creasing distance from the fovea and disappears completely at about 40 degrees from the fovea. A similar pattern holds for sensitivity to red and yellow light, with color responses disappearing in the order green, red, yellow, and blue as distance from the fovea increases. In the far periphery of the retina, you are totally color-blind. The exact distance, however, depends on the size of the stimulus—you can discriminate the colors of larger stimuli farther out on the peripheral retina (Johnson, 1986). To see how your own color discrimination varies across the retina try Demonstration Box 5-3.

Opponent-Process Theory

The German physiologist Ewald Hering (1878/1964) was not completely satisfied with a trichromatic theory of color vision. It seemed to him that human observers acted as if there were four, rather than three, primary colors. For instance, when observers are presented with a large number of color samples and asked to pick out those that appear to be *pure* (defined as not showing any trace of being

---

DEMONSTRATION BOX 5-3.   Color Sensitive Zones on the Retina

Color perception is best in the central region of the retina (excluding the small central region of the fovea, which is blue-blind). You can observe the changes in color discrimination for different parts of the retina by taking a small orange piece of paper and placing it on a gray surface. Now keeping your head fixed, look off to the side of the orange target. If you keep moving your eyes outward (away from the target), you stimulate more peripheral parts of the retina.

Eventually you will reach a point where the orange will look yellowish, meaning that you have now imaged it beyond the red sensitive zone. If you continue moving your eyes outward you may even hit a point where the orange no longer looks colored at all, but merely appears gray. Your eye will have to move farther to get these changes in color appearance if the orange patch is larger (see Johnson, 1986).

---

a mixture of colors), they tend to pick out four, rather than three, colors. These unique colors almost always include a red, a green, and a blue, as trichromatic theory predicts (Fuld, Wooten & Whalen, 1981); however, they also include a yellow (Bornstein, 1973).

Boynton and Gordon (1965) showed that with the color names red, yellow, green, and blue, English-speaking observers can categorize the entire range of visible hues (some stimuli seem to require a combination term containing two primaries, such as yellow-green). The way adult observers distribute their hue names is shown in Figure 5-14, which indicates four overlapping hue name categories corresponding to red, green, blue, and yellow. These results cannot be attributed simply to learning or language use. For example, Bornstein, Kessen, and Weiskopf (1976) showed that 4-month-old infants tend to see the spectrum as if it were divided into four hue categories. They did this by repeatedly presenting a given wavelength of a light until the infants became visually bored and stopped looking at the light (a process called **habituation**). They next monitored how much time an infant spent looking at a second wavelength of light. They found that when the second wavelength was selected from another hue name category (based on the adult data) the infants spent more time looking

at it than they did at a wavelength selected from the same hue category. The infants acted as if stimuli in the same hue category were more similar than those from different categories; hence it seems they were categorizing hues into the same four groups that the adults do.

Hering looked at another aspect of the subjective experience of hue. He noted that certain color combinations are never reported by observers, for instance, a yellowish blue or a greenish red. This led Hering to suggest hypothetical neural processes in which the four primaries were arranged in opposing pairs. One **opponent process** would signal

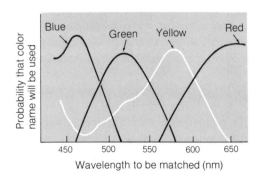

FIGURE 5-14   **The relationship between color names and wavelengths.**

the presence of red or green, and a separate process would signal blue or yellow. An example of such a process would be a single neuron whose activity rate increased with the presence of one color (red) and decreased in the presence of its opponent color (green). Since the cell's activity cannot increase and decrease simultaneously, one could never have a reddish green. A different "opponent-process" cell might respond similarly to blue and yellow. A third process was suggested to account for brightness perception. This was called a *black-white opponent-process,* after the fact that black and white are treated psychologically as if they were "pure colors" (see Quinn, Wooten & Ludman, 1985). But we need not limit the discussion to speculation based on color appearances alone, since physiological evidence exists that bears directly on the issue of opponent-process coding of color information.

Physiological Basis of Opponent-Process Theory

At the time Hering first suggested an opponent-process mechanism for the neural encoding of hue information, there was no physiological evidence to support such a speculation. Perhaps the single most important finding of 20th-century sensory physiology was that neural responses are subject to both excitatory and inhibitory influences caused by interaction between neighboring units. We introduced you to several such systems in Chapters 3 and 4. In fact, in Chapter 4 you saw that many brightness phenomena can be explained by the presence of a *spatially* opponent mechanism on the retina, where excitation in one region might cause inhibition in another. If we could also find *spectrally* opponent organization, where stimulation by one wavelength of light causes excitation in a cell, and stimulation by a wavelength in another region of the spectrum causes inhibition of that cell's neural response, then we would have a physiological unit that corresponds to the mechanism postulated by Hering.

The first evidence that different wavelengths

of light could cause opponent effects in neural response was offered by Svaetichin (1956), who inserted an electrode into the retina of a goldfish. When he recorded the responses to light transmitted by the horizontal cells (units at the first cellular layer beyond the cones, as noted in Chapter 3), he found that responses varied depending on the wavelength of the light reaching the cones. These neural responses were not in the form of the typical action potential found in most neurons but rather were graded shifts in the electrical polarization of the cells. Svaetichin found not only that the strength of response varied as the wavelength changed but, more importantly, that the electrical sign of the response was different for long and short wavelengths.

Figure 5-15 shows the pattern of responses recorded by Svaetichin and MacNichol (1958). Notice that the spectral sensitivities of the first two units are exactly what we would need for a blue-yellow cell and a red-green cell. For instance, the cell marked *red-green* would respond with a large positive signal if the unit is stimulated with a long-wavelength light (around 675 nm). This positive response could signal red. If the unit is stimulated with a greenish hue (around 500 nm), it would give its peak negative response, thus signaling the presence of green. If we simultaneously stimulated this unit with both a red and a green stimulus, the positive and negative responses would cancel each other and no signal would result. Thus, red and green oppose each other, and the same unit can never simultaneously signal both red and green. Such graded potentials are usually called **S potentials** after their discoverer, Svaetichin, and the cells that give these responses are called *C-type* horizontal cells (where the *C* stands for *color*). Also notice that there is another form of cellular response shown in the figure; it is marked *luminance.* This type of cell responds to the intensity of the light regardless of the wavelength. These *L-type* horizontal cells could be the basis of the black-white response hypothesized by Hering.

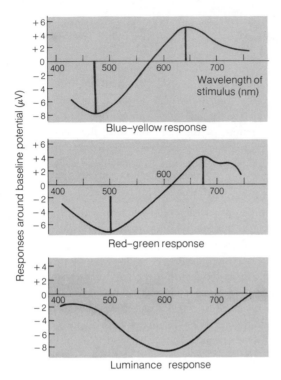

FIGURE 5-15   **Graded response of retinal cells to various wavelengths of light.** (Based on Svaetichin & MacNichol, 1958)

When we reach the level of the retinal ganglion cells, there is clearly an opponent-process coding; however, there is also a spatial distribution to these responses (Boynton, 1979; De Monasterio, 1978). The general form of this encoding involves the center-surround organization of receptive fields that we discussed in Chapter 3. Suppose we shine a tiny red spot on the eye while recording from a retinal ganglion cell. In some cases, as the size of the spot increases, the vigorousness of the neural response increases up to a point. After that, further increases in the size of the red spot have no further influence on the cell's response, Notice that this is very different from the type of response seen when white light is used (as in Chapters 3 and 4), where increasing the size of the spot starts to produce a

reduction of response rate as the spot begins to enter the inhibitory region of the receptive field. If we repeat the experiment with a green spot, we find that the cell appears unresponsive when the green spot is in the center of the receptive field; however, as the spot becomes larger, or it is moved into the surround field, the resting level of activity is reduced. Thus, we have a cell that has the property of being exited by red and inhibited by green, if the stimulus is the appropriate size and in the appropriate location on the retina. Of course, an equal number of cells with the opposite organization (green excitatory center, red inhibitory surround) plus cells in which the centers are inhibitory and the surrounds are excitatory are also found. The visual system, once having come upon a particular organizational scheme, seems to like to exhaust all possible combinations (see Gouras & Zrenner, 1981; Jacobs, 1986).

Further along in the visual system at the lateral geniculate nucleus, this particular arrangement can easily produce cells that generate a spectrally opponent signal with appropriate stimulus arrangements. In Chapter 3, we discussed some of the work of DeValois and his co-workers (DeValois & DeValois, 1980). They found that cells in the lateral geniculate of monkeys were also color-coded, similar to the color-coded retinal ganglion cells. These units showed a resting level of activity (in terms of neural responses per unit time) even in the absence of any light stimulation. When the eye was stimulated by large spots of light the response pattern changed. Some cells responded more vigorously when the eye was stimulated with short wavelengths of light, and decreased their response rate below their spontaneous (dark) activity level for long wavelengths of light. Other cells acted in exactly an opposite manner. As with the S potentials, two different classes of cells were reported. Each had different patterns of response as a function of wavelength, similar to what is needed for a red-green cell and a blue-yellow cell. Since the lateral geniculate receives its input directly from the retinal ganglion cells, this is exactly the pattern of results that we would expect. Thus, returning to our example above, if we have a red excitatory center in a receptive field, we should get increased response for a large area red light while the green inhibitory surround would completely ignore its presence. Conversely, a large green spot would cause an inhibitory response and be ignored by the red excitatory center, and so forth.

Typical responses from lateral geniculate cells can be seen in Figure 5-16. There are three cell types. One responds differentially to short and moderately long wavelengths (blue-yellow), one responds differentially to moderately short and long wavelengths (green-red), and one does not show different opponent processing, but rather responds

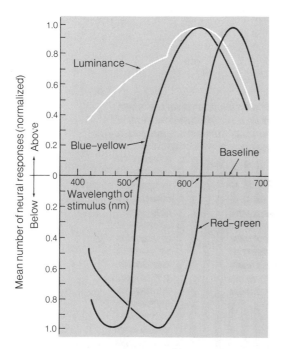

FIGURE 5-16 The neural response rate for cells in the lateral geniculate relative to their resting response rate, for stimulation by lights of different wavelengths. (Based on DeValois & DeValois, 1975)

simply to the amount of luminance reaching the eye. The spectrally tuned cells code both chromatic and spatial information in the responses. This means that whether a given wavelength will produce an increase or a decrease in neural response may also vary as the spatial position of the stimulus spot is varied within the receptive field of the cell.

The understanding of the processing of color information in the visual cortex has now become somewhat clearer, although much remains to be learned. Hubel and Wiesel's (1968) pioneering study, which recorded electrical responses from single cortical cells, showed that some cells in the monkey cortex respond differently as a function of the color of the test stimulus. Since then, evidence suggests that perhaps 50 percent or more of cortical cells are color-sensitive (Jacobs, 1976). This responsiveness to color appears in addition to the responsiveness to orientation, motion, and so forth, found in both simple and complex cortical cells (DeValois & Jacobs, 1984; Kruger & Gouras, 1980; Michael, 1981). Thus, in one complex cell, we might find that the largest response is for a red line of a particular orientation moving in a specific direction, whereas another cell might show its maximum response for a green line. An interesting demonstration of the way orientation and color responsiveness are intertwined can be seen behaviorally in the McCollough aftereffect (Harris, 1980; McCollough, 1965; Stromeyer, 1978). Demonstration Box 5-4 allows you to see this effect for yourself.

As we saw in Chapter 3, visual coding in the cortex seems to be highly organized, both across and down into the cortical surface. Similar organization is found for color-coding. Penetrating into the cortex, there are vertical columns, or slabs, where all the cells will be color-responsive, whereas in others no color responsiveness appears (Michael, 1981). Within a color column all cells show color sensitivity, however each might be tuned to different colors, orientation, or eye of input.

DEMONSTRATION BOX 5-4.   McCullough's Demonstration of the Interaction between Color and Form

The idea behind this demonstration is that through repeated exposure to colored stimuli at a particular orientation, the cortical cells that are tuned to that combination of color and orientation will become fatigued. When we next show a set of white stimuli at the same orientation, to which all color systems typically respond equally, the fatigued cells respond more weakly, causing a color aftereffect. The particular color seen is complementary to the adapting color. Thus, for instance, if you fatigue the green response, normally white light will appear tinged with red, fatigue of the blue response will produce a yellow aftereffect, and so forth. Of particular interest here is the fact that these aftereffects are also orientation-specific and seem to be caused by the selective fatigue of cortical cells tuned to color *and* orientation, although other explanations of this phenomenon have been suggested (see Skowbo, 1984).

To perform this demonstration, first notice that the figure in this box is completely achromatic. Now turn to Color Plate 6 and notice that there are two colored grids there, one containing vertical green lines and the other horizontal red lines. To selectively adapt the cortical cells, simply look at the green grid for about 5 seconds, then shift your gaze to the red grid for another 5 sec, then back to green grid again for 5 sec, continuing this alternation for about 2 or 3 minutes. When that inspection period has passed, look back at the figure in this box and you will find that it appears to be colored. Now the vertical white bars appear reddish (the green response to white vertical lines has been weakened) and the horizontal bars appear greenish (the red response to white horizontal lines is diminished). Notice also that turning the book sideways, or tilting your head so that the orientation of the lines changes on your retina, will change the colors of the lines. This demonstration indicates the intimate relationship between color and form predictable from our knowledge of the cortical coding of color and orientation.

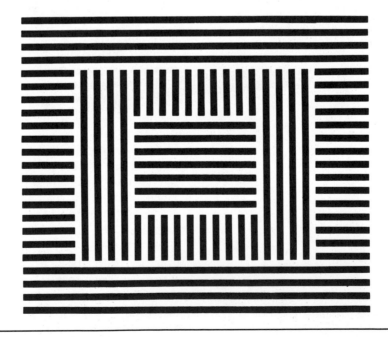

Penetrating the cortex vertically, we find types of cells that show an increase in response when the eye is stimulated with some colors and a decrease in response when stimulated with others. Once again, there is a spatial factor in this response. For example, stimulating the center of the cell's receptive field with red light would cause the cell to increase its activity, whereas stimulating the flanks with green light would cause the cell to decrease its activity. In Layer 4 of the cortex, there are cells

that have a *double* opponent process. Such a cell might increase its activity when the center of its receptive field is stimulated with red light, but actually decrease its firing when the surround is stimulated with red light. The opposite organization is seen for responses to green light in the same cell, with a green spot on the center of the receptive field producing a decrease in response and a green spot on the surround producing an increase in firing (Michael, 1985). Typical receptive fields of these types are shown in Figure 5-17. Such double opponent-process cells would respond most vigorously to contrasting colors placed next to each other, such as a red surrounded by a green. We still have much to learn about color processing in the central nervous system. However, a schematic outline of the arrangement of color processing in a section of striate cortex, as we currently know it, is shown in Figure 5-18.

Models of Color-Coding

How can a four-primary, opponent-process (or "push-pull") system exist when we already have provided physiological and psychophysical evidence indicating that the retina operates with a

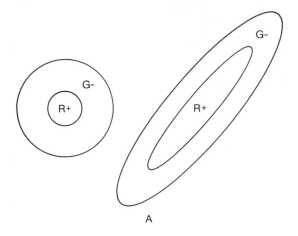

A

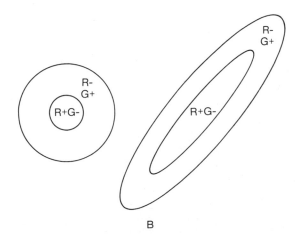

B

FIGURE 5-17 Receptive fields of typical color-opponent (A) and double-opponent (B) cells, recorded in the cortex.

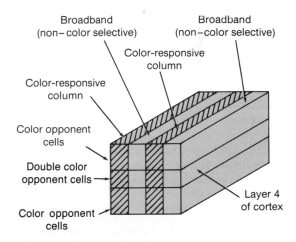

FIGURE 5-18 Arrangement of color-responsive cells in the striate cortex.

three-color pigment system? Hurvich and Jameson (1974) have suggested a *neural wiring diagram* that indicates the way cones, each containing only one of three pigments, could produce opponent responses at the postretinal level. An example of how such a wiring diagram might work is shown in Figure 5-19. It requires only that certain cones excite cells further along in the system, and that other cones inhibit the response rates of those cells. Engineers hit on a similar system when they designed color television transmission. The color in the original scene is first analyzed into its red, green, and blue components by the camera, and then transformed into two color-difference (or opponent-process) signals (plus an intensity signal). After reception at its distant location, the signals are reconverted into red, green, and blue signals by the television set. This technique was selected because

it required considerably less information to be transmitted through each channel, thus providing good fidelity and increased economy. Perhaps similar considerations of economy and fidelity underlie the organization of our visual systems.

An alternative neural coding theory for color was first suggested by Troland (1921) and recently revived. It claims that separate neural channels may not be needed for the various primary hues. Instead, information may be sent through common channels, with the color information carried via a sort of neural Morse code. Here, specific patterns of neural responses creating specified time intervals between bursts of firing could signal various colors. If this is the case, then it should be possible to create the subjective impression of color by flickering white light on and off in a pattern that mimics the usual neural code. Several investigators have been able to do exactly this, namely, generate the appearance of colors by pulsing white lights on and off (Festinger, Allyn & White, 1971; Jarvis, 1977; Piggins, Kingham & Holmes, 1972). Young (1977) has even managed to do this by pulsing tiny electric currents into the eye to simulate the supposed neural code. One phenomenon that this theory can explain very well is the appearance of **subjective colors.** These are colors perceived in the absence of the appropriate wavelengths of light, which can be made to appear in certain flickering black and white displays. A procedure for creating subjective colors for yourself is shown in Demonstration Box 5-5. Interestingly, people who show color defects for real colors also show the same color defects for subjective colors (White, Lockhead & Evans, 1977).

Most researchers today accept the fact that several mechanisms may be involved in color perception. It seems that there is an initial trichromatic coding at the level of the cones, followed by opponent processing at the higher neural levels with, perhaps, some additional information provided by the time relationships in the overall patterns of neural response.

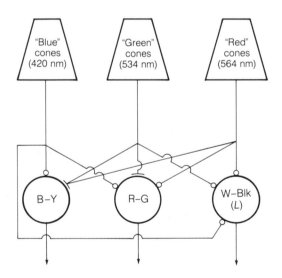

FIGURE 5-19 Schematic diagram indicating how a three-pigment system might be connected to produce opponent-process neural responses. The lines represent the connections. The round and flat connections differ in that one is excitatory and the other is inhibitory (which is which is arbitrary). Numbers indicate the wavelength of maximum sensitivity.

DEMONSTRATION BOX 5-5.   Subjective Colors

You have already encountered subjective colors in Demonstration Box 1-2, where colors appeared in a stationary stimulus. A more powerful set of subjective colors, produced by flickering black-and-white patterns, began as a toy invented by C. E. Benham in 1894. It was painted on a top and meant to be spun; hence the pattern is often referred to as **Benham's top.** The pattern is shown in the figure. Cut out this pattern (or carefully reproduce it), and mount it on a piece of thin cardboard. Punch a hole in the marked center region and insert a nail or a round pencil. Now spin the pattern as shown. Colors should appear when the pattern is spun at a moderate speed. If you are

spinning it clockwise, the inner bands should be slightly red, the next yellow, then green, and the last blue or violet. The order of the colors should reverse if you spin the pattern counterclockwise. The color effects arise because of the specific patterns of flickering white and black set up by each band. These patterns mimic the flashing on-and-off light patterns used to study subjective colors in a laboratory setting.

If you alter the adaptive state of your eye by staring at a white surface for a minute, you will notice that the perceived colors on each line will be different (Karvellas, Pokorny, Smith & Tanczos, 1979).

COLOR PERCEPTION

The wavelengths of light that are present are not the only factors that determine our perception of hue, as was demonstrated by the existence of subjective colors. A number of factors, such as stimulus intensity and duration, as well as the characteristics of surrounding stimuli, can also alter the perceived color.

Intensity and Duration

Increasing evidence suggests that color and brightness information are carried by different visual channels (Boynton, 1978, 1988; Favreau & Cavanagh, 1981). Perhaps the best evidence for this is the fact that their time courses are much different—responses to color changes are much slower than responses to brightness changes (Bowen, 1981).

However, it is also clear that the perception of hue may interact with the intensity of the stimulus (e.g., Emmerson & Ross, 1986). If intensity levels are low, only rods will be active and no color will be seen. But even beyond the cone threshold the perceived hue of a stimulus will change depending on the stimulus intensity. Specifically, if we increase the intensity of red or yellow-green stimuli, they not only appear brighter but begin to take on a more yellow hue. Similarly, blue-greens and violets begin to appear bluer when the intensity is increased. This phenomenon is called the **Bezold-Brucke effect,** in honor of its two discoverers. It is quite easy to demonstrate, as is shown in Demonstration Box 5-6. Although the basis of the Bezold-Brucke effect is not yet fully understood, it is clearly neural in its origin (Coren & Keith, 1970; Nagy, 1980). This effect may come about because the red-green opponent-process cells are slightly more sensitive than the blue-yellow cells. Thus, we can discriminate between red and green at lower intensity levels. Because the blue-yellow units become more active at higher intensity levels, hues tend to be dominated by these colors when stimuli are bright (Hurvich, 1981).

Prolonged exposure to colored stimuli also produces a shift in the perception of hue. For instance, if you viewed the world through a deep red filter for a sufficient period of time, you would find that when the filter was removed the world would take on a blue-green tint. This fatiguing of a specific color response is called **chromatic adaptation.** It is believed that these adaptation effects are due either to selective bleaching of one particular photopigment or to the fatigue of one aspect of the neural response of an opponent-process system (e.g., Vimal, Pokorny & Smith, 1987). Suppose you look through the red filter for a long period of time. The red-catching pigment becomes bleached, or the red response in the red-green opponent-process cells becomes fatigued. Now, when you view a white surface, the absence of red pigment (or the weakness of the red response) causes the blue and green systems to account for a greater proportion of the total activity. This gives the white a cyan (blue-green) tint. When such fatigue effects due to prolonged stimulation are localized (that is confined to one region of the retina), they are called **afterimages.** Demonstration Box 5-7 provides a stimulus for the production of color afterimages. You

---

DEMONSTRATION BOX 5-6.   The Bezold-Brucke Effect

For this demonstration you will need three pieces of colored cellophane, glass, or celluloid to serve as color filters. One should be a red, the other a green, and the last a yellow. Take a white sheet of paper that is brightly illuminated with room lighting, and cast a shadow over one-half of the paper. Looking through the red filter, you will notice that the hue of the red seen on the bright half of the paper is noticeably yellower than the hue seen on the shadowed portion. When you peer through the green filter, you should experience the same effect. However, looking through a yellow filter should not cause an apparent change in hue. Thus, the brighter you make a red or a green, the more yellow it will appear. This is a

demonstration of the hue shift, associated with increasing stimulus intensity, called the Bezold-Brucke effect.

Another way to see this effect is to simply look at an incandescent light bulb (60–100 W) through the red or the green filter. You will notice that the light bulb appears to be yellow, despite the presence of the filter. Since the red filter only allows the long (red) wavelengths of light to pass, and the green only allows the middle (green) wavelengths through, no yellow is reaching your eye. The yellow appearance of the bulb is caused by the Bezold-Brucke hue shift that occurs when the intensity of the stimulus is high.

DEMONSTRATION BOX 5-7. Color Afterimages

You can easily demonstrate negative or complementary color afterimages using Color Plate 7. Here you see four square patches of color: red, green, blue, and yellow. Notice that there is a black *x* in the middle of this pattern. Stare at the black *x* for about 2 minutes while keeping the plate under reasonably bright illumination. At the end of this period, transfer your gaze to the black *x* to the right of the figure. You should see a pattern of colored squares that is the exact complement of the pattern originally viewed. Where the red patch was, you will see green; where the green patch was, you will see red; where the blue patch was, you will see yellow; and where the yellow patch was, you will see blue. These are the complementary color afterimages caused by the fatiguing of the various color responses during the time you were staring at the color patches.

---

will notice when performing this demonstration that the hue of the afterimage tends to be a complementary hue of the stimulus producing the afterimage.

Spatial Interactions

In Chapter 4 you learned that the brightness of a stimulus could be affected by the intensity of adjacent stimuli. The general nature of the interaction was inhibitory, so that a bright surround made a central area appear dim. Inhibitory interactions between adjacent color systems can also occur and they result in hue shifts. The phenomenon is called **simultaneous color contrast.** Consider Color Plate 3. Notice that this figure has four brightly colored patches, each of which surrounds a small central square. The square on the red patch appears to be slightly green, and that on the green appears to be slightly red. The square on the blue patch appears to be slightly yellow, and that on the yellow patch appears to be slightly blue. However, each square is exactly the same gray. You might be able to increase the strength of this effect by viewing Color Plate 3 through a sheet of tracing paper or thin tissue.

Jameson and Hurvich (1964) suggested that simultaneous color contrast arises from mechanisms similar to those that cause brightness contrast, namely, an active neuron tends to inhibit the responding of adjacent neurons. In the case of the gray square on the red background, for example,

we have a situation where the red response systems exposed to the surround are highly activated. In turn these active neurons will inhibit the red response in the neurons exposed to the central gray patch. Since the red and green responses are usually in balance, inhibition of the red response results in the emergence of the complementary, or opponent, green response in this region. A tinge of green hue is then seen in the gray. As one might expect, if this is truly an inhibitory interaction such as we observed in brightness effects, it is even possible to produce colored Mach bands (Ware & Cowan, 1987).

Contrast-induced colors act very much like real colors in their ability to produce other perceptual effects. For instance, Anstis, Rogers and Henry (1978) induced very strong contrast colors on surrounded gray patches (as in Color Plate 3) and found that observers developed negative afterimages to the contrast colors, just as though they had been viewing real colors!

Age and Physical Condition

An individual may have normal color vision when tested at one stage in the life span, but may show color discrimination defects when tested at a later stage. Aging seems to alter color vision. Perhaps this is because the crystalline lens of the eye grows more yellow as an individual ages; hence we look through a gradually darkening yellow filter (Coren & Girgus, 1972a). Other effects, such as the loss of cone pigment with age (Kilbride, Hutman, Fishman & Read, 1986), may also account for changes in color vision. Generally speaking, aging seems to bring about a gradual deterioration of blue vision (Lakowski, 1962; Verriest, 1974). Most individuals are unaware of such changes because the onset is quite slow; however, the effect gradually accumulates. Since the perception of hue is subjective, you seldom have opportunities to assess whether your hue perception agrees with that of others. Does your red appear to be the same as that of your friends? Clearly, this is an unanswerable question.

Physical conditions can also result in losses in the ability to discriminate colors. Such acquired color vision losses are called **dyschromatopsias.** There are several diseases or physical conditions that lead to such dyschromatopsias. The most commonly observed losses are for sensitivity to blue (see Pokorny & Smith, 1986), which are observed in diabetics (Lakowski, Aspinall & Kinnear, 1972), individuals with glaucoma (Lakowski & Drance, 1979), and alcoholics (Reynolds, 1979). These color losses can be aggravated by a number of factors. For instance, diabetic women who take oral contraceptives show significantly greater discrimination losses in the blue range (Lakowski & Morton, 1977). Acquired problems with the red-green system are rarer and usually are associated with cone degeneration or optic nerve diseases (Pinkers & Marre, 1983).

Cognitive Factors in Color Perception

Although color is a basic sensory experience, there are also nonsensory factors that affect the perceived color of an object. In addition, color may interact with other nonperceptual behaviors.

Memory Color

The remembered color of familiar objects often differs from the objects' actual color. When observers are shown color samples and later asked to match them from an array of colored chips, systematic errors are made. Observers tend to pick chips of greater brightness when asked to remember bright colors and greater darkness when asked to remember dark colors (Bartleson, 1960; Newhall, Burnham & Clark, 1957). When asked to remember and match colors of familiar objects with characteristic hues, we remember apples or tomatoes as being more red than the actual objects, bananas are more yellow in memory than in the bunch, and remembered grass is greener than it is on the lawn. Because of this memory effect, many film manufacturers have chosen to modify the spectral reproduction ability of color film so that the reproduced colors are richer than they are in nature. Since television engineers have not made a similar correction, color memory distortions may account for part of our feeling that the picture reproduced on a color television set is an unfaithful reproduction of real color.

Memory color effects tend to creep into certain other matching tasks. For instance, if you are asked to match the color of a Valentine's Day heart or an apple, both of which have been cut out of orange paper, you will match them with a redder hue than you would use to match an oval or a triangle cut out of the same material. A banana-shaped figure, or one labeled *lemon,* is matched with a yellower hue. It seems as if the remembered color blends with the observed stimulus, altering the percept toward the ideal, or prototypical, color of an object (Bruner, Postman & Rodrigues, 1951; Delk & Fillenbaum, 1965; Harper, 1953; White & Montgomery, 1976). The color you remember is probably "better" than the color that is present; however, the color you see now may be tinged by your memory's hue.

Culture and Color

As we noted earlier, an English speaker is content to describe hue differences using four basic categories: red, yellow, green, and blue. This is not the case for many other languages, some of which have no separate names for green and blue, or the same name for yellow and green, or red and yellow. There are some languages that only distinguish red as a separate color and have no names for the other hues. It is often argued that there is an interaction between language and perception, and that when separate names for separate sensory experiences exist, these labels make discriminations easier. In other words, the Lakuti tribe, who only have a single term for blue and green, may see the two colors as being more similar to each other than English speakers, who have separate words for these stimuli (Whorf, 1956). The suggestion that different language terms for colors indicate different perceptual abilities has been presented in many different forms. For instance, Robertson (1967) suggested that there has been an evolutionary development in both the color-perceiving ability of humans and in the color terms encoded in the language. He suggested that the first discriminations were between red and green, then the discrimination ability for yellow evolved, and finally that for blue. He analyzed a number of ancient languages and found such evolutionary trends. One could conclude from such evidence that the ancient Greeks were relatively weak in their ability to perceive colors because their language had only a limited set of color names.

Actually, when the ability of individuals to match, discriminate, or reproduce colors (rather than just to name colors) is measured directly, the picture changes. It seems as if the number of color names in a language does *not* affect the ability to make such discriminations (Berlin & Kay, 1969; Bornstein, 1973, 1975). These findings indicate the danger, in the absence of perceptual measurements, of assuming that language usage directly reflects perceptual abilities.

Color Impressions

Color does more than provide us with additional information about stimuli, it has emotional conse-

quences. It delights and depresses. It makes humans feel warm or cold, tense or relaxed. For instance, a manufacturer of detergent found that the color of the detergent box made a difference in how the user evaluated the strength of the detergent. Women were given the same detergent in three boxes, which differed only in color. When the detergents were rated after use, the women felt that the detergent in a yellow-orange box was too strong, and supposedly had ruined some of the clothes. The detergent in a blue box was too weak, whereas the one with both blue and yellow-orange flashes seemed to be most effective (Kupchella, 1976).

Color can even produce sensory impressions that are characteristic of other senses. It is almost universal to call the short-wavelength (blue) colors "cool," and the longer wavelengths (yellow) "warm." Perhaps these labels arise because the cool of the night is first broken by the red of the dawn, with midday characterized by the yellow of sunlight and warmth. As the yellow begins to disappear and the blue of twilight begins to predominate, temperatures again grow cool. Many years and many generations of such an association might stamp this warm-cool relationship into our languages. In an era when the conservation of energy is important, it is interesting to note that people will turn a heat control to a higher setting in a blue room than they will in a yellow room, as if they are trying to compensate thermally for the coolness that has been visually induced (Boynton, 1971). Similarly, Alexander and Shansky (1976) have shown that dark saturated colors are perceived as being associated with a greater sensation of "weight" or "heaviness." All these findings emphasize that color is a psychological achievement, not simply a direct effect of the physical variation of wavelengths of light. If you still doubt this statement it will probably be instructive to turn back to Demonstration Box 1-2 or 5-5 to see colors develop in your mind where no physical variations in wavelength exist.

GLOSSARY

The following definitions are specific to this book.

Additive color mixture   A color mixture resulting from the addition of light of one wavelength to light of another, e.g., the projection of a blue light on top of a red light on a screen to produce magenta.

Afterimage   A visual sensation that appears after an intense or prolonged exposure to a stimulus.

Anomalous trichromatism   A defect in color vision in which color matches made by an individual are systematically different from normal, although the three primary color systems are still functioning.

Benham's top   A black-and-white pattern that when rotated produces subjective colors.

Bezold-Brucke effect   The shift in the apparent hue of a color as the intensity is changed.

Brightness   The psychological impression of light intensity.

Chlorolabe   Green-sensitive cone pigment.

Chromatic adaptation   A weakened response to a color stimulus due to previous exposure to other chromatic stimuli.

CIE chromaticity space   A variant of the color triangle system, using three imaginary ''super'' primaries.

Color atlas   A book in which each page represents a horizontal or a vertical slice through a color space.

Color blindness   A condition in which individuals lack the ability to make discriminations on the basis of wavelength of light.

Color circle   *See* Color wheel.

Color solid   *See* Color spindle.

Color spindle   A three-dimensional model of color appearance in which the relationships between hue, brightness, and saturation are depicted.

Color wheel   A circular scheme in which colors are represented according to hue, with complementary colors placed directly across from each other.

Complementary colors   Color pairs whose mixture produces an achromatic gray or white.

Cyanolabe   Blue-sensitive cone pigment.

Deuteranomaly   A condition in which an individual's color matches require more green than those of a color-normal individual.

Deuteranopia   A form of color blindness associated with the confusion of reds and greens due to insensitivity in the green system.

Dichromats   Individuals whose color vision is defective, allowing all hues to be matched with two rather than three primaries.

Dominant wavelength   The wavelength of a monochromatic stimulus that best approximates the hue of a color mixture.

Dyschromatopsias   Acquired color-vision losses.

Erythrolabe   Red-sensitive cone pigment.

Habituation   The process by which an observer ceases to respond, or reduces the magnitude of a response, to a repeated stimulus.

Hue   The term denoting the psychological dimension most clearly corresponding to the wavelength of light and most often termed *color* in common language.

Metameric colors   Colors that appear to be the same but are composed of different wavelengths.

Microspectrophotometer   A device for measuring the amounts and wavelengths of light emanating from microscopic target areas.

Monochromatic stimuli   Stimuli that contain only one wavelength of light.

Monochromats   Individuals who see color as mere gradations of intensity, because of the absence of any functioning cones.

Opponent process   Neural process that signals the presence of one color by increasing its activity and of an opposing color by decreasing its activity.

Primaries   Three monochromatic light sources that when combined in appropriate amounts can match any other hue.

Protanopia   A form of color blindness resulting in the confusion of reds and greens due to insensitivity in the red system.

Protanomaly   A condition in which an individual's color matches require more green than those of a color-normal individual.

Purity   A spectrally pure stimulus is composed of only one wavelength.

S potentials   Graded electrical retinal-cell responses that vary in direction and strength depending on the wavelength of the stimulus.

Saturation   The psychological attribute of a color associated with ''how much'' of a hue is present.

Simultaneous color contrast   A process in which inhibitory interactions between adjacent color systems cause hue shifts.

Spectral colors   Pure monochromatic stimuli, such as those in a prismatic spectrum.

Subjective colors   Colors that are consciously experienced, but not associated with any wavelength change in the physical stimulus.

Subtractive color mixture   A color mixture resulting from the subtraction or absorption of light of various wavelengths, e.g., the mixture of yellow and blue pigments to produce green.

Trichromatic theory   The theory that color vision is based on three primary responses.

Tristimulus values   The combination of the stimulus hue and brightness used in the CIE color system for determining any color stimulus.

Tritanopia   The color defect in which yellows and blues are confused due to reduced blue sensitivity.

CHAPTER
6

The Auditory System

It is one of those strange historical occurrences that while studying the physiology of the ear in order to help the deaf deal with the world of sound, Alexander Graham Bell developed the telephone. Perhaps the leap was not too great however, for if the eye is our window to the world then the ear must be our microphone. Just as an understanding of the physical nature of light and of the anatomy and physiology of the eye is important to understanding the psychology of vision, an understanding of the physical nature of sound and of the anatomy and physiology of the auditory system is crucial to our understanding of hearing.

The ear is a remarkable physical instrument. An engineer trying to duplicate the function of the ear would have to compress a sound system of immense complexity into a space of approximately 2 cubic centimeters (Stevens & Warshovsky, 1965). For example, the major functional part of the ear, the cochlea, has over 1 million moving parts (Hudspeth, 1985). So much complicated apparatus suggests that the path of sound waves, from their origin in the external environment to the final stage where we ''hear'' a sound, involves several different mechanisms and stages of information processing.

SOUND

Sound is a form of mechanical pressure. If you have ever attended a rock concert, you probably have felt the actual mechanical pulsations, especially those from the bass instruments, that may cause the floor, seat, or the air about you to vibrate. You are feeling the results of the movements of air molecules being pushed forward in waves by the cones of the speakers. It may be easier to understand this phenomenon if we consider what happens when we pluck a guitar string, causing a sound. We can see the string vibrate, moving rapidly back and forth in space. This movement causes the strand of steel or nylon to collide with the air molecules around it. These molecules in turn collide with others, causing air compression as the string moves forward and rarefaction as it moves back. This movement results in a **wave** of mechanical energy, as is shown in Figure 6-1.

Sound waves are alternations of rarefaction and compression of an elastic medium (e.g., water, air, or walls) in which they travel and are created by rapid movements of a source in mechanical contact with the medium. The medium acquires some of the movement energy of the source and transfers it to other parts of the medium by means of collisions between the molecules of the medium. Sound waves can be transmitted for great distances, although the individual air molecules simply move back and forth over very small distances. The collisions of molecules, of course, are not perfectly efficient in transferring the original collision energy, so a sound wave tends to become less intense as it moves farther away from the original source. Consequently, its ability to move or vibrate other objects decreases. Since sound involves the vibration of parts of the medium through which it travels, it cannot pass through a vacuum. The necessity of a medium for the existence of sound waves was demonstrated by Robert Boyle in 1660, when he pumped the air out of a jar and then failed to hear the sounds made by a watch suspended by a thread in the jar.

The speed of sound varies according to the medium in which it travels. The elasticity and density of the medium are important, with sound traveling faster in a denser or more elastic medium where molecules are closer or more strongly connected to each other. The speed of sound is rather slow compared to that of electromagnetic waves such as light, being approximately 340 m/sec in air and about 1,360 m/sec in water.

A Simple Sound Wave

Any sound wave may be described by specifying certain values. The simplest wave is *sinusoidal,* so-called because the trigonometric sine function describes it mathematically. Figure 6-1 shows the

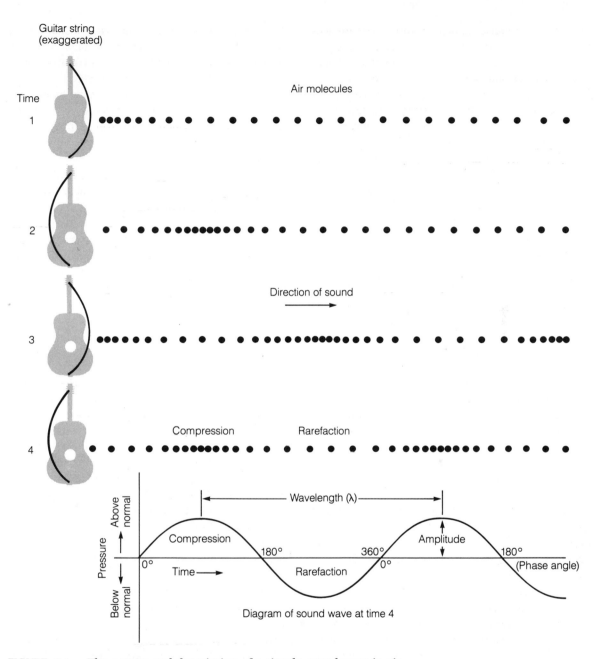

FIGURE 6-1   The nature and description of a simple sound wave in air.

alternate compressions and rarefactions of air molecules over time from the vibrating string of a guitar. When we plot the air pressure as it varies over time we get the wave shown in the figure. Its **wavelength** (represented by the Greek letter *lambda,* λ) is the distance from one peak to the next peak, representing a single **cycle** of the wave. The **frequency (f)** of the wave, by convention, is the number of cycles the wave is able to complete in one second. The unit used to measure frequency is the **hertz (Hz),** named after the German physicist Heinrich R. Hertz, one hertz being equivalent to one **cycle per second.** The frequency of a sound wave is important to our later discussion, since it is related to (although not the same as) the perceived pitch of the sound. The range of frequencies that seem to have pitch for most people is from about 20 to 20000 Hz. Sounds below 20 Hz are sensed as vibration, whereas sounds above 20000 Hz are not heard at all except by young children. Other animals, such as bats or dolphins, can hear frequencies several times as high as the upper limit for humans.

The intensity of a sound wave is related to its **pressure amplitude.** This is a measure of compression or rarefaction in the air or other medium at the peaks or valleys of the sound wave. For a sine wave in air, the pressure amplitude is the maximum amount by which the wave causes the air pressure (force per unit area expressed as dynes/cm^2) to differ from the normal atmospheric pressure (which is about 1,000,000 dynes/cm^2). The maximum *pressure variation* the ear can tolerate is about 280 dynes/cm^2 above or below atmospheric pressure, whereas the minimum pressure variation detectable (average for young adults) is about 0.0002 dynes/cm^2. For these threshold-level sound waves, the air molecules are displaced (on average) about 0.0000000001 cm, which is about one-tenth the diameter of an average air molecule. Obviously the ear is an extremely sensitive organ with a broad response range.

In order to express conveniently this wide range of sound sensitivity, we use some special measures. When dealing with sound in terms of energy units, we can speak of the difference between two levels by asking by how many powers of 10 (the logarithm) one energy level exceeds another. If one energy level is 1 million times greater than another (10^6 times greater), we say that it is 6 **bels** greater (a measurement unit named after Alexander Graham Bell). It is more convenient, however, to speak in terms of **sound pressure level (SPL),** which represents the actual force against the ear, than in terms of sound energy. Because of the nature of the mathematical relationship between energy and pressure amplitude, the number of bels is doubled when we speak of ratios of sound pressure levels. Since a bel is a rather large unit relative to normal hearing levels, the most common unit used is the **decibel (dB),** which is one-tenth of a bel. The formula for decibels is

$$\text{Number of dB} = 20 \log (P/P_0)$$

where P is the sound pressure level we wish to express in decibels, and P_0 is the standard reference level. The standard reference level is psychologically meaningful, since it is the average value of the threshold for sound (0.0002 dynes/cm^2) measured in young adults at 1000 Hz. Decibels are particularly suited to express the relationships between sound pressure levels since they compress the large range of possible pressures into more manageable units. Table 6-1 gives typical values of sound pressure levels expressed in decibels for some representative sounds. The table shows that as the measured intensity of a sound increases, subjective loudness also increases. Intensity is related to (but not identical to) loudness.

A final important parameter of sound waves is **phase,** which is important when two or more simple waves are compared. Phase refers to the particular part of the compression-rarefaction cycle a wave has reached at one instant of time. If two waves are at exactly the same part of their respective cycles at the same instant (so that their peaks and valleys coincide), they are said to be **in phase.**

Table 6-1. Sound Pressure Levels (intensity levels) of Various Sound Sources

Source	Sound Level (dB)
Manned spacecraft launch (from 45 m)	180
Loudest rock band on record	160
Pain threshold (approximate)	140
Large jet motor (at 22m)	120
Loudest human shout on record	111
Heavy auto traffic	100
Conversation (at about 1m)	60
Quiet office	40
Soft whisper	20
Threshold of hearing	0

If their peaks and valleys do not coincide, the two waves are **out of phase.** How much they are out of phase is expressed in terms of **phase angle.** A single cycle is assigned 360 degrees (as in circular motion); thus, a portion of a cycle can be specified by number of degrees from 0 to 360 (see Figure 6-1). If one wave is at its 90-deg point (its peak) when another wave is at its 180-deg point (crossing the zero pressure-difference line), then the two waves are 90 deg out of phase.

If we remember that these waves simply describe increases and decreases in mechanical pressure at various moments in time, it should be clear that different sound waves (patterns of pressure) that occur at the same time can interact with each other. If two same-frequency waves are perfectly in phase (0 deg out of phase), their peak and minimum pressures coincide; hence, they add strongly to each other's intensities. When two waves of the same frequency are 180 deg out of phase, one reaches its minimum when the other is reaching its maximum and they cancel each other's effects; therefore, we would not be able to hear the interacting sound waves.

Typically, everyday sounds are more complex than the simple sine waves we have been discuss-

ing. Only a few sound sources, such as tuning forks or electronic instruments, produce "pure" sounds, which are composed of a simple sine wave variation of compression and rarefaction. Sounds produced by musical instruments, the human voice, automobiles, waterfalls, and so on, have enormously complex cycles of compression and rarefaction. These complexities result from the interaction of many different waves of different frequencies and phases. Such complex waveforms produce the **timbre** of sounds (see Chapter 7 for a discussion of how this occurs). We can differentiate among the sounds of a trumpet, a clarinet, a piano, and a violin quite easily, because the wave forms they produce, even when they are playing the same musical "note," are quite different. You can see in Figure 6-2 that instruments produce very complicated waveforms. Demonstration Box 6-1 provides a method by which you can experience our extraordinary ability to recognize complex sounds through their timbre.

Complex sounds, such as those in Figure 6-2, can be described most usefully by analyzing each

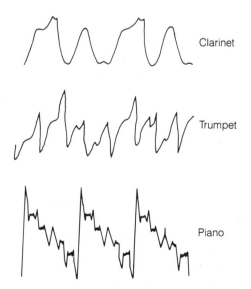

Clarinet

Trumpet

Piano

FIGURE 6-2   Complex sound waves produced by three musical instruments.

DEMONSTRATION BOX 6-1.   Perception of Timbre

Perhaps the most primitive musical instrument is the human hand, used (usually in pairs) to clap rhythms. As in any musical instrument, the shape and orientation of the surrounding parts will alter the complex components of the resultant sound, hence the *timbre* that we hear. There seem to be only a few basic ways of clapping, and people have the remarkable ability to distinguish which is occurring from the sound alone (Repp, 1987). Try holding your hands in the configuration shown in part A of the figure so that your hands are aligned and flat. Clap a few times, listening closely to the sound. Now hold your hands in configuration B, with your hands oblique and slightly cupped. Clap a few times, again listening closely to the sound. Position B generates more low frequency sounds in the mixture than position A. You should be able to distinguish the different claps quite clearly. You can also hear differences if the palms are crossed while clapping, or if you clap with your fingers around your palm, and so forth. It might be fun to have someone else now clap while you are not looking, and see if you can approximate what their hand positions are. If you can, you are responding to the timbre of the sounds, and performing some form of analysis of the complex sounds actually present into their constituent components, which then allows you to recognize their source.

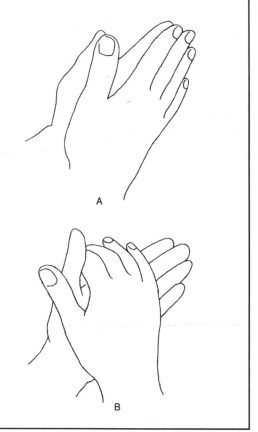

one into a set of simpler sine waves, which when added together would produce the more complicated waveforms. This method was invented by the French scientist Jean B. J. Fourier in the course of his studies of heat conduction. Fourier proved a mathematical theorem that states, in essence, that *any* waveform that is continuous and periodic can be represented as the sum of a series of simple sine waves with appropriate wavelengths, phases, and amplitudes. As it turns out, these simple waves often have frequencies related to each other by simple mathematical ratios. Figure 6-3 shows an example of the decomposition of a complex waveform into its **Fourier components.** Speech sounds may also be analyzed into their Fourier components, with results that are very useful for the understanding of speech perception (see Chapter 12). The ear itself acts as a sound analyzer, decomposing complex sounds into their individual components. This fact is known as **Ohm's acoustical law** after the physicist George Ohm. You may demonstrate this effect for yourself using Demonstration Box 6-2.

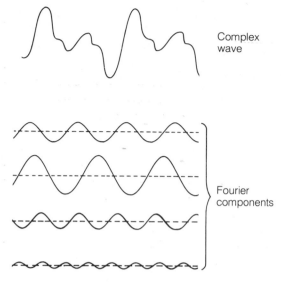

Complex wave

Fourier components

FIGURE 6-3   Fourier components (sine waves) of a complex sound wave.

THE STRUCTURE OF THE EAR

Evolution and Anatomy of the Ear

The human ear is a complex piece of biological engineering, yet biologists have traced its origins to simple organs in quite primitive animals (Steb-bins, 1980; van Bergeijk, 1967). All vertebrate ears seem to have evolved from the sense of touch. Whether primitive or advanced, they seem to be specializations of groups of cells with protruding hairs, much like those found on the skin of your arm. In fact, we can use the skin to demonstrate a number of phenomena associated with human hearing (Bekesy, 1960).

One of the first steps in the evolution of the modern mammalian ear is the *lateral line*. The lateral line is a linear array of nerve endings in the skin of fish and some amphibians from which protrude jellylike masses in which are embedded sensory hairs. Often these hairs are pigmented and form a horizontal line that runs the length of the animal's body. As the water moves or vibrates because of sounds made by prey or predators or other stimuli these sensory hairs bend. In a sense the fish does not so much "hear" sound as "feel" it. The lateral line system is especially useful under conditions of low light levels, such as in the Arctic or Antarctic during the winter. For example, the lateral line system in one Antarctic fish is tuned very precisely to the sounds made by the plankton it feeds on (Montgomery & MacDonald, 1987).

In addition to the lateral line system, some types of fish have primitive internal ears that work

---

DEMONSTRATION BOX 6-2.   Ohm's Acoustical Law

This demonstration is done with a piano or a guitar, but if neither is available use three glasses filled with water to different heights so that they produce a fairly high note, a middle note, and a low note when tapped with a butter knife. Now have some friends strike the high, middle, and low notes simultaneously a few times. Without telling you, have them drop out one note, sounding only two a few times, then put it back in. Notice that it is quite easy to determine which of the three notes was added or subtracted, despite the fact that the chord formed by these notes is quite a complex sound pattern. Notice that the individual sounds do not lose their identities, and can be discriminated from the others in the complex sound. With enough practice a person can learn to separate as many as six or seven different components of a complex chord or "clang." The separation of sound components by the auditory system is known as *Ohm's acoustical law*.

on much the same principles as do human ears. It is believed that these internal ears evolved from a specialized, deeply sunken part of the lateral line system. In such fish, vibrations in the water cause similar vibrations in an air bladder in the fish's body cavity. From there the vibrations are passed on to a series of small bones, derived from some of the vertebrae and ribs, and then to a complex organ called the **labyrinth,** whose looping passages are filled with fluid. This fluid contains hairs that are sensitive to the movements of the liquid in the labyrinth caused by the vibrations picked up by the air bladder. These hairs send the auditory information to the fish's brain by way of sensory nerves. In many of its elements, this system is quite similar to that found in humans, even to the composition of the fluid in the labyrinth. Many other animals have ears that are considered to be developments from these primitive versions. An interesting transition form is that of the frog. A tadpole has a hearing apparatus similar to those of fishes. Sound waves are picked up by the (not fully functional) lung and transmitted to the labyrinth. During metamorphosis into a frog, however, the ear changes. It develops an external membrane (the eardrum) that takes the place of the lung in the tadpole hearing system.

Another major component, which is common to all mammals and birds and also appears in the crocodilian reptiles, is the **cochlea.** The cochlea is a specialized development of the labyrinth that contains a long membrane covered with sensory cells from which (of course) hairs protrude. Its name (which means ''shell'') is derived from its coiled seashell appearance in mammals.

All mammalian ears have the same basic parts, although they differ somewhat in proportions (with the elephant of course having one of the largest). There are also differences in sensitivity. Bats, dolphins, and dogs have extraordinarily keen hearing over a very wide range of frequencies. The ears of mammals differ from those of birds, reptiles, and fish in that mammalian ears typically have three small bones to transmit vibrations to the labyrinth, rather than the single bone found in these other species. Bekesy (1960), in a series of detailed studies, established that all these various types of ears function in a similar manner. He was able to link many of the performance differences with differences in the physical properties of the ears (such as in the length of the cochlea). Thus, the human ear, with which we will be concerned in the remainder of this chapter, is a part of a large family of roughly equivalent organs. This fact makes it possible to extend the results of studies of other mammalian ears to the human auditory system.

Physiology of the Human Ear

We shall now follow a sound wave through the structure of the human ear, and trace the neural pathways to the cortex of the brain. The ear can be divided into three major parts, the **outer, middle, and inner ears.** Figure 6-4 is a schematic representation of the human ear. The outer ear consists of the **pinna,** which is the fleshy part of the ear visible from the outside. Only mammals have pinnae, and they are thought to function mainly to channel the sound waves into the **auditory canal,** although they may also be involved in the localization of sound (see Chapter 7). Some mammals, such as bats and dogs, have highly mobile pinnae that allow them partially to select the direction from which sounds are received. The sound waves that enter the auditory canal are channeled along it until they encounter the **eardrum** (or **tympanum**). The eardrum vibrates in resonance with incoming sound waves, moving back and forth at a high rate for high-frequency sounds, and more slowly for low-frequency sounds. As we mentioned when discussing sound, these vibratory movements are quite small. For frequencies in the middle of the audible range (1000–6000 Hz), the shape of the auditory canal helps to concentrate the sound and to increase its force against the eardrum.

The middle ear consists of a set of three tiny bones (**ossicles**): the **malleus** (''hammer''), the **incus** (''anvil''), and the **stapes** (''stirrup''). These

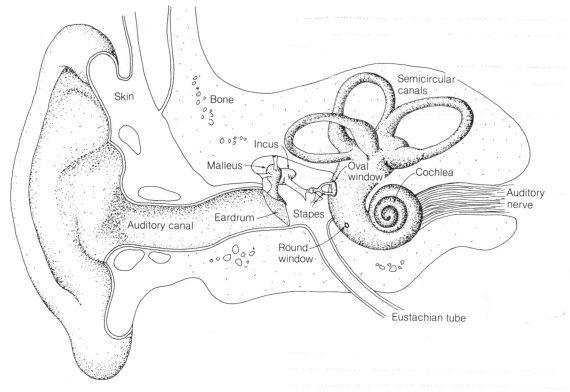

FIGURE 6-4   The human ear. (Based on Lindsay & Norman, 1977)

bones transmit the vibrations of the eardrum to the transducer mechanism located in the inner ear. Some interesting and important subtleties of operation of this part of the ear may help explain why the complex system of ossicles evolved. The middle ear amplifies sound waves in two ways as it transmits them to the cochlea. First, the energy of a sound wave may be approximately doubled by its transmission through the ossicles since they operate mechanically as a system of levers. Second, the area of the oval window is only about 1/15 that of the vibrating area of the eardrum. Elementary physics tells us that a given force applied to two surfaces of different areas yields a greater force per unit area on the smaller surface; thus, the forces applied to the oval window by the stapes are an additional 15 times greater than those at the ear-

drum. In total, the middle ear amplifies sounds by a factor of about 30. This amplification is needed because the tiny motions of the air molecules caused by the sound wave ultimately must cause the entire body of cochlear fluid to vibrate. Without this amplification, only very intense sounds would be heard.

A second important aspect of the operation of the middle ear is the ability of the ossicle system to selectively *decrease* the amplification it provides in order to protect the ear from damage by intense sounds. This is accomplished by means of a change in its relative orientation against the oval window. Sounds in the normal range of intensity cause the stapes to push directly on the fluid in the cochlea. For very intense sounds, however, the angle at which the stapes moves changes and the effect of the stapes on the cochlear fluid is greatly reduced. In addition, a muscle attached to the stapes contracts via a neuromuscular reflex when intense low-frequency sounds strike the ear, while another muscle attached to the eardrum contracts to stiffen the eardrum. These mechanisms make the eardrum less able to vibrate in sympathy with sounds in the canal, and, taken together, all these mechanisms tend to protect the ear from long-lasting excessive stimulation by loud sounds.

The bones of the middle ear are surrounded by air. The air pressure is kept approximately equal to that of the surrounding atmosphere by means of the **eustachian tube,** which opens into the back of the throat. The equalization of pressure on either side of the eardrum is important since a pressure differential would cause the membrane to bulge and stiffen, resulting in less responsiveness of the eardrum to the sound striking it. If the eustachian tube were not present, the pressure on the inner side would gradually drop because of absorption of the air by the surrounding tissue. However, the eustachian tubes (one for each ear) open briefly every time we swallow, allowing air to flow into the middle ear cavities from the mouth and lungs. This process equalizes the air pressure on both sides of the eardrums. Sometimes, for example when we have a head cold, the eustachian tubes become blocked, and the pressure in the middle ears cannot adjust to that of the outside air. Also, when we climb to cruising altitude in a commercial jetliner, the cabin pressure may become considerably lower than the pressure within our middle ears at the time of takeoff. Such inequalities in internal versus external air pressure can cause you to experience temporary hearing loss and even some pain.

We have already noted that the footplate of the stapes rests on a membrane called the **oval window.** This is the only part of the inner ear directly receiving mechanical vibrations. The oval window is at one end of one of the three canals that run the length of the **cochlea,** as can be seen in Figure 6-5. Two of these, the **vestibular** and the **tympanic canals,** are connected at the apex of the cochlea by an opening called the **helicotrema.** They are filled with a fluid resembling salt water. Since this fluid is relatively noncompressible, a point is needed where the pressure from the vibration of the stapes at the oval window is released. This release point is provided by the **round window,** which is a

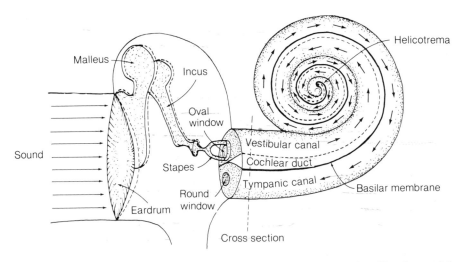

FIGURE 6-5   Movements of the eardrum in response to sound are transmitted by the ossicles to the fluid in the canals of the coiled cochlea.

membrane at the base of the tympanic canal that opens onto the middle ear. When a movement of the stapes causes the fluid to move away from the oval window, the round window bulges. This indicates that some fluid has been displaced, and the resulting pressure change has been transmitted through the helicotrema into the tympanic canal and to the round window at its base. Of course, this system allows any vibration of the stapes to set up similar vibrations in the internal fluid in the cochlea. This is why so much amplification of the sound energy in the middle ear is needed. The amplification is necessary to allow small and relatively weak displacements of the eardrum to cause the entire body of cochlear fluid to vibrate in the same fashion as the eardrum (Schubert, 1978).

The third canal of the cochlea, the **cochlear duct** (or *scala media*), is relatively self-contained. It neither opens to the middle ear nor joins the vestibular or tympanic canals. It is formed by two membranes that run the length of the cochlea: **Reissner's membrane** and the **basilar membrane.** Together they form a rough triangle with the wall of the cochlea (Figure 6-6). The cochlear duct is filled

with a different, more viscous fluid. Reissner's membrane is very thin (only two cells thick) and has no function other than to form one wall of the cochlear duct. The basilar membrane is the functionally important one. In humans it is about 3 cm long and varies in width from about 0.08 mm near the base (where the windows are) to about 0.5 mm at the apex (where the helicotrema is), and is about 100 times stiffer at the base than at the apex. A third membrane within the cochlear duct is also important. The **tectorial membrane** extends into the cochlear duct from Reissner's membrane, and touching it are some of the hairs of the **organ of Corti** (Figure 6-7). This is the part of the cochlear duct that accomplishes the final transduction of the mechanical energy of a sound wave into electrochemical energy interpretable by the nervous system.

The organ of Corti rests on the basilar membrane along its entire length. It is composed of about 23,500 cells, which resemble the cells of the skin in that hairs protrude from them. A single row of about 3,000 **inner hair cells** is found on the inner side (left side in Figure 6-7) of the **tunnel of**

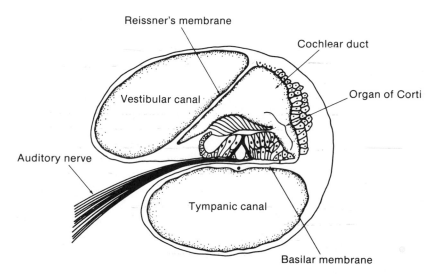

FIGURE 6-6   Cross section of the cochlea reveals its three canals and the organ of Corti, the auditory receptor.

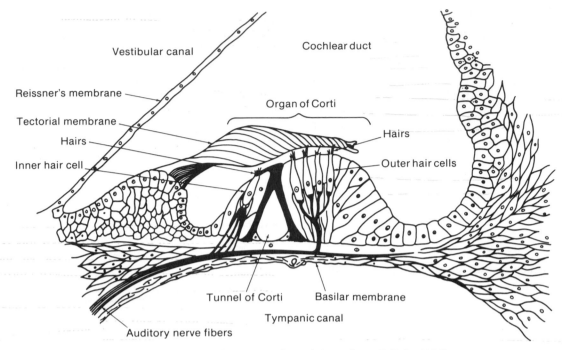

FIGURE 6-7   The detailed structure of the organ of Corti. (Based on Gulick, 1971)

Corti, and three or four rows of **outer hair cells** are located on the outer side. Inner hair cells have about 40–60 hairs each, which extend into the viscous fluid that fills the cochlear duct under the tectorial membrane but which apparently do not touch the membrane (Lim, 1980). Each outer hair cell may have as many as 100–120 very tiny hairs protruding from it. The tallest of these hairs are firmly embedded in the tectorial membrane; the shorter hairs apparently do not touch the membrane. In both kinds of hair cells, a graded set of hairs forms a **hair bundle.** Each hair bundle contains hairs that are connected to a shorter hair on one side and a longer hair on the other. All of the hairs in a hair bundle tend to move, or bend, as a unit.

About 30,000 nerve fibers, whose cell bodies are located in the **spiral ganglion,** form synaptic connections on the bases of the hair cells. About 95 percent of them, called **radial fibers,** make single connections with the inner hair cells (about 10

per inner hair cell). The other 5 percent of the fibers from the spiral ganglion, called **outer spiral fibers,** each make synaptic contact with about 10 outer hair cells. No outer hair cell receives more than about four such contacts (Spoendlin, 1978). Figure 6-8 shows a general picture of how the fibers of the spiral ganglion cells innervate the cochlea. The radial fibers have a large diameter and are probably myelinated, whereas the outer spiral fibers are smaller in diameter and probably unmyelinated, hence they have slower neural conduction speeds. In addition, the two types of fibers come from ganglion cells that have a noticeably different shape (Kiang, Rho, Northrop, Liberman & Ryugo, 1982). Given so many structural differences, it is likely (though as yet undetermined) that these two different sets of fibers carry different types of auditory information. The axons of these spiral ganglion cells make up the auditory nerve, which is the neural pathway to the brain.

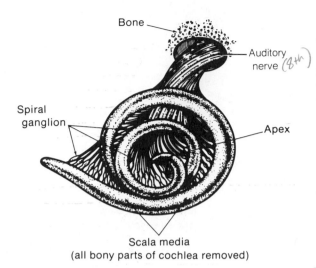

FIGURE 6-8   A view of the cochlea with the bone and other covering removed leaving only the soft membrane and neural tissue.

Wave Motion on the Basilar Membrane

Sound waves cause the bones of the middle ear to vibrate, and the vibration of the last of these bones (the stapes) causes the oval window, and thus the cochlear fluid, to move back and forth at the same frequency. This movement causes pressure differences across the cochlear duct and movements in the basilar membrane, stimulating the sensory cells of the organ of Corti. There are two important as-

pects of the transduction of mechanical energy into electrochemical energy accomplished here. The first is the movements of the basilar membrane that result in the stimulation of the sensory cells, and the second is the actual transduction mechanism itself. We discuss each of these in turn.

The movements of the cochlear fluid cause mechanical waves to travel down the basilar membrane from the base (near the oval window) to the apex. Such a wave is really a traveling bend or kink that moves down the length of the membrane, much like the motion when you crack a whip. Figure 6-9 is a schematic drawing of such a wave. The existence of these traveling waves was demonstrated by Georg von Bekesy (e.g., 1960), who received the Nobel Prize for his work on the mechanics of the ear. The waves themselves travel very quickly, going from the base to the apex in about 3 msec (Kitzes, Gibson, Rose & Hind, 1978). Each wave begins in the stiffer, narrower part of the basilar membrane and travels toward the looser, broader part.

The variations in elasticity and width of the basilar membrane are responsible for the direction and the speed of the traveling wave. They are also responsible for differences in the size or amplitude of the wave. Bekesy was able to demonstrate that the basilar membrane reacts differently to sound stimuli of different frequencies. Although the entire membrane vibrates for any given stimulus, the

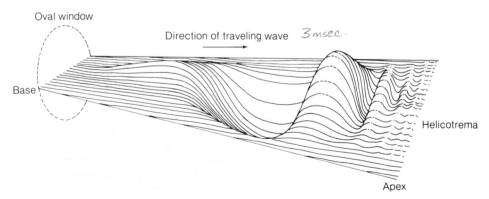

FIGURE 6-9   A traveling wave on the basilar membrane.

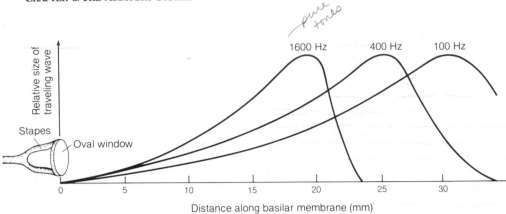

FIGURE 6-10   A graph of the relative sizes of traveling waves along the basilar membrane for three different frequencies of tone. Notice that as the frequency increases, the waves reach their maxima nearer the oval window and stapes (base).

traveling wave reaches a maximum at a different place along the basilar membrane for each different sound frequency. Traveling waves caused by low-frequency sounds grow steadily in size as they travel toward the apex of the membrane, and do not reach a maximum until they are near the apex. High-frequency sounds, however, cause traveling waves that reach their maximum near the base of the basilar membrane and then quickly dissipate, causing little deformation of the membrane near the apex. This is shown in Figure 6-10, which displays the amplitudes of traveling waves at different places along the basilar membrane for pure tones of several different frequencies. This characteristic action of the basilar membrane in response to sound provides a basis for the frequency analysis of complex tones, as well as for the more basic ability of distinguishing between pure tone stimuli of different frequencies. Demonstration Box 6-3 shows you how to demonstrate the differences in the ability of low and high frequencies to travel down a membrane.

DEMONSTRATION BOX 6-3.   **The Skin as a Model for the Basilar Membrane**

The basilar membrane is set into vibration by incoming sound stimuli. How the membrane vibrates, however, depends on the frequency of the sound input. Low frequencies tend to cause vibrations of significant magnitude along the entire length of the membrane; high frequencies cause vibrations that are significant only near the base. You can easily demonstrate the frequency-specific nature of the vibration by using your finger as a model of the basilar membrane, since skin has about the same resiliency and elasticity. Place your finger in your mouth, resting your finger tip firmly against the front of your teeth. Now make a loud, low sound (try to imitate the low sound of a foghorn), and notice that your entire finger seems to vibrate, perhaps all the way down to the knuckle at its base. Next make a high pitched sound (try to imitate the whistling of a teakettle or the test tone on a TV station that has ended the day's broadcasting). Notice that the feeling of vibration covers only a tiny region, perhaps your fingertip, or down to the first joint. In a similar fashion, lower sound frequencies induce waves that extend over the length of the basilar membrane, whereas higher frequency waves are restricted spatially in their effects.

Mechanisms of Transduction

We have been discussing the ear as if it were a purely mechanical device. The organ of Corti, which rests on the basilar membrane, is the site of the transduction of sound energy from its mechanical form into the electrochemical energy that is the communication medium of the nervous system (see Appendix). The movements of the basilar membrane described above cause the basilar membrane and the tectorial membrane to move laterally with respect to each other. Since the outer hair cells are attached at their base to structures connected to the basilar membrane, and the longest of their hairs are embedded in the tectorial membrane, a shearing force is applied to these hairs, causing them to bend. The inner hair cells may be bent in a somewhat different way. Since they appear not to make contact with the tectorial membrane, they are not subject to the shearing force applied to the longest hairs of the outer hair cells. It is possible that they do make contact with the tectorial membrane as a result of the movements of the basilar membrane and are bent when they rub against it (Crane, 1982). However, it is also possible that they are bent by the flow of the viscous fluid in the cochlear duct caused by these same movements (Dallos, 1978). Although this seems to be a less efficient way of producing bending, there appear to be no differences in the absolute sensitivities of the inner and outer hair cells (Dallos, Santos-Sacchi & Flock, 1982).

The mechanism by which the bending of hairs is transduced into electrical changes in the hair cells is still not fully understood (see Dallos, 1981). However, recent work suggests that flexing the hairs causes parts of the outer membrane of the hair to function like little "trap doors." Bending causes these to open and allow potassium ions to flow into the interior of the hair cells (see Hudspeth, 1985). Figure 6-11 shows this graphically. In the model suggested by Hudspeth (1985) each hair has such a trap door, which is attached to the next longer hair by a very thin filament. Ordinarily the trap door "rattles around," and is open only

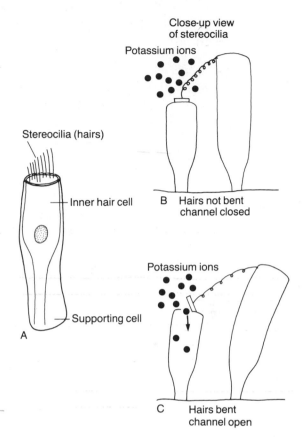

FIGURE 6-11   Model of transduction in hair cells. (A) A typical inner hair cell. (B) and (C) Illustration of operation of a typical transduction channel in the hairs. (Based on Hudspeth, 1985)

about 20 percent of the time. Potassium ions, which have a positive charge, flow into the cell whenever these pores are open. The inward flow of positive charge is just balanced by the outward flow of positive charge caused by other "pumps" elsewhere in the cell, maintaining the cell's resting membrane potential at about −60 millivolts (see Appendix). When the hair is bent in the direction of the tallest hairs, however, the filament attached to the trap door pulls on it and keeps it open more of the time, allowing more positive charge to flow into the cell. This causes a depolarization (making the potential more positive) of up to 20 mV, which in turn is thought to release transmitter substances from the synaptic cleft at the bottom of the hair cell. When these transmitter substances are received in large enough quantities by the spiral ganglion cells making the synapses with the hair cells, the spiral cells generate action potentials that then travel up the auditory pathways.

This model is very successful in accounting for many properties of the auditory system. For example, because the trap doors are constantly opening and closing, response to a sound can be very rapid, as data indicate it is (less than 1 msec). Moreover, because the process is probabilistic (hair bending simply increases the probability that the door will be open at a given instant), it is capable of responding to very low levels of sound (of the exceedingly small vibration distances mentioned above) if averaged over a sufficiently long time. All in all, this seems a very good candidate for the correct model of transduction.

ELECTRICAL ACTIVITY OF THE AUDITORY NERVE

We have followed sound energy to the point where it is converted into patterns of electrical activity in the auditory nerves. These signals are *spike potentials,* hence we can use the same techniques of electrophysiological recording that we used to investigate the visual system to study the neural processing of auditory information. If you have forgotten what these procedures are specifically, now would be a good time to glance back at the Appendix, which provides this information. Basically, the technique involves inserting electrodes into cells in the auditory pathways and recording the electrical activity of individual neurons in response to a variety of sounds.

As a first guess, we might suppose that the auditory system would be responsive mainly to simple physical aspects of a sound, namely frequency and intensity. Actually, some cells seem to mimic visual processing in that they are quite selective, responding to complex aspects of the stim-

ulus or specific stimulus "features." When we record the responses of single axons in the auditory nerve, we find that some respond only to complex noises and are completely unresponsive to pure tones. Others respond only to brief transient sounds such as clicks. Still others respond to a wide variety of different frequencies of pure tones. Apparently, auditory encoding is very complex even at this peripheral level. Thus, in much the same way that we found selective analysis taking place early in the visual system, similar selectivity seems to be characteristic of audition.

Although neurons possessing a great many different types of response characteristics are present in the auditory nerve, one type of neuron is extremely common. Such a neuron is often called a **tuned neuron,** in analogy to the way we "tune in" a radio station to its broadcast frequency. Figure 6-12 shows the absolute thresholds (minimum intensity of sound that stimulates a neuron to fire above its resting rate) of some typical neurons of this type. The results are called **threshold response curves,** and as can be seen from the figure each neuron has a best, or characteristic, frequency for

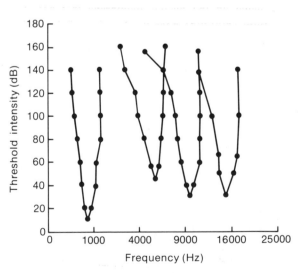

FIGURE 6-12   **Threshold response curves for auditory nerve fibers in the cat. (Based on Whitfield, 1968)**

which its absolute threshold is lowest. The sensitivity of tuned neurons decreases (the threshold is higher) as we move away from the best frequency in either direction. Another way of looking at the tuning of such an auditory neuron is simply to present a tone varying in frequency but fixed in intensity. A graph of the response rate of a tuned neuron treated in this way is often called a **tuning curve,** shown in Figure 6-13. In the auditory nerve there are neurons tuned to frequencies over the entire range of hearing.

The tuned nature of these cells probably comes about because of the mechanical properties of the basilar membrane (Khanna & Leonard, 1982). Most of the tuned auditory nerve fibers that have been studied are connected to inner hair cells (Kiang et al., 1982; Liberman, M.C., 1982), and there are more spiral ganglion cells synapsing with each hair cell the closer the hair cell is to the base of the cochlea (Keithley & Schreiber, 1987). Remember that different parts of the basilar membrane vibrate maximally to different frequencies of sound, and it is this vibration that causes the hair cells to bend and in turn initiate the neural response. A hair cell will respond most strongly when a tone of a certain frequency creates a traveling wave on the basilar membrane that has its maximum amplitude near the location of that hair cell. The frequency of this tone will be the frequency to which the neuron that synapses with that hair cell is "tuned." Other frequencies of sound of this same intensity will cause less vigorous movement of the basilar membrane at that location, which in turn results in less vigorous bending of the hair of the hair cell, and finally less vigorous responding of the neuron.

This passive mechanical tuning of the basilar membrane may not be the entire answer to the question of how neural tuning occurs. Most measurements of the mechanical tuning curves of the basilar membrane (similar to those of Figure 6-10) give curves that are less sharp (change less steeply with frequency) than the tuning curves measured in auditory nerve fibers (see Dallos, 1981). One explanation for this difference might be that the outer hair cells help to sharpen the auditory nerve tuning curves, because destruction of such cells results in broader tuning curves (Lynn & Sayers, 1970; Schmiedt, Zwislocki & Hamernik, 1980). These outer hair cells might actually act mechanically on the basilar membrane, dampening activity everywhere but at the maximum of the traveling wave and thus sharpening the mechanical tuning (see Hudspeth, 1985). This active cochlear process is being studied intensively, and several plausible models of how it could operate have been suggested (Jen & Steele, 1987; LePage, 1987a, 1987b; Zwicker, 1986). Such an active process has been used to explain why complex vibrations are found in the cochlea in the absence of any sound inputs at all (Brownell, Bader, Bertrand & de Ribaupierre, 1985; Hudspeth, 1985).

Further evidence for interaction between inner and outer hair cells comes from a finding called **two-tone inhibition** (Rose, Galambos & Hughes, 1959; Sachs & Kiang, 1968). This phenomenon is seen when recording from an auditory nerve fiber that is stimulated by its characteristic frequency and is responding vigorously. If a second tone of a different frequency, which is moderately close to the tuned frequency, is now briefly presented, the response rate in the tuned neuron drops. Such an inhibitory response may result from the action of outer hair cells (Javel, 1981). This is supported by the fact that two-tone inhibition disappears when outer hair cells have been selectively damaged by a drug (Schmiedt et al., 1980). Such inhibition

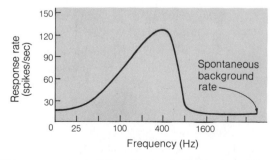

FIGURE 6-13 Tuning curve of a typical auditory nerve fiber. (Based on Lindsay & Norman, 1977)

provides an alternate means to sharpen tuning curves, since it involves the suppression of responses to frequencies other than the tuned one.

What is the nature of the information about intensity and frequency carried from the ear to the brain? One suggestion is that low frequencies may be encoded directly in the number of spike potentials in the neural response (Johnson, 1980; Rose, Brugge, Anderson & Hind, 1967). Thus, if the frequency of the stimulus is 100 Hz, the firing in the auditory nerve will tend to be approximately 100 Hz. This does not mean that any given individual neuron fires at this frequency. Rather, individual neurons seem to fire at fixed points in the cycle of the sound wave. For example, one neuron may fire at every second peak of the wave (and thus at 50 Hz), whereas another may fire at every fifth peak (and thus at 20 Hz). This is called **phase-locking.** For a great many neurons firing out of phase with one another there will tend to be a spike (or several) occurring at every peak of the wave and thus a composite response rate of 100 Hz could be achieved. This ability of the auditory nerve to follow the frequency of the stimulating sound wave (up to about 4000 Hz) has been a central component of several theories of pitch perception (e.g., Wever, 1979) that will be discussed in Chapter 7. The important factor to be noted is that the pattern of response of the whole auditory nerve rather than the responses of individual neurons may be significant in conveying frequency information to the brain.

The importance of pattern of response in the auditory nerve cannot be overestimated. Even though many cells in the auditory nerve may be tuned to the same characteristic frequency, they may still vary in terms of their threshold intensities over a range of about 20 dB (Evans, 1975). Once the intensity of a sound has exceeded a cell's threshold, further increases in intensity up to a level 30–50 dB above the threshold value will increase its rate of response. Intensity increases beyond this point (30–50 dB above threshold) will not cause the neuron to increase its rate of response; the neuron is firing as fast as it can and is

said to be **saturated.** These facts imply that for a sound of a given intensity and frequency there will be a population of neurons all firing at different response rates. This situation is represented hypothetically in Figure 6-14A, for two levels of intensity. Stimuli of different frequencies tend to cause different populations of neurons to fire above their background rates, as is shown in 6-14B. As the intensity of the stimulus increases, other neurons, tuned to nearby frequencies, may also be recruited, resulting in an increase in the number of neurons responding, as well as an increase in their response rates. Thus, the entire pattern of auditory activity changes with changes in the stimulus. Frequency seems to be indicated by *which* neurons are firing, whereas intensity seems to be roughly indicated by *how many* are firing, and to a minor extent *how fast* they are firing (Whitfield, 1978).

Our increasing understanding of how the auditory nerve encodes frequency and intensity has allowed some people with hearing disabilities to recover some auditory ability. If the hair cells do not function, either because they were damaged or congenitally malformed, a person is deaf. Recently, otologists have been able to implant in the ear devices (known as **cochlear implants)** that stimulate the auditory nerve electrically in response to external sounds (see Schindler & Merzenich, 1985). Modern cochlear implants first analyze the frequency composition of the sound into ranges of stimulus frequencies. The implant itself involves a series of electrodes that have been implanted at different points along the basilar membrane. These different regions of the basilar membrane are then stimulated, based on the initial analysis of the frequencies, in an attempt to mimic the way the traveling wave on the basilar membrane stimulates the hair cells. Deaf patients with such devices can discriminate the frequencies of different sounds (Townshend, Cotter, Van Compernolle & White, 1987) and can even recognize speech sounds quite well, especially when a speech preprocessor is attached to the cochlear implant to isolate certain speech-relevant frequency changes (Blamey, Dowell, Brown, Clark & Seligman, 1987). There is

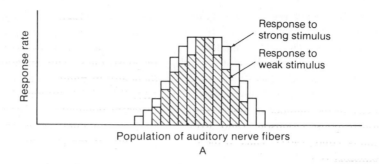

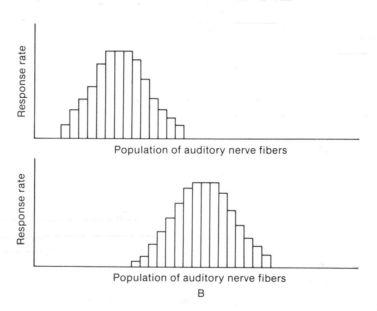

FIGURE 6-14   Hypothetical distributions of response rates for the population of auditory nerve fibers firing in response to (A) weak versus strong stimuli of the same frequency and (B) stimuli of the same strength but of different frequencies.

some promise that, in future, such devices will allow nearly a full range of hearing experience for people with this form of deafness.

THE AUDITORY PATHWAYS

Figure 6-15 diagrams the principal pathways taken by auditory information in the brain. The auditory pathways are somewhat more complex than the vi-

sual pathways. First, the axons of the spiral ganglion cells make up the auditory nerve, which projects to the **cochlear nucleus,** located in the lower back part of the brain. As shown in the figure, the auditory nerve fibers enter the **ventral** (front) **cochlear nucleus,** where each divides into at least two branches. One branch synapses with cells in the ventral cochlear nucleus, and the other proceeds to the **dorsal** (back) **cochlear nucleus.** The cells of the ventral cochlear nucleus send about half their axons to the **superior olive** on the oppo-site side of the brain and half to the one on the same side. The cells of the dorsal cochlear nucleus send all their axons to the opposite side of the brain, eventually to terminate in the **inferior colli-culus.** Thus, most of the information from the right ear is sent to the left side of the brain, and vice versa. The cells of the two superior olives send most of their fibers to the inferior colliculi (which are located just below the superior colliculi, dis-cussed in Chapter 3). At the level of the inferior colliculus, considerable fiber crossing takes place from one side of the brain to the other, so that each inferior colliculus has full information about what is going on in the other.

Most cells in the inferior colliculi send axons to the **medial geniculate,** although a few go to the su-perior colliculus as well. Since the superior collicular pathway has been implicated in visual localization, perhaps the auditory fibers that go there also carry in-formation about location. This sound localization in-formation could then be related to visual data to yield a more complete "picture" of space (see Chapter 7). From the medial geniculate, fibers project to a part of the temporal cortex that is often called the **primary auditory projection area,** or Brodmann's *Area 41.* The adjacent Brodmann's *Area 22* also receives ax-ons directly from the medial geniculate, although fewer of them (these regions of the brain were pic-tured in Figure 3-13).

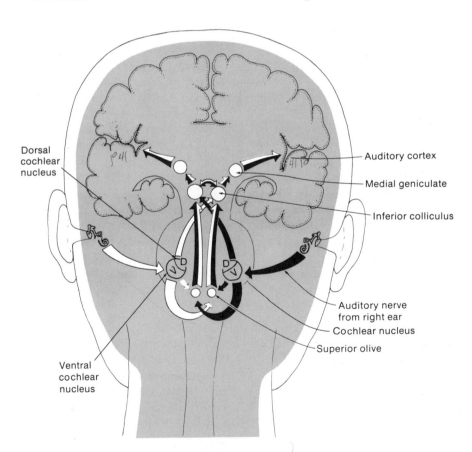

FIGURE 6-15   **The major auditory pathways in the brain. (Based on Lindsay & Norman, 1977)**

Electrical Activity of the Lower Auditory Centers

We have already mentioned that many of the response patterns found in the fibers of the auditory nerve suggest that there is some form of auditory feature analysis going on. Although some of these neurons respond only to clicks or other stimuli that are not pure tones, the majority of the fibers are axons from "tuned" neurons. Tuned neurons respond to a range of frequencies of pure-tone sounds, but each has a "preferred" band of frequencies to which it is most sensitive and to which it produces its maximum response. Similar tuned neurons are found in the cochlear nucleus, superior olive, inferior colliculus, and medial geniculate. Also, as described above for the auditory nerve, there is a region of nearby frequencies that produces an inhibition of response (as in two-tone inhibition) in these same cells.

In addition to the frequency tuning of cells in the more central nuclei of the auditory pathway, a number of more complex neural response patterns appear. When Pfeiffer (1966) recorded from single neurons in the cochlear nucleus of adult cats, he found a variety of different types of neural responses to a simple tone. **On neurons** gave a burst of responses immediately after the onset of the tone burst and then ceased responding, no matter how long the tone persisted. **Pauser neurons** exhibited a similar burst of firing at the onset of a tone, but this was followed by a pause and then a weaker sustained response until the tone was turned off. **Choppers** gave repeated bursts of firing followed by short pauses, with the vigor of successive bursts decreasing. **Primarylike neurons** gave an initial vigorous burst of firing when the tone was turned on, then the firing rate decayed to a lower level that was sustained for the duration of the tone. These primarylike neurons have been shown to be capable of encoding some critical aspects of speech sounds (Palmer, Winter & Darwin, 1986).

In addition to these response patterns, a response analogous to the **off responses** observed in the visual system seems to exist. These cells actually reduce their response rate below their spontaneous activity level at the onset of a tone, and then give a burst of activity at its offset. An interesting variation of this is the presence of tuned cells that *reduce* their activity level when a stimulus different from the "best" one is present. Of particular interest is a set of cells that are reminiscent of the on-center/off-surround cells observed in the visual system (Chapter 3). Rather than having a receptive field that consists of a region in space, these cells have a receptive field consisting of a band of frequencies. For instance, there are cells in the medial geniculate with "W-shaped" receptive field patterns. These neurons respond above their background rate of firing to a particular best frequency, and below the background rate for frequencies close to that frequency on either side. The firing rate gradually returns to background level for frequencies progressively more removed from the best frequency and its surrounding "worst" frequencies (see Webster & Atkin, 1975).

This type of correspondence between properties of neurons in different sensory systems is very common, although each sensory system also displays coding principles idiosyncratic to its own stimulus modality. We seem to be dealing with basically the same kinds of neural units at the electrophysiological level, regardless of the sensory system considered. It is as though some master technician found a useful biological coding scheme for stimuli, and simply modified it to fit the various requirements of different sensory systems.

Because different points along the basilar membrane vibrate most strongly for different frequencies of sounds, we refer to the response of the basilar membrane as **tonotopic** (from the Greek *tono* for "tone" and *topus* for "place"). This means we are actually representing sound frequencies with a sort of spatial code. This spatial encoding also seems to be preserved at other points in the auditory system. In the cochlear nucleus of the cat, Rose, Galambos, and Hughes (1960) recorded the responses of single cells to pure tones as a microelectrode was moved through the tissue. As the electrode was pushed along, the frequency of stimulus that gave the best response (highest rate of firing) changed systematically from high near one edge of the nucleus to low near the other. This indicated that the cells were arranged in an orderly spatial layout, with cells tuned to similar frequencies lying closer together in the nucleus than those tuned to different frequencies. Similar tonotopic arrangements of cells have been reported for the auditory nerve and other noncortical nuclei (Gulick, 1971; Webster & Atkin, 1975). In general, the tonotopic organization of the basilar membrane is preserved even up to the cortex, where we find cells that respond to high frequencies clustered in some areas, and cells that respond to low frequencies clustered in other areas. You can see this clustering for the cat auditory cortex in Figure 6-16 (where the high- and low-frequency areas are marked, and the intermediate frequencies fall in between).

This result has been confirmed in humans by some ingenious measurements of the magnetic field created in the brain by its electrical response to sounds (Romani, Williamson & Kaufman, 1982). The maximum brain activity observed in the auditory centers of humans varies in depth as the frequency varies. Responses to high frequencies are deep, whereas those to low frequencies lie near the surface of the brain. A similar result has been obtained using the technique of *positron emission tomography,* which allows researchers to visualize areas of the brain that are most active during various activities, such as listening to sounds of different frequencies (Lauter, Herscovitch, Formby & Raichle, 1985). These results are consistent with the idea that the frequency of sound waves is coded mainly by place (which neurons are firing), both on the basilar membrane and in the central auditory system.

THE AUDITORY CORTEX

Studies of nonhuman animals have provided us with most of the information we now possess about the physiology of sensory systems. For the lower levels of analysis we can be fairly confident in generalizing the concepts to humans. When we begin to discuss the cortex, however, we are on shakier ground. The human cortex is more complex than that of the most common experimental animals (such as the cat, the preferred subject of such studies), so that generalization of findings to humans is more tenuous. Nonetheless, animal studies have yielded a significant amount of useful information on the activity of the auditory cortex. Figure 6-16 shows the wide variety of areas on the cat cortex that have been shown to be responsive to sound stimuli. In this chapter we have been concerned mainly with the primary auditory areas, but a large number of nonauditory areas also respond to sound stimuli, especially association and visual areas. Presumably, similar responses occur in the human cortex, especially in the speech and general association areas.

Cells in the auditory cortex exhibit a variety of complex responses to sound stimuli. In the approximately 60 percent of the cells that respond to pure tones, there occur *on* responses, *off* responses, *on-off* responses, and more general *excitatory* and

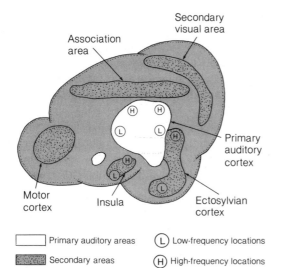

FIGURE 6-16   **Auditory areas of the cat cortex.**

inhibitory responses (see Figure 6-17). These responses, of course, resemble the response patterns of cells in the visual system. The other 40 percent of the cells seem to respond selectively to more complex sounds, including noise bursts, clangs, or clicks.

Another complex type of neuron found in the auditory cortex of the cat is the **frequency sweep detector** (Whitfield & Evans, 1965). These cells respond only to sounds that change frequency in a specific direction and range. Some cells respond only to increases but not to decreases in frequency in the same range. Others respond to decreases in frequency but not to increases. A third type responds only to increases in frequency for low-frequency tones. Since these types of stimuli are often encountered in speech and music, such detectors, if present in humans, could have an important role in speech and music perception. Certainly they

have obvious utility for the cat, whose "war cries" and "love calls" consist of just these types of sounds.

These cortical neurons respond to sound patterns in much the same way that visual cortical neurons respond selectively to light patterns. There are even auditory analogues to the highly specific visual cells (face and paw detectors) observed in the temporal cortex (see Chapter 3). Swarbrick and Whitfield (1972) found cells in the auditory cortex of the squirrel monkey that are sensitive to the vocalizations of other squirrel monkeys. Some of these cells are unresponsive to the presentation of simple tones, although they respond vigorously to the presentation of extremely complex vocalizations (Funkenstein, Nelson, Winter, Wolberg & Newman, 1971). Watanabe and Katsuki (1974) found cells in the cat auditory cortex that in addition to being tuned to a specific band of frequencies

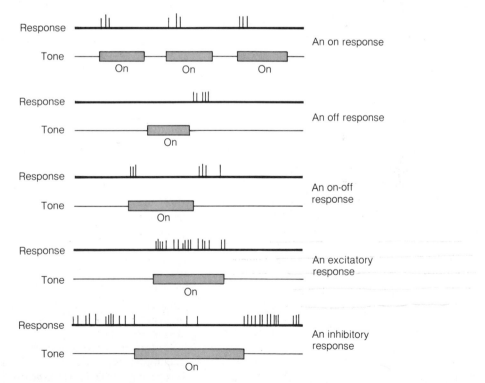

FIGURE 6-17 **Different types of response to pure tones recorded from neurons in the auditory cortex of the cat. (Based on Whitfield, 1967)**

also responded with a unique pattern of activity to recordings of cat vocalizations. Interestingly, these cortical cells did not respond with the same pattern of activity to any of the individual components of the cat vocalization. This indicated that the cells were integrating the outputs of cells from lower levels of the auditory pathway that do respond to simpler components of the sound pattern. We could say that the lower level cells were detecting the various features of the vocalization and the cortical cell was responding only to the combination of all of the features (Whitfield, 1980).

Although these physiological findings are quite intriguing and suggestive, the ultimate test of any hypotheses about the significance of neural encoding or analysis of auditory patterns rests on data about an individual's actual auditory percepts. In Chapter 7 we consider *what* is heard and try to integrate it with our present knowledge of *how* it is heard.

GLOSSARY

The following definitions are specific to this book.

Auditory canal   The canal conducting sound waves to the eardrum.

Basilar membrane   The membrane within the cochlea of the ear on which the organ of Corti lies.

Bel   The basic unit used to measure the relative intensity of a sound wave.

Chopper   A neuron that gives repeated bursts of impulses followed by short pauses, with the vigor of successive bursts decreasing, in response to presentation of a pure tone.

Cochlea   A snail-shaped part of the labyrinth of the ear that contains the auditory receptors.

Cochlear duct   One of the three canals in the cochlea; also called the *scala media*.

Cochlear implant   A device implanted in the cochlea that electrically stimulates the auditory nerve similarly to how it is stimulated by hair-cell activity.

Cochlear nucleus   A structure in the lower back part of the brain that receives input from the auditory nerve.

Cycle   In sound, the completion of a full sequence of air compression and rarefaction.

Cycles per second   The unit to measure frequency of sound waves, now usually referred to as *hertz*.

Decibel (dB)   The unit used to measure sound intensity; one-tenth of a bel.

Dorsal cochlear nucleus   The back half of the nucleus in the lower back part of the brain where the auditory nerve fibers end.

Eardrum   The membrane at the end of the auditory canal that vibrates in resonance with incoming sound waves.

Eustachian tube   A channel from the back of the throat to the middle ear; when we swallow it opens and allows the air pressure in the middle ear to equalize with the outside.

Fourier components   Simple sine waves that add together to form a complex waveform.

Frequency   The number of cycles a sound wave completes in one second.

Frequency sweep detector   A neuron that responds only to sounds that change frequency in a specific direction and range.

Hair bundle   A graded set of hairs protruding from a hair cell in the cochlea and tending to move, or bend, as a unit.

Helicotrema   An opening, between the vestibular and tympanic canals, at the apex of the cochlea.

Hertz (Hz)   The unit (cycles per second) used to measure frequency of sound waves.

In phase   When the peaks and valleys of different sound waves coincide over time.

Incus   One of the three middle bones involved in sound conduction to the cochlea. Also known as the *anvil*.

Inferior colliculi   Auditory processing centers in the midbrain that are the termini for cells of the superior olives.

Inner ear   The part of the ear containing the cochlea.

Inner hair cells   Cells found on the inner side of the tunnel of Corti.

Labyrinth   A structure of fluid-filled canals and chambers in the head that contains organs of hearing and the vestibular senses.

Malleus   The inner ear bone that is attached to the eardrum; also called the *hammer*.

Medial geniculate   The brain structure that receives inputs from the inferior colliculus and sends axons to the auditory cortex.

Middle ear   The part of the ear consisting of the ossicles (malleus, incus, and stapes) that transmit the eardrum vibrations to the inner ear.

Off responses   Neural responses that commence with the termination of stimuli.

Ohm's acoustical law   The auditory system separates complex sounds into simple (Fourier) components.

On neurons   Neurons that fire immediately and exclusively after the onset of a tone.

Organ of Corti   The part of the cochlear duct that transduces mechanical sound wave energy into electrochemical energy interpretable by the nervous system.

Out of phase   When the peaks and valleys of different sound waves do not coincide over time.

Outer ear   The pinna, the auditory canal, and the eardrum.

Outer hair cells   Cells found on the outer side of the tunnel of Corti.

Outer spiral fibers   Fibers extending from the spiral ganglion to the outer hair cells.

Oval window   A membrane in the cochlea that receives sound vibrations from the stapes.

Pauser neurons   Neurons, similar to on-response neurons, that exhibit an initial response to stimuli, followed by a pause, and then a weaker, sustained response until the stimulus stops.

Phase   The particular point in the compression-rarefaction cycle of a sound wave at one instant of time.

Phase angle   The degree to which one sound wave is out of phase with another, considering a complete cycle as 360 degrees.

Phase-locking   The tendency of individual neurons to fire at fixed points in the cycle of a sound wave.

Pinna   The fleshy visible part of the outer ear.

Pressure amplitude   A measure of the degree of compression or rarefaction at the peaks or valleys of a sound wave.

Primary auditory projection area   The area of the temporal cortex that receives most of the fibers from the medial geniculate; also known as *Brodmann's Area 41*.

Primarylike neuron   A neuron that gives an initial burst of firing in response to a stimulus, and then continues firing at a lower level until the stimulus stops.

Radial fibers   Fibers extending from the spiral ganglion to the inner hair cells.

Reissner's membrane   One of two membranes making up the cochlear duct.

Round window   The membrane at the base of the cochlea facing the middle ear.

Saturated   The state in which a neuron cannot fire any faster, even if stimulus intensity is increased.

Sound pressure level (SPL)   The log-relative pressure amplitude of a sound wave, measured in decibels.

Spiral ganglion   The cells whose axons form the auditory nerve.

Stapes   The bone in the chain of middle ear ossicles that makes contact with the oval window; also called the *stirrup*.

Superior olives   The brain termini for axons leading from the ventral cochlear nuclei.

Tectorial membrane   Within the cochlear duct, the membrane, extending from Reissner's membrane, in which some of the hairs of the organ of Corti are embedded.

Threshold response curve   A graph of neural absolute threshold as a function of sound frequency.

Timbre   A sound attribute associated with the components of a complex sound wave.

Tonotopic   Characteristic of the place of response to a sound depending on the frequency of the sound.

Tuned neuron   A neuron that responds optimally to tones of a characteristic frequency.

Tuning curve   A graph showing the rate of firing of an auditory neuron for different tone frequencies; it usually has a single peak.

Tunnel of Corti   A structure in the cochlea.

Two-tone inhibition   Inhibition of neural response to a characteristic frequency of sound that occurs when a second tone of a different frequency is presented; inhibition occurs during and for a brief period after the presentation of the second tone.

Tympanic canal   One of three canals running through the cochlea.

Tympanum   *See* Eardrum.

Ventral cochlear nucleus   The front half of the nucleus in the lower back part of the brain where the auditory nerve fibers end.

Vestibular canal   One of three canals running through the cochlea.

Wave   The pattern of air molecule motion that characterizes sound.

Wavelength   The distance from one peak to the next of a sound wave.

CHAPTER
7

Hearing

The moon was yellow and full in the night sky. Tamara and Scott crouched nervously under the large old oak tree and stared at the ancient mansion. Giving each other a reassuring glance, they advanced to the edge of the porch. They weren't sure what to expect, but the sound that greeted their arrival was utterly chilling: it sounded exactly like someone scraping metal claws across a piece of slate. The grating shriek shattered their determination and sent them racing toward home in a panic. Inside the mansion, a timid, but very reclusive hermit gave thanks that he had paid attention when his introduction psychology instructor had given the lecture about the sounds most feared by people. Perhaps he had bought himself another few years of seclusion. He ardently hoped so.

No one knows why the sound of metal (or fingernails) on slate is so aversive to so many people; it isn't the high frequencies present because removing them makes little difference (Halpern, Blake & Hillenbrand, 1986). Perhaps it is an ancient memory of sounds made by predators or fellow primates in distress. Whatever the reason, the phenomenon demonstrates the powerful effect sound can have on behavior and the richness of the psychological experience of sound. In this chapter we investigate some of this richness, concentrating on the more basic sensations associated with our perception of sound (in Chapter 12 we deal with the more complex phenomena of speech and music perception). Every sound gives rise to a number of perceived qualities including location, duration, loudness, pitch, timbre, volume, and density. Although some of these sensory qualities seem to be associated with particular aspects of the physical stimulus, as is often the case in many kinds of perception, our sensation from a sound is often not directly predictable merely from knowledge of the physical nature of the stimulus.

DETECTION OF SOUNDS

Clearly, the minimum auditory experience is the detection of the presence of a sound. What is the minimum sound intensity we can hear? In deter-

mining an observer's absolute threshold for sound presented through earphones we measure the sound pressure level (see Chapter 6) associated with the threshold stimulus very close to the eardrum. This value is called the **minimum audible pressure.** We might argue that this is a rather artificial situation, since the sound wave at the eardrum has already been somewhat amplified and distorted during its travel through the ear canal. Another, perhaps more natural, procedure would be to determine the absolute auditory threshold for an observer sitting in an open space that is free of echoes and other distortions. In this situation, sounds are presented by a speaker placed at various angles to the observer's ear and the intensity of the threshold stimulus is measured at the location of the observer's head. This measurement of threshold is called the **minimum audible field** (indicating that the intensity of the threshold stimulus was measured in a free field rather than at the eardrum).

In a classic study at Bell Telephone Laboratories, Sivian and White (1933) systematically varied the frequency of a pure-tone stimulus as they took a series of threshold measurements under carefully controlled conditions. Their results are shown in Figure 7-1. Notice that the absolute threshold is different for different frequencies of sound. The ear appears to be most sensitive to sounds with frequencies between 1000 and 5000

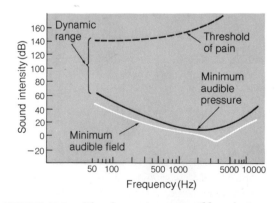

FIGURE 7-1   The dynamic range of hearing, from minimum audible intensities to the threshold of pain. (Based on Sivian & White, 1933)

Hz, being about 100 times less sensitive to a sound at 100 Hz than to a sound at 3000 Hz. Notice that the minimum audible field measurements are considerably lower than the minimum audible pressures. The reasons for this are rather complex. Probably the most important is that the free-field situation allows resonances and amplifications from the shape of the pinna (the outer cup of the ear) and the ear canal to come into play. This is supported by the fact that we are most sensitive to sounds of 3000–4000 Hz in free-field presentation, which is also in the range of the natural resonance frequency of the external ear canal. From an adaptive point of view, the benefit that humans derive from increased sensitivity in this particular range of frequencies may at first seem obscure, although some important frequencies found in speech are in this range. Another, somewhat macabre possibility is, as Milne and Milne (1967) speculate, that we leave a ''channel open—as though reserved for emergencies—for any high-pitched scream.'' In fact, screams of agony or terror, especially those of

females, do sometimes have peaks in the 3000-Hz range. You can demonstrate for yourself the effect of frequency on your ability to detect sounds using Demonstration Box 7-1.

The lower limit of sensitivity for the ear seems to be determined by the sound of blood rushing through the tiny vessels in the middle and inner ear (or perhaps the random noise generated by motion of the air molecules; see Hudspeth, 1985), whereas the upper limit is determined by the stimulus intensity that produces pain. The difference between the absolute threshold and the pain threshold for a particular frequency of sound waves defines the **dynamic range** of the ear for that frequency (see Figure 7-1). For stimuli with frequencies between about 1000–5000 Hz the ear has a dynamic range of up to 150 dB, which is equivalent to a 7.5-millionfold increase in sound pressure from the weakest sound detectable to the most intense sound tolerable. Few stereo systems can approach the dynamic range with which you were born.

The dynamic range of the ear is distinct from

DEMONSTRATION BOX 7-1.   Sound Frequency and Threshold

Many people are aware of the problems associated with replaying recorded music so that it sounds as it did when it was recorded. Recording techniques reproduce the frequencies produced by musical instruments, but the replay is often at a lower intensity. Most of the sounds of musical instruments lie in frequency ranges where the absolute threshold is most affected by changes in frequency. Thus, unless you listen to recordings of an orchestra at reasonable intensity levels, you will not hear many of the frequencies produced by the instruments. Many high-quality audio amplifiers have been modified to include circuits that compensate for such psychological mechanisms. These circuits are set to emphasize very low and very high frequency sounds.

For this demonstration you will need a radio or another sound source that produces orchestral music. A cheaper unit, such as a portable radio or your car

radio, both of which lack loudness compensation circuits, would be perfect. Find a station (or a record) where a full orchestra is playing. Turn down the sound and listen to the instruments you can hear. Now, gradually turn up the sound. As you do this, you will find that you become more aware of the bass violin and cello, the larger brass pieces, such as the tuba, and some of the lower notes of the harp or bassoon, as well as some of the higher tones from the violins, flutes, and piccolos. When the volume has been considerably increased so that you can hear the entire orchestra and many of the pieces (placing your ear close to the speaker helps), gradually turn down the volume again. Now, many of the lower and higher frequency instruments seem to disappear as certain frequencies they produce drop below threshold. The middle frequencies of the orchestra, however, are still quite audible.

the frequency range over which our ears respond to sound. Young adults can hear sounds between about 20 and 20000 Hz, and some young children can hear sounds with frequencies up to 27000 Hz. Unfortunately, with age a progressive loss in sensitivity occurs, particularly for higher frequencies, so that this range gradually decreases as we grow older (see Chapter 16). Demonstration Box 7-2 provides a simple test for the upper range of your own hearing.

Temporal, Frequency, and Binaural Interactions

A number of factors other than frequency and intensity determine our ability to detect sounds. One of these factors is the duration of the stimulus. The auditory system seems to act as if a fixed amount of sound energy is necessary to stimulate the ear sufficiently so that we hear a sound. It doesn't seem to matter if this energy comes at a high intensity over a short time interval or at a lower intensity over a longer time interval. We can describe this relationship algebraically as

$$T = I \times D$$

where I is the intensity of the sound, D is its duration, and T is a constant value necessary to reach threshold. This simple formula says that brief sounds must be more intense than longer sounds in order to be detected with the same (threshold) likelihood. This relationship is a good approximation for threshold sounds up to a duration of about 200 msec. Beyond 200 msec, increasing stimulus duration does not seem to improve our ability to detect sound. Notice the strong similarity to Bloch's law, which shows a similar relationship between time and intensity in the visual system, as we discussed in Chapter 4.

We may also increase the likelihood that a sound will be heard by increasing the number of different tones, or frequencies, that are presented together. Suppose we present an observer with two tones, neither of which would reach threshold by itself. Even if each tone is only about half the intensity needed for threshold, a sound will still be heard. It seems the nervous system adds the neural responses of different tones, producing a composite response based on the sum of the intensities of the various single stimuli. The tones should not differ in frequency by too much, however, or their energies will not sum, and the threshold intensities will be the same as if we presented each tone alone. Just as there was a critical duration beyond which temporal summation did not occur, there is a critical band of frequencies beyond which adding tones does not facilitate detection (Scharf, 1975). This critical band is not the same width for all frequencies, being much narrower for low frequencies than

---

DEMONSTRATION BOX 7-2.   High-Frequency Hearing Limits

You can make a simple test of your own high-frequency hearing using your television set. Turn it on and then lower the sound completely. Now lean over the back of your set and listen for a soft, high-pitched whine. If you can hear it, this means that you can detect frequencies on the order of 16000 Hz. Now, try this test on someone who is considerably older than you are and then with someone who is much younger. You should find that the older individual cannot hear this sound, whereas the younger one can. You might also try moving away from the set (if possible) until you can just hear the sound. This is your *threshold distance*. Now have your other observers do the same and determine their threshold distances. The greater your threshold distance, the more sensitive your ear is to these high-frequency sounds.

it is for high frequencies. Thus, if we start with a 400-Hz tone, adding a tone between 350 and 450 Hz will improve our ability to detect the sound, but adding a tone beyond these limits will not. If we started with a 5000-Hz tone, however, any added tone between about 4500 and 5500 Hz would improve our ability to detect the sound. The bandwidth has increased from 100 Hz in the lower frequencies to 1000 Hz at the higher. Figure 7-2 demonstrates how the critical bandwidth varies with frequency.

An additional factor affects our ability to detect the presence of sound stimuli. When sounds are presented to both ears, as opposed to only one, absolute thresholds are lowered. Presentations to one ear are called **monaural** (from the roots *mon* for "one" and *aural* for "ear"); presentations to two ears are called **binaural** (from the root *bi* for "two"). At first it was believed that this was only because one of the ears was more sensitive than the other, and the most sensitive ear determined the absolute threshold (Sivian & White, 1933). However, later work demonstrated that the threshold for two-ear stimulation is about one-half of that for one-ear stimulation (Chocolle, 1962). An interesting aspect of the interaction between the ears is that the two stimuli do not have to occur simultaneously in the two ears. If the tones are presented to the ears one at a time, and the total stimulus duration of the combined input is less than 200 msec, the pair of tones will be detected even if each individual tone is only about one-half of the intensity needed to reach threshold when presented monaurally (Schenkel, 1967).

In addition to lowering the absolute threshold, presentation of the same stimulus to the two ears causes the subjective impressions of loudness from each ear to add together (see e.g., Marks, 1979b). Thus, a binaural presentation will sound about twice as loud as a monaural presentation of the same tone. If you have a sound source nearby such as a radio or a television, you can demonstrate this for yourself by assessing the loudness when you hear the source with two ears, then covering one ear and noting how the apparent loudness diminishes.

Auditory Masking

We have all been in a noisy meeting, convention, or theater and found that we could not hear or understand a speaker very well. When the crowd quiets down, however, we find that the speaker's voice is audible immediately. This illustrates that whether a particular sound can be heard or not depends not only on its own intensity but also on the presence of other sounds in the environment. We just discussed how sounds can interact to facilitate detection; in the present situation the effects are reversed. Now we present an observer with a sound, which is audible by itself, and then add another sound only to find that the target tone can no longer be heard. We usually say that the second tone (the **masker**) is **masking** the first (the **target**). When target and masker are presented at the same time, we have **simultaneous masking.** A masking sound does not simply make all other tones more difficult to hear. Masking sounds act rather selectively.

A set of experiments demonstrating this was done by Zwicker (1958), who masked target tones

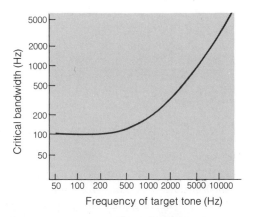

FIGURE 7-2 **The relation between critical bandwidth, within which added tones will facilitate detection, and frequency of target tone.**

using a narrow band of noise with a middle frequency of 1200 Hz. He measured the threshold intensity for a listener to detect a target tone with and without the masking stimulus. When he measured the amount of masking for several different frequencies of target tone, he obtained the results shown in Figure 7-3. As you can see from the figure, as the intensity of the masking stimulus is increased, the intensity of the test tone also must be increased for it to be audible. The most striking aspect of these data, however, is the asymmetry of the masking effect. Of course, the greatest masking is found for tones that have frequencies that are very similar to the masker itself (the thresholds are highest for tones of frequencies around 1200 Hz). But there is still a great deal of masking of tones higher in frequency than the masking sound (the threshold curves fall relatively slowly to the unmasked threshold curve on the right side of Figure 7-3), whereas tones of a lower frequency are relatively unaffected (the threshold curves fall quickly to the unmasked curve on the left of Figure 7-3).

Why does the added noise most effectively mask tones higher in frequency than itself? The answer may lie in the physiology of the ear. Turn

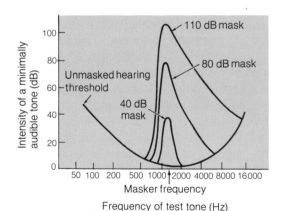

FIGURE 7-3 Thresholds for a pure-tone target in the presence of a narrow band of masking noise centered at 1200 Hz. The higher the curve, the higher the threshold, hence the more effective the masking. (Based on Zwicker, 1958)

back to Figure 6-10 in the previous chapter, which shows how the vibration pattern of the basilar membrane varies with the frequency of a pure tone. Notice that tones of low frequencies produce a very broad vibration pattern, extending over much of the membrane, whereas tones of higher frequencies produce vibration patterns nearer to the oval window and not extending as far along the membrane. Now look at Figure 7-4. Notice that when we have a weak test tone, and the masking noise is of a higher frequency than the target, the pattern of vibrations set up in the basilar membrane by the masking noise only extends part way up the membrane. Because the lower frequency target tone vibrates more of the membrane, the target's pattern extends beyond the flank of the vibration pattern produced by the masker. Thus, the target is detectable. However, the vibration pattern produced by the target tone when the noise is of a lower frequency than the target is completely covered by the masker's vibration pattern, and it is thus not detectable as a separate tone. The intensity of the higher frequency test tone in the presence of low-frequency noise must be increased (to the ''intense'' level in Figure 7-4) before its own vibration pattern at last extends beyond that of the masker and can be detected as a separate tone. You can experience some aspects of the frequency-specific effect of a masker by performing Demonstration Box 7-3.

Although sound-masking effects seem to be largely explained by the interaction of the patterns of vibration on the basilar membrane, this explanation is not adequate for all masking phenomena. For example, consider what happens if target and masker are not presented at the same time. If the masker is presented first, followed after some **interstimulus interval** by a brief target, the decreased ability to hear the target is called **forward masking.** Many studies (see Zwislocki, 1978) have found, as you might expect, that the forward masking effect increases as the intensity of the masking sound increases, and decreases as the interstimulus interval increases. For interstimulus in-

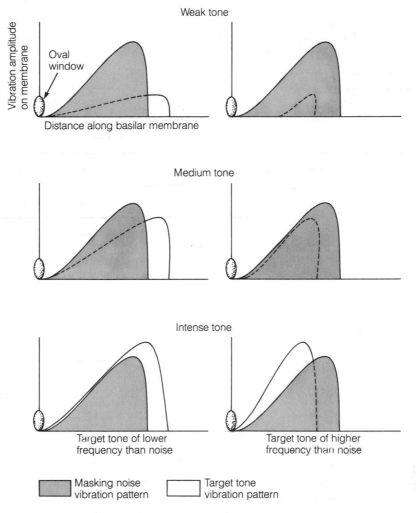

FIGURE 7-4 **The interactions of patterns of vibration of the basilar membrane resulting from a target and a noise stimulus. (Based on Scharf, 1964)**

tervals longer than 300 msec there is no measurable forward masking. Also, in general, the lower the frequencies of *both* the target and mask pair, the more masking takes place (Jesteadt, Bacon & Lehman, 1982). In addition, the same asymmetry we discussed above for simultaneous masking shows up in forward masking: there is little masking of target tones with frequencies lower than the masker, but a great deal for target tones of frequencies

higher than the masker. It is unlikely, however, that we can explain these effects by interaction of excitation patterns on the basilar membrane, since the excitation of the masker is not present when the target is presented at a later time. Some sort of interaction of more central neural processes must be involved. For the situation discussed above, it is likely that the masker is lowering the sensitivity of the hair cells, or their synapses with auditory nerve

---

DEMONSTRATION BOX 7-3.   Auditory Masking

To experience several different masking phenomena you need two major sources of sound, one for a masking sound, and one for the target sound that will be masked. Good sources are the noise of a car engine for a masking sound and the car radio for a source of target sounds. If you have a car with a radio, get into it and turn on the radio without starting the engine. Find some music with a good range of frequencies. Classical music is best, but any music will do. Modern music with a lot of steel guitar (country) or electrically amplified guitar (rock) is also good. Take particular note of the high and the low frequencies. Turn the volume knob on the radio to an intensity where you can just barely hear these frequencies. Now start the car motor. Press on the accelerator (with the car out of gear!) to make the engine turn over at high revolutions per minute. This creates a source of intense broad-band masking noise. Now listen for the high and the low frequencies that were clearly audible in the music before you started

the car engine. Turn up the volume until the high and low frequencies (which should now be masked) are just barely audible again and take notice of the difference between the volume settings before and after the noise was introduced. You could map out a masking curve for particular frequencies in a piece of music by varying the revolutions per minute of the motor to vary the intensity of the noise and by varying the frequency of the sounds whose audibility you are using as a criterion for radio volume adjustment. Note that even with intense masking noise, you can still hear the middle frequencies, where most of the singing is, while the higher and lower frequencies are masked. This is a reflection of the superior sensitivity of the ear to these frequencies. You also experience *speech masking* in your car. When the masking noise is of sufficient intensity (be careful not to damage your engine), even the middle frequencies (where most speech sounds occur) are masked, and you cannot understand the singer or the radio announcer.

---

fibers, to stimulation by the target tone, thus raising the threshold for that tone.

What happens when the target tone precedes the masker? Nothing, you might think; how could a tone that *follows* another affect our perception of the first tone, which has already been processed? Yet **backward masking** does occur, albeit somewhat differently from forward masking. For instance, your ability to hear a click may be reduced if another click follows it by as long as 25 msec (for loud masking clicks). Backward masking is more difficult to measure for tones than for clicks, because tones must extend longer in time, but it does occur. When a tone is masked with noise, the masker may have some effect on the threshold of a tone that begins up to 400 msec before the masker is turned on (Wright, 1964). The explanation of these backward masking effects is still not clear. One possibility is that inhibition caused by the

masker could build up faster than excitation caused by the target tone, thus overlapping with it in time and cancelling it to some extent, even when the target occurs appreciably earlier than the masker.

In addition to separating target and masker in time, we can separate them by presenting a target sound to one ear and a masking sound to the other. This is called **central masking,** since again there can be no interaction of the sounds on the basilar membrane and the masking is therefore assumed to take place in more central brain areas. In this situation the masker must be about 50 dB more intense than when a masking sound is presented to the same ear as the target tone. Under these conditions it can be shown that the effect of the mask is usually much more symmetrical and does not spread so widely as we vary the frequency of the test tone (Zwislocki, Damianopoulos, Buining & Glantz, 1967). Only when the frequency of the masking sound is quite low (less than 200 Hz) is there appreciable asymmetry of masking (Billings & Stokinger, 1977).

Interaction between the two ears can give rise to some strange and interesting phenomena. For example, Hirsh (1948) presented a pure tone plus a broad-band noise (that is, one containing many frequencies) to the same ear. He adjusted the target so that it could just be heard above the background noise. Next he presented some additional noise to the other ear, so that the two noises were in phase (meaning that the peaks and valleys of sound pressure coincided, as we discussed in Chapter 6). Under these circumstances the target tone, instead of being more difficult or perhaps impossible to hear, became more clearly audible. To reach the threshold value again, it was necessary to *lower* the target's intensity. What seemed to be happening was that the two masking tones were masking each other. Again, since the two noise masks were coming into different ears and did not share the same basilar membrane, the interactions must have been occurring more centrally, that is, in the brain.

Such central interactions become very important when we consider the processing of more complex and meaningful sounds, such as speech (see Chapter 12). Interestingly, it is sometimes impossible to ignore components of complex sounds that are far from the target in frequency, resulting in what is called *information masking*. When a masking sound made up of several different frequencies chosen at random is presented simultaneously with a target, the target is more difficult to detect even if none of the frequencies is particularly close to the target frequency (Neff & Green, 1987).

Sound Discrimination

In some respects the problem of masking is really a discrimination problem, of much the same sort as that discussed in Chapter 2. Basically, the observer's task is to discriminate the target sound from the masking sound. We may simplify this problem somewhat by asking the basic discrimination question in respect to the perception of sound: "How different must two sounds be in order for the difference to be detected reliably?" To answer this question precisely, we must separate two of the physical dimensions along which a sound stimulus may differ, namely, intensity and frequency.

Let us begin by considering our sensitivity to intensity changes. A good deal of care must be taken when studying such abilities, since turning a tone on or off, or changing its frequency or intensity abruptly, can cause the perception of a "click." In a threshold situation an observer might respond to this click rather than to the actual intensity or frequency change in which we are interested. Because of this, Riesz (1928) at the Bell Telephone Laboratories resorted to a rather elaborate technique based on a phenomenon known as **beats.** When we simultaneously listen to two tones that are similar in intensity but slightly different in frequency, we may perceive the occurrence of beats—a throbbing quality or an alternating rising and falling in loudness of the sound, much like the vibrato of a singer. The frequency with which the loudness fluctuates is the frequency difference between the two tones that are combined. The air compressions and rarefactions in the sound waves will add when the maximum of one wave is occurring at the same time as the maximum of the other, and subtract when the maximum of one wave coincides with the minimum of the other. For example, when two tones differ by 3 Hz, the maxima of the two sound waves will coincide (add) three times each second. The sound will thus seem to wax and wane at 3 Hz (three times per second). As the frequency difference becomes larger, the discriminability of the beats decreases. At a large enough difference between the two tones, the sound begins to take on a harsh or rough and grating quality. Figure 7-5 shows how two sound signals can combine to form a separate beat frequency.

Riesz (1928) used the perception of beats to determine the limits of intensity discrimination in an observer. He first presented a tone that was clearly audible by itself (say, at a frequency of

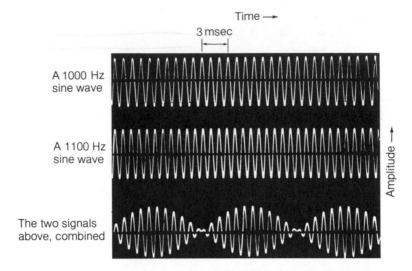

FIGURE 7-5   A 1000-Hz sine wave is added to a 1100-Hz sine wave to give a beat frequency of 100 Hz. This means that the beat pattern repeats every 10 msec as the overall envelope of sound pressures varies. (From Lindsay & Norman, 1977)

1000 Hz). He next presented another tone that was close enough in frequency (say, 1003 Hz) so that it would cause the perception of beats if it were intense enough. He gradually increased the intensity of the added sound until the listener first detected the fluctuation in loudness caused by the beating. On the basis of this he could compute the difference threshold, without contaminating the sound with the "click" caused by sudden changes in intensity at onset or offset of the stimulus.

You will probably recall from Chapter 2 that one measure of our ability to discriminate between two stimuli is given by the Weber fraction. We defined the Weber fraction as $\Delta I/I$, where ΔI equals the intensity change necessary to be just noticed, and I is the standard stimulus from which the change is taken. This fraction represents the proportion by which a stimulus must be changed in order for us to detect that change. Thus, a Weber fraction of 0.5 means we must increase (or decrease) the intensity of a stimulus by 50 percent in order to discriminate the change.

We can use the Weber fraction as a measure of our ability to discriminate sounds from one another. Figure 7-6 shows Riesz's (1928) results for how the Weber fraction varies as we vary the intensity of the standard (I) stimulus. Notice that we have plotted four different curves for four different frequencies. As you can see, the size of the Weber fraction is smallest (discrimination is best) for stimuli in the middle range of frequencies. Increasing or decreasing the frequency results in a decrease in our ability to discriminate intensity changes, although such variation in discrimination with changes in frequency are not always found to be as large as those shown here (see e.g., Jesteadt, Wier & Green, 1977), nor is the Weber fraction always found to drop off so smoothly with intensity (Long & Cullen, 1985). For moderate stimulus intensities and frequencies, however, the Weber fraction is rather constant. It would, of course, be perfectly constant if Weber's law were completely true, as we discussed in Chapter 2. More modern measurements (using pure-tone stimuli that were turned on and off gradually in order to avoid the spurious click we mentioned above) seem to indicate even

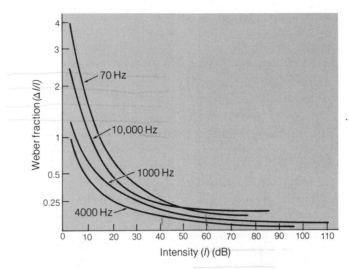

FIGURE 7-6   Intensity discrimination measured in terms of the Weber fraction for various intensities and frequencies of standard stimuli. (Based on Riesz, 1928)

less of a violation of Weber's law, with much less of a rise in the Weber fraction at lower intensities (Green, Nachmias, Kearny & Jeffress, 1979; Hanna, von Gierke & Green, 1986). Figure 7-6 shows that the auditory system is capable of detecting an approximately 10 to 20 percent change in stimulus intensity (5% under optimal conditions) across a broad range of frequencies and intensities, covering the stimulus range where most of our everyday hearing takes place.

We have discussed only studies of sound discrimination where the stimuli were presented to a single ear (monaural presentation). You might expect that, just as is the case with detection, it would be easier to discriminate intensities of sounds presented to both ears (binaural presentation) than those presented only to a single ear. In fact, intensity difference thresholds are about 33 percent smaller when the stimuli are presented simultaneously to both ears than when they are presented only to one or the other ear alone (Jesteadt & Wier, 1977). This is probably because the binaural presentation gives the observer two chances to hear the difference (one in each ear) rather than just the sin-

gle chance available when monaural presentation is used. Similarly, the intensity difference threshold is smaller the longer the duration of the stimuli, over a range of 2 msec to 2 seconds (Florentine, 1986). The longer stimulus durations give more information about the stimulus difference and thus more opportunity to detect it.

A similar, but special, case of intensity discrimination arises in what has been called **profile analysis** (Green, 1987). In this situation, a listener is presented with a complex sound made up of many different frequencies (often more than 20 of them) and is asked to discriminate a slight change in the intensity of one of the component sounds. For example, say a complex sound (a standard "flat" profile) consists of pure tones with frequencies of 250, 500, 1000, 2000, and 4000 Hz, all with amplitudes of 60 dB. A comparison sound could consist of tones with the same frequencies and amplitudes except, for instance, the 1000-Hz tone, which has been raised to an amplitude of 65 dB. A listener would be asked to say whether the standard or comparison tone complex has occurred at a particular time. Under these conditions intensity thresholds can be much smaller than for single tones. Thresholds actually decrease as the number of component frequencies is increased from 3 to 21 (see Green, 1987). The auditory system seems to carry out a "profile analysis," which is a comparison of the relative intensities of components in a complex sound, and seems better able to detect "bumps" in the profile (changes in a single component) when there are more component frequencies present. It is probably not surprising that listeners must practice for many trials before they can detect these profile differences. Once they can, however, the thresholds so obtained are robust and consistent with thresholds obtained with older methods. For example, profile discrimination is best when the intensity increment is added to components of intermediate frequencies, as in the example above (Bernstein & Green, 1987).

Thus far, we have dealt with the question of discrimination of differences in intensity of sound stimuli. We may also ask, "By how much must two tones differ in frequency for this difference to be noticed?" Again, the classic study was done at the Bell Telephone Laboratories, this time by Shower and Biddulph (1931) (you might guess that

the telephone company would have an interest in discovering the limits of our ability to discriminate sounds). The basic experiment involves presenting an observer with a tone of a given frequency and intensity and then varying (modulating) the frequency of the tone by larger and larger amounts until the observer is just able to detect a change in pitch. Again, we may measure the limits of discrimination using the Weber fraction. In this case, however, the fraction consists of $\Delta f/f$, where f represents the frequency of the standard tone, and Δf represents the change in frequency necessary to be just noticed as different from the standard. Figure 7-7 shows Shower and Biddulph's measurements of the Weber fraction for frequency discrimination for a number of different intensity levels and a broad range of frequencies. Notice that above 1000 Hz the Weber fraction is constant, and quite small for most intensity levels (around 0.005). This means that if we presented a listener with tones of 1000 Hz and 1005 Hz, this small difference in frequency (1/2%) would be detectable. At lower intensity levels our discrimination of frequency differences is not quite this good.

As was the case for intensity discrimination,

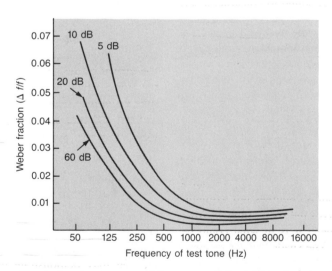

FIGURE 7-7 Frequency discrimination measured in terms of the Weber fraction for various intensities and frequencies of standard stimuli. (Based on Shower & Biddulph, 1931)

more recent studies of the effect of intensity and frequency on the frequency difference threshold have used as stimuli tones that are turned on and off gradually and that are only on for a brief duration (500 msec or so). The method of constant stimuli (see Chapter 2) applied to these tones then yields a measurement of the difference threshold. The most comprehensive of the modern studies was done by Wier, Jesteadt, and Green (1977). Their results were similar to those of Shower and Biddulph (1931), that is, the Weber fraction for frequency depended on both frequency and intensity in a way similar to that shown in Figure 7-7. Finally, as was the case for intensity discrimination, binaural frequency difference thresholds are about 33 percent smaller than are monaural ones (Jesteadt & Wier, 1977).

Sound Localization

Sounds are usually perceived as having a location in space, as emanating from sources to the right or left of, in front or behind of, above or below our bodies. Some sounds appear to come from close by, others from a distance. Our auditory systems use a variety of aspects of sound to construct a sort of auditory space, with our bodies at the center, within which sounds can be localized and their sources approached ("Hey Jill, nice to see you!") or avoided ("Grrrrooowwwlll").

Direction Cues: Simple Tones

When a sound comes from some distance away and from a particular angle to the listener, a number of cues indicate the direction to the right or left, the **azimuth,** of the sound source. Figure 7-8 shows a typical situation when a sound is coming from a source positioned at about 45 degrees left azimuth. Notice that one ear receives the sound directly from the source while the other ear is in what could be called a **sound shadow.** The shadowed ear receives only those sounds from the source that are *bent* around the head, or *diffracted* by the edge of the head. The presence of a sound shadow means that

the sound intensity at one ear is less than the intensity at the other ear.

Measurements have been made of **intensity differences** between the ears as both the azimuth of the sound source and the frequency of the emitted sound are varied. These show that the intensity difference between the ears increases as a sound source is moved toward one side. In addition, although low-frequency sound waves (those less than 3000 Hz) bend around the head very readily, high-frequency tones tend to rush right past the hidden ear unless deflected into it. This exaggerates the intensity differences caused by the presence of a sound shadow for higher frequency sounds. The changes in intensity difference as the angle of the sound source changes can serve as a cue to direction. A large intensity difference between the two ears indicates that the source of the sound is positioned to one side; the greatest intensity difference occurs when the sound source is located at 90 degrees azimuth. The ear receiving the loudest input is perceived as closest to the sound source.

When a sound source is at an angle, sound must travel different distances to reach the two ears. This is always the case unless the sound source is positioned at either 0 or 180 degrees, when the ears are at equal distances from the source of the sound. Because sound takes time to travel through space, there is a **time difference** in the arrival of the sound at the two ears. For example, for a sound at 0 degrees azimuth, there is no time difference between the stimulation of the right and the left ears since they are at equal distances from the sound source. For a sound at 90 degrees azimuth in either direction, however, the ear closer to the sound is stimulated approximately 0.8 msec earlier than the hidden ear. Intermediate azimuths result in intermediate values for this time difference (see Figure 7-8). Such a time difference may be a cue to the location of the sound source and may result in the experience of an apparent direction for it. You may demonstrate the effects of this time difference on direction perception for yourself using Demonstration Box 7-4.

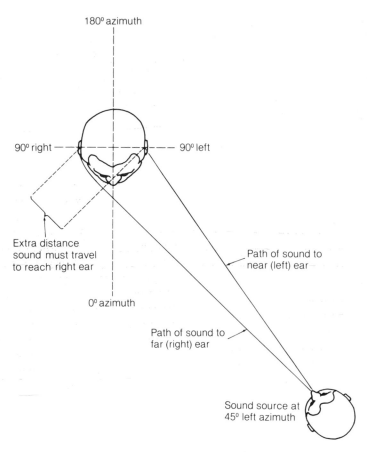

180° azimuth

90° right — 90° left

Extra distance
sound must travel
to reach right ear

0° azimuth

Path of sound to
near (left) ear

Path of sound to
far (right) ear

Sound source at
45° left azimuth

FIGURE 7-8 **The path of sound to the two ears for a sound source at 45 degrees left azimuth. (Based on Lindsay & Norman, 1977)**

Under certain circumstances, the time difference between the stimulation of the two ears results in a **phase difference.** If a sound is arriving earlier at one ear it will be in a different portion of its cycle of compression and rarefaction of the air molecules than the sound arriving at the other ear (this aspect of sound is discussed fully in Chapter 6). This is especially true for low-frequency sounds, where the time taken to complete one cycle is more than the maximum time difference of the arrival of sound at the two ears. For example, it takes a 1000-Hz tone exactly 1 msec to complete one cycle. If such a tone arrived 0.5 msec earlier

at one ear (as it would if the sound source were positioned at about 62 degrees azimuth), it would always be 0.5/1 or 1/2 cycle ahead of the sound arriving at the opposite ear.

Although phase difference could be a cue to sound direction, it provides ambiguous information when we consider the full range of sound frequencies. For instance, with a tone of 10000 Hz at 62 deg azimuth, the time difference between the arrival of the sound at the two ears would once again be 0.5 msec. However, a 10000-Hz tone takes only 0.1 msec to complete one cycle. This implies a phase difference of 0.5/0.1 or 5 cycles. Thus the

DEMONSTRATION BOX 7-4.   Time Differences and Auditory Direction

For this demonstration you will need a length of rubber hose or flexible plastic tube. Hold one end up to each ear as shown in the figure. Now, have a friend tap the tube using a pencil. At the point where she taps, a sound wave starts moving in both directions down the tube. If she taps so that there is a longer section of tube on one side, the sound must travel farther before reaching one of your ears. This delay is perceived as a shift in direction of the sound. Notice how the sound seems to change direction as different parts of the tube are tapped, causing different patterns of sound delays.

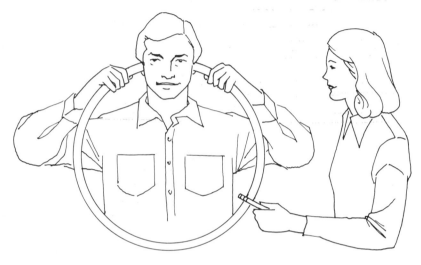

sound at the ear closest to the source is 5 cycles ahead of the sound arriving at the more distant ear. However, every cycle is identical. Therefore, how can the observer tell just what the phase difference may be? It could be 5, 4, 3, 2, or 1 cycles. Even at the lower frequencies, where potentially the phase difference cue could be more useful, the same phase difference is characteristic of sounds positioned directly opposite to one another (in reference to a line drawn through the head in any direction).

Finally, it has also been argued that the *pinnae* (the fleshy parts of the ears outside of the head) delay (Batteau, 1967) or amplify (Butler, 1987; Flannery & Butler, 1981) sounds of different frequencies by different amounts. Such differential delays and amplifications apparently provide cues to the location of complex sound sources, especially their elevation (Oldfield & Parker, 1984), since a positive relation exists between the apparent location of sounds and the amount of delay or amplification provided by the pinnae (see also Oldfield & Parker, 1986).

In 1907, Lord Raleigh proposed a dual, or two-process, theory of sound localization. He suggested that we localize low-frequency sounds by using time or phase differences, or both, at the two ears, and that we localize high-frequency sounds by using the intensity differences at the two ears caused by the sound shadow and differences in their distance from the sound source. This notion has been confirmed by later research. For example, Stevens and Newman (1934) had observers with their eyes closed make judgments as to the direction of a sound source. They played sounds of different frequencies from a variety of azimuths and recorded the listener's errors of localization for each sound. Their data are shown in Figure 7-9. The solid line in this graph represents a summary of the data they collected, with errors averaged over all the locations at a particular frequency. As you can see, most errors occur in the region of 1500–3000 Hz. Fewer errors occur above or below this frequency range. We can interpret this as indicating the efficient use of at least one cue in the low- and high-frequency ranges. Performance is worst in the midrange, however, where neither cue to localization is particularly useful. This interpretation has been confirmed by Mills's (1958) work on the **minimum audible angle,** which is the smallest amount of movement of a sound source that can just be detected. The minimum audible angle also varies as a function of frequency and location of a sound source; the variations are consistent with those observed in experiments like those of Stevens and Newman (Mills, 1960).

Direction and Distance Cues: Complex Sounds

When we are in an ordinary room, the sound from any source may go bouncing around the room, reflecting from the walls, ceiling, and floor many times before it reaches our ears. Figure 7-10 illustrates this phenomenon. Why do we not experience an overwhelming auditory confusion as these sounds ricochet around us? Typically, we respond only to the first of the many replicas of a particular complex sound in echo-producing surroundings. We do not respond to the echoes that arrive several milliseconds later. In fact, we do not even experience echoes until the reflecting surface, which hurls the sound back at us, is far enough away so that the echoes take a substantial time to reach us (more than 35 msec or so). Groups of sounds that arrive at interstimulus intervals of less than 35 msec are fused together into one sound. The first arrival appears to be the major determinant of where in space we perceive the sound source to be. This phenomenon is called the **precedence effect** and has been

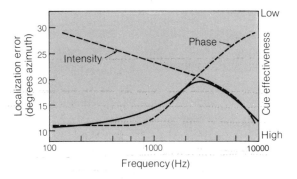

FIGURE 7-9 Relative cue effectiveness in arbitrary units for interaural intensity and phase differences (dashed lines) as a function of frequency. The solid line shows mean localization errors as a function of frequency. (From Gulick, 1971. Copyright 1971 by Oxford University Press, Inc. Reprinted by permission. Data from Stevens & Newman, 1934.)

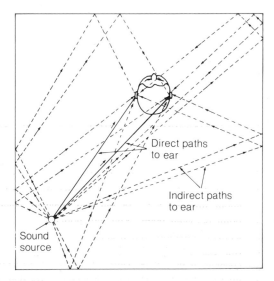

FIGURE 7-10 Some of the echoes produced by sound reflecting from the walls of a room. Unless the walls are quite far away, the echoes are not perceived. (From Lindsay & Norman, 1977)

extensively studied (see Rakerd & Hartmann, 1985; Wallach, Newman & Rosenzweig, 1949; Zurek, 1980). The experiments of Wallach et al. (1949) indicated that the earlier of a pair of fused sounds (separated by 2 msec) was 6–10 times more important than the later of the pair in determining the perceived direction of the sound source. Wallach et al. (1949) also pointed out that the precedence effect is an important part of our ability to listen selectively to one source of sound out of a larger group of competing sounds (see the discussion of the cocktail party problem in Chapter 15). You can experience the effects of precedence on the localization of sound by using Demonstration Box 7-5.

Under appropriate conditions, echoes can be important to the judgment of the location of sounds. For example, blind individuals apparently use echoes to help them locate obstacles and thus avoid them (Supra, Cotzin & Dallenbach, 1944; Worchel & Dallenbach, 1947). Animals such as bats and whales have highly developed **echolocation systems,** similar to sonar, which they can use to locate objects with the same facility with which we use our eyes (see Neuweiler, Bruns & Schuller, 1980 for a review). They may even have special auditory brain pathways analogous to the tectopulvinar visual pathway (serving visual localization, see Chapter 3) to control scanning head move-

ments, which in turn may help to build up a representation of the immediate environment (Kobler, Isbey & Casseday, 1987). We might call this representation "auditory space" to distinguish it from our more familiar perception of space based on vision.

There are a number of other cues to the spatial location of complex sounds. As we suggested above, head movements are important in building up our representation of auditory space. They serve to resolve ambiguities of location, such as whether the sound is in front of or in back of the listener (Noble & Gates, 1985; Wallach, 1939). They also provide information indicating that the sound is really "out there" as opposed to one generated inside the head, such as the ringing in the ears called *tinnitus* that some people experience if they take too much aspirin or have a bad head cold.

Distance information is also carried by complex sounds. One major source of this information is the relative intensity of a sound, with nearer sources being more intense. Changes in sound distance are thus reliably coded by changes in sound intensity (Mershon & King, 1975). Of course, it is always possible that the more distant source is actually emitting a stronger intensity signal, making this cue unreliable in determining the absolute distance of a sound source unless the sound is a

---

DEMONSTRATION BOX 7-5.   Precedence and the One-Speaker Stereo Illusion

For this demonstration you will need a radio, phonograph, or tape recorder that has stereo speakers located about 2 m apart. Turn on some music and stand about midway between the two speakers, facing a point between them. You will notice that the sound seems to envelop you. It comes from both sides, and you can clearly identify sounds coming from one speaker or the other. Take a few steps (you need not go very far) toward one side where a speaker is located. After only a step or two you will suddenly find that all the sound seems to be coming from the

speaker nearest you. You no longer get any sensation of sound coming from the more distant speaker (although it still affects sound quality as you can demonstrate by turning it off). A few steps to the other side will reverse this effect, making it appear as though all the sound is coming from the other speaker. As you move toward a speaker, you alter the time that it takes for the sound to reach your ears. The precedence process then takes the sound arriving first and emphasizes it, giving you the impression that all the sound emanates from that source.

familiar one. Through experience we build up memories of what a phone bell or a car engine sounds like when these sounds are made at different distances from us. In later encounters we can use this knowledge to judge how far away a sound source may be based on the remembered loudness of other similar sound sources.

Another important source of distance information is the relative amount of **reverberation** in the impinging sound. As we stated above, sound reaches our ears both directly from a source and after being reflected from (*reverberating* from) various surfaces such as walls (see Figure 7-10). In general, as a sound source gets further away from an observer, the amount of sound that directly reaches the ears decreases more rapidly than the amount reaching the ears after reverberation. Thus, the relative amount of "reverberation sound" (which has a distinct quality, like an echo) is a cue to the distance of a sound source from an observer. Bekesy was one of the first to investigate this cue systematically. In 1938 (Bekesy, 1960), he showed that altering the proportion of reverberant sound alters judgments of perceived distances of sounds. More recent work (Butler, Levy & Neff, 1980; Mershon & Bowers, 1979; Mershon & King, 1975) has confirmed and extended this earlier work.

Another cue to distance that seems to be as compelling as the amount of reverberation is the frequency makeup, or *spectrum*, of a complex sound. Sounds composed mostly of high frequencies seem to come from quite nearby, and the more the sound is dominated by low-frequency components the farther away its source seems to be. Butler et al. (1980) suggested that this is because more distant sounds typically are more dominated by low-frequency components, perhaps because the high-frequency components are so easily blocked by intervening obstructions. Again, our previous experiences may play a role in determining how far away we judge a sound to be based on the frequency spectrum.

A final important cue to the distance of a sound source is the presence of a compelling visual object that *could* be the source. Thus, the ventriloquist's dummy seems to be talking because its mouth moves and the ventriloquist's does not (if the ventriloquist is a good one). Of course, echoes and reverberation do not play a role in this effect (Mershon, Desaulniers & Amerson, 1980). In addition, the illusion that a sound is coming from a likely visual object can be so compelling that it can affect the perceived loudness of the sound. If the sound seems to emanate from far away, it sounds louder than if it seems to emanate from close by (Mershon, Desaulniers, Kiefer & Amerson, 1981). Observers seem to correct for the fact that actual sound intensity diminishes rapidly as the distance from the sound source increases, a phenomenon termed *loudness constancy* (see Chapter 14 for a discussion of the constancies).

Physiological Mechanisms

The auditory system seems to contain neural units that respond to both time and intensity differences between the two ears, which may, in turn, signal the location of a sound source. For instance, some neurons in the superior olives, inferior colliculi (Semple & Kitzes, 1987), and auditory cortex of various birds and mammals respond best to binaural stimuli that reach the two ears at slightly different times or intensities (see Erulkar, 1972 and Phillips & Brugge, 1985 for reviews). Different neurons have different "best" interaural time differences, or different "best" interaural intensity differences. In other words, different neurons are "tuned" to different time or intensity differences between the two ears. Since these differences are cues to the location of sounds, we could say that these tuned neurons encode sound location much as neurons tuned to sounds of different frequencies encode frequency. It is possible that such neurons constitute a kind of map of auditory space, with each neuron having a region of auditory space to which it responds best, a sort of "auditory receptive field" much like the visual receptive fields discussed in Chapter 3.

There are problems with this idea, however. The major one is that the tuning of the neurons is too gross to account for the accuracy with which animals, including humans, can localize sounds. In other words, the auditory "receptive fields" of these neurons are too large to account for the degree of accuracy shown in actual behavioral data. In some species, such as the barn owl, much smaller, more intricately organized auditory receptive fields have been found using electrophysiological recording techniques (Knudsen & Konishi, 1978a). An interesting nuance in the barn owl is that the receptive fields of these neurons have a center-surround organization (Knudsen & Konishi, 1978b). That is, not only do these neurons fire above their background rate in response to stimuli in their best areas of space but also they are inhibited in their response by sounds in areas outside their best areas, thus resembling, in many ways, the center-surround organization of neurons at various levels of the visual system (see Chapter 3) and other parts of the auditory system (see Chapter 6). So far there has been no direct evidence that such center-surround neurons exist in the auditory systems of mammals, but it is possible that the time and intensity difference detectors are preliminary stages leading to such neurons. Interaction of time and intensity difference detectors that have a center-surround organization could give rise to higher-level neurons that have relatively restricted receptive fields and might allow a fairly accurate mapping of auditory space.

SUBJECTIVE DIMENSIONS OF SOUND

Up to now we have concentrated on describing our ability to detect the presence of a sound, or to discriminate one sound from another. However, such analyses do not deal directly with the subjective quality of a sound as we experience it. Early in the history of the psychological investigation of audition, experimenters were inclined to believe that

there would be a direct correspondence between the experienced qualities of the sensation and properties of the physical stimulus. For a long time it was taken for granted that every *qualitatively different psychological variable* would reflect almost perfectly some corresponding *quantifiable physical variable*. For example, it was firmly believed that the subjective dimension of **loudness** was a direct reflection of the physical dimension of *amplitude* of the sound-wave stimulus. In similar fashion it was believed that the subjective dimension of **pitch** (whether a sound appears to be high or low in tone) was simply the psychological experience of the *frequency* of the sound wave. This sort of mechanistic viewpoint has been opposed by many investigators, who have pointed out that we should separate concepts and expressions that describe our conscious or phenomenal experience from those that describe the physical stimulus. The subjective qualities of loudness and pitch are complex perceptions that depend on the interaction of several physical characteristics of the stimulus, as well as the physical and psychological state of the observer.

The deeply rooted older view maintained that at best the observer could be expected to distinguish only two phenomenal dimensions (loudness and pitch) because there are two predominant physical dimensions (intensity and frequency). Actually, we can differentiate many qualitatively different experiences arising from sound stimuli. These include not only pitch and loudness but also the **perceived location** of a sound (where it seems to come from), its **perceived duration** (how extended in time it appears), its **timbre** (that complex quality that allows us to distinguish a note played on a clarinet from the same note played on a violin), its **volume** (the sense in which it fills space and seems large or small), and its **density** (a complex feeling of the compactness or hardness of the sound), as well as **consonance** or **dissonance** (how two tones seem to "go together" or "clash"). Our auditory experience is composed of these and other sensory qualities—not simply the registration of the frequency and the intensity of the stimulus. We have already discussed sound localization above; we discuss some of the other subjective qualities in more detail in the sections that follow.

Loudness

We cannot predict a subjective experience totally from a single physical dimension. However, the experienced loudness of a sound is affected greatly by stimulus intensity. If everything else is held constant, it is fair to say that as we increase the amplitude of the sound stimulus, we increase its apparent loudness. The experience of loudness, however, is *not* identical to stimulus intensity, and decibels are *not* measures of phenomenal loudness.

In order to study loudness, we must use psychophysical scaling procedures such as the magnitude estimation techniques we discussed in Chapter 2, or the matching of one stimulus to another on a different sensory continuum (cross-modality matching). Stevens (1956) did a classic study of this type using magnitude estimation. He gave an observer a standard stimulus tone and a set of tones that varied in intensity but had the same frequency (1000 Hz) as the standard. The standard tone was assigned a value of 100 units of loudness. The observer simply assigned numbers to the variable tone on the basis of its perceived loudness. Thus, a tone that sounded twice as loud as the standard would be called 200 units, and a tone that sounded half as loud would be called 50 units. Stevens found that the perception of loudness varied according to a simple equation:

$$L = aI^{0.6}$$

[handwritten: apparent loudness]

where L is the apparent loudness, I is the physical intensity of the sound (in units of pressure amplitude), and a is a constant. The loudness of the stimulus was increasing as approximately the 0.6 power of the physical sound pressure. Other exponents have also been found depending on the specific stimuli used and the test conditions employed (Marks, 1974). For example, the exponent of the

power function varies with stimulus frequency, being somewhat larger for frequencies lower than 1000 Hz (Scharf, 1978).

On the basis of his and others' work, Stevens suggested a new unit by which to measure loudness. He called this unit the **sone.** One sone is defined as the loudness of a 1000-Hz stimulus at an intensity level of 40 dB. For most of the stimulus range a linear relationship exists between the loudness measured by the logarithm of the number of sones and the intensity measured in decibels. To double the loudness (for instance, from 1 to 2 sones) we have to increase the intensity of the sound by about 10 dB. For very weak sounds (below 30 dB), however, the change in apparent loudness is much more rapid with increases in intensity (see e.g., Canevet, Hellman & Scharf, 1986). This relationship is shown in Figure 7-11, which also indicates the loudness in sones of some typical sounds.

Sound intensity does not provide a full description of loudness. For example, our perception of the loudness of a tone is also affected by its frequency. A typical procedure to measure the re-

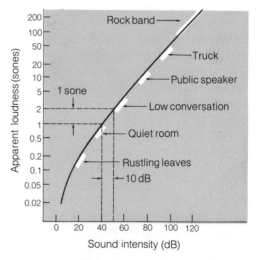

FIGURE 7-11   The relationship between loudness (measured in sones) and stimulus intensity (measured in decibels).

lationship between frequency and loudness involves presenting an observer with a standard tone of a given frequency and intensity. She is then asked to adjust the intensity of another tone (differing in frequency) until it matches the loudness of the first. When this is done for a number of comparison tones, we can plot a curve that describes the intensity at which tones of varying frequencies appear to be equally as loud as the standard tone. Such a curve is called an **equal loudness contour.**

A series of such equal loudness contours is shown in Figure 7-12. Each curve represents a different sound intensity for the standard tone in decibels. Notice that the lines are not flat. If sounds of various frequencies sounded equally loud when they were the same intensity, all of the curves would be straight lines. The fact that the contours rise and fall with frequency (much as the graph of absolute threshold varies with frequency) means that tones of equal intensity but of different fre-

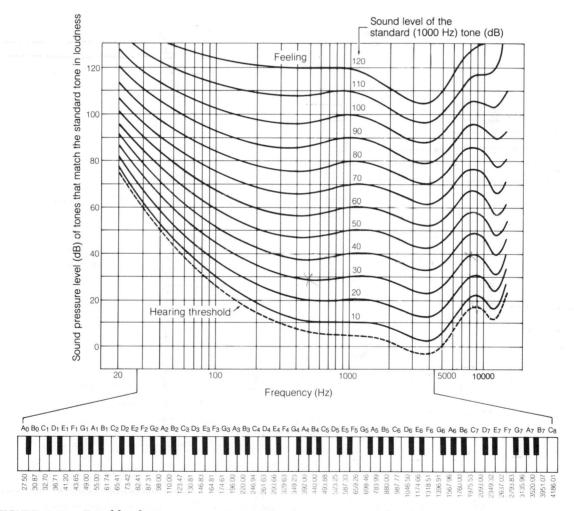

FIGURE 7-12   **Equal loudness contours.** (From Lindsay & Norman, 1977. Data from Robinson & Dadson, 1956.)

quencies appear to differ in loudness. Tones of less than 1000 Hz, or greater than 6000 Hz, must be considerably more intense to match the loudness of tones between 1000 and 6000 Hz. Thus, tones in the middle range of frequencies sound considerably louder than equally intense tones outside this range.

What if we wished to compare the loudness of tones of frequencies other than 1000 Hz, say an 8000-Hz, 40-dB tone and a 400-Hz, 30-dB tone? Figure 7-12 shows that both tones fall nearly on the 30-dB contour. This means they are both approximately equal in loudness to a 1000-Hz, 30-dB tone, and thus they also match each other in loudness. We could be more precise and specify their loudness in sones by finding the loudness in sones of the 1000-Hz, 30-dB tone. By graphical (see Figure 7-11) or computational methods we find this to be about 0.46 sone. Thus, both the 8000-Hz, 40-dB tone and the 400-Hz, 30-dB tone have a loudness of 0.46 sone. Table 7-1 summarizes essential aspects of sones and other audiometric units discussed in this chapter.

Duration also influences the apparent loudness of a tone. For tones briefer than about 200 msec, we must increase intensity to match the loudness of a longer tone. We could create an equal loudness contour, of a type similar to that for variations with frequency, by having a standard of fixed duration and requiring an observer to match its loudness with comparison tones of different durations. When we do this we get a curve similar to that shown in Figure 7-13. Thus a 2-msec burst of sound must be 15 dB in order to sound as loud as a 90-msec burst at 5 dB. This sort of finding suggests that the auditory system may sum all the inputs coming in over a 200-msec window of time (Gulick, 1971).

Other sounds occurring at the same time, or just before, a sound to be judged can also affect apparent loudness. For example, if a continuous tone is played to one ear and an intermittent tone to the other, the loudness of the continuous tone appears to diminish with time (Botte, Canevet & Scharf, 1982). The reduction in apparent intensity for a continuously presented stimulus is called **auditory adaptation.** Adaptation is weak for a continuous tone alone, but can be quite dramatic when different tones are presented to the two ears. The apparent loudness of the continuous tone actually diminishes to zero if the tone in the other ear is close to it in frequency and is played for 40 sec (Botte, Baruch & Scharf, 1986).

A related phenomenon, called **auditory fatigue,** is caused by exposing the ear to very intense sounds. The resultant reduction of loudness of other stimuli presented after the intense sound ceases may persist for a considerable period of time, depending on the intensity and duration of the fatiguing stimulus. For instance, Postman and Egan

Table 7-1. Audiometric Units

Audiometric term	Unit	What is measured	How measured
Pressure amplitude	Dyne/cm^2	Variation of sound pressure from atmospheric	Measure peak compressive force per 1 cm^2 area
Sound pressure level	Decibel (dB)	Ratio of pressure amplitudes of two sounds	$20 \log(P/P_0)$
Frequency	Hertz (Hz)	Number of cycles of compression/rarefaction	Count cycles per second
Loudness	Sone	Subjective impression of sound intensity	1 sone = loudness of 1000-Hz tone at 40 dB
Pitch	Mel	Subjective impression of sound frequency	Pitch of 1000-Hz tone at 40 dB is 1,000 mels

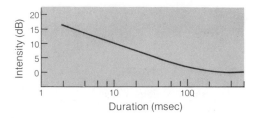

FIGURE 7-13 Equal loudness contour showing the changes in intensity needed to maintain a constant loudness as the duration of the standard is varied. (From Gulick, 1971. Copyright 1971 by Oxford University Press, Inc. Reprinted by permission.)

(1949) exposed observers to an intense sound (115 dB) for 20 min. They then measured the sensitivity of their observers over a period of several days. The results are shown in Figure 7-14. The horizontal line represents pre-exposure sensitivity, and the other curves represent the hearing loss, which could be interpreted as a reduction in loudness, for varying periods of time following the exposure to the stimulus. As you can see, the largest hearing loss immediately follows the exposure to the intense noise; however, it persists to measurable extent over a period of 24 hr. You can experience an interesting analog to this experiment using Demonstration Box 7-6.

Another factor that influences our perception of loudness is the complexity of the stimulus. Most of the sounds we hear in our everyday environment are made up of mixtures of a large number of different frequencies of sound. We can create a different kind of equal loudness contour by asking listeners to adjust the intensity of a pure tone of 1000 Hz until its loudness matches that of some complex sound. Suppose we take a complex sound composed of a group of frequencies centered around 1000 Hz. We can systematically increase or decrease the range of frequencies included. We usually refer to the range of frequencies as the **bandwidth.** As the bandwidth of the sound is increased, the intensity of each of the component frequencies is decreased in order to keep the overall intensity of the sound the same. Figure 7-15 displays an equal loudness contour for such a complex sound. Notice that when only a small band of frequencies makes up the complex sound, increasing the bandwidth does not affect our perception of the loudness of the stimulus. This is reasonable, since the overall intensity of the sound is not changing but only the number of different frequencies included in it. Notice, however, what happens when the frequencies reach a critical bandwidth of about 160 Hz. From this bandwidth onward, loudness

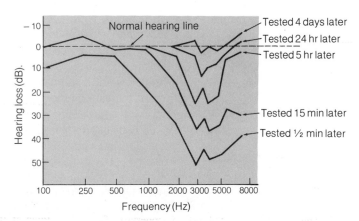

FIGURE 7-14 Prolonged reduction of loudness following exposure to an intense (115-dB) sound for 20 min. (Based on Postman & Egan, 1949)

DEMONSTRATION BOX 7-6.   Auditory Fatigue

During an average day you are exposed to many noises and sounds, from individuals who talk with you, from stereos, televisions, radios, and numerous other sources. Set a radio or a stereo to an intensity level where the sound seems comfortable for listening in the evening before you go to bed. At the day's end, your auditory system has become fatigued by the ongoing, persistent noise of the day. When you awaken in the morning, however, you may find that the radio, set to the same sound level, will appear to be too loud. During the night your ears have recovered from the auditory fatigue caused by exposure to the sounds you heard during the previous day. The quiet of the night has given you a chance to recover your sensitivity, hence all sounds now seem louder. This may explain why an alarm clock, whose bell seems low and pleasant when bought one evening in a department store, will seem so jarring and loud the following morning.

---

begins to increase as we include a greater number of frequencies, although the overall intensity of the sound is unchanged (Cacace & Margolis, 1985; Gulick, 1971; Scharf, 1978).

Pitch

Every time you sing or play a musical scale, you are varying the subjective experience of **pitch.** Your *do, re,* and *mi* differ in this tonal quality. The most important physical determinant of our perception of pitch is the frequency of the sound stimu-

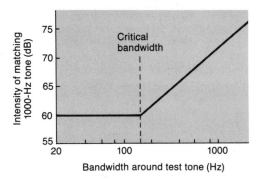

FIGURE 7-15   **The effect on loudness of increasing the bandwidth of frequencies in a complex tone. (Based on Gulick, 1971)**

lus—the high notes on a piano have higher frequencies than the low notes. For instance, the dominant frequency of A_4 (the 49th key on the extended piano keyboard pictured in Figure 7-12, counting from the left to the right) is 440 Hz; the dominant frequency of the A note one octave higher (A_5 or the 61st key from the left) is 880 Hz.

Perhaps the first demonstration of the relationship between frequency and pitch was performed by Robert Hooke in 1681. Hooke placed a card against a wheel that had teeth notched in it, and then spun the wheel. The spinning teeth hit the card and the resultant vibrations sent out a sound wave—a sort of rough, buzzing musical note. When the speed of rotation was increased the frequency of vibration of the card increased, and so did the pitch of the note. The relationship between frequency and pitch had been established. For centuries thereafter, the terms pitch and frequency were used interchangeably on the assumption that pitch rises and falls in exact step with frequency.

The most commonly used measure of the pitch of a sound is probably the musical scale, which is basically logarithmic in nature. Any note one octave higher than another note of the same name has exactly twice the frequency of the lower note. Thus, the note A_3 (the 39th key from the left in Figure 7-12) has a frequency of 220 Hz, whereas

A_4 (the 49th key from the left) is one octave higher and has a frequency of 440 Hz. The musical scale has undergone very little change over the years, although some attempts have been made to adjust the spacing between the notes in an attempt to represent more accurately the pitches of different musical notes. For example, there is a version of the musical scale called the **equal temperament scale** (W. D. Ward, 1970). Here each octave is divided into 12 standard intervals (representing equal logarithmic steps) between the musical notes. These intervals are called *semitones* and each semitone can be further divided into 100 *cents*. Thus, an octave consists of 1,200 cents, and the pitch of any tone can be precisely described in terms of what octave it is in and how many cents it lies above the lowest tone in that octave. This scale has proved to be quite useful for musicians, although there are still arguments about the spacing of the standard intervals within an octave. The reason for such arguments seems to lie in the fact that the musical scale is not a direct representation of the psychological scale for pitch.

The most useful psychological scale for pitch to date is the **mel** scale proposed by Stevens, Volkman, and Newman (1937). Like the sone scale of loudness, the mel scale can be created by various psychophysical scaling techniques. For instance, in one experiment the researchers created a sort of electronic piano with 20 keys and 20 corresponding knobs set above the keyboard. Turning a knob varied the tone produced by the corresponding key through a wide range of frequencies. Listeners were asked to sit before the keyboard and to tune the "piano" to produce pitch intervals that appeared to be equally wide. The results were somewhat surprising. Subjects did not tune the piano to equal steps on the frequency scale, nor did they tune them to equal steps on a logarithmic scale of musical intervals.

As in other psychophysical scaling techniques, a standard must be designated against which all other items will be scaled. By definition, a sound with a frequency of 1000 Hz and an intensity of 40 dB has been assigned a pitch of 1,000 mels (see Table 7-1 for a summary of measures of frequency and pitch). This frequency lies between the notes B_5 and C_6 on the extended piano keyboard in Figure 7-12 (the 63d and the 64th keys from the left). When we compare the mel scale with the musical scale, we find several large discrepancies. For instance, the one-octave difference between C_3 (Key 28) and C_4 (Key 40) is 167 mels, whereas the one-octave difference between C_6 (Key 64) and C_7 (Key 76) is 508 mels. Such measurements confirm the feelings, often expressed by musicians, that the higher musical octaves sound "larger" than the lower ones. It is as if there is more "psychological distance" between the keys at the high end of the piano than at the low end. The relationship between the musical scale and sound frequency is shown in Figure 7-16A, and is roughly linear, whereas the relationship between the perceived pitch (in mels) and sound frequency, shown in Figure 7-16B, is clearly quite different.

Just as a variety of factors other than sound intensity affect the perceived loudness of a sound, factors other than frequency affect its perceived pitch. The very existence of the mel scale and a glance at Figure 7-16B demonstrate that pitch is not identical to frequency. This is verified by the fact that when asked to find a sound that is half the pitch of a standard sound, a listener does not produce a sound that is half the frequency of the standard. Perhaps the major physical factor, other than frequency, that affects the perceived pitch of a pure tone is its intensity. There is a classic demonstration, first performed over a quarter of a century ago, in which an investigator struck a tuning fork tuned to middle C (C_4 or 262 Hz) a few feet from the ear of a trained singer. She was asked to sing the note she heard, and she reproduced the sound with reasonable accuracy. Next, the investigator held the same tuning fork a few inches from her ear. This increased the intensity of the sound reaching her ear, but it left the frequency unchanged since a tuning fork (when properly struck) produces sounds of only a single frequency. Nonetheless, the

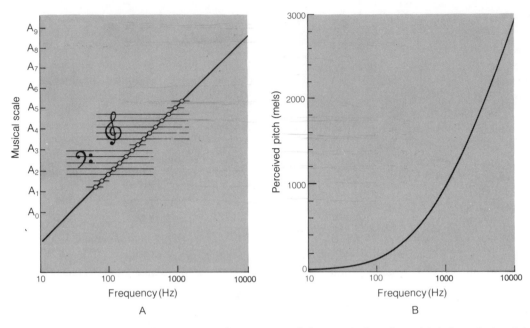

FIGURE 7-16   **(A) The relationship between frequency and the musical scale and (B) the relationship between mels and frequency.** (From Lindsay & Norman, 1977)

pitch the singer heard did change. She now sang a note that was considerably lower in pitch than middle C, clearly demonstrating that sound intensity affects perceived pitch.

Using an experimental technique similar to that used in producing equal loudness contours, we can produce **equal pitch contours.** The listener can be asked either to adjust the intensity of one of two tones that differ in frequency until the two tones match in pitch (Stevens, 1935) or to adjust the frequency of one of two tones that differ in intensity until it matches the other in pitch (Gulick, 1971). Figure 7-17 shows the results from one listener measured by Stevens (1935). The graph shows the percentage change in the frequency necessary to keep the pitch constant as intensity is changed. The ordinate was chosen so that lines curving upward mean that the pitch is increasing (sounds higher) and lines curving downward mean that the pitch is decreasing (sounds lower). As the figure shows, varying the intensity of the tone alters its perceived

pitch. For higher-frequency tones the pitch tends to rise as intensity increases, whereas for lower-frequency tones an increase in intensity tends to lower the pitch.

Another factor that affects our perception of pitch is the duration of the stimulus. A pure tone that lasts for only a few milliseconds is always heard as a click, regardless of the frequency. Before a tone is perceived to have the quality of pitch, one of two conditions must be met. For high-frequency tones (greater than 1000 Hz), the minimum length of time the stimulus must be sounded is around 10 msec. For low-frequency tones (less than 1000 Hz), at least 6–9 cycles of the sound wave must reach the ear before it is perceived to have pitch, meaning that most lower-frequency tones must last for considerably longer than 10 msec before they have pitch (Gulick, 1971). Even for tones that exceed the minimum duration for number of cycles, the tonal quality continues to improve as the duration is increased up to about 250

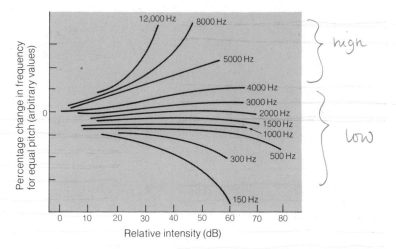

FIGURE 7-17   The relationship between apparent pitch and stimulus intensity for one listener. (Based on Stevens, 1935)

msec. Listeners are better able to discriminate between tones of different frequencies when their duration is longer. You may recall that the loudness of a tone also increases as we increase stimulus duration up to around 200–250 msec. Perhaps a quarter of a second represents some sort of fundamental time period for sensory systems such as the ear. Our phenomenal impressions of the world in many modalities seem to be based on averages or sums of energy changes taken over this small window of time.

Theories of Pitch Perception

The realm of pitch perception has proved to be a testing ground for the major theories of auditory perception. Several tests have been based on some interesting characteristics of our subjective impressions of sound. Suppose we created a complex sound by adding together several different sinusoidal sound waves. The auditory system conducts its own waveform analysis of the complex sound, and we are able to perceive the pitch of the various components separately. For instance, if two tones are played at the same time, you perceive a musical

chord containing two distinct pitches—you do not hear a single, unitary sound (as you discovered in Demonstration Box 6-2).

When we are considering a complex stimulus composed of several sound-wave frequencies, the lowest (usually most intense) frequency sound wave is called the **fundamental.** Musical instruments tend to produce complex sounds in which **harmonics** (frequencies higher than the fundamental) occur at whole number multiples of the fundamental frequency. For example, we have already noted that a sound wave of 220 Hz corresponds to a musical note that we call A (it would be A_3, or the 37th key from the left in Figure 7-12). When a musical instrument sounds this note, the complex waveform produced will also contain some sound energy at frequencies of 440 Hz, 880 Hz, 1320 Hz, and so on. These would be called *high even harmonics* (because they represent frequencies of 2, 4, and 6 times the fundamental frequency). The characteristic sound of a particular instrument depends on the specific harmonics it produces, a quality called its **timbre.** Different instruments emphasize different higher harmonics (sometimes called *overtones*). The number of higher harmonics, or overtones, and their strength determine the complex phenomenal perception that allows us to distinguish between a note played on a piano and the same note played by plucking a violin or guitar string. Thus, the pitch of a sound is greatly determined by the frequency of the fundamental, whereas the timbre is determined by the harmonics. Helmholtz's (1863/1930) summary of the various subjective experiences pertaining to the composition of a complex tone is shown in Table 7-2.

Because the fundamental frequency is the greatest common denominator of all the harmonics present in a complex sound, we could correctly determine the fundamental from our knowledge of the way harmonics work. For example, if we had harmonics of 600, 900, and 1200 Hz, the fundamental frequency would be 300 Hz. As just noted, a complex waveform normally contains both a fundamental frequency and several higher harmonics. For experimental purposes it is possible (through the use of special electronic filters) to remove the fundamental frequency without changing the higher harmonic structure. Alternatively, we could present together a set of pure tones that had a particular fundamental without presenting the fundamental (for example, 600-, 900-, and 1200-Hz tones without the 300-Hz fundamental). Such an artificial sound complex, from which the fundamental frequency is missing, is called a stimulus with a **missing fundamental.**

An interesting and puzzling problem comes from a particular illusion associated with the missing fundamental. Suppose you are presented with two complex sounds. One contains the fundamental and the higher harmonics and the other contains only the higher harmonics. The illusion lies in the fact that the pitch of both sounds appears to be that of the fundamental frequency, even though the fundamental frequency is not physically present in the waveform of the second sound (it is a *missing fundamental*). This unusual phenomenon of hearing plays an important role in a test of the two major theories of pitch. The first is based on the **place principle** and the second is based on the **frequency principle.**

More than one hundred years ago, Helmholtz became intrigued by the fact that the ear could separate a complex sound stimulus into its component simple frequencies. He observed that since the basilar membrane consists of many fibers stretched across its triangular shape, we could think of it as a harp with strings. He suggested that the longer strings resonate to (that is, vibrate in sympathy with) lower frequency tones, whereas the shorter strings resonate to tones of higher frequency. Thus, if we sounded a complex tone it would be automatically decomposed into its component frequencies on the basilar membrane. Each different tone would cause a different *place* on the membrane to vibrate. This is the *place principle.*

Table 7-2.   Sound Composition and Timbre (based on Helmholtz, 1863/1930)

Makeup of complex tone	Subjective impression
Fundamental alone	Soft
Fundamental plus first harmonic	Mellow
Fundamental plus several harmonics	Broad or full
Fundamental plus high harmonics	Sharp
Fundamental intense, harmonics less intense	Full
Harmonics intense, fundamental less intense	Hollow
Odd harmonics (for example, 1, 3, 5) dominating	Nasal
Frequency ratios of 16:15, 9:8, 15:8, 7:5, or 7:6	Rough or screeching

This basic idea was later supported and modified by Bekesy in a series of precise experiments that ultimately won the Nobel Prize for him (see Bekesy, 1960). His basic procedure was to cut tiny holes in the cochleas of guinea pigs and to observe the basilar membrane with a microscope as the ear was being stimulated by tones of different frequencies. He discovered that high-frequency tones maximally displace the narrow end of the basilar membrane near the oval window, and tones of lower frequencies cause displacement further toward the other (wider) end of the basilar membrane. The action of the basilar membrane was not quite as simple as Helmholtz's resonance notion, however, since low-frequency tones activated the entire membrane (see Chapter 6). This fact, together with the result that tones of intermediate frequency also displace a fairly broad area of the membrane, made it unlikely that differential displacement or vibration of the basilar membrane is sufficient to fully explain our ability to discriminate pitch (at least for lower to intermediate frequencies).

The place theory also has difficulty explaining the phenomenon of the missing fundamental. Helmholtz attempted to deal with this by suggesting that the transduction process in the middle ear distorts the sound waves before they affect the cochlea. This distortion creates the fundamental frequency, so that the fundamental is present inside the cochlea even though it is missing in the stimulus that contacts the outer ear. Bekesy (1960) modified this notion somewhat so that the distortion became part of the response of the basilar membrane, which was said to respond "as if" the fundamental were also physically present.

Unfortunately, several experimental results throw doubt on this distortion hypothesis for the missing fundamental. The basic form of such experiments (Patterson, 1969) involves the presentation of pairs of tones, such as 2000 Hz and 2400 Hz, which would produce a missing fundamental of 400 Hz. If a low-frequency band of noise, centered around 400 Hz, is now added to the complex

wave, we would expect that when the noise is sufficiently intense it would be very effective in masking the fundamental tone, since it is stimulating approximately the place on the basilar membrane that is said to be vibrating by the place theory. Nevertheless, despite the presence of this noise, the pitch of the complex wave is still perceived to be that of the fundamental frequency. Since the missing fundamental phenomenon cannot be explained by distortions in the ear, or the local response of the basilar membrane, it presents a problem for a place theory.

The second major class of theory is based on the *frequency principle.* It also has a long history, having been championed first by August Seeback in the 1840s (Green, 1976) and then carried forward to the present by Wever (1970) and in a modified form by Goldstein (1973). This theory argues that the vibrations of the basilar membrane reproduce at least partially the vibrations of the incoming sounds. The frequency of the sound is transmitted by the pattern of neural excitation resulting from this vibration. This situation is analogous to the microphone end of a telephone transducing the pattern of vibrations into variations of electrical signals as it vibrates in unison with your voice. According to this theory, pitch is determined by the frequency of impulses traveling up the auditory nerve. The greater the frequency, the higher the pitch. Some studies have shown that for tones of up to about 4000 Hz, the electrical response of the auditory nerve tracks the frequency of the tone (see Chapter 6). A tone of 500 Hz produces a pattern of response that contains some 500 bursts of electrical responses per second in the nerve, and a tone of 1000 Hz produces twice as many responses.

Such a theoretical position could explain the missing fundamental. Since there are many harmonics but only one fundamental frequency, masking the region of the fundamental should not appreciably change the overall pattern of sound excitation. The low frequency of the fundamental may actually be signaled by the neurons that respond to the higher harmonics, since it is these neurons that convey most of the information about the pattern of excitation. This may seem somewhat topsy-turvy in that we are saying that the fundamental is *not* fundamental, yet consider the example we used earlier in this discussion. Given a sound wave with harmonics of 600, 900, and 1200 Hz, the fundamental is inferred to be 300 Hz. In much the same way that we *infer* the fundamental from knowledge of the harmonic structure, a higher auditory center could infer the fundamental from the pattern of excitation reported by neurons that respond to higher frequencies (see Goldstein, 1973; Javel, 1981; Srulovicz & Goldstein, 1983). This can be verified to a certain extent by the following experiment. We again present an individual with a pair of tones, such as 2000- and 2400-Hz, tones to produce a missing fundamental of 400 Hz. If we now introduce a high-frequency band of noise, centered at about 2200 Hz and extending for several hundred Hertz on either side of it (which should mask the higher harmonics), the missing fundamental is no longer heard (Patterson, 1969).

Additional experiments give a similar picture. If we present one component of a complex tone, say 600 Hz, to one ear, and another, say 800 Hz, to the other, a missing fundamental corresponding to 200 Hz is perceived (Houtsma & Goldstein, 1972). Here there could be no activity on either basilar membrane corresponding to that created when a 200 Hz pure tone stimulates it, since each membrane was stimulated only by a single tone far from 200 Hz. Missing fundamental pitches seem to be perceived using a different mechanism than that used for the pitch of pure tones.

A number of problems still exist with a frequency theory for pitch perception. One difficulty is that an individual neuron cannot fire at high enough rates to account for the perception of high-frequency signals. Actually, an individual neuron can conduct only about 1,000 impulses per second. Thus, the ability of the auditory nerve to track frequencies above this point (up to about 4000 Hz; see the discussion of phase-locking in Chapter 6) has

to be explained in terms of a **volley principle** (Wever, 1970), which describes cooperation between neural fibers so that they fire in groups or squads. While one neuron is "reloading" (actually resting between impulses), its neighbor can discharge. The overall effect is that the pattern of neural firing is in direct correspondence to the frequency of the stimulus, since if we count the total number of discharges, or volleys, per unit of time, they correspond to the frequency of the stimulus. An example of how this can work is shown in Figure 7-18.

A major problem with a volley or frequency principle of pitch perception is that we are requiring the frequency of neural firing to encode both the intensity and the frequency of the sound. Although at first this seems impossible, one way to resolve the problem is to differentiate a concept of overall *density* of neural activity from one of a *number of volleys* (or bursts of firing) per unit time. The density of neural firing is the total number of neurons responding in each volley, or the number of "shots" being fired in each volley down the auditory nerve. An increase in the intensity of the sound, although not changing the volley frequency, could increase the number of neurons joining in the firing, or cause the rate of each individual neuron to increase somewhat. If all the neurons were connected to some higher center that ascertained pitch by the frequency of volleys and loudness by the number of responses per volley, the problem would be solved. An example of how this could work is also shown in Figure 7-18.

Since both the place principle and the frequency principle seem to be supported by some data, it seems likely, as Wever (1970) has suggested, that the ultimate explanation of pitch will include some aspects of both theories. Wever has proposed that in humans pitch is coded by the frequency principle for frequencies lower than about 4000 Hz (the theoretical upper limit for volleying). The use of this volley mechanism for the perception of lower pitches may be supported by an individual's learning and experience (Hall & Peters,

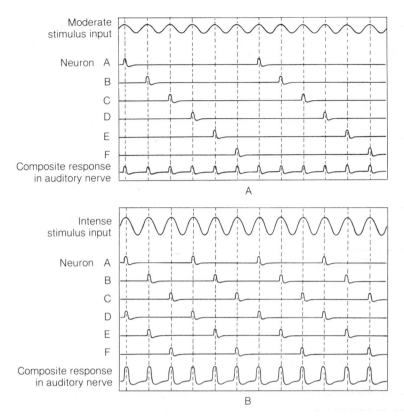

FIGURE 7-18   The volley principle. Note that the composite neural response follows the frequency of the stimulus. However, for the weaker stimulus (A) fewer neurons are firing in each volley than for the stronger stimulus (B).

1982; Terheardt, 1974). For frequencies from 500 to 20000 Hz, the place principle seems capable of explaining pitch perception. However, below 500 Hz the vibration pattern on the basilar membrane seems too broad to explain our excellent pitch perception. Notice that for frequencies between 500 and 4000 Hz, both principles are operating. This could explain the superior performance of the ear for sounds in this range as compared to sounds of higher or lower frequencies. For frequencies outside this range we must rely on only one mechanism, hence performance is poorer.

The place-frequency compromise is supported by a good deal of research (see e.g., Srulovicz &

Goldstein, 1983). In one of the most intriguing studies, Simmons, Epley, Lummis, Guttman, Frishkopf, Harmon, and Zwicker (1965) placed electrodes in the auditory nerve corresponding to different parts of the basilar membrane of a subject's deaf ear. They found that electrical stimulation at different locations produced perception of different pitches. Similarly, modern cochlear implants (see Chapter 6) produce perceptions of pitch differences by electrically stimulating different places in the cochlea (Townshend et al., 1987). This, of course, supports the place principle. When Simmons et al. (1965) varied the frequency of the electrical stimulus from about 20 to 300 Hz, however, the appropriate changes in pitch perception were produced, regardless of the place where the stimulating electrode was located. This supports the frequency principle. Clearly both mechanisms are needed to explain such data.

GLOSSARY

The following definitions are specific to this book.

Auditory adaptation   Transient reduction in auditory sensitivity due to prior or concurrent exposure to sound stimuli.

Auditory fatigue   Prolonged reduction in auditory sensitivity following exposure to very intense sounds.

Azimuth   The direction of a sound source indicated as degrees right or left around a horizontal circle, with 0 deg straight ahead of and 180 deg directly behind an observer.

Backward masking   Masking of a sound by another sound presented later in time. *See* Masking.

Bandwidth   The range of frequencies (frequency *band*) making up a complex sound.

Beats   Fluctuations in loudness of a complex sound caused by interactions of the simple sound waves composing it.

Binaural   Sound presentation to both ears simultaneously.

Central masking   Masking resulting from presentation of target sound and masking sound to different ears.

Consonance   The quality of two tones blending or "going together."

Density   The quality of compactness or hardness of a sound.

Dissonance   The quality of two sounds being discordant or "clashing."

Dynamic range   For a particular frequency, the difference between the absolute threshold and the pain threshold, measured in decibels.

Echolocation system   System used by some animals, such as bats and whales, to locate objects by analyzing self-emitted sound waves reflected from them.

Equal loudness contour   A curve describing the intensities at which tones of varying frequencies appear to be equally loud.

Equal pitch contour   A curve describing the frequencies at which tones of varying intensities appear to have the same pitch.

Equal temperament scale   A version of the musical scale in which each octave is divided into 12 intervals, called *semitones,* that are further divided into 100 *cents.*

Forward masking   Masking of a sound by another sound presented before it in time. *See* Masking.

Frequency principle   Asserts that sound frequency is encoded by the overall frequency of firing in the auditory nerve.

Fundamental   The lowest, usually most intense, frequency sound wave in a complex stimulus.

Harmonics   Frequencies that are whole-number multiples of the fundamental frequency in complex sounds.

Intensity difference   A difference in sound intensity at the two ears caused by the presence of a sound shadow; cue to localization of higher-frequency sounds.

Interstimulus interval   The time span between the end of one stimulus and the beginning of the next.

Loudness   The subjective experience of the magnitude or intensity of sound.

Masker   A sound that, when presented, makes perception of another sound more difficult.

Masking   When a usually audible sound can no longer be heard because of the presentation of another sound close to it in time.

Mel   A scale used to measure apparent pitch; the unit of that scale—a 1000-Hz tone at 40 dB has a pitch of 1,000 mels.

Minimum audible angle   The smallest amount of movement of a sound source that can be detected.

Minimum audible field   The threshold intensity of a sound stimulus presented and measured in a free field.

Minimum audible pressure   The threshold stimulus intensity for sound stimuli presented through earphones and measured at the eardrum.

Missing fundamental   When a complex sound has a fundamental frequency that is not actually present in the sound.

Monaural   Sound presentation to one ear.

Perceived duration   The length of time a sound appears to last.

Perceived location   Where in space a sound seems to come from.

Phase difference   The difference in the phase of a sound wave between the two ears caused by the different distances the sound wave has to travel to reach each ear; cue to localization of lower-frequency sounds.

Pitch   The psychological attribute of sound most closely associated with sound frequency, described by the words *high* or *low.*

Place principle Asserts that sound frequency is encoded by what *place* on the basilar membrane vibrates most to each frequency.

Precedence effect The first of a group of sounds (for example, a sound and its echoes) to arrive at the ear is the major determinant of where in space the sound source is perceived to be.

Profile analysis Detection of an intensity increment (''bump'') or other difference between complex sounds that differ in their profiles (amplitudes at the various frequencies making them up).

Reverberation A cue in determining the distance of a sound source; reverberant sound is sound that reaches the ears after having bounced off some surface.

Simultaneous masking When a sound is masked by another sound presented at the same time.

Sone A scale used to measure the apparent loudness of a sound; the unit of that scale—a tone of 1000 Hz at 40 dB has a loudness of 1 sone.

Sound shadow An area in which only sounds diffracted by the edge of the head are received by the ear, resulting in lower intensity especially for sounds of higher frequencies.

Target The sound to be detected in a masking situation.

Timbre A sound attribute associated with the harmonics or overtones of a complex sound.

Time difference The difference in the time taken by a sound wave to travel to the two ears when starting from an azimuth other than 0 or 180 deg; a cue to the direction of a low-frequency sound source.

Volley principle The theory that neural fibers fire in groups, one group of neurons firing while another group ''recharges.''

Volume The sound quality associated with the degree to which a sound fills space and seems large or small.

CHAPTER
8

Taste and Smell

The jungle man stopped and looked at the fresh gash in the tree. He touched his tongue to it. The lingering taste of metal verified that humans were near. He turned and sniffed the wind. There it was—the faint scent of two men. He could tell by the scent that they were city people. He could also tell by the message in the wind that *she* was with them.

Do you know anyone who tastes or smells this keenly? Probably not. Such accounts are common only in fiction. We humans are quite inferior to many other animals in our abilities to taste and smell; we rely more heavily on sight and hearing. Nonetheless, chemical sensitivities are important in many ways. The flavor of your favorite dessert, the acrid taste of a broken aspirin on your tongue, the smell of fresh coffee, cut grass, or roses, all evoke intense feelings and guide our behaviors in many ways.

More important than aesthetics, chemical senses serve a survival function. A reasonable rule of thumb, at least for natural substances, is that things that taste bad are likely to be harmful, indigestible, or poisonous, whereas things that taste good are apt to be digestible and contain substances the body can metabolize. When you eat a hot pepper, you usually experience a "burning" sensation in addition to (or masking completely) the flavor of the pepper. Some cultures, such as Mexican, Indian, or Szechwan, use this effect as a major flavor ingredient, and most people, whatever their native culture, appreciate "hot" foods. In this, humans are unique in the animal kingdom in ignoring the warnings (the burning sensation) of the *common chemical sense* and continuing to ingest, even finding enjoyable, foods that burn (Rozin, Ebert & Schull, 1982).

Smell has similar survival functions, since foul odors often signify danger in the sense of putrefied or spoiled substances that are no longer safely edible. Smell also helps the species survive by conveying sexual and social information. Although often we are not consciously aware that we are responding to smells, even in humans some odors serve to identify individuals and to convey information between members of our species.

THE GUSTATORY (TASTE) SENSE

Presumably, life began in the giant bowl of chemical soup that we call the sea. Various substances suspended or dissolved in water were important to the survival of primitive living things. Some substances provided food, some gave warning, some caused destruction. The most primitive, one-celled organisms clearly could not use anything like visual or auditory sensory systems, which require large numbers of specialized cells. They relied on chemical or mechanical interactions with their environment mediated by the cell's outer membrane. This was the first primitive "sensory system" used by living things. As life evolved, multicelled animals could afford a "division of labor" among the many cells composing their bodies. Specialized cells were grouped together to pick up chemical information from the surroundings. For example, fish have pits lined with cells responsive to a variety of chemical and mechanical stimuli. Insects and other invertebrates have such cells located on their antennae.

Although two anatomically separate systems developed, in the sea there was little differentiation between taste and smell. All important chemical stimuli were dissolved or suspended in the same substance, water. When life moved on to land, the two existing chemical receptor systems came to serve different functions. The taste system became a "close-up" sense, which provided the last check on the acceptability of food. Smell turned out to be useful as a distance sense, although it also retained an important function in dealing with food (see Rozin, 1982; and later in this chapter).

Taste Stimuli

The physical stimuli for the taste system are substances that can be dissolved in water, although the extent to which they can be dissolved in lipids (fats) may be more important to how they taste (Gardner, 1979). As is usual for physical stimuli, the amount of a chemical substance present is related to the intensity of the taste we experience.

However, which property (or collection of properties) gives rise to the various different taste qualities is still unknown in detail. There are several possibilities, such as the size of the individual molecules of the substance, how the molecule breaks apart when it is dissolved in water, or how the molecule interacts with cell membranes. Unfortunately, just which aspects of a stimulating substance cause its characteristic taste will be known only when we agree on the basic dimensions of taste (cf. Erickson, 1985).

There is general agreement that there are at least four primary taste qualities: *sweet, salty, sour, and bitter*. These taste qualities are associated with some general types of molecules. A sweet taste is generally associated with so-called organic molecules, which are made up mostly of carbon, hydrogen, and oxygen in different combinations. These organic molecules are commonly called sugars, alcohols, and so forth. Other sweet substances, like saccharin, are also organic chemicals, but they are quite different from ''natural'' sweeteners, such as sugars, in their molecular structure. Many sweet-tasting substances have a particular structure in common, termed the **AB,H system,** that consists of two negatively charged atoms (represented by the letters *A* and *B*) and a positively charged hydrogen atom (*H*) arranged in a special way. It is thought that this molecular structure selectively interacts with special parts of some taste receptors to cause them to respond (see Bartoshuk, 1979).

Bitter taste is closely related to sweet taste. Many substances that taste sweet in small amounts taste bitter in large amounts (e.g., saccharin). Also, a number of chemicals containing nitrogen (such as strychnine, caffeine, quinine, and nicotine) taste bitter. The relationship between sweet and bitter is further strengthened by the fact that bitter-tasting molecules also often contain an AB,H system. In bitter substances, however, the components have a different spatial arrangement than they do in sugars.

A salty taste is elicited by molecules that, when dissolved in water, break into two electrically charged parts called *ions*. For example, common table salt is composed of two atoms, one sodium (Na) and one chlorine (Cl). When dissolved in water, the atoms break apart. The sodium atom is now a positively charged ion, and the chlorine atom is a negatively charged ion. The ratio of the weights of these positively and negatively charged ions may be related to how salty a substance tastes. When the ratio is relatively low, substances taste salty. A high ratio is associated with substances that taste bitter (see Wyburn, Pickford & Hurst, 1964). In very low concentrations, salts tend to taste sweet.

Sour substances also break into two parts when in solution, but they are usually acids (such as hydrochloric, sulfuric, acetic, and nitric) rather than salts. In all these substances, hydrogen is the positively charged ion. The behavior of the hydrogen seems to be directly related to the sourness of such acids, but other properties must also be important because most acids taste sweet or bitter instead of sour. Thus, although we can relate some aspects of chemical stimuli to the tastes they produce, this relationship is not simple. Any given taste is probably the result of the interaction of several different properties of the physical stimulus with the properties of the receptor cells (see Faurion, Saito & MacLeod, 1980).

Taste Receptors

The tongue is covered with little bumps called **papillae.** The major receptors for taste are groups of cells called **taste buds** that are found in three types of papillae (see Figure 8-1). *Fungiform papillae* are shaped like little mushrooms *(fungi)* and are found at the tip and the sides of the tongue. *Foliate papillae* make up a series of folds *(folia)* along the sides of the rear portion of the tongue. *Cirumvallate papillae* are shaped like a flattened hill with a circular trench or valley surrounding it and are located at the back of the tongue. The *filiform papillae* are shaped like rough, tapered arrowheads or blades of grass. Filiform papillae contain no taste buds, but serve the purpose of abrading the food into smaller bits that will dissolve more easily. There are also some taste receptors scattered over

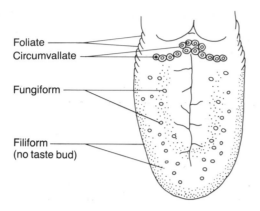

Foliate
Circumvallate

Fungiform

Filiform
(no taste bud)

FIGURE 8-1   A diagram of the human tongue showing the locations of the different types of papillae.

10,000 taste buds in your mouth when you are young, although their number decreases with age.

Within each taste bud, the individual cells are continually developing. Each cell has a life span of only a few days, so that the composition of the taste bud is always changing, with some immature cells (around the outside), some mature cells (near the inside), and some dying cells always present (Beidler & Smallman, 1965). No one knows why these cells have such a short life span; perhaps it is because they are somehow damaged when they respond to substances in the mouth. Each taste cell in the taste bud is leaflike and resembles a skin cell (from which it probably evolved). A slender projection from the top end of each cell lies near an opening onto the surface of the tongue called a **taste pore.** It is thought that the actual reception mechanism for taste is located in these slender processes (called *microvillae*).

parts of the mouth other than the tongue, such as on the *soft palate* (which is the back portion of the roof of your mouth). Figure 8-2A shows how the taste buds are distributed within a circumvallate papilla. Each taste bud consists of several receptor cells (perhaps up to 30) arranged like the closed petals of a flower (Figure 8-2B). There are about

A number of theories have been proposed for how the receptors interact with the stimulating molecules to generate the electrical current that ultimately results in action potentials in the taste nerves (see Teeter & Brand, 1987, for a review). There are probably several transduction mecha-

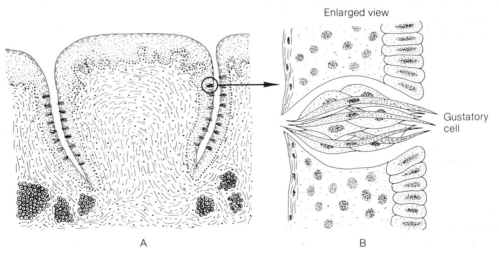

Enlarged view

Gustatory
cell

A

B

FIGURE 8-2   (A) A typical papilla with taste buds (one is circled); (B) enlarged picture of a single taste bud. (From Wyburn et al., 1964)

nisms, perhaps different ones for different classes of taste stimuli. In one proposed mechanism, salt ions, such as sodium or lithium, directly penetrate the cell membrane of the microvillae, causing electrical current to flow across the membrane. Another theory suggests that reversible chemical bonds form between specific parts of the taste stimulus molecule (e.g., the AB,H system) and receptor molecules in the cell membrane. These bonds, either directly or through causing chemical reactions inside the receptor cell, change the flow of ions across the cell membrane, thus generating an electrical current. Finally, it is possible that some taste stimulus molecules alter the electrical properties of the cell membrane itself, causing an electrical current. In all of these mechanisms, the final result is the release of a neurotransmitter across the synapse of the receptor cell with the taste nerve cell, causing spike potentials to travel up the taste nerves (see the Appendix for more about spike potentials).

Neural Responses in Taste

Three large nerves (the *chorda tympani, vagus,* and *glossopharyngeal*) carry fibers from the taste buds. They run from the tongue to the several nuclei in the **solitary tract,** which is located in the medulla (the place where the spinal chord widens to form the brainstem). In addition, there is information carried from the *common chemical sense.* In humans this consists mostly of the *trigeminal nerve* of the head and its various nerve endings in the mouth and nasal cavity. The common chemical sense responds to a wide variety of different stimuli, including and of particular interest to humans several popular spices such as peppers and ginger (see Silver, 1987).

From the nuclei in the solitary tract, taste information is carried via a set of pathways called the **medial lemniscus** to the taste center of the **thalamus,** which is situated at the top, rear, central portion *(ventral posterior nuclei)* of the thalamus. The thalamic taste area projects to three areas in the brain. Two are regions at the base of the primary somatosensory cortex (near where information from touch for the face is projected) and the third is the **anterior-insular cortex,** which is a part of the frontal cortex under the front end of the temporal cortex.

As in vision and audition, most of our knowledge of the electrical activity of the taste system has come from studies of nonhuman animals. A variety of studies has shown that taste fibers respond to increasing intensity (concentration) of the stimulus by increasing their overall rate of firing. One of the few studies that actually used human subjects for direct recording (Diamant, Funakoshi, Strom & Zotterman, 1963) capitalized on the fact that taste pathways from the front of the tongue must be cut during a certain kind of ear operation. Electrical activity in response to taste stimuli was recorded from this nerve during the operation. The data from these patients show that the amount of neural response grows as the logarithm of the intensity of the stimulus (in this case, table salt), much like the responses in vision and audition to increasing stimulus intensity (see Chapters 3 and 6). As in most modalities, the neural code for intensity seems to be the overall amount of firing of all the sensory fibers.

How is taste *quality* encoded? At first it was thought that there would prove to be "sweet receptors" and "salt receptors," and so forth, one for each taste quality, perhaps even corresponding to the different categories of papillae. However, most receptor cells seem to respond to all of the four basic kinds of taste stimuli although at different rates (Arvidson & Friberg, 1980; Kimura & Beidler, 1961). This seems appropriate given the different transducer mechanisms described above. The same sort of responsiveness to most stimulus types has been found in the solitary nucleus mentioned above and in the thalamus as well (Doetsch, Ganchrow, Nelson & Erickson, 1969; Scott & Erickson, 1971).

Actually, there is no theoretical need for specialized taste receptors as long as the various neural units have different stimulus-specific response rates. If this condition is met, then the code for taste quality could be an **across-fiber pattern** of neural activity (Erickson, 1985; Erickson & Schiffman, 1975; Pfaffman, 1955). Figure 8-3 shows how this might work. Notice that although all of the fibers respond to all taste inputs to some extent, the pattern of firing across the four diagramed fibers is different for each quality. Thus for a sugar stimulus (S), we find fiber *A* responding vigorously, *B* moderately, and *C* and *D* only weakly. For salt (NaCl), *A* and *D* respond weakly, whereas *B* responds strongly and *C* nearly as vigorously. Erickson (1963) was able to show such distinct across-fiber pattern differences. These patterns become somewhat less distinct in the thalamus (Doetsch et al., 1969; Scott & Erickson, 1971).

Although there do not seem to be taste receptors that respond only to one of the four basic taste qualities, different gustatory nerve fibers do seem to be "tuned" to certain taste stimuli, much as auditory nerve fibers are tuned to certain frequencies of sound (see Chapter 6). Such fibers respond most vigorously to their "best" substances and less vigorously to others. Eventually, it may be possible to classify such fibers into a few classes, corresponding to the basic taste qualities (Frank, 1975, 1985; Pfaffman, Frank & Norgren, 1979). The response patterns shown in Figure 8-3 could thus also be interpreted as those characteristic of such tuned fiber types. On the basis of such data, Pfaffman (1974) proposed the **labeled-line theory** of taste quality encoding. The basic idea is that each taste fiber encodes the intensity of a single basic taste quality, that associated with its best stimulus. To the extent that a stimulus activates the "sweet" fibers, it tastes sweet; to the extent it activates the

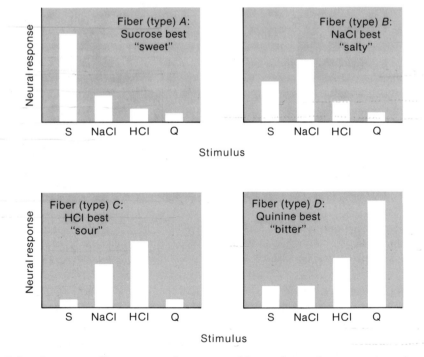

FIGURE 8-3 Using the across-fiber pattern theory, consider each graph to represent the response of a unique taste fiber to the various stimuli. Using the labeled-line theory, consider each graph to represent the average response of a group of more-or-less equivalent taste fibers.

"bitter" fibers, it tastes bitter. This means that "simple" stimuli such as NaCl could have a complex taste if they activated several types of fibers, and this seems to happen. For example, salts tend to taste both salty and sour (Bartoshuk, 1978). This theory is compatible with the across-fiber pattern approach, except that here the code for taste quality is a profile across a few fiber types rather than a pattern across many thousands of unique fibers (see also Scott, 1987; Smith, 1985).

Although it is unknown whether labeled-lines exist along the entire taste pathway, cortical neurons most responsive to the four basic tastes do seem to be localized in different parts of the taste cortex (Yamamoto, Yayama & Kawamura, 1981). Furthermore, it is likely that some recoding of the taste information takes place in the cortex. There may be specific cortical cells that give an "on" response to some taste stimuli and an "off" response to others, similar to the feature-specific cells in the visual cortex discussed in Chapter 3 (Funakoshi, Kasahara, Yamamoto & Kawamura, 1972).

Taste Thresholds

What are the limits of a human's sensitivity to taste? It is difficult to study the thresholds for taste stimuli, since there are so many different stimuli to consider. Also, we find that thresholds vary with the viscosity of the mixture to be tasted (Paulus & Haas, 1980) or with its temperature (Paulus & Reisch, 1980). The study is further complicated by the fact that the various parts of the tongue and mouth are not equally sensitive to different stimuli.

Let us begin by seeing how we can measure physically the amount of a taste stimulus present at any moment. Although there is some debate on the appropriate measurement procedures for taste stimuli, one useful measure is the **molar concentration** of a substance (Pfaffman, Bartoshuk & McBurney, 1971). Molar concentration is based on the weight of a substance dissolved in a given amount of a solvent (usually water when we deal with taste). A solution is said to have a concentration of 1 *mole*

if the molecular weight of the substance (in grams) is added to enough water to make one liter of solution. Different solutions with the same molar concentrations have the same number of stimulus molecules in a given volume of liquid.

Once we have decided how to specify the stimulus concentrations, we can begin to measure thresholds. We must be careful to note, however, that the region of the mouth or tongue stimulated also affects our sensitivity. For many years it was thought that the back of the tongue was especially sensitive to bitter taste, the front more sensitive to sweet and salty stimuli, and the sides of the rear most sensitive to sour stimuli. Work by Collings (1974) altered this picture. She used as a stimulus a tiny piece of filter paper that had been soaked in a stimulus solution. This gave precise control over the location of the stimulus on the tongue. Figure 8-4 shows a summary of her results for four differ-

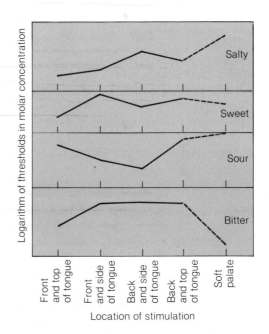

FIGURE 8-4   Average absolute thresholds for four different taste stimuli at four locations on the tongue and at a location on the soft palate. (Based on Collings, 1974)

ent parts of the tongue and the soft palate. For the bitter substance the lowest threshold on the tongue is at the front. For this substance, however, an even lower threshold occurs on the palate. The tip and back of the tongue are most sensitive to sweet, whereas the front and sides are most sensitive to salt. There is also differential sensitivity of parts of the mouth to "hot" tastes, such as those associated with chili peppers. Demonstration Box 8-1 helps you explore these differences.

Individuals often differ in marked ways in their sensitivity to certain tastes. This was shown in a study by Blakeslee and Salmon (1935), who tested the taste thresholds for 47 people using 17 different substances. Figure 8-5 summarizes some of their results. Most substances, such as table salt or saccharin, have a narrow range of thresholds for different people. For others, however, such as vanillin or **PTC** (phenylthiocarbamide), large individual differences in sensitivity exist. These latter two substances are interesting because some people are apparently "taste-blind" to them. That is, at ordinary concentrations some people cannot taste these substances at all. PTC produces a bitter taste for those who are sensitive to it, but many can't taste it even at high concentrations. If the stimulus is intense enough, however, even the taste-blind can taste PTC, as Figure 8-5 shows. One similarity between taste blindness for PTC and color blindness (discussed in Chapter 5) is that both appear to have a genetic component and tend to run in families.

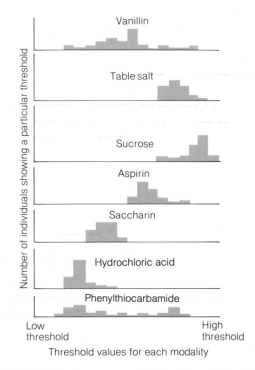

FIGURE 8-5   Frequency distributions of absolute thresholds of 47 observers to various taste stimuli. Phenylthiocarbamide (PTC) and vanillin have particularly wide ranges of thresholds, and PTC clearly shows two modes—tasters with low thresholds and nontasters with high thresholds. (Based on Blakeslee & Salmon, 1935)

DEMONSTRATION BOX 8-1.   Variations in Taste Sensitivity

Although you have all probably experienced spicy hot foods on numerous occasions, you may not know that sensitivity to hot spices varies over the mouth. For example, the tip of the tongue is most sensitive to red and black peppers, and the anterior (hard) palate and cheek are least sensitive (Lawless & Stevens, 1988). You could demonstrate this for yourself by placing several drops of Tabasco sauce or Louisiana style hot sauce (both of which contain hot red peppers) on the tip of a cotton swab or a bit of paper napkin twirled around a pencil or toothpick. Touch this "taste stimulator" to different parts of your mouth and tongue, and notice how the sensations differ in strength for different locations.

You might be surprised to learn that another substance associated with taste blindness is caffeine, the stimulant found in coffee (Hall, Bartoshuk, Cain & Stevens, 1975). For caffeine, the taster and nontaster groups are not as distinct as they are for PTC, but the range of thresholds is still quite large and two groups clearly appear. Furthermore, tasters of PTC tend to be tasters of caffeine and vice versa, indicating that a common mechanism may be responsible for this threshold variation. This is not simply a general "bitter" taste mechanism, for in the same study Hall et al. (1975) found that thresholds to two other bitter-tasting substances were unrelated to thresholds for PTC and caffeine. Similar results have been found for the bitter and sweet tastes of saccharin (Bartoshuk, 1979). In general, the attempt to explain such cases of taste blindness by attributing them to deficiencies in some particular taste system (as is often possible for color blindness) has not succeeded very well.

Taste Adaptation

Taste thresholds can also be affected by stimuli that have reached the tongue prior to the threshold test. The taste system adapts very readily to continued stimulation of the same type, and this adaptation temporarily raises the absolute threshold for the particular substance to which it has been adapted. Figure 8-6 shows an example of the effects of previous stimulation on absolute threshold. Here both the adapting stimulus and the test stimulus were table salt (NaCl). As you can see from the figure, the absolute threshold varied both with how long the tongue had been exposed to the adapting stimulus and the strength of the stimulus (Hahn, 1934; O'Mahony, 1979). Similar results can be demonstrated for the effects of adaptation on sensory intensity (Gent, 1979). This sort of adaptation explains why at dinner some people resalt their food again and again. As they eat, they adapt to the salty taste and come to need more salt to experience the taste at the same level. You can avoid

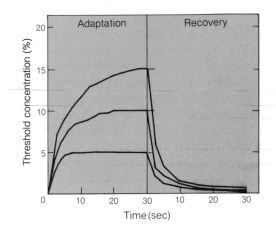

FIGURE 8-6   Adaptation and recovery from adaptation to continued stimulation of the tongue with table salt (NaCl). The three curves represent three different adapting concentrations. The time axis represents the amount of exposure to the adapting concentration, or recovery time, before determination of absolute threshold. Note the resemblance to dark adaptation curves (see Chapter 4). (Based on Hahn, 1934)

resalting your food if you eat something that is not salty between bites of salty food (see Halpern & Meiselman, 1980). As Figure 8-6 shows, recovery from adaptation is virtually complete in about 10 sec, no matter how much salt was eaten previously.

Adaptation to one substance can also have an effect on the threshold for (and the subsequent taste of) different substances. This is called **cross-adaptation.** For example, adaptation to one salt will raise the threshold to other salts. Similarly, exposure to a sour substance will raise the threshold to other sour stimuli. In some cases, exposure of the tongue to one stimulus may actually *lower* the threshold to another taste stimulus (or make its taste more intense). This special case of cross-adaptation is called **potentiation.** Thus, adaptation to an acid, while reducing the sourness of another acid may increase the sweetness of a sugar. Adaptation to urea (the bitter substance contained in human urine) will increase the intensity of salty sensations (McBurney, 1969). Perhaps the most striking phenomenon associated with cross-adaptation is the variability of the taste of ordinary tap water with adaptation to various substances. In fact, all four of the basic tastes can be induced in water by previous adaptation to a suitable taste stimulus (McBurney & Bartoshuk, 1972). Interestingly, "off" responses to pure water have been recorded in the human chorda tympani nerve (Oakley, 1985); such neural responses may partly mediate our experience of the taste of water. You can experience these tastes for yourself by trying Demonstration Box 8-2.

Taste Intensity and Qualities

Our ability to discriminate intensity differences in taste, regardless of the stimulus tested, is really quite poor. The Weber fraction (which measures the fractional amount by which two stimuli must differ for them to be discriminated as being different, as we discussed in Chapter 2) ranges from a relatively poor 1/10 to an awful 1/1, making taste the least sensitive of the senses by this criterion (Pfaffman et al., 1971).

To see how the sensation of taste grows as we increase the stimulus intensity, a number of investigators have used the magnitude estimation technique discussed in Chapter 2. In general, they have found that the sensation increase is described by a typical power function of the form $S = aI^n$, where S is the sensation, I is the intensity of the stimulus, a is a constant, and n indicates the rate at which the sensation increases. The exponent n is usually approximately 1 (i.e., for table salt it is 0.91, for quinine hydrochloride it is 0.85, for hydrochloric acid it is 0.99, and for sucrose it is 0.93) (Meiselman, Bose & Nykvist, 1972; Norwich, 1984). An exponent of 1 means that sensation grows linearly with stimulus intensity, that is, changes in stimulus intensity of the same size cause changes in sensation intensity of the same size no matter how intense the stimulus. Contrast this with vision and hearing, where the corresponding exponents are less than 1 and changes in weaker stimuli are perceived as greater than changes in more intense stimuli. An important caution here is that we must be careful to specify exactly the conditions under which such exponents are measured, for they are greatly affected by adaptation. For example, O'Mahony and Heintz (1981) found an exponent for NaCl of only about 0.7 under conditions some-

---

DEMONSTRATION BOX 8-2.   The Taste of Water

Water has a distinctive taste, especially when you have been eating or drinking some other substance before you taste the water. In this demonstration, you will be able to make water taste sweet, bitter, sour, or salty. Although you may not be able to (or want to) try all of the demonstrations, be assured that all of them work under the carefully controlled conditions of the laboratory (Bartoshuk, 1974).

The most pleasant of the demonstrations requires that you eat a few cooked artichokes of any variety (canned, fresh, or frozen) and then taste a sip of water. Be sure to thoroughly mash the artichoke onto your tongue and palate while eating it. Water tasted after eating the artichoke usually tastes sweet. Another way to obtain the sweet taste is to swish a mouthful of strong (caffeinated) coffee on the tongue for 30 sec before tasting tap water. To make water taste bitter or sour, take some very salty water and swish it around in your mouth for 30 sec and then spit it out. Afterward, taste some tap water. Something that has been tried in the laboratory but that you may not want to try is to swish some urea (a major component of urine) on the tongue for 30 sec. Tap water tasted after this treatment tastes salty.

what different from those used by other investigators (see also Meiselman et al., 1972).

Several studies have compared the changes in the rate of neural response with changes in stimulus intensity to the psychophysical data. They have shown that the two types of response vary with stimulus intensity in a similar fashion (Borg, Diamant, Oakley, Strom & Zotterman, 1967; Diamant & Zotterman, 1969). It seems likely that our sensation of the intensity of a taste is directly related to the overall amount of neural activity evoked by the stimulus, which in turn depends on the intensity (molar concentration) of the stimulus (see Norwich, 1984, for a theoretical discussion of this relationship). However, the situation is rather complex since our sensation of the intensity of any one taste stimulus may be affected by the presence of other taste stimuli. Demonstration Box 8-3 provides one way you can explore this complex interaction between tastes.

Modern psychophysical scaling techniques have also been used to look at the relationships among taste *qualities*. In 1916, Henning proposed that we could specify the qualities of all tastes using a specially shaped three-dimensional geometrical space,

in much the same way we specified colors in Chapter 5. He proposed that this space would be in the form of a pyramid, with the primary tastes at the corners. Intermediate tastes would be represented by points on the surface of (or within) this space, which is shown in Figure 8-7A. Schiffman and Erickson (1971) used a sophisticated mathematical technique to test whether this notion actually describes the way people perceive taste stimuli. The technique is based on the judged similarity between stimuli. Using a procedure called *multidimensional scaling,* observers' similarity judgments can be converted into a set of distances between points in a geometric space with the smallest possible number of dimensions. Figure 8-7B shows their results. Notice that Henning's taste pyramid fits reasonably well into this space. This has been verified in another study using a larger set of stimuli (Schiffman & Dackis, 1975).

Such techniques have also been used to explore the relationships between the tastes of more similar substances, such as sodium salts (Schiffman, McElroy & Erickson, 1980) and sweeteners (Schiffman, Reilly & Clark, 1979), and to try to discover the physical and psychological properties

---

DEMONSTRATION BOX 8-3. Putting Out the Fire

You may have had the experience of putting too much pepper or other hot spice in your mouth and finding the burning too much to bear. Or you may have been prevented from eating some tasty dish because it was "too hot." These are circumstances in which you want to reduce the intensity of sensations arising from stimulation of your common chemical sense. Surprisingly, the effectiveness of swishing various liquids in your mouth to put out the fire depends to some extent on how they taste (Stevens & Lawless, 1986). The most effective liquid has a sweet (e.g., soda pop) or sour (e.g., lemon or other citrus juice) taste, and is at a cool temperature. Bitter-tasting substances (e.g.,

quinine, or possibly beer) don't seem to help any more than simply waiting for the burning to cease, and salty substances are intermediate in effect. The cool temperature explains some but not all of the cooling effect, since different tastants at the same temperature have different effects. If you are daring, you might try swishing some *diluted* Tabasco sauce around in your mouth until it begins to burn and then experimenting with different quenching substances to see whether you can confirm these results. Remember to leave plenty of time between trials for the burning sensation to fade completely.

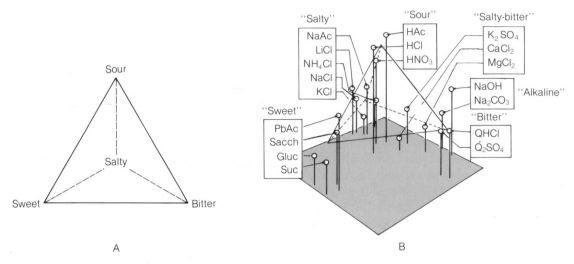

FIGURE 8-7 (A) Henning's taste pyramid. (B) Multidimensional scaling results for similarity judgments of taste stimuli. Henning's taste pyramid is superimposed on the three-dimensional space to show the correspondence. (From Schiffman and Erickson, 1971)

that underlie the similarity judgments. In general, multidimensional scaling does provide results that are consistent with the existence of the four primaries—sweet, salty, sour, and bitter, as shown in Figure 8-7—although there is some controversy about other relevant facts (see Erickson, 1985; Erickson & Covey, 1980; McBurney & Gent, 1979). It seems likely that investigators will continue to refer to four basic taste qualities because they provide a useful summary of most of our research findings in taste. However, their interpretation may change. For example, it has been suggested that each of the basic tastes should be considered to be a separate sensory modality, much as the skin senses can be separated into touch, warmth, cold, and pain (McBurney & Gent, 1979).

THE OLFACTORY (SMELL) SENSE

All of us are familiar with the sight of a dog or cat sniffing at some object, clearly processing information provided by their sense of smell. Since we never see a human being sniffing the ground to find out who had been there recently, or exploring a new room by sniffing the furniture, we tend to think that smell is unimportant; it is often referred to as a "minor" sense. Although much of our perceptual processing of odors is unconscious, our sense of smell plays a role that is far from minor. For example, it is very difficult to recall smells, or to name them, but the experience of a particular smell at a particular moment can stimulate a flood of memories of episodes in which that smell was present (Engen, 1982, 1987). These memories of our past are often rich in emotional tones. Thus, the scent of cinnamon might evoke feelings of joy associated with your mother baking apple pies, or the scent of ether might evoke the memory and fears associated with a childhood visit to the hospital.

In many common situations, smell works in conjunction with taste. When we have a bad head cold food seems flavorless, yet our nasal passages are most affected by the cold, not our mouths where the taste receptors are located. A major part of the experienced flavor of food and drink is caused by the odor of the substance (Brillat-

Savarin, 1825/1971; Hyman et al., 1979; Murphy & Cain, 1980). When our nasal passages are clogged with mucus our olfactory (smell) receptors cannot function properly. This affects our ability both to smell and to experience flavor, since much of the richness and subtlety of our experiences with food and drink come from their odors. When we cannot smell, our ability to identify foods by taste alone is significantly inferior, unfortunately for some of the most preferred foods, as Figure 8-8 shows. And this happens often. In an informal survey conducted by *National Geographic* magazine, it was found that over two-thirds of the analyzed returns reported occasional loss of the sense of smell, many of them quite often (e.g., every time a head cold occurred) (Gilbert & Wysocki, 1987). Many people over 70 years of age also experience major loss of the smell sense (Gilbert & Wysocki, 1987; Rabin & Cain, 1986) with similiar consequences for the experience of flavor (see Chapter 16). Demonstration Box 8-4 allows you to experience this for yourself in a controlled way (i.e., you don't have to wait for a head cold).

Actually, smell acts as if it has two separate modes of action that may result in different perceptual experiences, and different forms of information extraction (e.g., Rozin, 1978). One mode, which we have already mentioned, is associated with the experience of the flavors of food. The second is as a distance sense, responding to molecules that float about in the air carrying information about the objects or organisms from which they have become detached. For instance, we leave molecules of ourselves on the ground and in the air near the ground whenever we take a walk. Insects and some higher animals secrete volatile chemicals (*pheromones*) whose molecules waft through the air to other members of the species. The specific molecules secreted can carry messages about fear and sexual availability, among other things. Species that possess sensory systems that respond to these low concentrations of molecules in the air can take advantage of this information, hence improving their ability to survive (see Gibbons, 1986, for a popular review). It is interesting to note that there are times when the "distant smell" and "food

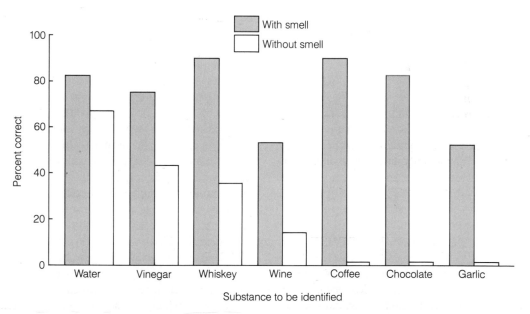

FIGURE 8-8   Identification of some common foods with and without smell. (Based on Mozel et al., 1969)

DEMONSTRATION BOX 8-4.   Flavor without Smell

The simplest way to experience flavor without smell is to pinch your nostrils closed before coming close to the substance to be tasted, and then put some of that substance into your mouth and swish it around while paying attention to its flavor. Then release your nostrils, open your mouth slightly, and breathe in gently through both mouth and nose. You should experience a significant change in the flavor when you do this. Try it for the various substances listed in Figure 8-8 and any others you can think of. Your experiences with nose pinched approximate those of elderly people who have experienced large deficits in their sense of smell.

It is rather easy to show that food identification is impaired when the sense of smell is absent. You simply need to get a friend to help you. First prepare several different substances to be identified—the ones listed in Figure 8-8 will do. They should be in a liquid state (i.e., mash up the garlic and mix it with water). Then seat your friend at some distance from the solutions and blindfold him or her. For each substance, first ask him to pinch his nose and when he has done that, put some of the solution in his mouth and ask for its name. After he has tried that, tell him to release his nostrils and again attempt to name the substance. Repeat this for each substance, and several friends if you can, and see how closely the results match those of Figure 8-8.

---

smell'' functions give different perceptual experiences. For instance, Limburger cheese has a long-distance smell that is quite strong and, most people think, offensive, but whose ''smell'' when in the mouth contributes in a positive way to the flavor of the cheese, which many people find quite pleasing.

Smell Stimuli and Receptors

Which aspects of a molecule give it the quality of evoking the sensation of smell? First, it must come from a volatile substance (one that has a gaseous state at ordinary temperatures—in other words, something that can evaporate), since air currents carry the molecules to the smell receptors in the nose. However, the most volatile substances do not necessarily smell the strongest. Water, which has a high volatility, has no smell at all (if it is pure). In fact, the extent to which a smell stimulus separates itself chemically from water (hydrophobicity) is highly correlated with the perceived intensity of that stimulus (Greenberg, 1981). Conversely, musk (a secretion obtained from some deer and beavers) has a low volatility, yet it is a very powerful odor-

ant and is used in making some of our most expensive perfumes.

In general, any molecule may be described as having a specific size, weight, shape, and vibration frequency. This last property has to do with the fact that atoms in a given molecule often are not held firmly in place but move around in a characteristic pattern, at predictable speeds that are different for different substances (Wright, 1977, 1982). In addition, the particular atoms that make up a molecule, and the number of electrons available for chemical bonding with other molecules on the smell receptors, are probably important components of smell stimuli. As yet there is no consensus as to which of these factors is critical; given the large number of molecules that can be smelled, it is likely that several of them are important.

The receptor cells that interact with the smell stimuli are located in a relatively small area in the upper nasal passages (see Figure 8-9) called the **olfactory epithelium,** which translates to ''smell skin.'' The actual receptor cells are oval in shape. Each sends a long extension (called the **olfactory rod)** toward the surface of the olfactory epithelium,

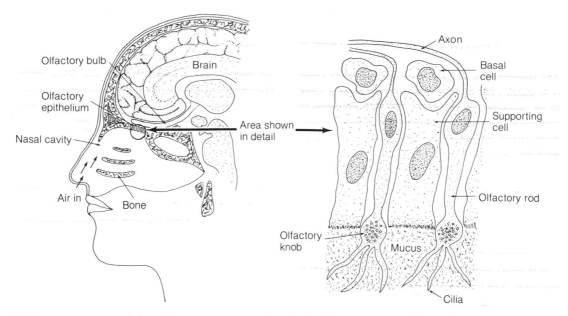

FIGURE 8-9   Anatomy of the olfactory system and a detail of the structure of the olfactory epithelium.

and in addition sends its axons toward the brain. Thus, the receptors are actually specialized neurons. Remarkably, the receptor cells only function for about four to eight weeks before deteriorating; new cells are continually being produced by the basal cells (see Figure 8-9 and Costanzo & Graziadei 1987). These are one of the few types of neuron in adult mammals that can regenerate.

The olfactory rod of the receptor cell reaches up toward the surface of the epithelium, where it expands to form a knob. From this knob protrude a number of **olfactory cilia,** which are hairlike structures embedded in mucus secreted by a set of special glands found nowhere else in the nasal passages. These cilia are probably the receptor elements that actually make contact with the smell stimulus (Cagen & Rhein, 1980). Both the number of cilia per receptor and the total number of receptors seem to be correlated with olfactory sensitivity. Animals that have more receptors and more cilia per receptor have keener senses of smell. Humans are at the lower end of the scale of smell

sensitivity. For example, a dog has about 200 million olfactory receptors as opposed to only about 10 million in humans. Also a dog has 100–150 cilia per receptor as opposed to a paltry 6–8 cilia in humans (Brown, 1975).

As is the case with the other senses, the mechanism by which the stimulus molecules cause an electrical response in the receptors of the olfactory epithelium is still something of a mystery. There are probably at least two classes of transduction mechanisms (Gesteland, 1986; see also Getchell & Getchell, 1987). One is made up of highly selective processes in which specific receptor-cell proteins form reversible chemical bonds with specific parts of odorant molecules. These then trigger generator potentials either directly or through other biochemical processes inside the cell. The generator potentials of course produce the action potentials that travel up the axons of the receptor cells. Notice that in this theoretical formulation the specific receptors are *specialists* for a specific odorant. Such selective processes may be distributed unevenly over the epithelium as well as being located on specific parts of the cilia. The second class of mechanism consists of less selective processes, in which various chemicals directly affect the receptor cell membrane anywhere they contact it, causing ions to leak in or out, thus producing generator potentials. These processes are the same for all receptor cells and may constitute what may be called *generalist* smell receptors. Some insects seem to possess both specialist and generalist receptors in their olfactory system (D. Schneider, 1969), and it is likely that mammals do too.

Two particular theories of the more selective mechanisms have been popular among psychologists. The **lock-and-key theory** maintains that variously shaped molecules fit into special sites on the receptor membrane like a key into a lock. When a molecule fits into a receptor site, a change in the structure of the cell membrane results, allowing ions into or out of the cell and generating an electrical current (Amoore, 1970). The **vibration theory** maintains that the stimulus molecule ruptures certain chemical bonds in the cell membrane, causing the release of stored-up energy, which in turn generates an electrical current. Which bonds are ruptured in which cells depends on the unique vibration frequency of each stimulus molecule (Wright, 1977, 1982).

Neural Responses in Smell

The olfactory receptor cells send their axons through tiny holes in a bone at the top of the nasal cavity to form the **olfactory nerve.** The nerve goes straight to the **olfactory bulb,** which is located in front of and below the main mass of the brain (see Figure 8-9). The axons of the receptors and the dendrites of cells from the olfactory bulb form complex clusters of connections in the bulb. These clusters may be grouped according to the type of receptor or type of stimulus molecule involved (Kauer, 1980, 1987). One type of olfactory bulb cell seems to send axons directly to the primary sensory cortex for smell, which is located in the temporal lobe of the cortex. Another type of cell sends axons to a variety of lower brain centers, especially the limbic system (which is involved in our experience of emotion and memory), as well as to the smell cortex. The number of fibers leaving the olfactory bulb is *much* smaller (about a thousand times smaller) than the number entering it, so presumably many receptor cells contribute to the activity of each of the cells in the olfactory bulb and later centers (Allison, 1953). The major route of information from the olfactory bulb to the smell cortex is called the **lateral olfactory tract.** After the primary smell cortex the neural pathways become extremely complex, including projections to the thalamus and several other cortical areas (see Price, 1987).

The study of the electrophysiology of the smell system is still in its infancy. As we mentioned earlier, however, a number of studies have found that the intensity of the neural response varies directly with the intensity of the stimulus. Most contemporary investigators have focused on the more subtle problem of how different smell qualities are signaled to the brain. They have tried to find evidence of specific types of receptors for different types of stimuli. One major early study was that of Ottoson (1956), who measured the electrical response of the entire olfactory epithelium to various stimuli. He discovered that passing a puff of odor-laden air across the epithelium resulted in a unique type of electrical response, a slow change in the electrical charge of the receptor cells. This change is thought to generate spike potentials in the axons of these cells.

With improved experimental techniques, Gesteland, Lettvin, Pitts, and Rojas (1963) were able to record the responses of single receptors in the olfactory epithelium. They recorded both the slow potential response to stimuli and the spike potentials generated in the axons of the receptors by the same stimuli. These two types of electrical responses are shown one on top of the other in Figure 8-10. As you can see in the figure, this particular receptor responded vigorously to a musky odor,

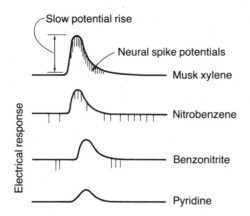

FIGURE 8-10 **Slow potential and spike potential responses of olfactory receptor cells to four different smell stimuli. (Based on Gesteland et al., 1963)**

less to nitrobenzene, hardly at all to benzonitrite, and not at all to pyridine. Gesteland et al. (1963) thought these responses indicated the existence of the sought-after receptor types, although they were cautious in making this interpretation. Such caution seems to have been well founded, since later recordings from single cells in the epithelium, olfactory bulb, and in cortical and lower brain centers that receive olfactory information have found that each neural unit responds to a broad range of stimuli (Cain & Bindra, 1972; Giachetti & MacLeod, 1975; Kauer, 1987; MacLeod, 1971; O'Connell & Mozell, 1969).

The same sort of across-fiber patterns that are found in taste seem to be present in the olfactory system, and it is likely that the "code" for smell qualities will be found in these patterns (Erickson & Schiffman, 1975; Kauer, 1987). At present there is no evidence of olfactory fibers falling into groups as the taste fibers seem to, although some investigators have proposed that receptors sensitive to the same stimuli send their axons to the same part of the olfactory bulb (see Kauer, 1987). Furthermore, a *labeled-line theory,* such as the one we discussed for taste, would be somewhat cumbersome for olfaction, requiring many more types of labeled lines

than for taste. This is due to the fact that there is no small list of primary smells for olfaction as you will see below.

Smell Thresholds

A dog's sense of smell can be amazingly acute. Droscher (1971) tells the story of a dog trainer who had worked with dogs for years. This trainer brought his dog to a university professor for testing, claiming that the dog's ability was "supernatural" since it could track people by scent even if they were wearing rubber boots! Actually, the dog was simply using its acute sense of smell to detect the millions of sweat molecules that leaked through the rubber boots. Why can't we humans smell such things? The sensitivity of each smell receptor is in fact about the same for humans and dogs. The really important difference is that a dog has many more smell receptors than a human, with more hairlike cilia projecting from each, as we mentioned earlier.

In the early 1960s, Stuiver studied the absolute sensitivity of human smell receptors by making a model of the nasal passages around the olfactory epithelium. He used this model to calculate just how much of an olfactory stimulus actually arrived at the surface of the epithelium (see Figure 8-11). When threshold stimuli were considered, he found that it takes 8 molecules at most to stimulate a single receptor in the human. Considering all aspects of the manner in which molecules of odor stimuli are distributed in the nose, it can be argued that a single receptor cell needs to be contacted by one stimulus molecule in order to respond (De Vries & Stuiver, 1961). Quite clearly this is the greatest sensitivity that any single olfactory receptor cell could have, hence a dog's (or any other animal's) receptors can't be more sensitive than a human's. Because the dog has more receptor sites, the likelihood that a very weak stimulus will actually stimulate the olfactory receptors and produce a noticeable sensation is greater for the dog (see Marshall & Moulton, 1981).

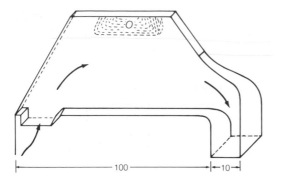

FIGURE 8-11   **A model of the nasal passage used by Stuiver to calculate the proportion of molecules in a smell stimulus that reaches the olfactory epithelium** *(O)*. **Air follows the path indicated by the arrows (measurements of distances are in mm). Stimulus molecules reach** *O* **via eddy currents (like the eddies in a stream).**
(From De Vries & Stuiver, 1961. Copyright 1961 by the MIT Press.)

More traditional attempts to determine the absolute thresholds for various odors encounter problems similar to those found when measuring taste sensitivity. Thresholds vary across methods. They seem to depend on the purity of the odorant, the way it is delivered to the olfactory epithelium, and how the stimulus intensity is measured. Different substances also have different thresholds.

In much the same way that we found individual differences in taste sensitivity, there are also individual differences in smell sensitivity (see Rabin & Cain, 1986), with some individuals relatively ''odor-blind'' to certain substances (see Engen, 1982). Amoore (1969, 1975; Amoore, Pelosi & Forrester, 1977) has reported the results of an extensive search for instances of odor blindnesses as a part of his plan to identify the primary odors. By 1975 he was able to report 76 different **anosmias** (odor blindnesses) ranging from the smell of skunk to the smell of vanilla. Some of these are quite common; for example, about 1 out of 3 individuals can not smell a strong stimulus of 1,8 cineole, which produces a camphorous odor (Pelosi & Pisanelli, 1981). Conversely, some anosmias are quite rare, as when only 4 people out of 4,030 couldn't smell a strong stimulus of n-butyl mercaptan, which has a foul, putrid odor. Amoore was able to divide these 76 anosmias into about 31 classes, each of which might represent a primary odor quality. Such specific anosmias are consistent with the idea that humans have two classes of olfactory receptors, the specialists and the generalists that we mentioned above (Wright, 1978a).

Smell Adaptation

As in most sensory systems, adaptation (from prolonged exposure to a particular stimulus) affects smell thresholds and the perceived intensity of an odor. It even affects the pleasantness of odors (Cain & Johnson, 1978). One of the great disappointments of wine tasting is that the aroma and the bouquet of the wine seem to last only for a few sniffs. The rich complexity of a great wine soon fades into a bland, featureless odor, even for the most experienced ''smeller,'' unless frequent breaks of about 15 sec are taken. Luckily, the odors of sweaty bodies and rotten eggs, and the sulfurous smell of air pollution, also soon fade away if you continue to sniff.

An important early study of adaptation of the smell sense was that of Moncrieff (1956). He studied the effects of previous exposure to an odorant on the threshold for that odorant (**self-adaptation**). He also studied how exposure to one odorant affected the threshold for different odorants (**cross-adaptation**). As you might expect, the largest loss of sensitivity was found for conditions of self-adaptation. Cross-adaptation effects varied with the similarity of the smells of the two stimuli. Stimuli with similar smells gave large cross-adaptation effects; those that differed in smell gave smaller effects. Surprisingly, all the adapting odors had some effect on observers' sensitivity for the others. This means that it was not possible to classify the various stimuli into a small number of primary classes based on adaptation data, which is similar to Amoore's conclusions based on anosmias. You can experience self- and cross-adaptation for yourself by trying Demonstration Box 8-5.

Color Plate 1

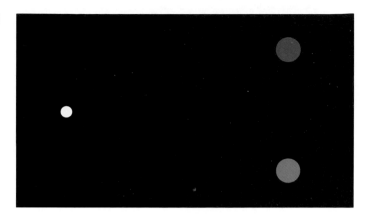

Color Plate 2

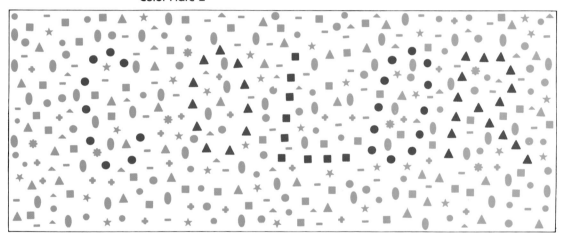

Color Plate 3

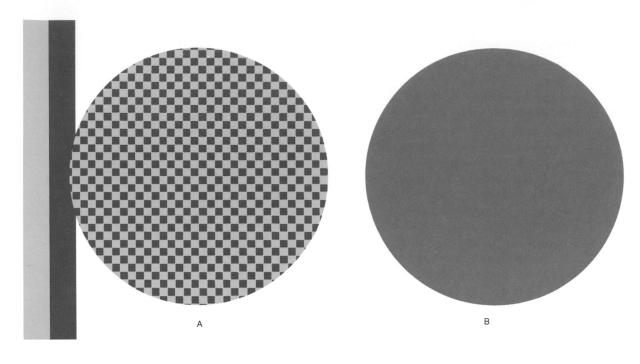

A   B

Color Plate 4

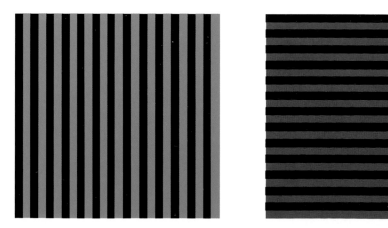

Color Plate 5

50°   40°   30°   20°   10°   0°

Color Plate 6

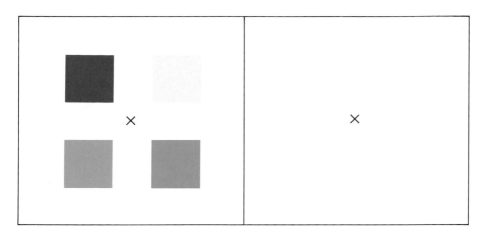

Color Plate 7

A Read through this list of color names as quickly as possible.
Read from right to left across each line.

RED	YELLOW	BLUE	GREEN
RED	GREEN	YELLOW	BLUE
YELLOW	GREEN	BLUE	RED
BLUE	RED	GREEN	YELLOW
RED	GREEN	BLUE	YELLOW

B Name each of these color patches as quickly as possible.
Name from left to right across each line.

C Name the color of ink in which each word is printed as quickly as possible.
Name from left to right across each line.

RED	BLUE	GREEN	YELLOW
YELLOW	BLUE	RED	GREEN
BLUE	YELLOW	GREEN	RED
GREEN	BLUE	YELLOW	RED
BLUE	YELLOW	RED	GREEN

Color Plate 8

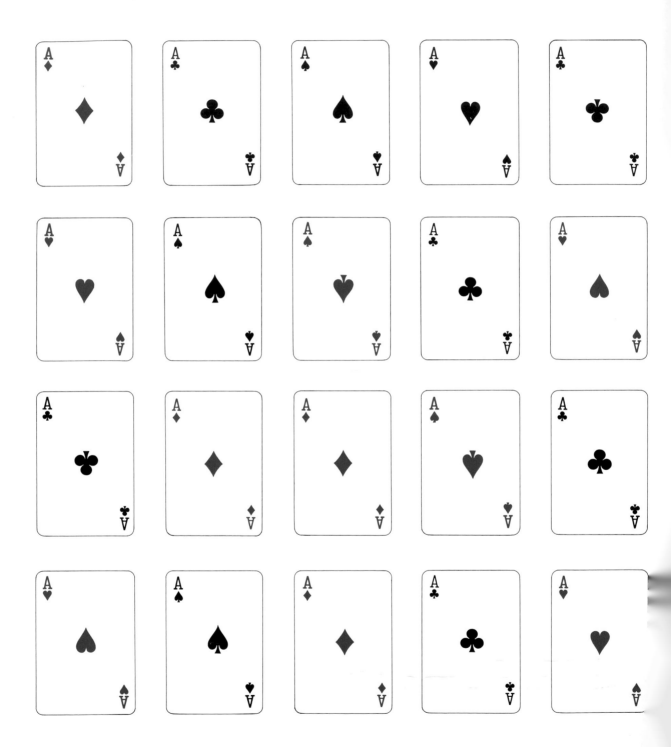

Color Plate 9

DEMONSTRATION BOX 8-5.   Smell Adaptation

You experience self-adaptation of odorants every day. The next time you notice a strong odor, take several deep sniffs and then take a more usual sniff and pay close attention to the intensity of the odor as compared to what you at first experienced. You should notice a significant decrease in sensation intensity. Alternatively, prepare yourself a cup of coffee or aromatic tea, keeping your nostrils pinched while you do. When the steaming cup is in front of you, release your nostrils and take a gentle sniff, noting the intensity of the odor. Then take several deep sniffs followed by another gentle sniff and compare the odor intensity during the final gentle sniff to that during the first gentle sniff.

It is a bit more difficult to demonstrate cross-adaptation, since the effects are weaker and not sys-

tematic. You should use your own judgment and explore a range of odorants using the general method described here. When two odorants you wish to test have been obtained, first step into another room, where you can't smell them, and take several deep sniffs. Then approach the odorants with pinched nose. Release your nostrils near the first (test) odorant, take a gentle sniff, noting the intensity of the odor. Then take several deep sniffs of the other (adapting) odorant, and return to the test odorant and take another gentle sniff. Compare the odor intensity on this sniff to the first one. If it is less intense, you have experienced cross-adaptation, if more intense you have experienced facilitation, as sometimes happens with biologically significant odors (see Engen, 1982).

Cain and Engen (1969) looked at the effects of adapting stimuli on the perceived intensity of odorants. They used a magnitude estimation procedure (such as described in Chapter 2), and found that the higher the concentration of the adapting stimulus the greater the reduction in the apparent intensity of the test stimuli presented afterward. This relationship does not hold for extreme test stimulus values, however, since *very* intense test stimuli all appeared to arouse about the same sensory response, regardless of the state of adaptation.

Smell Intensity and Qualities

When we consider how the intensity of an odor varies as stimulus intensity is varied, we again find it useful to refer to the exponent of the psychophysical power function to describe this relationship. The exponents of power functions fitted to magnitude estimations of odor intensity differ across the various odors scaled. Cain (1969) found that exponents ranged from about 0.7 to a low of about 0.15. Remember that the higher the exponent the faster the sensation increases as we increase

stimulus intensity. Cain reported that the size of the exponent is directly related to the degree of water solubility of the odorant, with exponents for completely water-soluble odorants about 2.5 times as large as those for non-water-soluble odorants. More recent work by Wright (1978b, 1978c) showed that the exponents for various odorants can be predicted from specific ways in which the odorant molecules interact with receptor cell membranes.

In *absolute* terms the sense of smell is remarkably acute, but for a long time it was thought that humans could not *discriminate* between different odor intensities very well. Most recent measurements, however, indicate that the olfactory system is actually more sensitive than the taste system in this regard. In fact, the olfactory system may be as sensitive as the visual or auditory system in discriminating changes in intensity, with Weber fractions as low as 0.05, meaning that a change in intensity of only 5 percent can be detected about half the time (Cain, 1977).

As in all of the other sensory modalities, attempts have been made to isolate a small set of "primary" smell qualities. If such could be found then all olfactory sensations could be predicted as the result of a combination of these primary responses. As we have already seen, the data from adaptation and anosmias do not suggest such a small cluster of primaries for smell. The classical attempt to describe smell primaries was that of Henning (1915). Figure 8-12 shows his "smell prism," which had six primary qualities arranged at its corners.

Although it was a standard representation of the "smell primaries" for quite some time, Henning's prism apparently does a poor job of describing the perceived relationships between odorants. When multidimensional scaling techniques are used to provide a geometrical representation of odor-similarity judgments, in much the same way as for taste judgments, neither Henning's smell prism nor any other readily identifiable classification scheme emerges. Figure 8-13 displays some representative results from this kind of study. This type of result has led some investigators (e.g., Erickson & Schiffman, 1975; Southwick & Schiffman, 1980) to speculate that only a complex set of physiochemical considerations could account for the interrelationships shown in the qualities of smell stimuli. Such results seem consistent with

Amoore's (1975) suggestion that there may be as many as 31 primary odors. Some of these particular primaries seem to be associated with receptor systems that respond to odors produced by the human body. These are the same types of odors emitted by most animals in various situations relevant to the survival of the species, such as danger and sexual contact, and humans seem to respond to this class of stimuli as well.

Sensitivity to Pheromones

Some smells have been said to have a special biological significance for humans. Around the turn of the century Ellis (1905) noticed that both men and women often emit strong odors during sexual excitement, and some researchers contend that some human behavior may be under the control of these olfactory stimuli (e.g., Comfort, 1971). Chemicals secreted by animals that transmit information to other animals (usually of the same species) are called **pheromones.** Although it has long been recognized that such olfactory signals are important for many animal species, the possibility that scents affect human behavior has been entertained only recently. As you might expect, manufacturers of colognes and perfumes, ever searching for ways to enhance the sales of their products, have immediately responded to this suggestion. In fact, a number of products are now on the market that contain *alpha androstenol,* which is known to be an effective sexual pheromone for pigs and also occurs in some human secretions.

Before we discuss the data available on humans, it will be useful to put the problem in context by describing some of the work done on other animals. Pheromones were first studied, indeed discovered and named, in insects (see Wilson, 1971). There are two major types: **releasers,** which on reception by an animal "release," or automatically trigger, a specific behavioral response; and **primers,** which trigger glandular and other physiological activities in the recipient. Most of the aspects of the lives of insects, particularly social insects

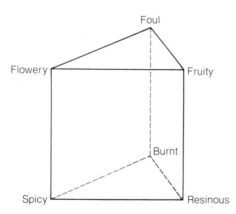

FIGURE 8-12   Henning's smell prism. Six "primary" odors are at the corners; the surfaces represent stimuli that resemble more than one primary.

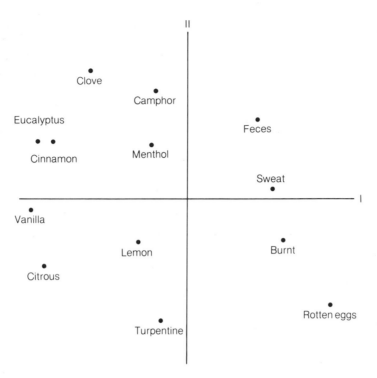

FIGURE 8-13   A composite replotting of selected odors from multidimensional scaling of similarity judgments of odor pairs (Schiffman, 1974). Dimension *I* is thought to be "pleasantness." This mapping bears little resemblance to Henning's smell prism (Figure 8-12).

like ants, bees, and termites, are regulated via communication by pheromones. Insects attract their mates, recruit fellows for food gathering or fighting, and recognize each other and their own species via releasers. Queen ants, bees, and termites control swarming, new-queen production, proportion of types of workers, and so on, using primers. The important thing to remember about insect pheromones is that usually a *specific chemical,* produced by a *specific gland,* and detected and recognized by a *specific (or specialist) receptor* is involved in such communication. Insect behavior is directly under the control of these pheromones.

Mammals, of course, are more complex animals than insects, and the effects of such olfactory stimuli are more subtle. Many pheromone-related effects have been found, however, in several spe-

cies, including rodents, dogs, and monkeys (see Brown & MacDonald, 1985a, 1985b, for a review). Mammalian releaserlike effects include the mutual recognition of mother and young offspring. Male and female sexual attraction is also affected by such scents, as is easily demonstrated by observing the effect of the odor of a female dog in heat on the male (Goodwin, Gooding & Regnier, 1979). Other pheromones elicit aggression in males, inhibit aggression in females, and are used for signaling purposes, such as trail marking or defining territorial boundaries. Primerlike effects include effects of scents on the estrous cycle of females, the age at which puberty is attained, and even the likelihood of becoming pregnant.

Some effects of pheromones have been observed in species rather close to humans on the evolutionary scale, namely monkeys. However, here the story becomes even more complex. Some early research studied the effect of vaginal secretions from female monkeys in estrus (that is, those that are sexually receptive) on the copulating behavior of males. Early work seemed to indicate that a powerful pheromone was involved. Normally, male monkeys seldom attempt to engage nonestrous females sexually. Such behavior could be elicited, however, if the females' sexual skins had been rubbed with the secretions of the sexual skins of females who were in estrus. These secretions, presumably containing pheromones, were dubbed *copulins* (Michael & Keverne, 1968; Michael, Keverne & Bonsall, 1971). Later work indicated that the suspected releaser pheromone was not as powerful as had been thought, and that monkey sexual behavior was under the control of many interacting factors, only one of which was the smell of the partner's sexual skin (Goldfoot, 1981; Goldfoot, Kravetz, Goy & Freeman, 1976; Keverne, 1978). In fact, odor cues are not necessary at all, for anosmic male monkeys show normal mating behavior (Goldfoot, Essock-Vitale, Asa, Thornton & Leshner, 1978). In all of the pheromonelike effects studied with mammals, communications delivered by chemical means, although often very important, have not been found to be as imperative as they are with insects. Mammals have more complex brains and their behavior is influenced by many different environmental factors, only one of which is odorants (see MacDonald & Brown, 1985).

When we consider humans, the behavioral effects of pheromones seem to be most subtle, since social and learning factors influence our behavior even more than they do that of other mammals. Some very interesting results, however, indicate that smells may play an important, although probably subordinate, role in many aspects of human social behavior. First, several studies (McBurney, Levine & Cavanaugh, 1977; Russell, 1976; Schleidt, Hold & Attili, 1981) have demonstrated

that people can reliably detect their own body odor from among a set of similar stimuli contributed by other people. The actual stimuli were collected by having people wear T-shirts for several days. When asked to rate the pleasantness of the body odors and to describe the individual whose odor they were smelling, there was a remarkable degree of consistency across people. In general, the shirts having unpleasant odors were usually described as if the individuals also would be likely to have socially undesirable traits. They were supposedly dumb, ugly, fat, and unhealthy. The more pleasant odors were described as coming from people with more desirable traits (McBurney et al., 1977).

People seem to be able to discriminate reliably the sex of an odor donor. In one study, the odors of males were characterized as "musky" whereas female odors were described as "sweet" (Russell, 1976); other studies have found that the stronger (and more unpleasant) odors are more likely to be attributed (correctly) to males (Doty, 1985; Doty, Green, Ram & Yankell, 1982; Doty, Kligman, Leyden & Orndorff, 1978). Similar results are found in different cultures (Schleidt et al., 1981). Males and females can also be discriminated on the basis of hand odor (Wallace, 1977) and breath odor (Doty, et al., 1982). Females do better at this (Doty et al., 1982; Wallace, 1977) and in fact do better than males at odor identification in general (Doty, Applebaum, Zusho & Settle, 1985). You can try your nose at some of these tasks using Demonstration Box 8-6.

Human sensitivity to human odors seems to be present from an early age. For instance, Russell (1976) found that a small sample of 2-week-old babies reliably responded to the odor of their own mother's breast and not to that of a strange mother; this ability may exist as early as 6 days after birth (MacFarlane, 1975). Breast-feeding babies (but not bottle-feeding babies) of the same age can also recognize their mothers' armpit odor (Cernoch & Porter, 1985). Actually, female (but not male) neonates (less than 2 days old) develop a prefer-

---

DEMONSTRATION BOX 8-6.   Social Significance of Human Odor

This demonstration is a bit complex, but is worth the effort. It is designed to see whether you or your friends can discriminate male from female body odors. The most important factor here is to eliminate the effects of perfumes and deodorants, which is difficult since almost all commercial products now contain scents. Ivory soap is one product that does not, so it is advisable to have odor-donors wash themselves with this soap before contributing the odor, or to simply soak for a period of time in clear water. The same should apply for the clothing mentioned below. The simplest experiment involves having a

group of friends put on scent-free T-shirts and wear them for at least 24 hours. At the end of the time period, put the T-shirts (with paper labels under them to indicate the sex and identity of the donor) into clean plastic bags. You now have your odor stimuli. Have each friend sniff at the opening of each bag and indicate whether the sample came from a male or a female. You might also want to have them try to guess whose T-shirt it is, and which one is their own, and you might even want to ask for a rank order in terms of pleasantness. When all have done this, tabulate the results and see how well everyone did.

---

ence for an artificial odorant simply by being exposed to it (Balogh & Porter, 1986).

One of the necessary conditions for most odor identification, at least in adults, seems to be a lot of experience with the odor and its source (Cain, 1979; Rabin & Cain, 1984). Certainly the relationship between parents and children contains much such experience. We might thus expect that parents could recognize the odors of their own offspring, and that perhaps siblings could recognize each others' odors as distinct from those of other children. This seems to be the case, raising the possibility that smell plays an important role in interactions among humans from the same family (Porter, Balogh, Cernoch & Franchi, 1986; Porter & Moore, 1981).

A second line of research with humans has been aimed at finding a sex attractant based on releaserlike pheromone action. The most promising candidate for such a substance is the substance alpha androstenol mentioned above, which causes a sow to become immobile, and thus receptive to a boar's sexual advances, when the boar secretes it in his saliva. Since alpha androstenol is also present in human apocrine (a gland in the underarm

region) sweat, it may play a role in human sexual attraction, especially since humans have been shown to reliably discriminate among axillary (underarm) odors. A few published studies have found positive effects. For example, androstenol affects ratings of various social characteristics of hypothetical applicants for a job, and affects male and female ratings differently (Cowley, Johnson & Brooksbank, 1977). Similarly, women in photographs were rated as more sexually attractive by both men and women wearing surgical masks impregnated with androstenol than by those wearing control masks (Kirk-Smith, Booth, Caroll & Davies, 1978). Finally, more women and fewer men (than in a control condition) used a seat in a dentist's waiting room that had been sprayed with androstenone (Kirk-Smith & Booth, 1980).

Such results are exciting to perfume manufacturers (and, perhaps, to the sexually deprived) but they may not be easy to interpret. Rogel (1978) critically reviewed a number of such studies along with those of monkeys, and concluded that although it is possible that olfaction does influence many aspects of social behavior, it would be wrong to believe that human behavior could be *controlled,* to the extent seen in lower mammals and insects, by such pheromones. This means that human sexual choice, contrary to the claims of some perfume manufacturers, is apt to be more a matter of higher mental processes than of primitive responses to sexual odors.

The most recent work on pheromonelike effects in humans has been more promising but less dramatic. It has been found that regular (weekly) intimate contact with a male, or even with male underarm secretions, causes the female menstrual cycle to become more regular in length (Cutler, Preti, Krieger, Huggins, Garcia & Lawley, 1986). Regular contact with other females, or with their underarm secretions, causes female menstrual cycles to become more synchronized (Preti, Cutler, Garcia, Huggins & Lawley, 1986; see also McClintock, 1971). These are primerlike effects, since they involve physiological changes and not specific behaviors. They can be important—for example, menstrual regularity is associated with healthy reproductive functioning and fertility—but they are not direct and powerful influences on human behavior.

GLOSSARY

The following definitions are specific to this book.

AB,H system   A chemical structure consisting of two negatively charged atoms (A,B) and a positively charged hydrogen atom (H) arranged in a special way; involved in sweet and possibly bitter tastes.

Across-fiber pattern   A pattern of neural activity in which various neural units have different stimulus-specific response rates.

Anosmia   Relative insensitivity to an odor.

Anterior-insular cortex   The cortical center for taste information.

Cross-adaptation   A phenomenon in which exposure to one tastant (or odorant) affects the absolute threshold or sensation intensity of other tastants (or odorants).

Labeled-line theory   A theory of taste in which each taste fiber encodes the intensity of a single basic taste quality.

Lateral olfactory tract   The main route, composed of axons, from the olfactory bulb to the smell cortex.

Lock-and-key theory   A theory of smell mechanism in which variously shaped molecules fit into holes in the walls of olfactory receptor cells like a key into a lock, causing an electrochemical change that in turn causes an action potential in the axon.

Medial lemniscus   The pathway that conveys taste information from the solitary nucleus to the thalamus.

Molar concentration   A measure of the amount of a tastant present; 1 *mole* equals the molecular weight of a substance in grams added to enough water to make 1 liter of solution.

Olfactory bulb   A complex brain nucleus where the axons of olfactory receptor cells terminate; sends axons to various brain centers including the olfactory cortex and limbic system.

Olfactory cilia   Hairlike projections extending from the knoblike end of the olfactory rod, protruding through the surface of the olfactory epithelium.

Olfactory epithelium   The small area of oval-shaped cells in the upper nasal passages that respond to smell stimuli.

Olfactory nerve   The bundle of axons of smell receptor cells that passes through the top of the nasal cavity and terminates in the olfactory bulb.

Olfactory rod   A long extension from smell receptor cells toward the surface of the olfactory epithelium.

Papillae   Small bumps on the tongue in which taste buds are located.

Pheromones   Chemicals secreted by animals that transmit information to other animals, usually of the same species.

Potentiation   A case of cross-adaptation in which exposure to one taste stimulus lowers the threshold to another taste stimulus.

Primers   Pheromones that trigger glandular and other physiological responses.

PTC   Phenylthiocarbamide, a substance that shows large variations in absolute threshold across different individuals; some people are "taste-blind" to it.

Releasers   Pheromones that trigger specific behavioral responses.

Self-adaptation   A phenomenon in which exposure to a tastant (or odorant) raises the absolute threshold or decreases the sensory intensity of the same tastant (or odorant).

Solitary tract   The region of the brain stem that receives information from cranial nerves about taste.

Taste buds   The group of cells in which the major receptors for taste are located, on the tongue and parts of the mouth.

Taste pore   An opening in the surface of the tongue leading to the taste cells extending from the taste bud.

Thalamus   The region of the lower brain that relays impulses to the cortex.

Vibration theory   A theory of smell mechanism in which a stimulus molecule ruptures chemical bonds in the cell membrane of olfactory receptor cells, causing a release of stored energy that generates an electrical current and action potentials.

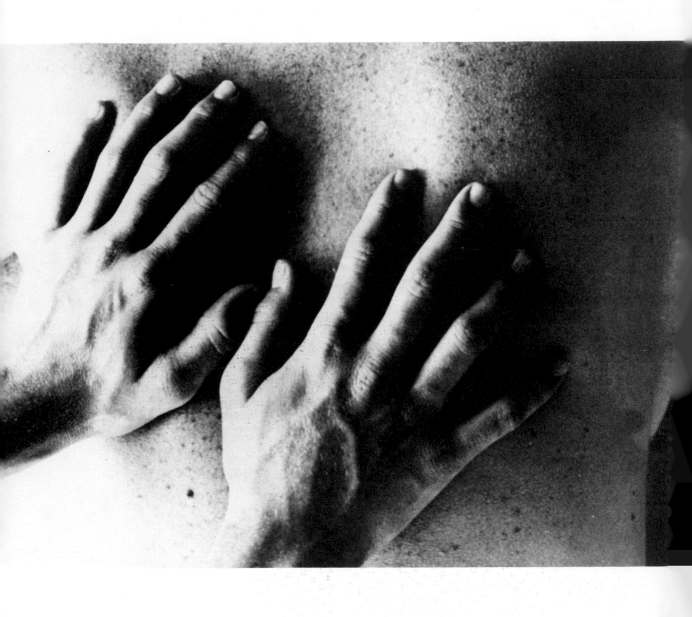

CHAPTER
9

Touch and Pain

"I guessed vaguely from my mother's signs and from the hurrying to and fro in the house that something unusual was about to happen, so I went to the door and waited on the steps. The afternoon sun penetrated the mass of honeysuckle that covered the porch, and fell on my upturned face. My fingers lingered almost unconsciously on the familiar leaves and blossoms which had just come forth to greet the sweet southern spring. I did not know what the future held of marvel or surprise for me. . . . We walked down the path to the well-house, attracted by the fragrance of the honeysuckle with which it was covered. Someone was drawing water and my teacher placed my hand under the spout. As the cold stream gushed over one hand . . ." (Keller, 1931, pp. 21–22).

Did it occur to you, as you read the passage above, that its author was blind and deaf? Helen Keller's perceptual world was restricted to smells, tastes, touches, and feelings of warmth and cold and pain. Her teacher taught her to communicate by finger taps on each others' palms, demonstrating that as long as we have normal skin we are not cut off from the richness of language. Although we are amazed and heartened by the accomplishments of someone like Keller, it is true that many species of animals rely almost exclusively on the so-called minor senses for information about the world. We have already described the senses of taste and smell in Chapter 8. Here we deal with the skin senses, kinesthesis (which is closely related to touch), and pain, which can be felt anywhere but is most clearly understood in relationship to the skin.

THE SKIN SENSES

All living things have a "skin" of some kind. Probably the most important function of the skin is to *define* the organism, that is, to set boundaries in space, inside of which exists the organism and outside of which exists the environment. The skin is an *interface* (a place where two systems meet) between the organism and the environment, and it is in intimate contact with the outside world. In the most primitive one-celled organisms, the skin is the cell membrane, and it is responsible for all the organism's contacts with its environment. These contacts include such functions as taking in food, excreting waste, isolating the inside of the cell from damaging outside substances, and responding to all sorts of external stimuli. Although more advanced organisms, such as mammals (including humans), have more specialized sensory organs to handle these tasks, their skins are also important and complex organs. The skin plays a role in respiration, temperature regulation, and protection. It also has a wide variety of sensory functions, and produces the sensations of touch, warmth or cold, and pain.

Skin Stimuli and Receptors

The skin responds to a variety of physical stimuli. When we press an object against the skin, it deforms the surface and we experience the sensation of touch, or pressure. When an object makes contact with a hair, causing it to bend, we also experience touch. The temperature of the object with which we touch the skin also elicits a sensation. Whether it is warmth or cold depends both on the temperature of the stimulus and on the temperature of the skin. Finally, the skin responds to electrical stimulation. For mild electrical stimuli, a type of touch sensation is usually felt, although temperature can also be experienced. When electrical stimulation becomes intense, the sensation usually becomes painful.

In humans the skin has a very complex structure. Figure 9-1 is a diagram of the most important structures in **hairy skin,** which covers most of the human body. A different kind of skin, found on the palms of the hands, soles of the feet, parts of fingers and toes, and other places, has no hairs protruding from it and is called **glabrous skin.** Although there is a thick outer layer of dead cells in glabrous skin, there are also many free nerve endings embedded in this layer. This makes such skin effective protection but also extremely sensitive to stimulation. All skin consists of two basic layers. The outer layer, called the **epidermis,** consists of several layers of tough dead cells on top of a single layer of living cells. The living layer divides constantly to generate the dead protective layers above. The inner layer, called the **dermis,** contains most of the nerve endings in the skin. Under these two layers is usually a layer of fat cells. In addition to these layers, the skin contains a variety of hairs, muscles, glands, arteries, veins, and capillaries. Some of these are also shown in Figure 9-1.

Figure 9-1 also shows some of the most common nerve endings in the skin. It has been difficult to specify exactly which ending is responsible for which of the skin sensations. In fact, all the endings seem to respond somewhat to all the different types of stimulation. Recently, some progress has been made in associating various receptor types with nerve fibers that have different response char-

acteristics (e.g., receptors that respond selectively to mechanical, thermal, or painful stimuli). In particular, most ''corpuscular'' endings—nerve endings with small bodies or swellings on the dendrites, including the *Pacinian corpuscles, Meissner corpuscles, Merkle disks,* and *Ruffini endings*—seem to be associated with various types of fibers that are particularly responsive to touch stimuli, whereas ''noncorpuscular,'' or so-called **free nerve endings** in subcutaneous fat are associated with pain fibers (see Vierck, 1978). Free nerve endings projecting into the epidermis may be associated with cold fibers (Hensel, 1981) or pain fibers (Perl, 1984). Modern electrophysiological and histological techniques may eventually succeed in identifying the nerve endings associated with the several types of nerve fibers that exist further along in the neural pathways (e.g., Torebjork, Ochoa & Schady, 1983). Much progress has already been made with regard to Merkle disks and Pacinian corpuscles (Gottschaldt & Vahle-Hinz, 1981).

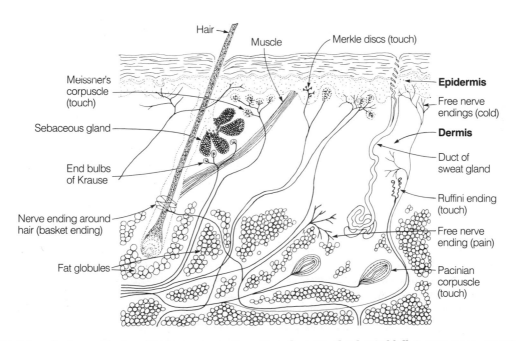

FIGURE 9-1   A piece of hairy skin in cross section. (Based on Woolard, Weddell & Harpman, 1940)

As an example of how a skin receptor responds to stimulation, consider the **Pacinian corpuscle** (see Figures 9-1 and 9-2). It has been well studied because it is large, easily accessible, and occurs in nearly all animals that have complex nervous systems. The elegant work of Loewenstein and his colleagues (see Loewenstein, 1960) involved peeling away the surrounding layers of the cell (much as we would peel an onion) to allow the researchers to touch the axon itself. Thus they were able to show that a mechanical stimulus operates directly on the axon of the nerve by deforming its membrane. This mechanical action causes numerous tiny holes in the membrane to open, allowing electrically charged particles (ions) to flow from one side of the membrane to the other, which in turn causes an electrical current to flow between the point of stimulation and another point on the axon. Finally, this electrical current generates a *spike potential* that jumps along the axon and carries the message of stimulation to the brain (see the Appen-

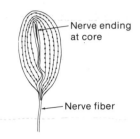

Nerve ending at core

Nerve fiber

FIGURE 9-2   A Pacinian corpuscle.

dix for information about ion flow and spike potentials). The surrounding layers of material in the Pacinian corpuscle seem to be present simply to make the effect of the stimulus less intense. Temperature could act in a similar way, perhaps by controlling chemical reactions that would affect the ability of electrically charged particles to cross the cell's membrane. Electrical stimuli probably trigger spike potentials directly. We do not know whether all the cutaneous nerve endings operate similarly,

---

DEMONSTRATION BOX 9-1.   Inhibitory Interactions on the Skin

In this demonstration you will see how skin sensations interact. You will need two fairly sharply pointed objects such as two toothpicks or two bristles from a hairbrush. The demonstration will work better if you ask a friend to control the stimuli. Do not use anything like a knife, for you will be pushing the point quite strongly against your skin. First, try pressing one point against the skin of your palm. Notice the spread of sensation around the stimulated point. Now put the two points as close together as you possibly can. Push them together on the same place on your palm. Notice that you feel only one point, although two are present. Now move the two stimulating points slightly apart. You should *still* feel only one point. Repeat this procedure several times, moving the points apart by a little more each time and paying careful attention to whether the sensation feels

like two points or one on your skin. If you are pushing hard enough and paying close attention to your sensations, at just about the separation where the two points begin to feel like two distinct points on the skin, you should have a surprising experience. The magnitude of the sensation from the two points should diminish greatly, perhaps vanish altogether for a short time. The sensation should be very faint, even though two toothpicks (or brush bristles) are pushing with some force against the skin. As you then move the points even farther apart, you will perceive two distinct, full strength sensations, appropriately separate on the skin. This phenomenon is explained by the overlapping of regions of excitation and inhibition in adjacent receptive fields of the skin, as shown in the accompanying figure.

but it is reasonable to suppose that they do. It is also possible that each nerve ending may utilize more than one of the several possible transduction mechanisms, as seems to be the case in taste (see Chapter 8).

Neural Pathways and Responses

Because there are so many different types of nerve endings in the skin, you might think that the nerve pathways to the brain would be hopelessly complex. They *are* complex, but there is an organizational plan we can understand. The plan depends on two major principles associated with the *type of nerve fiber* and *the place of termination* of the pathway in the cortex.

The *type of nerve fiber* is important because different types of nerve fibers carry different types of information to the brain. Fibers can be classified in at least three ways: (1) according to the type of stimulus that most easily excites them (mechanical, temperature, or noxious), (2) according to the way they respond to those stimuli (slow- or fast-adapting), and (3) according to whether they have large, ill-defined receptive fields or small, well-defined ones. By *receptive field* here, we mean much the same thing that we did for vision (see Chapter 3), only here it refers to that region of the skin that, when stimulated, causes responses in a particular neural fiber. These receptive fields can be quite complex. They are organized in such a way that sensory activity in one region can interact with sensory activity in nearby regions. If the distance between two stimuli is appropriate, a reduction in the perceived magnitude of the sensation may even occur. This seems to indicate that the receptive fields in the skin have the same sort of excitatory-center, inhibitory-surround organization that we observed in the visual system (Bekesy, 1967; Gardner, 1983). Demonstration Box 9-1 shows how you can demonstrate this organization for yourself with touch stimuli.

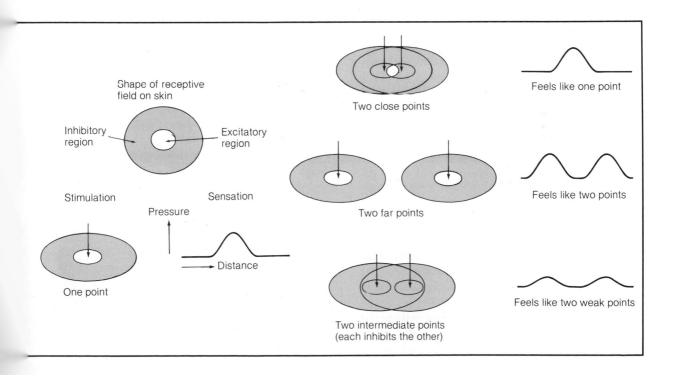

Using the three classification criteria described above, humans have been shown to have at least four different types of fibers that respond to mechanical deformation of glabrous skin: (1) rapidly adapting fibers with small, well-defined receptive fields, (2) slowly adapting fibers with similar receptive fields, (3) slowly adapting fibers with large, ill-defined receptive fields, and (4) rapidly adapting fibers with similar receptive fields (Vallbo, 1981). Such fibers are reminiscent of the sustained and transient pathways associated with the X and Y fibers that leave the retina of the eye (see Chapter 3).

The second major principle is that *where on the skin* a particular nerve ending is found determines *where its information goes in the brain,* regardless of the type of fiber it represents. All the sensory information from the skin is passed on to the spinal cord through 31 pairs of nerves (1 member of each pair for each side of the body). These nerve paths enter into the back portion of the spinal cord, hence are called the *dorsal roots.* There are also 4 cranial nerves that collect cutaneous information from the head region. These inputs are gathered into 2 main pathways to the brain, each of which seems to carry different types of information. Figure 9-3 shows various aspects of these pathways.

The first pathway is called the **medial lemniscus.** The nerve fibers that comprise it are large, conduct information quickly, and mostly receive inputs from the large, myelinated, fast-conducting Aβ fibers terminating in corpuscular endings in the skin. The pathway ascends the spinal cord on the same side of the body until it reaches the brain stem, where most of the nerve's fibers cross over to the other side. The pathway then continues to the **thalamus** and finally arrives at the **somatosensory cortex,** which is located in the **parietal** region of the brain (the upper central region, shown in Figure 9-4). Thus, the pathway terminates in the somatosensory cortex on the opposite side of the body from where it started. This system has fibers that respond mostly to touch and movement, al-

though temperature fibers have also been found (Hensel, 1981).

The second major pathway is called the **spinothalamic pathway.** This pathway is rather slow, and is made up of many short fibers instead of a few long axons. At the brain stem, it divides into two branches, the **paleospinothalamic** (*paleo* means "old") and the **neospinothalamic** (*neo* means "new"). The paleospinothalamic pathway is evolutionarily older and seems specialized for signaling dull or burning pain—it probably receives most of its input from the small, unmyelinated, slow-conducting, C fibers that terminate in free nerve endings in the skin. The neospinothalamic pathway seems specialized for signaling sharp or pricking pain and probably receives most of its input from the small, myelinated, slow-conducting Aδ fibers that terminate in free nerve endings in the skin. It also receives input from the large, fast-conducting Aβ fibers. (Aβ, Aδ, and C fibers are described in more detail in the "Pain" section of this chapter.) The two spinothalamic pathways ascend on the opposite side of the spinal cord from where their input fibers terminate in the skin and then innervate several areas of the brain, the most important being the thalamus and the **limbic system** (responsible for emotion and memory). Fibers from these areas then go to the somatosensory cortex. This pathway seems to carry information about temperature and touch as well as pain.

The somatosensory cortex is divided into two main parts, labeled *SI* and *SII,* and SI has several identifiable layers, labeled *1, 2, 3a,* and *3b* (see Kaas, 1983). Thalamic neurons project mainly to one or more layers in SI, depending on where they came from. SI neurons then project to SII (Pons, Garraghty, Friedman & Mishkin, 1987). This organization is very similar to that of the visual cortex (see Chapter 3).

The relationship between where a stimulus is applied to the skin and where neural activity occurs in the somatosensory cortex is quite regular. One classic "map" of this relationship was created by Penfield & Rasmussen (1950). These investigators

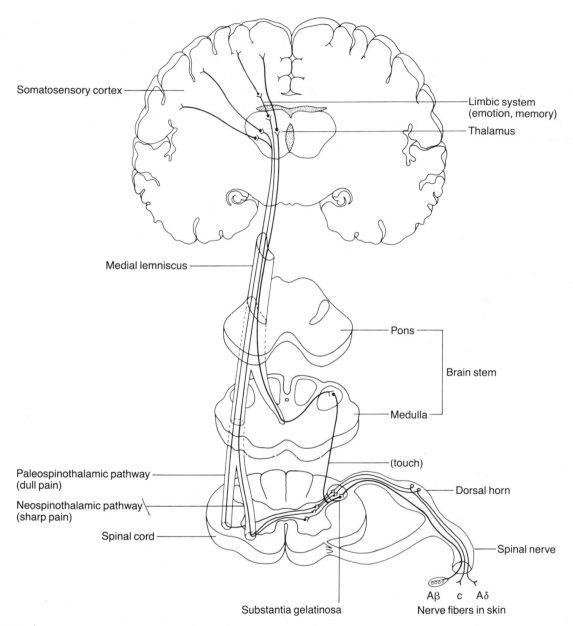

Somatosensory cortex

Limbic system
(emotion, memory)

Thalamus

Medial lemniscus

Pons

Brain stem

Medulla

(touch)

Paleospinothalamic pathway
(dull pain)

Dorsal horn

Neospinothalamic pathway
(sharp pain)

Spinal cord

Spinal nerve

Aβ   c   Aδ

Substantia gelatinosa

Nerve fibers in skin

FIGURE 9-3   Schematic drawing of some of the important neural pathways from the skin to the brain. The sections of the spinal cord and brain stem are horizontal; that of the brain is vertical.

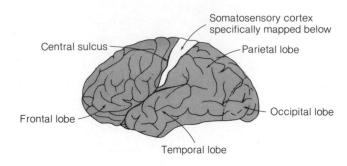

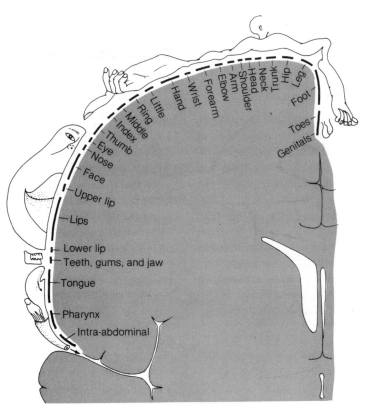

Sensory homunculus

FIGURE 9-4   Penfield and Rasmussen's (1950) topographic map of projections of "touch" nerve fibers on the somatosensory cortex. The length of the line next to the drawing of each body part is proportional to the area of somatosensory cortex subserving that body part. (From W. Penfield and T. Rasmussen, *The Cerebral Cortex of Man.* Copyright 1950 by Macmillan Publishing Co., Inc., renewed 1978 by Theodore Rasmussen.)

electrically stimulated the somatosensory cortex of patients during brain operations. As various points on the cortex were stimulated, the patients reported the sensations that they felt, which might be the tingling of one leg and so forth. The resulting somatosensory map of the body is shown in Figure 9-4. Notice that the spatial location of stimulation on the skin is preserved in the spatial location of activity in the cortex. More recently, details of how the cells in the somatosensory cortex encode information about touch stimuli have become clearer. For example, these cells respond to movement of ridges across the skin in much the same way that cells in the visual cortex respond to moving edges in the visual field (Darian-Smith, Sugitani, Heywood, Karita & Goodwin, 1982; Gardner, 1983; Leinonen, 1983; Whitsel, Dreyer, Hollins & Young, 1979). You can experience one of the consequences of a cortical map that encodes the stimulation of adjacent regions of the skin into adjacent regions of cortical activity by trying Demonstration Box 9-2.

TOUCH

Given the fact that any point on the body's surface can evoke the sensation of touch, it is surprising how often this modality is ignored. For instance, we seldom consider that major components of most sexual experiences are touch sensations. The very act of touching another person, in Western society, is considered to be an act of considerable intimacy, whether it is the gentle touch of a friend or lover or the violent punch of an aggressor.

Touch Thresholds

One of the most striking aspects of our sense of touch is how our sensitivity varies from one region of the body to another. Figure 9-5 shows the absolute touch thresholds for several different regions of the body (excluding most of the erogenous zones, which probably contain some of the lowest thresholds). Such thresholds are obtained by applying a small rod or hair (pig bristles were used in

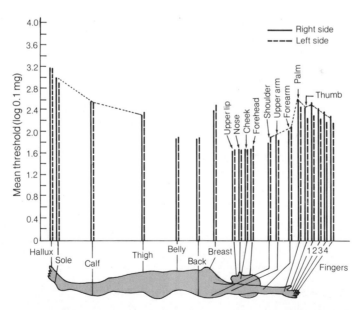

FIGURE 9-5   Average absolute thresholds for different regions of the female skin. Relative values for males are similar but higher overall. (From S. Weinstein, in D. R. Kenshalo, ed., *The Skin Senses*, 1968. Courtesy of Charles C. Thomas, Publisher, Springfield, Illinois.)

DEMONSTRATION BOX 9-2.   Aristotle's Illusion

The famous Greek philosopher-scientist Aristotle noticed an interesting illusion of touch that is quite easy to demonstrate. Hold your fingers as shown in Figure A and touch the point between them with a pencil, as shown. Notice that you feel one item touching you and the sensation of one single touch. Now cross your fingers as shown in Figure B, touching yourself again with a pencil in the place indicated between the fingers. Notice that you feel two distinct touches. The effect may be stronger if you close your eyes during the touches. The simplest and most plausible explanation of the illusion is that when the pencil is stimulating the inside of the two fingers (Figure A), the touch information is being sent to overlapping or adjacent areas of the touch cortex, resulting in the sensation of one touch. When the pencil is stimulating

the outsides of the two fingers because of your finger contortions, the information is being sent to two separate areas of the touch cortex, allowing you to experience two distinct touches. Such a cortical mapping is quite reasonable, since commonly a single object between two fingers would be expected to stimulate adjacent skin surfaces, hence should be encoded as a single touch source. It is normally not possible, however, for a single object to stimulate the outsides of two different fingers, and so two different touches should be experienced in these circumstances. The cortical mapping reflects these common situations. It seems that whether the fingers are actually crossed or not, all processing makes the assumption that they are uncrossed (Benedetti, 1985).

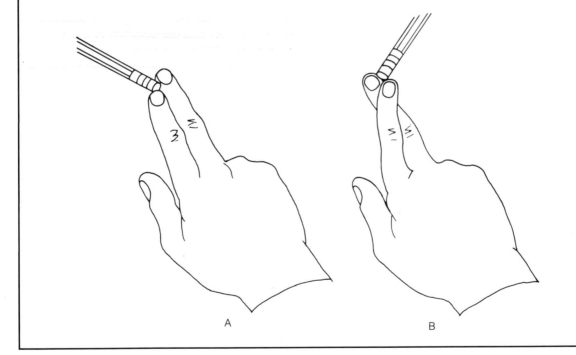

A   B

some of the earliest work) to the surface of the skin with differing amounts of force. When an investigator continues to use the same hair, these thresholds can be expressed in terms of the amount of force applied to the hair, as they are in Figure 9-5. Thus, the higher the bar, the greater the force needed, and the lower the sensitivity. It is probably best, however, to express absolute thresholds in units of force per unit area, since the actual stimulus is the change in the amount of tension in the skin and not the force itself (Frey & Kiesow, 1899). At any rate, it is apparent in Figure 9-5 that absolute thresholds vary considerably over the body surface.

Even more dramatic variations of threshold exist within a relatively small area of skin, say, the surface of the arm. If you explore a 2 × 2 cm area on your forearm with a toothpick or hairbrush bristle, pressing with the same light pressure every time you touch the skin (just enough to make the bristle bend slightly), you will discover a number of spots that respond to this stimulus with a distinct sensation of touch. You will also find a large number of places that will give only a faint sensation, or none at all.

The sensitivity of the skin is often tested using a *vibrating* stimulus, which alternately applies and releases a force to the same small surface region at frequencies ranging from 20 to 20000 Hz. Generally, vibrating the touch stimulus results in a lower absolute threshold; that is, when the stimulation is intermittent (on again, off again) the skin seems to be more sensitive. This is reasonable, since the change in the tension in the skin is the stimulus for touch sensation and vibrations cause these changes repeatedly. The threshold for touch sensation depends on the frequency of vibration of a vibrotactile stimulator on the skin much as the threshold of hearing depends on the frequency of a sound wave. Also, similar to responses of the ear, the skin is sensitive only to a limited range of vibration frequencies. The range most investigators agree on is from about 40 to about 2500 Hz. However, some researchers have claimed that under special conditions sensations can result from stimuli of frequencies up to 20000 Hz (Verrillo, 1975). Absolute thresholds for vibration also depend on skin temperature; they are usually lower the higher the temperature. This effect is restricted to vibration frequencies over 100 Hz for glabrous skin, but occurs at all frequencies for hairy skin, for example, that of the forearm (Verrillo & Bolanowski, 1986). Cooling also increases absolute threshold on the tongue, at least for intermediate frequencies of vibration (Green, 1987).

There seems to be an absolute minimum threshold measurable for touch, similarly to vision. Vallbo (1983) reports experiments that determined that 1 nerve impulse in 1 rapidly-adapting fiber from the hand could be detected (he was recording the nerve impulse from a subcutaneous electrode inserted into the nerve of an awake human volunteer). This single impulse was stimulated in this case by a 10-μm movement of a tiny probe placed on the skin. This is a very small movement indeed. Certainly, we can expect no greater sensitivity at the neural level than the detection of a single spike potential as a touch sensation.

One aspect of all tactual stimuli is that each touch sensation seems to be located at a particular place on the skin. Our ability to localize a sensation accurately varies across different regions of the skin, but seems to be directly related to the amount of neural representation each area has in the touch cortex. In general, the greater the representation of a particular area, the smaller are the errors of localization for that area (the relative cortical representation of areas of the body was shown in Figure 9-4). One way of measuring our sensitivity for localization is to introduce a second stimulus and to measure the **two-point threshold**. This refers to a fact discovered by Weber in the 1830s, who found that two-touch stimuli (such as the points of a drawing compass) will be felt as a single touch if they are close enough together. The two-point threshold is a measure of how far apart the stimuli must be before they are felt as two separately localizable touches. It was during investigations of this kind that Bekesy (1967) discovered inhibitory interaction in the skin (see Demonstration Box

9-1). A comprehensive determination of two-point thresholds was provided by Weinstein (1968), and a summary of his results is shown in Figure 9-6. Notice the remarkable differential sensitivity of the lower face and the hands, and even the feet. Presumably this reflects the use of these areas in the manipulation of objects. The high sensitivity of the feet may be a leftover from our primate ancestors, who could manipulate objects with their feet! Another interesting aspect of touch localization is studied in Demonstration Box 9-3.

Touch Adaptation

Touch sensations adapt, as do all other sensations. This can be shown by simply applying a stimulus to the skin and observing the gradual disappearance of the sensation. For example, when you first get dressed in the morning you may be (uncomfortably) aware of your belt or waistband, but after a while you no longer are consciously aware of the sensa-

tion from it. Zigler (1932) measured touch adaptation using several different areas of the body. He reported that the heavier the stimulus, the longer it took for the sensation to disappear, but that the larger the area covered by the stimulus, the less time it took for the sensation to disappear. You can demonstrate this result using Demonstration Box 9-4.

Another technique for measuring adaptation is to present a stimulus for some period of time and then introduce a second stimulus. The observer is asked to adjust the intensity of the second stimulus until the sensation associated with it matches that associated with the first. Since adaptation has reduced the sensation intensity of the first stimulus, the difference between the magnitudes of the two stimuli is a measure of the amount of adaptation that has taken place. This technique assumes that the two stimuli would be equal in sensation magnitude if they were equal in intensity. Using this technique, Frey and Goldman (1915) determined that adaptation to touch stimuli is similar to that for

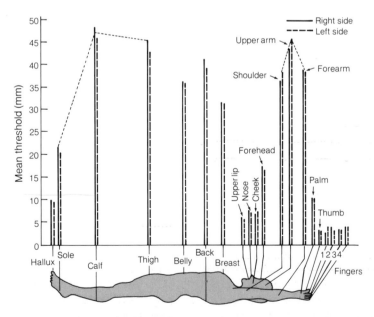

FIGURE 9-6   Average two-point thresholds for different regions of the male skin. Relative values for females are similar but lower overall. (From S. Weinstein, in D. R. Kenshalo, ed., *The Skin Senses*, 1968. Courtesy of Charles C. Thomas, Publisher, Springfield, Illinois.)

DEMONSTRATION BOX 9-3.   Touch Localization

Bekesy has studied localization in all the major sensory modalities and has discovered similar phenomena in all of them. One of the most striking is the discovery that a touch can be localized as being outside of the body under the appropriate circumstances (Bekesy, 1967). We will demonstrate a somewhat simpler phenomenon that apparently depends on the difference in arrival times of neural impulses from different parts of the skin surface to the primary sensory areas of the brain.

Touch your two index fingers together. Try to concentrate on experiencing *where* the sensations of touch are felt, that is, on which of the two fingers. Most people report sensations of about equal intensity from both fingertips. Now touch your fingertip (either one) repeatedly to your lower lip with light, quick touches. When asked to say where the sensation is, most people report that they feel it mostly on the lip and little or not at all on the fingertip, even though both are of about equal sensitivity and are being

stimulated approximately equally. Now use the same finger to touch, with the same light, quick touches, your little toe or your ankle. Most people now report that the sensation seems to be located mostly in the finger, rather than in the toe or the ankle, even though both are being equally stimulated. As it turns out, it takes somewhat more than 1 msec longer for the nerve impulses to travel from the fingertip to the brain than for them to travel from the lip to the brain. Similarly, it takes more than 1 msec longer for impulses to travel from the foot to the brain than from the finger to the brain. The impulses that arrive at the brain first (providing the difference is more than 1 msec) seem to dictate where the sensation will be experienced, even though the two places on the skin are being stimulated equally. The various other parts of the body fall in between these extremes, but in all cases the localization depends on the relative lengths of the pathways from the touching parts to the brain.

---

other modalities. The adaptation is very rapid for the first second or so and then gradually slows down. After 3 sec, the sensation level has decreased to about 1/4 of the beginning value.

Bekesy (1959) used this same technique to measure the time course of adaptation for vibratory stimuli, which generally takes longer than adapta-

tion for static stimuli. Again, different parts of the body respond differently. On the lip adaptation is complete after about 20 sec; for the forearm, however, loss of sensation is more gradual, and adaptation is not completed even after 60 sec. These longer adaptation times are consistent with the greater effectiveness of the vibratory stimulus.

DEMONSTRATION BOX 9-4.   Touch Adaptation

For this demonstration, you will need a watch with a sweep second hand, two pieces of cardboard (cut into small circles with diameters of about 1 cm and about 4 cm), and a friend. Lay one piece of cardboard on the skin of your friend's back and record the amount of time before the sensation of touch disappears. Re-

peat this with the other piece of cardboard. Try the experiment again, only this time press gently on each cardboard. Notice that the lighter touches and the larger surface area stimulations disappear faster from consciousness. Thus, they show faster adaptation.

Touch Intensity

When measuring the subjective intensity of touch stimuli, vibrating stimuli are often used because, as we just noted above, they do not adapt as quickly. A study by Stevens (1959) demonstrated that magnitude estimations of the intensity of a 60-Hz vibratory stimulus on the fingertip followed the standard psychophysical power function. The apparent intensity increased with increasing physical intensity with an exponent of about 0.95, suggesting that there was almost a one-to-one relationship between the sensation magnitude and the magnitude of the stimulus. More recent measurements using single mechanical pulses applied to the skin of the hand found that magnitude estimates produce similar results for both hairy and glabrous skin, but that exponents were somewhat lower for glabrous (about 0.70) than for hairy (about 1.05) skin (Hamalainen & Jarvilehto, 1981).

We mentioned earlier that the action of a vibratory stimulus on the skin is quite similar to that of sound on the ear in that sensitivity is greatest for certain stimulus frequencies (see also e.g., Gescheider & Verrillo, 1982; Marks, 1979a). This means that for a given physical pressure, some vibration frequencies give a more intense touch sensation than others. This can be seen in Figure 9-7, which shows a set of equal-sensation curves for a vibrating stimulus on the skin that are highly similar to the equal-loudness contours presented in Figure 7-12. Here, maximum sensitivity seems to be in the region of 200–400 Hz, with sensitivity decreasing dramatically as frequency declines. Notice that stimulus intensity in Figure 9-7 is measured in decibels (compared to a displacement of the vibrator surface by one millionth of a meter, which then represents 0 dB). This makes the vertical scale a logarithmic scale similar to the logarithmic decibel scale used in hearing (see Chapter 6).

Tactile Pattern Perception

The sense of touch has the ability to discriminate and recognize complex stimulus patterns (see e.g., Klatzky, Lederman & Metzger, 1985), although it

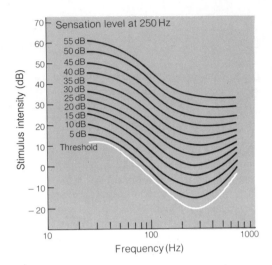

FIGURE 9-7   Equal-sensation contours for a vibrating stimulus. These contours are quite similar to equal-loudness contours over the same range of frequencies (see Figure 7-12). (From Verrillo, Fraioli & Smith, 1969)

tends to respond best to different aspects of stimulus patterns than, for example, the visual system does (Klatzky, Lederman & Reed, 1987). Most of you have probably heard about Louis Braille's tactile pattern alphabet, by which blind people can read any suitably translated book or paper. In this alphabet, patterns of raised dots on paper play the role of the patterns of ink on paper that sighted people use for letters. The speed with which an experienced blind person can read with this alphabet is a testimony not only to long hours of practice (as is any form of reading) but also to the remarkable sensitivity of the touch system. Of course, the final interpretation of these patterns of touch stimuli involves a number of complicated cognitive processes (Krueger, 1982).

Braille is not the only method by which pattern information is used to convey information through touch. Alternate methods have been invented by those who wanted to more directly substitute patterns of touch for those of vision. White, Saunders, Scadden, Bach-y-Rita, and Collins (1970) developed a **vision substitution system** in which a television camera is used to scan a visual pattern. The information gathered by the television camera is then converted into a pattern of vibrating points on the skin of the back of an observer (see Figure 9-8). The observer can move the camera to view different parts of the visual scene. When visual stimuli are presented tactually in this way, observers can identify a wide variety of different stimulus patterns (up to 25). Remarkably, the relative distance of several visual objects in a scene can be perceived from the tactile pattern, and even visual illusions can be experienced. These types of findings raise questions similar to those raised by visual and auditory pattern perception; for example, we might ask if there are also feature detectors for touch. The findings also point to the importance of higher-level cognitive processes in even the simplest types of perceptual experiences.

Reading in Braille requires that the paper or book be translated into Braille. This is especially difficult to do with newspapers and magazines, which are published in large numbers. The **Optacon** (Bliss, Katcher, Rogers & Shepard, 1970) works similarly to the vision substitution system except that the size of the visual field scanned is about 1 printed letter, and the pattern of vibrations corresponding to each letter is formed on the fingertip instead of the back. After approximately 50 hours of training, blind users can read untreated material at about 20 words per minute. Experienced users attain rates as high as 60 words per minute. In 1977, nearly 2,000 blind people were using the Optacon for reading (Craig, 1977).

The Optacon and similar devices are now being used for research into the mechanisms of tactile pattern perception (see e.g., Craig, 1981, 1983b; Loomis, 1981; Schneider, Hughes, Epstein & Bach-y-Rita, 1986). One particularly active area involves the interaction between successively presented patterns. If the presentation of one pattern

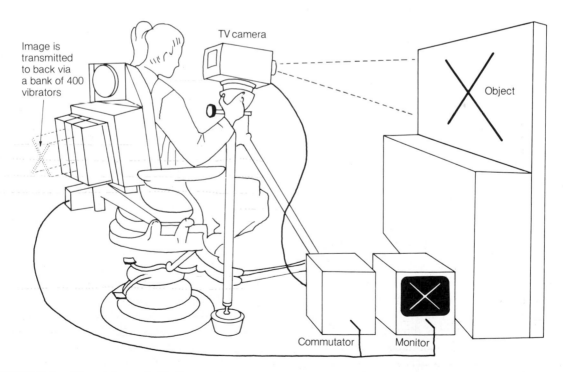

FIGURE 9-8   The vision substitution system. (From White, Saunders, Scadden, Bach-y-Rita & Collins, 1970)

on the skin makes it more difficult to identify another pattern we refer to this as *masking* (see Craig, 1978). For example, if a letter pattern is presented on the Optacon and then followed immediately by a rectangular pattern, observers have a harder time identifying the letter than if no masking pattern is presented. This is called **backward masking,** since the masking pattern seems to act backward in time to interfere with the perception of the earlier target. **Forward masking** also occurs with tactile patterns; here, the masking pattern is presented first, followed by the target. As in audition and vision (see Chapters 7 and 11), masking studies often reveal basic mechanisms of tactile perception. For example, there is usually more backward masking when the time interval between target and mask is short and more forward masking when the time interval is longer (Craig, 1983a). This is consistent with the idea that the perceptual representations of tactile features persist for about 1,200 msec (Craig & Evans, 1987; Evans & Craig, 1986), and reveals something about how those representations are integrated over time (Evans, 1987). These masking effects do not depend very much on where on the body the patterns are presented, although pattern discrimination and identification in the absence of masking does vary with location on the body (Cholewiak & Craig, 1984).

WARMTH AND COLD

Are you cold right now? Are you warm? Probably you are feeling rather neutral, that is, comfortably unaware of any temperature sensations. Our bodies contain a remarkable system of thermal sensors that trigger reflexes regulating the flow of blood in the blood vessels in our skin, the activity of the sweat glands, and the tiny muscles located around the roots of hairs in the skin. When our internal body temperature is too high (above 37 deg C), the blood vessels of the skin dilate, allowing more blood to flow and thus radiating more heat into the air. We also begin to sweat, losing heat both by the con-

duction of the overheated sweat to the surface of the skin where it can radiate more efficiently and by the cooling of the skin surface through evaporation. When we are too cold, the blood vessels in the skin contract, thereby slowing heat loss, and we begin to shiver, which generates more heat from our muscles. The thermal sensitivity of the skin plays a major part in this complex, mostly reflex-operated temperature-regulating system that keeps our internal body temperatures around 37 deg C (98.6 deg F) (see Hensel, 1981). Usually the system functions so well that we do not notice any temperature sensations, at least in temperate environments. The ability of this system to regulate body temperature is limited, however, and when the limits are exceeded the body needs to take more dramatic steps, such as changing clothing or starting a fire. Such actions bring the temperature of the skin's environment within its safe limits again. Such necessities are signaled by the conscious sensations of warmth and cold.

Neural Coding of Temperature

Temperature seems to be sensed in the skin by nerve endings that are quite similar in appearance to those sensitive to mechanical contacts. Two types of nerve fibers respond when the skin is cooled or warmed. **Cold fibers** respond to cooling of the skin with an increase in firing relative to their resting rate, and to warming with a firing decrease. **Warm fibers** respond to warming with an increase in firing rate and to cooling with decreased firing (see Hensel, 1981). Also, after an initial change in firing rate in the direction appropriate to the type of stimulus and the type of receptor, both types of fibers gradually adopt a steady rate of firing. This ''resting'' rate is related to the *absolute* temperature of the skin (and thus of the receptor).

Cold and warm fibers have different patterns of response over a broad range of skin temperatures. This is shown in Figure 9-9, which is from the work of Zotterman (1959). As you can see in the figure, the cold fibers respond in the range from

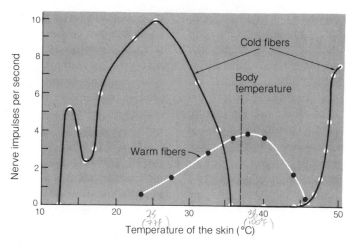

FIGURE 9-9   Steady-state discharge of cold and warm fibers in the cat as it varies with skin temperature. (Based on Zotterman, 1959)

about 13 to 35 deg C (55 to 95 deg F) and again from about 46 to 50 deg C (113 to 122 deg F). Above this limit the receptors become damaged and the response ceases. Notice that the cold fibers have two response peaks, one at about 25 deg C (77 F) and another at about 50 deg C (122 deg F). Warm fibers respond from about 23 to 46 deg C (73 to 117 deg F) with a peak at about 38 deg C (100 deg F—just above body temperature). These *steady-state* responses provide us with information about the absolute temperature of the skin. This information is quite important, since internal body temperature must be maintained within a narrow range of values around 37 deg C (98.6 deg F) (see Hensel, 1981). Demonstration Box 9-5 allows you to experience the consequences of having both cold and warm fibers stimulated optimally, something that wouldn't happen under normal conditions.

Thermal Thresholds and Adaptation

Because the skin works to maintain a constant internal body temperature, sensations of warmth or cold are generally caused by departures from a particular reference skin temperature called **physiological zero.** Thus, to talk about feeling "cold"

means a stimulus has caused the *skin temperature* to drop below physiological zero. This reference temperature is a floating neutral point, based on the temperature to which the thermal receptors in the skin have adapted. There is a **neutral zone** around physiological zero, within which no sensation will be felt if a stimulus within that temperature range is applied to the skin. This zone is seldom more than a couple of degrees on either side of physiological zero, but it varies in width depending on what the physiological zero is, where on the body the change occurs, and what kind of stimulus is applied. A good average value for physiological zero in a temperate environment (room temperature) would be around 33 deg C (91 deg F). At room temperature such a skin temperature maintains the normal internal body temperature of about 37 deg C.

The measurement of absolute thresholds for warmth and cold sensations is complicated by the fact that relatively complete adaptation to thermal stimuli takes place over a range of temperatures, and that thermal sensations are relative to the temperature to which the skin has become adapted. Several techniques have been used to measure adaptation. Typically, an area of the skin is exposed

DEMONSTRATION BOX 9-5.   The Heat Grill

For this demonstration you will need two pipe cleaners bent as shown in Figure A. Be careful to bend the pipe cleaners so that they fit together closely when both are laid on a table, as shown in Figure B. Place one pipe cleaner in a glass of cool water and the other in a glass of very warm (not unpleasantly hot) water. Take the pipe cleaner out of the glass of cool water, and place it on a flat surface. Working quickly, take the pipe cleaner out of the glass of warm water and arrange it to form the configuration shown as Figure B. As soon as this is done, place your forearm over the set of pipe cleaners and press down as shown in Figure C. The temperature sensation you receive will probably be quite surprising. Although the stimulus consists of alternately cool and warm surfaces,

you will feel no coolness. Observers usually get a sensation of an intense stinging heat. Some people may find the heat sensation sufficiently intense to cause them to withdraw their arms. The temperatures of the pipe cleaners are such (if you followed directions faithfully) that receptors of both cold and warm fibers in the same general area of the skin are being stimulated near their optimum. Usually this does not happen. When it does, you mislead your brain by making both the cold and the warm fibers fire near their maxima. The brain processes this information as emanating from a single, very hot stimulus. (Note in Figure 9-9 that for very hot stimuli, the cold fibers would be firing vigorously.)

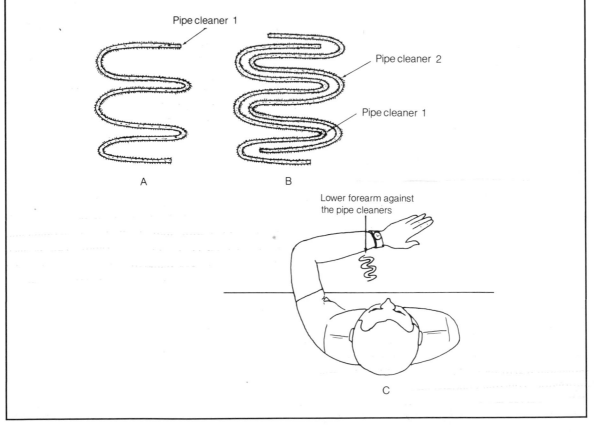

Pipe cleaner 1

Pipe cleaner 2

Pipe cleaner 1

A

B

Lower forearm against the pipe cleaners

C

to very high or low temperatures for some period of time (usually by dipping it in water at the required temperature), and then a threshold for warmth or cold is determined. In a different technique, observers are exposed to a particular thermal stimulus and asked to report when they no longer feel any thermal sensation at that temperature. For instance, Kenshalo and Scott (1966) had observers change the temperature of a sophisticated thermal stimulator just enough to maintain a detectable sensation, while they adapted the skin to a given thermal level. The stimulator started at the previously measured temperature of the observer's skin. Adjustments were made every minute at first, and then every 5 min for up to 40 min. Figure 9-10 shows the results obtained for four observers. Using this technique, Kenshalo and Scott (1966) found that complete adaptation occurred over a range of about 4 to 8 deg C centered around the average skin temperature. This then serves as an experimental measurement of the neutral zone around the physiological zero set by adaptation. Notice that when adaptation has not fully occurred (early in the period), the neutral zone is actually quite narrow (perhaps about 2 deg), but it widens as the adaptation becomes more complete.

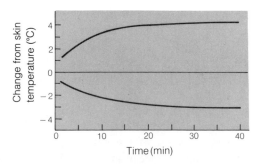

FIGURE 9-10   **Adaptation to thermal stimuli. Each curve represents the average amount of adjustment by four observers to maintain a just noticeable warm or cool sensation with a thermal stimulator. Thermal changes closer to the 0 line than the curves are felt as having neutral temperature. (Based on Kenshalo & Scott, 1966)**

Overall, the sensation of warmth or cold caused by stimuli with temperatures near 33 deg C is determined largely by the temperature to which the skin has been adapted before the stimulus is applied. You can experience this in Demonstration Box 9-6. Absolute thresholds for these sensations can be defined as the amount of temperature change (from the adapting temperature) necessary to cause an experience or a report of warmth or cold. Absolute thresholds differ for upward and downward changes in temperature depending on the adapting temperature (Kenshalo, Nafe & Brooks, 1961). Sensitivity to lowering of temperature is greater when skin temperature is colder, but it is greater for rises in temperature when skin temperature is warmer, as can be seen in Figure 9-11. Thus, at relatively high or low skin temperatures we are more sensitive to fluctuations in temperature, especially those changes that indicate greater deviation from our normal body temperature. This makes sense, since very low or very high temperatures can be dangerous for the body, hence the detection of thermal changes is more important when the stimuli are more extreme. The minimum threshold values obtained are about 0.1 deg C of temperature change from the adapting temperature.

As in other aspects of touch, the place on the body surface to which the stimulus is applied also affects our sensitivity to warmth and cold. The head is the most sensitive to warm stimuli, with the limbs least and the trunk intermediate. Conversely, the trunk, particularly the back, is the most sensitive to cold stimuli, with the limbs intermediate and the head least (J. C. Stevens, 1979). This is easy to demonstrate for yourself using pieces of metal that have been dipped in water of different temperatures (pay attention to the intensity of the sensations aroused by the stimuli on the various parts of your body). The mouth seems to be more sensitive to increases in temperature than to decreases (Green, 1986).

There are significant differences in sensitivity to warmth and cold even over a small patch of skin. If the thermal stimulus has a small area

---

DEMONSTRATION BOX 9-6.   The Dependence of Thermal Sensation on Physiological Zero

For this demonstration, you will need to create three water baths of different temperatures. You can use a meat thermometer to measure the temperatures or try the following formulas.

Assuming that your tap water has temperatures of 10 deg C (cold) and 60 deg C (hot), you can make a 30 deg C bath by adding 3⅔ cups of cold tap water and 2⅓ cups of hot tap water to a bowl. A 35 deg C bath requires 3 cups each of hot and cold tap water. For a 40 deg C bath, use 2⅓ cups of cold water and 3⅔ cups of hot water. It is best to have a friend help with preparing the water baths and with keeping them at a nearly constant temperature (by adding a little hot water every minute or so). Your friend can then try the demonstration while you make the baths.

First prepare the 30 deg and the 40 deg C baths. Place one hand in the 30 deg C and one in the 40 deg C bath. Keep the hands in the baths for about 5 min. Under these conditions most people report that after 5 min there is no longer any sensation of warmth or cold, although the cooler bath initially felt cold

(as it should have relative to your average skin temperature of about 33 deg C) and the warmer one felt warm. Now prepare the 35 deg C bath (quickly, if you are doing it by yourself), and plunge both hands into it at once. The hand that was in the 30 deg C bath should now feel as if it is in warm water while the other hand (40 deg C) will feel as if it is in cool water. Since the water is actually the same for both hands, but their physiological zero has been changed by the previous 5 min adaptation period, the sensations of warmth and cold must be caused by the relationship of the stimulus temperature to the current temperature of the skin (physiological zero). You can experiment with this phenomenon further by trying out more extreme adapting temperatures and adapting to them for longer times. See if you can find points beyond which all stimuli feel either warm or cold. Changes in temperature near these points only result in changes in the intensity of that sensation, rather than resulting in a change in sensation quality (Kenshalo & Scott, 1966).

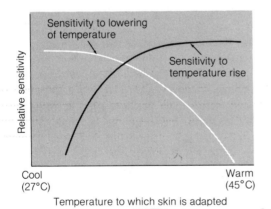

FIGURE 9-11   Sensitivity to increases and decreases in temperature varies as a function of the adaptation temperature of the skin.

(perhaps the size of a pin head), it is possible to find some spots that yield only sensations of warmth and others that produce only sensations of cold. There are also regions that produce no temperature sensations at all (although they may respond to touch). Figure 9-12 shows a set of maps of such warm and cold spots from an area of 1 cm^2 on the skin of the upper arm (Dallenbach, 1927). The spots were mapped on four successive days so that the permanence of the spots could be determined. As you can see from the figure, the spots tend to be in the same places from day to day. Since all these spots are innervated only by free nerve endings, the difference between the cold and warm spots probably has to do with the type of nerve fiber generating these nerve endings. Cold fi-

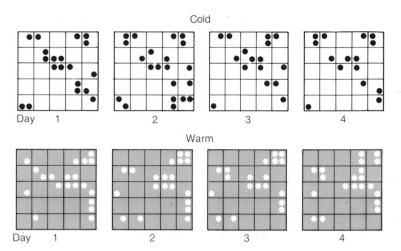

FIGURE 9-12   Maps of cold and warm spots on a 1 cm² area of the skin of the upper arm of a single observer on four successive days. Notice how the spots tend to be in the same places from day to day. (From K. M. Dallenbach, *American Journal of Psychology*, 1927, 39. Copyright by the University of Illinois Press.)

bers are typically larger in diameter and myelinated whereas warm fibers are smaller and unmyelinated (Hensel, 1981).

Thermal Intensity and Qualities

Because of the complexity of the situations under which warmth and cold sensations occur, it would seem to be difficult to measure the apparent intensity of thermal stimuli. We can, however, measure these sensations using direct scaling techniques such as those discussed in Chapter 2. For instance, Stevens and Stevens (1960) had observers make magnitude estimations of the thermal sensations caused by the application of warm or cool pieces of aluminum to the skin of the forearm. They used stimuli above the average skin temperature (about 33 deg C or 91 deg F) for warmth sensations, and stimuli below this temperature for cold ones. They found that warmth and cold sensations also follow the psychophysical power law when measured in this way, with exponents of the power functions for warmth around 1.6 and for cold about 1.0. Similar power functions have been found for the skin of the

lips and tongue, although the exponents differ under different conditions and locations, especially for cold (Green, 1984). In general, however, the sensation of warmth grows somewhat more rapidly with stimulus intensity than does that of cold.

Because of the close relationship between the sensations of warmth and cold, it should not surprise you to learn of some very interesting and somewhat paradoxical phenomena associated with thermal stimuli. One of these, called **paradoxical cold,** was discovered by Max von Frey in 1895. He found that if cold spots (such as those illustrated in Figure 9-12) are touched with a very warm stimulus above 45 deg C (113 deg F), a sensation of cold will result. The opposite phenomenon, *paradoxical warmth*, has been much sought after but never convincingly demonstrated. This asymmetry is consistent with the tendency of nerve fibers that respond to cooling (cold fibers) to respond both in the range of temperatures between about 12 and 35 deg C (54–95 deg F) and in that between 46 and 50 deg C (113–122 deg F). Warm fibers respond only in the range between about 25 and 46 deg C (77–117 deg F) as shown in Figure 9-9. When the skin temperature rises above 46 deg C (117 deg F), only the cold fibers respond. Therefore, very high temperatures actually result in neural activity equivalent to that caused by very cold temperatures, and both are felt subjectively as cold.

KINESTHESIS

We have been talking about receptors that respond to information generated by the world around us when contact is made with our skin. There is also a vast amount of mechanical information generated within our own bodies. This information indicates whether we are moving or stationary (see also "Motion" section of Chapter 13), and informs us of the position and movement of our body parts. The neural processing of this information, and the sensations we feel, called collectively **kinesthesis,** bear striking resemblances to touch.

One of the things distinguishing animal from plant life is the ability to move about in the world. In higher organisms, specialized receptor systems inform the brain about the position of the limbs or the orientation of the body. The bodies of such organisms (including humans) are literally enmeshed in a web of sensory receptors, which accurately monitor the positions of various parts so that appropriate action can be initiated. In many cases the signals of these sensory systems are not consciously perceived, but rather used in controlling reflex actions that maintain an upright posture. When these signals are perceived, they give rise to the sensations of force or weight, which are often used to help guide our voluntary movements, as in sports or other skilled motor performances.

Kinesthetic Stimuli and Receptors

The overt physical stimulus to which the kinesthetic system responds is *movement* (the root *kine* is from the Greek word for "movement"). Some information about position is available, however, even when no movement is taking place. This information is generated by our continual battle against gravity. Both movement and postural responses involve tension, compression, or twisting forces on the muscles, tendons, or joints of limbs. These physical forces should be considered the stimuli for kinesthesis. Any position of the body, even supine and fully relaxed, results in a complex pattern of muscular tensions and compressions, and consequent mechanical forces acting on tendons and joints. The relative intensities of the various forces, or changes in those intensities over time, signal body movement and posture.

Just as in the surface layers of the skin, a great many other touch and stretch receptors are scattered throughout the body. First, at least two types of nerve endings exist in the deeper layers of tissue beneath the skin: free nerve endings and Pacinian corpuscles. The free nerve endings are thought to be responsible for pain sensations. The Pacinian corpuscles provide our sense of deep pressure (which can be felt even when the overlying skin has been anesthetized). Although the visceral organs themselves are rather insensitive to touch, temperature, or pain stimuli (with the obvious exception of stretching or twisting forces that cause, for example, gas pains), these organs are surrounded by muscle. This muscle is supplied with a variety of nerve endings that are responsive to the movements of the viscera. Finally, several types of nerve endings are located in and around our joints in the muscles that move our limbs.

Matthews (1933) divided the receptors in the muscles into three major types, two of which are shown in Figure 9-13. His first type is called the *A endings,* which have two subtypes. The A_1 endings are often called "flower-spray" endings because they look like a bouquet of flowers against the muscles where they synapse. Endings of the A_2 type are wound around strands of muscle fibers called *muscle spindles*. Both subtypes respond to stretching of the muscle and therefore have been called **stretch receptors** or **spindle organs,** since they both attach to muscle spindles. This type of nerve ending is found also in great numbers in the

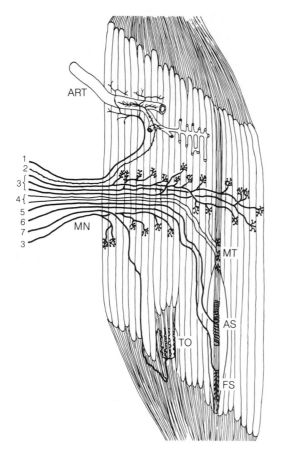

FIGURE 9-13 Nerve endings in muscle. (1) Free nerve endings around an artery *(ART)*; (2) efferent nerves that regulate the size of the artery; (3) motor nerves *(MN)* that cause the muscle to contract; (4) more motor nerves; (5) Matthews type A$_2$, or annulospiral *(AS)*, nerve endings on a muscle spindle; (6) Matthews type A$_1$, or flower-spray *(FS)*, nerve endings on the same muscle spindle; (7) Matthews type B, or Golgi tendon organs *(TO)*, nerve endings on a muscle tendon *(MT)*. Matthews type C endings, or Pacinian corpuscles, are not shown. (From Creed, Denny-Brown, Eccles, Liddell & Sherrington, 1932)

joints between limbs. Matthews's second type, the *B endings*, look much like the flower-spray endings but are attached to the tendons that connect the muscles to the bones. B endings are also called

Golgi tendon organs. They seem to respond to both stretching and contracting of the muscle, whereas the spindle organs respond only to stretching. Matthews's third type of receptor, which he labeled *C,* is thought to be the Pacinian corpuscle (Geldard, 1972). Although it is important in the cutaneous senses, it probably plays little role in kinesthesis. There seem to be few such Pacinian corpuscles in muscles or near joints. In addition to all of the above, muscles and joints are well-supplied with free nerve endings that may be responsible for pain sensations that occur in these areas.

Neural Responses in Kinesthesis

The various receptors send their messages to the brain via the two major neural pathways described previously for touch: the medial lemniscus and the spinothalamic pathways. Most of the fibers follow the medial lemniscus, except for the free nerve endings, many of which follow a spinothalamic pathway. There are also a great many branchings and interactions of these two pathways with others of less importance. The nerves that terminate on muscles or tendons and in joints also project to the somatosensory cortex. Thus, information about stimuli touching the skin of the arm and about the position and movement of the arm are both projected onto the same general area of the cortex. However, the cutaneous information is kept separate from the position and movement information even at the cortical level (see Vierck, 1978).

Let us look at the signals generated by these kinesthetic receptors. Figure 9-14 shows an electrophysiological recording from a nerve fiber that terminates in the knee joint of a cat. The limb was repeatedly bent and returned to its original position. The movement of the limb is signaled by a sudden change in neural response rate, the size of the change indicating the speed of movement. The static position of the limb is signaled by the resting level of neural response. These are slow-adapting fibers because after a limb movement it takes sev-

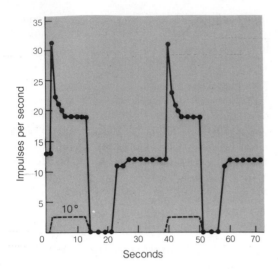

FIGURE 9-14   The response of a single nerve fiber that terminates in the knee joint of a cat. The dotted lines represent bendings of the knee joint by 10 degrees. The slow-adapting fiber gives a large initial burst of impulses to the bending, which then gradually declines to a stable rate of firing above background (no bending). When the limb is "unbent," there is an inhibition of responses, so that nerve firing is below background rate, and then firing climbs back to the background rate. (From Boyd & Roberts, 1953)

eral seconds for them to reach a new resting rate of firing corresponding to a new limb position. Cells with similar response characteristics are also found higher up in the kinesthetic system at sites in the thalamus and cortex (Mountcastle, Poggio & Werner, 1963; Mountcastle & Powell, 1959). In addition, more rapidly adapting fibers and "postural neurons" (which respond only when a joint is in a particular position) have been found in monkey somatosensory cortex, along with neurons that act much like feature detectors for the different limb components of particular postures (Costanzo & Gardner, 1981; Gardner & Costanzo, 1981). Virtually all positional and movement information comes from the receptors located in the joints (Adams, 1977). The other kinesthetic receptors

may serve to give us the sensation of strain when lifting something, or of pain. Their major role seems to be to provide information to control our postural reflexes, automatically adjusting our muscle tension to the requirements of whatever load we are carrying.

Perception of Weight and Force

The sensations of weight and force can be described psychophysically much as other sensations have been (see Jones, 1986, for a review). In fact, the discrimination of lifted weights was the first and the most generally used technique in the early days of psychophysics. Weber was the first to study it experimentally, and Fechner did an enormous number of experiments testing Weber's law with lifted weights (see Chapter 2). Weight discrimination is about as good as discrimination of sound intensity or light intensity, with a typical Weber fraction of about 0.08 (meaning that an 8% change in stimulus magnitude can just be detected).

Force and weight can be scaled by direct scaling methods. Judgments are affected by many factors, for example the size-weight illusion in which a larger-sized object feels lighter than a smaller object of the same weight. Physiological factors also play a role, such as fatigue, which makes everything feel heavier. Because of this there is disagreement about the exact form of the psychophysical function. Sensations of force or weight seem to increase as a power function of stimulus intensity, but differently for lifted weights with a moderate range (exponents near 1.0) versus grip or squeezing force generated on a dynamometer (in which changes are more easily sensed, with exponents of 1.5–2.0).

Gravity also affects the perception of weight. During parabolic flight, which provides periods of 0 gravity at the apex and about 1.8 gravity at the nadir, magnitude estimates of weights were lowest during 0 gravity, next lowest during 1.0 (ordinary) gravity, and highest during 1.8 gravity (Ross &

Reschke, 1982). Interestingly, the value of the Weber fraction approximately doubled under conditions of prolonged weightlessness (or 0 gravity) in the U.S. Spacelab (Ross, Brodie & Benson, 1984). Actually, of course, everything weighs nothing under such conditions, but objects still have mass and, therefore, momentum. The Weber fraction obtained in 0 gravity was really a Weber fraction for mass, obtained by having the astronauts shake the stimulus objects in order to generate forces that could be perceived.

You might try demonstrating some of these effects for yourself by repeating Demonstration Box 2-2 while riding in an elevator. The starting and stopping of an elevator, especially one of the fast ones now in use in tall buildings, also generates short periods of lessened and greater than normal gravity. As you ride the elevator, also pay attention to the magnitude of the sensation of weight of the objects you are trying to discriminate. Do they feel heavier as the elevator comes to a stop after a drop from the 10th to the 1st floor? Did they feel lighter as the drop began?

PAIN

The shrill squeal of the siren seemed to pierce his head like a knife. The pain was exquisite. Then came a brilliant flash of light; he blinked, trying to somehow relieve the savage pain flooding in through his eyes. He stumbled, barking his shin on a log, and another bright, fierce pain penetrated his consciousness. On top of all this, the old World War II shrapnel wound in his hip began to throb with a dull, sickening ache. Finally, he found the water, diving into a dark, cool world that promised to soothe his battered body. But something was wrong with the water; instead of cooling it was burning. His head seemed to explode as the caustic liquid burned its way along his nasal passages and forced its way between his lips. Finally, and almost gratefully, he lost consciousness, his body

succumbing to an assault it was never meant to experience.

Pain is a complex experience. It is usually associated with damage to the body of an animal, and, in humans, it is usually accompanied by myriad emotions and thoughts. Some sensory psychologists consider it to be a sensation in its own right; other psychologists argue that pain is not a sensation at all, but rather an emotion, or even a bodily state akin to hunger or thirst (e.g., Wall, 1979). Perhaps the best view is a compromise. There certainly seem to be identifiable sensory characteristics to the experience of pain. Pain apparently has absolute and differential thresholds, it adapts, it may have definable and separate physiological pathways, and it can be measured in a variety of ways. Thus, pain acts much like a separate sensory system, and we will therefore treat it as a separate sensory modality. We must be aware, however, that interactions with other sensations and with more complex cognitive and emotional processes are important for a complete understanding of pain phenomena.

Pain Stimuli and Receptors

The evolutionary significance of pain may be twofold. First, it is essential that an animal be able to respond appropriately to environmental situations that could destroy it. It must respond by avoiding such situations in the future or terminating the ongoing dangerous stimulus. Light, sound, touch, and temperature, when they occur at very high intensities or for prolonged durations, can destroy the receptors that are specialized to receive them. If such potentially damaging intensities are not signaled quickly to the brain, the organism will be damaged beyond repair. This is often the unfortunate fate of those humans who are born without a well-functioning pain sense (see Sternbach, 1963). Second, pain seems to have the effect of requiring a person to cope appropriately with an injury if it does happen. Many people who receive serious injuries do not feel pain until quite a while, sometimes several hours, after they occur (see Melzack, Wall & Ty, 1982). Their pain seems to have the function of inducing them to be still in order that healing may occur, or to seek treatment for the injury. When an injury first occurs, more important responses than pain may be appropriate, for example escape or fighting for life. In this view, the biological significance of pain lies in its ability to promote healing (see Wall, 1979). During the recovery phase, the stimulus for pain is the injury itself, and the function of the pain is not to warn but to promote recovery.

All pain does not arise from overstimulation or serious injuries. Certain kinds of painful experiences come from only moderately intense stimulation, such as a pinprick or salt touching an open wound. Conversely, overstimulation can sometimes occur without eliciting pain. For instance, pain is not experienced as one increases the concentration of sugar stimulating the tongue. At present it is difficult to say exactly what stimulus properties are responsible for the experience of pain. Intense stimulation and tissue damage are certainly only part of the story.

The best candidates for pain receptors are the free nerve endings with which the skin and the rest of the body are particularly well supplied. As we mentioned earlier in this chapter when discussing the skin senses, free nerve endings in the subcutaneous fat under the dermis of the skin have been found to be connected to nerve fibers associated with pain (see Vierck, 1978). The position of these endings in the subcutaneous fat makes them respond only to higher intensity stimuli, whether mechanical or temperature. Other pain fibers terminate in the epidermis; these endings are wrapped in a Schwann cell sheath (see Appendix), that allows them to retain a high threshold even in this more exposed location (Perl, 1984). Modern methods promise to reveal even more about the nerve endings that respond to noxious stimuli.

Another view puts less emphasis on the receptors than on the nerve fibers that carry information away from the stimulated site on the body. There are at least three major classes of such nerve fibers. Large, myelinated fibers, called *Aβ fibers,* seem to respond especially well to light touch stimuli. These fibers conduct nerve impulses at high speed (as fast as any in the nervous system, at least 40 m/sec) and connect with both the medial lemniscus and the spinothalamic pathways. Smaller myelinated fibers ($A\delta$) and small, unmyelinated fibers (*C*) are much slower conducting (about 5–20 m/sec for $A\delta$ and less than 2.5 m/sec for C), have higher thresholds, and respond only to noxious stimuli such as pinches, pinpricks, or extreme temperatures (see Willis, 1985). The $A\delta$ fibers seem especially sensitive to noxious mechanical stimuli, whereas the C fibers respond to all kinds of noxious stimuli (they are often called *polymodal nociceptors*). These fibers typically terminate in free nerve endings, either in the subcutaneous fat or epidermis of the skin (as mentioned earlier) or deep in muscles and joints, and the Aβ fibers typically terminate in corpuscular endings. $A\delta$ and C fibers connect mainly with the spinothalamic pathways, and are now generally acknowledged to be "the" pain fibers (see Figure 9-3). Apparently the fast fibers and pathways (e.g., Aβ fibers and the medial lemniscus) are specialized for highly discriminative, complicated processing of information, whereas the slower fibers and pathways (e.g., $A\delta$ and C fibers and spinothalamic pathways), which are also the more primitive ones, carry less complicated information such as pain, temperature, and rudimentary touch, as Henry Head (1920) first suggested.

This view is appealing on physiological grounds, and is consistent with some interesting psychological phenomena. Consider, for example, the phenomenon called **double pain.** This is the experience of two distinct peaks of pain, differing in quality and separated in time, arising from a single pain stimulus. It is now generally accepted that the first, sharp or pricking pain arises from the response of the somewhat faster $A\delta$ fibers to the noxious stimulus, whereas the second, dull or burning pain arises from the slower-conducting C fibers

(Cooper, Vierck & Yeomans, 1986; Torebjork & Hallin, 1973; Willis, 1985). You may be able to experience this for yourself if you try Demonstration Box 9-7.

Neural Responses to Pain Stimuli

The electrophysiology of the pain system(s) has been studied by applying noxious stimuli (such as electric shock, pinching, or pricking) to animals and recording the responses of neurons at various levels of the nervous system. It is assumed that these stimuli cause pain for the animals, as they usually do for humans, but this may not always be the case. Unfortunately, simply knowing that a particular stimulus was present cannot guarantee that a particular sensation was present. Thus, injured humans, particularly those engaged in some demanding activity such as war or athletics, often do not feel pain although horribly wounded, presumably because of conflicting and more urgent responses. We do know, however, that certain nerve fibers appear to fire only when their receptive fields are stimulated by noxious stimuli. For example, Poggio and Mountcastle (1960) found such neurons in the cat's thalamus, and Casey and Morrow (1983) found them in the thalamus of awake monkeys. Such neurons also have been found in area SI of

---

DEMONSTRATION BOX 9-7.   The Production of Double Pain

This demonstration uses the method of Sinclair and Stokes (1964) to generate two pains for the price of one. Double pain is experienced only under certain conditions. When these conditions are met, people report a first, sharp stinging sensation, followed about 1 second later by a more intense burning pain that may spread to a wider area and fades more gradually. Although most people, under the appropriate conditions, experience this sequence without being told what to expect, we are telling you now so that you will have a good chance to experience it. For this demonstration you will need to find a source of hot water, something to measure its temperature, and two medium-sized bowls to hold it in. You need to produce two water baths: one at 35 deg C (95 deg F) and one at 57 deg C (135 deg F). If you have access to a thermometer (a meat thermometer is fine for this demonstration), this would obviously be the best way to measure the temperatures of the baths. If you don't have a thermometer, simply mix 3½ cups of very hot tap water with 3½ cups of cold tap water for the 35 deg C bath. To keep it at about this temperature, add a little hot water every minute or so. To create the 57 deg C bath, combine 6⅔ cups of hot tap water with ⅓ cup of cold tap water.

Immerse your entire hand in the 35 deg C bath for about 10 minutes. When this time has elapsed, mix the 57 deg C bath, and carefully insert your finger into it until the water comes up past the second joint of the finger. Count "one-thousand-one" to yourself, and then withdraw your finger. Pay careful attention to the sensations you experience. Notice that first you feel a sharp stinging and then about a second later a burning feeling. You may try the experiment again and again without fear of any damage if you immerse your hand in the 35 deg C bath between trials, and always limit your immersion in the 57 deg C bath to 1 second. If you wish, you can try varying the temperatures of the two baths to find the limits of the conditions under which the phenomenon will occur. Also, in calculating the formulas for the two baths, we assumed that the cold tap water in your area has a temperature of about 10 deg C (50 deg F), and the hot tap water a temperature of about 60 deg C (140 deg F). If your water temperatures vary significantly from these, you will have to adjust the proportions of each to make up the baths.

the somatosensory cortex of rats (Lamour, Willer & Guilbaud, 1983) and monkeys (Kenshalo & Isensee, 1983), and may also occur in area SII (see Willis, 1985). It is clear that both the thalamus and the somatosensory cortex play roles in pain perception. Just what these roles are, however, is far from clear. Probably there are many brain areas that participate in the pain experience (see Casey, 1978; Willis, 1985).

Perhaps the most interesting electrophysiological fact about pain is that the several types of nerve fibers involved in pain and in other cutaneous and kinesthetic sensations interact, sometimes in opposition to each other. Melzack and Wall (1965, 1982) devised an ingenious conceptual model of pain, called the **gate-control theory,** based on the interaction of two of these fiber types. This theory provides the foundation for most modern accounts of a variety of pain phenomena, so it is important to understand it thoroughly at this point. Figure 9-15 presents the theory diagrammatically. Let us go through it step by step, since there are several aspects to keep in mind.

First, notice in Figure 9-15 that both fast (e.g., Aβ) and slow (e.g., Aδ and C) fibers have connections with the **substantia gelatinosa** (a group of neurons in the spinal cord; see also Figure 9-3) and with the first **transmission cells (T cells).** These T cells are part of the set of slow fibers that make up the spinothalamic pathways and send pain information up the spinal cord to the brain. The fast fibers also have a direct connection (the medial lemniscus) to the brain (or "central control," to use Melzack and Wall's terminology), which can in turn send information back down the spinal cord to the gate-control system. Notice in Figure 9-15 that the connections of both the fast and the slow fibers to the T cells are marked with a plus sign, meaning that they increase neural activity in, or excite, those cells. The actions of these fibers on the substantia gelatinosa cells are different, however. The fast fibers excite the neurons in the substantia gelatinosa (+), whereas the slow fibers inhibit their action (−). When the T cells are sufficiently active, we experience pain. A normal stimulus, say a touch, would mostly stimulate the fast fibers, which have lower thresholds. This would excite the substantia gelatinosa neurons, thus causing them to inhibit the T cells, keeping them below the activity level that is sensed as pain. A noxious stimulus, however, would stimulate the higher-threshold slow fibers as well as the fast fibers. Because the slow fibers inhibit the substantia gelatinosa cells, canceling their excitation by the fast fibers, the substantia gelatinosa neurons no longer inhibit the T cells, which fire more vigorously, and pain is experienced. The substantia gelatinosa is the "gate" for the activity of the T cells—the fast fibers close this gate and the slow fibers open it.

Generally speaking, chemical anesthetics act to inhibit the slow fibers, but do not affect the fast fibers. This allows the substantia gelatinosa to inhibit the T cells and close the pain gate. Melzack and Casey (1968) suggested that the central pathway to the gate can also be responsible for closing it, so that other perceptions, cognitions, and emotions could be responsible for changing the nature of a potentially painful experience. Certainly there is good evidence of these descending pathways inhibiting responses of spinal cord neurons to noxious stimuli (e.g., Dickhaus, Pauser & Zimmerman, 1985; Willis, 1983; Zimmerman, 1983).

Pain Thresholds, Intensity, and Adaptation

To treat pain as a sensation it is first necessary to define a pain threshold. Usually this is taken to be the intensity of a stimulus that will just barely produce a sensation of pain. Obviously, thresholds will vary across the different conditions under which they are measured, since pain can be aroused in so many different ways. As in the case of touch and thermal sensitivity, there are specific tiny points on the skin that respond selectively to pain. These points will give the sensation of pain for stimuli that do not produce painful sensations when applied to places other than "pain points." In gen-

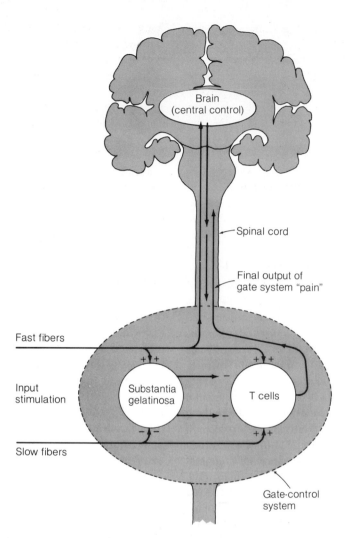

FIGURE 9-15 An illustration of the *gate-control theory* of pain.

eral, pain points seem to correspond to receptive fields of the small, slow-conducting pain fibers (see Willis, 1985). The distribution of such pain points over the body seems quite variable, as can be seen from Table 9-1. Pain thresholds vary in the oral-facial regions as well, with the tongue and inside of the lip being less sensitive than other parts to heat-induced pain (Green, 1985).

One major advance in the standardization of conditions for measuring pain thresholds was made by Hardy, Wolff, and Goodell (1943). They used a device that focused an intense beam of light on the ink-blackened forehead of a subject in order to produce a painful heat stimulus. Since the device used radiant heat as a stimulus, the stimulus could be precisely controlled and measured. They called the device **dolorimeter,** from the latin *dolor,* ''pain,'' and *meter,* ''to measure.'' This development

Table 9-1.   Distribution of Pain
Sensitivity

Skin region	Pain points/cm^2
Back of knee	232
Neck region	228
Bend of elbow	224
Shoulder blade	212
Inside of forearm	203
Back of hand	188
Forehead	184
Buttocks	180
Eyelid	172
Scalp	144
Ball of thumb	60
Sole of foot	48
Tip of nose	44

Based on Geldard, 1972

permitted the investigation of the various conditions that affect the level of the pain threshold. The exact thresholds measured in this way are of little importance to us here, since the units of any pain threshold stimulus vary with the pain-producing device or stimulus modality. However, Hardy et al. (1943) were able to show that pain thresholds acted very much like the thresholds for other sensations. Pain thresholds were shown to be relatively stable as long as the conditions were stable, but they varied systematically with changes in the neurological, pharmacological (drugs), or psychological state of the individual. These results have been replicated many times, and more recently even social situations have been shown to affect pain thresholds (Craig, 1978).

Whether two pains are the same or different in intensity can be discriminated, indicating that pain has a differential threshold, too. The first good measurement of the differential threshold was done by Hardy, Wolff, and Goodell (1947) using a modification of the dolorimeter. Since the authors felt the knowledge was important, they served as their own subjects and as a result experienced both a large amount of pain and considerable tissue dam-

age. They even moved the site of the painful stimulation from the forehead to the forearm because the latter was more easily cared for when blistered by the pain stimuli. These rather extreme measures resulted in some very important results. Hardy et al. (1947) found that the differential threshold could be measured for pain, and that it is reproducible under constant conditions. Moreover, they also found that the Weber fraction remains remarkably constant (as Weber's law would assert) at about 0.04 (a mere 4% stimulus change) over quite a large range of stimulus intensities. This indicates that we are quite sensitive to variations in pain intensity. Weber fractions begin to increase dramatically at only the highest stimulus intensities. At the extremes, however, the data were not very reliable, because the skin damage sustained made it difficult for the observers (the authors themselves) to concentrate on the pain intensities.

Hardy et al. (1947) also created the first scale of pain intensity. Since they had established the validity of Weber's law for pain, they merely added up *jnds*, as Fechner had done (see Chapter 2), to create a scale of pain intensity based on the discriminability of painful stimuli. They appropriately called this scale the **dol scale** (again based on the latin *dolor*). Later scales of pain intensity were created by more direct methods (see Chapman, Casey, Dubner, Foley, Gracely & Reading, 1985, for a review of pain measurement). For example, Stevens (1961) obtained magnitude estimations of the intensity of pain produced by electric shocks. He found that the magnitude estimations were a power function of the stimulus intensity with an exponent of about 3.5, making pain produced by electric shock the sensory modality with the largest power function exponent. This implies that the sensation of pain grows faster with increasing stimulus intensity than does any other sensory experience. The actual size of the exponent varies as a function of a variety of stimulus and even social factors (Craig, Best & Ward, 1975; Sternbach & Tursky, 1964), and more recent studies have typically obtained somewhat lower exponents, usually under 2.0 (e.g., Rollman & Harris, 1987).

Being able to measure pain is important to understanding pain phenomena. For example, it has recently been observed that pain summates, that is, different pains add together to produce a higher intensity of experienced pain than either one alone. This is true both within modalities and across modalities. Thus, stimulating two teeth at the same time lowers the pain threshold compared to stimulating a single tooth, and turns mild discomfort into pain (Brown, Beeler, Kloka & Fields, 1985). Also, pain from shock and loud noise experienced together is roughly the linear sum of the pains experienced separately (Algom, Raphaeli & Cohen-Raz, 1986).

If we want to argue for a sensory basis for the experience of pain, we must ask if pain sensations adapt as do all other sensations. Dallenbach (1939) demonstrated that pain caused by needles, heat, and cold does adapt. Heat-induced pain was studied by Hardy, Stolwijk, and Hoffman (1968) by having observers judge the degree of experienced pain as they sat with their hands in hot water over a period of time. As can be seen from Figure 9-16, adaptation is complete for the lower-temperature pain

stimuli, which were only mildly painful, and less complete for the more painful stimuli. Adaptation may not take place at all for extremely painful stimuli, although recently it has been shown that even dental pain adapts (Ernst, Lee, Dworkin & Zaretsky, 1986).

Analgesia and Endogenous Opiates

Because pain is unpleasant we seek to minimize it. After it has served its function of warning that the body is about to be, or already has been, damaged, the pain signal is no longer necessary or desired. Yet strong pain signals often persist, or indeed may occur for the first time, well after the damaging stimulus is gone. This may be because the pain induces us to remain relatively immobile, so that healing may proceed optimally (Wall, 1979). However, humans are not content to simply accept this immobilizing pain, nor do they desire to experience the pain from surgery or illness. Thus, we have assembled an impressive array of analgesics and anesthetics to rid ourselves of pain. The major focus of much pain research seems to be the

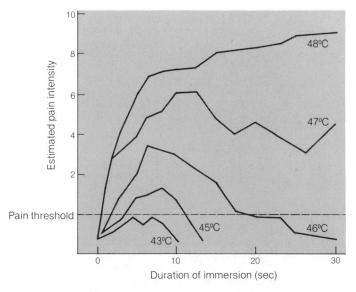

FIGURE 9-16   Average estimations of pain intensity from hot-water immersions of different temperatures at different durations.

discovery of new ways to induce analgesia. The most potent and reliable method of pain alleviation involves chemicals that are eaten (such as aspirin) or are injected into nerves or muscles (such as the novocaine used by dentists). We can even buy sprays or tubes of salve that contain substances that cause a temporary analgesia on cut or burned skin. For more severe pain we resort to narcotic drugs (such as morphine, an opium derivative) or opt for unconsciousness (as with ether or chloroform).

While studying how some of the more powerful opium-based drugs produce analgesia, researchers made a discovery that helped advance our understanding of how our bodies control pain naturally. Opiates interact with specific receptors in the brain to produce their analgesic and intoxicating effects. Since the brain has receptors for this family of chemicals already, it seemed likely that there must be a class of chemicals naturally present in the body that also interacts with these receptors. Presumably, these **endogenous opiates** (meaning opiates generated from within) should exhibit analgesic properties similar to those of opium derivatives. Several such substances were discovered by biochemists in the early 1970s (see Kosterlitz & McKnight, 1981; Snyder, 1977). At least two major classes of internally generated chemicals, the **enkephalins** and the **endorphins,** have significant analgesic effects, and seem to react with the same sites that opiates do (see Millan, 1986; Yaksh, 1984). When bodily levels are artificially raised (by administration of extra amounts of these substances), the endorphins seem to be the more potent and longer lasting. The opiumlike action of these endogenous substances is further demonstrated by the fact that their analgesic effect can be blocked by the administration of *naloxone,* a potent antagonist of opiates such as morphine, which is often administered to those who have taken overdoses. Administration of naloxone by itself makes people who are under stress more sensitive to pain, presumably because it blocks the effectiveness of endogenous opiates released naturally under these circumstances (Schull, Kaplan & O'Brien, 1981).

Specific sites in the brain seem to be respon-sible for both the generation of endogenous opiates, and for their analgesic effect. For example, electrical stimulation of certain parts of the thalamus can produce strong analgesic effects. This analgesia is reversible by naloxone and less strong for individuals who have developed a tolerance or relative insensitivity to morphine, thus suggesting that this part of the brain may be one site where endogenous opiates are produced (see Akil & Watson, 1980). It is interesting to note that sufferers of chronic pain have lower than normal levels of some endogenous opiates in their spinal fluid, and electrical stimulation of the brains of such people produces both analgesia and dramatic increases in the levels of endorphins in their spinal fluid (Akil & Watson, 1980; Terenius & Wahlstrom, 1975).

Our conscious experience of pain intensity is affected not only by the magnitude of the pain stimulus but also by these chemical regulators, generated internally and acting directly on specific areas of the central nervous system. Study of endogenous opiate systems may also provide clues as to the mechanisms involved in the nonchemical methods for the reduction of pain. For example, there are many instances where purely psychological factors seem to cause reduced sensitivity to pain. Willer, Dehen, and Cambier (1981) found that the psychological stress caused by the anticipation of a painful shock actually resulted in analgesic effects. Presumably the stress triggered the endogenous opiate system (see also Lewis, Terman, Shavit, Nelson & Liebeskind, 1984). Similarly, women during the last two weeks of pregnancy experience significant increases in pain thresholds, which reduces their discomfort (Cogan & Spinnato, 1986). Since pregnant rats experience the same threshold increases, and since the effect is much reduced when the rats are given naltrexone (another opiate antagonist) (Gintzler, 1980), it is likely that the endogenous opiate system is involved.

Similar factors seem to be involved in some of the more "mysterious" reports of reduced pain sensitivity. For example, placebo effects are sometimes reversible by naloxone, suggesting that some opiate system is involved. Perhaps even more mysterious is the traditional Chinese technique for alleviating pain called *acupuncture* (from the Latin *acus* meaning "needle" and *pungere* meaning "to sting"). In this technique, long thin needles are inserted at various sites on the body (see Figure 9-17). These needles may be twirled, heated, or have electrical current passed through them. Although Western doctors have been cautious about accepting acupuncture as a valid means of reducing pain, most studies support its effectiveness (see P. E. Brown, 1972; Chapman, 1978; Cheng, 1973; Clark & Yang, 1974). A large number of studies

have now established that pain reduction achieved through acupuncture is mediated by release of endogenous opiates (Akil & Watson, 1980; He, 1987; He, Lu, Zhuang, Zhang & Pan, 1985; Kosterlitz & McKnight, 1981).

The brain-chemical interaction we have been discussing provides only an incomplete picture of the factors influencing our perception of pain. For instance, many forms of pain reduction, such as that achieved via hypnosis, do *not* appear to be mediated by endogenous opiates (Akil & Watson, 1980; Kosterlitz & McKnight, 1981). It is therefore not the case that all forms of "mysterious" analgesia can be explained by endogenous opiates. The most recent evidence suggests that humans have at least two pain control systems, and that only one of them involves endogenous opiates (Akil & Watson, 1980; Mayer & Watkins, 1984; Watkins & Mayer, 1982).

Some of the most interesting analgesic procedures involve cognitive processes. These include such techniques as suggestion, attitude, concentration of attention, and social modeling (see Craig, 1978; Weisenberg, 1984; Wolff & Goodell, 1943). The efficacy and interpretation of these techniques vary, but there is no doubt that they are real—pain thresholds can be affected dramatically. For instance, social modeling, where observers see another person's reactions to painful stimuli before judging the painfulness of the same stimuli for themselves, has been reported to affect both d' and physiological reactivity to painful electric shocks (Craig & Coren, 1975; Craig & Prkachin, 1978). Demonstration Box 9-8 provides an opportunity for you to assess the effectiveness of one form of cognitive control of the perceived intensity of pain.

Quite clearly, the perception of pain is complex, involving a number of different levels of control. You can see how these many levels may be integrated into one system by considering the gate-control theory of pain that we discussed earlier. According to this theory, pain is experienced when the T cells are firing at a high enough rate. The theory describes not only a spinal gate controlled by fast and slow conducting fibers, but also allows

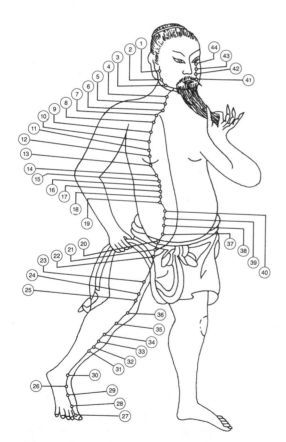

FIGURE 9-17   **A typical acupuncture chart. The numbers indicate sites at which needles can be inserted, and then either twisted, electrified, or heated. An impressive analgesia results in many cases.**

DEMONSTRATION BOX 9-8.   Cognitive Effects on Pain: The Lamaze Technique

A cognitive technique to alleviate the pain of childbirth is taught in many places in North America and Europe (see Beck & Siegel, 1980). The basic idea was that of a French medical doctor named Fernand Lamaze. One demonstration of how this technique works requires a friend to assist you.

Have your friend grasp your leg just above the knee with a hand. Have your friend squeeze gently at first, then with steadily increasing force until you can feel a fairly severe pain. This should convince you that the stimulus is actually painful. Now you have three things to practice simultaneously. First, you have to breathe in a particular way. To do this you must take five short panting breaths in a row, followed by a strong blow outward (pant-pant-pant-pant-pant-*blow*). Repeat this pattern during the entire period during which the painful stimulus might occur. Do not breathe too quickly for you might hyperventilate and get dizzy. If you do get dizzy, stop for a moment and then start up again at a slower place. Second, you

must count the breaths (1-2-3-4-5-*blow*) or say a short poem or nonsense sentence over and over again to the rhythm of your breathing (''Am I a bird or *plant?*''). Third, you must concentrate your visual attention on (look intently at) some clearly visible object during this entire period. Practice these behaviors until you feel fairly confident of your ability to maintain them for a couple of minutes. Then have your friend give you the gradually increasing pressure on the leg, while you do your breathing. Under these conditions, if your concentration is really intense, you might not feel the pain (or the pressure) at all, or at least it will be of much less intensity. According to the Melzack-Wall-Casey (Melzack & Casey, 1968; Melzack & Wall, 1965) approach to pain, what is happening here is that your central control system is closing the pain gate. Thousands of mothers claim that this basic technique of concentrating on something removed from the source of the pain effectively alleviates the pain and distress of childbirth.

---

inputs from higher levels of the nervous system to open or close the gate. Thus, cognitive factors, motivational states, attentional factors, or other stimulation such as high-intensity hissing noises, electricity, or music could all be responsible for controlling the gate via the pathway *descending* from the brain to the spinal cord gate (Willis, 1983, 1985). These descending pathways seem to be strongly implicated in analgesia caused by release of endogenous opiates. Perhaps activation of the descending pathways causes release of endogenous opiates into the spinal cord, thus closing the pain gate (Watkins & Mayer, 1982). However, the mechanism involving the substantia gelatinosa does *not* seem to use endogenous opiates to produce its effects.

We do not understand fully the story of the perception of pain. However, we now have a hint of why the 2nd-century physician Galen prescribed the shock from an electric fish for a headache, a

12th-century English doctor prescribed the wearing of a copper bracelet on the left hand to relieve a pain in the right hand, and a modern Chinese doctor twirls needles stuck through the skin of an appendectomy patient—all claiming successful analgesic results. Perhaps each was stimulating one of the several pain control systems we possess, rather than simply engaging in ''empty superstition.''

GLOSSARY

The following definitions are specific to this book.

Backward masking   When a masking pattern interferes with the perception of a target presented earlier in time.

Cold fibers   Neurons that respond to cooling by firing more rapidly and to warming by firing more slowly.

Dermis   The inner layer of skin, containing most of the nerve endings.

Dol scale   A scale of pain intensity based on the discriminability of painful stimuli.

Dolorimeter   A device that delivers precise quantities of radiant heat; used to measure pain thresholds.

Double pain   The phenomenon of two distinct peaks of pain, differing in quality and separated in time, from a single pain stimulus.

Endogenous opiates   Analgesia-inducing opiates produced naturally in the brain and other areas of the body.

Endorphins   One of the major groups of endogenous opiates.

Enkephalins   One of the major groups of endogenous opiates.

Epidermis   The outer layer of skin.

Forward masking   When a masking pattern interferes with the perception of a target presented later in time.

Free nerve endings   Noncorpuscular, branching nerve endings in skin, joints, etc., that may be receptors for pain and temperature.

Gate-control theory   A conceptual model of pain based on the interaction of slow, high-threshold nerve fibers and fast, low-threshold nerve fibers via the substantia gelatinosa (the "pain gate").

Glabrous skin   A type of skin that has no hairs (e.g., on lips); it is highly sensitive to stimulation.

Golgi tendon organs   Nerve endings attached to tendons that respond to both stretching and contracting of muscle.

Hairy skin   Covering of the human body from which numerous hairs protrude; it is both a protective and stimulus-sensitive covering. *See* Glabrous skin.

Kinesthesis   Sensations of force, weight, and limb position and movement.

Limbic system   A part of the brain, evolutionarily old, involved in emotion and memory.

Medial lemniscus   A part of the spinal cord composed of large, rapidly conducting nerve fibers that conduct touch information from the skin to the brain.

Neospinothalamic pathway   A part of the spinal cord, evolutionarily more recent, that conducts information (representing sharp, pricking pain, temperature, and rudimentary touch) from the skin, muscles, and joints to the brain.

Neutral zone   A temperature range surrounding physiological zero. Stimuli within this range feel neither warm nor cold.

Optacon   A system, similar to the vision substitution system, that converts printed letters into vibration patterns on the fingertip.

Pacinian corpuscle   A corpuscular nerve ending found in skin and joints, sensitive to mechanical deformation.

Paleospinothalamic pathway   A part of the spinal cord, evolutionarily older, that conducts information (representing dull, burning pain, temperature, and rudimentary touch) from the skin, muscles, and joints to the brain.

Paradoxical cold   The phenomenon of cold spots in the skin responding to warm stimuli with a sensation of cold.

Parietal cortex   The upper central region of the brain housing the somatosensory cortex.

Physiological zero   A neutral point in the perception of heat and cold, usually taken to be the skin temperature.

Somatosensory cortex   The part of the cerebral cortex, located in the parietal lobe, that receives input from the thalamus and other brain regions representing touch, temperature, pain, and kinesthesis.

Spindle organs   *See* Stretch receptors.

Spinothalamic pathway   A slow pathway of short fibers in the spinal cord that conducts information (representing pain, temperature, and rudimentary touch) to the brain from the skin, muscles, tendons, and organs.

Stretch receptors   Nerve endings attached to muscle spindles that respond to stretching of the muscle.

Substantia gelatinosa   The part of the spinal cord implicated in pain transmission through the gate-control theory.

Thalamus   The region of the lower brain that relays nerve impulses to the somatosensory cortex.

Transmission (T) cells   In the gate-control theory of pain, these transmit pain impulses to the brain.

Two-point threshold   The minimum distance necessary between two pointed touch stimuli (such as two toothpicks) so that they will be felt as two distinct sensations.

Vision substitution system   An instrument that converts a visual pattern from a television camera into a pattern of vibrating points on the skin of the back; used for the visually impaired.

Warm fibers   Neurons that respond to warming by firing more rapidly and to cooling by firing more slowly.

CHAPTER
10

Space

In 1621 Robert Burton noted, "All places are distant from heaven alike." Perhaps for a clergyman-philosopher such a description of spatial relations was sufficient. Yet for you, a simple mortal trying to pick up a cup of coffee from the tabletop, much more precision is needed. You must be able to judge how far the cup is from your hand with a good deal of accuracy, lest you end up with a messy puddle of hot fluid. Your very life may depend on your precision in judging depth and distance, as when you sense that you are near the edge of a cliff. You must know how close you are lest you fall, and you must also know the direction of the edge from your body lest you step toward it rather than away from it. We cannot get cut by a knife edge pictured in a flat photograph, but the real blade extending toward us in space can produce painful contact. Thus, our daily tasks and our safety depend on the accuracy of our spatial perception.

TYPES OF DEPTH AND DISTANCE PERCEPTION

Your perception of space consists of at least two different aspects. One aspect involves the perception of the actual distance of an object from you, such as how far away a pencil is on your desk. This is an estimate of **absolute distance,** which involves a process called **egocentric localization.** Most of us are familiar with the word *egocentric* in its everyday use—you are egocentric if you are concerned only about your own activities and their effect on yourself. In the context of space perception, *egocentric* means that we have a good sense of where our bodies are positioned relative to other objects in the external environment. We encounter a different aspect of space perception when we ask whether the pencil is lying nearer to the book or to the coffee cup, which are also on the table. This is the judgment of **relative distance,** requiring the

observer to make **object-relative localizations,** which are estimates of the distances between objects in the environment. The judgment of relative distance is also involved in the perception of whether an object is flat (as in a two-dimensional picture) or solid (three-dimensional), in that this requires estimation of the spatial relationships between parts of an object.

The accomplishment involved in seeing objects in depth is quite amazing considering that the basic information available to the nervous system is just a flat image on our retinas. The question of how we convert this two-dimensional image into our three-dimensional conscious impression of the world has stimulated a number of different theoretical approaches. One is called **direct perception** (Michaels & Carello, 1981) and is characterized by the work of J. J. Gibson (e.g., 1979). Direct perception has had its major influence by stating several viewpoints. The first is that all the information you need to see three-dimensionally is present in the retinal image, or in relationships among parts of the retinal image. The second is the concept that the visual scene is analyzed in terms of objects, textures, and surfaces, rather than in terms of specific stimulus components. Finally, direct perception suggests that the impression of depth or distance arises immediately in the observer, and needs no further computation or any additional information based on inferences or experience.

An alternative approach, which contains some of the flavor of direct perception, was proposed by a number of theorists who were influenced by developments in artificial intelligence (a part of computer science that attempts to make machines perform human tasks). These include efforts to develop computer programs that will allow machines to interpret visual information in the same manner that a human observer might. Such theorists, including Marr (1982), began with the general assumption made in direct perception, namely, that all the information you need to derive three-dimensionality is present in the visual inputs, but added the suggestion that this interpretation might require the detection of fairly subtle aspects of the stimulus, and might also require a number of computations and several stages of analysis. This added feature, and the assertion that these computations can be described precisely mathematically, have resulted in the label of **computational theories** for this approach. (See Chapter 11 for more on computational theories.)

The last major approach is based on the assumption that our perceptual representation of the world is much richer and more accurate than might be expected on the basis of the information contained in the visual image alone. This approach, which might be called **intelligent perception,** originated with Helmholtz in 1867 and is today best exemplified by Rock (1983). It suggests that perception is like other logical processes in that, in addition to the information available at the moment, we can also use information based on our previous experience, our expectations, and so forth. In other words, our visual perception of space may involve other sources of information, some nonvisual in nature, some based on our past history and cognitive processing strategies. Because of this combination of several sources of information, these theories have been called **constructive theories** of perception.

Although it is quite likely that each of these approaches is true for some aspects of the perceptual process (cf. Coren & Girgus, 1978; Uttal, 1981), theorists who favor particular approaches will tend to try to isolate different factors when they consider the perception of depth or distance. Some will concentrate on isolating structures within the sensory systems themselves, others on the properties of the physical world and the way our sensory systems interact with it, and still others on the cognitive interpretive processes called into play when we interpret the three-dimensional nature of the world. All of these approaches, however, usually begin by attempting to isolate the **cues** for

depth. These are stimulus characteristics of which we are often consciously unaware, but that function to shape our perceptual responses.

PICTORIAL DEPTH CUES

When you look at a realistic painting or a photograph you find it quite easy to perceive the spatial relationship among the various items portrayed. Your impression of the relative distances in such scenes is based on a set of cues, appropriately called **pictorial depth cues.** These cues are also called **monocular cues,** since they appear in pictures (which are two-dimensional) and only require one eye to register (remember a camera has only one eye), and in order to distinguish them from cues that require two eyes. To understand these depth cues we must first recognize that our visual experience usually depends on the transfer of light reflected from an object in the external world to the eye of the observer. A number of depth cues depend on characteristic ways in which light travels to the eye, and on ways in which it interacts with the medium (usually air) through which it passes or interacts with other objects, and on some specific aspects of the geometry of images.

Interposition or Overlay

The vast majority of objects in the world are not transparent. Since light reflected from distant objects cannot pass through opaque objects that stand between them and the observer, a nearer object tends to block the view of a more distant one. This depth cue is called **interposition,** or **overlay.** It is easy to see that the cat in Figure 10-1 is nearer to you than the man's leg because your view of the leg is partially covered by the image of the cat. Notice that interposition is a cue for relative depth only, indicating that the cat is nearer than the man's leg, but not how far away the cat itself is from you.

FIGURE 10-1   Interposition as a depth cue is illustrated by the fact that the cat is seen as closer than the man's leg since it partially blocks your view of the leg.

Shading

The fact that light cannot pass through most objects gives rise to the interposition cue. The fact that light usually travels in straight lines gives us another cue for relative depth. This is based on the fact that the lower part of an in-going ''dent'' will catch some of the light from above, whereas the upper part will be in shadow. This is illustrated in the ''muffin tin'' in Figure 10-2, in which the cups are clearly pushed in relative to the surface. If the shadow pattern is reversed, with bright on the top and shadow on the bottom, we perceive the same pattern as an out-going ''bump.'' You can see this by rotating the book 180 degrees and looking at

FIGURE 10-2   Shading makes it clear that we are looking at a muffin tin with the cups pushed in. Inverting the figure reverses the shadow pattern and now makes it appear that the cups are pushed out toward you.

Figure 10-2 again. Now it should look like an inverted muffin tin, with the bottoms of the cups pointed toward you (cf. Berbaum, Bever & Chung, 1984). Clearly, for this shading cue to work consistently in this example, we must be assuming that the light is coming from above. If the light were coming from another position the shading pattern would be different. Observers do seem to use their knowledge or presumptions about the location of the light source to help them accurately perceive the three-dimensional nature of objects using the shading cue (Berbaum, Bever & Chung, 1983; Ramachandran, 1988).

Aerial Perspective

The partial or complete blockage of light gave us our first two pictorial cues for relative depth. A cue for absolute depth emerges from the fact that the air is filled with light-absorbing and light-scattering molecules, even on the clearest of days. As light passes through the air, it tends to be absorbed and somewhat scattered by these minute particles of dust and moisture. Large particles (such as dust) scatter the light uniformly, causing a uniform distribution of light or a blurring of the image. For particles that are small in comparison to the various wavelengths of light (such as minute bits of water vapor), the degree of scatter depends on the specific wavelength, with shorter wavelengths (blue) undergoing more scatter than longer wavelengths (Uttal, 1981). The combined effect of these phenomena produces the cue called **aerial perspective,** in which the image of a very distant object, such as a distant mountain, will be slightly bluer in hue and hazier in appearance than the images of nearer objects. Such changes in appearance can provide information about the absolute distance of relatively faraway objects. In some geographic regions (such as the prairies of the United States and Canada), this can lead to considerable errors in distance judgments, since the clear dry air reduces aerial perspective. Thus, a plateau that appears to be only 1 or 2 miles away on a clear day, when looking across a dry sector of Wyoming, may actually be 20 or 30 miles distant. Conversely, this explains why objects seen in the morning fog or a mist appear to be farther away than when seen in bright midday sun (Ross, 1975).

There is an interesting variant of the aerial perspective cue that is usually referred to as **relative brightness.** The luminance of a lighted surface or object does not decrease with distance, but the light from more distant objects must travel through the atmosphere for a greater distance. Therefore, increased absorption or scattering of the light by the particles in the air could account for the perception of a diminished brightness with increasing object distance, even though the distances may not be as great as those described in the context of the usual aerial perspective cue (Uttal, 1981). Certainly, in the absence of any other cues, you will tend to see the brighter of two identical objects as closer (Ittelson, 1960).

Retinal and Familiar Size

As an object moves farther away from you, its **retinal image size** begins to diminish. One country song captured this effect in its lyric, "If you see me getting smaller I'm leaving." The geometry of this situation is shown in Figure 10-3, where the more distant person is casting a smaller retinal image. We tend to use these relative differences in retinal image size as a cue for relative distance, as in Figure 10-4, where we see a row of puppy dogs that seem to recede in distance from us because of their decreasing image size. Thus, the comparison of the sizes of objects in the visual field, relative to each other, is an important part of the process of perceiving relative distance.

Retinal image size is a cue used by both direct perception and computational theories of perception. There is, however, another size cue that is important in constructive theories. This has nothing to do with image size but rather with your previous

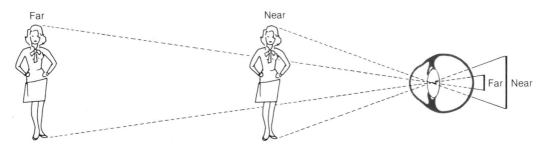

FIGURE 10-3 Objects of the same physical size produce smaller retinal angle sizes with increasing distance from the observer. Thus, relatively speaking, smaller images are perceived to be more distant.

experience with the usual or **familiar size** of the object. For example, playing cards all tend to be the same size. Ittleson (1951) presented to observers three playing cards, under **reduction conditions.** This is usually a darkened room with all other depth cues removed. One of the playing cards was normal in size, a second was twice normal size, and a third was one-half normal size. He found that observers tended to judge the double-sized playing card as being much closer to them and the half-sized card as being much more distant than the normal-sized card. This is the same process that causes you to see the dogs in Figure 10-4 as receding into the distance. You presume that all of these images are about the same "dog size" and use this familiar size information in conjunction with the changing retinal size to gain the impression of changes in relative distance.

As long as the objects are commonplace, and the distances not too extreme, familiar size can give you absolute depth information, not merely relative depth information (Epstein & Baratz, 1964; Fitzpatrick, Pasnak & Tyer, 1982). Thus, if we see a very tiny elephant, we can use our knowledge that elephants are relatively large creatures to deduce that the elephant has not shrunk in size but rather has moved away from us and is now more

distant. You may demonstrate the effect of familiar size for yourself by following the instructions in Demonstration Box 10-1.

Linear Perspective

There is a well-known pictorial depth cue that may be seen as an extension of the retinal image size cue to distance. This cue is **linear perspective.** For example, look at Figure 10-5, which is adapted from a book on how to depict perspective in drawings authored by Jan Vredeman de Vries in 1604 (de Vries, 1604/1968). In this schematic scene we notice that physically parallel lines, such as those defining the paving blocks making up the floor, seem to converge as objects become more distant. So do the hypothetical lines that connect all the tops and all the bottoms of the pillars, all of which are actually the same size. This means that physically parallel lines, such as railroad tracks, appear to converge and objects appear to get smaller in a systematic fashion as their distance from you increases. Eventually they will reach a **vanishing point,** where all the perspective lines will converge and objects will diminish to invisibility. This point is usually on the horizon, as shown in the figure. This is a simple geometric effect that occurs in the

FIGURE 10-4   Relative size differences are interpreted as cues for relative distance. Thus, we see a row of puppy dogs that seem to recede in distance because of their decreasing image size.

DEMONSTRATION BOX 10-1.   Familiar Size and Distance

Look at Figure 10-4. Notice that the row of puppy dogs seems to recede into the distance. Off to the right is a ball. If we told you that it is a tennis ball or a baseball, you would have no difficulty in deciding which dog is at the same distance away from you as the ball. After you decide this, return to this box.

Now, suppose we told you that the ball is really a volleyball or a basketball. Which dog is the same distance as the basketball? Notice that the ball apparently "moved backward" in depth when you assumed that it was a larger object. This shows how knowledge of the size of an object can affect our judgment of the distance of the object, giving us the *familiar size* cue to distance.

FIGURE 10-5   An example of linear perspective, in which physically parallel lines seem to converge as they grow more distant. Notice that the lines have been extrapolated to show a vanishing point on the horizon.

real world, and when we project a three-dimensional scene onto a two-dimensional surface. It provides a powerful relative depth cue. Hence, it is easy to determine that pillar *B* is farther away from you than pillar *A* by utilizing the perspective cue.

Texture Gradients

J. J. Gibson (1950) suggested an interesting way of combining both linear perspective and relative size information into one cue, which he referred to as **texture gradient.** A texture is any collection of objects (Caelli, 1982), and the gradient (continuous change) is the change in the relative size and compactness of these object elements. The more distant parts of the texture have smaller elements that are more densely packed together (Gibson, 1950). This cue is sometimes called *detail perspective*. Figure 10-6A shows a texture of lines. Since the texture is uniform, it shows little depth, and looks much

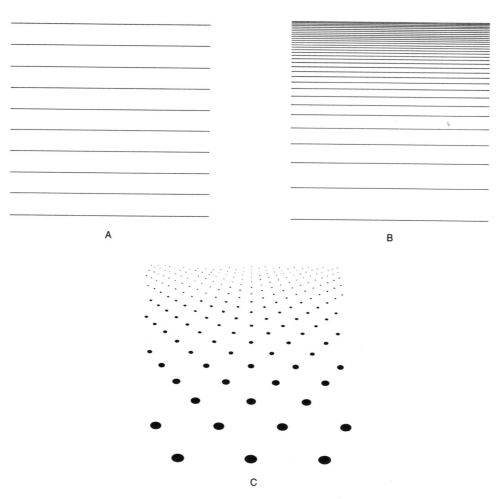

A

B

C

FIGURE 10-6   Examples of texture gradients in B and C, which appear as surfaces receding in depth. In *A* there are no decreases in element size or spacing and thus the perception is of a flat surface.

like a flat wall or garage door. If we introduce a gradient, however, as is done in 10-6B, with the lines becoming more compact as we move toward the top, we now get an impression of depth. An even stronger impression of depth appears if we allow the gradient to appear in the horizontal placing of elements as well as the vertical, as can be seen in the texture of dots in 10-6C. One important type of information contained in texture gradients emerges from the fact that sudden changes in texture usually signal a change in the direction or distance of a surface. Thus, Figure 10-7A shows how the gradient changes when we shift from floor to wall, and 10-7B shows how the gradient changes at a cliff or step down. The perception of depth obtained from texture gradients can be quite striking. Texture helps us to define the shapes of objects (Todd & Akerstrom, 1987; see also Chapter 11) as well as delicate variations in distance, as shown in the undulating surface depicted by texture cues alone in Figure 10-8.

Height in the Plane

There is another cue to distance that depends on the relationships between objects as their images are projected onto our retinas. This cue is **height in the plane,** or *relative height,* and refers to where an object is relative to the horizon line. In Figure 10-9, post *B* seems farther away than post *A* because its base is closer to the horizon line. Hence it is said to be "higher in the plane," or "higher in the picture plane" if we consider this as a two-dimensional representation. The reverse holds for targets above the horizon. Bird *C* seems farther away than bird *D* because it is "lower in the picture plane." In other words, proximity to the horizon line signals the greater distance.

Motion and Motion Parallax

We have been considering only depth cues that could also be represented in a photograph or a

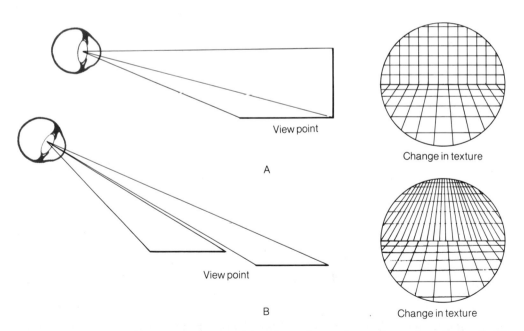

View point

A

Change in texture

View point

B

Change in texture

FIGURE 10-7   How texture changes at a corner (A) and an edge next to a sharp drop in depth (B).

FIGURE 10-8   This rippling or undulating surface is defined completely on the basis of variations in texture density.

FIGURE 10-9   Height in the plane and proximity to the horizon will determine which elements in the diagram are perceived as more distant. In this case, B and C are seen as being farther away because they are closer to the horizon line.

painting, but when we add motion to the incoming visual pattern we provide some additional opportunities for depth cues to appear. One of these movement cues concerns the motion pattern of an object as you travel past it. Suppose you are traveling in a car or bus and looking at the scene in Figure 10-10. Suppose also that your direction of movement is from right to left and that you are gazing at the spot marked ''Fixation point.'' Under these conditions, all the objects closer to you than the fixation point will appear to move in a direction opposite to your movement, while objects that are farther away will appear to move in the same direction you are moving. Not only the direction but also the speed of movement varies with the objects' proximity to you and to your point of fixation. This cue to distance is called **motion parallax.** Motion parallax

can also be generated by swinging your head back and forth while your body is stationary. The motion parallax from head movements also gives very good information about the depth of objects if they are not too distant from you (Ono, Rivest & Ono, 1986).

A special form of motion parallax occurs when an object moves or rotates. The relative pattern of movement of parts of the object can give us information about its three-dimensional shape (e.g., Carpenter & Dugan, 1983; Doner, Lappin & Perfetto, 1984). The fact that motion cues can give us information about the relative depth of parts of an object has been called the **kinetic depth effect** (Gibson, 1966; Kaufman, 1974; Rock, 1975). Demonstration Box 10-2 allows you to see this phenomenon for yourself. In Chapter 13 you will

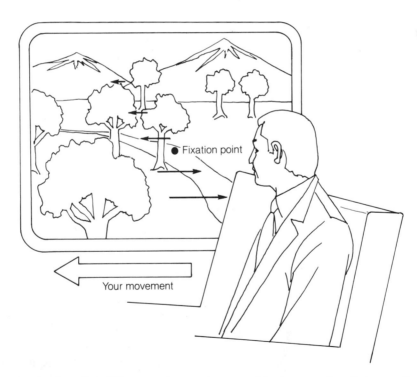

● Fixation point

Your movement

FIGURE 10-10   Motion parallax. When an observer moves, objects at varying distances from the observer will move in different directions at differing speeds. These differences can serve as cues for the relative distance of the objects.

DEMONSTRATION BOX 10-2.   The Kinetic Depth Effect

To see how subtle motion parallax effects can create the impression of a three-dimensional form in a two-dimensional pattern, you will need a candle and a piece of stiff wire (a coat hanger or a long pipe cleaner will do). Bend the wire into a random three-dimensional shape. Now light the candle and darken the room. Place the bent wire so that it casts a shadow on a blank wall as shown in the figure. Notice that when the shape is absolutely motionless, the shadow is seen as a flat pattern of lines. Now if you rotate the shape with your hand, the shadow suddenly changes perceptually, becoming a three-dimensional object that cannot be seen as flat, despite the fact that you are viewing a two-dimensional shadow.

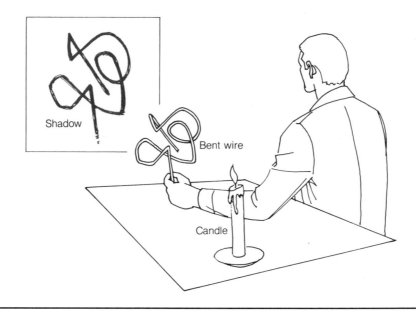

also learn how motion parallax can give you information about the direction of your movements through space.

PHYSIOLOGICAL CUES FOR DEPTH

Up to now, we have only considered cues for depth that can be found in the retinal image itself. There are other cues for distance that come about because of the way the visual system responds to or interacts with the visual stimulus. These may be called **structural** or **physiological cues,** since they tend to arise from muscular responses and adjustments of the eye.

Accommodation

When we discussed the physiology of the eye in Chapter 3, we described how the crystalline lens responds to targets at different distances from us. Basically, we noted that the lens must change shape (actually it changes its amount of curvature) in order to keep the retinal image in clear focus (Dalziel & Egan, 1982). This process is called **accommodation.** There is only one particular curvature that will clearly focus the retinal image of an object viewed at a particular distance from the eye. Relaxed accommodation, where the lens is relatively flattened, is necessary if distant objects are to be clearly focused on the retina, whereas a strongly curved lens is needed to image closer objects on the retinal surface. As we change the tension on the ciliary muscles, which control the lens shape, feedback from these muscular changes can provide us with some additional, nonvisual, information about the distance of the object we are looking at.

In addition to feedback from the act of accommodation, the presence or absence of blur due to an object being out of focus can serve as a cue for relative distance. It has been shown that in the absence of all other depth information observers can judge that two spots of light presented in complete darkness are at different distances. This is probably because accommodation cannot be correct for two stimuli at different distances at the same time; hence, one of the lights will be slightly blurred and out of focus, suggesting that the targets are not equidistant (Kaufman, 1979).

Accommodation is rather limited in the range of observer-to-object distances over which it is useful (Graham, 1965). At a distance of around 3 meters, the lens has fully relaxed accommodation and doesn't flatten out any further, regardless of how far away an object is. There is a similar limit for close objects. If a target is within 20 centimeters of your face, your lens has reached its point of maximum curvature. Within the range of 20 to 300 cm, however, accommodation may provide a useful, if not very precise, auxiliary cue for distance (Hochberg, 1971).

Convergence and Divergence

Another potential distance cue comes from the fact that we have two eyes. Two-eyed perception is referred to as **binocular,** from *bi,* meaning "two," and *ocula,* meaning "eye." Since (as we learned in Chapter 3) the best visual acuity is obtained

when the image of an object is focused on the fovea, eye movements are executed to bring the image to this region of the eye. If the eyes move in different dircctions these are called **vergence movements.** If an object is close to you, you must rotate your eyes inward (toward the nose) in order to focus its image on the fovea. Such movements are called **convergence** (the root *con* means "toward"). When a target is farther away, the eyes must move away from each other in an outward rotation (toward the temples), hence these movements are called **divergence** (from the root *di* meaning "apart"). Different degrees of convergence are illustrated in Figure 10-11.

Each target distance, up to about 6 m, is associated with a unique angle between the eyes called the *convergence angle,* as indicated in Figure 10-11. To achieve each eye position, a unique pattern of muscular contractions must occur. Feedback from such vergence movements could be useful in determining the distances of objects, although there has been some controversy about how useful and reliable such information is as a depth cue (Gogel, Gregg & Wainwright, 1961; Hochberg, 1971). Recent evidence, however, suggests that convergence and accommodation together may provide quite accurate absolute depth information, even when the only visible stimulus is a single point of light whose distance observers are asked to judge (Morrison & Whiteside, 1984).

PHYSIOLOGICAL CUES FOR DIRECTION

Distance is only one aspect of our perception of space. The perception of the location of an object will also include its direction relative to our bodies. There are actually two types of directional judgments that we integrate in a complex fashion to give us our sense of up, down, right, and left (Howard, 1982). The first one we call **bodycentric** direction. It uses as a reference location the midline

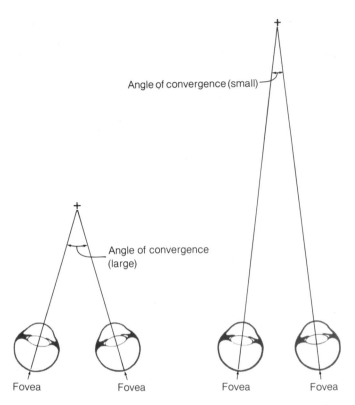

Angle of convergence (small)

Angle of convergence
(large)

Fovea   Fovea   Fovea   Fovea

FIGURE 10-11   Convergence angle changes as a function of fixation distance. This may provide some information about target distance.

of the body, an imaginary vertical line parallel to the spine passing vertically through the naval. This can be contrasted to **headcentric** direction where the midline of the head is used as another reference location for right and left. This is an imaginary vertical line running up and down, centered on the nose. Of course, bodycentric and headcentric directions are potentially different since it is possible to rotate your head independently of your body. The distinction between these two aspects of direction is shown in Figure 10-12.

Most of the research on direction has concentrated on one aspect of headcentric perception we can refer to as the *visual straight ahead*. Generally speaking, we tend to define our notion of "straight ahead" as a direction in front of us, oriented

around the midline of the head, regardless of eye position. The visual **egocenter** is the position in the head that serves as our reference point for the determination of headcentric straight ahead. In some respects, this is a very complex judgment, since we seem to ignore the directions that the eyes are pointing, and to compute a straight ahead that seems to be located in front of the middle of the head. Researchers often refer to this compromise direction as the location pointed to by a hypothetical **Cyclopean eye,** a name derived from the mythical Greek giant Cyclops who had a single eye in the middle of his forehead. Demonstration Box 10-3 shows how you can experience for yourself the referring of the visual direction of the two eyes to this common egocenter.

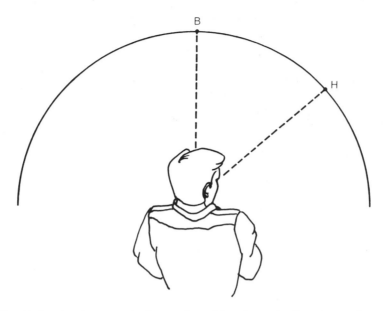

FIGURE 10-12   The distinction between bodycentric and headcentric directions. The point *B* is straight ahead of the body midline, whereas *H* is straight ahead of the midline of the head. Notice, however, that these two straight ahead directions can be two different points in visual space.

Eye Movements and Direction

A number of variables affect our sense of the direction of objects. Stimulus factors are, of course, important; the more stimuli available, the more stable our directional judgments, which accounts for the fact that our ability to judge direction is much less stable in the dark. Also, specific visual configurations influence the judgment of direction. For example, if you are looking at a square or rectangle that is not exactly centered in your visual field, there will be a tendency for you to judge the straight ahead direction as the center of this displaced square or rectangle. It is as if the perceptual system confuses what is straight ahead of the observer with what is centered with respect to the other contents in the visual field (Roelofs, 1935). However, nonvisual factors also play a role in directional localization.

In the previous section we saw how eye movements, in the form of convergence and divergence, conveyed information about the distances of objects. It would also seem reasonable that feedback from eye movements could help in determining the visual direction of an object. At least two sources of eye movement information could be used to compute the direction of an object in space. The first arises from the movement commands sent to the eye muscles (the **efference copy**); the second (the **afference copy**) arises from the eye movement that is planned or intended (although not necessarily executed, e.g., Hershberger, 1987). There is a good deal of controversy about which of these types of movement information is more important (e.g., Matin, 1982; Shebilske, 1976; Stark & Bridgeman, 1983), but it seems clear that eye movement information does play a role in localizing targets in space.

There are many examples demonstrating how eye movements affect our localization of targets.

DEMONSTRATION BOX 10-3.   The Common Visual Direction of the Two Eyes

You can experience how the visual directions of the two eyes are referred to one common direction in the center of the head. First, take a sheet of stiff cardboard (20 × 27 cm will do) and place it in front of the eyes as shown in the figure. Put a dot in the middle of the far end of the cardboard and stare at it while a friend marks the exact center position of each of your pupils on the end of the cardboard closest to your face. Next, draw lines from these marked points until they form an angle, or *V* (as pictured). Finally, reposition the cardboard in front of your face at a point slightly below your eyes. Now, stare at the far point where the two drawn lines intersect, and you should see, in addition to the two lines you have drawn, an additional, somewhat more shadowy line running between them. This "new" line is the fusion of the views of the two eyes and should appear to point directly at a spot close to the midline of the head. This demonstrates that, although the direction of each eye's view is different (as shown by the spatial separation between the two drawn lines converging on the far point on which you are fixating), the visual direction of the combined binocular view is referred to a common point between the eyes. This point is called the *egocenter,* or the *Cyclopean eye.*

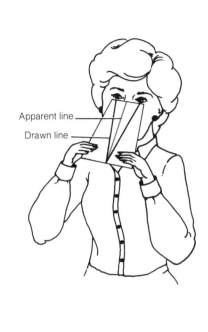

Apparent line
Drawn line

The information about target localization seems to be associated with where the eyes are pointing at any given moment. Imagine that the fovea of the eye serves as a reference point. In the absence of other information you localize a target as being in the direction that your fovea is pointing when you try to look at it. This means that if you accurately image the target on your fovea you will accurately perceive the direction of the target. If, on the contrary, you inaccurately point your eyes, such as when the eyes lag behind a moving target that you are trying to track (see Chapter 13), you should inaccurately localize the target. There is a good deal of evidence that this is exactly what happens (e.g., Coren, Bradley, Hoenig & Girgus, 1975;

Festinger & Easton, 1974; Honda, 1984; Mack & Herman, 1972).

The role of eye movements in target localization can be quite subtle. For example, there is a suggestion that the eye movement does not actually have to be made, but that the eye movement you compute in order to move the eye at some later time may bias your perception of direction (e.g., Coren, 1986). Furthermore, information may be passed from one response system to another. Thus, Mather and Fisk (1985) were able to show that the information you obtain from looking at a target can aid you in accurately pointing to the target. Conversely, information obtained from pointing can assist the eyes in accurately looking at other targets.

DEMONSTRATION BOX 10-4.   Sighting Dominance and the Straight Ahead Direction

The visual straight ahead may depend on a single eye (Porac & Coren, 1976, 1981; Walls, 1951). Try the following demonstration to see how this works. Stand in front of a wall at a distance of about 3 m. Pick a point on the wall that is directly in front of you (a small crack or bump will do). Now, with both eyes open, *quickly* stretch out your arm and align your fingertip with the point on the distant wall. When the alignment has been completed, alternately close each eye. You will find that the point on the distant wall will shift out of alignment for one of the eyes. However, the other eye will seem to be aligned with the point on the wall whether one or both eyes are opened. The eye that maintains the alignment is called the *sighting-dominant eye*. You will notice that regardless of which hand you use to perform the alignment, you will tend to line up a near (your fingertip) and a distant (the point on the wall) target in terms of the same eye. The presence of a sighting-dominant eye, and our tendency to make a straight ahead alignment in terms of this eye, indicates that the locus of the egocentric straight ahead direction may be shifted toward the side of the sighting-dominant eye.

Eye Dominance and Perceived Direction

We have considered eye movements of either eye to be interchangeable, but there is some data that suggest that the two eyes are not used equivalently in the computation of visual direction. Before we consider this evidence, it is important to understand that there are some tasks we habitually do with one eye. In sighting tasks where only one eye can be used at a time (such as in looking through a telescope), 65 percent of all observers consistently use their right eye, whereas the remainder consistently use their left (Coren, Porac & Duncan, 1981). The preferred eye for such tasks is usually called the **sighting-dominant eye** (Porac & Coren, 1981; Ruggieri, Cei, Ceridono & Bergerone, 1980). Demonstration Box 10-4 shows how you can determine which eye is your sighting-dominant eye.

For the purpose of our discussion of the perception of direction, sighting dominance is important because the visual direction associated with straight ahead is more strongly influenced by the dominant eye (Porac & Coren, 1976, 1981). This certainly does not mean that only one eye is used to determine visual direction (Ono & Weber,

1981). Rather, it means that the location of the egocenter, or Cyclopean eye, is biased toward the side of the sighting-dominant eye (Barbeito, 1981). For instance, Porac and Coren (1986) tested observers in a totally darkened room and had them set a point of light so that it appeared to be visually straight ahead. Whether observers used only one or both eyes, they tended to set the point so that it was closer to the side of the dominant eye, rather than midway between the two eyes.

BINOCULAR DEPTH PERCEPTION

Except for vergence movements, all the cues to depth we have discussed work just as well with one eye as they do with two. Nevertheless, having two eyes confers a great advantage in trying to estimate relative depth. For example, in many common tasks involving judgments of relative depth, such as threading a needle, inserting items into slots, or even placing cards behind alphabetic dividers in a box, people perform up to 30 percent faster and more accurately when using both eyes than they do with one eye alone (Sheedy, Bailey, Burl & Bass, 1986). Demonstration Box 10-5 allows you to see

---

DEMONSTRATION BOX 10-5.   Binocular versus Monocular Depth Perception

For this demonstration, which was suggested by Sekuler and Blake (1985), you will need two sharp pencils. Hold one in each hand at a relaxed arm's length, so that their tips are pointed toward each other but separated by about 10 cm. Now close one eye, and slowly bring the two pencils together so that the two points touch each other. Now try this with both eyes open. You will probably find that you were much more accurate with both eyes open than with one eye alone. However, not all of you will show this improvement with binocular viewing, since between 5 and 10 percent of the population do not have **stereopsis,** which is the term used to describe the ability to see depth based on binocular disparity.

---

how much better your depth perception is under binocular (two-eyed) conditions, as compared to monocular (one-eyed) viewing.

Cues for Stereopsis

The cues for binocular depth perception (**stereopsis**) depend on the fact that, in humans and other animals, the two eyes are horizontally separated. In humans, the distance between the two pupils may be up to 6.5 cm. Because of this separation, each eye has a different direction of view and, hence, a different image of the world. We call the differences between the two eye's images **binocular disparity.** You can see how different the images may be by following the instructions in Demonstration Box 10-6.

The process by which we merge these disparate images into a single unified percept is called **fusion.** As a process, however, fusion is fairly limited in its range of operation and many parts of the total visual image do not fuse. This failure of the two eyes' views to merge completely gives rise to double vision, or **diplopia.** Under normal viewing conditions you are usually not consciously aware of this diplopia, however you can readily learn to see the double images in the unfused portion of the visual field. Demonstration Box 10-7 shows how this is done.

In Demonstration Box 10-7, you should have noticed that the pattern of double images is different depending on whether the unfused image is in front of or in back of the target you fixated. In the demonstration we defined these patterns as **crossed** versus **uncrossed disparity.** Objects more distant than the point of fixation are seen in uncrossed disparity, whereas closer objects are seen with crossed disparity. Hence, we can use the type of double image as a cue to relative distance. Only objects at about the same distance as the target we are fixating will be fused and seen singly. When we map out all the points where targets are at about the same convergence or fixation distance in visual space, we trace out an imaginary curved plane called the **horopter.** A narrow region on either side of this hypothetical plane includes all points in visual space that are fused into single images. It is called **Panum's area.** Figure 10-13 contains a diagram of the horopter and Panum's area. The size and shape of Panum's area actually changes a bit with varying fixation distances. However, it always remains the zone in the visual field where the disparate images are seen as fused into a single object.

The process of fusion has also been looked at in terms of **corresponding retinal points.** These are areas on the retina that represent a common direction in the visual areas of the brain. The foveas of each eye are corresponding retinal points and, according to this conceptualization, the horopter represents the zone in visual space that stimulates corresponding retinal points for one fixation distance.

DEMONSTRATION BOX 10-6.   Binocular Disparity

You can see the difference between the views of your eyes by holding a pencil up near your nose, as shown. The tip of the pencil should be toward you and angled slightly downward. Now alternately close each eye. The pencil seems to swing back and forth. With your right eye open, it appears angled toward the left; with the left eye open, it appears angled toward the right. With both eyes open, the fused view is of a pencil straight ahead of your nose.

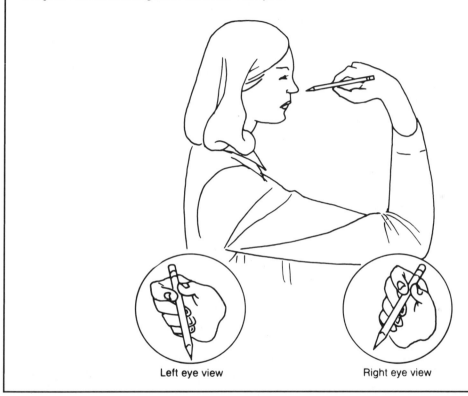

Left eye view   Right eye view

The Process of Stereopsis

In the 1830s two physicists, Charles Wheatstone and Sir David Brewster, independently created a technique to recreate the impression of depth from flat pictures using only the binocular disparity cue (see Wade, 1984). Basically, this involves recreating the disparate views each eye would see and representing them to the eyes in the form of draw-ings or photographs. Thus, in Figure 10-14A, we have two rods at different distances from the observer. If we drew the image each eye sees, we would get something like Figure 10-14B. Notice that the images are disparate, since the rods are more widely separated in the right eye's image than in the image in the left eye. Now the resulting images are viewed in an optical instrument known as a **stereoscope,** which places different stimuli into

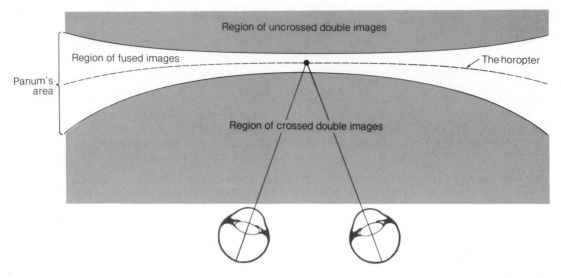

FIGURE 10-13   The horopter and Panum's area for one fixation distance. The regions of fusion and disparate images are shown. Crossed disparity is present at distances closer to the observer than the fixation distance; uncrossed disparity is present beyond the fixation distance. The presence of disparate images may provide a cue to distance.

the two eyes simultaneously, as shown in Figure 10-14C. When this is done, the disparate images fuse and the objects are seen as if they were an actual three-dimensional scene. For a period of time, every Victorian living room had a stereoscope and a set of travel pictures of famous places that had been taken using a two-lensed camera. This produced the "visual magic" of depth from flat images. Unfortunately, the trend toward more prurient photographic subjects relegated the stereoscope to unsavory establishments, although it did not end the interest in stereoscopic depth.

Understanding how stereopsis is achieved is more difficult than setting up the conditions that allow us to see binocular depth. There have been several computational approaches to this problem, most of which involve selecting a particular location in space, then comparing and computing the relative positions of parts of the images, and on the basis of this deriving the relative depth of the objects being viewed (e.g., Marr & Poggio, 1979;

Mayhew & Frisby, 1980). From a physiological viewpoint, however, the initial breakthroughs in understanding began in the late 1960s, when investigators began to find disparity-tuned detectors in the visual cortex of the cat (see Pettigrew, 1978a).

These detectors are cells that are finely tuned to small differences in the relative horizontal placement of images in the two eyes (Bishop, 1981). For example, suppose there is no disparity in the images of the two eyes and a particular cell responds maximally to this condition. This particular neuron would represent a spatial position that lies on the horopter, or the zone of fused images in external space. In a like manner, other neurons may be tuned to particular disparities that represent locations in space that lie in front of or behind the horopter. There is even evidence that there are different cells that respond to crossed versus uncrossed disparities (Mustillo, 1985). Each of these neurons seems to be tuned to only one particular

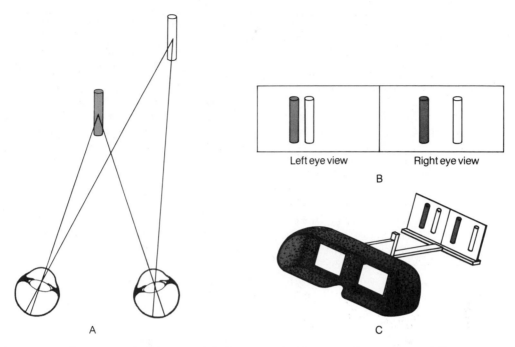

Left eye view   Right eye view

B

A   C

FIGURE 10-14   Disparate retinal images. (A) The two retinal images of a scene are different because the two eyes view the world from slightly different directions. (B) A *stereogram* is a flat representation that mimics the differences between the two retinal images. (C) A stereogram is viewed in a stereoscope that allows for the separate but simultaneous stimulation of the two eyes. The phenomenon is called *stereopsis.*

disparity value. Some seem to be responsive only to stimuli that lie close to the horopter; others are tuned to large disparities or to stimuli that lie far from the horopter (Aslin & Dumais, 1980; DeValois & DeValois, 1980). This means that rather large populations of cortical neurons are needed to represent all the possible disparity values in the visual scene.

It has been suggested that the existence of disparity-tuned detectors is not enough to explain stereoscopic depth perception. The problem arises in situations like that in Demonstration Box 10-8, which contains a random-dot stereoscopic display. These displays were first introduced by Julesz (e.g., 1971), who used them to demonstrate the notion of **global stereopsis.** If you follow the instruc-

tions in Demonstration Box 10-8, you will see a dotted square floating in front of the background of random dots. This perception comes about because of disparity cues built into the dot patterns. Figure 10-15 shows how this disparity, which consists of a horizontal shift in a group of these random dots, is created.

You might suppose that since there is disparity built into the random-dot stimulus, neurons tuned for such information should be capable of detecting depth from these arrays. The problem comes about because the stimulus is composed of identical dots, rather than discrete and identifiable contours. If stereopsis is based on the action of disparity-tuned detectors, each of which responds to one disparity value in the array, any dot potentially could be

DEMONSTRATION BOX 10-7.   Double Images and Disparity

Find a piece of transparent colored material like cellophane (any hue will work). Place it before your right eye. If you wear glasses you can affix it to the frame over the lens in front of your right eye; if not, use a piece of tape to hold it to your forehead. Now align two index fingers directly in front of your nose with the closer finger about 10-20 cm from your nose and the farther finger about 8 cm behind the closer one.

Now that you have arranged the appropriate situation, fixate your nearer finger. However, simultaneously try to pay attention to what the far finger looks like. This is a pretty difficult feat to accomplish at first, but with practice you should be able to fixate one target while simultaneously paying attention to what is going on beyond the fixated area. When you fixate the near target, you will notice that two images of the far target will be seen. The fact that one eye is viewing the image through a colored filter should help make the presence of double images beyond the fixation point more apparent. If you switch your fixation to the farther object, the closer of the two targets will appear as a double image. Targets that lie away from the area surrounding the point of fixation are not fused into a single image. They produce *disparate* retinal images. Disparate, unfused images are always

present in the visual field; however, we are usually not aware of them unless forced to attend to them as in this demonstration.

Once you have become comfortable with this procedure, fixate the near target and then close your right eye. You should notice that the image of the far target (the uncolored image) appears to lie to the left of the nearer, fixated object. Now close the left eye and open the right and you will notice the opposite. The image of the far target (the colored image) now appears to lie to the right of the closer, fixated target. The fact that the right eye is seeing the right disparate image and the left eye is seeing the left disparate image means that when both eyes are open the far target is seen in **uncrossed disparity.** The opposite will happen if you change your fixation to the far target. Now the closer object appears as *diplopic* (double). If you once again alternately close each eye, you will notice that the right eye is now seeing the image that lies to the left of the fixated target (the colored image), while the left eye is viewing the image that lies to the right. In the case of double images that lie closer to us than the point of fixation, we have a situation of **crossed disparity.** As the text explains, these differences in disparity may be a cue to distance.

---

combined with any other dot, with each of the many possible combinations producing a different depth. For this reason there must be a method of eliminating or avoiding false combinations and selecting only correct disparity pairs. Marr (1982) has suggested a very sophisticated computational scheme that would allow one to program a computer to do exactly this. However, some investigators have looked for physiological solutions that assume that detectors tuned to the same disparity cooperate, whereas those tuned to different disparities inhibit each other. With a population of neu-

rons working together in this fashion, only one depth solution would be common to this facilitatory-inhibitory process and only one global stereoscopic view would be seen (Julesz & Schumer, 1981). In any event, the solution used by the neural system probably involves a good deal of computation, since it often takes a good deal of time for observers to actually see the depth in random-dot stereograms. It has been suggested that stereoscopic information may be integrated over intervals of up to a half second in length (White & Odom, 1985).

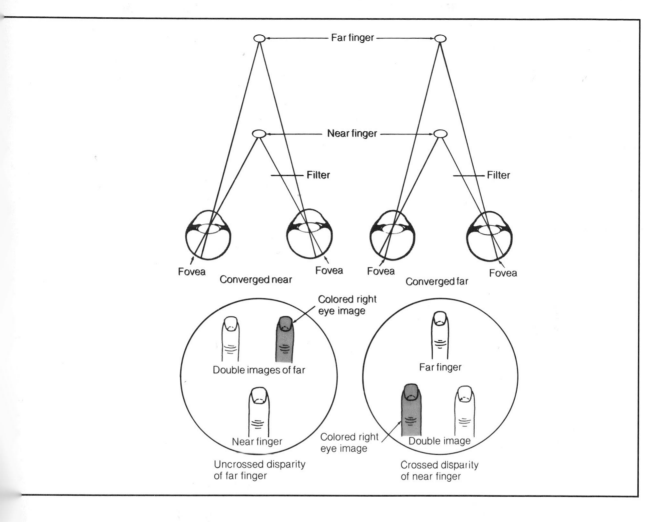

Far finger

Near finger

Filter   Filter

Fovea   Fovea   Fovea   Fovea
Converged near   Converged far

Colored right
eye image

Double images of far   Far finger

Near finger   Double image
                Colored right
                eye image

Uncrossed disparity   Crossed disparity
of far finger   of near finger

INTERACTION OF CUES

Although it is the case that each of the cues for depth we have discussed is sufficient, by itself, to give the conscious impression of a three-dimensional arrangement in space, the accuracy of our perception of distance often depends on the interaction of a number of cues. Under normal conditions, if a cue such as interposition suggests that your friend Fred is standing closer to you than your friend Maria, other cues, such as relative size, height in the plane, and binocular disparity, will tend

to confirm this relationship. Chaotic and conflicting cues, such as those shown in William Hogarth's 1754 engraving *False Perspective* (Figure 10-16), virtually never occur in "real world" settings.

How do cues for depth combine? Jameson and Hurvich (1959) suggested that an observer's sensitivity to a difference in distance when several cues are available is approximately the arithmetic sum of the sensitivities obtained with each cue alone. This has been demonstrated experimentally by van der Meer (1979), who found that information from binocular disparity and linear perspective added

DEMONSTRATION BOX 10-8. Random-Dot Stereograms and Global Stereopsis

You may demonstrate how depth cues can bring about the perception of a binocular form by using the accompanying figure. You will need a pocket mirror, which should be placed on the dotted center line of Figure B while you hold your head as shown in Figure A. Adjust the images until the two views seem to overlap and the frames around the outside seem to be at the same distance. Viewing it in this way, you will see a square form emerge, floating above the background, created completely by the depth cue of binocular disparity. Notice that this square simply can't be seen in either monocular view alone.

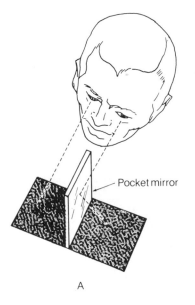

Pocket mirror

A

B

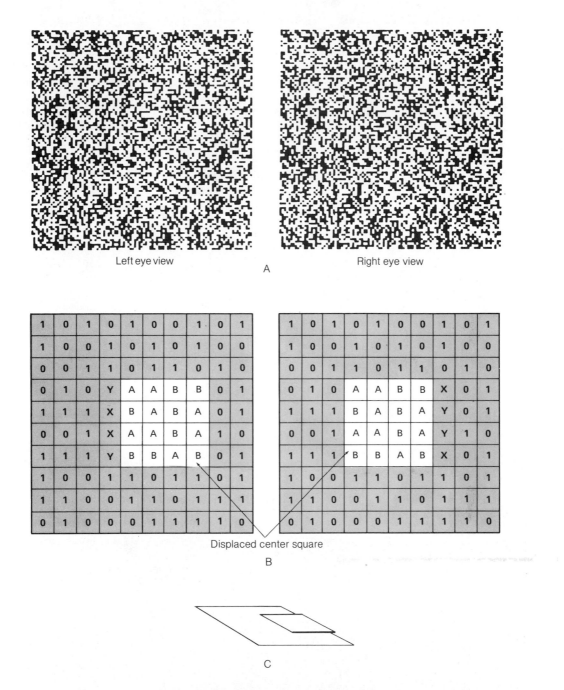

Left eye view   Right eye view

A

Displaced center square

B

C

FIGURE 10-15   Figure A is a random-dot stereogram. Figure B shows how A is constructed, and C illustrates that a central square is seen floating above the background when the two views are combined in a stereoscope. (From B. Julesz, *Foundations of Cyclopean Perception.* Copyright 1971 by the University of Chicago Press.)

FIGURE 10-16   Ambiguity of depth cues gives a confusing, difficult interpretation to a scene, as shown in Hogarth's 1754 engraving *False Perspective*. The more you study this figure, the more contradictory depth cues you find.

together in the final judgment of perceived depth. Although we cannot prove that there is a simple addition of information from various cues to distance, it is certainly the case that the more cues available, and the more consistent they are, the stronger the perception of depth (Berbaum, Tharp & Mroczek, 1983).

Another important aspect of the interaction of depth cues is the fact that absolute and relative depth cues may help calibrate each other. For example, binocular disparity is most effective as a relative depth cue, indicating whether one target is nearer or farther than another, rather than how close they both are to an observer. The geometry of the situation, however, is complicated by the fact that if we keep the relative distance between two targets constant but move both targets farther away from you, the amount of disparity in the image grows smaller. Nonetheless, our perception of the relative difference in the depth of these targets remains the same, a phenomenon sometimes called *stereoscopic depth constancy* (Ono & Comerford, 1977). Apparently, this adjustment of the relative depth obtained from binocular disparity comes about as a consequence of using other cues for absolute distance. In other words, we recalibrate our interpretation of the magnitude of depth difference signaled by a particular amount of binocular disparity by using other information about absolute depth (Cormack, 1984).

The phenomenon of stereoscopic depth constancy reveals a problem with depth perception originally noticed by Brunswick (1952, 1956). He argued that each separate distance and depth cue is ambiguous under certain conditions, such as those depicted in Figure 10-16, and that sometimes any single cue may lead us to an incorrect interpretation of depth or distance within a scene. The importance we assign to a particular cue will be determined by its reliability and our past experience with its accuracy. Simply shifting our attention to a given depth cue seems to increase its power in determining how we perceive three-dimensional space (Kawabata, 1986). If we accept such an argument, we are, in effect, accepting a constructive theory of

depth perception, in which our ability to decipher and to combine depth cues may be a learned ability that becomes more efficient with experience. It is on the issue of whether there is a learned component in the perception of depth that direct and constructive theories of perception have focused much of their argument. In the older literature this has been referred to as the "*nativist* versus *empiricist*" question (Hochberg, 1972). The nativists argue that these perceptual abilities and our capacity to use them are inborn and automatically invoked by stimulation, whereas the empiricists maintain that interaction with the world, through which we learn about its properties and organization, is crucial to our spatial awareness and abilities. Let us now consider this issue briefly.

DEVELOPMENT OF SPACE PERCEPTION

One of the most common ways to assess whether there is a constructive aspect to space perception is to observe the behavior of young organisms when they are placed in situations that call on their abilities to perceive distance or direction. Since infants and young animals have limited experience with the world, their abilities to deal with such situations should shed some light on the role of inborn versus learned components in the perception of visual space.

Species Differences

The evidence is quite clear that in certain simpler animals the perception of direction and distance is inborn. For example, in salamanders it is possible surgically to rotate the eye 180 deg, thus inverting the retina. When this is done, animals consistently swim and snap in the opposite direction when presented with a food lure (Sperry, 1943). Since the same results occur when similar operations are performed during the animals' embryonic stage, it is clear that visual direction is related innately to the location of retinal stimulation in this species (Stone, 1960). Similarly, immediately after birth chicks peck at small objects with reasonable accuracy. When experimenters optically displaced the images of the targets to one side (using special lenses attached to hoods), the chicks proceeded to peck systematically to one side. This pattern of inaccuracy showed little improvement over time, suggesting that this response to the apparent direction of stimuli was not changeable by experience (Hess, 1950). In higher animals, such as mammals, experience may play a larger role.

To allow more exact determination of which factors may be influenced by experience, investigators frequently use controlled-rearing procedures, such as rearing an animal in total darkness from birth until testing. Such dark-rearing eliminates all externally-generated visual experience. If experience with various visual depth cues is necessary for the development of normal depth perception, these dark-reared animals should have measurable deficits when required to respond to distance cues. If depth perception simply matures as the animal ages, then restricting the animal's visual experience should not affect its behavior and the only important variable should be its chronological age.

A simple and popular procedure for measuring depth perception in young animals uses an apparatus called the **visual cliff** (Walk & Gibson, 1961). A diagram of a typical visual cliff arrangement is shown in Figure 10-17. Basically it consists of two sections, divided by a ''start platform.'' Each section provides a different depth impression. The ''shallow'' side is a piece of glass that lies directly over a patterned surface. The ''deep'' side has the same type of patterned surface, but looks like a sharp drop since the surface is placed at some distance below the glass. For testing, a young animal is placed on the central starting platform that separates the apparently shallow and deep surfaces. It is assumed that from this position the animal can see that the shallow side is safe, whereas the deep side, with its simulated cliff-like drop-off, would be perceived as being dangerous. Investigators make the presumption that if the animal consistently chooses the shallow over the deep side, then it can perceive the difference in apparent depth and is attempting to avoid a fall.

A number of different types of animals have been tested on the visual cliff, including rats,

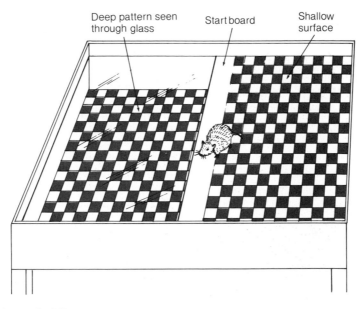

FIGURE 10-17   The visual cliff.

chickens, turtles, goats, sheep, pigs, cats, dogs, monkeys, and humans (Walk & Gibson, 1961). In all cases, even when testing very young animals, there was a preference for the shallow over the deep side of the cliff. There were some interesting species differences, however, which seemed to be related to the habitat features of the natural environment for the various species (Sloane, Shea, Procter & Dewsbury, 1978). For instance, aquatic animals, such as certain turtles, did not show the marked preference for the shallow side that the other, more landbound species displayed. Perhaps the survival value of cliff avoidance may not be as pronounced in animals that spend much of their lives swimming, since changes in depth of water are not as perilous as sudden sharp drops on land.

Experience and Depth Perception

Although the cross-species differences observed in depth perception are of interest, the visual cliff apparatus has been used primarily to generate data concerning the development of depth perception. A combination of controlled rearing followed by observations of behavior on the visual cliff has been the experimental technique most commonly used in animal studies. In general, the findings have suggested that experience and innate factors interact to produce an animal's ability to perceive depth. For example, when cats or rats are initially reared in the dark they show little depth discrimination on the visual cliff when first tested. However, as they receive more and more experience in a lighted world their depth discrimination rapidly improves until they are indistinguishable from normally reared animals (Walk & Gibson, 1961; Tees & Midgley, 1978).

When the visual experience takes place also seems important. There seem to be **sensitive periods** in an animal's development, referring to the fact that there are particular ages and particular durations of time when depriving an animal of a particular type of visual experience may produce the largest perceptual deficits (Aslin, 1981b; Mitchell, 1981; Timney, 1985). For instance, a study by

Tees (1974) shows how deprivation of visual experience during a sensitive period can affect later depth perception. Dark-reared rats were compared to light-reared rats on their preference for the deep versus the shallow side of the visual cliff. The amount of time that the animals were dark-reared was varied, and in addition, the strength of the depth information was varied by varying the distance to the bottom of the deep side of the visual cliff. In this study, the age of the animal, the amount of distance information, and the amount of visual experience all interacted. It was only among animals that had been dark-reared for a comparatively long time (60 to 90 days) that the effects of rearing conditions revealed themselves. For these animals, although depth could be discriminated when the drop-off was large, there was an insensitivity to weaker distance cues. These data indicate that there may be inborn components in the ability of rats to discriminate depth on the visual cliff. These are probably sharpened through experience with depth cues in the environment, a finding supported by other research as well (e.g., Kaye, Mitchell & Cynader, 1982).

The developmental time course and the effects of experience seem to be different for the various depth cues. Binocular depth perception develops quite early, since evidence for the use of binocular disparity for a depth cue may be found in 3- or 4-month-old infants (Birch, Shimojo & Held, 1985; Braddick, Atkinson, Julesz, Kropfl, Bodis-Wollner & Raab, 1980; Hutz & Bechtoldt, 1980; Petrig, Julesz, Kropfl, Baumgartner & Anliker, 1981). Infants at this age are too young to crawl and cannot be tested on the visual cliff, so other techniques must be used. For example, Fox, Aslin, Shea, and Dumais (1980) presented random-dot stereograms, similar to those in Figure 10-15, to infants between 2 and 5 months of age. When viewed with special glasses, these infants saw a square floating in front of a background only if they could combine the disparate information from the two eyes' views. (You saw in Demonstration Box 10-8 that such patterns are meaningless unless you can make use of the disparity cues hidden in each monocular view.) This square was made to move. When infants could see the square in depth, they tended to follow it with their eyes. An alternative technique for measuring depth perception in young infants capitalizes on the fact that infants tend to reach for objects that appear to be near them (Granrud, Yonas & Pettersen, 1984). Results using this technique verified the finding that binocular depth perception is present by 4 months of age (Granrud, 1986), suggesting either an innate or a rapidly learned process. This may be contrasted to earlier animal work, which suggested that the use of monocular cues for depth is much more dependent on specific experience (Eichengreen, Coren & Nachmias, 1966).

The ability to use kinetic depth information seems to develop at about the same time that the ability to use binocular depth information appears, at roughly 3 to 5 months of age (Kellman, 1984; Owsley, 1983; Yonas & Granrud, 1985b). One biologically important aspect of depth perception, namely sensitivity to information about object motion toward the body (which may indicate an impending collision), seems to be present at an even earlier age. It has been measured at ages as young as 2 to 3 weeks (Ball & Vurpillot, 1976; Yonas, 1981). Even at this young age, infants will blink their eyes when presented with an object that seems to be moving closer and seems to be growing close enough to strike them in the face.

Studies that have looked at sensitivity to pictorial depth cues have shown a slower developmental process, by about 3 to 4 months. For example, several studies have shown that 6- to 7-month-old infants respond to linear perspective information (Kaufman, Maland & Yonas, 1981; Yonas, Cleaves & Pettersen, 1978) or to familiar size (Granrud, Haake & Yonas, 1985). Use of more complex cues, such as the perception of relative depth in a picture, based on the direction of shadows cast in the pictorial representation, may not appear until the age of 3 years (Yonas, Goldsmith & Hallstrom, 1978).

Developmental studies indicate that the perception of depth and distance cannot be fully understood unless we allow some components to be explained by inborn factors, whereas others may require active experience to emerge. These studies suggest that adhering strictly to either a direct perception or constructive perception viewpoint might be too limiting. Innate components of perception must mature, and certain types of experience can help or hinder the achievement of a high level of perceptual functioning. In much the same way, some aspects of depth perception seem to be given directly, and others require memory and experience to allow them to function properly.

GLOSSARY

The following definitions are specific to this book.

Absolute distance   The distance of an object from the observer.

Accommodation   The change in focus of the lens of the eye, which may serve as a depth cue.

Aerial perspective   A distance cue in which objects appear hazy, less distinct, and bluer the farther away they are, because of the interaction of light with dust and moisture particles in the air.

Afference copy   Information about eye movement arising from an intended or planned eye movement.

Binocular   Pertaining to two eyes.

Binocular disparity   The difference in the monocular views of the two eyes.

Bodycentric   Direction with the midline of the body used as a reference point.

Computational theories   Theories involving the presumption that certain perceived qualities must be computed from stimulus information and that these computations can be precisely described mathematically.

Constructive theories   Theories maintaining that perception may involve the integration of several sources of information, and may be affected by cognitive factors and experience.

Convergence   The inward rotation of both eyes toward the nose as a fixated object becomes closer.

Corresponding retinal points   Areas in the two retinas that share a common visual direction when the two monocular inputs are processed in the brain.

Crossed disparity   A cue for relative distance, where, when there are double images, the unfused image in the right eye appears on the left and that in the left eye on the right.

Cues Features of visual stimuli that prompt the perception of depth or distance.

Cyclopean eye An imaginary point midway between the eyes thought to be used as a reference point for the straight ahead direction.

Diplopia Double vision.

Direct perception The idea that all the information needed for the final conscious percept is in the stimulus array and is apprehended directly.

Divergence The outward rotation of both eyes away from the nose as a fixated object becomes more distant.

Efference copy Information about eye movement arising from the commands issued to the ocular musculature to rotate the eye.

Egocenter The position in the head that serves as the reference point for the determination of headcentric straight ahead.

Egocentric localization The awareness of where our bodies are positioned relative to other objects in the external environment.

Familiar size The known or remembered size of objects.

Fusion The process by which disparate views are synthesized into one percept.

Global stereopsis Stereopsis that is not dependent on local contour elements (e.g., as in random-dot stereograms).

Headcentric Direction judged using the midline of the head as a reference point.

Height in the (picture) plane A cue for distance referring to where an object is relative to the horizon.

Horopter An imaginary plane in external space used to describe the region of fused images.

Intelligent perception The presumption that cognitive processes and experience can affect perception.

Interposition The depth cue based on the blocking of an object from view by another closer object.

Kinetic depth effect The perception of the three-dimensional qualities of an object based on cues generated by the object's motion.

Linear perspective The apparent convergence of physically parallel lines as they recede into the distance.

Monocular cues Depth cues requiring only one eye to be used.

Motion parallax The apparent relative motion of objects in the visual field as the observer moves his head or body.

Object-relative localizations The estimation of the relative positions of objects (other than the observer) within the environment.

Overlay *See* Interposition.

Panum's area The region around the horopter where all images in space are fused.

Physiological cues *See* Structural cues.

Pictorial depth cues Cues for distance that can be found in photographs and pictures.

Reduction conditions An experimental procedure in which an attempt is made to eliminate or reduce most depth cues.

Relative brightness A depth cue in which the brighter of two otherwise identical objects will be seen as closer.

Relative distance Distances of objects relative to one another.

Retinal image size A potential depth cue based on the size of the image on the retina.

Sensitive period An age range during which the development of a perceptual ability may be strongly influenced by the presence or absence of relevant stimulation or experience.

Sighting-dominant eye The eye whose use is preferred in monocular tasks such as looking through a telescope.

Stereopsis The ability to see depth based solely on the disparity of the two retinal images.

Stereoscope An optical instrument enabling two different images to stimulate the two eyes simultaneously to produce an effect of depth.

Structural cues Depth and distance cues arising from adjustments of the eye(s) in interaction with the visual stimulus.

Texture gradient Distance cue based on variations in surface texture as a function of distance from the observer.

Uncrossed disparity A cue for relative distance in which, when there are double images, the unfused image in the right eye appears on the right and that in the left eye on the left.

Vanishing point In linear perspective a point on the horizon at which converging parallel lines seem to meet.

Vergence movements Movements of the eyes in which the two eyes move together but in opposite directions, either converging or diverging.

Visual cliff A table with shallow and deep sides overlaid by a sheet of glass; used for measuring depth perception in young animals.

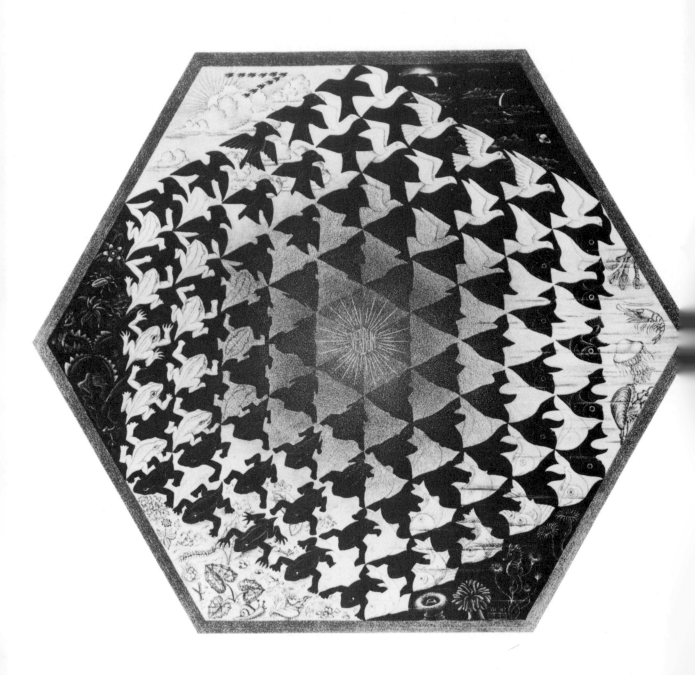

CHAPTER
11

Form

"When I lift my eyes from the paper on which I am writing I see the chairs and tables and walls of my room. . . . I see, from my window, trees and meadows, and horses and oxen, and distant hills. I see each of its proper size, of its proper form, and at its proper distance; and these particulars appear as immediate transformations of the eye. . . . How, then, is it that we receive accurate information, by the eye, of size and shape and distance?" (Mill, 1829, p. 97)

Look around you, as John Stuart Mill did. You will be struck, as he was, with how filled the perceptual world is with *objects*. When you enter your room you see a desk, a chair, some books, and so forth, not patches of light, brown, gray, red, and green, which is the actual stimulus on your retina. You not only *see* these patches as objects but also identify them as members of particular classes of objects, and can recall whether you have seen them before. This is a common everyday form of perceptual achievement that we each do automatically and easily, yet describing how we manage to accomplish this has turned out to be very difficult. In this chapter, we tell you something of what we now know about the perception of form (Mill's other questions, about size and distance, are dealt with in Chapters 10 and 14, respectively). We describe first the information about the world that is present in the distribution of light on our retinas, and then we describe how the visual system transforms that into "perceptual objects." Finally, we discuss how we recognize and identify these perceptual objects. In several places in the chapter, the traditional psychological approach to the perception of form is contrasted with the newer "computational" approach.

THE VISUAL FIELD

The eye receives information in the form of reflected light from the environment. The total of all the parts of the environment that stimulate your eyes at any given moment is called the **visual field.** Figure 11-1 portrays the visual field as seen by the left eye of the physicist/psychologist Ernst Mach, as he lay on the couch in his study in Prague, Czechoslovakia, sometime around 1885. Reflected light from the visual field forms a **retinal image,** consisting of a two-dimensional distribution of light of various intensities and wavelengths on his retina. This distribution carries information about objects in the environment, because light is altered uniquely by each object it falls on. Some of the light may be absorbed before being reflected to the eye; this will alter the intensity of the image on the retina, so that, for example, his shoes will look darker than the couch on which he rests. When light of certain wavelengths is selectively absorbed, areas of the image appear colored (see Chapter 5); thus, if one of his books absorbs all but light of the

FIGURE 11-1   **The visual field as seen by the left eye of Ernst Mach. (Based on Mach, 1959/1886)**

longer wavelengths, the portion of the retinal image that corresponds to it will contain only red-appearing light. The process of getting from the flat patches of light that make up the retinal image to the world of objects about us is the major problem in the perception of visual form.

CONTOUR

At the most basic level, the visual system divides the visual field into **shapes,** sometimes called "blobs," separated by **contours.** A contour is a place in the retinal image where the light intensity (or wavelength composition) changes abruptly. Examples of contours include a black line on a sheet of white paper, the edge of a blackboard, and the outline of the moon against the night sky. Generally speaking, shapes are regions in the retinal image that are surrounded by contours. Under appropriate circumstances we may interpret these blobs in the retinal image as objects in the real world; however, since this is an interpretation, at times we may be wrong.

Contour and Change

Contours are the basic building blocks of visual perception; in their absence we actually lose our ability to see. We can demonstrate this by looking into a **Ganzfeld** (German for "whole field"). A Ganzfeld is a visual field that contains no abrupt luminance changes and thus no contours. When observers look into a Ganzfeld, they usually report seeing "a shapeless fog that goes on forever." Any hint of color soon fades to gray, even if the entire field is illuminated with, say, green or blue or red light (Cohen, 1958). Many observers even experience perceptual *blank out,* a feeling that they *can't see,* after prolonged viewing. This feeling quickly disappears the instant any kind of luminance change is introduced into the visual field (Avant, 1965; Cohen, 1958).

Blank out can occur in natural environments as well. For instance, *snow blindness* is a kind of natural blank out, caused by the lack of contour in the retinal image when the visual field contains a lot of snow and ice. The snow and ice scatter much of the light in all directions, and together are often very uniform in texture, which creates a kind of natural Ganzfeld. You can experience some of these sensations for yourself by trying Demonstration Box 11-1.

For vision to occur, there must be not only local variations in the intensity of light, such as contours, but also variation in the pattern of illumination on the retina over time. This can be demonstrated using a **stabilized retinal image.** In this technique, the retinal image is made to stay in one place on the retina, in spite of where or how the eye moves. Normally, the retinal image is continually in motion, because of saccadic eye movements made as we look around the environment, smooth tracking movements, and drifting movements. There are also *microsaccades* (tiny, involuntary eye movements) that keep our eyes shivering in their sockets. These microsaccades occur many times a second, and cause the retinal image to shift from place to place on the retina even when we are trying to hold our eyes completely still. The effect of the microsaccades, combined with other forms of eye movement, is to constantly move any contours across a number of different retinal receptors. This causes temporal variations in the stimulation of any given receptor (in the form of "on" times followed by "off" times) as contours are swept across the retina.

When we do manage to stabilize the retinal image, usually by having an observer wear a special contact lens that moves with the eye and has a mirror or a tiny projector mounted on it, the stabilized image soon fades from view (e.g., Pritchard, Heron & Hebb, 1960; Riggs, Ratliff, Cornsweet & Cornsweet, 1953; Yarbus, 1967). The contours disappear in chunks, and the color also fades away. If we now flicker the stabilized image on and off, it

DEMONSTRATION BOX 11-1.   The Ganzfeld

Although Ganzfeld situations have been produced with elaborate laboratory equipment, there are several simple ways to produce a Ganzfeld that will allow you to experience this contourless field for yourself. You can take a table tennis ball and cut it in half, placing one half over each eye, or you can use two white plastic spoons (like those probably available in any campus cafeteria) to produce a Ganzfeld by placing the bowl of a spoon over each eye as shown in the accompanying figure. Direct your gaze toward a light source (a fluorescent lamp, say) prior to placing the objects before your eyes, so that your field of view will be flooded with diffuse, contourless light. Stay in this position for a few minutes and monitor any changes or alterations in your conscious perceptual experience. If the light originally had a tint, you will soon notice that the color will fade into a gray. After a while you will suddenly feel that you cannot see. This feeling of blindness is called ''blank out.'' It seems that in the absence of contours in the field, vision ceases. If a friend now casts a shadow over part of the field (say, with a pencil across the spoons), vision will immediately return with the introduction of this contour.

Spoon

will reappear and, if the flicker rate is high enough, it will not fade (Cornsweet, 1956). Flickering the image has re-introduced the temporal changes in light intensity usually caused by the eye's movements. The disappearance of our perception of patterns when the retinal image is stabilized, and its reappearance when the retinal image is flickered, supports the idea that constant temporal change in the stimulation of the individual receptors is a necessary condition for vision. Without this constant change, receptors soon cease to respond differently from neighboring receptors, hence we lose the signal that should be present if a contour is in the image (cf. Norwich, 1983). In the absence of signals indicating that a contour is present, much like our experience in the Ganzfeld, our perception of patterns will fade and disappear from consciousness.

You may experience the reappearance of a stabilized image that has disappeared by trying Demonstration Box 3-3 (see Chapter 3) again. In that demonstration you mapped the pattern of blood vessels that lie above your retina. Ordinarily you don't see these blood vessels because they create a stabilized image on your retina as light passes through them. They are always in the same place so they create no temporal changes in stimulation of the receptors. By moving a flashlight placed at the corner of the eye, however, you cause their shadows to move across the retina, making them visible. You will note that as soon as you stop moving the flashlight (thus stopping the temporal change), the blood vessels disappear, since their image is now stabilized again.

Contour Emergence

Temporal factors are important to our perception of contours in another way. We are not immediately aware of a contour when it appears on our retinas. It takes some time for the contour information to be processed and the perceived contour to emerge into our consciousness. If anything interferes with that processing before we see the contour, it may never become visible. The first demonstration of this was by Werner (1935) and it created an experimental technique that is now used to investigate many other phenomena. Werner presented observers with a brief view of a black disk on a white background (the *target*) and then, after a variable amount of time (called the *interstimulus interval*), presented a brief view of a black ring (the *mask*) in the same place in the visual field. The inner contour of the ring was exactly the same size as the outer contour of the disk, so the procedure resulted

in two opposite contours appearing in the same place on the retina separated by different intervals of time. Figure 11-2 contains a diagram of this situation and also summarizes the results of the experiment, which were quite striking.

For very short interstimulus intervals, less than 100 msec, observers tended to see only a large black disk, a combination of the disk and the ring. It was as if the two had merged, or added together. For long interstimulus intervals, greater than 200 msec, observers saw both of the stimuli clearly, the disk before the ring. But for interstimulus intervals between 100 and 200 msec, observers tended to see only the ring. It was as if the disk had not been presented at all, although it stimulated the retina exactly as it had at other interstimulus intervals. Werner interpreted this *masking* of the disk by the ring to mean that the later-appearing contour had interfered with the processing of the earlier one, preventing its appearance in consciousness. This kind of masking is called **backward masking** since the mask appeared after the target and seemed to be acting backward in time. A more general term, used to refer to any situation in which contours on adjacent parts of the retina interfere with one another, is **metacontrast.**

Studies of masking have helped shed light on several aspects of form perception, such as how contours interact in the visual system (e.g., Kahneman, 1968; Lefton, 1973). One interesting suggestion is that for each contour detected the visual system produces both *excitation,* to indicate the existence of the contour, and *inhibition* of contours detected nearby. If two contours are detected closely enough in time and are spatially close to each another, then the inhibition produced for one (e.g., the ring) may cancel the excitation produced for the other (e.g., the disk; see Weisstein, 1968; Weisstein, Ozog & Szoc, 1975). Another suggestion is that if the visual system does indeed decompose the retinal image into spatial frequency components (as suggested in Chapter 4), different components may be processed in different channels (see Graham, 1981). Because of this separation, contours composed of similar

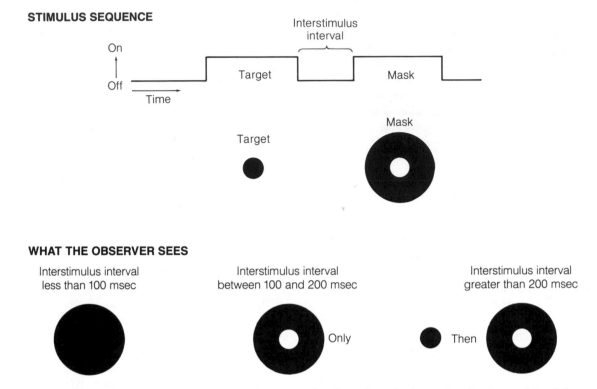

FIGURE 11-2   A typical metacontrast experiment. Notice that when the interstimulus interval is of the appropriate length, the target is often not seen at all.

spatial frequency components will mask one another, whereas those composed of different components will not (Weisstein, Harris, Berbaum, Tangney & Williams, 1977).

THE PERCEPTUAL OBJECT

The quotation from Mill beginning this chapter emphasizes that the visual world is filled with *objects*. That is, under normal viewing conditions, our visual systems operate to produce **perceptual objects** from the array of blobs and contours contained in the distribution of light on the retina. There are no perceptual objects on the retina, they exist only in our minds, and only as the result of many levels of processing and interpretation applied to the retinal image. The miraculous thing is that the perceptual objects so closely resemble what physics tells us is the nature of the "real" objects "out there" in the world. An apple to our consciousness is very like an apple "out there." How does this come about? The best guess at this time is that the perceptual object is *constructed* in focal attention from a group of features (or attributes) detected at a particular spatial location. In what follows we discuss how this happens.

Figure and Ground

The simplest perceptual object is a two-dimensional **figure** on a two-dimensional **ground.** A figure is simply an integrated group of contours. A shape can be a figure, but shapes can also form part of the background (or *ground*) from which the figure emerges. Thus, a ball resting on a field of grass is a figure (here a round shape) resting on a ground consisting of many elongated shapes (the blades of grass). How can we tell the difference between a figure and its ground? For example, how can you tell the book you are reading apart from the table on which it rests, or the printed words apart from the page? On your retina the blobs of contours that make up figures and grounds are all run together, intersecting and overlapping, but somehow the visual system separates the book from the table and the words from the page.

To begin with, this separation is a psychological achievement, as can be seen in Figure 11-3B. This is the famous Rubin (1915, 1921) face-vase ambiguous figure. When you look at this figure you might see a pair of silhouette faces gazing at each other or you might see an ornate vase. The vase appears white against a black ground, whereas the faces are black against a white ground. Notice that as you look at 11-3B for a few moments the two pattern organizations alternate in consciousness, demonstrating that the organization into figure and ground is in your mind, not in the stimulus. Notice also that the faces and the vase never appear together. You "know" that both are possible but you can't "see" both at the same time. It is impossible for a given part of a visual pattern to be simultaneously interpreted as both figure and ground. Gen-

erally speaking, the smaller an area or a shape is, the more likely it is to be seen as figure (see Weisstein & Wong, 1986). This is demonstrated in Figure 11-3, where it is easier to see the vase when the white area is smaller (11-3A) and easier to see the faces when the black area is smaller (11-3C).

Once a particular interpretation has been arrived at, for example the vase, figure and ground take on distinct properties. When the white area is seen as the vase, it appears to be "in front of" the black area seen as the ground, and the contours in the pattern seem to "belong" to the vase. However, when the interpretation changes, the contours are now seen to belong to the faces, and the faces seem closer than, and in front of, the white background. Furthermore, figures appear to be more "thinglike" and appear to have a shape whereas the ground appears formless. Figures are seen as "richer" and more meaningful and are remembered more easily. Figures also contrast more than the ground, appearing brighter or darker than equivalent patches of light that form part of the background (Coren, 1969). Finally, work based on the relative ability of figures and ground to mask other stimuli in a metacontrast-type of experiment suggests that stimuli seen as figures are processed or registered more quickly than stimuli seen as ground (Weisstein & Wong, 1986).

Figure-ground organization affects many other aspects of how we respond to the visual world, as

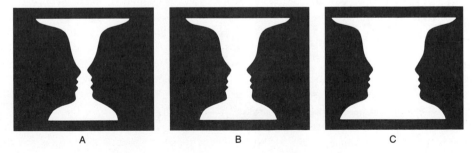

FIGURE 11-3 (B) A reversible figure-ground stimulus in which a pair of black faces or a white vase (or perhaps a birdbath or goblet) are seen alternately. When the white area is smaller (A) the vase is easier to see; when the black area is smaller (C) the faces are more easily seen.

has been demonstrated by a series of experiments by Naomi Weisstein and Eva Wong. Wong and Weisstein (1982) reported that the tilt of a short, straight line was easier to discriminate when it was flashed on a part of an outline version of Figure 11-3B that was currently being seen as figure (either the face or the vase), than when flashed on a part currently being seen as ground (e.g., the white part when the faces are figure). This finding is consistent with the notion that figures are usually given some processing priority over ground.

Not only can separation into figure and ground result in perceptual effects affecting other variables but it appears that other forms of perceptual processing can affect our perception of figure and ground. Figure 11-4A illustrates how form (and figure) can emerge from a two-dimensional array because of the existence of depth cues in the figure (see Chapter 10). In this case the cue is interposition, where an object apparently blocking another object is seen as closer than the occluded object. Despite the compelling percept of a white rectangle, which is brighter than the white making up the other parts of the figure, there is in actuality no rectangle drawn in here. The implicit depth cues cause you to conclude that such a figure should be present, and you then reorganize the perception of the array to perceive a figure (the white rectangle)

that actually is not present (Coren, 1972). The contours bounding the rectangle are called **subjective contours** or **illusory contours** because they exist only in your mind and are not physically present on the retina.

Although many factors can contribute to the formation of subjective contours (e.g., Halpern, 1981; Ware, 1981), the presence of depth cues seems to provide a powerful impetus to organize parts of the field into simple figures, even when they are not defined by physical contours. This is consistent with the fact that observers do report that subjective figures created by subjective contours appear to lie in front of their backgrounds, even when all other depth cues are carefully removed (Coren & Porac, 1983b). Figure 11-4B shows another subjectively contoured figure in the form of a white triangle in which the triangle clearly appears to stand out in front of the other elements in the figure. We saw another example of subjective contours created by depth information in the random-dot stereograms created in Demonstration Box 10-8.

Interestingly, subjective contours act very much like real contours, to the extent that they can mask real contours (Lehmkuhle & Fox, 1980; Weisstein, Matthews & Berbaum, 1974), improve judgments of the position of a dot (Pomerantz, Goldberg, Golder & Tetewsky, 1981), and cause

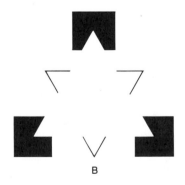

A   B

FIGURE 11-4   The white rectangle across the word *STOP* in A and the white triangle in B are bounded by subjective contours. They actually do not exist in the stimulus. (From Coren, 1972. Copyright 1972 by the American Psychological Association. Reprinted by permission.)

motion aftereffects (Smith & Over, 1979). They can even meld with, or "capture," real contours superimposed upon them (Ramachandran, 1986). Subjective contours, then, are one example of how certain factors interact to segregate the perceptual field into figure and ground (see Petry & Meyer, 1987, for a full review of subjective contour research).

Figural Organization

Most forms or objects we see are composed of a number of elements. We have already found that the organization of elements into perceptual objects involves an active constructive process. We can see the action of this "urge to organize" in Figure 11-5, where the many possible organizations of the elements seem to alternate in a rapid unstable manner.

The general question of how all perception comes to be organized into patterns, shapes, and forms was central to a group of psychologists (Max Wertheimer, Kurt Koffka, and Wolfgang Kohler were the most influential) who formed the **Gestalt**

School of psychology. *Gestalt* is a German word that can be translated to mean "form," "whole," or even "whole form." They were interested in processes that cause certain elements to seem to be part of the same figure or grouping and others to seem to belong to other figures or groups. They formulated several laws of perceptual organization that govern the emergence of a visual figure (Wertheimer, 1923). Their basic observation was that elements within a pattern do not seem to operate independently. At the phenomenal level, there appear to be attractive "forces" among the various elements that cause them to form a meaningful and coherent figure, much as gravity organizes the planets, sun, and moons of our solar system. They described how certain regular properties of elements within a pattern bring about the emergence of stable figures.

A Gestalt principle is illustrated in Figure 11-6A, which is usually seen as two clusters of dots. Although the array actually contains 12 individual dots, perceptual processes organize them into an experience of two groups. This is an example of

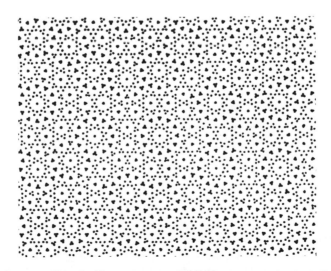

FIGURE 11-5   A stimulus revealing the "urge to organize." There are many possible organizations of the various small elements, and the visual pattern you see is continually changing as you shift from one organization to another.

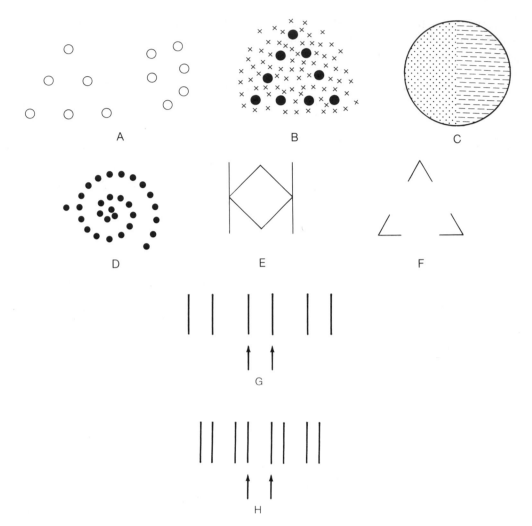

FIGURE 11-6   Examples of the Gestalt principles of figural organization: (A) grouping by proximity; (B) and (C) grouping by similarity; (D) good continuation; (E) an extreme example of closure in which two common figures are hidden; (F) closure; (G) and (H) the distortion of the distance between elements (the distances marked by the arrows are the same) by the principle of proximity.

the **law of proximity,** which states that elements close to one another tend to be perceived as a unit or figure. Figure 11-6B is normally seen as a triangle composed of black dots on a background of (or surrounded by a swarm of) X's. This is an example of the **law of similarity,** which maintains that similar objects tend to be grouped together.

Another example of this law is seen in Figure 11-6C where the two halves of the circular field appear quite separate because of grouping by similarity (for a more advanced analysis of such effects see Julesz, 1981). Figure 11-6D is viewed usually as a spiral of dots with one standing outside. This is an example of the **law of good continuation,** which states that elements that appear to follow in the same direction (as in a straight line or simple curve) tend to be grouped together. Figure 11-6E is an example of the **law of closure,** which states that when a space is enclosed by a contour it tends to be perceived as a figure. Most people see a diamond between two vertical lines here. Actually, Figure 11-6E also could be seen as a letter *W* stacked on a letter *M,* or a normal *K* and a mirror-image *K* facing each other, were it not for the compelling nature of closure. Closure also allows us to complete broken contours as in Figure 11-6F, which is seen as a triangle rather than as three separated acute angles.

The Gestalt principles are so powerful they may even be responsible for visual illusions. For example, distances between parts of a pattern that are organized into the same group, or figure, are underestimated relative to the same distances when the same parts belong to different groups (Coren & Girgus, 1980). Figures 11-6G and 11-6H illustrate this effect. The figures show two different groupings formed by operation of the law of proximity. The distance between the two lines pointed to by the arrows in each figure is identical, yet that distance seems larger in the lower figure, where the lines are parts of two different groups. Such distortions support and enhance the operation of the Gestalt laws to form perceptual objects from discrete parts of the visual array.

All the Gestalt laws operate to create the most stable, consistent, and simple forms possible within a given visual array. The Gestalt psychologists called this process the **law of Pragnanz,** which states that the organization of the visual array into perceptual objects will always be as ''good'' as the prevailing conditions allow. Here the meaning of *good* encompasses concepts such as *regularity, simplicity,* and *symmetry.* The law of Pragnanz is also a way of saying that the perceptual systems work to produce a perceptual world that conveys the ''essence'' of the real world, that is, to assure that the information about the real world is correctly interpreted. In fact, the German word *Prag-*

nanz means approximately ''conveying the essence of something.'' Because prevailing conditions are sometimes not ideal, as in line drawings or on a foggy night, the essence can be ''better'' than the reality. Seeing complex patterns of contours as perceptual objects makes further processing of the vast array of information in the retinal image simpler and faster. For example, it would take you less time to count 12 dots if they were organized into two triangles of the sort shown in the left half of 11-6A, than if the 12 dots were randomly grouped in a single cluster (Oyama, 1986). Demonstration Box 11-2 allows you to explore the concept of Pragnanz further.

Information, Symmetry, and Good Figures

Although the notion of ''figural goodness'' seems intuitively reasonable, it has proved difficult to obtain a precise definition of it for purposes of testing the law of Pragnanz in various situations. Suggestions have been made, but there still seems to be no consensus. One important suggestion was that figural goodness can be defined in terms of the *amount of information* needed to describe a particular organization (Hochberg & Brooks, 1960). Hochberg and Brooks gave a formula to compute figural complexity, based on the number and sizes and varieties of angles and line segments in the organized figure, where these aspects are considered to be the information needed to specify the organization. They argued that the organization with the lowest figural complexity would be the most likely one to be seen, and provided evidence that this is true.

Another way of looking at the amount of information in a figure, and its consequences for perception, was offered by Attneave (1955). He proposed that quantifying patterns in terms of information theory (see Chapter 2) would help in understanding figural goodness. To see how information theory applies to patterns, consider Figure 11-7, which is an image of a woman's right eye as it might appear as an enlargement of a newspaper photo. Notice

DEMONSTRATION BOX 11-2.   Pragnanz

Look at the accompanying figures for a moment and (without looking back again) draw them on a separate piece of paper. When you have finished, return to this box.

Now carefully compare the figures you drew to the actual figures. Did you pick up the fact that the ''circle'' is actually a tilted ellipse? that the ''square''

contains no right angles? that the ''triangle'' has two rounded corners and an open one? that the ''X'' is actually made up of curved lines? Look back at your reproductions. If you drew (or remembered) just a good circle, square, triangle, and X, your percepts have been ''cleaned up'' by the action of Pragnanz.

that the picture is made up of a number of dots, each of which can be either black or white. We can analyze any figure into such an array. Consider Figure 11-8, where we have broken up square visual fields into separate, smaller squares called *cells* or *pixels* (we call the whole array a *matrix*). Notice that we can construct a variety of patterns by simply filling in cells, as we have done in 11-

FIGURE 11-7   An example of a figure made up of dots that can be either black or white.

8A. Suppose we asked you to guess the figure present, without actually seeing it, by simply guessing whether each cell was black or white. Since each guess deals with two alternatives, the answer to each contains one bit of information, as we pointed out in Chapter 2. If we filled in the pattern randomly, in order to guess the complete pattern you would need 64 guesses (1 for each cell) or 64 bits of information (1 for each guess needed). If we told you that the left side was the mirror image of the right side, called a *vertically symmetrical* pattern since the mirror images are symmetrical around a vertical line, you would only need to guess 32 cells either on the right or on the left in order to guess the pattern, thus reducing the amount of information to 32 bits. Therefore, a vertically symmetrical figure, such as 11-8B, contains less information than an asymmetrical figure, such as 11-8A. Figure 11-8C, which is symmetrical around both the vertical and horizontal axes, contains even less information than the other two patterns (16 bits), since only one corner (16 cells) must be known before the entire pattern can be derived.

Since good figures are generally symmetrical

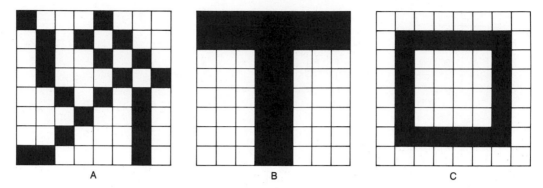

FIGURE 11-8 Examples of symmetry in patterns: (A) no symmetry; (B) symmetry around a vertical axis; (C) symmetry around both horizontal and vertical axes.

and regular, we can now see that they also contain less information. This means that they should be easier to remember and easier to recognize. Attneave (1955) found that this was so. More recently, Freyd and Tversky (1984) found that symmetrical forms were often matched to even more symmetrical forms, indicating a perceptual bias towards symmetry in the representation of forms. They argued that detection of overall symmetry in a form led to the assumption that it is symmetric in its details as well, which might explain the results you got when you tried Demonstration Box 11-2. Yodogawa (1982) has given a mathematically rigorous measure of pattern symmetry, based on information theory, that nicely predicts perceptions of pattern symmetry and pattern complexity.

A final suggestion about goodness that has been influential was made by Garner (1962, 1974), whose definition of the amount of information in a pattern is somewhat different. It depends on the number of possible alternatives that a figure could be drawn from, much like the definition for the difficulty of recognition that we used in Chapter 2 when we introduced the concept of information. Garner argued that the smaller the set of possible alternatives that could be created from a figure by rotation and reflection, the less the information and the better the figure. Figure 11-9 shows the set of alternative patterns for three different dot patterns.

Clearly, Figure 11-9A is the "best" and 11-9C the "worst" under this definition. Since Figure 11-9A is unique, it is the least informative about its set of alternatives (which has no members); Figure 11-9C, in contrast, is one of eight patterns that can be created by reflection and rotation. Seeing it indicates that the other seven alternatives did not appear, and thus conveys three bits of information (since, as you learned in Chapter 2, the amount of information is equal to $\log_2$ of the number of stimulus alternatives). Garner and his colleagues (Garner & Clement, 1963; Handel & Garner, 1965) found that the smaller the set of possible alternatives, the more likely an observer was to rate a pattern as "good" (the observers didn't see the set of alternatives). This approach, and the others described above, all support the conclusion that good figures are simple and contain less information. In this sense it doesn't matter which approach we prefer, the law of Pragnanz is the same in all of them.

Texture Segregation

Shapes and figures can be formed by changes in the stimulus pattern other than of intensity or wavelength. For instance, object boundaries may be defined by areas of the visual array that differ in **visual texture.** Visual textures are collections of tiny contour elements or shapes. For example, if you look

Set of all possible unique rotations and reflections

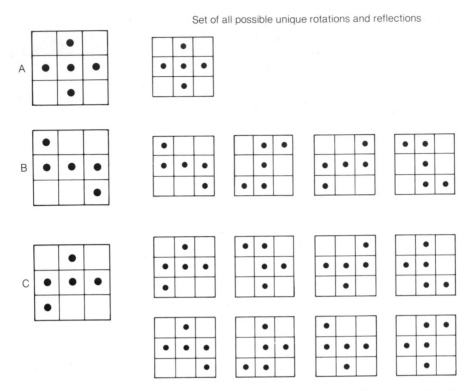

FIGURE 11-9   Relationships between figural goodness and the set of possible alternative stimuli that can be created by rotations and reflections: (A) is the "best" figure and (C) is the "worst." (Based on Handel & Garner, 1965)

back at Figure 11-6C you will see two regions defined by different textures—one a texture of dots, the other a texture of dashes. Notice that there is apparently a boundary, or contour, between these regions. This contour is a form of subjective contour, since it is not actually present in the stimulation, and is generally referred to as a **textural contour.** Perhaps the most common shapes formed by such textures are the pictures in newspapers, which are formed by arrays of thousands of tiny dots that differ in size forming textures that define the shapes of people, buildings, and other objects in the photographs reproduced there, such as the one in Figure 11-7. In a sense, all shapes are defined by textures, since the retinal image is effectively made up of

millions of tiny points of light as a result of the retina being made up of millions of tiny receptors with gaps between them.

The ease with which you can make out shapes defined only by textures depends on the nature of the textural elements. It has often been suggested that the segregation of parts of the field on the basis of textural elements is really an example of grouping by similarity, which we discussed above. Although the number of dimensions in which groups of textural elements differ from one another is indeed quite important, predictions based on a simple definition of grouping by similarity are often not confirmed. A good example is shown in Figures 11-10A and 11-10B. Although people judge the

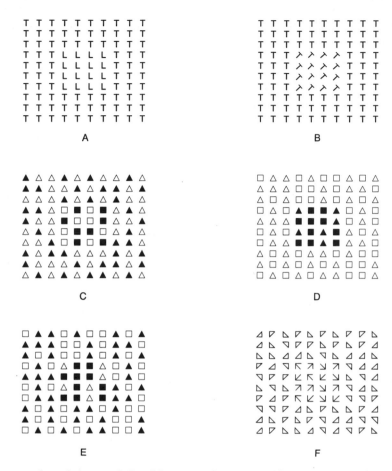

FIGURE 11-10   Examples of shapes defined by textural contours of varying strength.

tilted *T*'s to be more similar to the upright *T*'s than are the *L*'s, the square shape created by the tilted-*T*/upright-*T* boundary is much more apparent than is the shape created by the *L/T* boundary (see Beck, 1966, 1982). Apparently the orientation of small contours is an important aspect of their contribution to texture.

Texture segregation is usually easy and automatic when there are differences in the number, density, or type of a few classes of local elements that are generically called **textons** (Julesz, 1981; Julesz & Bergen, 1983). These include elongated blobs of a particular color, length, width, or orientation, line ends *(terminators)*, or line crossings *(intersections)*. For example, the square shape that appears in Figure 11-10F is defined by a boundary between elements that have no terminators and elements that have three terminators. Notice that all of the textons are made up of the same parts, a slanted line in two different orientations and a "corner" shape in four different orientations. The local texture elements differ only in how these parts are put together.

Although Julesz' theory and demonstrations

are convincing, they must be modified somewhat. To begin with, all textons are not equally powerful in their ability to define textural contours. This is demonstrated in Figure 11-10C and D. In C the central square is formed by a shape difference, whereas in D it is formed by a color difference. Notice that the color difference seems much more dramatic, and that color differences between elements actually make the shape boundary harder to see in C. Color differences are clearly dominant over shape differences in forming textures, and this differential salience strongly affects texture segregation (Callaghan, Lasaga & Garner, 1986; Enns, 1986; Gurnsey & Browse, 1987). Certain higher-level factors, such as closed versus open figures, can often act as a texton when the closed figures are very different from the background figures (Enns, 1986). The best suggestion seems to be that texture segregation is determined by the degree to which textons unique to a particular region of the visual field are salient in the context of textons in other, surrounding, regions (Enns, 1986; cf. Olson & Attneave, 1970; Beck, 1982).

Finally, the number of stimulus dimensions involved is important. Treisman and Gelade (1980) showed that although texture segregation was easy and automatic when either shape or color of elements differed, forming a boundary, it was impossible when particular conjunctions (pairings) of shape and color differed. For example, look at 11-10E. Is there a central square here? Actually there is, but only *conceptually*, not *perceptually*. It is formed where the outside elements are only empty squares or filled triangles and the inside elements are only empty triangles or filled squares. But because the element boundary is defined only by differences in *conjunctions* of basic properties, the textural contour does not emerge. To find the boundary you must scrutinize the shapes one by one. Apparently the form of grouping by similarity that results in textural contours depends on elements that differ in only a single dimension, and doesn't work when you require combinations of dimensions or properties (see Treisman, 1986b).

Spatial Frequencies and Figural Organization

Several investigators have tried to combine certain aspects of figural organization with suggestions that come out of a consideration of textural segregation and of spatial frequency analyses (such as we discussed in Chapter 4) to produce a multiprocess, multilevel explanation of how the perceptual object is formed. In the context of the separation of figure and ground, for example, Julesz (1978) argued that texture segregation and a kind of "early warning" to detect regions requiring finer analysis were accomplished by background processes, whereas the finer, more detailed analysis of important shapes was accomplished by figure processes. This would mean that figural analysis would involve *higher spatial frequencies* (e.g., finer details) and would require more stability, but would be slower to emerge. Ground processing, in contrast, would involve lower spatial frequencies (e.g., a crude "blob detection"), but would require less stability and would be faster.

These speculations have been confirmed. For example, Calis and Leeuwenberg (1981) found that ground processing is faster than figure processing. Weisstein and Wong (1986; Wong & Weisstein, 1987) reported several experiments that demonstrate that simply flickering different regions of a uniform field of dots can make the flickering area stand out as figure or ground, depending on the flicker rate. Usually, a rapid flicker rate induces a perception of ground, whereas a slower flicker rate causes the flickering area to be seen as figure. Finally, Klymenko and Weisstein (1986) reported that when regions of a visual field were defined by different spatial frequency sine wave gratings, the region containing the higher spatial frequency grating was more often seen as figure and the one containing the lower frequency grating was more often seen as ground. This is demonstrated in Figure 11-11, where the faces are much easier to see as figure because they are filled with high spatial frequency gratings. Thus, there is evidence of a low temporal/

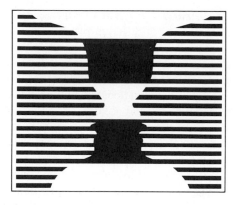

FIGURE 11-11 A reversible figure-ground stimulus in which the faces are easier to see than the vase because they are filled with relatively high spatial frequency gratings. (Based on Klymenko & Weisstein, 1986)

high spatial frequency processing system for figure and a high temporal/low spatial frequency processing system for ground.

Features

The shapes that emerge into our consciousness from the retinal image can be said to possess **features** that differentiate them from other shapes. For example, letters consist of combinations of lines of various orientations and curvature. Sometimes these lines intersect, sometimes they touch without crossing. A given letter may be printed in red ink, or may be an outline. The relevant features of the letters are those that help to differentiate a given letter from other letters, or from numbers or other similar shapes (Garner, 1974). Some of these features may be textons, such as an intersection. Others may be unique to letters, such as a "bend" in a particular line. Whatever they are, we will often speak of shapes being different in their features, especially when we look at how they are recognized and identified. The strength of using a set of features to describe a shape is that the features appear in our consciousness; they can be seen directly and thus talking about them is easy. The weakness

in this approach is that the feature set is arbitrary and it may change as the shapes we wish to differentiate change.

An exception to the above characterization of features is when they can be traced to more fundamental units, such as textons, or line or angle "detectors" in the visual cortex. One such approach, dealt with in the previous section, involves specifying the spatial frequency components that make up a shape as its "features." As was pointed out in Chapter 4, the two-dimensional distribution of light on the retina can be completely described in terms of simple sine wave gratings (making some simplifying assumptions). One suggestion has been that these Fourier components are the features used to identify perceptual objects (e.g., Campbell & Robson, 1968; Pollen, Lee & Taylor, 1971). It has now been shown that this approach cannot work if the Fourier analysis is applied over the entire visual field (e.g., Caelli, 1984; Cavanaugh, 1984; De-Valois & DeValois, 1987), but it may be useful if the analysis is done over smaller regions, around the size of cortical receptive fields.

Unfortunately, the spatial frequency approach is really different from other forms of feature analysis in more ways than simply being describable in terms of mathematical equations. First, the spatial frequency components are not apparent to consciousness, and thus are not useful in describing what we see. Second, they are not related to texture segregation, since regions of the visual array that are clearly different in their Fourier components cannot be seen as a shape (Julesz, 1981; Julesz & Bergen, 1983). However, this approach does have the advantage that the set of possible Fourier components is not arbitrary and does not change with the set of shapes, so it may ultimately be made useful through some modifications.

Some idea of the complexity of feature analyses of forms appears when we begin to re-analyze the principles of figural organization. The early Gestaltists thought of a whole figure as composed of parts "glued" together by the attractive forces we described in our discussion of figural organization. However, recent attempts to describe in more detail the way the Gestalt laws actually operate have questioned this conclusion. For example, Pomerantz (e.g., 1986) has demonstrated that when parts configure into wholes an **emergent feature** is usually created. In effect, this suggests that something like closure might be considered a feature rather than an organizing principle. Thus, if you look at a figure like 11-6F, and a similar closed triangle (without the gaps), they look different, because one has the feature of being closed and the other does not. This kind of analysis suggests that features may result from higher-level processes, not simply relationships among contour elements.

Feature Integration Theory

In our discussion so far, although we have referred to the perceptual object being *constructed* from the information available in the retinal image, we have perhaps given the impression that all the constructive activity happens automatically, without any effort and for all parts of the visual field at once. This is probably not the case. Quite a bit of evidence is accumulating that we can construct only one perceptual object at a time (as noticed in a reversible figure) and that usually we must focus our attention on a particular location in "visual space" in order to synthesize a perceptual object from all the information coming from that location.

A particularly attractive version of this viewpoint is Treisman's **feature integration theory** (Treisman, 1986a, 1986b, 1988). The theory asserts that there are two major stages to the construction of a perceptual object. First, **preattentive processes** (those that happen without active attention playing a part) operate on the information in the retinal image to produce shapes and register their features. A crucial assumption about this stage is that features such as color, the various linear features (e.g., line orientation, closure), and three-dimensional location are registered separately from one another in special processing systems (e.g., carried separately in the geniculostriate and tecto-

pulvinar systems, or registered in different "maps" of the visual field in different places in the cortex; see Chapter 3). The second stage of the process consists of active **focal attention** (see Chapter 15) selecting a spatial location and integrating the features registered at that location into a perceptual object. This perceptual object, or *object file* in Treisman and Kahneman's terms (see Kahneman & Treisman, 1984), consists of a temporary representation of the current appearance of the object that is constantly updated as new information is obtained. When attention shifts to another object, because the current one disappears or in the process of scanning the environment or being distracted, the old object file vanishes and is replaced by a new one at a different location. This view explains how objects in the "real world" can be seen as enduring and solid, even though the information about them we receive changes drastically from moment to moment, since each object is associated with a particular location in space. This is somewhat reminiscent of earlier speculations by Ames (1955) that the minimum properties of any perceived stimulus are its *thereness,* referring to its location in space, and its *thatness,* referring to its object properties.

A lot of data have been accumulated to test these ideas. One of the most intriguing findings is the discovery of **illusory conjunctions.** Feature integration theory predicts that if attention is overloaded, so that it is difficult to integrate separable features into a perceptual object, the features might combine incorrectly, giving rise to the perception of an object that is not really there (an illusory conjunction). For example, an observer may be exposed briefly to a red *O* and a blue *X*, but may see a red *X*, which wasn't really there (Treisman & Schmidt, 1982). A simple analogy to this is if you meet a man named Fred, who is an architect, and another named George, who is an accountant, then in recounting your experiences to a friend you might end up recalling Fred, the accountant. The name and the occupation are features, which you assign to the particular stimulus (the person) sepa-

---

DEMONSTRATION BOX 11-3.   Figural Integration

It is rare that we see an object in its entirety. Either we or the object is moving about, resulting in glimpses that are partially occluded by other objects (e.g., a dog running though some trees), yet we have no difficulty identifying the object. Parks (1965) studied this phenomenon by moving a shape behind a narrow window, or slit. His surprising result was that a wide variety of shapes could be easily recognized, even though the shape was never seen except as a series of fragments. Because of one of the shapes Parks used, the phenomenon of easy recognition of shapes presented by moving behind a slit has come to be called ''Parks's camel.''

In order to experience ''Parks's camel'' for yourself, arrange to have a friend pass various objects (including himself or herself) behind a narrow slit created by a door that is slightly ajar (Shimojo & Richards, 1986). Try varying the size of the slit and the speed with which the object passes across it. You will find that over a surprisingly wide range of size and speed conditions the object will be identifiable. Also, pay attention to the strength of the feeling you will have that the *entire* object is present, even though at any moment you are only receiving a fragmentary view of it. When the conditions are optimal, that impression is very strong. This demonstrates the importance of the integration over time required to create the perceptual object out of a chaotic and constantly changing retinal image.

---

rately. In the perceptual synthesis, however, the objects don't even have to be similar for their properties to be exchanged in this way. For example, color is exchanged among dissimilar-shaped objects (e.g., a triangle and a circle) just as easily as it is among similar-shaped objects (e.g., two small outline triangles) (Treisman, 1986a). This is possible because the individual features are processed separately and then synthesized with reference to a given place in space via a different process.

Just how the Gestalt principles interact with the feature integration process is an interesting, and still controversial, question. Prinzmetal (1981) found evidence that illusory conjunctions were less likely when the components came from different Gestalt groupings of visual contours than when they came from the same grouping. He argued that perceptual organization prevented the illusory conjunction of features from groups of contours that were likely to be parts of different objects (see also Butler & Kring, 1987). Also, Prinzmetal and Millis-Wright (1984) found that illusory conjunctions were more likely to occur within letter strings that formed pronounceable words than in random, un-

pronounceable letter strings. Again, the preattentive analysis of the contours in the retinal image into shapes that may signify objects in the real world seems to constrain feature integration. Since we learn through experience with the world which features are likely to go together, feature integration is less subject to error when we know which objects to expect (Treisman, 1986a). One role played by the feature integration process seems to be to maintain the continuity and coherence of the perceptual object in the face of the constantly changing array of visual information about it. Demonstration Box 11-3 allows you to experience the coherence of the perceptual object in a somewhat different way.

OBJECT RECOGNITION AND IDENTIFICATION

Look at Figure 11-12 and study it for a minute or so. You have never seen it before, because it was especially constructed for this book. It is clearly an object, but what is it? Now look at it again. You

FIGURE 11-12   **An object you have never seen before. (Based on Biederman, 1987)**

recognize it because you have seen it before (just a minute or so ago), although you still are not able to identify it (it is not a "real" object). You experience familiarity, but the object makes no sense. Now study it a little longer. Eventually you may begin to be able to classify it into some object class or other, perhaps it resembles a distorted version of a streetside hot dog vendor's cart, or perhaps a child's toy. The longer you look at it, the more associations it generates, although it still doesn't have a name. If we told you that it was a "Horned wheeler," the name might suggest that it is an apparatus for conveying or transporting things, although how or why still might be a puzzle.

Every day, practically every moment, you recognize and identify perceptual objects like the one in Figure 11-12, although they are seldom as novel. But the ability to see a stimulus as an object is not sufficient. Our very survival may depend on our recognition of an object as something we have seen before, and on our labeling (really categorizing) that object so that we can retrieve information about its likely behavior or the behavior we should perform in its presence. In this section we discuss what we know about how these feats are accomplished.

Recognition versus Identification

The first thing we must do is make our terminology clear. In what follows, when we refer to object **recognition** we mean the experience of "perceiving something as previously known" (Mandler, 1980). Object **identification** means naming an object, correctly classifying it in some categorization scheme, knowing in what context it is usually encountered, knowing its relation to other concepts, and so on—in short, remembering something more about it than merely having seen it before. According to Mandler (1980), the experience of familiarity comes about because the more exposure you have to a perceptual object, the more you have organized the various processes that create and maintain that object out of a particular combination of critical features. The process of feature integration leaves memory traces, which are then experienced as familiarity the next time that particular conjunction of features is encountered. The more times an object file is constructed for an object or event, the more detailed that file can become, and the more familiar it will seem when it is next encountered.

Identification, however, clearly requires some sort of retrieval process. The representation of the perceptual object created for the moment, the object file, must be compared to other representations in memory, along with the connections these other representations have to other information stored in memory. Most investigators agree on this much. What they don't agree on is the composition of this representation that is compared to the memory, whether it is features of some sort, or spatial frequency components, or another system. We investigate some of these proposals in the next section.

Data-driven versus Conceptually-driven Processing

Feature integration theory and most other modern theories of visual object recognition and identification assume at least two major types of psychological processing. One type is referred to as **data-driven processing,** which begins with the arrival of sensory information at the receptors. This type of processing is characterized by the processing of information, or data, directly in terms of some fixed set of rules or procedures. In a sense, the data themselves *drive* the processing, since the rules usually concern the registration of particular patterns in the data. In terms of visual object recognition, data-driven processing would be involved in the registration of distinctive features, such as luminance differences in the image, line orientations, intersections, or other attributes that distinguish the pattern from others. The first stage of preattentive processing in feature integration theory is supposed to be data-driven.

The other type of processing is called **conceptually-driven processing.** In this type of processing, higher level *conceptual* processes, such as memories of past experiences, general organizational strategies, and expectations based on knowledge of the world and previous events or the surrounding context, guide an active search for certain patterns in the stimulus input. An example of conceptually-driven processing is the feature integration stage of feature integration theory, where focal attention selects a locus in space and integrates the features there into a perceptual object, perhaps in conjunction with prior hypotheses as to what to expect. Thus, a dark thing flashing through the air on a playground might be seen as a ball someone has thrown, whereas in a quiet park it might be seen as a bird flying by, because of prior expectations. Both conceptually- and data-driven types of processing may occur together, or in sequence, but both must occur. If only conceptually-driven processing occurred, we would see only what we expected to see, and would make too many mistakes to survive. If only data-driven processing occurred, we would not be able to take advantage of our tremendous amount of experience with the visual world to enhance our perceptual functioning, especially in poor environments, and to distinguish the relevant from the irrelevant in the flux of information on our retinas.

Since in data-driven processing the emphasis is on detection of predefined patterns in stimulus input, one place to look for evidence of such processing is in the physiology of sensory systems. In Chapter 4 we discussed how neurons in the visual system interact through lateral inhibition, and we showed how these interactions could be responsible for enhancement of contours, even creating some illusions. In Chapter 3 we discussed cortical cells that respond to specific features, such as contour orientation, in the retinal image. These seem to be parts of the visual system that do data-driven processing.

An interesting source of evidence for data-driven processing of patterns on the basis of extracted features from the retinal image comes from work on stabilized images (a technique we discussed earlier in the chapter). As you recall, when we stop the movement of the image on the retina it fades out of consciousness. This fading is not by a gradual, uniform disappearance of the whole figure, nor is it by the disappearance of little random bits of the pattern; instead the stabilized image fades out by features, such as whole lines or angles (Evans & Wells, 1967; Heckenmueller, 1965). Figure 11-13 contrasts the fadeout by features (A), which does happen, with a fadeout by random bits (B), which doesn't happen.

Global versus Local Processing

Because there is considerable evidence for physiological feature detectors, most approaches to data-driven processing emphasize the role of **local** features in object recognition and identification. Local features may be viewed as the small-scale or detailed aspects of a figure, but there is a bit of a conceptual problem with our definition of what a local feature is. Just how small-scale must a feature be to be called ''local''? What if a form has no features of this particular scale? Does it thereby lack local features? At least we can easily contrast local features with the overall or **global** aspect that gives the whole form its apparent shape. In Figure 11-14B, we see the global shape of a letter *H* made up locally of small *S*s. Each small *S* is made up in turn of local features (e.g., the curved line segments) and each of these features could be subdivided into even smaller local features (such as microdots of ink) if we had a large enough

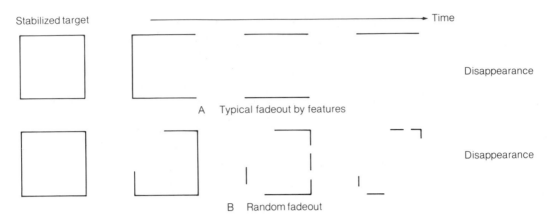

FIGURE 11-13   Typical feature-by-feature fading of a stabilized retinal image is shown in (A) as opposed to what would be expected if disappearance were random in its time course, shown in (B).

magnifying glass. Thus, the terms *local* and *global* are relative; we must specify what level of detail we are referring to when we use them. You can see for yourself the importance of local features in object identification by trying Demonstration Box 11-4.

```
H              H              S              S
H              H              S              S
H              H              S              S
H              H              S              S
H H H H H      H              S S S S S      S
H              H              S              S
H              H              S              S
H              H              S              S
H              H              S              S

       A                            B


H              H              S              S

H              H              S              S

H   H   H                     S   S   S

H              H              S              S

H              H              S              S

       C                            D
```

FIGURE 11-14   Examples of stimuli that have two distinct levels of detail.

An interesting issue arises with respect to global and local levels of detail in visual forms. In a seminal paper, Navon (1977) argued that the detection of more global (larger-scale) aspects of a form with several levels of detail would always be faster than the detection of the more local details. This position resembles the Gestalt position, in that whole forms that are grouped by Gestalt processes seem more immediately available to our consciousness than do the more local constituents that have been so grouped. Navon (1977) did several experiments to test this proposition and one in particular was provocative. In this experiment, observers were asked to name forms like those in Figures 11-14A and 11-14B at either the global level (e.g., *H*) or the local level (e.g., *H* for 11-14A, *S* for 11-14B) as fast as they could. In addition, sometimes the name of the form was the same as that of its constituents (11-14A) and sometimes the names at the two levels were different (11-14B). The first result was that regardless of what the stimuli were like observers were always faster in naming the global level form than the local level forms. Moreover, when naming the global level form, it didn't matter whether the local constituents had the same name as the global form or not; observers were equally fast. However, when naming the local con-

DEMONSTRATION BOX 11-4.   The Role of Local Features in Pattern Recognition

Harmon (1973) and Harmon and Julesz (1973) have presented an interesting set of demonstrations that illustrate how local features can interfere with a more global percept. One of their demonstrations is presented in the figure, a computer-processed block representation of a photograph. The brightness information from this scan is then locally averaged, so that the brightness value in each of the squares is an average of a number of brightness samples taken in that area of the picture. This technique can be used to see if such local brightness information can elicit the percept of the orig-

inal photograph. To try this, look at the figure at normal reading distance. Do you recognize the person? Try again, viewing from 2 m this time. (It will also help if you squint your eyes.) If you follow these instructions, you should be able to identify this block portrait as a very famous historical person. If not, the name of the individual is printed upside down in the bottom right-hand corner of this page. (From Harmon & Julesz, 1973. Copyright 1973 by the American Association for the Advancement of Science. Used by permission.)

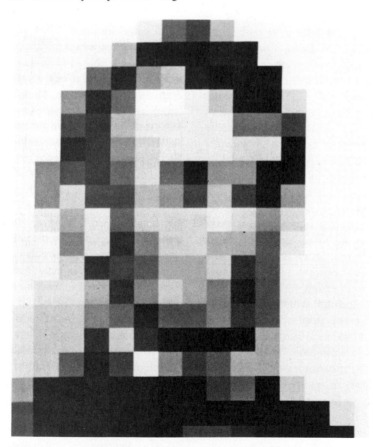

Abraham Lincoln

stituents, observers were greatly slowed down if the global form had a different name. Based on these data, Navon argued for *global precedence*, the idea that detection of the more global aspects of a visual form will always be faster than detection of the more local aspects.

Although Navon (1977) did demonstrate one set of conditions under which global forms have **processing dominance** (see Ward, 1983) over local forms, other studies suggest that local and global features are detected simultaneously (in parallel) and at approximately equal speed (Boer & Keuss, 1982; Hughes, Layton, Baird & Lester, 1984; Paquet & Merikle, 1984). More specifically, it seems that global processing dominance for visual forms seems to hold only for a specific set of conditions. When the global form is made a bit harder to see, for example, by spacing out the local features as in Figures 11-14C and 11-14D, the results are reversed (Martin, 1979). Now the smaller letters are named more quickly and the naming of the larger letter is slowed down when the smaller constituents have different names, as in Figure 11-14D. The *absolute* size of the figure is also important in determining whether global or local features are processed more easily. When the stimulus is much larger (for instance, when you hold Figures A or B close to your eyes), you will notice that now the smaller letters are much more salient and easier to see and the larger letter is more difficult to see. In the laboratory, observers can tell which of two smaller letters is present in such a display more quickly than they can tell which of two larger letters is present when the display is larger than about 7 deg of visual angle. When the display is smaller than this (try holding the book at arm's length to view A or B) the larger letters are more quickly discriminated (Kinchla & Wolfe, 1979). Why is absolute size so important in determining processing priorities? Perhaps because of the fact that various feature-sensitive cells in the cortex are "tuned" for specific-sized stimuli (see Chapter 3). Thus, the visual system may be biased toward a faster reaction to groupings of local features of a particular size (e.g., Hughes et al., 1984).

All the factors above are affected by how an observer distributes attention to the figure. Observers are able to voluntarily direct their attention either to global or local aspects of the figure, and thus give that level processing dominance (Hoffman, 1980; Kinchla, Solis-Macias & Hoffman, 1983). If they are forced to switch attention from one level to the other, however, this tends to slow and interfere with their ability to process either level of features (Ward, 1982b, 1985).

Integral versus Separable Stimuli

Processing dominance has also been studied from perspectives other than global versus local processing. For example, Pomerantz, Sager, and Stoever (1977) showed that in groupings of simple linear features those that form closed, "good" figures are much easier to recognize than those composed of the same features in a different arrangement. These data seem to indicate some kind of direct (faster or earlier) perception of such good figures. Perhaps it is the case that figural goodness is itself treated as if it were a feature or collection of features. If it were a perceptually dominant feature then it might be extracted earlier than nondominant features, and hence be responded to more quickly.

There are some aspects of good figures that do seem to make them special. For instance, they have a certain unitary wholeness, that is, they appear to be coherent and not easily broken into components. One analysis of processing dominance that incorporates this idea introduces the concept of an **integral stimulus,** which is a stimulus that is seen in all of its aspects simultaneously. A light bulb is such a stimulus since it is seen to have shape and color all at once (Lockhead, 1966). Integral stimuli have many characteristics reminiscent of good figures. In contrast, we have the concept of a **separable stimulus,** which is a stimulus that has features that cannot be easily integrated. An example of a separable stimulus is one of the matrices in Figure 11-9, in which the dots and the lines forming the grid don't seem to be parts of a coherent figure. It has been argued that integral stimuli are processed first as blobs at a global level before they are analyzed into their component parts (Lockhead, 1972, 1979; Lockhead & King, 1977; Monahan & Lockhead, 1977). Some separable stimuli, however, hang together better than others. These are said to contain a **configural feature** (usually something like the Gestalt qualities of closure or symmetry). Thus, a pair of parentheses like () is seen as more of a figure than one like ((and is processed more quickly, even though it still remains a separable configuration of two components (Garner, 1978).

In our discussion of global versus local processing we noted that processing dominance may be affected by attentional factors. Attention also seems to interact with figural goodness in determining how well we process certain patterns and pattern components. Many patterns are not really very good (and are certainly not very integral). These include the compound letter stimuli in Figure 11-14 (see Pomerantz, 1983). Such stimuli tend to be synthesized into perceptual objects by attentional factors, as well as by the Gestalt principles. According to feature integration theory we need to pay attention to a particular place in visual space in order to join the separately extracted features of a pattern into a proper perceptual object. This would explain why dividing attention between aspects of a pattern slows identification at all levels. The less attention paid to features at a given level, the more difficult (and slower) it would be to combine those aspects into a perceptual object. Since there is much evidence suggesting that our attention is usually "caught" by good figures, or the best aspects of figures, this would also explain why better features are more easily and quickly joined into perceptual objects. Gestalt processes operating on the entire pattern would produce groups of elements that would be easy to join together into a perceptual unit (Prinzmetal, 1981; Treisman, 1982). The relationship between attention and the Gestalt principles of perceptual organization is thus like that of a train engine to its track. Although the force and movement is provided by the engine (attention), the path that it must follow, if it is to go anywhere at all, is determined by the pattern of the track (the principles of organization). Of course, the fuel that powers the engine is data-driven feature extraction.

Context and Identification

As you have seen in the discussion above, we could not talk about data-driven processing without mentioning attention, an aspect of conceptually-driven processing. Any time your perceptual processes are influenced by your expectations, previous experience, hypotheses, or any global organizing principle, you are demonstrating the operation of conceptually-driven processing. There are many other examples of the importance of conceptually-driven processing in the formation, recognition, and identification of perceptual objects. Look at Figure 11-15. Most people would see there two lines of characters, the top line being *A, B, C, D, E, F* and the bottom one being *10, 11, 12, 13, 14*. Now look closely at the forms you saw as *B* and *13*. They are identical; the same form was interpreted as a letter *B* in the context of other letters, and as a number *13* in the context of other numbers. Notice that the data (the actual stimulus input) are identical for both the perceptual organizations representing the *B* and the *13*. Your identification of those perceptual objects, however, has been affected by conceptually-driven processing based on knowledge and assumptions, mostly obtained here from the other stimuli that form the context.

A,B,C,D,E,F
10,11,12,13,14

FIGURE 11-15   The effect of context on pattern recognition. The *B* and the *13* are identical figures.

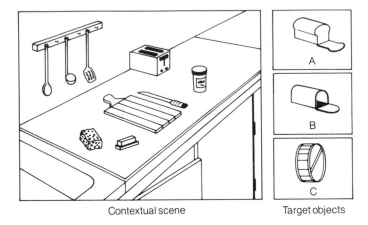

Contextual scene   Target objects

FIGURE 11-16   Context and target stimuli used by Palmer (1975a).

Another example of the effect of context on identification comes from a study by Palmer (1975a). Palmer asked observers to identify objects presented after they had seen either an appropriate context or an inappropriate context for that object. For example, in Figure 11-16, the loaf of bread (A) would be appropriate in the context of the kitchen counter displayed there, but the mailbox (B) or the drum (C) would be inappropriate. Objects presented after an appropriate scene were more readily identified than were the same objects presented after an inappropriate scene. It seems that what you see immediately before the presentation of a stimulus evokes a series of expectations about objects likely to be present. When the next object seen matches these expectations identification is easier, whereas incongruous or unexpected items become harder to identify.

It should be clear by now that the final interpretation of a visual scene depends on both data-driven and conceptually-driven processing (cf. Norman, 1976; Palmer, 1975b). Palmer (1975b) demonstrated this notion in relation to face perception. Look at Figure 11-17. Notice that when seen as part of a face, any bump or line will suffice to depict a feature. When we take these features out

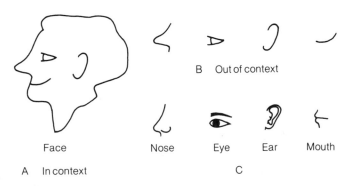

Face   Nose   Eye   Ear   Mouth

A   In context   C

B   Out of context

FIGURE 11-17   Facial components are easily recognized in context (A), but out of context they are much less identifiable (B) unless they are made more detailed (C) (Palmer, 1975b). (From Norman, Rumelhart & the LNR Research Group 1975. Copyright 1975 by W. H. Freeman and Co. Used by permission.)

of context, they do not really portray the objects very well. We actually require more of a detailed presentation (such as in Figure 11-17C) to identify facial features unambiguously when presented in isolation. Thus, in this situation the conceptually-driven contextual expectations compensate for lack of detail in the data-driven feature extraction.

THEORIES OF OBJECT IDENTIFICATION

Many different types of theories have been offered to explain how perceptual objects are identified. We have already encountered parts of a few of them in our discussion. One recurring pattern, common to several of these theories, is the presumption that during the first stage of perception information in the retinal image is processed to detect simple features, which are then combined into perceptual objects at a second stage and compared to memories of other perceptual objects at a third stage to determine the identity of the stimulus. Expectations and context play their role at the stage of comparing the input to memories; the match required for identification doesn't need to be as good if a particular object is expected either because of the context or because it is being searched for. The major disagreements arise in specifying just what aspects of the perceptual object (the features) are used in the comparison process.

Pandemonium

One very successful theory of this type emphasizes data-driven feature extraction processes. It is called **pandemonium,** because each stage of the analysis of an input pattern was originally conceived of as a group of *demons* shouting out the results of their analyses (Selfridge, 1959). Figure 11-18 shows how the theory works. In the first stage, an *image demon* passes on the contents of the retinal image to each of a set of *feature demons*. These feature demons shout when they detect ''their'' feature in the input pattern. These shouts are listened to by the *cognitive demons,* each of which is listening for a particular combination of shouts from feature demons. As the information is analyzed by the feature demons, the cognitive demons start ''yelling'' when they find a feature appropriate to their own pattern, and the more features they find the louder they yell. A *decision demon* listens to the ''pandemonium'' caused by the yelling of the various cognitive demons. It chooses the cognitive demon (or pattern) that is making the most noise as the one that is most likely to be the pattern presented to the sensory system.

Pandemonium is one of many similar models that depend on data-driven analysis of simple features much like those to which cortical cells are tuned (see Chapter 3). In general, such models can account for many aspects of object identification, such as the mistakes people make when trying to identify alphabetic characters (see Ashby & Perrin, 1988; Keren & Baggen, 1981; Townsend & Ashby, 1982). Variations of the basic theory can be constructed to account for between-letter confusions that either do (Sanocki, 1987) or do not (Friedman, 1980) depend on minute details of the letters such as size, type style, and the like.

Identification-by-Components

Although pandemonium is a successful theory, it has several shortcomings. One of these is that the set of features used to characterize perceptual objects is really rather arbitrary. This problem has been addressed by a more recent approach based on the idea that objects can be represented by what these researchers feel is a nonarbitrary, primitive set of parts or modules (cf. Brooks, 1981; Guzman, 1971; Marr, 1982). According to this theory, there are some simple properties of visual geometry that generally remain constant even though the image and the observer are moving and changing in various ways. From these properties, the researchers derived a set of simple components of which all perceptual objects are said to be composed

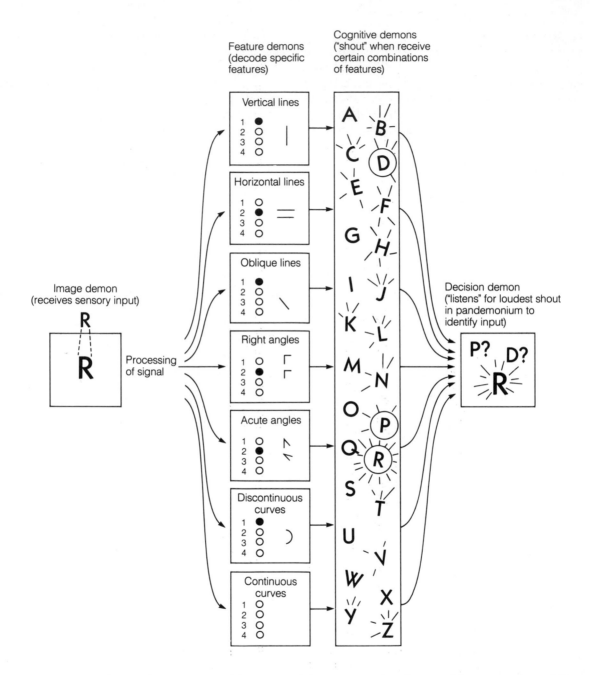

FIGURE 11-18   The pandemonium model in action. The number of each type of feature registered by the feature demons is indicated by which circle is blackened in each box and by the number of times the feature is printed in the box.

(Biederman, 1987). All of the components, called **geons,** are (at a mathematical level) variations of a generalized cylinder. Figure 11-19A displays some of these geons and something of the variety of shapes that can be derived from just one of them. Figure 11-19B shows how various combinations of the simple geons give rise to various perceptual ob-jects (see also Figure 11-12). Biederman (1987) calculated that a very small set of such geons (no more than 36) can generate over 150 million 3-geon objects, ample to describe even the richness of human object perception.

Not only does this theory provide a set of primitive features (the geons) with which to

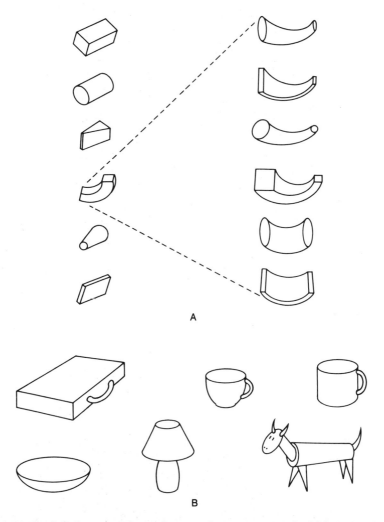

FIGURE 11-19   (A) On the left is a partial set of geons, from any one of which many variants can be created (as on the right for one of them) by varying the basic parameters. (B) Some of the objects that can be created from geons. (Based on Biederman, 1987)

describe an object but it also accounts for some of the major phenomena of object identification. The importance of geons can be seen from the fact that if you degrade a pattern but still permit an arrangement of as few as two or three geons to be seen, it doesn't hinder object identification (Biederman, 1987). The idea is that the description of an object in terms of its geon components is compared to other remembered (geon) descriptions. Moreover, even if you've never seen the form before, as in Figure 11-12, it can still be analyzed into its geon components, and even tentatively placed into a category. Finally, this approach also emphasizes that the law of Pragnanz applies to the geons that make up an object and not to the whole object. We tend to see the best *geons,* which will then give rise to the best object.

Computational Approaches

There is a class of theories of object perception and identification that arises from a very different viewpoint and tradition. It began with the desire to develop machines that can ''see'' and identify patterns. Perceptual researchers soon recognized that this line of endeavor might lead to some useful insights about alternative ways in which biological organisms see forms, since, at the very least, in order to program a machine to perform this function we must be very specific about the way information is selected and processed.

Probably the most influential version of this approach has been that of Marr (1982), who first analyzed the problem of creating such a ''seeing machine'' into three levels. The first required a *computational theory,* which attempts to specify in formal terms (usually mathematical) exactly what the nature of the visual problem is, the information that may be available, and the information required to ultimately achieve the correct identification. The second level, called *representation and algorithm,* has to do with the various ways the required information could be represented and the necessary calculations made. Finally, the third level, *hardware implementation,* describes the actual implementation of a given algorithm in some device. The device was originally meant to be a computer, but speculations are often made about whether the same principles might work in a brain.

This *computational approach* is quite different from the usual psychological approach. For example, perceptual psychologists typically deal only with the second level (representation and algorithm), and even then usually do not use mathematical language to specify their theories. A good example of the psychological approach is that of Treisman (e.g., 1986b). She defines the task of object perception in terms of three domains: the physical domain (physics's description of the real world), the phenomenological domain (what we experience, the perceptual object), and the functional domain (the various processes that connect the other two domains). Really, all of Treisman's domains are within Level 2 of the computational approach, as shown in Figure 11-20.

Not all computational approaches to object identification follow Marr, but all do have in common the emphasis on being able to compute the solution to an identification problem (that is, having a computer do it). In Marr's own approach, the computational theory stage discussed above is broken down into computable problems. First, a set of routines computes from the retinal image what Marr called a *primal sketch.* This is an abstract representation of where various contours (described mathematically) are located, along with a rough grouping of contours into shapes (blobs) that may belong together. From the primal sketch is computed the *2½-D sketch,* which contains a description of the orientation and approximate depth relationships of potential surfaces in relation to the viewer. Finally, a *3-D model* is computed from the 2½-D sketch. This model, corresponding to what we have called the perceptual object, represents shapes and their spatial organization in terms of their relationship to each other and in terms of modules similar to geons. This set of de-

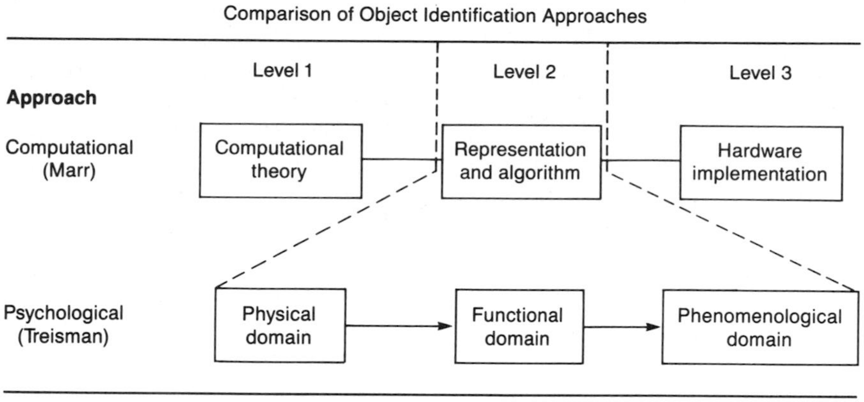

Comparison of Object Identification Approaches

FIGURE 11-20 An indication of the different concerns, and levels of analysis, of computational and psychological approaches to object perception.

scriptions constitutes the computational theory of object representation (when it is expressed formally, that is), although we don't provide you here with the mathematical procedures for accomplishing these computations. Many investigators are still working both to refine the computational theory and to construct representations and algorithms that will do the computations (see, e.g., Ullman, 1986). Ultimately, however, the usefulness to psychology of such approaches will depend on whether they provide us with any insights as to how the brain actually processes the visual information in a biological system, such as in humans.

It is truly humbling to realize that understanding the simple act of recognizing that you are looking at a pencil, and that the pencil is not part of the desk on which it rests but is a separate object in its own right, remains a problem about which there are many theories but still no final answer.

GLOSSARY

The following definitions are specific to this book.

Backward masking   The phenomenon whereby exposure to a second stimulus interferes with the perception of an initial stimulus presented at a critical interval previously.

Conceptually-driven processing   Perceptual information processing that is guided by conceptual processes, such as memories and expectations concerning the nature of the incoming stimulation.

Configural feature   A stimulus whose aspects can be seen separately but still produce an emergent feature, such as closure, that dominates processing.

Contour   Any place in the retinal image where the light intensity changes abruptly.

Data-driven processing   Perceptual information processing that responds directly to properties of the incoming stimuli according to fixed procedures and without influence from memories, expectations, or the like.

Emergent feature   A feature that characterizes a particular configuration of parts rather than others, and is at least as perceptually salient as any of the parts.

Features   Attributes of a shape that distinguish it from other shapes.

Feature integration theory   A theory of how features are integrated to form perceptual objects; it assumes that features are extracted in parallel and automatically, but that attention must be paid to a particular spatial locus in order for perceptual objects to be formed from the features.

Figure   Integrated visual experience that "stands out" in the center of attention.

Focal attention   Active attention focused on a particular spatial location.

Ganzfeld   A visual field that contains no abrupt luminance changes and thus no visible contours.

Geon   One of the primitive components from which perceptual objects are constructed in identification-by-components theory.

Gestalt   A concept and school of psychology emphasizing the notion of a meaningful and coherent form, or "whole."

Global   The overall arrangement of parts of a figure, as opposed to the local details.

Ground   The background against which figures appear.

Identification   Naming a perceptual object and knowing something about it.

Illusory conjunction   Percept consisting of an incorrect integration of features from separate objects into a single perceptual object (e.g., seeing a red X when only a red O and a green X are present).

Integral stimulus   A stimulus that is experienced in all of its aspects at once and inseparably.

Law of closure   The Gestalt law stating that contours that form a closed region tend to be attracted to each other and form a figure.

Law of good continuation   The Gestalt law stating that figural elements that form smooth curves tend to be grouped together.

Law of Pragnanz   The Gestalt law stating that the psychological organization of the percept will always be as "good" as prevailing conditions allow.

Law of proximity   The Gestalt law stating that elements close to one another tend to be grouped together.

Law of similarity   The Gestalt law stating that the more similar figural elements are, the more likely they are to be grouped together.

Local   The detailed aspects of a figure as opposed to the global aspects.

Metacontrast   Interference (e.g., masking) between two contours that are adjacent but not necessarily overlapping.

Pandemonium   A computer model of pattern identification based on a series of successive stages of feature analysis and recombination.

Perceptual object   The perceptual experience of a part of the retinal image forming a whole entity, an "object," that usually corresponds to a real world object.

Preattentive processes   Perceptual processes that operate to produce shapes and register their features without the need for focal attention.

Processing dominance   When some aspects of a form are processed faster than, or are more immune to interference from and interfere more with, other aspects of the same form.

Recognition   The experience of perceiving something as previously known.

Retinal image   The two-dimensional distribution of light of various intensities and wavelengths on the retina.

Separable stimulus   A stimulus that has single features that cannot be easily integrated.

Shape   A region of the retinal image surrounded by contours.

Stabilized retinal image   An image whose retinal position remains constant regardless of eye movements.

Subjective (or illusory) contours   Contours that are consciously experienced, but not associated with physical stimulus change.

Texton   Elongated blobs of a particular color, length, width, or orientation, line ends, or line crossings; differences between regions of the visual array in the textons they contain define textural contours.

Textural contour   A contour created by a boundary between two areas differing in visual texture.

Visual field   All the parts of the environment that are sending light to the eyes at any moment.

Visual texture   Aggregates of many small luminance contours or dots of different colors in the retinal image.

CHAPTER
12

Speech and Music

MUSIC

If a classical pianist sits down to play a concerto by Bach, the result is undoubtedly music. If a small child sits down at the piano, having never studied the instrument, his best efforts at playing produce auditory stimuli politely describable as random sounds but perhaps more accurately called noise. This is in spite of the fact that there are only 88 notes on a standard piano, which is all that, say, Arthur Rubinstein had to work with, and that anyone can sound each note, although not necessarily in the sequence suggested by Bach. What, then, distinguishes between a mere collection of sounds, varying in intensity, pitch, timbre, and duration, and the stimuli we experience as music? The answer seems to be that music is created by the context, or relationship of each sound to those preceding and following it. A child's random striking of the keys on the piano, or your experience when presented single stimuli in a pitch judgment experiment, lacks the relationships that would transform the stimuli into music. Once you perceive a sequence of sounds as music, however, an entirely new set of phenomena emerges, and even the perception of individual sounds will be different (Krumhansl & Shepard, 1979).

Musical Tones

One of the most striking examples of the perceptual phenomena that differentiate musical perception from other forms of auditory perception is the difference between musical pitch and acoustic pitch. In Chapter 7 we introduced the mel scale for acoustic pitch. This scale shows that when subjects are asked to adjust a set of pure tones differing in frequency so that the intervals between "notes" are equal steps, the results are not the same frequency intervals that correspond to our common (equally tempered) musical scale. For both the mel scale and the musical scale, sounds vary along the dimension musicians call **tone height,** which is simply whether a sound appears to be of higher or

lower pitch. In musical scales, however, there are other relations between the pitches of sounds that help to describe what we hear.

One relationship that is important for musical perception involves the concept of the *octave*. In the common scale—*do, re, mi, fa, sol, la, ti, do*—the second *do* is one octave higher than the first *do*. To get a tone one octave higher than another, you simply double the frequency of the first sound. Thus, middle C on a piano has a frequency of 261.6 hertz (Hz) and the C one octave higher is 523.2 Hz. Sounds separated by an octave seem more similar than do sounds separated by less than an octave (such as C and G, or *do* and *sol*). In other words, as you ascend the musical scale all of the *do*s sound similar to each other, as do the *re*s and so forth, regardless of how many octaves apart they are.

This tendency for tones separated by octaves to sound musically similar means that a simple one-dimensional scale (with low notes at the bottom and high at the top) will not suffice to describe our perception of musical pitch. As we ascend the scale, each note seems to reappear periodically, cycling through again with a different quality. This is reminiscent of the situation we discussed in Chapter 5 for color. There, when dealing with the dimension of hue, we found that we seemed to be moving around a circle, recycling from red through yellow, green, blue, and purple, then back to red. In color we could independently vary the intensity dimension linearly, without changing the identity of the hue. In music we can vary the tone height without changing the identity of the tone. Thus we can have a high *do* and a low *do* that sound similar, although one is clearly of a higher pitch. To represent this relationship graphically we have to use a three-dimensional scheme, much as we did for color. In 1846, Drobisch proposed that musical pitch might be represented as a helix, an idea that has persisted until the present (see Shepard, 1982). Figure 12-1 shows this representation of tonal qualities.

The additional aspect of musical pitch repre-

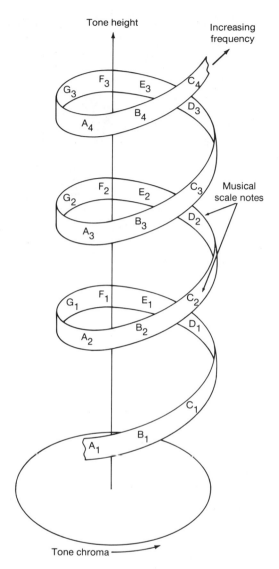

FIGURE 12-1 A regular helix represents the two aspects of musical pitch, height and chroma.

circle. It can be seen in Figure 12-1 as the circular component of the helix, whereas tone height is represented by the vertical component. One complete turn of the helix (a 360-degree rotation in the horizontal plane) represents a single octave, and all notes with the same name fall on a line drawn down the helix onto the same point on the chroma circle at the bottom and all sound similar. For convenience, we have labeled the spiral with some names of musical scale notes corresponding to the white keys on the piano rather than using tone frequencies. Thus, A_1 is the lowest A note on the piano, A_2 is one octave above it, and so on.

Although the usual laboratory experiment in pitch perception is able to isolate tones that seem to vary only in tone height, it is also possible to produce a series of sounds that vary only in tone chroma (move around the chroma circle in Figure 12-1) yet seem to ascend in height (Shepard, 1964; but see also Burns, 1981; Pollack, 1978). You can try this for yourself in Demonstration Box 12-1. An interesting variant of this illusion was reported by Deutsch (1986). She found a circular pattern of tones that is heard as ascending when played in one musical key but descending when played in another, which is contrary to the experience in music that a melody sounds the same when transposed to another key.

Although the musical helix represents the major aspects of musical pitch, it doesn't tell the whole story. Although confirming the importance of the chroma circle, much work has indicated that other relations between musical tones are also quite important (see Krumhansl & Kessler, 1982; Shepard, 1982). For example, when one tone is exactly 1.5 times the frequency of the other (a 3-to-2 ratio, or a perfect fifth musically) the two tones seem to ''go together'' or sound better together than when the tones are separated by other frequency steps (save for the octave step where tones sound similar). This and other relations between tones and between keys (a particular group of notes that comprise the musical scale used for a particular melody) require a much more complicated

sented in the figure is called **tone chroma,** a name that shows its similarity to hue in the realm of color perception. Thus, all *do*s have the same chroma, as do all *re*s, and so forth. More precisely, all tones with the same name (e.g., C or G) share the same chroma. Like hue, tone chroma is represented by a

DEMONSTRATION BOX 12-1.   The Tonal Staircase

Shepard (1964) invented a series of complex tones generated by a computer that when listened to in sequence seemed to continually increase in pitch. That is, each step between tones was perceived as being a step upward in pitch. Shepard, however, used a trick in generating this series of sounds and in fact the series ended where it had begun, completing a journey around the chroma circle (see Figure 12-1). The continuing rise in pitch was an illusion. It is rather difficult to produce Shepard's series of sounds without complex equipment, but it may be possible for you to hear the illusion anyway. First, fill a glass partially full of water; a crystal glass would be best, perhaps a wine glass, but any glass with a "ring" should do. Now tap the glass gently with a knife or other implement to make it ring. Continue tapping gently to produce a series of complex sounds. Each sound will be slightly different from the others in its frequency components because of variation in the way the knife strikes the glass. The series of sounds produced this way can often be heard to ascend or descend in pitch continuously, much in the way Shepard's sounds did,

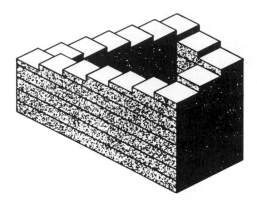

even though the sounds are highly similar and the fundamental frequency probably does not change. In Shepard's demonstration, this illusion is quite similar to the visual staircase illusion shown here. The stairs seem to climb endlessly but never get anywhere. This is probably the most striking demonstration of the reality of the quality of tone chroma in musical sounds.

representation, and agreement on what that might be has not yet been reached (see Krumhansl & Kessler, 1982; Shepard, 1982). What is certain, however, is that such relations play an important role in music theory and do have a perceptual reality, at least for the musically inclined. Since these relations must be taken into consideration in any description of music perception, it is much more difficult to generate a *musical space* than it was to generate a color space to represent our perceptions (see Chapter 5).

How well can people identify musical notes? In music contexts, we frequently hear of individuals who have *perfect pitch*. Such musicians are able to identify a musical note that is played on an instrument even when it is presented in complete isolation from other notes (although they do occa-

sionally misidentify the octave where it is located because of the perceptual similarity we have already discussed). However, when these same musicians are presented with pure, sine-wave tones they can identify the notes correctly only about half the time (Lockhead & Byrd, 1981). This is still a lot better than those without perfect pitch, who tend to be correct on only about 8 percent of the trials, but it is nowhere near "perfect." Remember from Chapter 7 that the perception of the pitches of a set of tones is predominantly determined by the frequency of the fundamental, or lowest tone, in the set. When a note is played on a musical instrument, though, different harmonic frequencies (multiples of the fundamental) are also sounded, giving the *timbre,* or complexity, to the sound. Clearly, the musicians who have perfect pitch are using more than the fundamental frequency of the musical notes to identify them; they are probably using these higher harmonics (e.g., in a piano note) to aid in identification. From their self-reports, these musicians judge chroma by comparing the test note with an internal (remembered) standard for each note, whereas the people without perfect pitch simply seem to guess at chroma.

The spacing between tones or notes is called a **musical interval.** In music of the Western world, scales have been arranged with logarithmic musical intervals. This is because frequency intervals that are equal on a logarithmic scale are perceived as being approximately equal intervals of musical pitch. For example, if you heard an interval generated by a pair of notes with frequencies of 200 and 400 Hz and another generated by a pair with frequencies of 2000 and 4000 Hz, they would seem to be about equally large (since $\log 400 - \log 200 = \log 4000 - \log 2000 = 0.3$). One implication of this is that any pair of steps between notes of the musical scale that are separated by the same number of intervening notes will appear to be the same size. In the preceding example we were dealing with octaves, a separation of eight notes (from *do* to *do,* excluding sharps and flats), which are always separated by 0.3 log units. When you subtract logarithms of frequencies you are performing the equivalent of division on the frequencies. This means that when we are talking about the logarithmic intervals between musical notes we are also talking about the ratios between frequencies of tones.

When three or more musical tones are played at the same time, we have a **chord.** Chords give much of the characteristic sound to what we call music (see e.g., Krumhansl, Bharucha & Kessler, 1982). Formal music theory provides a somewhat complicated system for naming chords, which we won't go into here. Suffice it to say that chords too are defined in terms of the ratios of the frequencies of the tones that constitute them. Chords whose respective components stand in the same frequency relationship are given the same name, no matter what octave they are from. For example, an E major chord is composed of the notes E, G#, and B no matter whether the notes are three octaves up from the lowest on the piano (E_4, $G\#_4$, and B_4) or six octaves up (E_7, $G\#_7$, and B_7). This aspect of musical pitch also is consistent with the helix shown in Figure 12-1, if spacings between the notes are logarithmic, since the intervals between the notes remain the same regardless of tonal height or absolute frequency.

Musical Forms

So far we have described a few of the most important local, or individual component, aspects of musical sequences or combinations of notes. That is, we have described music at the level of the particular frequencies of the notes that make up the music. Any sequence of notes also has global properties, however, that give an overall pattern to the sound sequence and are very important to its musical character since they comprise the aspect of music called *melody.* These properties include the sequence of pitch changes, the proportion and sizes of the various ascending and descending intervals, and so on. They are global properties because they are perceived in relationship to one another, rather than as individual features (Cuddy, Cohen & Mewhort, 1981; Deutsch, 1978). In fact, melodies can even be recognized on the basis of such global properties alone, although performance is better when the local cues are also available. These global cues are often collectively described as the **contour** of a piece of music. Contour means much the same thing here as it does in visual pattern perception. It is the general shape of the musical sequence of sounds, defined in terms of rises and drops in frequency instead of in terms of changes in direction of a line in space. Figure 12-2 shows some examples of musical passages that share a contour even though they are in different positions on the musical scale.

A typical piece of music consists of a rather long sequence of different notes and chords, similar

FIGURE 12-2   When a melodic sequence is transposed to different positions on the musical scale (A) it still retains the same contour (B).

to a long string of sounds uttered by a person making a speech. Just as we perceive a complicated hierarchy of words, phrases, and sentences as we listen to someone speaking, we also organize music in a hierarchical fashion. Combinations of notes form *motives* (pronounced ''mo-*teevs*''), combinations of motives form *phrases,* and so on (Deutsch, 1978).

How are these combinations formed perceptually? It turns out that notes, motives, and phrases are grouped together according to principles that very strongly resemble those that govern visual pattern perception, suggesting that the perception of music and melody is a form of auditory pattern perception. Of particular interest in this regard are the Gestalt laws of grouping that we discussed in Chapter 11.

There are three major principles that tend to group notes or chords together in a listener's consciousness (see Deutsch, 1978). The first of these is based on pitch range. This principle says that notes that are close together in pitch are perceived as part of the same perceptual unit, whereas notes that are far apart in pitch are perceived in separate groups. This principle is related to the Gestalt law of *proximity,* and its visual equivalent can be seen in Figure 11-6G. Whenever the same instrument plays both a melody and an accompaniment, they are played in different pitch or frequency ranges so that the melody will be the figure (the part that stands out perceptually) and the accompaniment will be the ground (the background against which the melody is imaged). An example is in folk-guitar playing, where the performer often keeps a steady accompaniment going on the bass strings of the guitar while playing a melody on the treble strings.

Another principle of grouping is based on timbre (see Chapter 7). Different types of musical instruments play the same notes with different timbres, which gives them their characteristic sounds and allows you to identify which instrument is playing any given note. When several instruments are playing simultaneously, the observer tends to group those of similar timbre into units, in a way analogous to the Gestalt law of *similarity* (see Figure 11-6B or C). In symphonic music, this principle is used to separate phrases that have a similar fundamental frequency range but a different musical message. Also, timbre provides an additional principle of grouping to that of pitch range when different instruments play different parts of a piece (as in the lead and rhythm guitar parts of a piece of modern rock music).

The third principle is based on the concept of *good continuation* in direct analogy to the Gestalt principle of that name (again, Figure 11-6D provides a visual analogue of this principle). Sequences of frequency changes in the same direction (e.g., rising up the scale) tend to be perceived as part of the same sequence, whereas changes in direction between sequences of notes tend to act as boundaries between segments (Deutsch & Feroe, 1981). A good illustration of this is the illusion shown in Figure 12-3, first described by Deutsch (1975). Two different sequences of tones are presented, one to each ear, as in the left panel of A. Seventy percent of Deutsch's listeners heard the sound sequences represented in the right panel of A; apparently good continuation created an auditory "stream" of notes (see Bregman, 1978) in each ear that was illusory. Later data indicated that such sequences are ambiguous figures, as in Figure 11-3, that have competing organizations (Smith, Hausfeld, Power & Gorta, 1982). However, some cases are compelling enough to be used by composers of music, as in Figure 12-3, B and C. In B, two violin sections play the left phrases of music but the audience hears the notes as if the right

phrases were being played. A similar phenomenon occurs for the music in C played by two pianos. Dowling and Harwood's (1986) book includes a taped demonstration of this and many other musical phenomena that you might wish to obtain from the library and try for yourself.

So far, we have concentrated on variations in the frequency of musical notes or combinations of notes, neglecting the other major dimension of musical sounds, their duration. You probably learned in grade school that written sequences of musical notes indicate not only tone height (frequency) but also tone length—a quarter note is held for half the duration of a half note, and so forth. Both the duration and height of notes are vital in determining our perception of melody. You can clearly see this in Figure 12-4, which presents three musical excerpts. All have the same tonal contour. They differ only in the time that the notes are held, but this causes a tremendous difference in the melody you perceive. The first is the beginning of the familiar American folk song "Red River Valley," the second is the opening of Mozart's Serenade in D, and the third is the beginning of the second movement of Beethoven's Symphony No. 5. If you play a musical instrument you might want to try these phrases for yourself, just to hear how different they sound.

A sequence of sounds of various durations possesses **rhythm** and **tempo.** Tempo is the perceived speed associated with the presentation of the sounds, and rhythm is their perceived organization in time. When listeners are presented with a sequence of sounds they spontaneously organize it into sub-sequences consisting of an accented sound followed by at least one and sometimes several unaccented sounds (Bolton, 1894). This is why the ticking of a clock seems to go "*tick,* tock, *tick,* tock," despite the fact that every ticking sound emitted by the clock is identical. This spontaneous organization happens when the sounds are presented at rates between 10 per second and 1 every 2 seconds and seems to be optimal at rates of 2 to 3 sounds per second. Under some circumstances the percept may vary in the degree of accenting of

FIGURE 12-3   Three examples of the Deutsch illusion. In all cases, the left part of the figure shows what is played, the right shows what is usually heard. (A) The original, from Deutsch, 1975. (B) From Tchaikovsky, Sixth Symphony, last movement. (C) From Rachmaninov, Suite for Two Pianos, Opus 17, second movement.

sounds so that a fairly complex rhythmic structure is perceived despite a physical stimulus that is absolutely regular. In the perception of music, these perceptual rhythms are superimposed on a deliberately manipulated rhythmic structure according to principles of grouping similar to the Gestalt-like principles mentioned above. This rhythmic organization interacts with the organization induced by the variations in pitch of the musical notes, making it easier to perceive the melodic structure of the music (Deutsch, 1978; Handel & Oshinsky, 1981). Actually, the most recent evidence indicates that the principles associated with determining an apparent melody and those determining your perception of rhythmic structure add together to produce a coherent musical pattern (Palmer & Krumhansl, 1987). Demonstration Box 12-2 shows how sounds may be grouped together by varying the rhythm or timing between them.

Music is an important part of every culture

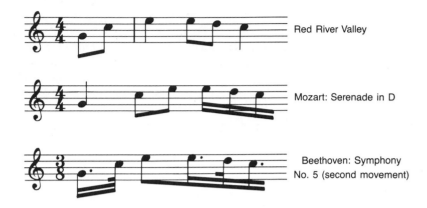

FIGURE 12-4   Three musical phrases in which the melodic sequence of tone height is the same, and the tones differ only in duration.

DEMONSTRATION BOX 12-2.   Rhythmic Grouping

In this demonstration you will produce a series of tapping sounds as stimuli. In order to indicate how your taps should be distributed in time, let us establish a sort of rhythmic notation. Whenever we present a *V* it indicates a tap, whereas a hyphen indicates a brief pause. First, tap this simple sequence *VV-V*. Listen carefully, and notice that the first two taps seem to "go together" or form a unit, but the last seems to stand alone. Now, repeat this sequence of taps several times and try to mentally change this organization so that you have two groups with the first tap (*V*) forming one and the last two taps (*V-V*) forming the other. Notice that no effort of will allows you to do this. The two taps that are close together in time seem to go together and the other does not. This is analogous to the Gestalt principle of grouping by proximity that we discuss in Chapter 11.

Next, try the sequence *VVV-V-V-VVV-V-V-VVV*, and so on. Notice that this is a repetition of three quick taps, followed by two slow taps. Notice that now the three taps form one group, and the two slow taps form another, perceptually. It is virtually impos-sible to hear this any other way. This is analogous to the Gestalt principle of similarity (the visual analogue is shown in Figure 11-6).

While you are tapping, you can see that perceptual groups or clusters can be formed by frequency or timbre differences despite the absence of rhythmic differences. Begin by steadily tapping a surface with your pencil. Make sure that the tapping rhythm is steady and unchanging. Now take a piece of paper and slip it between the surface and your pencil and notice that the sound quality changes. Without chang-ing your rhythm, slip the paper in and out so that you are tapping *table, table, paper, paper, table, table,* and so on. Notice that the sounds seem to take on a grouping, with the table taps together and the paper taps together, and it seems, despite the fact that you are tapping quite steadily and monotonously, that the sounds have a rhythm that goes *table, table,* pause, *paper, paper,* pause, *table, table,* and so forth. Here, grouping by perceived similarity has imposed an ap-parent rhythm on the sound sequence.

and it has many more aspects than those few we have space to cover here. Several recent books (Dowling & Harwood, 1986; Howell, Cross & West, 1985; Pierce, 1983; Sloboda, 1985) and a special issue of the journal *Perception & Psychophysics* (Dowling & Carterette, 1987) cover these other aspects in some detail. In addition, we are now beginning to find that certain neural mechanisms may be critical to music perception. Perhaps comparisons between the musics of different cultures may yield some insight into which aspects of music perception depend on learning the musical vocabulary of a particular culture and which depend on mechanisms that characterize all human beings (Deutsch, 1982). Until such data are available we will continue to listen to a symphony of theories and speculations.

SPEECH

''I just can't understand it,'' Consuela muttered to herself as she strolled down the Champs Élysées at dusk. ''I've given myself practically a Berlitz course in French. I can read French fluently. Signs and papers are no problem at all. Yet every time I try to talk to someone in a store, or on the street, and especially when I go to a student party to try to find out where the excitement is, I can't understand a word anyone is saying. It all sounds like noise.'' She sighed as she turned into the street where her hotel was located. ''I guess I just don't have an *ear* for French.''

Consuela's problem is not unique among those learning a second language. We seldom think about how remarkable an accomplishment speech perception is until we are in a situation like hers, where we listen to a stream of nearly continuous speech without understanding it. In our native language we can understand speech at rates of up to about 50 discrete sound units per second, although speech usually proceeds at about 12 units per second (Foulke & Sticht, 1969). This is quite amazing, since listeners can only determine the order of non-

speech sounds when they occur at rates of less than 1 unit every 1.5 seconds (2/3 unit per second) (Warren, Obusek, Farmer & Warren, 1969). Remember, we are discriminating not only various units of sound but also their order of occurrence (as when we discriminate between the words *tab* and *bat*). Advertisers often take advantage of our ability to process rapidly occurring speech sounds by having announcers in commercials speak much faster than usual speech. Our ability to interpret speech sounds much more quickly than the identity or order of nonspeech sounds suggests to some researchers that speech may involve some special form of perceptual processing, although this suggestion leads to controversy.

Simple knowledge of the nature of sound signals may well not be enough to allow us to understand how people interpret speech sounds so accurately, since we can understand speech even when the signal is grossly distorted or transformed (see Remez, Rubin, Pisoni & Carrell, 1981). Examples of distorted but understandable speech are found when you speak with an accent, with a mouthful of food, or while holding your nose. Devices like telephones and radios also produce distortions of the sound signal that don't greatly affect the intelligibility of speech. Telephones allow only a limited range of frequencies to pass along the wire, yet normal conversation is possible over the telephone (but try it in a foreign language that you don't know very well and you will see how this distortion may render the conversation difficult to understand). Other transmission systems can severely *clip* the speech signal (turn it into a series of *on* or *off* pulses) yet still only marginally affect its intelligibility (although it *will* sound different). You can also easily understand conversations despite a background of noise, even when the noise level is only 6 decibels less than the speech intensity. In fact, even if the utterances and noise are the same intensity we can identify about 50 percent of single words, and we can understand speech even when it is less intense than the noise if it is about a familiar subject.

As a first guess, you might think that speech perception is merely another form of auditory pattern perception and as such should follow principles similar to those of music perception. To a certain extent this is true. However, because its function is to convey information, and because speech plays such an important role in so many aspects of human behavior, you will find that the way we conceptualize speech identification problems and mechanisms will be quite different from the ways we treated simple sound stimuli, or even music. Also, we should warn you in advance that there will be no final answers presented here. Speech is one of the most controversial areas of perception research and we are moving only slowly toward the best way to think about the difficult problems that exist.

The Speech Stimulus

When we dealt with visual pattern perception in Chapter 11, we suggested that the major task for the observer centered around the construction of perceptual objects that in turn carry information about the environment. Speech perception is similar, only in this case the objects are words, or phrases, that carry linguistic information. As Liberman and Mattingly (1985) put it, "the objects of speech perception are the intended phonetic gestures of the speaker" (p. 2). This simply means that the ultimate goal of the speech perception process is to put into your consciousness an accurate representation of what the speaker *intended to say*.

Given the intimate association between speech and language it was probably inevitable that linguists were the first to set up procedures to describe the speech stimulus. Their description depends on the analysis of speech sounds in terms of how they are produced *(phonetics)* and how specific sounds distinguish words *(phonemics)*. Such descriptions are universal, in the sense that speech production and the methods of distinguishing linguistic units follow the same rules in every human language, although the specific sounds and the rules for com-

bining them may be quite different (see Clark & Clark, 1977; Ladefoged, 1975). Although our discussion will be limited to the English languge, you should be aware that a similar analysis can be conducted in any language.

Consonants and Vowels

In the English language, the vocal apparatus produces two basic types of speech sounds: **vowels** and **consonants.** They are produced by alternating sequences of opening and closing the vocal tract (the air passages in our throats, mouths, and nasal areas) while air from the lungs flows through it. Typically, closing movements produce consonants and opening movements produce vowels.

Consonants can be classified along three major dimensions, corresponding to the ways in which they are produced. First, consonants can be *voiced* or *unvoiced*. Voiced consonants consist of a constriction of the flow of air out of the mouth followed very closely in time (less than 30 msec) by vibration of the vocal folds (vocal cords). For an unvoiced consonant, the vocal folds don't begin vibrating until a longer time after the constriction, usually more than 40 msec. Demonstration Box 12-3 allows you to experience an exaggerated version of voiced and unvoiced consonants for yourself.

The other two classifications are by how *(manner)* and where *(place)* in the vocal tract the constriction of the airflow occurs. There are three manners in which the constriction can be produced. *Stop consonants* are formed by completely stopping the flow of air from the lungs and then suddenly releasing the flow. The p in "pea," the t in "tea," and the k in "keep" are examples of stop consonants. *Fricatives* are formed by stopping the flow through the nasal passages but leaving a small opening in the mouth and forcing air through it, producing some variety of "hissing" sound. Examples are the s in "best," the z in "buzz," and the f in "fricative." *Nasal consonants* are produced through the nose, as you might have guessed. For these sounds the mouth is closed and the air from

---

DEMONSTRATION BOX 12-3.   Voiced and Voiceless Fricatives

Consonants in the English language are produced by a combination of vocal fold vibration and variations in the passage of air through the oral cavity. Fricatives are a class of consonants that are formed when the mouth moves to a position that nearly blocks the flow of air, so air is forced through the tiny hole. However, fricatives also differ in whether they are voiced (accompanied by vocal fold vibration) or voiceless (have no vocal fold vibration). To illustrate this interaction between the flow of air and the quality of voicing, try the following demonstration suggested by Brown and Deffenbacher (1979). Make the sound

of a *z,* such as in the word "zip." Now try producing a tune (for example, "Oh, Susannah") while you sound the *z.* You should be able to do this easily; in fact, it will sound something like a kazoo. However, now try the same thing while making the sound of an *f,* such as in the word "fat." *F* is a voiceless fricative; therefore, the lack of vocal fold vibration should make it impossible for you to produce a melody (remember, just produce the sound of *f,* do not hum simultaneously). The quality of voicing, or vocal fold vibration, allows one type of fricative to be "melodic," whereas the other is lacking in that quality.

---

the lungs flows through the nasal passages. Examples are the *m* in "mean" and the *n* in "nose."

There are two areas in the vocal tract where most of the constrictions occur. In one, the lips or the lips against the teeth control the flow of air from the lungs; consonants produced by such constrictions are called *labial* (*labium* is Latin for "lip"). Examples of labial consonants are the *b* in "bat" (voiced, stop), the *v* in "vat" (voiced, fricative), and the *m* in "mat" (voiced, nasal). The other area of constriction is inside the mouth. Here the tongue is positioned at various places, most often at the ridge behind the teeth *(alveolar),* against the hard palate *(palatal),* or against the velum (the soft palate at the top of the throat, *velar*). Examples are the *t* in "tin" (unvoiced, stop, alveolar), the *n* in "gnat" (voiced, nasal, palatal), and the *c* in "cot" (unvoiced, stop, velar). Try producing these sounds and paying attention to where your **articulators** (the parts of the vocal tract used to produce speech sounds, such as teeth, tongue, lips, and palates) are while you are doing it.

Vowels are produced in a very different way from consonants. In general, as we mentioned above, vowels are produced by vibrating the vocal folds as air moves out of the lungs through the open mouth. Here also, which vowel is produced

depends on the relative positions of various parts of the vocal tract. First, the position of the tongue in the mouth is important, whether front, center, or back, and so is its relative height. Changes in tongue position and height change the shape of the resonating chamber in your mouth, resulting in the various vowels. For example, the *ee* in "beet" is produced with the tongue at the front and quite high up in the mouth, the *a* in "sofa" is produced with the tongue central and of middle height in the mouth, and the *o* in "pot" is produced with the tongue at the back and low down in the mouth. Try saying these sounds and pay attention to where your tongue is. Second, the degree of rounding of the lips is important in vowel production. The *o* in "who" is called a *rounded* vowel since the lips must be rounded in order to produce it, while the *e* in "he" is *unrounded* since the lips are flat when it is produced.

Phonemes

Linguists have also worked out a descriptive system of speech units that is sufficient to describe any utterance in any language. In this system, the basic unit of speech sound is the **phone.** A phone that is used in a language to distinguish one word from another is called a **phoneme.** Every language has its own group of necessary phonemes; some have only a few (Hawaiian has 11), whereas others require as many as 60 (some African dialects) in order to distinguish all the words. North American English has 40 basic phonemes (excluding regional dialects such as drawls and nasal twangs). Table 12-1 lists the major phonemes of American English and the symbols used by the International Phonetic Association (IPA) to refer to them. Phonemes are usually set off from text by a pair of slashes (e.g., /p/ or /θ/), but to make things more natural we will simply italicize phonemes and give an example word in quotes (e.g., the *p* in ''pod''). You should try saying the various example words in Table 12-1, paying attention to how the sounds of the phonemes correspond to the way the sounds are produced (their articulatory features).

Every phoneme has a unique description in terms of its articulatory features (e.g., the *b* in ''bat'' is a voiced, bilabial, stop), so there is a one-to-one correspondence between the articulatory and phonemic descriptions of words. Unfortunately, if we look at the acoustic properties of the speech signal itself, it is sometimes impossible to isolate the sound features that correspond to a particular phone in a particular uttered phrase. This is due to the fact that when we speak we often move our articulators to produce sounds that provide information about several different phones simultaneously (this is called *coarticulation*). It is therefore difficult (some say impossible) to find a clear correspondence between acoustic features and perceived phonemes except in fairly specific, often simplified, instances.

Acoustic Properties of Speech

Since phones refer to speech *sounds,* it would seem useful to have a means of displaying the speech sound signal so that we can better analyze it, perhaps with an idea of trying to determine some aspects of the relationship between articulatory and acoustic features and the final perceived speech units. One popular way is based on the fact that any complex sound wave can be represented as the combination of a set of simple sine waves of different amplitudes and frequencies (see Chapter 6). For speech we must add the dimension of time, since the speech waveform is not periodic (repeating) but varies over time. The result of analyzing a sequence of speech sounds into its simple sine wave components on a moment-to-moment basis is displayed as a **speech spectrogram.** An example is shown in Figure 12-5. In all such spectrograms, the horizontal axis shows time in milliseconds from the onset of the speech signal, and the vertical axis shows the frequency (in Hz) of the simple sine-wave components at a given moment. The intensity of the sine-wave components is represented by the darkness of the smudges on the spectrogram: the darker the smudge the more intense the component. Notice in Figure 12-5 that there are very intense components from about 300 to 700 Hz in all of the syllables. These components last about 200 msec for the ''bab'' syllable and about 300 msec for the ''gag'' syllable.

Table 12-1. The Major Phonemes of North American English

Consonants				Vowels			
p	pea	θ	thigh	i	beet	o	go
b	beet	ð	thy	ɪ	bit	ɔ	ought
m	man	s	see	e	ate	a	dot
t	toy	ʒ	measure	ɛ	bet	ə	sofa
d	dog	tʃ	chip	æ	bat	ɜ	urn
n	neat	dʒ	jet	u	boot	ai	bite
k	kill	l	lap	ʊ	put	aʊ	out
g	good	r	rope	ʌ	but	ɔɪ	toy
f	foot	y	year	ɒ	odd	oʊ	own
ç	huge	w	wet				
h	hot	ŋ	sing				
v	vote	z	zip				
ʍ	when	ʃ	show				

Note: The phonetic symbol is to the left of each column and its sound corresponds to the part of the word represented in **bold** type. Some vowel and consonant combinations are also shown.

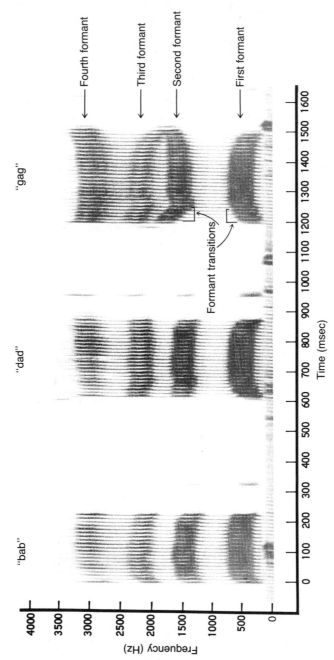

FIGURE 12-5 Speech spectrograms of the words "bab," "dad," and "gag," spoken with a British accent. (Based on Ladefoged, 1975)

The dark smudges in a speech spectrogram are called **formants.** Formants are bands of especially intense components that arise because the complex sound waves created by the passage of air from the lungs across the vocal folds and out through the mouth and/or nose are affected by the positions of the various parts of the vocal tract. For each mouth posture and airflow pattern certain ranges of nearby frequencies are enhanced and others diminished, and these show up as the pattern of smudges on the spectrogram. At least four formants can be distinguished for each of the syllables in Figure 12-5. The one at the lowest frequency (around 500 Hz in the figure) is called the *first formant* and is produced by the shape of the pharynx (wall of the throat). Any change in the shape of the pharynx produces a change in the frequency at which the first formant happens. The *second formant,* at about 1400 to 1500 Hz in the different parts of Figure 12-5, is produced by the shape of the oral cavity. Higher formants are produced by complex resonances of the vocal tract, including the nasal passages.

In general, vowels and consonants can be dis-tinguished in speech spectrograms. The relative positions of the various formants roughly correspond to the different vowel sounds. A special apparatus, called a *vocoder,* provides a sort of reverse spectrograph, re-creating the sounds for any pattern of sine-wave components it has been fed and even creating artificial speechlike sounds. Using artificial speech stimuli it has been shown that only the first two formants are needed to create sounds that listeners readily identify as vowels, hence in our presentation we will indicate only the first two formants. Figure 12-6 shows the first two formants for a set of vowel sounds spoken by an adult male. Since people have different-sized mouths, noses, and throat passages, they have different ranges of possible shape changes. This means that the first and second formants will appear at a range of different frequencies across different speakers. Figure 12-6 also shows, for comparison, one vowel spoken by a child. Notice that both formants are centered on higher frequencies for the child than for the adult.

Consonants are generally indicated by changes of formants over short intervals of time (usually

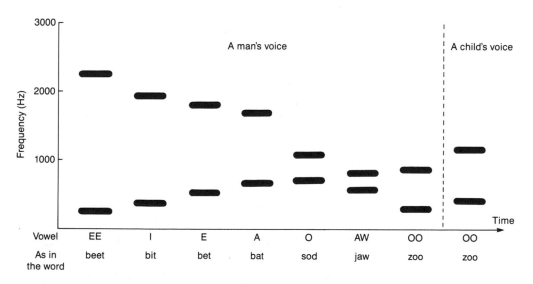

FIGURE 12-6 The first two formants for a series of vowel sounds made by an adult male voice. For comparison, the last vowel sound is shown also as it would be made by a child's voice.

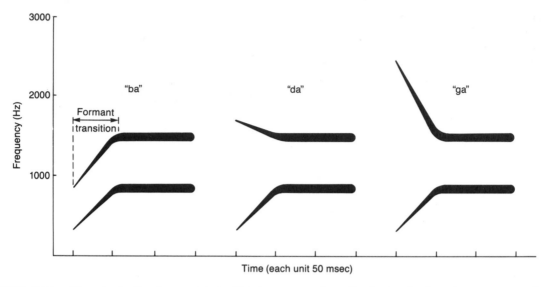

FIGURE 12-7   Changes in the formant transition cause a systematic change in the consonant sound heard for the same vowel. The vowel sound is the *o* in "sod."

less than 100 msec) called **formant transitions.** A typical formant transition is highlighted in Figure 12-5 and shown schematically in Figure 12-7. Notice in Figure 12-7 that as the formant transition changes the consonant changes from *b* to *d* to *g,* although the vowel (defined as the two formants) remains the *o* as in "sod."

The rate of change in the formant transition is also quite important in the perception of the phoneme. Figure 12-8 shows that if we begin with the *e* vowel as in "let," a short formant transition is heard as the consonant *b* and a slightly longer one as the consonant *w;* however, when it is made longer yet, it doesn't sound like a consonant at all,

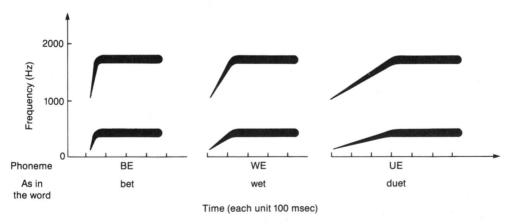

FIGURE 12-8   The duration of the formant transition affects what is heard. When it is short a consonant is heard; when it is long a shift between two vowels is heard.

but rather like the change between two vowels, as the *ue* in "duet."

Simple sounds of the sort described here do produce systematic perceptual responses, yet in natural speech the signal is not so regular. The theoretically expected components are often missing or distorted. Some individuals (such as Victor Zue) seem to be able to "read" speech spectrograms with an accuracy of about 90 percent (Cole, Rudnicky, Zue & Reddy, 1980), but this is a rare quality. In our usual conversational exchanges there is seldom a precise correspondence between the acoustic properties of the stimulus and the speech signal as it is heard. As we will see below, whereas it is possible to obtain a precise acoustic description of any utterance in terms of a speech spectrogram, it is not always possible to say exactly what aspects of that spectrogram are meaningfully related to speech perception. In some respects this is quite reasonable, suggesting that we should be looking for relationships or patterns rather than individual speech units. In music we can recognize a melody played on a piano in one key as being the same melody when played on the clarinet in another key even though no two acoustic signals corresponding to parts of the melody are ever the same. The melody is carried in the relationships among the individual sounds rather than in any sound pattern itself. Such a global analysis based on relationships instead of on individual acoustic components may be needed in speech perception as well.

Issues in Speech Perception

Our orientation thus far has been to view speech perception as a form of auditory pattern perception in which the listener's immediate task is to isolate phonemic units and integrate them into a meaningful whole, much like the perceptual object task we discussed in the chapter on visual form (Chapter 11). To this end, we have been looking at some features of the speech signal and their characteristics. However, because speech perception is studied by investigators from so many different disciplines—linguists, electrical engineers, and computer scientists as well as psychologists and speech and hearing scientists—there is a tremendous diversity of approaches to the field. One way to integrate these diverse views is to focus on the major problems, or issues, common to most approaches. We have chosen a few of these for discussion here.

Ambiguity and Invariance

Although we suggested earlier that we can find consistent features of the speech signal that correspond to our conscious perception of speech elements, this is actually an oversimplification that only holds under certain controlled circumstances. In natural speech we do not simply add together the various simple vowel and consonant components to produce the final complex utterance. Conversely, when we are listening to normal speech we may perceive a consonant in the absence of the expected formant transition, or hear a vowel that is not the one predicted by the actual formants present. Put simply, the problem is that specific features in the acoustic signal do not always predict specific perceptual interpretations of the speech stimulus.

There are a number of ways our perception of the speech signal differs from its acoustic properties. For instance, we hear speech in segments that we interpret as phonemes, words, or phrases separated by pauses. In actual fact, the acoustic signal is often a continuous stream, without any obvious breaks or other "markers" corresponding to these perceived subdivisions (e.g., Chomsky & Miller, 1963). Another feature the speech signal lacks is **linearity.** In terms of phonemes, linearity means that for each phoneme in an utterance we should be able to find a corresponding segment of the physical speech signal. Furthermore, linearity requires that the order of the segments in the physical signal must correspond to the order of phonemes. Neither of these criteria are met in the natural speech signal.

Another source of ambiguity comes from the fact that the speech signal lacks **acoustic-phonetic invariance.** Invariance refers to the notion that for each phoneme there must be some *constant set* of acoustic features associated with it whenever it is heard. In concrete terms, this might mean that there is a specific feature, say the formant transition representing a particular consonant, that must be present if we are to hear this consonant in the utterance. If this acoustic feature is present it means that the associated phoneme was intended, whereas its absence means that the phoneme was not intended. Unfortunately, such invariance is not found in the speech signal. The actual state of affairs is much more complex.

Figure 12-9 illustrates how very different acoustic signals can be perceived as the same phoneme. In this case the phoneme is *d*. Formant transitions usually convey information about consonants; the formants themselves contain information about the vowels. Here we have a set of consonant-vowel combinations in which the consonant remains *d*. As we saw in Figure 12-7, it was the change in the formant transition of the second formant that determined which consonant we heard. If that is the case, then at the acoustic level something strange is going on here: When we hear *d* in combination with the vowel *ee*, to form the complex *dee* as in "deep," the formant transition

in the second formant is a rise; when we hear *d* in combination with *o,* to form the sound *do* as in "dope," the second formant transition is a sharp drop; and when we hear the *d* in combination with *e,* forming the *de* in "deck," there is no second formant transition at all! This situation seems to violate linearity, since the information about *d* does not correspond to a specific segment of the speech signal. It also violates invariance, since the acoustic cue for *d* depends on the context (here the vowel it is paired with) rather than a specific set of invariant acoustic features. This lack of clear correspondence between phonemes and acoustic features makes it quite difficult to determine exactly what you will perceive given only the information present in the acoustic input. You can see this for yourself in Demonstration Box 12-4.

Is Speech Special?

In some respects, we must recognize that speech is quite special and different from other stimuli. The speech stimulus is produced by humans to communicate linguistic information, something only humans do naturally. Speech sounds special to the listener; there is a distinct difference between our

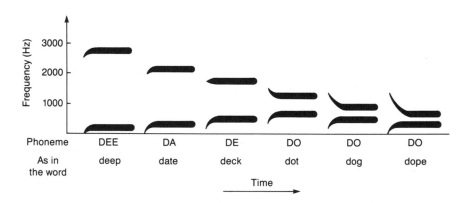

FIGURE 12-9   Despite the fact that the formant transition in the second formant changes from a rise to a drop, depending on the vowel, the same consonant phoneme *d* is heard. The fact that the first formant is largely irrelevant to the perception of a consonant suggests that there is no single feature corresponding to this phoneme, hence it demonstrates the lack of acoustic-phonetic invariance in the speech signal.

DEMONSTRATION BOX 12-4.   Segmenting the Speech Signal

To see how difficult it is to segment the nearly continuous speech signal into words purely on the basis of acoustic criteria, look at the two speech spectrograms in this box, both of which are adapted from Pisoni and Luce (1986). Before reading the next paragraph, look at each segment and try to figure out how many words or syllables are in phrase A.

Phrase A has five words and six syllables. It was made from a recording of the sentence "I owe you a yoyo." How successful were you? Even knowing the phrase in advance doesn't seem to help very much does it?

Now look at phrase B. It represents the spectrogram of the phrase "Peter buttered the burnt toast." There are five occurrences of the phoneme *t* as in "toy" in this phrase. If there is invariance and linearity in the speech signal you should be able to find five repetitions of the same signal representing this phoneme *t*. Can you find them? It may be of some comfort to know that speech researchers have the same difficulties, and they haven't solved them yet. A recent book devoted to this problem illustrates the variety of approaches that is being tried and provides an excellent summary of the current state of knowledge on this subject (Perkell & Klatt, 1986).

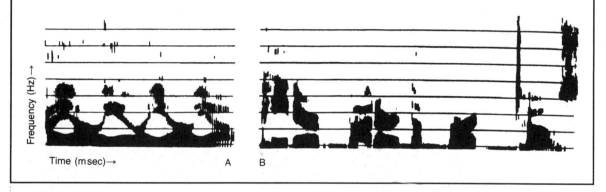

perception of speech and of other sounds. However, speech researchers usually mean something else by the question of this section. They refer to the proposal by a group of researchers that the perception of speech is accomplished by a specialized set of neural mechanisms in the human (e.g., Liberman, 1982). This is a major point of controversy within the speech research community and researchers often classify each other by where they stand on this issue. Several lines of research have been used to argue for or against the special quality of speech processing. We discuss a few of them in what follows. The arguments usually take the form of the "speech is special" forces obtaining a dramatic finding that appears to demonstrate a special

"speech mode" of processing, followed by the "speech is just a form of auditory pattern perception" forces showing that the same finding can be obtained using nonspeech stimuli and proposing a purely acoustic explanation for the phenomenon with both speech and nonspeech stimuli. The results have thus been much like a tennis match, with the players lobbing research findings and interpretations.

At the physiological level, there is a reason to suggest that speech is different from other aspects of auditory processing. It has long been known that in most humans the two hemispheres of the brain show some degree of specialization in their functioning. Damage to the left side of the brain is more likely to produce disruption in speech comprehension or production (e.g., Kolb & Wishaw, 1985), and a series of behavioral studies has also confirmed that speech processing is predominantly left hemisphere in nature. Such studies have either used *dichotic listening* procedures (where different messages are simultaneously presented to the two ears, and hence differentially activate the two hemispheres) or direct recording of brain activity while individuals are presented with various speech and nonspeech stimuli. The general pattern of data obtained shows that the left hemisphere is most strongly involved in speech processing, whereas the right hemisphere is most strongly activated when musical or other patterned auditory stimuli are presented (Bryden, 1982: Springer & Deutsch, 1985). Although this specialization is not exclusive and some language processing is also undertaken in the right hemisphere (Millar & Whitaker, 1983), and simple auditory stimulus processing seems to be bilateral, such specialization of function in different areas of the brain suggests that speech might receive a different form of perceptual processing than other forms of auditory pattern perception.

Categorical Perception   From a perceptual level, one of the first phenomena to suggest the possibility of a special speech mode of processing was that of **categorical perception** (Liberman, Harris, Hoffman & Griffith, 1957). An example of categorical perception uses the continuum of **voice onset time** for stop consonants discussed above. Basically, this refers to the fact that if voicing occurs shortly (say 20 msec) after a constriction of the airflow from the lungs is released, a *voiced* consonant (such as the *b* in "bad") is heard. If the voicing is delayed somewhat after the constriction is released, an *unvoiced* consonant (such as the *p* in "pad") is heard. The time at which the onset of voicing occurs can be viewed as a stimulus continuum, ranging from about 0 to 70 msec or so after the constriction is released. This might lead you to expect that as we varied the voice onset time we should get a gradual shading of the consonant from *b* to *p,* with perhaps some region in which the identity of the phoneme was ambiguous or a combination of the two. Perceptually, such a graded change does not occur.

As the voice onset time is changed you hear one consonant until, when the voice onset time exceeds some critical value, there is a shift in the percept and you now hear the other consonant—rather like what you might expect if there had been an abrupt shift from one category of stimulus to another. In studies using artificial speech sounds we find that for every voice onset time up to some particular value listeners report hearing only the voiced consonant (e.g., *b* in "ba"), as shown in Figure 12-10A. When the voice onset time is just a little longer than this they suddenly start hearing the unvoiced consonant (e.g., *p* in "pa"), as is also seen in Figure 12-10A, and hear only that for all longer voice onset times. The value at which this change in the phoneme seems to occur is called the **phonemic boundary** and is around 35 msec in the curve in Figure 12-10A. In other words, there is a sudden shift in the percept from the phoneme *b* to the phoneme *p* at the phonemic boundary. Moreover, if listeners are presented with pairs of sounds with voice onset times on the same side of the phonemic boundary (say 10 vs. 20 msec before voice onset) they have a very hard time discriminating them at all, whereas if the stimuli come from opposite sides of the boundary (say 30 and 40 msec) discrimination is very good. Consonants show this categorical perception, but vowels do not.

When these findings were first presented, it was thought that nonspeech stimuli didn't segregate into perceptual categories but rather produced much more gradual perceptual transitions as the stimulus changed. This led many researchers to assume that some special kind of mechanism must exist to process and categorize acoustic cues defining the various consonants. The data are not so clear now, however (see Pisoni & Luce, 1986, for a review). Several studies have shown that similar dramatic categorization effects can occur for nonspeech stimuli. For example, Cutting (1976) found a fairly sharp categorical boundary for "plucked" versus

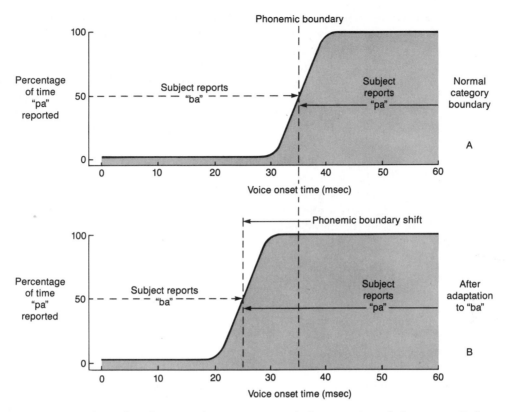

FIGURE 12-10   Typical results of an experiment on categorical perception of phonemes. Before adaptation the phonemic boundary is at about 35 msec voice onset time. After listening to "ba" for 2 minutes, the phonemic boundary is shifted to about 25 msec voice onset time.

"bowed" sounds (like those of violins), which differed only in their onset times. Other studies have shown similar categorization effects in nonhuman species such as macaque monkeys and Japanese quail, neither of which should be expected to have a special mechanism for speech processing (Kluender, Diehl & Killeen, 1987; Kuhl & Padden, 1983). Such data, although still quite controversial, seem more consistent with the notion that speech perception is a special case of auditory pattern perception, rather than a special perceptual process.

Categorical perception effects can actually be obtained for any perceptual continuum. The trick seems to be to use the *adaptation level* as the category boundary. You should recall from Chapter 2 that the adaptation level represents a sort of neutral

point in any perceptual continuum, which serves as a subjective reference point for judgments. Stimuli above the adaptation level seem to be qualitatively different from those below the adaptation level (e.g., hot vs. cold, loud vs. soft). For a variety of stimulus continua, discrimination of stimuli is considerably worse when stimuli are selected either all from below or all from above the adaptation level. This pattern of data is much like that observed in categorical speech perception (Streitfeld & Wilson, 1986).

Just as the adaptation level can be made to change because of previous experience with particular sets of stimuli, the phonemic boundary can be made to shift around. The phonemic boundary can be moved by presenting listeners repeatedly with a good example of a phoneme at one end of a continuum such as voice onset time, say the syllable *ba* with a voice onset time of 10 msec. After 2 minutes or so of listening to *ba,* listeners are now presented with the other voice onset time stimuli as before, such as those used to generate the curve in Figure 12-10A. This results in a category shift, as though the effectiveness of the original stimulus has been weakened. Thus, some stimuli that previously were heard as *ba* are now classified as *pa.* The boundary has been shifted in the direction of the adapting stimulus *(ba)* so that now a stronger (shorter voice onset time) stimulus is necessary to perceive *ba,* as shown in Figure 12-10B. Similar results have been obtained with other characteristics of speech stimuli, such as place of articulation and vowel pronunciation (see Diehl, 1981).

Originally, these findings were interpreted (by proponents of the ''speech is special'' view) as meaning that there were special speech feature detectors that were being fatigued or adapted (Abbs & Sussman, 1971; Eimas & Corbit, 1973; Lisker & Abramson, 1970). As a counter to this argument, the ''speech is just auditory pattern perception'' group obtained similar shifts in categorical boundaries with nonspeech stimuli, depending on the acoustic similarity of the nonspeech stimulus used for adaptation to the speech stimulus used for testing (Samuel, 1986; Sawusch, 1986). These results have been taken to suggest that no special speech feature detectors, or special speech processing, need to be postulated to explain the data; however, a fine-grain analysis of the patterns of adaptation actually obtained suggest that the situation may be more complex than originally thought (Samuel, 1986).

Duplex Perception   Yet another finding that has been interpreted as evidence for a special speech processing mode is a phenomenon called **duplex perception,** in which the same sound can be perceived as having both speech and nonspeech qualities (Rand, 1974). The most common technique used to demonstrate duplex perception is to present a group of synthetically generated formants, called the *base stimulus,* to one ear and present an isolated formant transition to the other ear. Typically, the base stimulus is heard as a particular syllable, say *da,* which either is heard this way or modified by the presence of the formant transition in the other ear (e.g., it might now be heard as *ga*). Duplex perception manifests itself when, in addition to hearing the speech sound, most observers also hear a nonspeech ''chirp.'' This chirp is actually the same sound you would hear if the isolated formant transition were presented alone. If observers are attending to the speech sound they show many of the phenomena usually associated with speech processing, such as categorical perception; if they are attending to the nonspeech chirp they do not show these phenomena. This result has been interpreted as suggesting that when you attend to speech stimuli you invoke a different mode of perceptual processing than you do for nonspeech stimuli (see Liberman, 1982).

It is also possible to produce duplex perception by presenting the same specifically constructed stimulus to both ears (Whalen & Liberman, 1987). In this case, the speech percept alone is heard at lower intensities, while at higher intensities both speech sounds and nonspeech chirps are heard. Interestingly, the ''duplexity threshold,'' at which both sounds are heard, is about 20 dB higher than the threshold for discriminating speech sounds in the same stimuli. At the least this indicates that speech processing dominates nonspeech processing, and is consistent with the idea of a separate speech processing mode. However, duplex perception does occur for nonspeech stimuli such as musical chords (Pastore, Schmeckler, Rosenblum & Szczesiul, 1983), providing evidence for an argument against interpreting these phenomena as arising from a special speech processing mode.

Cross-modal Integration   A final phenomenon that has implications for the ''is speech special?'' controversy is the **McGurk effect** (McGurk & MacDonald, 1976). This involves a form of cross-modal integration in which nonacoustic stimuli affect what the listener hears when listening to speech. In this effect, you listen to a string of speech sounds, like *da,* and at the same time look at a movie or video of a face articulating speech sounds in synchrony with the actual speech stimuli. Everything is fine as long as the sounds and the facial movements refer to the same syllable. Suppose, however, the sound reaching your ear is *ba* but the face is making the articulatory and mouth movements associated with saying *ga.* The visual input seems to alter your interpretation of the sound, and you hear a compromise sound, *da.* This suggests that in some fashion nonauditory information is used to aid in our interpretation of speech, and perhaps to resolve some of the ambiguities inherent in the acoustic signal. There is some evidence that the McGurk effect is strongest for syllables, not for complete words (Easton & Basala, 1982). This has been taken to mean that if there is a great deal of auditory and semantic information about what is being said, the visual cue is not powerful enough to overcome it. Only when

there is about an equal amount of information from each cue does the conflict produce the "in between" percept.

Of course, in normal speech the visual and auditory cues are usually consistent, hence the sight may be a useful means of augmenting the intelligibility of the sound. It is reasonable to suppose that speech perception would involve such a mechanism, since most linguistic communication takes place, and is learned by the child, in a face-to-face mode where both types of cues are available. However, we don't *need* visual cues to understand speech. For example, we understand speech on the radio, even at higher than normal presentation rates as in commercials. Also, other theories can account for such cue integration (e.g., Massaro, 1987). You can experience a similar effect caused by the cross-model integration of speech cues by trying Demonstration Box 12-5.

The McGurk effect has been interpreted as evidence that visual and auditory cues about what is being said converge at some abstract (special?) level of speech processing. Some data seem to be

---

DEMONSTRATION BOX 12-5.   Cross-Modal Integration of Cues

For this demonstration you need access to a TV set and a radio. Bring the radio into the same room as the TV set and turn them both on. Tune the radio to a point in between channels so that a hissing or roaring sound comes from the speaker. Tune the TV set to a newscast or other show where there is a person talking steadily, looking directly into the camera. Set the volume of the TV set to a medium setting, so that you can comfortably understand what is being said, but low enough so that when the radio noise is turned to a high level you can't hear the TV. Now, close your eyes and turn up the radio noise until you can't understand what the speaker on the TV is saying, then lower the radio noise until you can just barely understand the speaker, and finally raise it a bit so you can't again. Now, open your eyes. In the presence of

the visual cues as to what is being said, you will find that you now can understand the TV speaker when you see his or her face. The effect will be similar to turning down the noise slightly, except that all you did was to add the visual cues. When you close your eyes again, you should find it again impossible to understand the TV speaker's speech. The additional information you are obtaining visually by watching the speaker talk is clearly having an effect on the intelligibility of the speech. These visual cues are particularly important anywhere the intelligibility of speech is reduced by the presence of noise, such as at a noisy party or on a noisy downtown street or if your hearing is not very acute. Thus, many hearing-impaired people find it easier to understand speech when they are looking at a speaker's face.

inconsistent with this interpretation, however. For instance, Roberts and Summerfield (1981) set up conditions like those we described above (the sound was *ba,* the visual image mouthed *ga,* and the subject heard *da)* and repeated the presentation until subjects had adapted. Next the phonemic boundary was measured, as we illustrated in Figure 12-10. The question was, Does the phonemic boundary shift in a manner consistent with the phoneme the subject perceives (as a special process might predict) or in a manner consistent with the actual acoustic signal (as auditory pattern theory might predict). The answer was that the phonemic boundary seems to shift according to the acoustic signal *ba,* rather than the perceived signal *da.*

Let us now reiterate our original question, "Is speech perception a special process?" As you can see from the give-and-take nature of the data we have presented, a special process is a possibility, but a simple extension of auditory pattern perception processes cannot be rejected. Hence, this question is far from decided, and the controversy will probably go on for a while yet.

Development

Infants are born with a remarkable ability to respond to human speech in a special way (see Jusczyk, 1986; Kuhl, 1987). At birth, infants move their limbs in synchrony with connected adult speech but not with other sounds, such as tapping sounds or disconnected vowel sounds (Condon & Sander, 1974). In addition, infants show much the same patterns of responses that adults do. For example, Eimas, Siqueland, Jusczyk, and Vigorito (1971) found that infants as young as 1 month of age discriminated speech stimuli better across phonemic boundaries than within phonemic categories, showing categorical perception much the way that adults do. Since, at 1 month of age, infants have had only a little bit of exposure to speech sounds and their utterances consist only of cries, screams, and random babbles, they clearly have not yet learned language. Their ability to make speech dis-

criminations similar to those of adults has thus been taken as evidence of some innate mechanism for speech processing.

Another very impressive demonstration of infants' speech perception ability was made by Kuhl and Meltzoff (1982). They presented 4-month-old infants with two video displays of the same person's face speaking two different vowel sounds, as illustrated in Figure 12-11. At the same time, the baby was presented (from a loudspeaker midway between the faces) with the sound of the person's voice producing one or the other of the vowel sounds. The voice and the two faces were all in synchrony with each other, but the voice corresponded to only one of the faces' articulatory movements. From video recordings of where the baby looked during the tests, it was determined that the baby spent more time (about 73 percent of the total looking time) looking at the face that was articulating the vowel sound it was hearing. Thus, very young infants also demonstrate cross-modal integration of speech cues, just like adults do (e.g., the McGurk effect), even though they have had only limited experience with such cues and do not yet speak. Moreover, this ability is apparently a function of the left hemisphere of the brain in infants, just as speech production is a function of that hemisphere in adults (MacKain, Studdert-Kennedy, Spieker & Stern, 1983).

Although there is a good deal of evidence suggesting that from birth infants can discriminate the entire set of possible phonemes that the human vocal apparatus is capable of making, adults can not. Thus, a native Japanese speaker may say "ararm crock" when he actually means "alarm clock," not because of sloppy speech but because the Japanese language does not have the two separate phonemes *r* as in "run" versus *l* as in "look" and the adult speaker no longer has the ability to make this perceptual discrimination. As we discuss later (in Chapter 16), infants maintain their ability to discriminate phonemes present in the language that they hear in their environment. However, they soon begin to lose the capacity to discriminate phonemes

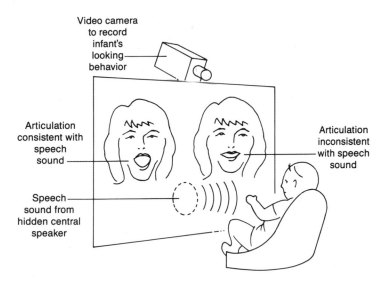

Video camera
to record
infant's
looking
behavior

Articulation
consistent with
speech
sound

Articulation
inconsistent
with speech
sound

Speech
sound from
hidden central
speaker

FIGURE 12-11 **Illustration of the setup of an experiment showing that infants can integrate phonemic information across auditory and visual modalities. (Based on Kuhl & Meltzoff, 1982)**

they are not regularly hearing. For instance, 6-month-old infants can still make discriminations in languages other than the one their parents speak, but by the time they are 1 year old they have lost this ability (Werker & Tees, 1984). It is as if our linguistic surroundings tune the mechanisms that will later be used to discriminate speech, with the end result that we no longer have the ability to perceive phonemes not found in our own tongue.

This inability may simply be due to the fact that different languages have different phonemic boundaries. Phonemes that sound different in one language might then be heard as the same phoneme in another and our experience may alter our placement of this boundary and hence our categorization of the phoneme. For instance, if you make a continuous z sound as in "zzzzz-oo," and then bring the tip of your tongue close to your teeth, the sound will change into an extended th as in "that." The distinction between z and th is determined by the tongue position, which sets the phonemic boundary conditions. This boundary is different for different languages. Thus, adult native French speakers will

make sounds that sound to their ears as if they have crossed the boundary from z to th, but that to native English speakers still appear to remain on the z side. That is why a French speaker is perceived by an English speaker as saying that she is going out to "walk ze dog."

Context

We mentioned above that a major problem in speech perception is the ambiguity of the speech signal due to the lack of an invariant set of acoustic features that correspond to the perceived speech units. We encountered this fairly graphically in Demonstration Box 12-4. One factor that helps interpret patterns, whether visual, auditory, or speech, is the context in which these patterns appear. The other stimuli in the environment assist our identification of the present stimulus. We saw this for visual patterns in Figure 11-15, where the same pattern elements were seen either as a letter or a number, depending on the context formed by the surrounding stimuli. In terms of the ultimate function of speech, which is to convey meaning, context is vital, since the same sound unit may signify different things. This occurs in the case of **homophones,** which are words that sound alike when spoken—such as *be* and *bee, rain* and *reign, no* and *know*—although they convey different meanings. Although there may be acoustic cues that differentiate these words, most often the surrounding context helps us tell which word was meant by the speaker.

Interestingly, there are other words that sound quite different to us, such as *married* and *buried,* that are produced by speakers using nearly identical movements of the mouth and lips. These are called **homophenes,** and are difficult for lip-readers to discriminate out of context. Clearly, if we are watching a speaker's face for some cross-modal information in a difficult listening context and if the word uttered is a homophene, we will not get much help from the visual image, but we may get help from the context provided by other words in the sentence. Demonstration Box 12-6 gives an example that demonstrates how context affects our ability to extract the meaning of speech stimuli.

The context effect in Demonstration Box 12-6 was based on identifying the general topic an utterance was concerned with. There are a great many other context effects in speech perception, many of them depending on the meaning attached to the speech sounds (see also Liberman & Mattingly, 1985; Sawusch, 1986). One interesting demonstration of this type of effect was provided by Day (1968, 1970). She presented sound sequences simultaneously to both ears of listeners. For example, if the left ear received *b-a-n-k-e-t* the right ear received *l-a-n-k-e-t.* Many of the listeners fused the two sequences into the word *blanket,* even when *lanket* preceded *banket* by several msec; other listeners heard only the separate sound sequences. But no one heard *lbanket,* which is a sequence of phonemes that does not occur in English. The expectations as to which sounds *can* occur in speech clearly provide a context that influences what is perceived.

The importance of context in speech perception is demonstrated by the fact that if trained listeners are asked to provide a phonetic transcription of spoken passages in an exotic language they do quite poorly, despite their training, simply because of the absence of an adequate semantic and syntactic context (Shockey & Reddy, 1974). Even if you know the language, your ability to identify isolated

---

DEMONSTRATION BOX 12-6.   Context and Speech Perception

In the absence of an appropriate context, even common words are often difficult to identify. To see how context interacts with speech perception, read the following phrase in a smooth, rapid, conversational style to a friend: "In mud eels are, in clay none are." Ask your friend to write down the phrase exactly as he or she heard it. Now you should provide a context by telling your listener that you are going to read a sentence from a book that describes where various types of amphibians can be found. Then read the above sentence again at the same speed that you did before. After your listener writes down what was heard this time, you can compare the sentences (or nonsentences) that were heard with and without the context. Without the context you might find responses such as "In middies, sar, in clay nanar" or "In may deals are, en clainanar" (Reddy, 1976). Here the words in the sentence are difficult to identify when presented rapidly, and a strange and largely meaningless set of segments is generated. When the proper context is supplied, however, the same speech sounds are correctly segmented into words, and interpreted as meaningful elements.

words taken from a stream of recorded speech is quite poor. Generally in such tests, listeners are capable of identifying less than half of the items presented in isolation (Pollack & Pickett, 1964). If the same words are presented surrounded by longer strings of the words in the original recorded utterance, identification is much better. Thus, the more acoustic, syntactic, or semantic context provided, the better the observers are at identifying the words.

The context of a sentence can actually induce a listener to supply missing parts of the stimulus to fill in a gap in continuous speech so that it is heard as if it were uninterrupted. Warren (1970) presented listeners with a taped sentence: "The state governors met with their respective legislatures convening in the capital city." The acoustic information corresponding to the first *s* in "legislatures" was deleted and replaced by the sound of a cough. Nineteen of 20 listeners reported nothing unusual about the sentence. They restored the missing phoneme, hence the effect was named the **phonemic restoration effect.** Again, the context of the sentence determined the speech sequence actually perceived. Apparently both meaning and acoustic cues play a role in such restoration of missing or obliterated components (Bashford & Warren, 1987; Samuel, 1981). This means that if we delete portions of common words or phrases, or present only the distinctive parts of words, the listener is more likely to "hear" the speech as being continuous and to accurately restore the missing portions in consciousness. In effect, we hear the speech units that the immediate context suggests should be in the phrase, even if they are not physically present.

Theories of Speech Perception

A great number of different theories have been proposed to explain various subsets of the phenomena we have discussed above. It is probably safe to say that no one theory has yet achieved a consensus of researchers that it is the most useful. In fact, many researchers feel that theory is an area of significant weakness in speech perception research (e.g., Pisoni & Luce, 1986). The many candidate theories of speech perception seem to be subdivided on the basis of their level of analysis, whether they are oriented toward the identification of phonemes or of words, and on the basis of whether they utilize **active** or **passive processing** (Nusbaum & Schwab, 1986). Passive processing involves a filtering or feature detection sequence of events that is relatively fixed in nature and works at a sensory level. After the message is sensed and filtered, it is then mapped fairly directly onto the acoustic or articulatory features of the language. Active processing involves a much more interactive sequence, in which the acoustic features are sensed but then a series of higher level processes involving analysis of the context (either meaning or phonetic) is considered, and in which expectations or even knowledge of speech production and articulation may play a role. In active processing the sequence of processing steps may not be fixed, but may vary depending on the results of earlier computations. Both active and passive models may use general acoustic processing rules or invoke "special" speech analysis units.

Many passive theories incorporate the notions of *feature detectors* or *template matching*. Feature detectors for speech are usually conceptualized as neurons specialized for the detection of specific aspects of the speech signal, much the way specific neurons in the visual cortex selectively respond to aspects of the visual stimulus such as line orientation (see Chapter 3). The concept of an auditory template may be viewed as a stored abstract representation of certain aspects of speech that develops as a function of experience and serves the same function as a feature detector. The use of feature detectors or templates in speech identification is often viewed as a process similar to the visual feature extraction model called "pandemonium" we discussed in Chapter 11, in that the signal is perceived on the basis of the template that it most closely matches or the phoneme or word that has the most features in common with it.

Some theories that are predominantly passive in nature stress that ordinary auditory processes are sufficient to explain speech perception at the level of phonemes (e.g., Fant, 1967; Massaro, 1987). These *auditory theories* usually postulate several stages of processing of speech sounds. The first stage consists of "ordinary" auditory processing, including analysis of a complex sound into its simple sine wave components, auditory feature analysis, and auditory pattern processing. For some theorists feature analysis occurs first, then pattern analysis, whereas for others they occur at the same time (in parallel). The next stage then applies more specialized (but not "special") rules to the output(s) of the first stage(s), integrating them to produce perception of phonemes. A good example of this approach that uses words, rather than phonemes, as the unit is Klatt's (1980) Lexical Access From Spectra (**LAFS**) model. In this model the listener does a spectral analysis of the input signal, matching the results of this analysis to a set of templates of features stored in memory. Words are then identified from the set of features detected in the input. In this model, there is no need to describe segments or phonemes or other linguistic entities; the speech input is directly matched to words in memory by a fixed process.

It is possible also to have a passive model that uses "special" speech units (for example, Eimas & Corbit, 1973). In such a model, the first stages would consist of detection of speech features by "special" feature detectors followed by integration of these features into percepts by (possibly) "special" rules. Figure 12-12A gives a schematic representation of a general passive speech perception theory that contains elements similar to many current models.

Active models of speech perception are somewhat more variable since they often involve analysis of the context in which the speech is occurring, the expectations of the listener, the distribution of attentional resources, and memory components. Since different researchers place different degrees of emphasis on these various mechanisms, active theories often differ dramatically from one another.

For example, Marslen-Wilson (1980) offered an active model of word identification called *cohort theory*. In this model the early passive stages of analysis initially extract the first phoneme(s) of a word. On the basis of this information all the words in memory that have the same beginning (e.g., all words beginning with *st,* such as "stop," "stall," "stride") are activated. These words constitute the "cohort" or group of possibilities to be considered. After the cohort is activated, other acoustic or phonetic information as well as higher-level expectations operate to eliminate all the candidates except one, which is identified.

Phonetic refinement theory (Pisoni, Nusbaum, Luce & Slowiaczek, 1985) is also concerned with word identification. It resembles cohort theory in that the initial feature processing activates candidate words that all sound alike along some dimensions (not just the first phoneme) that form what they call a *phonetic space*. The set of candidates is narrowed down through the application of additional information, both phonetic and contextual, until a single word is identified because it satisfies all the available constraints best and is hence most strongly activated. In this model, words can be identified even if there is only partial information available, since even that partial information may activate the correct word more than it does any other words.

Another active theory, which has been implemented as a computer model, is McClelland and Elman's (1986) **TRACE** model. This model begins with passive feature detection in three levels: (1) acoustic feature detectors whose output is the input to (2) phoneme detectors whose output is the input to (3) word detectors. The unique aspect of this model is that the various detectors and other processors, referred to in the computer model as *nodes,* are highly interconnected. Activating one node tends to activate all the nodes to which it is connected, both at the same level and at other

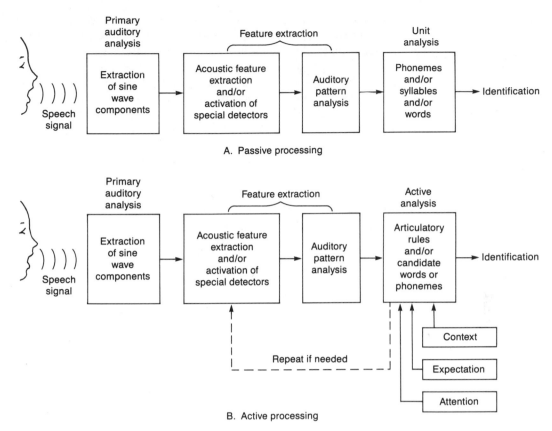

FIGURE 12-12 Diagrammatic representation of the difference between a typical passive model of speech processing (A) and a generalized active model of speech processing (B).

higher or lower levels. This is actually quite a complex model in which various levels may interact with one another in a looping fashion, with higher levels "tuning" or altering the weighting given to specific features.

All active theories have one thing in common. They all have higher-level decisional processes superimposed on the initial feature extraction results. Thus, the speech you "hear" may be determined by factors other than the actual acoustic signal. A diagram of a general active speech processing theory is shown as Figure 12-12B.

One of the first, and most influential, theories

of speech perception is difficult to classify as active or passive for it seems to have elements of both approaches. This is the *motor theory* proposed by Liberman, Cooper, Shankweiler and Studdert-Kennedy (1967) and recently revised by Liberman and Mattingly (1985). It is oriented toward the identification of phonemes considered as the intended phonetic *gestures* of a speaker, that is, what the speaker intends to say. In this theory, speech is clearly "special," in the sense that perception of speech sounds is accomplished by a specialized processing mode that is both innate and part of the more general specialization for language that humans possess. In particular, the theory assumes that the same adaptations of the mammalian motor system that made speech possible for humans also made possible a system for perceiving the sounds produced by the speech motor system based on the actual movement commands issued to produce the speech sounds. This system uses complex calculations to deduce the intended speech gestures from the acoustic signal based on an abstract representation of the articulatory movements the listener herself would have used to produce just such a speech signal.

An example of how this system might be involved in speech perception can be seen by looking back at Figure 12-9 and noting that the *d* in the composite *dee* as in "deep" is perceived as the same *d* as in *do* (in "dope") although they are quite different acoustically. According to motor theory, both are heard as *d* because the listener would use equivalent articulatory movements to produce the *d* phoneme for both utterances. The face that the actual sounds of the two *d*'s are not the same is irrelevant, just as the pitch of voice, speed of speech, and other sound-distorting factors are irrelevent.

A recent further development of this approach emphasizes the *modular* nature of the special and distinct system proposed to process speech sounds (Liberman & Mattingly, 1985). A module consists of neural circuits that perform special processing that provides higher cognitive processes with representations of events that have particular biological, ecological, or behavioral significance (see Fodor, 1983). We can have little awareness of what a module is doing, and its processing is automatic and dominates other processing of the same stimuli. In this sense the theory is a passive one: in it speech perception cannot be greatly influenced by conscious analysis. However, the processing involved is complex and flexible, taking account of the effects of expectations, context, and other important factors, just as the more active theories do.

No one theory or level of analysis has come to dominate speech perception. In fact, there is a gradual blurring of some of the distinctions. For instance, we have seen that active processing models begin with a passive-processing, feature-extraction component; some of the passive processing models may well allow active processing when the signal is degraded or conditions are difficult (e.g., Fant, 1967; Massaro, 1987); and motor theory doesn't fit especially well into either the active or passive category. In addition, some investigators have proposed that both general auditory processes and special speech processes are necessary to account for all the data (e.g., Pisoni, 1973; Werker & Logan, 1985). Certainly there can be no argument as to whether an auditory mode of processing exists. The problem speech theorists still must contend with is just how "special" speech perception is, and how much of what is heard is in the signal and how much is constructed in the mind of the listener.

GLOSSARY

The following definitions are specific to this book.

Acoustic-phonetic invariance   The idea that there must be some set of acoustic features associated with each phoneme in all contexts.

Active processing   Models of speech perception that incorporate the effects of expectations, context, memory, and attention. Processing may vary depending on previous computations.

Articulators   Parts of the vocal tract that are used to produce speech, such as teeth, tongue, lips, and palates.

Categorical perception   A phenomenon in which discrimination of stimuli within a perceptual category is worse than that across a category boundary.

Chord   Simultaneous presentation of three or more musical notes.

Consonant   A basic speech sound produced by closing the vocal tract.

Contour   The general "shape" of a musical sequence of sounds defined by the rises and drops in frequency of the notes.

Duplex perception   Perception of both speech and nonspeech sounds simultaneously from a single auditory stimulus.

Formants   Bands of especially intense components of a speech signal, seen as dark smudges on a spectrogram.

Formant transitions   Changes in formants over relatively short intervals of time (less than 100 msec) that are related to consonant sounds.

Homophenes   Different words that are produced by almost identical patterns of lip movements.

Homophones   Words that are pronounced similarly, but spelled differently.

LAFS   Acronym for Klatt's (1980) theory of word recognition: Lexical Access From Spectra.

Linearity   The idea that for each phoneme in an utterance there must correspond a segment of the physical speech signal.

McGurk effect   The perception of an "intermediate" phoneme when auditory and visual speech cues conflict.

Musical interval   The perception of the separation in musical pitch between two musical sounds.

Passive processing   A model of speech perception based on filtering the signal for features only, with no higher level interactions.

Phone   The basic sound unit used by linguists to describe speech.

Phoneme   A phone used in a language to distinguish one word from another.

Phonemic boundary   The point on a speech feature continuum where the perception of the phoneme changes from one category to another (e.g., from "ba" to "pa" as voice onset time increases past 25–35 msec).

Phonemic restoration effect   When a listener hearing a spoken sentence fills in a missing phoneme based on the context.

Rhythm   The perceived organization in time of a sequence of sounds.

Speech spectrogram   A representation of the speech signal in terms of the frequencies and amplitudes of its simple sine wave components as these change over time.

Tempo   The perceived speed with which a sequence of sounds is proceeding.

Tone chroma   A "circular" dimension of musical pitch that connects similar notes of different octaves.

Tone height   The simple "vertical" dimension of pitch in musical scales.

TRACE   McClelland and Elman's (1986) theory of word identification.

Voice onset time   The latency in producing a vowel sound following a stop-consonant sound.

Vowel   A basic speech sound produced by opening the vocal tract and vibrating the vocal folds.

CHAPTER 13

Time and Motion

The Nobel-prize-winning physicist Albert Einstein often thought about the meaning of time, ultimately to conclude that "the distinction between past, present, and future is only an illusion, however persistent" (Einstein & Besso, 1972). From the psychological point of view, a better conclusion might be that time and space are modes by which we perceive and think about our world, rather than physical conditions under which we live.

Your sense of the passage of time is a perceptual experience. Up to now we have seen that most perceptual experiences are more or less related to some physical stimulus continuum. However, in the case of time the situation is less clear. There certainly is no readily visible "time organ" for such stimuli to impinge on. Our notion of time may well be associated with some form of internal clock that we consult like a wristwatch to determine the span of an event, but it also seems to be tied to our experience of successive change (Fraisse, 1963). It is through the concept of change that time and motion become intertwined. Changes that occur in a sequence are often associated with a perception of time passing, whereas changes in location may, under the proper conditions, be perceived as movement. Time and motion thus represent dynamic qualities of perceptual experience.

TIME

The concept of time is fundamental to human beings. For example, every language thus far analyzed has separate tenses for past, present, and future, plus innumerable modifiers to specify *when* more precisely—*yesterday, today, recently, in an hour, while, during, after,* and hundreds more (Bentham, 1985). Despite this position as a fundamental experience the study of time is complex, since "time is not a thing that, like an apple, may be perceived" (Woodrow, 1951). In fact, there are two qualities of our perception that seem to be added to our consciousness, and do not seem to correspond to simple physical dimensions. These qualities are an awareness of a present moment and the impression that time passes. Let us call these the concepts of **now** and **flow,** respectively (Michon, 1985).

The concept of *now* is fairly unitary, and has been described by William James (1890) as the "saddle-back of time with a certain length of its own, on which we sit perched, and from which we look in two directions into time." Sometimes called the *subjective present,* it is the few seconds of our current experience of ongoing consciousness; all else is either past or future. Although *flow* is an equally fundamental perceptual attribute of time, it can be further subdivided into several measurable aspects of experience (cf. Poppel, 1978). Each of these additional aspects of time perception may be different from the others and may be maintained by different physiological or information processing mechanisms. First we have *duration estimation,* which is a report of the experience of how much time has elapsed between two events (for example, between when you turn on the heating element under a pot of water and when the water boils). We usually use units such as seconds or minutes to describe duration. Next, we have the perception of *order* or *sequence,* which involves the determination of which event came first, second, and so forth (such as the sequence of digits in a phone number someone has just read to you). There is a special case of the perception of sequence that involves determining the minimum time interval that must separate two events before they are perceived as occurring one after the other, rather than at the same moment. This judgment involves the discrimination between the experience of *simultaneity* versus *successiveness.* The last aspect of flow is somewhat less perceptual but still requires time estimation. It is the *anticipation* or *planning* of an ordered sequence of events before they occur, which is especially important in playing musical instruments, or in actions such as speech production where we automatically plan and execute an ordered sequence of sounds to produce meaningful utterances.

When we look for the mechanisms by which

we perceive time, we find that two general processes have been suggested. We may call these "clock" theories, since each gives a mechanism that determines how we monitor the passage of time. The first involves a **biological clock,** and assumes that there is a biological or physiological basis to our perception of time. Just as we have a sense organ that is sensitive to light (the eye), we also have a sense organ that accounts for our ability to keep track of time. The second involves a **cognitive clock,** where time is viewed as a purely cognitive process that is not tied to any objective or "clock" time, but rather is based on how much sensory information is processed, how many events occur within a given interval, or how much attention is paid to ongoing cognitive events. In this latter viewpoint time is constructed rather than simply monitored. Both of these types of clocks may exist, and each may be used for different types of time perception.

Biological Clocks

Many physical phenomena have their own rhythms or timing—there are day-night cycles, cycles of the moon, cycles of the seasons, and many others. Living organisms often display similar rhythmic activities—many flowers open and close at particular times of the day. In animals there are physiological and behavioral processes that cycle regularly. One proposal about the way time is perceived is based on the idea that the *flow* of subjective time is related to some body mechanism that acts in a periodic manner, with each period serving as one "tick" of the biological timer. Anything that alters the speed of our physiological processes would then be expected to alter our perception of the speed at which time passes.

Circadian Rhythms

One of the most obvious examples of an apparently timed behavior is the sleep-wakefulness cycle that runs through a regular daily rhythm. Another is the return of hunting and foraging animals to a partic-

ular area 24 hours after a successful hunt or food find there (Groos & Daan, 1985; Rijnsdorp, Daan & Dijkstra, 1981). There are also more subtle physiological processes that have their own periodic changes. For example, the pulse, blood pressure, and temperature of the body show day-night variations in humans as well as in many other animals; there is a more than 1 deg C difference in body temperature between the coolest point, which occurs during the night, and the warmest point, which occurs during the afternoon. These are all examples of a **circadian rhythm,** which comes from the Latin *circa,* meaning "approximately," and *dies,* meaning "day." Thus, a circadian rhythm is one that varies with a cycle of roughly 24 hours.

So much rhythmic activity in behavior suggests control by some internal *biological clock.* Alternatively, it may be that these repetitive 24-hour changes are simply a function of the regular changes in light and temperature that occur in the day-night cycle. Thus, an animal might become active in the presence of daylight when it can see more clearly and the temperature is a bit higher, and it is this activity that then alters the physiological function. The "built-in" approximately 24-hour cycle, however, can be demonstrated experimentally in the absence of light or temperature changes. For example, suppose that we find ourselves in a constant-light environment, where there are no changing cues that indicate the passage of time. Under these conditions our biological clock will "run free," gaining or losing time like a not-too-accurate clock. Although different people will have different cycle lengths, most of us will begin to live a "day" that is approximately 25 hours long (e.g., Aschoff, 1981; Wever, 1979).

If the internal biological clock is set for about 25 hours, why do our internal and behavioral rhythms continue on a 24-hour cycle? Why doesn't our daily activity cycle drift out of phase with local time? This is because there is a mechanism that synchronizes the internal timer with local time. From the behavioral point of view, the most salient aspect of local time is the alternation of light and dark cycles. To be an accurate reference against local time, a biological clock must be synchronized with the local day-night cycle, and it must have a stable period that is relatively free of unpredictable environmental fluctuation. This process of synchronization is called **entrainment.** If there were no such mechanism, traveling across the continent, where the sun might rise 3 hours earlier relative to the current setting of your biological clock, would leave you 3 hours "out of step" with your new environment. There is, of course, some disruption of your time sense from such trips in the form of *jet lag,* which accounts for the sight of newly arrived Europeans wandering through the lobbies of New York hotels at 4 or 5 A.M., looking for an open restaurant to have breakfast in. Because of their great speed of travel, their circadian rhythms are still set to Paris, Moscow, or some other European time. Body time does eventually adapt to the new time zone at a rate of 1/2 to 1 hour per day. This adaptation comes about through entrainment of the biological clock to the local environmental sunlight-to-darkness cycle.

To use the scientific term, we would say that light is the primary **zeitgeber** (German for "time giver"). There is much evidence, based on several species of animals including humans, that shows the internal clock is synchronized to light (e.g., Johnson & Hastings, 1986). A brief flash of light will reset the biological clocks of animals reared in constant darkness, either advancing it or retarding it, depending on when the flash occurs (Aschoff, 1979). If there is no regular light cycle, however, other environmental stimuli, such as daily fluctuations in temperature, may serve as zeitgebers to set the internal timer.

Is there a single physiological structure that might serve as the biological clock? Researchers have isolated a region in the hypothalamus that seems to be the basis of the circadian rhythm in animals and humans (e.g., Rusak & Zucker, 1979). It is called the **suprachiasmatic nucleus** (which we will abbreviate as the **SCN**), and it is located very near the optic chiasm, as can be seen in Figure

13-1. The timing function of this brain structure is easily demonstrated. For example, rats are nocturnal animals, sleeping during the day and foraging at night. Destroying the SCN abolishes this pattern. The animal still sleeps the same amount of time, but the circadian pattern is gone and it sleeps in random periods throughout the day and night (Stephan & Nunez, 1977). Tumors in this region have the same effect in humans (Fulton & Bailey, 1929). Furthermore, electrical stimulation of the SCN in animals will reset the biological clock, in much the same way that brief flashes of light do for dark-reared animals (Rusak & Groos, 1982). Because light is the primary zeitgeber for the circadian clock, we would expect that the SCN would receive inputs from the visual system, and it does (e.g., Groos & Meijer, 1985).

Short-Term Timers

It seems clear that our circadian rhythms are maintained by an internal biological clock, but we often make estimates of times that are considerably shorter than 24 hours. We can even accurately determine which of two time intervals was longer, when each was less than a second in duration. A "slow" circadian clock would probably be quite useless for this task, which suggests that there are probably several biological clocks in animals. For example, destroying the SCN does not affect the cyclic change in body temperature (Fuller, Lydic, Sulzman, Albers, Tepper & Moore-Ede, 1981), nor does it seem to affect some shorter-cycling biological rhythms. In much the same way that we might use a stopwatch to measure short intervals, our wristwatch to measure longer ones, and a calender to measure even longer periods of time, there seem to be different biological clocks for different aspects of behavior. Heartbeats, electrical activity in the brain, breathing, hormonal and metabolic activities, and even walking steps have at one time or another been suggested as candidates for an internal biological timing mechanism (Aschoff, 1981; Ornstein, 1969; Poppel, 1978; Treisman, 1963). Some

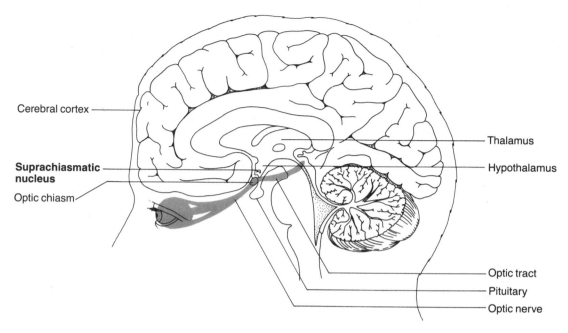

FIGURE 13-1   The location of the suprachiasmatic nucleus of the hypothalamus, which is thought to be the basis of the biological clock that maintains circadian rhythms.

of these might be useful as biological clocks to measure intervals shorter than the 24-hour circadian period. Hence, we might view the perception of time as occurring in a "clock shop" rather than in a single biological timer.

Rather than looking at long time intervals, some researchers have gone to the other extreme and asked what is the shortest time interval we can sense. Experimentally, they asked the question, What is the minimum time separation needed for two events to be perceived as occurring at different times (successively) rather than at the same time (simultaneously)? In effect, they were searching for the basic time unit in perception. This idea was discussed in some detail by Stroud (1955), who suggested that psychological time is not a continuous dimension but rather consists of discrete bits. These **perceptual moments** are the psychological unit of time. Based on a number of research findings, Stroud estimated that each moment is about 100

msec in duration, which would thus be the shortest perceived duration a stimulus can have. In addition, stimuli presented within the same moment either would be perceived as occurring simultaneously or, depending on the nature of the stimulus, would not be distinguishable from each other. Stimuli presented in different moments would be perceived as being successive. Efron (1967, 1973) demonstrated this aspect of the perceptual moment by looking at *micropatterns,* which are variations in a stimulus that occur so quickly that there is no corresponding change in the perception. For instance, a 20-msec stimulus composed of 10 msec of red light followed by 10 msec of green light is not perceptibly different from one in which the green comes before the red—both appear yellow (if visual persistence is eliminated; Yund, Morgan & Efron, 1983).

White (1963) attempted to measure the perceptual moment by having observers estimate the number of clicks they heard. He presented the clicks at different rates up to 25 per second. Observers were fairly accurate at rates of up to 5 per second; at the highest click rates, however, observers still estimated a presentation rate of about 6–7 clicks per second. This corresponds to a perceived rate of 1 stimulus every 150 msec. Thus, information could not be processed in "chunks" smaller than 150 msec, which would be the resolution limit of the internal timer. In another study, Efron (1967) presented two brief pulses of light and asked observers to say which one was longer. One of the flashes was always 1 msec in duration; the other was of a variable duration. Both flashes were always seen as being of the same length until the exposure time of the variable flash exceeded a value of 60 or 70 msec. At this duration, the variable flash was seen as being longer than the 1-msec flash. Efron concluded that the minimum duration of a stimulus in consciousness (which should be 1 perceptual moment) was around 60 or 70 msec.

It seems likely that the perceptual moment is different for different tasks and, perhaps, for different sensory modalities (e.g., Kolers & Brewster, 1985). For example, reaction time studies (where observers are asked to react as quickly as possible to a stimulus input) have indicated that short-term memory can be scanned at about the rate of 25–30 msec per item (e.g., Sternberg, 1975). The timing of well-trained motor tasks, such as typing or piano playing, also seems to support a 30-msec internal timing organization (Augenstine, 1962; Shaffer, 1985). Eriksen and Collins (1968) used a set of patterns that, if seen by themselves, seemed random. If, however, two patterns were superimposed, either physically or psychologically, they contained a word. They found that when observers were shown patterns sequentially, recognition for the word was highest when the interval between the presentations was about 25 msec. This implies that the perception of simultaneity is maintained over only a 25 msec interval rather than one that approaches 100 msec.

An interesting "reverse" demonstration of the perceptual moment comes from Intraub (1985), who presented a series of pictures to subjects at a rate of 1 every 111 msec. One of these pictures always had a frame around it, and observers were simply asked to indicate which picture had the frame. On 54 percent of the trials, subjects reported that the frame was around the picture that appeared before or after the correct one, probably because the two pictures fell within the same perceptual moment. All these data suggest that, depending on the specific task, the minimum perceptual duration (or the time between ticks of the fastest biological clock) is probably between 25 and 150 msec.

Biological Pacemaker

To the extent that there is a biological timer that serves as a sort of **pacemaker,** ticking away internal time, it would be reasonable to expect that it would speed up or slow down along with other physiological processes in the body. Hoagland (1933) verified this when his wife became ill with a high fever. He asked her to estimate the duration of 1 minute by counting to 60 at a rate of one number per second. When her body temperature was approximately 39 deg C (103 deg F), her perceived minute was only 37.5 sec by objective clock time. This suggests that at higher body temperatures the speed of physiological activities increases, and this causes the pacemaker to tick more rapidly than usual. Thus, when asked to reproduce a given physical time interval, a person with a high body temperature produces an interval that is too short. An alternate way of looking at this is to note how our perception of physical (clock) time will seem to change when psychological time is running quickly. A given physical duration will appear to be too long if the psychological clock is ticking faster than the physical clock, hence giving more ticks per unit time than normally occurs (see Figure 13-2).

If an increase in body temperature increases apparent duration, then lowering body temperature may have the opposite effect. This was found by

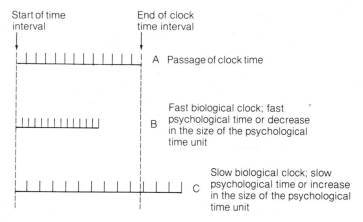

FIGURE 13-2   Each tick mark on these lines represents a unit of time. Those in A are clock time; those in B and C are ticks of the biological clock. Notice that in B the internal clock is faster, so that the same amount of clock time seems psychologically longer and time "drags by." For C, the internal clock is slower and so the same amount of clock time seems much shorter psychologically.

Baddeley (1966), who tested scuba divers diving in cold water off the coast of Wales. Like Hoagland, he asked his subjects to count to 60 at a rate of one number per second. After the dive, when their body temperature was approximately 1 deg C lower than it had been prior to entering the water, his subjects required approximately 70 sec to count to 60. This indicates that their pacemakers were ticking at a slower rate than the external clock. Count-

ing time using the slower ticking rate of their internal timer led them to underestimate the passage of time. In other words, when your internal clock is too slow, physical time seems to whiz by (see Figure 13-2). You may demonstrate the effects of temperature on your own time sense by trying Demonstration Box 13-1.

If we have an internal biological clock, then anything that affects the rate of physiological

---

DEMONSTRATION BOX 13-1.   Body Temperature and Time Perception

This demonstration is based on an experiment performed by Pfaff (1968). We know that our body temperature can fluctuate as much as 1 deg C during the course of a day. It is at its lowest point early in the day and tends to rise throughout the afternoon. Given this, try the following observations. On rising in the morning, try counting to 60 at the rate of what you perceive to be one number per second. You will probably need a friend to keep track of clock time for you so that you can relate your perceived minute to a clock

minute. Then take your temperature. (Do not take your temperature before you count, otherwise it may bias your counting rate.) Do this several times throughout the day, and keep a record of your results. If the theory is supported, you should find that your counting time will shorten (relative to a clock minute) as your body temperature increases. Thus, as the body clock speeds up, the passage of time tends to be overestimated and "clock" time seems to pass more slowly.

function might also affect our estimates of time. For instance, fatigue usually slows physiological functioning. Thus, the longer you are awake (or the greater the pressure for sleep) the slower your biological clock, and the more likely that when asked to estimate the passage of an hour your estimate will be longer than a physical clock hour because of shortened time experience (Aschoff, 1984; Daan, Beersma & Borbely, 1984). Similarly, general anesthetics lead to a shortening of time experience (Adam, Rosner, Hosick & Clark, 1971; Steinberg, 1955). Conversely, a number of investigations have found that drugs like amphetamines and caffeine (both of which are stimulants) lead to a lengthening of time experience (Frankenhauser, 1959; Goldstone, Boardman, & Lhamon, 1958). Drugs such as marijuana, mescaline, psilocybin, and LSD also seem to produce a lengthening of perceived time relative to a nondrug state (Fisher, 1967; Weil, Zinberg & Nelson, 1968). It has been argued that all these changes in time perception are caused by acceleration or deceleration of the physiological pacemaker that serves as our internal timer.

Cognitive Clocks

When you say that two minutes sitting on a hot stove feels like two hours, but two hours sitting with your loved one seems like two minutes, you actually are expressing the central aspect of most cognitive clock theories of time perception. These theories are based on the presumption that the perception of the passage of time is based not on physical time but rather on the mental processes that occur during an interval. In effect, time is not directly perceived, but rather "constructed" or "inferred" (Fraisse, 1963; Woodrow, 1951). This suggests that the tasks a person engages in will influence that person's perception of the passage of time. Given the variety of potential cognitive activities, it is perhaps not surprising that there are a number of different variables that affect the cognitive clock. Among the variables that have been

shown to affect the subjective perception of duration are: (1) the number of events occurring during the interval (e.g., Adams, 1977; Block, 1974; Poynter & Holma, 1985), (2) the complexity of stimulus events (e.g., Block, 1978; Ornstein, 1969), (3) the type of cognitive or information processing required (e.g., Hicks, Miller & Kinsbourne, 1976; Thomas & Weaver, 1975), and (4) the amount of attention given to the passage of time (e.g, Brown, 1985; McClain, 1983). All of these affect the perception of the *flow* or passage of time, and all are consistent with the idea that the rate at which the cognitive clock ticks is affected by how internal events are processed.

Change

One notion is that the ticking rate of the cognitive clock is dependent on **event processing** or **change monitoring.** The greater the number of events, or the more changes that occur, during an interval, the faster your cognitive clock ticks, and thus the longer is your estimate of the amount of time that has passed. Several studies seem to support this idea. A duration filled with stimulus events is perceived as being longer than an identical time period empty of any external events, a phenomenon known as the **filled duration illusion.** For example, if we fill a time interval with brief tones, this interval will be perceived as being longer than an identical time period in which no tones (or fewer tones) were presented. This is also true for such events as light flashes, words, or drawings (e.g., Avant, Lyman & Antes, 1975; Hicks, Miller, Gaes & Bierman, 1977; Ornstein, 1969; Poynter & Holma, 1985). Conversely, observers engaging in **restricted environmental stimulation technique** studies (where they remain anywhere up to 24 hours or more, reclining in a soundproof, darkened chamber with essentially all typical environmental stimulation removed) tend to drastically underestimate the amount of time they have spent in the chamber (Suedfeld, 1980). This underestimation occurs, presumably, because so few stimulus events have transpired during the interval.

Processing Effort

How difficult stimuli are to process, and the amount of memory storage they require, have also been shown to affect our perception of the duration of a time interval. For example, we tend to judge the brief presentation of a word to be longer in duration than a blank interval of the same length (Thomas & Weaver, 1975). Furthermore, the presentation interval of familiar words is judged to be shorter than the presentation interval of meaningless verbal stimuli (Avant & Lyman, 1975; Avant, Lyman & Antes, 1975) and presentations of non-familiar words appear to take longer than familiar words (Warm & McCray, 1969). In both instances, an increase in the amount of information processing required during the interval (a word versus a blank and a meaningless group of letters versus a word) leads to an increase in the estimated duration of the interval. This is consistent with a **processing effort model** of time perception. Similarly, the more items you store in memory during an interval of time, the longer you judge the time to be (Block, 1974; Mulligan & Schiffman, 1979), a notion sometimes referred to as the **storage size model** of time perception. Both are based on the presumption that the ticking rate of the cognitive clock is dependent on the amount of cognitive activity actually engaged in.

Temporal versus Nontemporal Attention

Both the *event processing* and *processing effort* mechanisms seem to affect our cognitive clock time, but the results are complicated by the way the observer is attending to the task. A simple example of this is given by the old homily "A watched pot never boils," which suggests that the more attention you pay to the passage of time, the longer the time interval appears to be (e.g., Block, George & Reed, 1980; Cahoon & Edmonds, 1980). This may be called the **temporal processing model** of time perception.

One of the best examples of the temporal processing model is the fact that, in general, when we are told in advance that we will have to judge the time that a task takes, we tend to judge the duration as longer than if we are unexpectedly asked to judge the time after the task is completed (e.g., Brown, 1985; McClain, 1983). Simply telling observers that they will later have to estimate the time that has passed causes them to pay attention to, and perhaps to order, internal events and external physical events in a manner that increases the perceived duration of the task.

Conversely, anything that draws our attention away from actually monitoring the passage of time should shorten our sense of "time passing." For instance, making the task we are working on more difficult makes it harder to attend to time directly. For this reason, we find that estimates of the duration of difficult tasks are usually shorter than estimates of the duration of easy tasks (e.g., Arlin, 1986; Brown, 1985; McClain, 1983). Sometimes, directing attention toward or away from the passage of time may even reverse the *filled duration illusion,* which we discussed earlier, since it is more difficult to process many events in an interval while at the same time attending to the flow of time itself (e.g., Miller, Hicks & Willette, 1978; Zakay, Nitzan & Glicksohn, 1983). Demonstration Box 13-2 shows how attention to time and task difficulty interact to affect our perception of the passage of time.

It should be clear from the discussion above that in the same way that there are a number of biological clocks that can interact in complex ways to give us a sense of the flow of time, there are also a number of cognitive clocks, or at least a number of ways to set the speed of a single cognitive clock. Even level of motivation can affect the apparent passage of time. For example, in one study subjects who were told that a desirable goal would be obtained on completion of their tasks tended to overestimate the passage of time relative to subjects who did not have this expectancy (Filer & Meals, 1949). In another study, observers who were placed in a stress situation (they were receiving electrical shocks) also overestimated the

---

DEMONSTRATION BOX 13-2.   Time Perception and Attentional Factors

For this demonstration you will need a stopwatch or a watch with a sweep second hand. Do each step *before* you read the instructions for the next one.

1. Sitting quietly, note the time and then, with your eyes closed and with no counting, estimate the passage of 30 seconds. Then open your eyes and note the actual amount of time that has passed.

2. Next, note the time, look away from the watch, and start to count backwards from 571 by threes (e.g., 571, 568, 565, etc.). Be sure that you count out loud. When you feel that 30 seconds has passed, stop counting and note the amount of time that has elapsed.

3. Compare the two time estimates. The first one should be shorter than the second one, because your cognitive clock was moving slower when you were attending only to the passage of time and faster when you were dividing your attention between the counting task and the monitoring of time (see Figure 13-2).

---

passage of physical time (Falk & Bindra, 1954). Given all these factors, the perception of time remains a complex and only partially understood phenomenon.

MOTION

Perception is not static, but changes continually over time. Some of these changes are like successive snapshots, such as glancing from one page to another or shifting your gaze from one building to another as you stand in the street, but many other changes are more continuous in nature, such as the sight of a car moving in the street beside you or a bird flying through the air. These latter perceptual experiences have the added quality of perceived motion.

Your initial feeling might be that the perception of motion is really quite trivial. You might expect that all you need for motion to be perceived is the image of a visual stimulus moving across your retina. Actually, motion perception involves some fairly complex interactions among a number of different systems (cf. Sekuler, Ball, Tynan & Machmer, 1982). For instance, it is possible for us to perceive movement when the image of the stimulus is not moving across our retina at all, such as when

we follow a moving car with our eyes and the image of the car remains fixed on the same retinal location. There are also times when we should see movement but do not. When our eyes move from one location to another the images of objects that are stationary in the environment are sliding across our retinal receptors, yet we perceive the world as remaining stationary. Thus, movement of the retinal image does not fully account for the perception of motion. Although it will be important for us to understand the visual stimulus conditions that elicit the perception of motion, you will soon see that there are also important nonvisual factors to consider.

Physiological Motion Detectors

It seems reasonable to begin our discussion of the perception of motion by first seeing if there are specific neural units for the detection of motion, much as there are for the detection of colors. The existence of such physiological mechanisms is suggested by clinical cases where patients can no longer perceive motion. Consider one case of bilateral brain damage where a woman reported that, although she could still recognize cars when she saw one, she could no longer judge their speed. The simple act of pouring a cup of coffee became virtually impossible since she could not see the dynamic flow of the fluid, nor the rise of the liquid level (Zihl, von Cramon & Mai, 1983).

In Chapter 3, we described how certain cells in the visual system respond differently to different stimulus properties. For example, we noted that there were two types of retinal ganglion cells, an X type, which seems particularly suited for detail perception in stationary targets, and a Y type, which responds to any change in stimulation. The Y type of cell seems particularly suited for the detection of motion. The fact that X and Y cells are differentially distributed across the retina (Y cells are more abundant in the peripheral retina) helps to explain why the apparent speed of a moving target might depend on where in the visual field it is (Campbell & Maffei, 1981). For example, you will probably recall from Chapter 4 that visual acuity diminishes with distance from the fovea (the number of X cells diminishes with increasing distance from the fovea). In a similar fashion, our ability to detect slow target movements (up to about 1.5 deg/sec) decreases with distance from the fovea (Choudhurt & Crossey, 1981; Lichtenstein, 1963; McColgin, 1960). For higher target velocities, however, this relationship reverses. At moderate to fast velocities, the peripheral retina seems better able to detect movement (because of the increased proportion of Y cells) even though the decrease in acuity may be so great that the observer may not be able to recognize what is moving (Bhatia, 1975; B. Brown, 1972).

At the level of the visual cortex, we find even clearer evidence for specialized cells tuned to stimulus motion. Specifically, there are numerous complex cells in the cortex of mammals that respond only to moving targets. Not only do these cells respond to motion, but they are tuned to the direction of stimulus movement, discharging strongly when a properly oriented stimulus drifts in one direction across the visual field and responding less strongly (or not at all) when the same stimulus moves through the field in the opposite direction (see Hubel & Wiesel, 1979). The degree of specificity of response to moving stimuli may be quite strong. Thus, there seem to be cells that respond not only to particular directions of movement but also to particular velocities of the moving targets (Maunsell & van Essen, 1983; Orban, Kennedy & Maes, 1981a,b). There are also some suggestions that the entire tectopulvinar pathway in vision may be specialized for the perception of movement and to control the direction of responses, such as eye movements, toward moving stimuli (Flandrin & Jeannerod, 1981; Guitton, Crommelink & Roucoux, 1980; Von Essen, 1979). Furthermore, there is recent evidence suggesting that there is a specific region of the cortex that contains many cells with very specific velocity tuning and directional characteristics. This region is not in the occipital cortex, which is the primary visual center, but is located in the temporal lobe of the brain (Allman, Miezin & McGuinness, 1985; Maunsell & van Essen, 1983).

Some of the information about the nature of motion-specific cells in humans comes from the use of a psychophysical technique called **selective adaptation** (Sekuler, 1975). The rationale of this technique is the same as the adaptation procedures we discussed in the spatial frequency section of Chapter 4. It involves exposing the eye to a moving pattern such as a field of stripes. Prolonged viewing of such a stimulus causes the motion-specific cells that have been responding to the direction of the pattern's movement to become less sensitive (e.g., Hunzelmann & Spillmann, 1984). When this happens, an observer's ability to detect the movement of other patterns, moving in the same direction and at the same speed as the previously exposed adapting pattern, is reduced. However, this drop in sensitivity does not carry over to faster or slower movements, nor does it generalize to movements in the opposite direction (Sekuler, 1975; Sekuler & Ganz, 1963; Wright & Johnston, 1985). Thus, the selective adaptation procedure gives results consistent with the idea that our brains contain movement-sensitive cells that are tuned to a particular direction and velocity. To experience an interesting illusion that researchers believe is caused by the fatigue of motion-sensitive cells, try the procedure in Demonstration Box 13-3.

Stimulus Factors in Motion Perception

Generally speaking, there are two principal mechanisms by which we perceive motion. The first involves detecting shifts in the relative positions of parts of the visual image; the second involves using our eyes to follow a moving target. Presumably these involve different perceptual systems, and for convenience we call the system that responds to image changes the **image-retina system** and the one that interprets motion from our eye and head movements the **eye-head system** (cf. Gregory, 1978). Since the image-retina system involves stimulus relationships, let us consider it first.

DEMONSTRATION BOX 13-3.   Motion Aftereffect

To experience a **motion aftereffect,** cut out (or trace) the accompanying stimulus and place it on the turntable of a record player as if it were a record. Let the stimulus rotate for about a minute, while you stare at the center. Stop the turntable and hold it so that it is completely stationary. While the turntable was moving, the spiral appeared to expand. Now it should appear to be (paradoxically) shrinking. This shrinking (without any apparent change in size) is an illusory movement, since the stimulus is no longer in motion. It is probably caused by fatiguing, or selective adaptation, of physiological motion detectors, produced by prolonged stimulation in one direction of movement. You can demonstrate that the cells are tuned for different stimulus velocities by changing the speed of your turntable and repeating the demonstration. You will notice that this will change the rate of shrinking in the aftereffect.

Perhaps the first question to ask is how much movement in the image is needed before we can perceive motion. To answer this question, we usually measure a movement threshold just as we measured thresholds for the minimum amount of light or sound needed for sensation (see Chapter 2). Our sensitivity to the movement of an external target depends on several variables. In experimental settings, movement thresholds have usually been studied using a small point of light that moves against some sort of stationary background, as in one of the earliest studies by Hermann Aubert (1886). He found that observers could detect the movement of a luminous dot in the dark, 50 cm from the eye, when it was moving at about 2.5 mm per second (which is about ⅕ of a degree of visual angle per second).

Target movement alone, however, is not enough to allow us to describe the motion thresholds. Our ability to detect that a target has moved is much more sensitive when there is some motionless reference, such as stationary features associated with the background, which we call the **visual context.** An example might be a stationary square frame surrounding the target. Under these circumstances we find that observers are much more sensitive (e.g., Palmer, 1986). The minimum movement that can be detected in the presence of a stationary visual context is about .25 mm per second (or ³⁄₁₀₀ of a degree of visual angle per second). This is an incredible degree of movement sensitivity. If a snail were to crawl across a desk 1.5 m wide at this rate, it would take it 1 hour and 40 minutes to go from end to end.

Our ability to judge the difference between two velocities is similarly facilitated by the presence of other stimuli that are stationary (Bonnet, 1984). Some researchers contend that the image-retina system really involves two different sources of motion information. The first is **subject-relative change,** where the only information is the movement of the target relative to the observer's position in space. The second is called **object-relative change,** which is the movement of one target relative to others and creates a sort of "configurational change" in the visible pattern and hence may involve processes similar to form perception (e.g., Mack, Heuer, Fendrich, Vilardi & Chambers, 1985; Wallach, Becklen & Nitzberg, 1985). In terms of the detection and discrimination of motion, we appear to be much more sensitive to object-relative change.

We have just seen how the addition of a visual context or background, in the form of stationary stimuli in the field, can increase our sensitivity to motion. Under certain conditions the relationship between the visual context and a target stimulus can also distort our perception of movement. For instance, Duncker (1929) displayed a bright dot in a dark room. When the dot was moved very slowly, observers were not certain whether or not it was moving. However, when a stationary dot was placed near the moving dot (in effect becoming the visual context), it became quite clear that one of the dots was in motion (due to the object-relative changes). Curiously, observers could not identify which of the two dots was moving. Duncker next changed the context stimulus by making it a rectangular luminous frame that was stationary and surrounded the dot. Under these circumstances there was no ambiguity and observers were able to tell that the dot rather than the frame was in motion. Duncker next varied the conditions so that the dot was stationary and the surrounding rectangular frame was moving. Under these circumstances an illusion appeared, in that observers reported that the stationary dot was moving rather than the frame. Duncker called this **induced motion,** since the perceived movement of the dot was induced or brought about by the real movement of the surrounding context. This is similar to the perception that the moon is moving behind the clouds, when actually the clouds are moving quickly and the moon moves much more slowly (relative to the earth) than we can detect. The clouds provide a surrounding context that is in motion and, consistent with the principle that Duncker discovered in the laboratory, they induce an apparent motion of the not-detectably-moving moon.

Induced movement effects are most dramatic

when the context is moving slowly rather than quickly (Wallach & Becklen, 1983). Square frame shapes are more effective than circular frames and large surrounds are more effective than small ones (Michael & Sherrick, 1986). Furthermore, in order to induce motion, the target and the background must be at the same distance from the observer (that is, apparently near each other). If the frame that supplies the context is too far in front of or behind the target, no motion will be induced (Gogel & Koslow, 1972). Actually, the appearance of induced motion seems to be controlled by the part of the visual context or frame that is closest to the target (Schulman, 1979). You can produce induced motion yourself by following the instructions in Demonstration Box 13-4.

Apparent Motion

Illusions of movement, such as induced motion, might seem to be merely interesting but not very useful curiosities. Yet every time you go to the cinema, you are paying to see two hours of a motion illusion. Each frame in the film you watch is actually stationary, being exchanged for a new frame about 24 times a second; television works in much the same way, with static frames changing about 30 times a second.

One of the early psychological researchers who systematically studied this phenomenon was Max Wertheimer (1912). Beginning with two lines separated in space that could be flashed on and off sequentially, he varied the time interval between the offset of the first line and the onset of the second (we call this variable period the **interstimulus interval**). When the interstimulus interval was very brief, observers saw two lines appear simultaneously. If the interval was long, the observers saw a line appear followed by a second line in a different location. However, for some intermediate interstimulus interval Wertheimer's observers reported that they saw a line appear and then *move* from the first position in space to the second. Although initially called *phi movement,* we now refer to this experience of movement between successively presented stationary stimuli as **apparent movement,** to distinguish it from **real movement,** where the stimulus actually moves in space. You can demonstrate this type of apparent movement for yourself by following the instructions in Demonstration Box 13-5.

The magnitude of the apparent movement experience is dependent on the interstimulus interval and also on the distance between the positions of the stimuli. Generally speaking, when the stimuli are separated by larger distances, longer time intervals between the stimuli are needed for apparent motion to be perceived (Farrell, 1983).

Several researchers have suggested that there are actually two separate perceptual systems that

---

DEMONSTRATION BOX 13-4.   Induced Movement

To induce movement in a stationary target, all you need is a sheet of clear cellophane or glass, and a sheet of white paper. In the middle of the white paper draw a small dot. On the clear cellophane draw a large rectangle, about 10 to 16 cm (4 by 6 in.), using a felt-tip marker or a grease pencil. Now lay the clear sheet over the paper so that the dot is enclosed by the rectangle and near one of its sides. Look steadily at the dot and *slowly* move the cellophane across the paper. You will notice that the dot appears to move in the direction opposite the motion of the rectangle. The effect is strongest when the dot is near the sides of the rectangle, where object-relative change plays a role. Increasing the speed of movement should reduce the amount of induced motion you perceive. Why?

DEMONSTRATION BOX 13-5. Apparent Movement

To see apparent movement similar to that described by Wertheimer, simply hold your index finger vertically a short distance in front of your nose. Look at any distant target (such as a mark on the far wall of the room). Relax your eyes and alternately wink each eye. You should see your finger in a different place with each eye. Now, begin to rhythmically open and close each eye in turn (remembering to keep your eyes relaxed). At slow rates you should see your finger "jump" from side to side; however, at some moderate rate of winking you should see the finger appear to actually "move" from one position to the other.

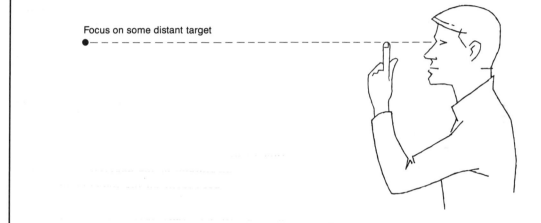

Focus on some distant target

bring about apparent movement. They are called, respectively, the **short-range process** and the **long-range process** (Anstis, 1978; Braddick, 1980). The short-range process encodes only small spatial target jumps as motion, perhaps 15 minutes of visual angle or less. It also responds only to fairly short interstimulus intervals, usually less than 100 msec (e.g., Baker & Braddick, 1985). This perceptual process probably detects only simple shifts of a contour, and is probably mediated by activity of some of the physiological motion detectors we discussed in the section of that name. This is supported by the observation that if we expose an observer to such short-range apparent motion in one direction for a while, a motion aftereffect much like the one produced in Demonstration Box 13-3 will appear (Vautin & Berkley, 1977).

The second system, the long-range process, responds to stimuli that are spatially separated by distances greater than 15 minutes of visual angle; this may include separations of many degrees across the visual field. The interstimulus interval needed to produce the perception of motion is also much longer, over 100 msec. This process seems to be based on more complex inferential procedures—for instance, the brain deciding that it is improbable that the disappearance of one stimulus should be followed so quickly by the sudden and independent appearance of an identical stimulus nearby, and therefore concluding that the original stimulus must have moved to this new location. In some ways this process seems to involve a form of "logic" or simplifying principle, which derives apparent motion as a reasonable interpretation of the stimulus changes observed (Hatfield & Epstein, 1985; Rock, 1983).

In some respects, the apparent motion obtained from the long-range process demonstrates a good deal of "tolerance" in its interpretation of movement. For example, suppose we present an apparent movement display, alternately flashing spatially separated stimuli at a rate we know produces the sensation of motion. Now suppose that the target on the right is red and the one on the left is green. Will we still see motion? The answer is that we will see a target both moving *and* changing color as it moves. We can get apparent motion not only between targets of different colors but between targets with different shapes, sizes, brightnesses, and orientations, and in most of these situations the target seems to be transformed while it is moving (Anstis & Mather, 1985; Bundesen, Larsen & Farrell, 1983; Kolers & Green, 1984; Kolers & von Grunau, 1976). Similarly, apparent motion is "flexible" in that it will adapt to the conditions in the visual field. If you place an object in the pathway of the apparent movement, the perceived path of motion will seem to deflect around that object (Berbaum & Lenel, 1983). If a particular pathway is suggested, by, for instance, briefly flashing a curved path between the two flickering stimuli, the apparent motion will seem to follow that pathway (Shepard & Zare, 1983). All these factors suggest that higher-level cognitive processing mechanisms play a role in the perception of apparent motion, at least when we are dealing with the long-range process (Rock, 1983).

Biological Motion

All the experiments we have thus far described tended to use rather simple stimuli, and we have mostly been concerned with the process by which we see motion in these stimuli. Movement patterns themselves, however, serve an important function in helping us identify objects in our environment. In a series of studies, Gunnar Johansson and his co-workers have shown how various perspective

transformations can predict the motion of differing objects, and how individuals can later identify these objects based on schematic movement patterns.

Perhaps the most interesting work is with **biological motion** (e.g., Johansson, 1976a). This refers to the intricate and coordinated set of movement patterns accomplished by the skeletal structure of the human body, for example, when walking across the room. Johansson began by asking, "Will an observer be able to identify these motions as the act of walking even in the absence of any other information, such as sight of the person?" To answer this question Johansson and his co-workers used the following technique. They attached small flashlight bulbs to the shoulders, elbows, wrists, hips, knees, and ankles of an individual (see Figure 13-3A). They then made a motion picture film of the person as he moved around in a darkened room. When observers later watched the film they only saw a pattern of lights moving about in total darkness. Nonetheless, observers were able to identify the pattern as a person walking or running, even when they only got to see the motion for as short an exposure as 200 msec (Johansson, von Hofsten & Jansson, 1980). Observers were also easily able to detect abnormalities, such as the simulation of a small limp. In another experiment, two people with similar arrays of lights were filmed while performing a spirited folk dance. Figure 13-3B shows a series of positions from the folk dance in which the black dots mark the positions of the lights. Once again, even with only a moving pattern of lights, observers had no difficulty identifying the motion as a dancing couple (Johansson, 1976b). Infants as young as 4 months of age seem to notice that biological motion is different from other forms of motion, and prefer to watch patterns of the sort we have been discussing, rather than random patterns of lights moving (Fox & McDaniel, 1982).

Our precision in identifying individuals based only on their biological motion patterns is really quite striking. For example, in one study research-

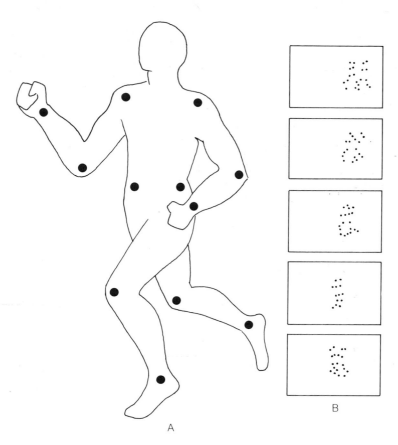

A

B

FIGURE 13-3   An example of the type of displays used by investigators to study patterns of humans in motion. A indicates the positions of lights affixed to individuals and B shows a sequence of movement positions made by a dancing couple.

ers photographed a group of people who were acquainted with one another. These people were photographed with only lighted portions of several joints visible. Several months later these same individuals were invited to watch the films and attempt to identify themselves and their friends in the motion picture. People were able to identify themselves and others correctly on a fair percentage of trials, although their performance was not perfect. The investigators also asked their observers how they went about making their identifications of various individuals in the film. People tended to mention a variety of motion components such as the speed, bounciness, and rhythm of the walker, the amount of arm swing, or the length of steps as features that allowed them to make their identification. In other studies, these same investigators found that observers could tell, even under these conditions, whether a person was a male or a female, despite seeing only a moving pattern of dots. In fact, it was not necessary for all the body joints to be represented in the light display for people to make correct identifications. Even when only the ankles were represented, observers could detect the sex of the walker. They could also make these gender identifications within about 5 sec of viewing

(Barclay, Cutting & Kozlowski, 1978; Cutting & Kozlowski, 1977; Cutting & Proffitt, 1981; Kozlowski & Cutting, 1977). Thus, different motion patterns characterize each sex and each individual.

Much work is being done to determine the nature of the information used to identify individuals, and from this some fairly sophisticated computer programs have been developed to create simulated biological motion patterns (Cutting, 1978; Runeson & Frykholm, 1983; Todd, 1983). For instance, Cutting, Proffitt, and Kozlowski (1978) proposed that the torso of the body acts like a flat spring with the limbs in symmetrical motion around it. This, along with certain individual differences in bodily dimensions (such as the relative widths of the shoulders and hips), provides a center of movement that is not necessarily associated with any body part; however, it organizes the coherent motion of

the body parts in an individual fashion making identification possible. Perhaps it is patterns of biological motion such as this that enable us to identify people in light too dim to allow us to see their faces. It also probably explains how you can identify people walking down the street, even though they may be too far away for you to make out their features or may have their backs to you.

Eye Movements and Motion Perception

Up to now we have focused our discussion mainly on the visual stimulus factors that contribute to our perception of motion, such as movement of the image across the retina. To that extent we have been concerned with the image-retina movement system (see Figure 13-4A). There are, however, aspects of

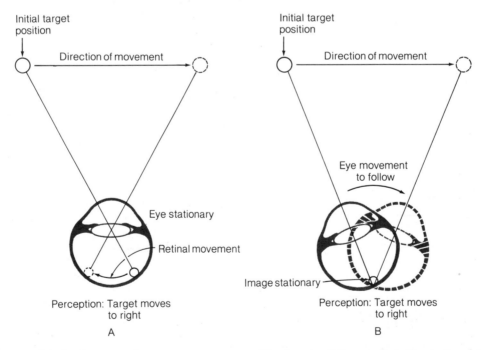

FIGURE 13-4 (A) The image-retina movement system. The image of the moving object stimulates the retina when the eyes are held stationary. This gives information about object motion, possibly as a result of the involvement of movement-detecting cells. (B) One of the functions of the eye-head movement system. When the eye pursues a moving target, the image remains stationary on the fovea of the eye but we still perceive the movement of the object.

motion perception based on information from sources other than the visual image. The most well researched of these alternative modes of motion perception involves the *eye-head movement system,* which we mentioned earlier. This system enables us to detect the movement of external objects even when the image remains in a fixed position on the retina. This most commonly occurs when we move our eyes to follow the path of a physically moving object, as when we track an automobile moving down the highway. Such eye movement, called **smooth-pursuit movement** and illustrated in Figure 13-4B, functions to keep the image of the target on the fovea (the most acute part of the retina). Suppose that the image of the target remains on the fovea and that there is no patterned background to provide object-relative information as to movement. This means that the only way the observer can know the path or the speed of an object is to monitor the speed and direction of the tracking eye movements (e.g., Epstein & Hanson, 1977; Rock & Halper, 1969). It should not surprise us to learn that spatial information is conveyed by eye movements, since we have previously (see Chapter 10) discussed how eye movements can provide us with information as to the size and location of objects (e.g., Coren, 1986).

Actually, there are two forms of smooth-pursuit eye movements. The first is **reflex pursuit movement,** which keeps images of objects relatively fixed in one place on your retina despite the fact that your head may be moving. An example of this is shown in Figure 13-5, where the individual is steadily looking at the lens of the camera. Notice that the eyes seem to remain stationary while the head seems to rotate around them, whereas actually the eyes are tracking in the direction opposite to the head movement. This automatic reflex movement is controlled by the *vestibular system* (see Parker, 1980), which we will discuss later in this chapter. The second type of smooth eye movement is **voluntary pursuit movement.** This type of eye movement (the one we showed in Figure 13-4B) tries to keep the image of the object fixed on the fovea, despite its physical movement across the visual field. This system is actually found only in animals that have foveas. It now seems clear that voluntary pursuit eye movements provide most of the information about target movements (Post & Leibowitz, 1985; Raymond, Shapiro & Rose, 1984).

To the extent that our perception of the motion of an object depends on information about the movements our eye has used to track the object, it

FIGURE 13-5   Reflex-pursuit eye movements are used to keep the image of an object fixed on your retina even though you move your head. Here the individual is looking at the camera while rotating her head. Notice how these vestibularly controlled movements keep the eyes fixed while the head seems to rotate around them.

seems reasonable that anything that alters the direction or speed of motion of the eye might also alter our perception of the movement of the object. This routinely occurs, since the eye does not pursue moving targets with perfect accuracy, but rather tends to follow some distance behind the target. The degree to which the eye lags behind is dependent on the speed of the target (Fender, 1971; Puckett & Steinman, 1969), and under some circumstances the eye never really catches up to the stimulus (Young, 1971). This may cause distortions in the size or the shape of the path the eye follows (e.g., Festinger & Easton, 1974). For example, Coren, Bradley, Hoenig, and Girgus (1975) have shown that the size of the circular path traced out by a rotating spot of light seems to shrink as the speed of the target increases. At slow speeds, where the eye can track accurately, or at speeds much too fast for even an attempt at tracking, the judgments are reasonably accurate.

Another example of the effect of tracking lag

is the **Aubert-Fleischl effect** (named for the two researchers who explored it). Aubert and Fleischl noted that when we track a target with our eyes while it moves relative to a stationary background, it appears to move more slowly than it would if we were to fixate steadily on the stationary background. This phenomenon is associated with several predictable perceptual distortions. Because of the lag in tracking, an observer will not only underestimate the velocity of a target that is tracked with the eye but will also tend to underestimate the distance the target has moved (Mack & Herman, 1972). Demonstration Box 13-6 allows you to see this effect for yourself.

There are some circumstances where our own eye or head movements produce movements of the visual image across our retina that are very similar to those that might occur if the scene were actually in motion. Another important function of the eye-head movement system is to compensate for such movements, so that we continue to see the world

---

DEMONSTRATION BOX 13-6.   The Aubert-Fleischl Effect

To experience the underestimation of both speed and distance moved when you track a target, begin by practicing a movement that will serve as your tracking target. With your eyes closed, swing your hand back and forth in front of you at a moderate speed and in a rhythmic fashion as shown in the figure. When you are moving with a nice regular tempo, open your eyes, look straight ahead, and judge the speed and the distance your hand is moving. Now look directly at your finger and track it. Notice that your hand seems to be moving more slowly, and the size of the back-and-forth movement (the path length) appears to be shorter. The apparent path length seems shorter probably because when you are tracking the target, information about the extent of the motion comes from the eye-head system, and your tracking movements lag behind the physical target, resulting in a slower overall velocity and a shorter eye-movement path length.

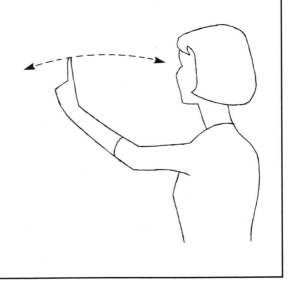

as being stationary despite the fact that we are moving. This process of compensating for eye movements is called **position constancy,** and the fact that objects seem to maintain a fixed position relative to us, despite rotations of both our head and eyes, is called **direction constancy.** We are quite accurate in our ability to distinguish image movements caused by target movements from those caused by our own movements (see Wallach, 1987). Although we do not know exactly how this movement compensation system works, it must include a system that monitors the changing position of the eye relative to the position of the head, either when we are tracking a moving target or when we are making eye movements to scan a stationary scene (Howard, 1982). Two classes of theory have been proposed to explain how the eye-head movement system accomplishes this.

Sir Charles Sherrington (1906) suggested that motion is detected via feedback information from the six extraocular muscles that control eye movements. This feedback information, called *proprioceptive* or *position information* (see Chapter 9), enables the observer to monitor eye position. The proprioceptive information tells the brain that the eyes have moved, and in turn this information allows the brain to interpret movement across the retina as being observer-generated rather than object-generated. In support of this theory, there is evidence that there are cells in the superior colliculus and visual cortex of the cat that monitor eye position (Berkley, 1982; Kurtz & Butter, 1980). These cells fire at different rates depending on the extent and direction of eye movement (Donaldson & Long, 1980; Kasamatsu, 1976; Noda, Freeman & Creutzfeldt, 1972). Sherrington's theory is often called an **inflow theory** because it is the information "flowing in" from the eye muscles to the brain that constitutes the crucial message for the interpretation of movement.

A different theory about how the eye-head system compensates for self-generated movements of the visual image was offered by Hermann von Helmholtz (1909/1962). He suggested that when the brain initiates an eye movement, efferent (motor) signals are sent out commanding the eyes to move. Copies of these signals, sent to central regions of the visual system, cancel the movement information coming from the retina as the eyes move. Since the interpretation of the origin of movement is based on information from the message sent out from the brain that initiates an eye movement, this is called an **outflow theory.** As in the case of inflow information, there seem to be some cells in the cerebellum and the cortex of monkeys that contain information about eye position. Since these cells respond before the actual movement takes place, they could represent the source of outflow information registering the *intention to move*, rather than the movements themselves (Miles & Fuller, 1975; Wurtz & Goldberg, 1971).

To see how outflow information might compensate for eye movements, try this little experiment suggested by Helmholtz. Place your hand over one eye and try tapping or pushing (through the eyelid) the side of your other (uncovered) eye very gently with your fingertip. This rotates the eye in a movement similar to one that could be initiated by the brain. However, in this case the brain has not sent a signal to move the eye. When the eye is rotated in this passive fashion, the visual field will seem to swing around in the direction opposite to the movement of the eye, and to the same extent that the eye actually moved (e.g., Miller, Moore & Wooten, 1984). Thus, the stability of the visual field holds only for eye movements initiated by signals from the brain. Passive eye movements result in an apparent movement of the visual field. It seems as though the action of the eye-head system requires that the signals to and/or from the eye muscles be compared to signals arriving from the retina indicating changes in retinal image position (Matin, 1982). Figure 13-6 illustrates the difference between the inflow and outflow theories; it seems likely that both inflow and outflow may be needed to provide a full explanation of the eye-head movement system. Table 13-1 gives a

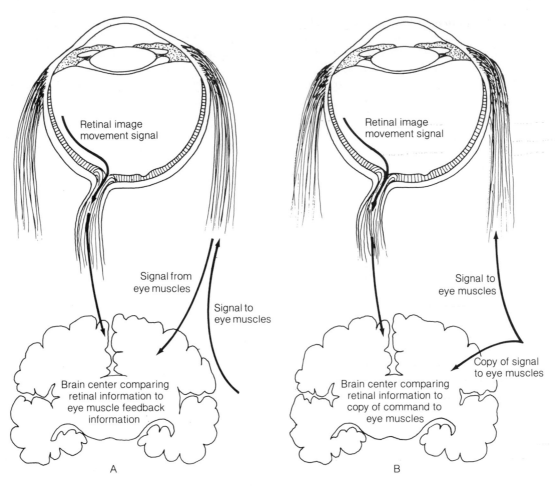

FIGURE 13-6 A major function of the eye-head movement system is to maintain the stability of the visual world during eye movements, thus achieving position or direction constancy. The inflow theory (A) states that this is accomplished by comparing movement signals from the retina with proprioceptive feedback from the eye muscles, which indicates that the eye has moved. The outflow theory (B) maintains that commands from the brain to initiate voluntary eye movements cancel the movement information coming from the retina as the eyes move.

summary of the relationship between the image-retina and eye-head movement systems. Demonstration Boxes 13-7 and 13-8 give other interesting examples that illustrate the relationships between eye movements, visual stability, and the perception of motion.

The Vestibular Sense

There is another sensory system that is primarily concerned with motion and motion-related matters, and tends to interact with visual stimulation to separate bodily motion from stimulus motion. This is

Table 13-1.   The Effect of Retinal Image Change and Voluntary Eye Movements on the Perception of Motion

Physical Target	Action of Eye	Retinal Image	Commands to Eye (Head)	Perception
Image-retina				
Moving	Stationary	Moves	None	Movement
Eye-head				
Moving	Tracks target	Stationary on fovea	Yes	Movement
Stationary	Moves	Moves	Yes	No movement
Stationary	Passively pushed	Moves	None	Movement in direction opposite to eye motion
Image stabilized on retina	Moves	Stationary on retina	Yes	Movement in same direction as eye motion

---

DEMONSTRATION BOX 13-7.   Afterimages and Apparent Movement

You can readily experience one of the ways in which the eye-head movement system differentiates external from observer movement. The first thing that is needed is to generate a *stabilized retinal image*. Ordinarily, the retinal image is in constant motion and stimulates varying groups of receptors at a rapid rate. However, by quickly satiating or fatiguing a single group of retinal receptors, we can generate an image that maintains its position regardless of eye movements. Many of you are probably familiar with the technique used to give rise to such an image if you have ever had your picture taken with a flashbulb attached to the camera. If you looked at the light while it flashed, you may have noticed a purple dot that tended to linger in your field of view for some time after the picture was taken. This purple dot is called an *afterimage*. It is one example of a stabilized retinal image. The afterimage does not shift position on the retina. It stays in a constant position regardless of how we move our eyes. We can use the afterimage to demonstrate the operation of the eye-head movement system.

Perhaps the easiest way to generate an afterimage is to look at a rather bright but small source of light for a brief period of time. Make a 1-cm hole in an index card and hold it up in front of a light bulb. Look at the hole for a few moments and this should provide a clearly visible afterimage when you look away from the light. Now notice that each time you move your eyes the afterimage seems to jump in the same direction. This apparent movement is due to the action of the eye-head system.

Commands have been issued to the eye to move, yet the image remains on the same place on the retina. This could only occur if the image had moved as much as the eye (see Table 13-1). You may also notice that the image sometimes seems to drift smoothly from place to place. Again, the image never moves; the movement is signaled from the movements of your eyes. This is one example of how the action of the eye-head movement system can lead to illusions of motion.

DEMONSTRATION BOX **13-8.**   The Autokinetic Effect

There is an interesting phenomenon in which movement is seen in the absence of any physical motion of the target. The word used to describe the occurrence is *autokinesis,* which means "self-moving." For this experiment, you will need a *very* dark room. No stray light of any sort should be visible. In addition, you will need a small dim point of light (a lighted cigarette works fine). Place the point of light about 2 m away from you and look at it steadily. After a few minutes it should appear to move, perhaps slowly drifting in one direction or another. Of course the light is still stationary; hence the movement is an illusion, which is called the **autokinetic effect.**

The autokinetic effect demonstrates the outflow principle that operates in the eye-head movement system. The visual system only monitors commands to initiate voluntary eye movements. However, these are not the only types of eye movements possible. Our eyes also exhibit involuntary movements. As you

may have guessed, these are not monitored by the visual system. One type of involuntary eye movement is *eye drift,* and this is the mechanism that has been implicated in the autokinetic effect (Matin & MacKinnon, 1964). When we steadily fixate or stare at a target, it is difficult for the eyes to maintain steady and accurate fixation on that one point in space (Ditchburn, 1973). The eyes will tend to drift off of the fixation point; however, the visual system does not monitor this movement until it exceeds a critical point. In the autokinetic situation, retinal image movement has been signaled in the absence of commands to initiate voluntary eye movements. This is the situation under which the movement of the retinal image is attributed to an externally moving object (see Table 13-1). There is no information that the eyes have moved, so illusory movement of the dim spot of light is seen.

the **vestibular system,** which functions to inform us about the motion of our body through space, to assist in the maintenance of an upright posture, and to control eye position as we move our heads while viewing various stimuli. For the most part, these operations take place outside of consciousness. Before we consider the higher-level interactions that involve this system, let us first consider its basic structure and physiology.

Some of the most primitive organisms have organs that are sensitive to changes in motion of the body. In primitive invertebrates such as the crayfish these are called **statocysts.** Each consists simply of a fluid-filled cavity that is lined with hair cells. In the cavity is a tiny stone, called a **statolith** or "still stone," that rests on the hairs. When the animal accelerates, the stone tends to lag behind because of its inertia, thus bending the hairs on which it rests. This action generates an electrical response to the movement. If the animal is tilted,

the stone rolls along over a number of different hairs, bending them and generating a different response indicating tilt. The function of such organs is to signal the animal's orientation with respect to gravity. More advanced invertebrates, such as the squid or octopus, have statocysts that approach vertebrate vestibular organs in complexity, with multichambered statocysts and the ability to detect acceleration in several planes (Stephens & Young, 1982).

Primitive vertebrates have organs that have a similar function; they are called **otocysts** and the bones they contain are called **otoliths.** Notice that these terms each contain the root *oto,* meaning "ear." These organs are usually closely associated with the ears, since both the auditory receptors and the vestibular organs probably evolved from pits on the surface of hairy skin. In mammals, these organs are protected by the skull from possibly damaging outside forces. In humans, the **bony labyrinth** in the head contains the cochlea (which is the auditory organ) and the **semicircular canals,** the **utricle,** and the **saccule,** which comprise the vestibular organs (see Figure 13-7 and look back at Figure 6-4).

Vestibular Stimuli and Receptors

The effective physical stimulus for any vestibular organ is change of rate of motion, or **acceleration,** which occurs whenever we move through space, whether we jump up and down, take off in a jet plane, or simply stand up and walk. The semicircular canals and their associated receptor organs seem particularly well suited for monitoring rotary acceleration (as when turning around or falling down). The other two organs, the utricle and the saccule, seem mainly to respond to linear acceleration (as when taking off in a plane).

The movement-receptive portion of the semicircular canals is called the **crista,** which is found in a swelling (called an **ampulla**) at the base of each semicircular canal (see Figure 13-7). The crista consists of an array of sensory cells from which tiny hairs protrude, as shown in Figure 13-8A. These hairs are embedded in a jellylike material called the **cupola.** When your head accelerates, the inertia of the fluid in the canals causes the cupola to move in the opposite direction. This in turn causes the hairs to bend, generating neural responses. As your head continues to move at a particular rate of speed, the cupola gradually comes back to its resting position, no longer bending the hairs, and no longer causing a response in the sensory cells. This is why the effective stimulus is acceleration rather than steady movement.

The receptor organ found in the utricle and the saccule is called the **macula,** shown in Figure 13-8B. It functions much like the statocyst we discussed before. As in the crista, tiny hairs protrude from the sensory cells in the macula. These hairs are embedded in a jellylike substance covered by a membrane containing otoliths, which lags behind

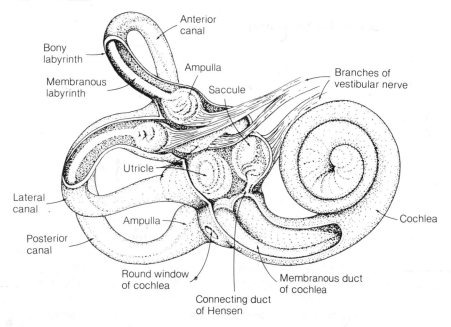

FIGURE 13-7 A diagram of the right inner ear showing the cochlea (which houses the auditory receptor), the semicircular canals, the utricle, and the saccule. (From Geldard, 1972)

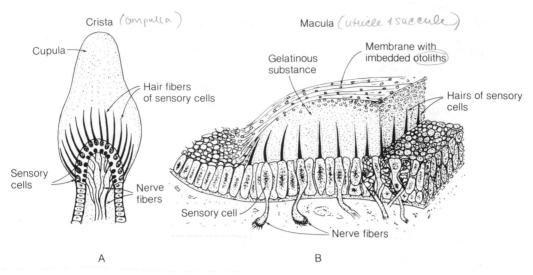

Crista (ampulla)

Macula (utricle & saccule)

FIGURE 13-8   (A) Diagram of the crista, the receptor found in the ampulla of each semicircular canal. (B) Diagram of the macula, the receptor found in the utricle and the saccule. (From Geldard, 1972)

when the head is accelerated, bending the hair cells and generating an electrical response. When the jelly-and-hairs catch up to the rest of the head, which would happen if the acceleration ceased and motion became steady, the hairs are no longer bent. This means no response would be generated, even though the head could be traveling at thousands of kilometers per hour relative to the earth.

Neural Responses in the Vestibular Sense

The hair cells from both the crista and the macula send their information to the brainstem via the eighth cranial nerve. From there most of the nerve fibers go to the **vestibular nuclei** (still in the brainstem). After this the sensory pathways become complicated and somewhat obscure. There are projections to the cerebellum and to the cortex, but they are different in different animals (see Correia & Guedry, 1978). It is important to note that most of the fibers leaving the vestibular nuclei are motor or **efferent fibers.** One major group of these fibers forms a pathway to the muscles that move the eyes. Szentagothai (1950) discovered that each pair of eye muscles receives fibers from a different semi-

circular canal. The arrangement indicates that muscles that move the eye in a particular plane are controlled by nerve fibers that originate in the one of the semicircular canals that responds to acceleration in that plane. Acceleration in a particular direction causes compensatory eye movements in the opposite direction. This allows the eyes to remain fixed on an object even though the head is turning in various directions. The relationship between eye movements and vestibular stimulation is shown in Demonstration Box 13-9.

Lowenstein and Sand (1940) performed a classic study that illustrates the electrophysiology of the vestibular system. They recorded the electrical activity of single nerve fibers from the crista of a ray (a kind of fish) while the entire labyrinth was rotated on a turntable. They found that as long as the head was accelerating, the fibers responded. The fibers increased their firing rate above the resting rate for acceleration in one direction, and decreased it below the resting rate when the acceleration was in the opposite direction. Thus, as in other sensory systems, both excitatory and inhibitory responses to physical stimuli occur. Lowenstein and Sand also showed that the magnitude of

---

DEMONSTRATION BOX 13-9.   Vestibular Stimulation and Eye Movements

For this demonstration you will need a friend and a little space. Have your friend hold her arms out and spin around (like a whirling ice skater) until she becomes dizzy. This continuous rotation sets up currents in the semicircular canals that trigger the compensatory eye-movement system. Now stop your friend from turning and look into her eyes. You will notice that the eyes drift steadily in one direction, and then snap back and start to drift again. This type of repetitive eye movement is called **nystagmus.** It is a reflex movement that is evoked automatically by the vestibular stimulation caused by fluid currents in the semicircular canals.

---

the response (impulses per second in single fibers) varies directly with the magnitude of the stimulating acceleration. So stimulus intensity seems to be encoded in a manner similar to that in other sensory systems. There are at least two other types of nerve fibers: one always responds to acceleration (regardless of direction) with an increase in firing rate, and the other only responds with a decrease in firing rate.

The fibers connected to the hair cells of the macula respond to their stimuli somewhat more simply. Two types of responses have been described. The first is an increase in the rate of neural firing when the head is tilted; the second is a rate increase when the head is returned to its original position (Wyburn et al., 1964). Although there have been some studies of cortical responses to acceleration of the head, little is known in detail about these responses. One fact that has emerged is that inputs from vestibular, kinesthetic, and visual systems converge in the cortex, so that our sensations of "turning" and the like depend in a complex way on all of these inputs (Mergner, Anastasopoulos, Becker & Deecke, 1981; Parker, 1980). One striking example of this complex interaction is the phenomenon of motion sickness, which is often caused by a mismatch between visual and vestibular or kinesthetic inputs. A great deal of effort is being put into studying this aspect of human reaction, especially because of its importance in space travel, which involves zero-gravity conditions.

Self-Motion

Back in the nineteenth century there was a fairground ride called the Haunted Swing. In this ride, people entered a boat-shaped enclosure and artificial scenery was slowly swung backward and forward outside the windows. This resulted in an incredibly strong illusion that the chamber was rocking, and people felt all of the bodily sensations of real motion, including a feeling of loss of their postural stability that made them sway, and even vertigo (Howard, 1982; Wood, 1985). There is an everyday example of this effect. Probably most of you have had the experience of sitting in a bus or a train parked next to another vehicle. All at once the adjacent vehicle starts to move. However, instead of correctly attributing the movement to the vehicle beside you, you have a powerful sensation of yourself in motion. This is a case of induced movement, such as we discussed earlier, however it is an *induced movement of the self*. It is important since it reflects the interchangeability of visual and vestibular factors in the perception of body motion.

If we were not aware of dynamic changes in the visual image as we move, we would probably bump into things much more often as we walk around, or not notice that our body has swayed or leaned until we actually incline too far and topple over. Our perception of **self-motion** depends on an analysis of the continually changing aspects of the retinal image as we move. Consider our most typical motion, which is forward in depth. For this kind of motion the visual array in front of us is a radially expanding pattern in the center of our visual field and a laterally translating pattern in our periphery. For example, consider the pattern shown in Figure 13-9A. Here the arrows represent the flow of the visual array as if you were moving toward the door marked A. Images of objects around Door A, that is, those stimuli to its sides or above or below it, expand radially outward and into the periphery as you move forward. This flow of stimuli has been called **streaming perspective** (Gibson, 1979). If your path were angled so you were going toward the door marked B, the optical transformation pattern would be similar to that in Figure 13-9B. In both cases, the center of this outward flow,

which is called the **focus of expansion,** indicates the direction of your movement. Although the specific patterns shown by the streaming perspective of targets in the field will vary as you move your eyes (Andersen, 1986; Cutting, 1986; Regan & Beverly, 1982), it is still easy to direct your movements by keeping the door you wish to reach in the center of the outward flow of stimuli.

If we present you with a steadily moving pattern that is the equivalent of a natural streaming-perspective pattern, you will feel as though you are moving. If the pattern is radially expanding, as in Figure 13-9, you will feel as though your body is moving forward. If the pattern is moved steadily to the side you will feel that you are moving (or starting to lean or tilt) sideways, or even rotating if the

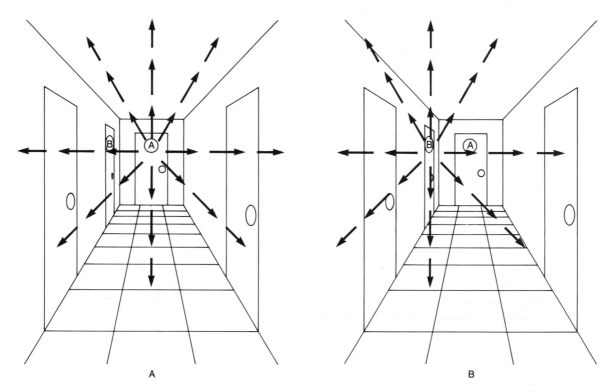

A   B

FIGURE 13-9   Streaming perspective. A shows the pattern of flow or expansion of stimuli as it would appear if you were moving toward Door A. The length of the arrows indicates the rate of change or speed of expansion, with longer arrows meaning faster change. B shows how the pattern of stimulus flow changes if you were now moving toward Door B, rather than straight down the hallway.

pattern surrounds you. Such induced motion of the self is usually called **vection** (Dichgans & Brandt, 1978). Generally speaking, there is a consensus that the central visual field is more specialized for object motion, whereas stimulation of the peripheral visual field is necessary to induce the feeling of self-motion. Thus, patterns that extend into the periphery tend to produce strong feelings of vection (e.g., Delorme & Martin, 1986; Held, Dichgans & Bauer, 1975). If the speed of flow is not too fast, and the pattern is correct, visually induced self-motion can be experienced even for smaller central patterns (Andersen & Braunstein, 1985; Stoffregen, 1985). Demonstration Box 13-10 shows how you may experience a form of induced self-motion.

The relatively greater contribution of the peripheral retina to vection may explain why the feelings of self-motion can be so strong when you view motion pictures with an oversized or wraparound screen. In fact, a modern version of the "haunted swing" illusion can be found in some fairs and amusement parks, where viewers are surrounded by

the projected pictures associated with riding down a roller coaster, flying in a helicopter, or hurtling down a raceway at high speed. Most viewers feel all the bodily effects normally associated with the equivalent self-motion, and they are sufficiently indistinguishable from actual movement that it suggests that the visual and vestibular inputs must have some common neural pathways and centers. This would be a sensible arrangement, since the vestibular system only responds to accelerations or decelerations of body motions. As we saw in the previous section, after any prolonged period of constant velocity the vestibular system would cease to respond and the only remaining indication of movement would be the motion in the visual array.

To the extent that vestibular and visual information can each produce similar feelings of self-motion, it should not be surprising to find that there are cells in the vestibular nuclei whose rates of firing are influenced by signals suggesting bodily motion, whether such signals come from the vestibular organs themselves or from visual motion (e.g.,

---

DEMONSTRATION BOX 13-10. Induced Self-Motion

For this demonstration you should have two small light sources (lighted candles will work fine) and a darkened room. Hold the candles out at arm's length and about at eye level, as shown in the figure. Look straight forward (remove your glasses or squint your eyes a bit so that you don't see the surrounding room too clearly). Now slowly move the candles back toward the sides of your head (not too close!). As you do so, you should experience an induced motion of your body so that you now feel that you are leaning forward slightly. If you move the candles slowly forward, you should get the impression that you have straightened up, or are now leaning backward somewhat. Next try the same arm movements with your eyes closed to see that this effect does not occur in the absence of the visual stimulation. This means that the feeling of body tilt produced in this situation is a form of vection caused by the streaming perspective

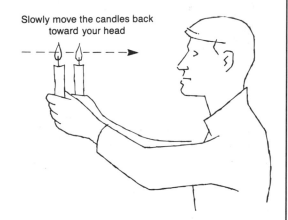

Slowly move the candles back toward your head

simulated by the movements of the lights, which suggested that at least the upper portion of your body was moving forward.

Henn, Young & Finley, 1974; Waespe & Henn, 1977). There seems to be a complex interaction between the visual and the nonvisual inputs to give us this feeling of self-motion (DiZio & Lackner, 1986; Henn, Cohen & Young, 1980).

The perception of motion, and to some extent the perception of time, are good examples of a process we will call **sensory convergence.** This is a process by which a number of inputs all combine to produce a single coherent perception, in which you may not be conscious of all the components that have gone into the computation. Thus, we have seen that the apparently *visual* experience of motion may contain proprioceptive inputs from eye movements and the vestibular sense, or copies of efferent commands issued to the eye muscles, even though your conscious impression remains strictly visual. The mechanism of sensory convergence may be quite simple, with various peripheral sources of information converging on a single group of neurons, or it may involve higher-level, central or cognitive integration, as we saw in our consideration of the factors influencing our perception of the passage of time. The final percept, as experienced in our consciousness, may be an amalgam of many sources, though to us it seems quite simple and pure.

GLOSSARY

The following definitions are specific to this book.

Acceleration   Change in rate of motion.

Ampulla   Swelling at the base of a semicircular canal containing the crista.

Apparent movement   Perceived movement of spatially separated static stimuli flashed successively at appropriate interstimulus intervals.

Aubert-Fleischl effect   A moving target being tracked with the eyes seems to move more slowly than when a stationary background behind the moving target is fixated.

Autokinetic effect   The illusion of movement of a stationary point of light viewed in an otherwise totally dark field.

Biological clock   A physiological mechanism that underlies our experience of time.

Biological motion   The movement patterns of the skeletal structure of a human engaged in activities such as walking or running.

Bony labyrinth   The structure inside the head that contains the cochlea and the vestibular organs. It is made of very hard bone.

Change monitoring   The theory that the tick rate of the cognitive clock reflects the number of events, or changes, that occur in an interval.

Circadian rhythm   A rhythmic biological cycle occurring over an approximately 24-hour period.

Cognitive clock   A cognitive mechanism that determines our experience of time.

Crista   Movement-perceptive organ found in the ampulla of the semicircular canal of the ear.

Cupola   Jellylike material in which the hairs of the crista are embedded.

Direction constancy   The stability of an object's perceived direction despite changes in eye position.

Efferent fibers   Neural fibers that carry outgoing commands from the brain to muscles or other action systems.

Entrainment   The process by which the biological clock is synchronized to physical time cycles.

Event processing   *See* Change monitoring.

Eye-head system   A movement-perception system that monitors and differentiates eye- or head-generated from object-generated movement of the visual image on the retina.

Filled duration illusion   An interval filled wth stimulus events is perceived as being longer than an identical interval without stimulus events.

Flow   The perception of time passing.

Focus of expansion   A point in space around which all other stimuli seem to expand. If you are moving forward, it represents the place toward which you are moving.

Image-retina system   A movement-perception system that detects movement within the retinal image.

Induced motion   An illusion of movement of a stationary object created by movement of the background or surround context.

Inflow theory   The suggestion that motion is detected via feedback information from the six extraocular muscles controlling eye movement.

Interstimulus interval   The time span between the end of one stimulus presentation and beginning of the next.

Long-range process   The perceptual system responsible for apparent motion when stimuli are separated by more than 100 msec in time and more than 15 min of visual angle in space.

Macula   The receptor organ of the utricle and saccule. It is responsive to linear acceleration.

Motion aftereffect   An illusion of movement that occurs in the direction opposite to a moving stimulus that an observer has viewed for an extended time.

Now   The interval of time that we interpret as "the present."

Nystagmus   A reflexive, jerky eye movement caused by stimulation of the vestibular organs (cristas) in the semicircular canals.

Object-relative change   The movement of objects in relation to one another.

Otocysts   In primitive vertebrates, fluid-filled cavities functioning to maintain balance and attitude to gravity. *See* Statocysts.

Otoliths   Bony bodies in otocysts.

Outflow theory   The suggestion that brain commands initiating eye movements enable the eye-head movement system to differentiate object-generated from observer-generated movement of the retinal image.

Pacemaker   The mechanism that sets the speed of the biological clock.

Perceptual moment   The hypothetical basic psychological unit of time, about 100 msec.

Position constancy   Stable perceived position of objects despite body, eye, or head movements.

Processing effort model   A theory that time is measured internally by the amount of cognitive work or processing that an individual does during an interval.

Real movement   Physical movement of a stimulus.

Reflex pursuit movements   Smooth eye movements, under vestibular control, that are made to keep the image of a target on the fovea despite head movements.

Restricted environmental stimulation technique   A procedure in which a subject remains in a dark, sound-deadened room for specified intervals of time.

Saccule   A vestibular organ contained in the bony labyrinth.

Selective adaptation   A psychophysical technique in which motion-specific cells in the visual system are fatigued, causing reduced sensitivity to other visual stimuli moving in the same direction and at the same speed as the previously exposed adapting pattern.

Self-motion   The perception that the body is moving through space.

Semicircular canals   Vestibular organs contained in the bony labyrinth, next to the cochlea of the ear.

Sensory convergence   The notion that several different sensory inputs, from different modalities and sources, combine to form an apparently simple perceptual experience.

Short-range process   The perceptual system responsible for apparent movement when stimuli are separated by less than 100 msec in time and less than 15 min of visual angle in space.

Smooth-pursuit movement   The continuous eye movement involved in following a smoothly and steadily moving object.

Statocysts   In primitive invertebrates, motion-sensitive cavities lined with hair cells.

Statolith   A tiny stonelike body resting on the hairs of statocysts and causing them to bend in response to the motion or change of position of an animal.

Storage size model   A model that contends that time is measured internally by the number of items processed and stored in memory during an interval.

Streaming perspective   The optical flow of stimuli as we move through space, centered around the direction of movement.

Subject-relative change   The movement of objects relative to the body.

Suprachiasmatic nucleus (SCN)   A center in the hypothalamus that is believed to be responsible for circadian rhythms.

Temporal processing model   The theory that your experience of the passage of time depends on the amount of attention that you direct toward monitoring time.

Utricle   A vestibular organ contained in the bony labyrinth.

Vection   An illusion of induced motion, in which you experience your body moving through space or tilting because of changes in the optical flow.

Vestibular nuclei   In the brainstem, way stations along the route of nerve fibers from the crista and macula to the cerebellum and cortex.

Vestibular system   The system that monitors the body's movement and orientation in space. Its receptors are located in the bony labyrinth.

Visual context   Visual stimuli that surround or accompany other stimuli.

Voluntary pursuit movements   The eye movements by which you voluntarily track a moving target.

Zeitgeber   The stimulus used to calibrate, or entrain, the biological clock.

CHAPTER
14

The
Constancies

When you look around at the world, your perception is of objects and surfaces. Each of these has a relatively enduring set of properties that are apparent to you, such as size, shape, and color. Now consider a very simple problem. Suppose you are presented with two rectangles made of cardboard and are asked to say which one is larger. If the difference in their physical size is not too small, you would probably have little trouble giving the correct answer. Now consider a second problem. How did you reach your conclusion? Many people would probably give an answer like this: "The larger rectangle produces a larger image in my eye." However, this answer would be quite wrong, as can be seen from Figure 14-1. There we have three different rectangles; the image of each is the same size on your retina, yet each is a representation of a diffent-sized cardboard rectangle "out there" in "the real world." The smallest of these pictured objects would be only a few centimeters on each side "out there," whereas the largest would be over a meter in width and length.

To paraphrase Albert Einstein, "We like to keep things simple, but not too simple." Up to now we have been treating perception in a fairly simple fashion, in that we have adopted the general position that for every distinct kind of perceptual experience—color, brightness, distance, size, or the like—there is some unique stimulus or type of stimulus information that affects our sense organs. Although we may not fully understand what that stimulus is, we believe that we could potentially discover it. We also have been assuming that our perception is related directly to the stimulus information that reaches us, with, perhaps, room for some minor adjustments caused by interactions with or limitations imposed by the nature of our sensory receptors, or the neural processes used to encode the information they receive. However, this assumption that a given identifiable stimulus dimension (such as the size of a retinal image) is related uniquely to a particular perceptual dimension (such as the apparent size of the object we are looking at) is "too simple."

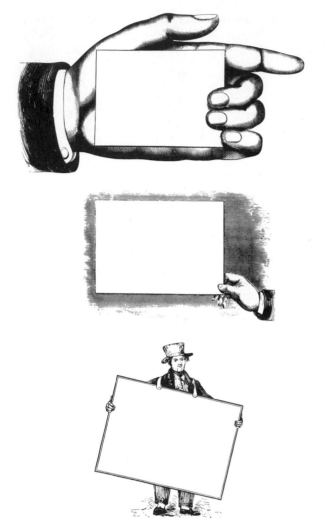

FIGURE 14-1   Three rectangles whose retinal images are all the same size, although each appears to be different in actual size from the others.

THE TASK OF PERCEPTION

Before we go any further in our discussion we must make some distinctions. To begin with, stimuli can be divided into two general classes: a **distal stimulus** is an actual object or event "out there" in the world; a **proximal stimulus** is the information our sensory receptors receive about that object. For example, a tree falling in the forest would be a distal stimulus, whereas the sound of its fall at our ears and the changing light reflected from it to our eyes would be proximal stimuli. The task of perception is to characterize accurately the distal stimulus, since that corresponds to an actual object or event in the real world (Brunswick, 1956; Coren, 1984a). The problems associated with doing this come from the fact that the proximal stimulus is, by itself, not always an ideal source of information about the distal stimulus, as we saw when we judged the size of the real-world objects depicted in Figure 14-1. Other factors such as the *context* in which the distal stimulus occurs, must be taken into account. In this sense, our perception of objects may be viewed as being a form of **multidimensional interaction** (Uttal, 1981).

There is a bit of controversy about the nature of multidimensional interactions. Consider how we go about judging visual size. One approach is called **direct perception,** a notion that began as early as the writings of Hering (1878/1964) and that has been well elaborated since then (Gibson, 1966, 1979; Michaels & Carello, 1981). In direct perception theories, the perception of visual size is completely based on information from the proximal stimulus, here the distribution of light on the retina. Certain features in the proximal stimulus determine perceived size. These features may be higher-level and fairly complex, such as the comparison of the size of the image of the object to the sizes of images of other objects that form its visual context. Presumably, if we look carefully enough, we should be able to isolate a set of *purely visual* stimulus factors that determine our perception of the size of an object.

The alternative approach is of equal vintage. It can be traced back to the works of Helmholtz (1909/1962), has many active supporters (e.g., Epstein, 1973; Rock, 1983; Uttal, 1981), and refers to a **constructive theory** of perception. In constructive theories, perception arises as a form of

unconscious inference, which is to say that it is derived or pieced together from a number of different sources of information. This information may come from other sensory inputs, such as feedback from eye movements, from prior experience that has given us a concept as to the usual size or shape of an object, or even from *expectations* and *guesses* as to the nature of the distal stimulus.

It is important to notice that both direct perception and constructive theories involve some form of multidimensional interactions. The major difference is that in direct perception theories the interactions do not involve any computation or inference and all occur within the same modality as the percept, whereas in constructive theories the interactions may involve other sensory modalities and some fairly complex deductive or inferential procedures. It seems likely that both a direct and a constructive process are ultimately involved in achieving the task of perception, which is to ascertain the actual properties of objects in the environment (e.g., Gogel & DaSilva, 1987a).

PERCEPTUAL CONSTANCIES

If the only information we had about nature were the proximal stimulus, such as the retinal image of an object, our world would be as chaotic as the Wonderland Alice found at the bottom of the rabbit hole. Since the retinal image is larger the closer an object is, an approaching friend would appear to grow larger as she grew nearer. A piece of white paper would appear black when viewed in the moonlight, since the amount of light in the retinal image is no greater under these conditions than in the image of a piece of coal viewed in normal room light. This same piece of paper would appear to change shape continually— the retinal image changing from rectangular to trapezoidal as the paper's angle of tilt was varied—and its color would appear to be blue under fluorescent lighting and yellow under incandescent lighting. Fortunately our perception of objects is much more *constant* than would be expected if the only information available were the proximal stimulus. Your friend remains the same size but changes her distance from you. The piece of paper remains a white rectangle, although you might sense the fact that the color or intensity of the light falling on it, or its angle of tilt relative to you, has changed. This illustrates a very basic aspect of perception, which is that *the properties of objects tend to remain constant in consciousness although our perception of the viewing conditions may change.* The fact that our perception of the world does not vary as much as fluctuations in the proximal stimulus would lead us to expect is what we mean by the *perceptual constancies.*

Although there are many varieties of perceptual constancies, they fall into three general classes. The first pertains to object properties, such as an object's size and shape; the second to certain qualities, such as the whiteness or color of surfaces; and the third to the locations of objects in space relative to the observer.

Each constancy has two major perceptual phases. The first phase involves **registration,** the

process by which the changes in the proximal stimulus are encoded for processing. There is no need for the individual to be consciously aware of this registration process. The second phase involves **apprehension,** the actual subjective experience. This is the conscious component that is available for you to describe. Normally, registration is oriented toward a **focal stimulus,** which is simply the object you are paying attention to. In addition, you also register a set of stimuli that are nearby, or occurring at the same time, which form the **context stimuli.** During apprehension you become aware of two classes of properties, the **object properties** of the focal stimulus, which tend to remain constant, and the **situation properties,** which indicate more changeable aspects of the environment, such as your position relative to the focal object or the amount or color of the available light, and which are derived from cues found in the context. The way these categories interact is shown in Table 14-1, which describes these variables for a number of constancies. If all this appears a bit complicated in

Table 14-1. The Relationships between the Registered and Apprehended Variables in Some of the More Common Perceptual Constancies.

| Constancy | Registered Stimulus (may be unconscious) | | Apprehended Stimulus (conscious) | |
	Focal Stimulus	Context	Constant	Changes
Size constancy	retinal image size	distance cues	object size	object distance
Shape constancy	retinal image shape	orientation cues	object shape	object orientation
Lightness constancy	intensity of light on the retina	illumination cues	surface whiteness	apparent intensity illumination
Color constancy	color of retinal image	illumination cues	surface color	apparent illumination color
Position constancy	retinal location of image	sensed head or eye position	object position in space	head or eye position
Loudness constancy	intensity of sound at the ear	distance cues	loudness of sound	distance from sound
Odor constancy	amount of odorant in the nose	proprioception from sniff	intensity of smell	strength of sniff

theory, in practice it is really quite straightforward. Let us look at some of the more common constancies to see how they work.

SIZE CONSTANCY

Before you can understand size constancy, you must understand what happens to the retinal images of objects as our distance from them varies. As the distance between the eye and the object grows larger, the size of the retinal image grows smaller. This relationship is shown in Figure 14-2. As you probably recall from Chapter 4, retinal image size is usually expressed and measured in terms of visual angle. The visual angle for S_1 (Stimulus 1) is α_1 and for S_2 is α_2. Like other angles, these are expressed in degrees, minutes, and seconds of arc. As an example, the image size of a quarter (25-cent piece) held at arm's length is about 2 deg, whereas at a distance of about 80 m the quarter would have a visual angle of 1 min of arc. At a distance of 5 km it would have the tiny retinal image size of only 1 sec of arc. Thus, as its distance from an observer increases its retinal image size decreases.

Consider what happens as you watch someone walk down the street. Suppose we perceived size only in terms of retinal image size. If such were the case, a man who is 180 cm (about 6 ft) tall would look like a small child when he was at a reasonable distance but would appear to "grow" as he approached us. Of course this does not happen. Instead, we perceive him to be "man size" regardless of his distance from us. This stability of perceived size despite changes in objective distance and retinal image size is called **size constancy.** In essence, it involves assigning a constant size to an object in consciousness, no matter what its distance or retinal size may be.

Size Constancy and Distance Cues

Size constancy, we have seen, is a process by which we "take into account" the apparent distance of an object, in order to "adjust" the perceived size to more accurately represent the actual physical size of the object. For example, in Figure 14-3A we see three men standing in a courtyard. All appear to be about the same size, even though the retinal image size of the apparently most distant individual is only about one-third that of the apparently nearest one. In other words, we estimate

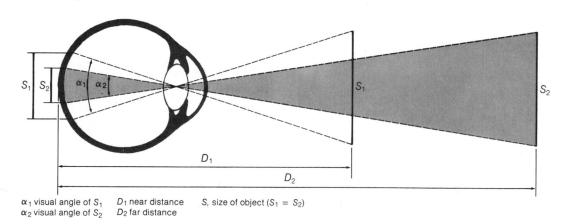

α_1 visual angle of S_1 D_1 near distance S, size of object ($S_1 = S_2$)
α_2 visual angle of S_2 D_2 far distance

FIGURE 14-2   The visual angle. Although the physical size (S) of the object does not change, changes in distance (D) will result in changes in the size of the visual angle (α). Here α_1 (the image of object S_1 close to the eye) is larger than α_2 (the image of object S_2 farther from the eye).

FIGURE 14-3   (A) Three men, whose retinal images grow smaller as they appear to be more distant; however, because of size constancy they appear to be the same size. (B) Here, when the images remain the same size, the more distant man appears to be larger.

distance and size together and adjust our perception of size in accordance with our distance judgment, perceptually "enlarging" more distant objects. You can see how this **constancy scaling** works by looking at Figure 14-3B, where all the images of men are exactly the same size. Here the constancy scaling correction makes the apparently farthest appear much larger. This suggests that changes in apparent distance should alter our perception of apparent size, which is a reasonable suggestion, as can be seen from Demonstration Box 14-1.

How does the perceptual system take depth into account? The simplest answer is that we utilize cues to the distance of the target that are available as part of the visual context. This would suggest that when we increase the number of distance cues constancy should be better, whereas reducing the number of cues should reduce our tendency toward constancy. Many experiments have demonstrated how the availability of cues in the visual array con-

tributes to the maintenance of size constancy, beginning with the early work by Holway and Boring (1941). Simply stated, the more cues, the better the size constancy (e.g., Chevrier & Delorme, 1983). For example, Harvey and Leibowitz (1967) asked observers to choose a size match for a standard target that was placed at various distances. There were two viewing conditions. One corresponded to natural situations with many distance cues, and the second involved the removal of the surrounding context by having the observers view the standard target through a small opening that blocked the view of everything but the target to be observed. Under natural viewing conditions, size matches conformed very well to the predictions based on the efficient operation of the size constancy mechanism. This was the case for all the observer-target distances used in this experiment. However, when the context was removed, size matches conformed to constancy predictions only at viewing distances

DEMONSTRATION BOX 14-1. Size Constancy and Apparent Distance

An easy way to demonstrate how apparent distance affects apparent size requires that you carefully fixate the point marked *X* in the accompanying white square while holding the book under a strong light. After a minute or so, you will form an afterimage (see Chapter 5) of the square. If you now transfer your gaze to a blank piece of paper on your desk, you will see a ghostly dark square floating there. This is the afterimage, which will appear to be several centimeters long on each side. Now shift your gaze so that you are looking at a more distant, light-colored wall.

Again you will see the dark square projected against the wall, but now it will appear to be much larger in size. Because of the nature of an afterimage, its visual angle does not change. But as you project it against surfaces at varying distances from you, its apparent size changes. It appears to be larger when it is projected on a distant surface. This is an example of how size and distance perception interact by means of the size constancy mechanism. The quantitative expression of the relationship is often called **Emmert's law.**

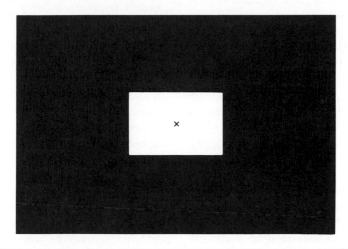

up to about 120 cm. After that, size matches began to deviate from the predictions based on size constancy. This experiment shows the role of distance context in the maintenance of size perception.

Why was there still constancy at the closer distances even though the depth cues were removed? Probably because the manipulation used removed only *visible* distance cues. As we discussed in Chapters 3 and 10, when we fixate objects at different distances, the lens of the eye changes shape to accommodate for changes in fixation distance. Simultaneously, the eyes either converge for near objects or diverge for distant objects

to produce stable binocular foveal fixation. When targets are relatively close to you, information about their distance can be gotten from feedback from the accommodation and convergence actions of the eyes. This suggests that these physiological cues to distance have been incorporated into the multidimensional mix of information resulting in the size constancy.

One important thing to notice in this example is that the source of the distance cues is not really important. The cues do not have to come from the visual array per se, but can come from other sources. We can show this by demonstrating that in the absence of any other information about the distance of the target (such as the pictorial cues to distance catalogued in Chapter 10), changes in accommodation and convergence result in changes in perceived size. This was confirmed by Leibowitz and Moore (1966). Their observers viewed a white triangle in an otherwise completely dark field. They matched the size of this stimulus by making size adjustments in a similar triangle. Accommodation and convergence were varied by inserting prisms and lenses before the eyes. This forced the subjects to adjust their convergence and accommodation to closer or farther distances when viewing the target, although the retinal size remained constant. If these depth cues help to stabilize the perception of size, this experimental manipulation should have resulted in changes in perceived size.

The prediction of these investigators was confirmed. The size of the target judged to be equal to that of the standard triangle increased as accommodation and convergence changes were manipulated to indicate increasing target distance (much as the size of the man increased with increasing apparent distance in Figure 14-3B). Hence, it seems that the state of the *oculomotor* (eye muscle) system, which varies with the distance of the distal stimulus, conveys information that helps to stabilize size perception. Since the perception of size seems to be linked to the perception of distance in

some way, this is one way in which structures within the visual system "take distance into account" in computing the size constancy correction.

Actually, any source of distance information can be used to obtain accurate size constancy. We have seen that visual depth cues trigger size constancy, as do accommodation and convergence. Adding binocular disparity, the depth cue involved in stereopsis (see Chapter 10), can also strengthen size constancy, as shown in Demonstration Box 14-2.

Direct and Constructive Aspects of Size Constancy

Earlier in this chapter we contrasted the *direct* and the *constructive* theories of perception. Direct theories of perception are based on the presumption that all of the information we need for such things as constancy can be found in the proximal stimulus. Geometric regularities, such as the convergence of parallel lines with increasing distance (linear perspective) or the increasing textural density of more distant fields of elements, serve as reliable cues for distance. Such cues may be sufficient to maintain size constancy (Gibson, 1950, 1979; Michaels & Carello, 1981).

For example, we can imagine two objects of the same size sitting on a surface at different distances from the observer. As you know from Chapter 10, the

---

DEMONSTRATION BOX 14-2.   Additional Depth Cues Strengthen Size Constancy

Hold out both of your hands with their backs toward you. One hand should be relatively near you (about 20 cm or 8 in. should do), and the other should be out at arm's length. At first glance, both hands should appear to be about the same size. Now, remove the binocular disparity depth cue by closing one eye. Keeping your hands at these different distances, and your head very steady (to prevent motion parallax as a further depth cue), move your distant hand to the side until its image appears to be just next to the near one. Now when you compare the size of the two hands it should be clear to you that the more distant one appears smaller than the near one, showing a clear weakening of size constancy. You can restore the size constancy by adding additional depth cues— open both eyes and swing your head from side to side, and your hands will again appear to be the same size.

fact that textured surfaces show denser gradations of coarseness as they recede into the distance is a very powerful distance cue. If two objects at different distances appear to cover the same number of textured elements (in other words, their relationship to the textured surface remains constant), they will remain perceptually the same size. This principle was first described in detail in 1604 by the artist Jan de Vries. In Figure 14-4 we have modified one of the drawings he used. You will notice that here we have two rectangular structures (A and B) that appear to be about the same size, but that appear to vary in distance. Despite the fact that their retinal image size differs, notice that each rectangular object is 3 texture elements long and 3 wide (here the texture elements are the square "tiles"), regardless of its location. Notice that this relationship holds even when the viewing angle is

different, as for object D. Different sizes are associated with different ratios between the textures and the objects themselves. Thus A, B, and D appear to be the same height (about 1 texture element), whereas C (whose height in the picture is actually smaller than A) appears to be a much taller object since it is about 4 texture elements high. Thus, according to direct perception, the observer could extract the physical size of the objects (which is simply our size constancy correction) by comparing the relative size of the objects to the size of the surrounding texture elements.

Constructive theories of perception allow for sources of information other than the proximal stimulus to shape the final percept. We have already seen how feedback from the accommodative and convergence movements of the eye might serve such a function. More important than this type of

FIGURE 14-4   Rectangles A, B, and D all appear to be the same size, since each covers the same number of texture elements. (Based on de Vries, 1604/1968)

information for constructive theories, however, is information generated by cognitive judgments and operations or from learned factors and expectations (e.g., Epstein, 1973; Rock, 1983; Uttal, 1981). In this type of theorizing it is probably inappropriate to speak of "cues." Rather, any factor that results in a change in one aspect of perception (here the distance of the object) can bring about a change in another aspect of perception (here the size of the object), regardless of the source of that information (see Hochberg, 1974). Let us see how some nonvisual sources of information can affect our perception of size.

Our experience with the world has already provided us with much information that assists us in maintaining size constancy. For example, we learn that particular objects have typical visual sizes. This *familiar size* information can be used in the absence of any other information to judge the size of an object once it has been identified, or to judge the distance of the object based on its retinal and familiar size, similarly to the situation in Demonstration Box 10-1. Simply put, we have an expectation that familiar objects, such as playing cards or coins, have typical sizes. If we were presented with a very tiny image of a playing card, we would maintain our size constancy by seeing this as a normal-sized playing card viewed from a long distance rather than a playing card that is much smaller than usual (cf. Gogel & DaSilva, 1987b; Higashiyama, 1985; Ono, 1969).

Our experience and expectations also explain an interesting breakdown of size constancy that occurs at very large target-observer distances. You need only to climb to the top of a tall building and note that people below appear to be tiny dolls and cars appear to be little toys. It seems likely that the unusual viewing conditions and exceptional distances are so unfamiliar that they simply do not trigger the size constancy mechanism in this instance (Day, Stuart & Dickinson, 1980). This is supported by the fact that the range of distances over which size constancy works is greater for adults than for children (e.g., Zeigler & Leibowitz,

1957), presumably because adults have had more experience with a greater variety of environmental viewing conditions.

A number of other considerations seem to support some constructive theory factors in size constancy. Some evidence suggests that you do not actually have to *perceive* the distance. Simply *knowing* the distance, such as being told how far an object is from you, seems to be enough to elicit the size constancy adjustment (Pasnak, Tyer & Allen, 1985). Furthermore, if your attention is directed elsewhere, so that the full measure of cognitive processing is not available, your size constancy processing begins to break down (Epstein & Broota, 1986). Demonstration Box 14-3 allows you to see how attention interacts with size constancy.

Neither direct nor constructive theories of perception seem adequate to explain all aspects of size constancy (nor any constancy, for that matter). It is more likely that both processes combine to produce the final perception of size and distance (e.g., Gogel & DaSilva, 1987a).

Size Constancy and Illusion

Size constancy provides stability in our perception of the world by giving our conception of particular objects a consistent set of properties despite variations in the retinal image size. This is usually useful, but under special circumstances it can lead to errors or illusions. To see how this comes about, consider a variation of Figure 14-3: in Figure 14-5A we see two logs lying in the middle of a road. Although they have been drawn to be two different sizes on the paper, the distance cues in the context (perspective, texture, and others) indicate that the upper log is more distant. Because of size constancy we see it as being the same-sized object as the closer log. In Figure 14-5B we have two logs that appear to be different in size, with the more distant one seemingly longer than the closer one, although they have been drawn to be exactly the same physical size. Once again, this merely represents the operation of size constancy. To the

DEMONSTRATION BOX 14-3.   Attention and Size Constancy

Begin with your right hand in front of you at arm's length. Now look directly at your hand and move it toward your face and away again several times. Although the retinal image size is changing, your hand appears to be the same size because of the operation of size constancy.

Next hold the index finger of your other hand up in front of your face (at about 20 cm) as shown in the figure. Look steadily at the finger. Now, while maintaining fixation on your fingertip, bring your right hand toward and away from your face. Try not to

move your eyes from your finger, but try also to pay some attention to the image of your hand as you move it closer and farther from your face. Under these conditions, where your attention is divided and pulled away from simply viewing the target, your size constancy should break down. Now the hand seems smaller when farther and larger when nearer to you, demonstrating that when attention is somewhat diverted we are more apt to experience the proximal (retinal) stimulus changes rather than apply the constancy correction.

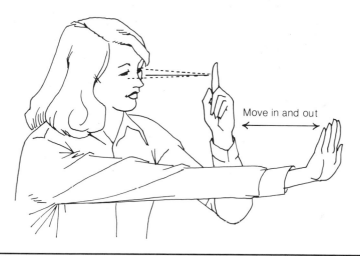

Move in and out

extent that the picture mimics conditions in the real world, the upper log appears to be more distant. In the real world, it could cause the same-sized retinal image as the lower log only under conditions where it was physically longer. Since in the picture the logs have been drawn the same size, the constancy scaling mechanism has correctly adjusted our perception.

The perceptual problem arises with Figure 14-5C, where we see two converging lines and two horizontal lines. Notice that the upper line appears to be slightly longer. Because, like the logs in Fig-

ure 14-5B, the two lines are physically equal in length, this perceptual difference is a visual-geometric illusion (usually called the **Ponzo illusion.** Actually, this is an illusion only in the sense that no context for depth or distance has been drawn into the figure. It is caused by the fact that there are *registered* cues for distance here (the converging perspective lines) that are sufficiently strong to evoke the size constancy mechanism, yet are not sufficiently strong to evoke the conscious *apprehension* of distance (Coren & Girgus, 1977; Gillam, 1980; Gregory, 1966). In some instances

FIGURE 14-5   (A) The two logs lying on the road appear to be at different distances. Therefore their apparent size is the same despite the fact that the apparently more distant log is physically smaller (on the page) than the other one. (B) The logs are identical in size; however, the one that appears to be more distant looks larger. The application of size constancy can lead to illusions of size, as seen in (C), which is the Ponzo illusion and is similar to (B) except that the context indicating distance and depth has been greatly reduced. (Based on Coren & Girgus, 1978)

there is a very fine distinction between a picture and a simple array of lines that produces a visual illusion. It is possible to imagine a child with poor drawing ability producing a figure like 14-5C when asked to draw 14-5B, where the converging lines were really meant to be depth cues!

Cues that are registered in sufficient strength to inappropriately elicit size constancy are often quite subtle. Consider Figure 14-6, where the vertical line marked A appears to be shorter than the vertical line marked B although they are equal in length. This distortion, which is called the **Mueller-Lyer illusion,** has also been explained in terms of size constancy (Coren & Girgus, 1978; Eijkman, Jongsma & Vincent, 1981; Gregory, 1966; Madden & Burt, 1981). For example, the wings turned toward the vertical line might mimic the perspective cues of the outside of a building (shown in dark lines in C), whereas the wings turned away from the vertical line might mimic an interior corner of a room (shown in D). Since the closest point in the array is the plane of the paper, it is easy to see that if the wings imply increases or decreases in distance away from that plane, the vertical shaft in B is more distant than that pictured in A. Hence, the operation of size constancy would enlarge the apparent length of B relative to A. Notice again that this is an illusion of size only in the sense that no depth or distance was intended; therefore, the application of size constancy is inappropriate in this situation.

Several other illusion distortions also seem to result from observers responding to implied depth cues in the configuration (Coren & Girgus, 1978; Ward, Porac, Coren & Girgus, 1977). Perhaps the most spectacular of these is the **moon illusion,** where the moon on the horizon appears to be larger than the moon when it is high in the sky, despite the fact that it is optically always the same-sized disk. One explanation of this phenomenon is based on size constancy (Kaufman & Rock, 1962). The notion is that the moon is seen as if it were on the ''surface'' of the sky. If the sky were a uniform hemisphere there would be no illusion. However, the sky actually appears to be a flattened bowl, with the horizon farther away than the zenith, as shown in Figure 14-7. This is because when you look toward the horizon you have many depth cues for distance (texture gradients, familiar objects, etc.), whereas when you look up there is only sky. This means that the moon appears farther away when on the horizon than when at zenith and, hence, by the action of size constancy, its apparent size is apprehended as being larger. Although size constancy does not account for all the effects in the moon illusion (see Hershenson, 1982; McCready, 1986; Reed, 1984), nor totally for all other illusions of size (see Coren & Girgus, 1978), it certainly seems to play a

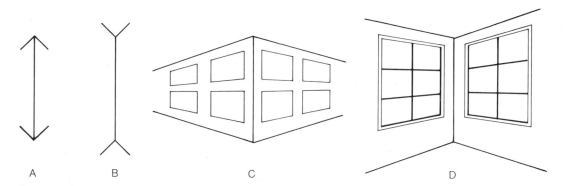

FIGURE 14-6   (A) The underestimated segment of the Mueller-Lyer illusion. (B) The overestimated segment. (C and D) The corresponding perspective configurations.

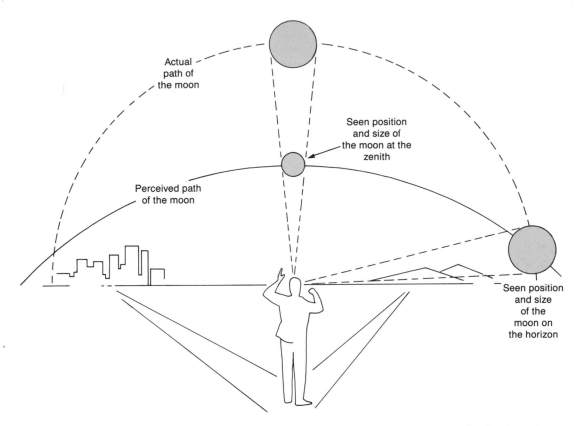

Actual
path of
the moon

Seen position
and size of
the moon at the
zenith

Perceived path
of the moon

Seen position
and size
of the
moon on
the horizon

FIGURE 14-7 The fact that the moon is registered to be more distant when it is at the horizon than when it is overhead helps to explain the moon illusion.

role in producing some interesting illusions of size, as well as correcting for normal variations in size of the retinal image that occur with the changing distance of viewed objects.

SHAPE CONSTANCY

We have spent a good deal of time describing size constancy because the other constancies have much in common with it. Each involves the registration of either environmental cues or cues about our relationship to an object in the environment, and the apprehension of the object properties as being con-

stant while the environment changes or our own relative condition changes. Thus, Epstein and Park (1964) have defined **shape constancy** as the relative constancy of the perceived shape of an object despite variations in its orientation. To see why such a form of constancy correction is necessary, consider what happens when you view a rectangular card from different angles, as in Figure 14-8. As we increase the tilt of the card, the retinal image becomes more like a trapezoid with the formerly vertical sides tapering outward. Yet the object still "looks" rectangular. The same happens when we swing a door outward. The large changes in the shape of retinal image are ignored, and the door

What the situation   Image seen from   Shape of the
is from the side   the front   perceived surface

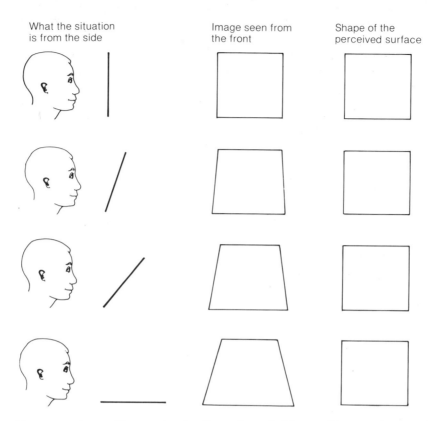

FIGURE 14-8   Shape constancy. Changes in the tilt or slant of objects will cause changes in the shape of the retinal image; however, perceived shape remains constant. (Based on Lindsay & Norman, 1977)

still appears to be rectangular. In achieving shape constancy, the perceptual system appears to compensate for changes in slant in a way analogous to the compensation for distance changes in size constancy. Follow the instructions in Demonstration Box 14-4 to see the operation of shape constancy for yourself.

There is an intimate relationship between size and shape constancy—both are related to distance perception. However, for shape constancy the distance information pertains to the relative distance of different parts of the object from the observer, in other words, its orientation in space or its slant. In unrestricted viewing, with many contextual cues

available, observers tend to perceive the shape and slant of objects with remarkable accuracy (Lappin & Preble, 1975). As in the size constancy situation, when observers are prevented from using contextual or depth information that would indicate the degree of slant, the operation of shape constancy becomes less effective and the percept comes to reflect the retinal situation rather than the actual object (Leibowitz & Bourne, 1956; Leibowitz, Wilcox & Post, 1978).

Observers use several strategies to assist in the judgment of orientation and to supplement contextual information. For example, in Figure 14-9A we have a shape (the letter *E*) that has a common or a

---

DEMONSTRATION BOX 14-4.   Shape Constancy

Look at the box in the accompanying figure. Most people believe that a dime will fit inside the top of this box. Try placing a dime (flat on one face) into the box. Does it fit?

The reason that the top surface of this box appeared to be large enough to accommodate the dime is because you made a shape (and size) constancy correction. The shape constancy correction changed the appearance of the top of the box into a square; the size constancy correction made the sides of the box top appear equal. Look back at the box and notice that its real physical shape is a parallelogram, not a square.

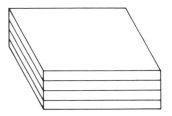

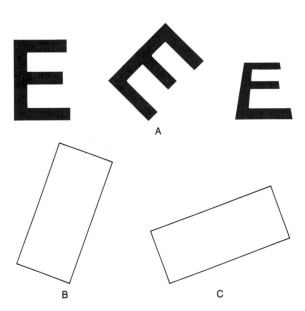

FIGURE 14-9   (A) We can tell how some shapes are tilted in space because of our familiarity with them. For less common shapes we assume that the longest axis indicates "upright"; hence, we will see (C) as more tilted than (B), although they are both tilted the same amount from the horizontal.

normative orientation based on our experiences with this form. We can use such normative information to infer whether the shape is upright, rotated, or tilted (e.g., Braine, Plastow & Greene, 1987; Rock, 1973). In the absence of such prior experience, we make certain presumptions about shapes. For example, we presume that the longest dimension (sometimes called the *principle axis*) represents the upright dimension. Thus, we are apt to consider the rectangle shown in Figure 14-9C as more tilted than that shown in Figure 14-9B (cf. Humphreys, 1983, 1984).

The way we approach the task of looking at objects may also affect the degree of constancy we obtain. For example, Carlson (1977) and Kaess (1980) asked observers either to report the sizes and shapes of the objects they were viewing (the **objective instruction**) or to report the sizes and shapes of their retinal images (the **projective instruction**). The objective instruction is closest to normal viewing, where the perceptual task is to derive what is ''out there.'' The projective instruction is similar to what an artist must do in trying to translate the scene being viewed onto a canvas consisting of sizes and shapes of colored regions that will represent objects in space when viewed by an observer. It has been shown many times (e.g., Gilinsky, 1955; Leibowitz & Harvey, 1969) that when observers are asked to adopt the projective viewing set they show less constancy, although it appears that they cannot completely turn off the constancy correction. Observers continue to make constancy corrections although the judgments become more like the retinal image (Lappin & Preble, 1975; Lichte & Borresen, 1967). There are other viewing factors that affect the degree of constancy obtained. For instance, Epstein, Hatfield, and Muise (1977) showed that, much like any cognitive task, the more processing time available, the more shape constancy is found. Epstein and Lovitts (1985) showed that, much like size constancy, the more attention you pay to the task, the better the shape constancy correction.

LIGHTNESS OR WHITENESS CONSTANCY

How light or white an object appears to be is also affected by a constancy mechanism. The amount of light at different points in our retinal image coming from an object (the **retinal illuminance**) is determined by two things. The first is the amount of light from any source, such as the sun or a light bulb, that falls on the object. This is called **external illuminance.** The second, called **reflectance,** is the proportion of light falling on the object that is reflected to the eye of the observer. The reflectance is the object property that most closely corresponds to how light or white a surface appears. For example, a white surface will reflect most (perhaps 80%–90%) of the light that falls on it. In contrast, a black surface will absorb a great deal of light, and the proportion reflected will be quite small (often less than 4%–5%). Roughly speaking, the amount of light reaching the eye can be obtained from the simple formula

light at eye = reflectance × external illuminance

Thus, if a surface that reflects 90 percent (or 0.9) of the incident light receives that light from a source with a physical intensity of 100 units, we would calculate a "light at eye" value of 90 units. Although not all of the light reaching the eye from a surface actually reaches the retina itself, since some is absorbed or reflected by the cornea, lens, and the like, the proportion of the "light at eye" that does reach the retina is a constant. Thus, retinal illuminance does depend directly on the amount of "light at eye."

Your impression of how light an object is, however, is relatively independent of the amount of light reaching your eye and, thus, of the retinal illuminance. A piece of white paper appears to be approximately the same shade of white whether it is viewed in dim light or bright light. A piece of coal viewed in bright sunlight will still appear black even though it may be reflecting a greater amount of light to the eye than would a piece of white paper viewed in ordinary room light (i.e., $0.05 \times 1,000$ units of sunlight falling on the coal, which equals 50 units of light reaching the eye from the coal, is greater than 0.9×50 units of room light falling on the paper, which equals only 45 units of light reaching the eye from the paper). This is an example of **lightness** or **whiteness constancy.**

Two types of explanation have been given for lightness constancy. The first is based on direct perception theory, in which constancy is maintained by stimulus relationships. In size constancy, the ratio or relationship between texture element size and the object size is significant. In lightness constancy, a similar ratio is suggested between regions of illuminance on the retina.

This constant-ratio notion works as follows. Suppose you are looking at two pieces of paper; one is white with a reflectance of 80 percent, and the other is gray with a reflectance of 40 percent. They are illuminated by a light source of 100 units of intensity. The amount of light reaching your eye would then be 80 and 40 units, respectively.

Suppose that we now reduce the intensity of the light by half to 50 units. Now the amount of light reaching your eye is 40 and 20 units, respectively. We might now predict that the white patch would appear to be gray, and similar in lightness to the gray patch viewed under the intense illumination. This, however, is not the case—the white still appears white and the gray appears gray. It is not the total retinal illumination that matters, but rather the ratio of the intensities of the two patches of light on the retina, which remains constant with that from the white surface twice as intense as that from the gray surface, regardless of the intensity of the external illumination.

The constant-ratio explanation of lightness constancy has received experimental support from a number of researchers, such as Wallach (1948, 1972), who verified it using the experimental setup shown in Figure 14-10. There have been a number of elaborations of this theory (cf. Cornsweet, 1970, 1985; Richards, 1977; Marr, 1974), and some suggestion that the mechanism might work via the operation of lateral inhibition, which we discussed in Chapter 4. Such a theoretical

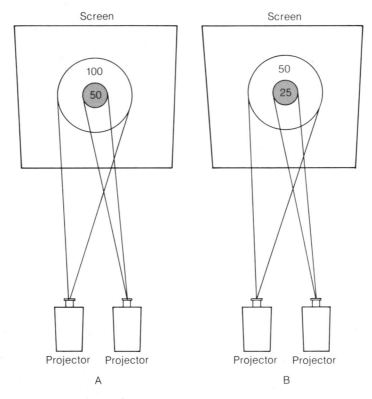

FIGURE 14-10   Relational determinants of lightness constancy. Wallach (1948, 1972) found that regardless of absolute physical intensity, equal lightness would be perceived when targets stood in an equal intensity ratio with their surroundings. In this example, which demonstrates the experimental technique used by Wallach, the central circles will appear to be equally bright because they both stand in a 1/2 to 1 intensity ratio with their respective surroundings. The numbers in the figure represent relative light intensity after a subject has made a match by adjusting the central target in B to match the central target in A.

mechanism would work if we assume that the amount of lateral inhibition increases as we increase the intensity of retinal illumination at any one point on the retina. This would result in lightness constancy, since the amount of stimulation and the amount of inhibition would both increase equally, leaving the overall response of the eye relatively unchanged.

One prediction made by the constant-ratio theory is that lightness constancy should depend on having several different levels of reflectance under the same illumination in close proximity in the visual field. This prediction is confirmed in the results of a classic experiment by Gelb (1929). He used a concealed light source to illuminate an object that was placed in a dimly lit field, as shown in Figure 14-11. The illuminated object was a black disk, but observers reported seeing a white disk in dim light rather than a very brightly lit black disk. Of course, this represents a complete failure of constancy. If constancy were operating, the observers would see the black disk as black even though it was very brightly lit. Gelb then tried a second manipulation. He placed a piece of white paper in front of the brightly lit black disk. As soon as this was done, observers reported that the disk looked black. In other words, with the addition of the reference white paper constancy returned. However, as soon as the piece of white paper was removed, the black disk returned to its former white appearance. Although these results appear to strongly support the direct perception notion of constant intensity ratios as the basis for lightness constancy, Gilchrist and Jacobsen (1984) have shown that other factors still must play a role, since we do maintain lightness constancy even in a world of one reflectance level, such as an all-white room!

A second explanation based on constructive theory would add a number of factors to the constant ratio explanation of lightness constancy. Such a theory would argue that the observer responds to cues indicating the nature of the illumination falling on the object, and adjusts the apprehended lightness of the object in consciousness accordingly.

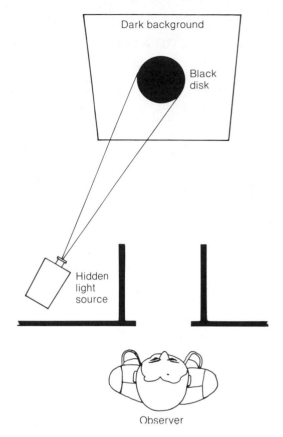

FIGURE 14-11   **Experimental situation used by Gelb (1929) to test for lightness constancy when a light source was hidden from view.**

Thus, in the Gelb experiment it could be argued that the introduction of the white piece of paper provides a cue indicating that there is an intense, hidden light source. This information evokes the formerly inoperative constancy correction.

Several such cues seem to be important in triggering lightness constancy. For instance, the presence of visible shadows produces a lightness correction (Gilchrist & Jacobsen, 1984; MacLeod, 1947). Also, cues as to the location of the object relative to the light source provide information to allow us to correct our perception of the whiteness or lightness of the object, despite the retinal illu-

---

DEMONSTRATION BOX 14-5.   Lightness Constancy

To a certain extent, lightness constancy depends on assumptions that the observer makes about the nature of the world. Consider the gray tube shown here. Notice that the gray of the interior of the tube appears to be lighter than the gray of the exterior. In fact, they are the same gray. Coren and Komoda (1973) suggested that this apparent lightness difference involves a cognitive adjustment based on presumptions that we make about the environment. If the tube were real, its interior would be likely to receive less light than its exterior. In the tube pictured here, however, the same amount of light reaches the eye from both the apparent interior and the apparent exterior surfaces. This could only happen if the interior surface reflects a greater proportion of the light that reaches it; in other words, the internal surface must have a greater reflectance. This demonstration shows one way in which lightness constancy operates. The visual system makes presumptions about the amount of light reaching surfaces and adjusts the perceptual experience so that the apparent lightness corresponds to the assumed relative reflectances rather than to the actual distribution of light reaching the eye.

Also notice one other interesting aspect of the tube shown here, namely that either the right- or the left-hand portion can be viewed as the interior or the exterior surface. A figure that can assume several different orientations depending on one's point of view is called a *reversible figure*. Notice how the apparent lightness difference between the two sides changes depending on whether you see the right or the left side as the interior surface. The apparent inner surface, regardless of whether it is the right or the left, appears to be the lighter one.

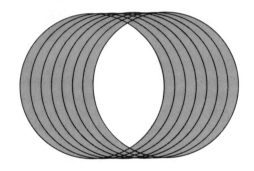

---

mination intensity (e.g., Beck, 1965; Flock & Freedberg, 1970; Hochberg & Beck, 1954). Even information about the relative spatial relationships among objects seems to contribute to this effect (Gilchrist, 1980; Mershon & Gogel, 1970). Demonstration Box 14-5 shows how your presumptions about the illumination falling on a surface can affect its apparent lightness.

COLOR OR HUE CONSTANCY

Similar to the size and intensity changes of the retinal image, there are systematic changes in the spectral composition of the retinal image that could

be registered as color or hue changes. Nonetheless, within limits, we can identify red as red whether it is viewed under fluorescent lights that have a dominant blue hue or incandescent lights that are basically yellow. **Color constancy** refers to our ability to maintain the percept of a particular hue throughout variations in the quality of the illuminance and the reflectance properties of an object's surface pigment. Based on our discussion of lightness constancy, we know that such variations will change the properties of the retinal image in terms of both luminance and wavelength. However, just as in lightness constancy, our perception of color is not based completely on the properties of the image on the retina but on the relative composition of sur-

---

DEMONSTRATION BOX 14-6.   Color Constancy

To carry out this demonstration you will need a re-duction screen, which is simply a ½ cm hole cut into the center of a dark piece of cardboard. In addition, you will need a fluorescent and a tungsten light source (such as your desk lamp and your room light, respectively) and a piece of colored paper (green works best). Hold the paper under the tungsten light. Notice its color. Next hold the colored sheet under a fluorescent lamp and notice that it still appears to be the same color under both light sources. Now look at the paper through the reduction screen, making sure that nothing else is visible through the hole except the patch of color. If you have used green paper, it should appear to be yellow-green under the tungsten light but blue-green when under the fluorescent lamp. In a full-cue situation with context information available, the operation of color constancy prevented you from seeing this hue change.

---

rounding colors in the field (e.g., Brou, Sciancia, Linden & Lettvin, 1986; Land, 1977) and also on our perception of the nature of the illuminant falling on a surface. An example of color constancy is shown in Demonstration Box 14-6.

OTHER CONSTANCIES

There are many other constancies, some well-known, some less obvious. For example, there is an auditory version of size constancy called **loudness constancy.** In this situation, the perceived loudness of a sound source remains constant, even though the sound level at your ear is diminishing because you are moving farther away from the source.

There are also several other visual constancies. We already encountered one class of these in Chapter 13. There we saw that despite the fact that the retinal image moves we do not experience the world as moving but recognize that this change is due to our eye movements. This phenomenon is known as **position constancy,** which we saw is controlled by feedback of some sort from our eye and head movements combined with the actual movements of the visual image across the retina. Similar, but not the same, is **direction constancy,** in which despite our head and eye movements the egocentric direction of objects (where they lie relative to our bodies) remains constant.

Position and direction constancy can be distinguished from each other in the following way. Eye movements do not change egocentric direction, but head and body movements can. For example, look at an object that is straight ahead of your body. Now shift your head to one side. Since we tend to use the head as the reference point for egocentric direction (see Chapter 10), the object no longer seems to be directly straight ahead. Although the object is now perceived to lie in a different direction, its position in space is the same as it was before the head movement. Position and direction constancy are related but still separable phenomena (Shebilske, 1977).

There is even a kind of **odor constancy.** When you are sniffing an object, a deep sniff will tend to pull more of the odorous molecules into your nose. We know that if we artificially give a large puff of some vapors to you, it will smell more intense than a smaller puff (e.g., Rehn, 1978). Yet when you actually sniff something, its "smelliness" remains constant despite the strength of your sniff, hence demonstrating odor constancy (Teghtsoonian, Teghtsoonian, Berglund & Berglund, 1978).

As we go through this list of constancies, a pattern ought to be emerging. The purpose of perception is to derive information about the nature of the external environment and the objects that inhabit it. The viewing conditions, our relationship to objects, and our own exploratory behaviors will very frequently change the pattern of the proximal stimuli at our receptor surface. The constancies, then, are a complex set of "corrections" that take into account the ongoing conditions and allow us to extract a stable set of object properties from the continuous flow of sensory inputs at our receptors. Were it not for such constancy corrections, objects would have no permanent properties in consciousness at all. They would continually change size, shape, lightness, color, and direction, with every move we make. Consciousness and sanity would be difficult to sustain in a world of such sudden and frequent changes.

GLOSSARY

The following definitions are specific to this book.

Apprehension   The conscious representation of a perceptual experience.

Color constancy   The phenomenon whereby the color of an object does not appear to change despite changes in the spectral composition of the light falling on it.

Constancy scaling   The process by which the size of a target is changed in consciousness in order to correct for registered viewing distance.

Constructive theory   An approach to constancy contending that perception may be altered by experience, or other factors not in the proximal stimulus.

Context stimuli   Stimuli that are near to, or occur at the same time as, the stimulus you are perceiving.

Direct perception   An approach to constancy maintaining that all aspects of the percept must be directly derived from components of the proximal stimulus.

Direction constancy   The stability of an object's perceived egocentric direction despite changes in eye or head position.

Distal stimulus   An object or event in the environment.

Emmert's law   The quantitative expression of the relationship between apparent size and apparent distance; objects appear larger when projected on a more distant surface.

External illuminance   The amount of light falling on an object.

Focal stimulus   The stimulus you are perceiving.

Lightness constancy   The process by which the apparent lightness of a stimulus remains unchanged, despite changes in physical illumination.

Loudness constancy   The process by which the apparent loudness of a sound source remains unchanged despite changes in your distance from it.

Moon illusion   An illusion in which the moon appears larger when near the horizon than when high in the sky.

Mueller-Lyer illusion   An illusion of length caused by placing inward or outward facing wings on the ends of lines.

Multidimensional interaction   Interactions between several stimulus channels or sources of information.

Object properties   The physical properties characterizing an object, such as size, shape, etc.

Objective instruction   Instruction directing an observer to report the sizes and shapes of real-world objects.

Odor constancy   The process by which odor intensity appears to be unchanged, despite variations in the strength of sniffing.

Ponzo illusion   A length illusion produced by registration of converging lines as distance cues.

Position constancy   Stable perceived position of objects despite body, eye, or head movements.

Projective instruction   Instruction directing an observer to report the sizes and shapes of parts of his or her retinal image.

Proximal stimulus   Information about a distal stimulus that reaches the receptors, such as visual image on the retina, or sound at the ears.

Reflectance   The proportion of light reflected from a surface.

Registration   Perceptual representation of information extracted from the proximal stimulus, but not necessarily consciously apprehended.

Retinal illuminance   The amount of light falling on the retina.

Shape constancy   The process by which the apparent shape of an object remains constant despite changes in the shape of the retinal image.

Situation properties   The conditions affecting the way objects are viewed, such as your distance from them or the amount of ambient light.

Size constancy   The stability of perceived size despite changes in objective distance and retinal image size.

Unconscious inference   A process by which information from a number of sources is unconsciously put together to create a perception.

Whiteness constancy   *See* Lightness constancy.

CHAPTER
15

Attention

My experience is what I agree to attend to. Only those items which I notice, shape my mind.

—WILLIAM JAMES (1890, p. 402)

Our ability to perceive, process, and interpret the numerous and diverse stimuli that continually bombard our receptors is limited. For this reason, we are forced to choose among all that is there to be looked at, listened to, felt, smelled, or tasted. The various ways by which we select among stimuli as we sense our world are often grouped together under the general label of *attention*.

VARIETIES OF ATTENTION

Attention has several different aspects. For example, think back to the last time you were reading this book and the various extraneous events that distracted you. You got a cramp in your foot and initiated a stretching movement; a fire engine screamed by outside and you listened until the siren stopped somewhere down the block; a flicker of movement in the periphery of your visual field

caused you to look toward the door to the room where your roommate was bringing you a midnight snack. In all of these cases important environmental events demanded an **orienting** response. That is, your attention was drawn, or pulled, to the source of a sudden change in your sensory world. Some events you gave only brief attention, as when you initiated the foot-stretch. Other events you listened to (the fire siren) or looked at (your roommate bringing the snack) for longer periods of time. While you attended to some stimuli you were also excluding many others, hence you were probably unaware of the goldfish swimming in its bowl or the humming of the refrigerator in the next room. Technically we would say that you were **filtering** out the extraneous events, attending to only one, or perhaps a few, **information channels** (distinct and separable sources of stimulus information).

As you continued to study this book, perhaps your attention wandered for a moment and you thought of the exam scheduled for tomorrow in calculus. You wondered where your notes were and looked up, scanning your room for the green binder you would be poring over in a few minutes. You were **searching** for a relevant stimulus in the environment, scanning your sensory world for partic-

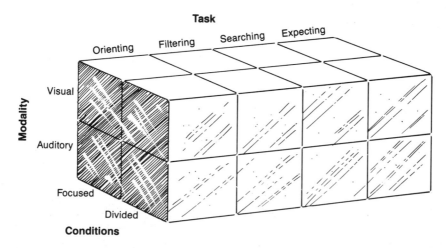

FIGURE 15-1   A representation of various perceptual attention situations dealt with in this chapter.

ular features or combinations of features. Finally, just as you were about to start studying your math notes, you paused, realizing that it was at about this time every night that the wolves in the zoo next door began to howl at the moon. You listened for a few moments. Yes, there they were, right on time. You were **expecting** something to happen and momentarily attended to "empty space" until it did. In all of these situations, different forms of attention were called on and each played a major role in determining your conscious perceptual experience.

In what follows, we describe in more detail some of what is known about how attention operates in these four tasks: orienting, filtering, searching, and expecting. Our attention is restricted to just the visual and auditory modalities, since the most work has been done on these, but our conclusions apply to the other modalities as well. By way of definition, it must be clear that each of the tasks can involve a single target or event (**focused attention**), or several (**divided attention**). Figure 15-1 is a summary of all the situations we discuss in this chapter.

ORIENTING

The simplest form of selecting among the stimulus inputs is to *orient* your sensory receptors toward one set of stimuli and away from another. In this sense we might say that you do not passively see or hear, but rather you actively look or listen.

Orienting Reflex

Whenever a sudden movement or loud sound happens in your environment, your attention tends to be drawn toward that event. You have all seen a dog or a cat prick up its ears and turn its head toward a sudden sound. The animal is performing the most primitive form of **orienting response**, which involves adjusting the sense organs so they can optimally pick up information about the event. Re-

sponses such as flicking the eye in the direction of a sound or peripheral movement occur automatically and are collectively referred to as the **orienting reflex.** This is such a reliable reflex (e.g., Butterworth, 1981; Muir & Field, 1979) that eye- and head-turns toward sounds have been used to test the hearing of newborn infants. The best stimuli to elicit the orienting reflex are often loud sounds and suddenly appearing bright lights, changes in contours, or movements in the peripheral visual field that are not regular, predictable occurrences. When these stimuli happen, the animal, or human, turns its eyes or ears so as to fixate the visual object or sound source, and often orients the head and body to face toward the event as well. A variety of other behaviors also occur, such as postural adjustments, skin conductance changes, pupil dilation, decrease in heart rate, a pause in breathing, and constriction of the peripheral blood vessels (see Rohrbaugh, 1984, for more details). In short, every resource is focused on the stimulating event, to allow its significance to be understood as quickly as possible.

The orienting reflex seems to be triggered by unexpected changes in our environment. It is as though we had an internal "model" of the immediate world of stimuli around us. When we notice a departure of stimulus input from that model, we reflexively attend to that stimulus in order to update that model (Donchin, 1981; Sokolov, 1975). This is consistent with the fact that the orienting reflex rapidly *habituates*. This means that it becomes weaker and less likely to happen if the same stimulus, no matter how strong and sudden, is repeated again and again. The response, however, recovers to full strength with any change in the nature or form of the stimulus.

Covert Orienting

Up to now we have been dealing only with *overt orienting* responses, which actually involve looking at or turning toward a stimulus. Although this is one of the most direct signs that we are attending to something, a number of researchers have pointed out that it is possible to attend to an event or stimulus without making any overt sign that we are doing so. For example, Helmholtz (1909/1962) observed that he could direct his attention voluntarily to any portion of an absolutely featureless dark field at will without the necessity of an eye movement or change in accommodation or convergence. This shift of attentional focus, which is dissociated from any visible change in overt eye/head/body orientation, is called *covert attention*. A common example of covert attention is when you become aware of a familiar voice and the conversation it is having somewhere else at a party even while you look at, nod at, even say "uh-huh" every once in a while to the person in front of you. Most modern research on attention takes for granted that overt orienting is not necessary for paying attention. Typically, in an experiment eye/head/body movements are strictly controlled, or they are made irrelevant by using headphones or such short stimulus presentations that there is no time to shift the eyes to fixate the stimulus. Such controlled presentations allow researchers to separate the effects of overt orienting from more covert shifts of attention. When your attention is involuntarily drawn to a stimulus, without any overt orienting response, we refer to this as **covert orienting.** It is similar to the orienting reflex in that in such instances we seem to have no choice about what we pay attention to.

There are many ways your attention can be seized by certain stimuli. A dramatic example capitalizes on the fact that visual stimuli seem to be more capable of drawing our attention than auditory stimuli. This is the phenomenon ventriloquists depend on, called **visual capture.** Demonstration Box 15-1 allows you to experience this for yourself.

An interesting experimental demonstration of how attention can be drawn to a stimulus was made by Yantis and Jonides (1984, Jonides & Yantis, 1988). They demonstrated that the abrupt appearance of a stimulus in the visual field captures visual attention and gives that stimulus an advantage in terms of how quickly or accurately it can be responded to. They asked observers to say whether a letter target, whose identity was indicated at the beginning of each trial, was present in a field of other distractor letters. On each trial, one letter appeared abruptly in the visual field while either one or three others appeared gradually by the fading of selected lines in figures that had been displayed previously, as shown in Figure 15-2. Sometimes the target letter was the abruptly appearing one, sometimes it was one of the gradually appearing letters. When the target appeared abruptly, observers detected it significantly more quickly than when it faded on. Moreover, it didn't matter whether there were two or four distractor letters to check when the target appeared abruptly. When the target was one of the gradually appearing letters, however, it took significantly longer to detect when there were four letters in the display than when there were two. The abruptly appearing stimulus seems to have been drawing attention to itself. If it was the target, a positive response could immediately be made; if it wasn't the target, then the other figures had to be checked for the target before a response could be made, slowing down that response. Even if the abruptly appearing figure wasn't the target, observers still covertly oriented toward it first, before they checked any of the other figures.

A similar phenomenon happens in the auditory modality. In the early experiments on divided attention, subjects were given a different message in each of their two ears by means of headphones. They were asked to pay attention to and repeat the message they were hearing in one ear (this procedure is called **shadowing**) while another message was delivered to the other ear. When an abrupt or distinctive sound was presented or an unexpected change, such as a switch from a male to a female voice, occurred in the nonshadowed ear, subjects tended to "stumble" or lose the continuity of their shadowing (see e.g., Kahneman, 1973). Appar-

DEMONSTRATION BOX 15-1. Visual Capture

Visual capture is a phenomenon in which attention is caught by a visual stimulus in a way that results in an illusion of auditory localization. Whenever you are listening to a sound, such as a voice talking, there is a tendency to try to identify visual events, or objects, that could be causing the sound. When the ventriloquist's dummy is moving its mouth and limbs, and the ventriloquist is talking without moving *his* mouth, then your visual attention is "captured" by the dummy's movements and you *hear* the ventriloquist's voice coming from its mouth, even though it is really the ventriloquist speaking.

You can demonstrate this effect for yourself by obtaining two television sets (or going to a store that sells them and asking to use two of theirs for a "scientific demonstration"). Place them side by side, about 500 centimeters apart, and tune both sets in to the same newscast, talk show, or other show in which

the sound is highly correlated with the picture. (You could also use a radio and a television set, tuning in to a simulcast show like some concerts.) Now turn off the sound on one of the sets and turn off the picture on the other. Move back a short distance and look at a place between the two sets while paying attention to the picture-displaying set. The sound seems to come from that set, even though its sound is turned off. It actually doesn't matter where you look, the sound will seem to come from the set with the picture. You could also try moving the sets apart to see how powerful the phenomenon is. You will be surprised at how far apart the sets can be before the actual sound source dominates. By the way, this also explains why when you are watching a film the sound seems to come from the actors' mouths, even though the speakers may be located at the side of the film screen, or even in the back of the room.

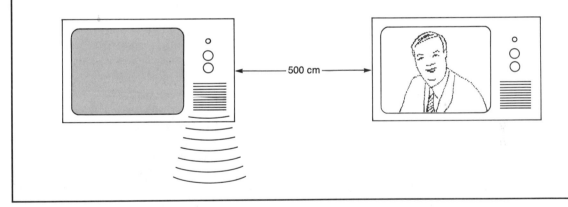

enty their attention was drawn involuntarily to the nonshadowed message, causing them to fail to hear what they were supposed to be attending to and thus to interrupt the smooth flow of the shadowing.

In both of the examples above, attention was drawn to some conspicuous stimulus somewhere in the visual or auditory field. We refer to such a stimulus as a **stimulus cue.** Orienting, filtering,

and searching all depend on the presence of one or more stimulus cues toward which attention is either drawn (orienting) or directed (filtering or searching). When we receive information in advance about where or when something is likely to happen, but there is no stimulus cue available toward which to orient our attention (we call this an **information cue**), attentional phenomena appear to be quite

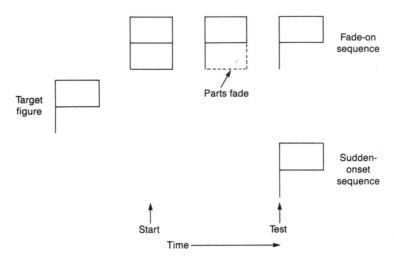

FIGURE 15-2   The upper sequence shows how a stimulus is gradually presented by fading lines as opposed to sudden onset of the stimulus in the Yantis & Jonides (1984) study. Sudden-onset stimuli were more easily detected.

different. This suggests that our expectations interact with how we direct our attention, a matter discussed in a later section of this chapter, Expecting.

The Attentional Gaze

A useful way of conceptualizing some of the findings in covert visual orienting, and in visual search as well, is a metaphor we will call the **attentional gaze.** Other terms have been suggested for this concept (e.g., a *zoom lens* by Eriksen & Hoffman, 1972, Eriksen & St. James, 1986, and Eriksen & Murphy, 1987; a *spotlight* by Hernandez-Peon, 1964, and Treisman, 1982; the *mind's eye* by Jonides, 1980), but attentional gaze is the most general. In this metaphor, we imagine that your attention can "gaze" about independently of where your eyes are looking. In the case of orienting, attention can be drawn to a stimulus cue anywhere in the visual field where there is adequate acuity and sensitivity to register it, either by an abrupt onset, as above, or by movement or other conspicuous changes (but see Jonides & Yantis, 1988). Such covert attentional shifts seem to take place as

though you are swinging your gaze through space with a fixed velocity of about 125 degrees per second—that's only 8 msec to move 1 deg (see Tsal, 1983). Notice that this implies that your attention does not "jump" from one stimulus to another, but rather that in shifting your attention from point *A* to point *B* your attentional gaze actually moves through all the intermediate positions (Shulman, Remington & McLean, 1979; but see also Murphy & Eriksen, 1987).

Auditory attention also acts as if it has a direction of gaze. It can be drawn to particular spatial locations in a way similar to that of visual attention. However, auditory attention moves at about 233 deg/sec, almost twice as fast as the shift of visual attention (Rhodes, 1987). Another difference is that for shifts of gaze greater than 90 deg the time it takes to move attention no longer increases with increasing distance; instead, auditory attention seems to "pop up" at the new location rather than systematically traveling through space.

One major limitation on both the visual and auditory attentional gaze mechanisms is that, like the movement of your eyes, your attention cannot be drawn simultaneously to more than one location in the visual field at any one instant (Eriksen & Yeh, 1985; Van Der Heijden, Wolters, Groep & Hagenaar, 1987; Yantis & Jonides, 1984). Thus, divided covert orienting would seem to be as difficult to accomplish as divided overt orienting, given that you can't point your head, body, or eyes in more than one direction at the same time.

There are three aspects of the attentional gaze that are important in the processing of sensory information. At any one moment attention may be described as having a *locus,* an *extent,* and a *detail set.* As noted above, the attentional gaze shifts around much as your eyes move to take in visual information. Once attention is located at a particular place, or **locus,** in the visual field, processing of stimuli occurring at or near that locus is improved. It is improved more if the locus is near the fovea than if it is in the more peripheral regions of the retina (Shulman, Sheehy & Wilson, 1986). The **extent** of the area over which attention is spread can be controlled by making the stimulus cue larger or smaller (LaBerge, 1983; Podgorny & Shepard, 1983). The greater the extent, the less the processing efficiency. Processing also becomes less efficient for stimuli that are farther away from the center of the attended region (Eriksen & St. James, 1986).

Finally, there is some evidence that the attentional gaze is set or calibrated for a particular level of detail at any one time. In the visual modality, for example, this **detail set** tends to direct the focus of attention to elements of a particular relative size. Several studies have shown that observers can focus selectively on either the more global (relatively larger) aspects or the more local (relatively smaller) features in a visual form. Thus, if we have a large figure made up of smaller distinct components (such as the large letter made up of smaller letters that we saw as Figure 11-14), you may be set to attend to either the larger figure or its smaller elements. When you are set to attend to one level of detail, your processing of features at the other level is poorer (Hoffman, 1980; Kinchla, Solis-Macias & Hoffman, 1983; L. M. Ward, 1985). An example of the effects of detail set is given in Demonstration Box 15-2.

FILTERING

Once we have oriented, either covertly or overtly, to a source of stimulation, we may continue to attend to (look at, listen to) that source to the exclusion of other things happening in our environment. Specifically, we are **filtering** out all stimuli except those that come from the region or channel we are attending to. How well can we do this? What factors affect how well we can select one information source and filter out others? And what happens to

---

DEMONSTRATION BOX 15-2.   Level of Detail and Attention

How many times in your life have you looked at a penny? Probably thousands of times. Take a piece of paper and, from memory, draw both sides of a penny. There is no need to be artistic, just try to represent all the figures, all the words, numbers, and dates on a penny, each in its proper place. Next, compare your drawings to an actual penny. It is likely that you will find at least one, and probably several, errors in the material you include and your placement of it. The reason for this is that it is possible to recognize a penny based on a fairly global set of characteristics, namely its size, shape, and color. So your *detail set* when attending to pennies has probably seldom been small enough to pick out the local characteristics, regardless of the thousands of times that you have looked at one.

information we don't attend to? At the level of awareness, it is apparent that things we attend to seem sharp and clear while things outside the attentional field are less distinct and more difficult to remember. It turns out that research confirms these informal impressions.

The Cocktail Party Phenomenon

Let us consider a noisy cocktail party. This is a good example of many possible sources of stimulation occurring at one time, which require attentional filtering for you to make any sense out of the proceedings. For example, there are often many conversations going on simultaneously, including the one in which you are involved. If you hear a significant or familiar voice you may orient to it. You may follow that conversation for a while, nodding occasionally to your own conversational partner. You may also suddenly be startled to notice the person to whom you had been "talking" give a sniff and walk away rapidly, obviously angry with you. You are puzzled, because you can't remember a thing that person has said in the last five minutes. However, you remember perfectly what your former sweetheart said in the conversation to which you *were* listening. Apparently you very effectively filtered out everything else, including whatever it was that caused your conversational partner to walk away.

Colin Cherry (1953), in a now-classic article, investigated some of the problems exemplified in the behavior we described above. He introduced the experimental technique called *shadowing* in order to control how his observers oriented their attention. In this technique, an observer is presented with two messages through two different information channels. For example, the two channels could be the two ears (one message to each ear, a technique called **dichotic listening**), or one message could be presented visually and the other auditorily, or the two messages could be presented at different locations in space. The observer must repeat aloud (that is, follow along with, or shadow) one

of the messages as it is presented. If the observer is allowed to lag slightly behind the message, and repeat entire phrases at once, the technique is called **phrase shadowing.** If the requirement is to repeat each syllable as it is presented, it is called **phonemic shadowing.** Cherry was the first to demonstrate that observers could orient to one message and filter out the other.

It is not equally easy to shadow all messages. For example, using the dichotic listening technique it has been shown that if the selected message is prose, such as a selection from a story, shadowing is relatively easy. Shadowing random lists of words is more difficult, and shadowing nonsense syllables (e.g., *orp, vak, bij*) is the most difficult of all. Phrase shadowing is considerably easier than phonemic shadowing. Clearly meaning and grammatical structure help us attend to one message and filter out others. Shadowing is also easier if the messages come from two different places in space, are different in pitch (e.g., one male voice and one female voice), or are presented at different speeds. For an example of how this works, try Demonstration Box 15-3.

What happens to the inputs you don't attend to, which we earlier suggested were "filtered out"? Cherry (1953) found that listeners could remember very little of the rejected message in the shadowing task. Moray (1959) found that in difficult shadowing tasks, even though they knew that they would later be asked about it, listeners were unable to remember words that had been repeatedly presented in the unshadowed message. Did the listeners simply not hear the unshadowed message, or did the shadowed message somehow interfere with their memory of the unshadowed message? Both Cherry and Moray had waited a little while after the shadowing task was completed to ask about the unshadowed message. Perhaps the unshadowed message was heard, maybe the words were actually recognized, but they were forgotten quickly because they weren't committed to a long-lasting memory. Perhaps we must pay attention to an input in order to remember it for longer than a few seconds. This idea was tested by interrupting listeners' shadowing

DEMONSTRATION BOX 15-3.   Selective Attention and the Precedence Effect

You may remember our discussion of the precedence effect from Chapter 7, where we listed some variables that affect our ability to localize the position of sound sources in space. When sounds are emitted in enclosed spaces, they tend to cause echoes as they bounce from walls, ceilings, and floors. However, we can still make a correct localization of the sound source because the sound emanating directly from this source will reach our ears before its echoes. The auditory system is sensitive to these time differences and can use this information in the localization of sound-producing sources. The direction of the sound emanating directly from the sound source takes precedence over other sounds in localization, hence the name *precedence effect*.

The precedence effect can also be helpful in selective attention, when we are attempting to process one of many simultaneously occurring stimulus events. A good example of this is found in cocktail party situations, where you may try to follow one of many competing conversations. This aspect of selective attention is helped by the spatial and temporal separation of the auditory inputs. You can demonstrate this for yourself with the aid of two friends (preferably of the same sex) and a doorway. First have your friends stand as shown in Figure A, while each reads passages from a book or newspaper simultaneously. Notice that even with your eyes closed you can easily separate and locate the two messages. Now stand out of the direct line of sight (and sound) of each friend, as shown in Figure B. In this situation the messages must travel indirectly out through the open door. This means that they will tend to reach you at the same time and come from the same direction. Now, again with your eyes closed, notice how difficult it is to locate the voices and to separate their messages.

to ask them to report what had just been presented to the unshadowed ear (Glucksberg & Cowen, 1970; Norman, 1969). When this happens, listeners can usually recall the last five to seven words, numbers, or whatever units are being shadowed. It seems that material in the unshadowed ear is actually perceived at some level and is available for processing, and attention, for a short while after it occurs, but unless it is attended to it is not entered into a long-lasting memory.

The Video Overlap Phenomenon

Although it happens rarely in this electronically sophisticated age, sometimes two powerful TV stations may be near enough that their signals encroach on each other, making it impossible to tune a television set to a single channel in some geographical areas. When this happens, there will be an overlap of video broadcast of two different programs, with one usually looking somewhat ghostly, or like a negative image. If you have ever experienced this, but wanted to watch one of the channels enough (your favorite soap opera), you may have experienced a visual phenomenon similar to the cocktail party phenomenon for sound. What you probably found was that it was possible to watch "your" program and filter out the other one, although of course it wasn't pleasant because you had to make an unaccustomed effort to do so.

An analog of the shadowing task described above has been used to study this kind of visual filtering (Neisser & Becklin, 1975). Overlapping video programs, one of a hand game and the other of a ball game, were presented to observers. In the hand game, the players tried to slap each other's hands, and observers who "shadowed" this game had to report each attacking stroke (but not feints). In the ball game, players threw a basketball to one another while moving about irregularly. Observers who shadowed the ball game had to report each throw of the ball from one player to another (but not fakes and dribbles). "Odd" events were also sometimes inserted in the programs (e.g., the hand-game players shook hands then resumed play, or the ball-game players threw the ball out of the picture, played with an imaginary ball for a few seconds, and then resumed playing with the real ball). Figure 15-3 shows examples of single frames from each game and the two frames superimposed.

The results of this study were remarkably similar to those from auditory shadowing experiments. Observers could easily follow the events in one program presented alone, as would be expected. They also had little difficulty following the events

of one program when the other one was superimposed on it, although they did make a few more errors in this condition. Moreover, the odd events in the shadowed programs were almost always noticed, whereas the odd events in the unshadowed programs were rarely noticed. For example, only 1 of 24 subjects noticed the handshake in the hand game while shadowing the ball game; no subjects noticed the ball disappear in the ball game while they were watching the hand game. The reports that did occur were vague and uncertain, and usually not correct. Generally, those few subjects felt that there might be something unusual about the unshadowed program but they didn't know what it was. Most subjects noticed nothing unusual at all. This indicates that, like auditory filtering, visual filtering allows little of the filtered-out information to make a lasting impression, a result that has been verified in many different situations (e.g., Rock & Guttman, 1981). You can experience a similar type of visual shadowing, and its effect on memory of the unshadowed message, by trying Demonstration Box 15-4.

Divided Attention

An important question relevant to perception is whether it is possible to attend to more than one source of information at the same time, and if so, whether performance suffers. In the visual filtering experiment just discussed, observers were asked also to *divide* their attention and to shadow both programs simultaneously. That is, they had to report both attacks in the hand game and throws in the ball game. When they tried to do this, performance deteriorated dramatically. Observers missed many more events and typically said the task was "demanding" or even "impossible" (Neisser & Becklin, 1975). Moreover, presenting the two programs to different eyes (**dichoptic presentation**) made the divided attention task no easier. The conclusion is that dividing visual attention between two (or more) sources is very difficult; we can look at only one thing at a time. Another example of

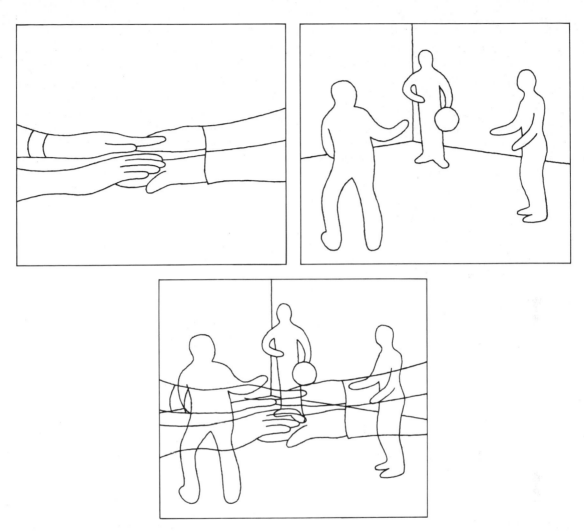

FIGURE 15-3 Outline tracings of isolated frames from the video overlap experiment. (A) Hand game only. (B) Ball game only. (C) Hand game and ball game superimposed. (From Neisser & Becklin, 1975)

what happens when we must divide our attention visually is demonstrated by the phenomenon of **binocular rivalry.** When the views presented to the two eyes are different enough, it is virtually impossible to hold both views in consciousness simultaneously. The two views *rival* each other for our attention. Thus we first see one eye's image while suppressing the other, and then the view alternates to that of the other eye. Demonstration

Box 15-5 allows you to experience this failure of divided visual attention for yourself.

Attempts to divide attention between two auditory information channels are similarly difficult. Of course, it is impossible to shadow two messages at once because we cannot say two things at once. Experiments have been done, however, in which people were asked to listen to messages (in this case word lists) in both ears and later distinguish

---

DEMONSTRATION BOX 15-4.   Visual Shadowing and Memory

In the accompanying passage, the relevant message is shaded and the irrelevant message is printed in the normal fashion. You are to read the shaded passage aloud as rapidly as possible, ignoring the irrelevant (unshaded) message. Now without cheating and looking back, write down all the words you remember from the irrelevant message. Go back and read the shaded passage again, but this time stop after each line to write down the words you recall from the irrelevant message (without looking back at it). You should find that the list of remembered words is longer when your reading is interrupted and you are not asked to recall all the irrelevant message at once. (From Lindsay & Norman, 1977)

In performing an experiment like this one a man attention car it house is boy critically hat important shoe that candy the old material horse that tree is pen being phone read cow by book the hot subject tape not pin the stand relevant view task sky be read cohesive man and car grammatically house complete boy but hat without shoe either candy being horse so tree easy pen that phone will cow attention book is hot not tape required pin in stand order view to sky read red it not too difficult

---

words they had heard from distractors (Levy, 1971, cited in Kahneman, 1973). Recognition performance was far poorer when listening to both ears than when listening to only one ear and filtering out the other. You may have had similar experiences at a cocktail party when trying to listen to two interesting conversations at once. It is possible to switch back and forth between them, but if they are at all demanding a great deal of the information of each one will be lost.

Divided attention is easier if the information channels are in different modalities, such as vision and audition, although performance still suffers in comparison to attention focused on only one channel whenever the filtering task is at all difficult (e.g., Treisman & Davies, 1972). Only when the task is very easy, such as responding to a simple signal as soon as it occurs in either of two modalities, is there no decline in performance under divided-attention conditions (e.g., Miller, 1982). An apparent exception to this rule is a study by Allport, Antonis, and Reynolds (1972) in which subjects sight-read music and shadowed a message at the same time without loss of efficiency compared to doing either task alone. This seems to imply that

there may be attentional resources that are unique to certain sensory modalities or perhaps even particular tasks (allowing better performance in dividing across modalities or tasks). However, in the vast majority of cases, divided attention performance is considerably worse than focused attention performance.

Finally, it is worth mentioning that dividing attention between two demanding tasks does become easier with extensive practice. You all have experienced doing two, or more, things at once, such as driving a car and carrying on a conversation, or reading a book, chewing on a sandwich, and scratching your head. It has been shown that a skilled typist can type at a high rate and shadow a message at the same time with almost no loss of efficiency at either task (Shaffer, 1975). What seems to be happening here is that extensive practice in typing has made that skill somewhat automatic for the typist. **Automatic processing** does not require conscious effort and little conscious attention is allocated for it, thus allowing more attention to be allocated to the less-automatic skill (shadowing, in this case). We discuss automaticity more fully in the next section.

DEMONSTRATION BOX 15-5.   Binocular Rivalry

You may demonstrate binocular rivalry by using the accompanying figure and a pocket mirror. Place the mirror on the center line of Figure B and hold your head relatively close as shown in Figure A. Adjust the mirror, and your head, so that the half of the figure seen in it appears to be at the same distance as when seen directly. The two halves of the figure should overlap, with one eye viewing the vertical and the other the horizontal stripes. Now look at the superimposed lines for a few moments. At first you will see one set of lines. Then they will be replaced by the other set as they rival each other, alternating in and out of your consciousness.

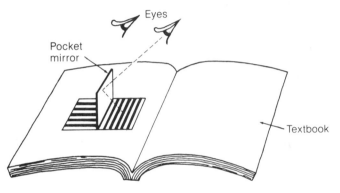

A   How to view the stimulus given below in order to experience binocular rivalry

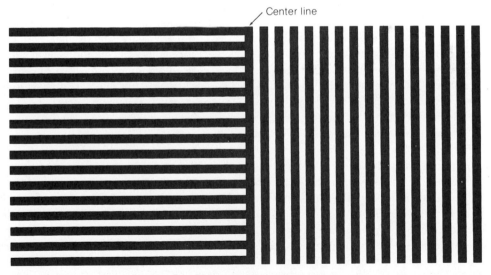

B   Binocular rivalry stimulus

SEARCHING

Imagine you are waiting in an airport for a loved one to arrive home from a trip abroad. The plane arrives and a flood of people comes through the exit door. Your eyes flick back and forth across the mass of faces, searching for that familiar face. You don't bother looking at people's clothes because you know she is wearing a new outfit, and you don't know what it looks like. You are looking instead for the peculiar combination of longish, coal black hair, large nose, and close-set eyes that you remember so well. Someone near you suddenly shouts to a large man in a bright orange suit, who waves in reply. The shouter confides to you that she always has an easy time finding her husband at the airport because he always wears that silly suit and "stands out like a sore thumb." We often know what we are looking or listening for and must search a field of "distractors" to find it. This situation has become one of those most used for studying attention, partly because it is easy to implement in the laboratory and partly because it has important implications for everyday life.

Eye Movements and Visual Searching

It is much easier to study looking-for than listening-for, since there is an obvious external indicator of visual searching—eye movements. Our eyes are constantly exploring the visual field with high-speed ballistic movements called **saccades.** "People scan the visual world actively and purposively. They know where to look and they know what to look for" (Rabbitt, 1984, p. 287). People can rapidly learn to inspect spatial locations in optimal order to detect targets that may be present. Although this is a fairly automatic process for adults, it does not appear to be fully developed (for some tasks) until children are about 6 or 7 years of age (e.g., Cohen, 1981; Green, Hammond & Supramaniam, 1983) and becomes much more difficult for the elderly (Rabbitt, 1984). In typical situations, people use their knowledge of the world to guide their searching. The ability to recognize a scene in a few

hundred milliseconds may allow people to retrieve previously stored search strategies that can then be used to find the important areas within the scene (Rabbitt, 1984).

There certainly is evidence that meaning and expectation can direct what we look at in a visual scene (Antes & Penland, 1981; Findlay, 1981; Stark & Ellis, 1981). For example, Yarbus (1967) recorded eye-movement patterns while observers looked at pictures with different intentions in mind. Figure 15-4 shows the eye-movement patterns observers made for a typical picture (A) when asked to estimate either the ages of the individuals in the picture (B) or their wealth (C). Clearly, people looked at different places in order to find information relevant to the different questions. Also, people have a harder time locating a target object, such as a bicycle, in a photograph of a natural scene if the scene has been jumbled by randomly interchanging different areas as has been done in Figure 15-5 (Biederman, Glass & Stacey, 1973). Moreover, we look at unusual objects in a visual scene longer when we find them (Antes & Penland, 1981; Friedman, 1979), even when we are motivated to distribute our attention equally over the scene (Friedman & Liebelt, 1981). Because of this, unexpected objects tend to be remembered and recognized more easily, and exchanges of one unusual object for another (a cow for a car in a living room) are noticed far more often than are exchanges of one usual object for another (a chair for a table in a living room) (Friedman, 1979).

Feature versus Conjunction Searching

A common laboratory task to study visual searching involves asking an observer to scan an array of letters, or other visual forms, in order to find a target letter or form. One relatively early study of this type was by Neisser (1967). Observers scanned, from top to bottom, an array of letters arranged in 50 lines of 6 letters each, and came to perform this search at great speed (as fast as 60 letters/sec). A number of factors, however, affected their search speed. For instance, when the target was an angular

FIGURE 15-4   Eye-movement patterns made when viewing the picture (A) vary depending on whether the viewer was asked the ages of the individuals in the picture (scan pattern B) or their wealth (scan pattern C). (From Yarbus, 1967. Copyright Plenum Publishing Company, reprinted by permission.)

letter *(W, Z, X)* and the other letters (distractors) were roundish *(O, Q, C)*, observers searched much more quickly than when the target was more similar to the distractors (e.g., a *W* when distractors were *K, Z, X, Y*). When the target differs from all of the distractors by possessing a feature they don't have (e.g., an angled line), we call this a **feature search.** When the only way to detect the target is to detect a conjunction (or particular combination) of features (such as the particular angles and their orientation that distinguish between a *W* and an *M*), we call this a **conjunction search.** In general, feature searches are much easier than conjunction searches. Thus, Neisser's subjects typically reported that when they were searching the list, particularly when the target was very different from the distractors, the nontarget letters were just a blur and they did not ''see'' individual letters. In fact the target often just ''popped out'' of the array.

Neisser (1967) argued that there is a ''preat-tentive'' level of processing that segregates regions of a visual scene into figure and ground, a distinction we discussed in Chapter 11. This suggests that when there are clear feature differences between the target and the distractor items, the target becomes readily visible because the distractors are lumped together as ground and the target stands out as a figure by the action of this preattentive process alone, without any further processing. The notion is that certain (usually similar) elements are grouped together automatically and the ones that don't fit seem to leap into consciousness. This isn't possible when the target and background items closely resemble each other as in a conjunction search. Here, closer attention and scrutiny are needed to detect specific elements (e.g., Julesz, 1980).

The differences between feature and conjunction searching have been extensively explored (e.g., Treisman, 1982, 1986a). The really striking

FIGURE 15-5   It is easier to find a target object in a coherent, natural scene (above) than in the same scene randomly jumbled (opposite page). (From Biederman et al., 1973)

result is that when feature search is possible the number of distractor items doesn't seem to affect searching speed. The target simply pops out of the display. However, when conjunction search is required the number of distractors does affect searching speed. This can be seen clearly in some prototypical data illustrated in Figure 15-6. In conjunction search we seem to be comparing each of the distractors, one at a time, with the image of the target and responding only when they match. Such an orderly and sequential set of comparisons is often referred to as a **serial search.** To explain this kind of data, Treisman offered a *feature integration theory*. It suggests that each feature of a stimulus (such as its color, size, or shape) is registered separately. When an object must be identified from a combination of features, a correct analysis can only be achieved if you focus your attention on one lo-

cation at a time. Recalling our discussion of attentional gaze, we might say that features occurring in a single attentional "glance" are combined to form an object. This combination and comparison takes time and effort. If your attention is diverted or overloaded, errors may occur, and you may attribute the wrong features to a particular item and either miss your target or select a wrong target (Prinzmetal, 1981; Treisman & Schmidt, 1982). Demonstration Box 15-6 gives you an opportunity to try feature and conjunction searches for yourself.

Automatic versus Controlled Searching

Searching can be improved by particular strategies that an observer adopts, and by practice. For example, a conjunction search may be treated as two simple feature searches under some circumstances

(Egeth, Virgi & Garbart, 1984). This would mean that in Demonstration Box 15-6 you might be able to look only at the white letters in array C, ignoring the black letters, while searching for the white *O*. In a sense, the figure-ground preattentive process is used to reject as ground all distractors that can be ruled out on the basis of a simple feature difference from the target, leaving you with only a second simple feature search to complete. Another strategy that sometimes helps is to group items together into smaller sets of stimuli. If stimulus sets are small enough (say two to eight items), attention operates as if all items are checked at the same time (**parallel search**), rather than sequentially as in serial search. Using such a grouping strategy, the smaller arrays may be searched in parallel for both features and conjunctions (Pashler, 1987).

When observers have been able to practice for

a very long time on a task that always demands the same response under the same conditions, the nature of the search process seems to change—searching time for a stimulus becomes much faster and seems to be relatively independent of the number of distractors present. Perhaps the most carefully designed research demonstrating this result was done by Shiffrin and Schneider (1977; Schneider & Shiffrin, 1977). In a typical study, some observers searched for a fixed set of targets (say the letters *H, S,* and *T*) among a fixed set of distractors (say all of the digits). At first, the more distractors in the display, the longer it took to find the target. However, after practicing for 14 days (over 4,000 searches) on the same task, the number of distractors in the display ceased to matter. It took the same amount of time to find the target regardless of the number of distractors. Figure 15-7 shows

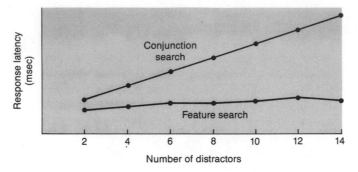

FIGURE 15-6   The relation between response latency to report the presence of a target and the number of distractor items that must be checked for feature and conjunction searches. (Based on Treisman, 1982)

this result graphically. Shiffrin and Schneider (1977) argued that at first the searching was a typical serial conjunction search (they called it **controlled processing**), but that after much practice in a consistent environment the searching became automatic, rather like a simple feature search. A similar result has been obtained for an auditory detection task (Poltrock, Lansman & Hunt, 1982), which indicates that automatic and controlled processing are not limited to vision but occur in other modalities as well.

So we see that with practice the direction of attention shifts from controlled to automatic processing (Schneider, Dumais & Shiffrin, 1984), and that this is accompanied by several changes in the nature of the searching process. For instance, it becomes more difficult to stop yourself from responding to targets that you are automatically set to search for, even if you wish to ignore them. You will be able to do other tasks at the same time that you are engaging in this automatic search, however, and these added tasks won't materially

---

DEMONSTRATION BOX 15-6.   Feature and Conjunction Search

In each of these arrays of visual forms there are targets to find. The target is a white *O*. Scan each array quickly, only once, and write down how many targets you see. Notice in each array how difficult or easy it is to find the targets. Do this before reading further.

Now you can know that arrays A and B required a feature search (in A the feature was brightness, in B it was shape), whereas array C required a conjunction search (for both brightness and shape). There were three targets in each array. Did you get them all? Most people find the conjunction search to be the most difficult of these tasks, and if they are apt to miss any targets it will be in array C.

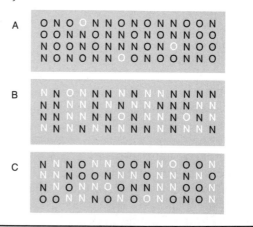

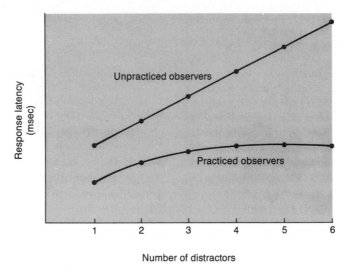

FIGURE 15-7 The relation between response latency to report the presence of a target and the number of distractors to be checked for unpracticed and practiced observers. (Based on Glass & Holyoak, 1986)

interfere with your automatic processing. Unfortunately, you won't be able to remember as well the things you found and responded to under automatic control. Many of these results have been documented in other studies (see Schneider et al., 1984). You can experience for yourself the powerfully automatic nature of reading words, and how this can interfere with other tasks, by trying the demonstration of the **Stroop effect** in Demonstration Box 15-7. Actually, many lapses of attention in everyday life can be traced to such seemingly automatic processes and their inevitable effects (see Reason, 1984).

We might take an extreme position, for the sake of argument, and suggest that when a process is truly automatic it requires no attentional resources at all (cf. Schneider et al., 1984). This is called *strong automaticity*. A number of results have discouraged this extreme position. For example, reading in the Stroop effect demonstrated in Demonstration Box 15-7 is supposed to be automatic. However, the Stroop effect is much weaker when the colored ink and the incompatible color name are spatially separated than when they occur

in the same place (see Kahneman & Treisman, 1984 for these and other similar data). Strong automaticity would require that as long as the word could be read automatically it wouldn't matter where it was, yet it seems that it is possible to filter out the incompatible color word if it isn't part of the same perceptual object but not if it is. This kind of result favors a weaker notion of automatic processing.

There are other similar data that confirm weaker automaticity. For example, it is easier to detect another stimulus while searching for an "automatic" target in a task like that of Shiffrin and Schneider (1977) if that stimulus is close to the spatial location of the automatic search target. Conversely, it is easier to detect the automatic target if it occurs near another stimulus that is also to be detected (Hoffman, Nelson & Houck, 1983). Also, it has been shown that extensive practice can dramatically improve visual searching even when the conditions and responses are not always kept constant, such as when the task demands that different responses have to be made to the same stimuli under different conditions and these conditions keep

---

DEMONSTRATION BOX 15-7.   The Stroop Effect

The **Stroop effect** is an interesting example of how well-learned material can interfere with our ability to attend to the demands of a task. In 1935, Stroop found that observers had difficulty screening out meaningful information even when it was irrelevant to the task. He devised three situations. In the first he recorded how long it took individuals to read a list of color names, such as *red* and *green,* printed in black ink. He then took an equal number of color patches and recorded how long it took observers to name each one of the series. Then he took a color name and printed it in a color of ink that did not coincide with the linguistic information (for example, the word *blue* printed in red ink). When he had observers name the ink color in this last series, he found that they often erroneously read the printed color name rather than the ink color name; therefore, it took them much longer to read through this last series. The Stroop effect demonstrates that meaningful linguistic informa-

tion is difficult to ignore, and the automatic expectations that have come to be associated with the presence of words often take over, resulting in difficulties in focusing attention.

Color Plate 8 is an example of the Stroop Color Word Test, so you can try this for yourself. Have a friend time you with either the second hand of a watch or with a stopwatch, if you have one, as you read each group. Start timing with the command ''Go'' and read across the lines in exactly the same fashion for each group. When the last response is made in each group, stop timing and note your response time. You should find that reading the color names will take the least amount of time, whereas naming the colors of the ink when the printed word names a different color will take you the most time. Naming the color patches will fall in between these two.

---

changing (Cooke, Breen & Schvaneveldt, 1987). However, even extensive practice in a consistent environment sometimes fails to produce automatic searching (e.g., Fisher, Duffy, Young, & Pollatsek, 1988).

A somewhat different approach to these same data emphasizes the development of **skill** in accomplishing various perceptual tasks (Neisser, 1976). Here the suggestion is that the effects of practice do not simply involve a switch from controlled to automatic processing, but rather that the task is being restructured (Cheng, 1985). That is, a different strategy is being used to accomplish the same task. A nonperceptual example would be adding a group of identical numbers, such as $2 + 2 + 2 + 2 + 2$. This could be accomplished by adding each of the numbers to a running sum, or more quickly and easily by simply multiplying 5×2. In this view, extensive practice allows a new strategy to be developed and learned, rather than causing a transition from controlled to automatic processing.

Vigilance

Sometimes we are asked to maintain a sustained level of attention, for prolonged periods of time, while we search for targets that may only rarely appear. An example is an observer watching a radar screen for the presence of a particular type of aircraft that flies by only occasionally, or a quality control inspector examining an assembly line where damaged or substandard items seldom appear. In these cases the observer is said to be performing a **vigilance** task. Research into vigilance began after it was noticed that radar operators during World War II tended to become fatigued after a time on duty, resulting in a decrease in their ability to detect enemy planes. After the war, experiments began in an attempt to understand how attention sustained itself, particularly in boring search tasks with infrequent stimuli.

The original experiments on vigilance required observers to watch a display similar to a clock face around which a clock hand moved in steps. They had to press a key each time the hand took a double step. After only ½ hour of watching, observers began to report fewer and fewer double steps, missing almost 25 percent of them (Mackworth, 1948). Physical fatigue didn't seem to be a reasonable explanation of the drop in performance since the work load was very light. Perhaps the visual system itself was becoming fatigued and thus less sensitive, or perhaps the observer was just as sensitive to the double steps but simply failed to respond on some occasions. It was important to decide whether one or the other or both of these explanations were correct.

The scene was set for the application of signal detection theory (see Chapter 2). If the visual system was becoming less sensitive it would be reflected in a decrease in d', the measure of the observer's sensitivity. If there was some change in how willing the observer was to report the double step it would be reflected in a change in β, the observer's criterion that indicates response bias. When this type of analysis was applied, it was found that sensitivity, or d', did not change over time but β did. Observers were becoming less willing to say yes, meaning that the rare event they searched for had actually occurred, the longer they had to maintain vigilance (Broadbent & Gregory, 1963, 1965). More recent research has indicated that extensive training can decrease or eliminate such vigilance decrements (Fisk & Schneider, 1981; Parasuraman, 1984). Apparently the setting of a criterion for responding in such tasks is a function of alertness, or the way available attention is allocated to the task at hand (Parasuraman, 1984).

Does sensitivity ever change in a vigilance task? Yes it does, for the worse, but only when the numbers of events per unit of time that must be monitored for the targets is very high and the targets are difficult to discriminate from the nontargets (Parasuraman, 1984; Parasuraman & Mouloua, 1987). Declines in sensitivity seem to be associated with prolonged high demand on attentional resources and do indeed result from a kind of fatigue.

A major part of maintaining overt attention seems to be a certain degree of physiological arousal. We adopt certain body positions, tense specific muscle groups, and have the feeling of ''concentrating'' whenever we are vigilant. Apparently most of us already believe that if we are highly aroused physiologically we will be better able to sustain attention, since we often attempt to raise our arousal level in vigilance situations with stimulants such as coffee. In order to understand how arousal affects vigilance, we should look at how arousal affects performance in general.

The relation between arousal and performance is perhaps most elegantly expressed in the well-known **Yerkes-Dodson law** (Yerkes & Dodson, 1908). Figure 15-8 shows this relation graphically. Contrary to what common sense might tell us, performance doesn't always get better the more highly aroused we are. In fact, overall performance of any task peaks at an intermediate level of arousal. This intermediate level is lower for difficult tasks than for easy tasks, perhaps because as arousal increases attention narrows, thus decreasing the number of inputs that can be monitored. This tends to decrease the number of distracting inputs processed, which would help in easy tasks. However, difficult tasks usually require that more inputs be attended to, so a narrowing of attention would actually hurt performance in such tasks (Easterbrook, 1959; Hockey, 1970). How does this relate to vigilance? The modern consensus is that physiological arousal is mainly responsible for the overall level of vigilance but pretty much unrelated to the decline in performance over time (Parasuraman, 1984).

EXPECTING

Knowing exactly when or where an important signal will occur is often difficult. For this reason we have orienting mechanisms that draw our attention to conspicuous stimuli. We also have search strategies that allow us to investigate likely locations where important stimuli might be. However, sometimes we get an advance cue about where or when something will happen. We call such a cue an

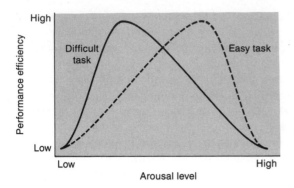

FIGURE 15-8 Yerkes-Dodson law. Performance is best at intermediate levels of arousal, and performance peaks at lower levels of arousal for difficult than for easy tasks.

information cue. For example, imagine you are back in the airport, this time trying to monitor two doors at once, through only one of which your beloved will arrive. Suddenly the loudspeaker announces that passengers disembarking from that flight will arrive through Gate 21, the left one of the two doors. Although you know that still doesn't guarantee it will be *the* door, you find yourself more often shifting your attention to the left door. You are actively **expecting** something to happen there, and it has affected your attentional state.

Costs and Benefits of Information Cues

Probably the best demonstration of the effects of information cues on performance was done for another reason. Posner (1980) was trying to demonstrate covert orienting by asking observers to press a key when they detected a flash of light either to the right or the left of a fixation point. In half of the trials (the *neutral* trials), observers fixated a plus sign in the middle of the visual field and the flash occurred randomly on one side or the other. In the other half of the trials, observers received an information cue in the form of an arrow pointing either right or left and located where the plus was located on the neutral trials. These were the *cued*

trials. In 80 percent of the cued trials the flash occurred on the side to which the arrow pointed (*valid* trials), and in the other 20 percent it occurred on the opposite side (*invalid* trials). The observers were not allowed to move their eyes away from either the plus or the arrow; they could only orient their attention. Figure 15-9A shows a summary of these conditions.

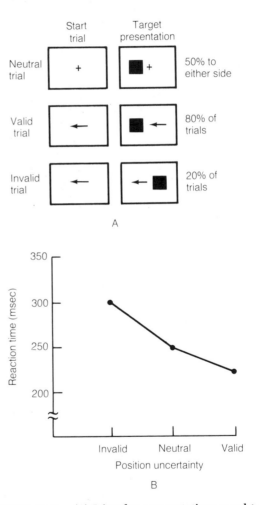

FIGURE 15-9 (A) Stimulus presentations used to study the effects of expectation on detection. (B) Results of reaction-time study of expectation showing the costs (invalid cue) and benefits (valid cue) of advance knowledge of stimulus location. (Based on Posner, 1980)

Figure 15-9B shows the results of Posner's experiment. Using the neutral trials as a baseline to indicate what performance level you would expect without any information cue, you can see that it took over 50 msec more to respond to the flash on invalid trials (a **cost** of the information cue being wrong), but about 30 msec less to respond to the flash on the valid trials (a **benefit** of the valid information cue). The costs and benefits of information cues have been interpreted by Posner (1980), and others, as indicating that attention can be covertly oriented by an information cue, even in the absence of a stimulus on which to focus the attentional gaze. Of course, it is possible that a more complex interpretation is called for; for instance, observers may be using different strategies on the neutral trials than they are on the cued trials (cf. Jonides & Mack, 1984). But for whatever reason, the data do demonstrate that a valid information cue allows you to detect a stimulus more rapidly than when there is an invalid information cue.

The effects of expectation and information cues on attention are somewhat complicated. For instance, we noted earlier that when stimulus cues are present it takes time to shift the attentional gaze from one location to another, and that the time it takes is longer when the distances between the starting and the new locations are greater (e.g., Tsal, 1983). When attention is shifted because of the presence of an information cue, however, it always takes the same time to shift attention to a new location (Remington & Pierce, 1984), at least under certain circumstances.

Hughes and Zimba (1985) repeated Posner's experiment but altered the display so that the flash didn't always occur in the same place in the visual field. Imagine a hypothetical line drawn vertically through the fovea that divides the field of view into a left and right half, or **hemifield.** In Chapter 3 we saw that each such hemifield projects its information to a different side of the brain. On both valid and invalid trials the flash could occur either in the usual position or sometimes in other positions in the same hemifield. It didn't matter where in the cued hemifield the flash occurred, the benefit was

the same. A similar result was obtained for costs on the invalid trials. Moreover, if both cued and uncued locations were in the same hemifield, there were no costs or benefits at all! Finally, it was found that with practice the benefits of the valid cue disappeared, whereas the costs of the invalid cue remained. Hughes and Zimba (1985) suggested that "attending to a spatial location acts primarily to inhibit the processing of signals that originate in the unattended hemifield" (p. 428). The costs result from this inhibition. This suggests an interaction between the physiological organization of the visual system and the way in which expectations affect the distribution of our attention.

Our expectations can help or hinder our detection of stimuli in sensory modalities other than vision. For instance, pretend you are expecting your mother to come home any minute now. You are expecting to hear her cheery "Hello" in her usual, rather high-pitched voice. At this moment your father shouts to you to come help him in the basement. You don't hear him calling and a minute later he storms into the room, demanding to know why you weren't responding to him. You might explain that you were listening for your mother's voice and simply didn't hear his much-lower-frequency voice (if he doesn't believe you, you can show him this book). There is lots of evidence that detection of sounds is more difficult, that is, there is a cost, when they are of uncertain frequency (Swets, 1963; Scharf, Quigley, Aoki, Peachly & Reeves, 1987). Moreover, if observers are told which frequency to listen for by an information cue, such as lights, tones, or even the early parts of tonal patterns, detection of the target sounds improves if the cue was valid but remains poor if it was invalid (Howard, O'Toole, Parasuraman & Bennett, 1984). Again, the information cue seems to lead to inhibition of the detection of the unexpected stimulus rather than better detection of the expected one.

Apparently, information cues act differently on attention than do stimulus cues (cf. also Briand & Klein, 1987). When a stimulus cue is present, the attentional gaze can be drawn or moved voluntarily to a particular spatial location, where it facilitates processing of perceptual objects and their properties. However, an information cue in the absence of a stimulus cue may cause us to suppress inputs from unexpected sources. Such suppression would enhance processing of expected inputs by lessening interference from unwanted inputs rather than by directly facilitating processing of expected inputs.

THEORIES OF ATTENTION

Ever since attention was first studied, investigators have attempted to construct a coherent theoretical account of the major phenomena. Unfortunately, because the concept of attention has meant so many different things to different people and has been studied in so many different ways, this has not yet been accomplished. At present there are several different approaches to understanding attention. We will try to give you the flavor of a few of the major approaches here, but you must remember that no one of these approaches seems adequate to explain all of the data described above, let alone the vast array of data we did not describe.

All the models attempt to explain why attention lets some information reach consciousness while screening other information out. Probably the earliest theoretical approach to have survived until now is the group of **structural theories.** As pointed out by Kahneman and Treisman (1984), the studies of stimulus filtering that were popular in the 1950s and 1960s seemed to imply that perceptual attention was *structurally* limited. The notion was that there is a bottleneck or a filter somewhere in the information processing system beyond which only one, or at most a few, stimulus inputs can pass at one time. The earliest studies suggested that this bottleneck occurs very early in the perceptual process, just after registration by the sensory system and before the meaning of an input can be determined (e.g., Broadbent, 1958). For example, if you are trying to listen to only one person in a crowded room full of talking people selection

would be accomplished based on the physical characteristics of the stimulus, rather than its meaning. While the sensory qualities, such as frequency and loudness, are registered for all of the voices, only the words associated with some particular physical characteristics, such as voice quality and location, are passed on to be processed for content and comprehension. This is called **early selection** and is depicted schematically in Figure 15-10.

The early selection models had difficulty with the fact that there is evidence that at least some analysis is done on information coming through unattended perceptual channels. This processing may affect our responses even if we are unaware of it (see Cheeseman & Merikle, 1984; Holender, 1986). A striking example is when someone in a conversation that you are not paying direct attention to mentions your name—you immediately become aware of the fact. This kind of evidence led to a set of structural theories that emphasized **late selection.** They hypothesized that *all* information entering sensory systems gets preliminary analysis and the bottleneck occurs at the stage of more or less conscious processing, when material is being entered into a longer-lasting memory (e.g., Deutsch & Deutsch, 1963; Norman, 1968). A schematic representation of this kind of model is shown in Figure 15-10. The debate between early and late selection still rages (cf. Pashler, 1984) and has spilled over onto other approaches as well.

A second general approach to attention has grown mostly from studies of search and expectation (cf. Kahneman & Treisman, 1984), especially studies involving comparisons of focused and divided attention. The general finding that dividing attention between two tasks or searching for more than one target usually is more difficult than focusing on one task or target has led to the notion that there are **attentional resources** that can be "used up" by a task. If there is more demand than there are resources available, then performance suffers. The first theories that assumed a limited capacity to attend thought of attention as a single "pool" of capacity (e.g., Kahneman, 1973). The operation of such a model is shown in Figure 15-11 A and B.

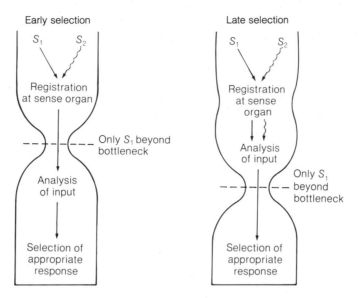

FIGURE 15-10   Schematic diagrams of two types of bottleneck models of attention. Both models assume that perceptual selectivity stems from a structural limitation on our capacity to process all the incoming stimulation (stimuli are indicated by S_1 and S_2). The early selection models see the limitation as occurring at the earliest stages; only limited amounts of stimulation are channeled along for further processing. The late selection models conceptualize stimulus selection (attention) as occurring at later stages of information processing.

All of the available capacity is used for one task in A, whereas in B involving divided attention the capacity must be shared, leaving less processing resources for each task.

Recently the attentional resource models have had to be revised. There have been some demonstrations of near-perfect divison of attention, for instance, when sight-reading music and shadowing at the same time. This has led some theorists to suggest that there may be multiple resources, as shown in Figure 15-11C (Navon & Gopher, 1979; Wickens, 1984). Some of these resources are probably specific to a particular modality, whereas others may be attributable to an "executive" that monitors inputs from the various modalities and controls access to response selection. Whether attention to one task interferes with attention to another would then depend on the characteristics of the tasks and the processing required. For example, monitoring and analyzing two prose passages read into the two ears will probably require that the same set of resources and analyzers be utilized, hence these two tasks would interfere with each other. In contrast, drawing a picture or doodling while monitoring someone speaking probably involves different types of mental capacity and one task will not compete with the other for mental resources. Recent research suggests that the bottleneck and capacity models can be combined, and it may make sense to think of selectivity and capacity limitations at both early and late processing stages (Dark, Johnston, Myles-Worsley & Farah, 1985).

Where does this leave us with the notion of attention and its role in perception? Simply put, that which we do not attend to, or which does not force us to orient toward it, has no more effect on us than a subthreshold stimulus. Attention is the gateway through which only selected stimuli, a few out of endless hordes impinging on our receptors, enter into the limited realm we call consciousness.

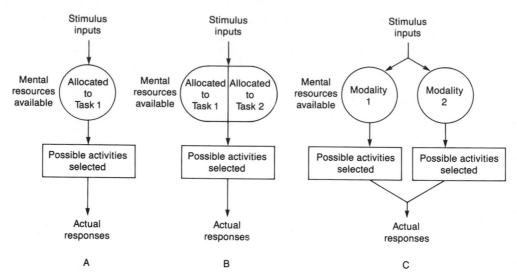

FIGURE 15-11   Attentional resource models. These models suggest that attention is limited by the mental resources available. Parts A and B show a single resource model. Notice that in B, where attention must be divided between two tasks, fewer resources are available for Task 1 than in A where attention is undivided. This would suggest decreased performance for Task 1 under divided attention. In C, we have a model where there are separate resources available for different modalities or task types. Whether tasks interfere with each other thus depends on whether they require the same or different modalities.

GLOSSARY

The following definitions are specific to this book.

Attentional gaze   A metaphor for how attention is drawn or directed to stimulus cues.

Attentional resources   The capacity for processing stimulus inputs that can be "used up" by a task, resulting in poorer performance in divided-attention situations.

Automatic processing   A type of information processing characterized by parallel, capacity-free, and involuntary comparison of stimulus items with target representations.

Benefit   When a valid information cue results in improved perceptual performance.

Binocular rivalry   If the views presented to the two eyes are different enough, we see only one or the other of them but not both.

Conjunction search   A type of search for a target defined by a conjunction, or particular combination, of features each of which is also possessed by some distractors.

Controlled processing   A type of information processing characterized by a serial, capacity-limited, voluntary comparison of stimulus items with target representations.

Cost   When an invalid information cue results in poorer perceptual performance.

Covert orienting   When attention is focused on a stimulus in the absence of an overt orienting response.

Detail set   The level of detail, for example the relative size of elements, for which the attentional gaze is set.

Dichoptic presentation   Presentation of different information to each of the two eyes.

Dichotic listening   A technique in which two different messages are simultaneously played through earphones, with a different message to each ear.

Divided attention   Attention directed toward more than one source of stimulus information or more than one perceptual task.

Early selection   Attentional selection occurs immediately following sensory registration, before the meaning of an input can be determined.

Expecting   When an observer is in possession of advance information about where or when a stimulus event will happen.

Extent   The area of the visual or auditory field over which the attentional gaze is spread.

Feature search   A type of search for a target when the target differs from all distractors by possessing a feature they don't have.

Filtering   Attending to a single information channel and attempting to ignore others.

Focused attention   Attention directed toward only a single source of stimulus information or a single perceptual task.

Hemifield   One half of the visual field, usually as divided vertically through the fovea.

Information channel   A separable source of stimulus information, such as each of the two ears or a particular spatial location in the visual field.

Information cue   Advance information about where or when a stimulus event will happen.

Late selection   All information entering a sensory system gets preliminary analysis and selection occurs at the stage where material is entered into longer-lasting memory.

Locus   A particular spatial location to which the attentional gaze has been drawn or directed.

Orienting   When attention is drawn toward a sudden change in the environment. Often accompanied by an orienting reflex.

Orienting reflex   A constellation of responses to a novel or dramatic stimulus, including the orienting response and various physiological changes such as pupil dilation and heart-rate decrease.

Orienting response   When an observer turns toward and orients sensory receptors toward a novel or dramatic stimulus.

Parallel search   A pattern of visual search in which all the items in an array can be compared to a target representation at the same time.

Phonemic shadowing   When a listener must repeat each syllable of a shadowed message as it occurs.

Phrase shadowing   When a listener is allowed to lag somewhat behind a shadowed message and repeat entire phrases at once.

Saccades   High-speed ballistic eye movements that facilitate exploration of the visual field.

Searching   Scanning the environment for particular features or combinations of features.

Serial search   A pattern of visual search in which items in an array are compared one at a time with a target representation.

Shadowing   When listeners are asked to repeat the verbal input they are receiving, usually in a particular ear; used to study filtering and divided attention.

Skill   An approach to attention that emphasizes learning how to process stimuli optimally, rather than shifting between modes of processing, as an explanation for good divided-attention performance.

Stimulus cue   A conspicuous stimulus somewhere in the visual or auditory field toward which attention can be drawn or directed.

Stroop effect   The difficulty of observers to eliminate meaningful but conflicting information from a task even when that information is irrelevant to the task.

Structural theories   Theories of attention that emphasize a structural limitation on the ability to attend to multiple perceptual inputs.

Vigilance   Maintaining overt attention to a perceptual task, often with infrequent stimulus events, for prolonged time periods.

Visual capture   When sound seems to be originating from a spatial location where visual movement is occurring, as in ventriloquism.

Yerkes-Dodson law   The principle that arousal and performance are related, with the best performance occurring for a medium amount of arousal.

CHAPTER
16

Development

The camp counselor turned to the newest arrival and asked, "And how old are you, son?"

"Well," said the boy, "it all depends. According to my latest set of anatomical tests I'm 7. According to my physical dexterity test I'm 10. I've got a mental age of 11, a moral age of 9, and a social age of 10. If you are referring to my chronological age though, that's 8, but nobody pays any attention to that these days."

Although you might not relish the thought of spending a summer with this child, his comments point out that there are significant changes in many of our physical and psychological characteristics as we age. Each of these changes has its own time course. Some changes simply represent physiological transformations occurring as the body matures (such as a person's anatomical age). Others represent patterns of behavior that are learned as the individual grows older (such as social or moral age). Still others may represent a combination of both learning and maturation (such as mental age). Although no one refers to a perceptual age, there are also changes in perceptual characteristics that occur as an individual develops and matures. These changes are usually improvements producing perceptual experiences that more accurately represent the physical environment. However, there are also some perceptual capacities that deteriorate with age.

In considering how an individual's perceptual functioning changes we can adopt two different perspectives. The first is long-term, viewing people over their entire life span. This is the **developmental approach,** which assumes that knowledge of a person's chronological age will allow us to predict many aspects of perceptual behavior. The other approach is short-term, viewing the changes that occur in perceptual responses as a result of a circumscribed set of experiences. This is the **perceptual learning approach.** It is based on the presumption that our interactions with the world can shape our percepts. These two approaches are not mutually exclusive; understanding the nature of perception often requires us to use both. Common

to both viewpoints is the conclusion that, despite the fact that you may not be aware of it, your perceptual behavior is continually changing. Your experience of the world differs from individuals who are 10 years older or 10 years younger than you. Because the developmental and perceptual learning approaches use different techniques and often address somewhat different theoretical issues, we deal with these areas in separate chapters, beginning here with the developmental approach and proceeding to the effects of learning and experience in Chapter 17.

PERCEPTION IN INFANTS

Before speaking about how perception changes as we age and develop, we must first know what perceptual capacities we had at the moment of birth. Unfortunately, newborn infants *(neonates)* are difficult to test. They sleep most of the time, and they do not respond to instructions or answer our questions in any direct verbal fashion. Finally, they produce only a limited range of observable behaviors. These problems require experimenters to be rather ingenious in devising measures of the perceptual abilities of the very young, and different techniques may produce somewhat different pictures of the developmental process (Teghtsoonian, 1987; Trehub & Schneider, 1987). These same problems also often force researchers to use animal subjects rather than humans, especially if direct physiological measures of functioning are desired.

Development of the Visual System

Let us begin by looking at the physiology of the infant's visual system. In comparison to the rest of the body, the size of the eye changes very little after birth. The body may increase in size about 20 times, but the eye merely doubles in volume, with the length from the cornea to the retina growing from about 16 to about 24 mm (Hickey & Peduzzi, 1987). The infant's retina contains rods and cones as does the adult's. Electrical measures indicate that these receptors are functioning from birth, although the responses may not yet exactly match those of older children or adults (Aantaa, 1970; Maurer, 1975). Anatomically, however, the retina still seems immature (Banks & Salapatek, 1983). For instance, the region of the central fovea is not well defined in a 1-week-old infant (Abramov, Gordon, Henderson, Hainline, Dobson & La Bossiere, 1982). Visual development seems to take place first in the central retina, with the peripheral portion maturing several weeks later (Banks & Salapatek, 1983; Russoff, 1979).

Knowledge of the status of the visual pathways in newborns and infants comes mostly from animal studies, with the cat providing most of the data. If we measure the physiological functions of the various sites in the visual pathways of the cat at the time when the animal first opens its eyes, we get results like those in Table 16-1 (see Hickey & Peduzzi, 1987; Imbert, 1985; Norton, 1981a). The table shows that a number of adultlike and immature response patterns coexist in the newborn cat. Thus, in the retinal ganglion cell, we find the expected center-surround arrangement of excitatory and inhibitory responses; however, the receptive fields differ in size from those of the adult and there is a general sluggishness in the response (e.g., Russoff & Dubin, 1977).

In Chapter 3 we discussed two different visual response types, sustained and transient, characterizing X- and Y-type retinal ganglion cells,

Table 16-1. The Functional Condition of Various Sites in the Visual Pathways of the Newborn Cat

Adultlike Responses	*Immature Responses*
Retinal Ganglion Cells	
Center-surround organization of receptive fields	Low activity level
	Overly large receptive fields
Adult percentage of on/off center	Slow responses to light and weak inhibition
	X vs. Y responses not clear
Lateral Geniculate Nucleus	
Normal visual-field mapping	Low activity and silent areas
Binocular separation of inputs	Large receptive field diameter
	Slow, sluggish, fatigable responding
Superior Colliculus	
Normal visual-field mapping	Slow, sluggish fatigable responses
Center-surround receptive fields	Large receptive fields
Adult percentage of on/off center	No movement direction sensitivity
Striate Cortex	
Normal visual-field mapping	Sluggish, fatigable responses
Adult separation of responses by eye of input	Many silent cells
	Fewer or absent orientation and direction-selective cells with broader tuning
	No binocular disparity cells

respectively. These appear to involve different types of information processing, with the sustained (X-cell) responses associated principally with detail vision and the transient (Y-cell) responses specialized for movement and rapid response. These two systems are characterized both by response pattern differences and by different pathways to the cortex. In the infant cat, however, the two response types are not as well defined, and the difference between the sustained response and transient response systems is much reduced (Hamasaki & Sutija, 1979; Mooney, Dubin & Russoff, 1979).

At the lateral geniculate nucleus, we do find the adult correspondence between retinal response location and geniculate response location, the separation of the inputs from the two eyes into clearly defined layers, and some evidence of the X-like sustained response types. However, many of the cells in the geniculate simply don't seem to respond to any sort of visual input, responses are generally slow and fatigue easily, and the transient Y-like responses appear to be absent (Daniels, Pettigrew & Norman, 1978). A somewhat similar pattern emerges for the superior colliculus, with the general topography resembling that of the adult and with a center-surround organization of responses. However, again, receptive field size is too large and responses are slow and weak and not particularly direction sensitive (Norton, 1981a).

Finally, at the level of the primary visual cortex, we find that the two eyes' inputs do separate into the expected columnar arrangement discussed in Chapter 3, and that directional and orientation-sensitive cells (both simple and complex) are sometimes present. However, there appear to be fewer of these feature-specific cells, and even when they are found, responses are slow and easily fatigable (Imbert, 1985). Binocular-disparity-sensitive cells seem to be almost absent until several weeks of age (Blakemore & van Sluyters, 1975; Fregnac & Imbert, 1978; Held, 1985). Overall, many of the characteristics of the adult system seem to be present or anticipated in the newborn visual system, but

the full adult pattern of response clearly is not present (Banks & Salapatek, 1983). Some of these statements are species specific, and humans appear to develop somewhat more slowly than cats do. Thus, whereas cats show separation of the two eyes into ocular dominance columns from birth, humans may take 4 to 6 months to develop similar complex neural structures (Hickey & Peduzzi, 1987).

It should be clear from this discussion that many of the characteristics of the visual system mature at different rates. The X pathways to the cortex may mature more quickly than the Y pathways (Maurer & Lewis, 1979). Also, the responses of the neonate are slower and less vigorous than those of the adult, suggesting that the quality of visual information reaching the higher centers of the newborn's brain may be somewhat poorer (see Movshon & van Sluyters, 1981). This leads to different perceptual functions appearing at different times during development, as we will see shortly.

In humans, we can determine how well the visual cortex of the infant is functioning by measuring what is called the **visually evoked potential** (often abbreviated **VEP**). This is a change in the electrical activity of the brain in response to a visual stimulus, which is correlated with some aspects of visual detection and pattern identification (Cannon, 1983). The VEP is usually recorded by fixing electrodes (generally flat pieces of silver) to the scalp and connecting them to very sensitive amplifiers. Almost all newborn infants (and even most premature infants) show some VEP, although it differs somewhat from the adult response in its pattern, size, and speed (Ellingson, 1968; Umezaki & Morrell, 1970). Over a period of about 3 months, the infant's electrical responses to visual stimuli come to look more and more like those of adults (Atkinson & Braddick, 1981; Banks & Salapatek, 1983; Harter & Suitt, 1970; Jensen & Engel, 1971). It is generally agreed that during the first year of life the visual system may continue to mature, and that, although it begins to show many adult capabilities by the end of the second year

(Ellingson, Lathrop, Nelson & Donahy, 1972; Movshon & van Sluyters, 1981), the brain continues to develop until the child is 10 years of age or older (Imbert, 1985).

Infant Visual Psychophysical Methods

Methods of testing infants' visual capacities must be very carefully devised, since we can't use verbal instructions or obtain verbal responses from them. The researcher's only recourse is to use existing behaviors, which, for perceptual research, usually involves attending behaviors. These include eye movements, head turns, visual following behavior, and other subtle indicators (Banks & Dannemiller, 1987). Given the limited response repertoire available to a young baby, we can appreciate the methodological breakthrough accomplished by Fantz (1961). His procedure, called **preferential looking,** involves first placing a young baby in a special chamber (either on its back or in an infant chair). Visual stimuli are then placed on the walls or the roof of the chamber, and there is a tiny hole through which the experimenter can watch the baby. An apparatus similar to Fantz's is shown in Figure 16-1. When the baby views one of a pair of stimulus patterns placed in the chamber, the experimenter determines which one by noting where the eyes turn and then triggers a timer that records how long the infant views each of the two stimuli. If the baby looks at one target longer than the other, this is taken as indicating a preference for it. The existence of a preference implies that the infant can discriminate between the patterns. Unfortunately, this simple result does not tell us why the baby preferred to look at one stimulus rather than the other, nor can we be sure that the absence of a preference means that the baby cannot discriminate between the two stimuli.

There have been many elaborations of this

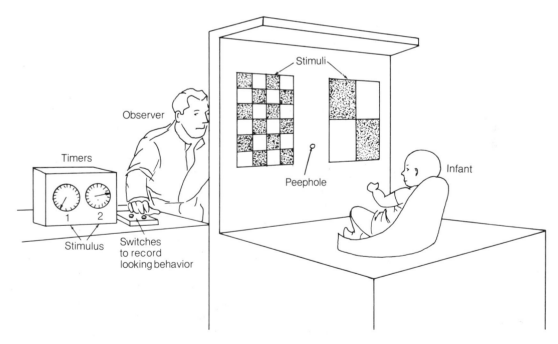

FIGURE 16-1   An apparatus for monitoring how long infants view particular stimuli.

technique, such as the one by Teller (1981) called the **forced-choice preferential looking** technique. Her procedure allows the investigation of the detection of stimuli as well as discrimination between stimuli. Here, the infant is presented with only a single stimulus, while its response is monitored by a hidden observer or TV camera. If, on the basis of the infant's head and eye movements alone, the observer can correctly tell whether the test target was presented to the left or right side of the screen, it is presumed that the information concerning the position of the target has been transmitted from the screen through the infant's visual system and behavior to the observer. At the minimum, this suggests that the infant can see the stimulus.

A further variation of monitoring an infant's looking behavior allows us to see if an infant can notice any difference between stimuli. Again, only one stimulus is presented and the viewing behavior is monitored. At first the infant will spend a good deal of time looking at the stimulus, but as time passes it will cease to pay any attention to it. This process is called **habituation.** If we now present a different stimulus, the baby will once again look. The presence of renewed looking at the stimulus suggests that the infant can see that something has changed, and that the present stimulus is different from the previous one (e.g., Kellman & Spelke, 1983; McCall, 1979).

These looking techniques in conjunction with the monitoring of eye movements and physiological responses (such as the VEP), and a few more esoteric methods, provide the main methods for measuring infant visual capacities (Banks & Dannemiller, 1987).

Eye Movements and Spatial Vision

In Chapter 10 we saw that certain aspects of spatial vision, such as the binocular perception of depth or distance, are not present at birth but take time to develop (e.g., Held, 1985; Yonas & Granrud, 1985a). The perception of direction, however, is

much better, as shown by the fact that infants can move their eyes so as to bring targets onto or close to their foveas. Thus, if we present a young infant (about 2 weeks of age) with a target that suddenly appears 15 deg or 20 deg from the fovea, he will turn his eyes in the direction of the stimulus (Tronick, 1972). As the infant grows older, he will direct his eyes toward targets that appear even farther away in the periphery (Aslin, 1987; Harris & MacFarlane, 1974). Furthermore, 3-month-old infants seem to be able to identify targets in the periphery of their visual field well enough to guide their eyes to selected or preferred stimuli (Maurer & Lewis, 1979).

Although infants will look at a target that flashes on to the side, or suddenly moves to one side, infants' eye movements are not exactly like those of adults. There are two types of voluntary eye movements, each taking time to develop fully. The first is **saccadic eye movements,** which are fast, sharp movements from one target to another that occur when you direct your attention toward a target. In adults, a saccade will start the eye moving toward a target displaced to the side within 200 to 250 msec, and usually come within 5 or 10 percent of the distance needed to center the image on the fovea in a single movement (e.g., Komoda, Festinger, Phillips, Duckman & Young, 1973). A typical adult eye movement to a target 30 deg to the side is shown in Figure 16-2. Infants are much slower to begin the saccade, and tend to make a series of small saccades, often not reaching the target for well over a second or more, as shown in Figure 16-2 (see Aslin, 1987).

The other type of eye movement is the **smooth-pursuit eye movement** used to track a steadily moving object, such as a ball flying through the air or a person on a swing, where the eyes track the target with a uniform and even motion. Smooth-pursuit eye movements do not appear in newborns, they use short, jumpy, saccadic eye movements to track smoothly moving objects. Thus, rather than keeping pace with the moving target infants seem to attempt to

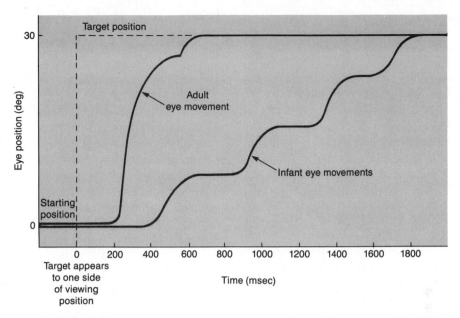

FIGURE 16-2   A typical adult eye movement to a target appearing 30 deg to one side of fixation will involve a single, fast, large saccade and a small corrective flick, whereas an infant will have a longer delay before moving, and the movement will involve a series of short eye movements.

grab a fixed glimpse of it, wait till it drifts from view, and then attempt to look at it again, so producing a set of little stepwise movements rather than a smooth tracking. The more adultlike pattern of smooth movement begins to emerge at 8 to 10 weeks of age (Aslin, 1981a).

The fact that infants move their eyes in response to moving or displaced stimuli can be used to measure other capacities in the newborn. For instance, if we show an adult observer a continuously moving pattern (such as a screen full of stripes all moving in one direction) we get a characteristic eye-movement pattern. The eye will smoothly track in the direction of the movement for a distance, and then snap back in the opposite direction. After this return movement the observer's eyes lock onto another stripe and follow it, and this process repeats itself while the observer views the array. This repetitive eye movement sequence in the presence of a moving pattern is called **optokinetic nystagmus.**

A generally similar (albeit not as smooth) pattern of eye movements is found in infants younger than 5 days (Kremenitzer, Vaughan, Kurtzberg & Dowling, 1979). In fact its appearance is so reliable that the absence of optokinetic nystagmus is used as an indication that there may be neurological problems (Brazelton, Scholl & Robey, 1966). This eye-movement pattern seems to be automatic or reflex in nature, rather than voluntary, and it seems to be controlled by the tectopulvinar system we described in Chapter 3 (Atkinson & Braddick, 1981; Hoffmann, 1979). The perceptual scientist can use these reflex movements to measure other aspects of visual function. If an infant cannot see a pattern of moving stripes (because they are not large enough or lack sufficient contrast), it will not be able to track the moving pattern. This technique has been used to study brightness discrimination, visual acuity, and motion perception (see Banks & Salapatek, 1983).

Visual Acuity

Many studies have shown that the visual acuity of infants is rather poor, but improves steadily with age. A number of different methods have been used in these studies. For instance, the optokinetic response can be used to test the visual acuity of infants by finding the narrowest width of stripes that will still produce the tracking response. Alternatively, one of the preferential looking procedures can be used. The levels of acuity found for infants may vary with the technique (Teller & Movshon, 1986) or the specific acuity stimuli used (Shimojo & Held, 1987), but there is a general agreement that visual acuity is originally quite poor, often around 20/800 (6/240 in metric units) for neonates (which is less than that needed to see the single big E on a standard Snellen acuity chart). Newborns act as if they had limited accommodative ability, with their lenses fixed somewhere around a focus point of 20 cm (White, 1971). The child's acuity increases steadily with age, finally reaching average adult levels at around 3 or 4 years of age, as shown in Figure 16-3. If you have access to a young infant you can see the effect of this limited accommodation by trying Demonstration Box 16-1.

Brightness and Color

A variety of techniques has been used to assess the basic sensitivity of infants to brightness and color. The findings show that 3-month-old infants are about 10 times less sensitive to light, both under dark-adapted (scotopic) and light-adapted (photopic) conditions, than are adults, and 1-month-old infants are about 50 times less sensitive (Peeples & Teller, 1978; Powers, Schneck & Teller, 1981). However, despite this difference, infants like adults are still exquisitely sensitive to small amounts of light. For example, in Chapter 4 we found that an adult can detect an input of as little as 6 quanta of light hitting anywhere in a patch of 1,300 rod receptors. In comparison, a 3-month-old infant would need an input of about 40 quanta of light over the same region, and a 1-month-old infant would detect an input of about 100 quanta of light (see Teller & Bornstein, 1987), still a very minimal amount of light.

A number of studies show that despite differences in absolute sensitivity, the relative sensitivity of infants and adults to different wavelengths of light is about the same. Both are most sensitive to middle wavelengths, and exhibit a gradual decrease in sensitivity to longer and shorter wavelengths

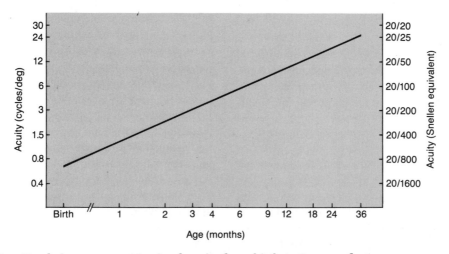

FIGURE 16-3   Steady improvement in visual acuity from birth to 3 years of age.

DEMONSTRATION BOX 16-1.   Infant Accommodation

To demonstrate that an infant's accommodation is limited to close objects, you will, of course, need an infant, preferably 2 months of age or younger. If you can find one, catch its attention and then slowly move a pencil from side to side near the infant's face. Use a distance of about 20 cm, or around 8 inches. Watch the child's head and eyes and notice that the infant will track, or at least try to track, the pencil. Now repeat this, only vary the distance to 1 or 2 meters away from the child. At this distance you should have exceeded the ability of the infant to accommodate and you should notice that little, if any, tracking occurs.

(Dobson, 1976; Moskowitz-Cook, 1979; Werner, 1979). This does not mean, however, that infants have color vision equivalent to that of adults. In general, young infants do show the ability to discriminate between colors (Bornstein, 1985; Werner & Wooten, 1979). However, color vision matures, and discrimination performance improves. Varner, Cook, Schneck, McDonald, and Teller (1985) reported that most 1-month-old infants fail to make a discrimination between a pair of short-wavelength stimuli, thus acting much like tritanopic color-blind individuals (see Chapter 5), whereas most 2-month-old infants do make this discrimination. Although there is good color discrimination between the long and middle wavelengths of light (red and green) for the 1-month-old infant, the short-wavelength (blue) discriminating mechanism seems to be immature (see Teller & Bornstein, 1987). Thus, at birth, infants do have brightness and color vision, but brightness sensitivity lags behind that of the adult and color perception is still in the process of developing.

Pattern Discrimination

The preferential-looking technique has been used extensively to explore pattern perception in infants. Using this procedure it is possible to show that premature infants, born 1 to 2 months prior to a full-term gestation, still often preferentially look at patterned stimuli rather than plain ones of equal average brightness, and also sometimes discriminate between different patterns (Fantz & Miranda, 1977). This means that the optical and neural bases of pattern vision do not abruptly become functional after the full term of pregnancy, the age at which babies can first be ordinarily observed, but rather have already matured to a reasonable degree of function prior to the normal birth time.

Preferential-looking studies have shown that young infants can discriminate among a variety of different types of patterns. For instance, in one experiment newborn infants were shown pairs of targets. These neonates showed a clear preference for viewing patterns of stripes over a simple square, and also preferred patterns with high contrast between the figures and the background. They showed a preference for larger patterns, indicating that they can discriminate size, and also preferred patterns containing many rather than few elements. In addition, they showed some ability to discriminate certain aspects defining contours, such as curvature, by preferring curved to straight-line elements. Figure 16-4 shows some sample forms, and the star indicates those most preferred by newborns for each pair (Fantz & Yeh, 1979).

Generally, infants prefer moderately complex stimuli over those that are very simple or very complex, although preferences do change with age (Karmel & Maisel, 1975). Younger infants prefer simple patterns with highly contrasting elements, whereas 5-month-olds can make more subtle distinctions in contrast and configuration (Fantz & Yeh, 1979). Banks and Salapatek (1983) suggested

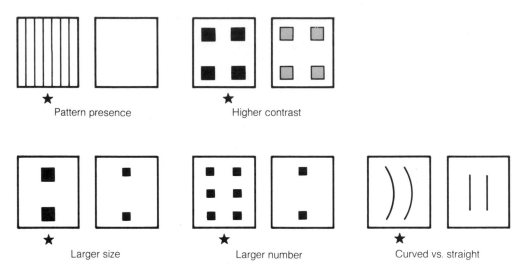

FIGURE 16-4   Patterns most looked at by newborns are indicated with a star for each pair of stimuli. **(Based on Fantz & Yeh, 1979)**

that pattern perception in infants reflects the developing ability to discriminate various spatial frequencies (see Chapter 4).

Preferences in viewing also show that some higher-level aspects of pattern perception are possible for the young infant. Infants can discriminate the orientation of patterns within the first few weeks (Maurer & Martello, 1980), and perhaps even on the first day of life (Kessen, Salapatek & Haith, 1972). Furthermore, they seem to be aware of certain forms of symmetry, or its absence (Bornstein, 1981). Although infants respond to both the size and position of stimuli, at age 4 months they are relatively insensitive to changes in the configuration of the stimuli (Humphrey, Humphrey, Muir & Dodwell, 1986). Furthermore, 3- to 4-month-old infants seem to pay attention to specific features (such as whether the dots making up a pattern are square rather than round) instead of to global changes in the configuration (such as the pattern the dots make); by 6 or 7 months they are responding to these global changes as well (Dineen & Meyer, 1980). Figure 16-5 summarizes the sensitivity of the 4-month-old infant to various aspects of visual patterns. It shows a pattern to which the infant is

habituated, and then some test patterns. The patterns accompanied by a plus sign are changes that the infant would be expected to notice; that with minus sign is a change that would not be noticed (see Dodwell, Humphrey & Muir, 1987).

Certain meaningful patterns receive special attention, even from neonates. A number of researchers have studied the response of infants to targets that approximate the human face. One common procedure is to use some targets that are only head-shaped, others containing only some facial features (such as a hairline or eyes), some containing scrambled facial features, and others that actually look like faces. Samples of such stimuli are shown in Figure 16-6. In general, it is found that by 2 months of age infants prefer to look at stimuli that contain facial features arranged in the normal configuration rather than scrambled facial stimuli, whereas children younger than 1 month do not make this discrimination (Carey, 1981; Haaf, 1977; Maurer & Barrera, 1981). Between 1 month and 4 months infants begin to take note of certain features in the facelike stimulus. By about 10 or 12 weeks, infants notice and recognize changes in the hairline and eyes, although changes in mouth and nose con-

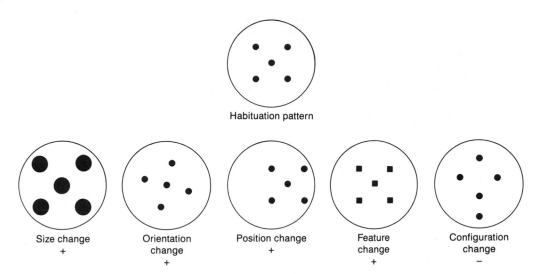

FIGURE 16-5   In a habituation experiment where 4-month-old infants habituate to the top pattern, they act as if they recognize changes in the pattern dimensions indicated by a plus (+) sign, but do not for the change in pattern indicated by the minus (−) sign.

figurations go unnoticed (Caron, Caron, Caldwell & Weiss, 1973). However, the configurational and specific features picked up by infants only 1 month of age do seem to be sufficient to permit the infant to discriminate its own mother's face from that of a stranger (Maurer & Salapatek, 1976), which suggests that young infants can discriminate among certain classes of fairly complex patterns.

A general summary of the child's increasing visual competence, when certain skills or the ability to resolve certain features or cues in the environment appear, is presented in Figure 16-7.

Infant Hearing

The ears of infants are functional at birth, but the auditory cortex is still rather immature and continues to develop over the first year (Kuhl, 1987). A number of studies have suggested that infants less than 6 months of age have higher absolute thresholds than those of adults (Berg & Smith, 1983; Trehub, Schneider & Endman, 1980). An interesting feature of these data is that the differences are most noticeable in the frequency range below 10000 Hz. The ability of adults to detect tones in

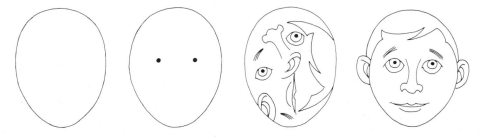

FIGURE 16-6   Schematic and scrambled facelike stimuli.

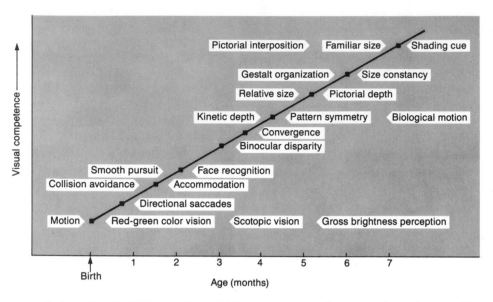

FIGURE 16-7   Various visual abilities, and sensitivity to various environmental or stimulus dimensions, appear at different ages.

this range is nearly twice as good as that of infants (Olsho, 1984). At the higher frequencies, however, infants show more adultlike sensitivity (Kuhl, 1987).

Newborns seem to be able to indicate their ability to localize the direction of a sound source by turning either their head or eyes (Butterworth, 1981; Muir & Field, 1979). Probably the youngest child tested for this ability was by Wertheimer (1961). A mere 3 minutes after birth, with the infant lying on her back, a loud click was sounded next to her right ear or left ear. Two observers noted whether the eyes moved to the infant's right or to her left, or not at all. On 18 out of the 22 times when the child's eyes moved, they moved in the direction of the click. When the experiment was completed the child was still only 10 minutes old; hence these data allow us to conclude that some directional aspects of auditory stimuli are accurately processed and are capable of guiding behavior from birth.

You probably recall from Chapter 7 that there are several binaural cues that help to indicate the direction of a sound relative to the listener. The two most important of these are the time differences in the arrival of low frequency sounds to the two ears (first to the closer ear), and the intensity differences between the two ears caused by the lack of bending of higher frequencies of sound around the head (see Green, 1976; Moore, 1977). Which of these cues is most effective for the infant? By directly controlling both the time differences between the ears and the intensity of sound reaching the two ears, Clifton, Morrongiello, and Dowd (1984) demonstrated that newborn infants, and those up to about 9 weeks of age, respond to intensity differences between the two ears by turning in the direction of the sound. At this age, the more complex time discrimination cue is not adequate to induce the child to turn its head in the appropriate direction, but by age 5 months both cues are effective and cause the child to look in the direction of

---

DEMONSTRATION BOX 16-2.   Auditory Localization in Infants

If you have access to an infant, auditory localization is easily demonstrated. Simply look squarely at the child and then make a sharp sound near one ear. Good sound sources are a rattle, a snap of the fingers, or a toy "clicker." Watch the infant's head and eyes. You should see the eyes flick in the direction of the sound, or you may see the head turn in the direction of the stimulus.

---

the sound source. If you have access to an infant, Demonstration Box 16-2 will show you how to demonstrate auditory localization.

Touch and Pain in Infants

Generally speaking, touch and heat sensitivity appear to be among the first sensory modalities to emerge during the course of fetal development (Hall & Oppenheim, 1987). This can be demonstrated through certain reflexes, which show the ability to feel and to localize touch stimuli immediately after birth. For instance, there is the **rooting response,** in which a child will reflexively turn its head in the direction of a touch to the cheek. This response helps the child to locate the breast for feeding. Demonstration Box 16-3 shows you how to elicit this directional response.

There is a widespread belief among many clinicians and other investigators that because the cortex is not fully developed in the neonate infants do not experience pain as severely as adults, nor is its impact believed to persist as long (e.g., Eland & Anderson, 1977). This has led to the practice of giving little treatment for pain to babies during or after major medical procedures and operations (see Liebeskind & Melzack, 1987; Owens, 1984). Unfortunately, recent evidence (e.g., Grunau & Craig, 1987) suggests that this is not the case, and infants appear to be just as susceptible to the perception of pain as adults.

Taste and Smell in Infants

Taste receptors start to form early in fetal life and are apparent as early as 13 weeks after conception (Bradley & Stern, 1967). In general, then, neonates appear to be as well equipped with taste receptors as adults. However, they respond to the taste primaries differently (Crook, 1987). Using sucking responses as an indicator, Lipsett (1977) found a preference for sweet stimuli in newborns. Even small differences in the concentration of sweetness produced differences in neonatal reactions. How-

---

DEMONSTRATION BOX 16-3.   The Rooting Response

The easiest method to show tactile sensitivity and localization in infants is to elicit the reflex called the *rooting response*. To see how early this ability exists, a very young baby of less than 2 months of age should be used (although the response can be elicited in older infants). To demonstrate tactile localization ability you should stroke the infant's cheek lightly with your finger. If you stroke the right cheek the infant should turn to the right. If you stroke the left cheek the infant should turn to the left.

ever, infants less than about 4 months of age seem to be insensitive to the taste of salt (Beauchamp & Cowart, 1985). If we use strong enough concentrations, we can get some indication of responses to sour and bitter stimuli by watching for differences in facial responses (Ganchrow, Steiner & Daher, 1983). Thus, we can probably summarize neonatal gustatory perception as clearly showing sweet sensitivity, with less sensitivity for sour and bitter, and very weak or absent salt sensitivity (Crook, 1987).

Work on infant smelling ability has involved presenting newborns with a cotton swab saturated with some olfactory stimulus. The swab is placed under the infant's nose and activities such as heart rate, respiration, and general bodily activity are monitored using a polygraph (i.e., Engen, Lipsitt & Kaye, 1963). These studies have shown that infants can detect a number of strong odorants, such as anise oil, asafetida, alcohol, and vinegar. However, infants seem to have more sensitivity to smells than originally thought. For example, newborn infants turn away from noxious odors and toward pleasant ones (Rieser, Yonas & Wikner, 1976). This turning response has been used to show that infants respond to odorants of human body origin. Babies less than 2 weeks old will orient toward an object carrying their mother's scent, such as a breast pad (Cernoch & Porter, 1985; Russell, 1976). There is even the suggestion that, in contrast to some of the other limitations on infant sensory capacities, children actually may be considered to be more responsive than adults to human body odors (Filsinger & Fabes, 1985).

PERCEPTUAL CHANGE THROUGH CHILDHOOD

Throughout childhood there is a general improvement in perceptual discrimination, identification, and information processing. Many of these changes occur fairly rapidly within the first year or two, and others continue over much longer time spans.

The most dramatic changes seem to occur at around the age of 2 months (Atkinson & Braddick, 1981; Maurer & Lewis, 1979), when there is a sudden improvement in the child's visual abilities. Acuity increases markedly (Braddick & Atkinson, 1979), tracking behavior becomes more adultlike (Atkinson, 1979), the ability to recognize individual elements surrounded by an enclosing contour appears (Milewski, 1976), and infants begin to show more adultlike eye-movement patterns when viewing figures (Hainline, 1978). By 3 months of age stereoscopic depth perception appears (Shea, Fox, Aslin & Dumais, 1980), and this ability continues to improve over the first 2 years (Fox, Aslin, Shea & Dumais, 1980; Held, 1985). The ability to discriminate depth based on binocular disparity also seems to improve throughout childhood and into early adolescence (Romano, Romano & Puklin, 1975).

Other basic visual processes also seem to develop rapidly over the first 2 years. Thus, visual acuity, which is originally quite poor, improves steadily into early childhood (Gwiazda, Brill, Mohindra & Held, 1980) and early astigmatic problems, which serve to lower visual resolution in infants, also disappear (Atkinson, Braddick & French, 1979; Ingram & Barr, 1979). By 5 years of age children seem to have fully developed scotopic and photopic visual systems, which show adaptation effects and sensitivities equivalent to those of adults.

A similar pattern is found for the other senses. Consider hearing as an example. Infants begin with a substantial low-frequency hearing deficit and a lesser high-frequency deficit. Over the first 2 years hearing improves quickly, especially for the low frequencies, and the improvement then continues more gradually until about 10 years of age (Kuhl, 1987; Trehub et al., 1980; Yoneshige & Elliott, 1981).

Attention and Search

In addition to changes in basic sensory processes, there appear to be changes in the patterns of attention and information encoding, which show up as developmental changes in perception. Theorists such as Hochberg (1981, 1982) suggest that what is happening during the developmental process is that the way information is integrated over time is changing. This notion of **integration** involves the construction of mental models of the perceptual situation called **schemata.** In addition, it involves the ability to select relevant information and to retain and compare this new perceptual information to the existing schemata. Simply put, this means that attention and memory come to play a role in the perceptual process.

As we learned in Chapter 15, one of the ways we can observe the pattern of overt attention is to monitor eye movements. Developmental theorists, such as Piaget (1969), have argued that patterns of eye movements provide some clues as to which stimuli are being selected and compared by individuals of different ages. For instance, we know that adults display a strong tendency to look at forms that are informative, unusual, or of particular functional value (Antes, 1974; Friedman & Liebelt, 1981; Loftus & Mackworth, 1978). Thus, by monitoring eye-movement patterns in children, we are observing the **search** component of visual attention. Information about search should be helpful in determining how children are viewing, and hence constructing, their visual world.

We have already seen that infants from birth to 2 months do make a variety of eye movements—such as fixating stationary stimuli, tracking moving stimuli, or guiding their eyes toward stimuli in the periphery—although not as precisely as do adults. More importantly, they typically do not move their eyes to the most informative parts of the stimulus (at least by adult standards) but rather seem to view only limited parts of the stimulus, usually around a border or corner (Day, 1975; Mackworth & Bruner, 1970). For instance, when there is a distinct contour within the visual field of an infant, its eye is drawn toward it. Infants of 1 month tend to direct their eyes toward one distinctive feature of a visual stimulus, such as the corner of a triangle (Haith, Bergman & Moore, 1977; Salapatek &

Kessen, 1973). Their eyes seem to be "captured" by the feature since they dwell on it for prolonged periods. Because the gaze of a 1-month-old infant is caught by the first contour encountered, most of the viewing time is spent focused on the external contours of a form. If the stimulus has internal features, they are ignored or missed. This changes by the age of 2 months. Now the infant scans the contours a little more and shorter periods are spent on each feature (Banks & Salapatek, 1983; Hainline, 1978; Salapatek, 1975). In addition, the infant dwells almost exclusively on the internal features of the stimulus, seemingly ignoring the overall pattern. These differences are shown in Figure 16-8.

The patterns of 3- and 4-year-olds are similar to those of a 2-month-old infant. Children of this

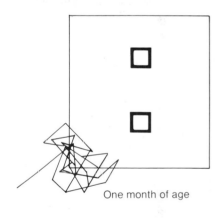

One month of age

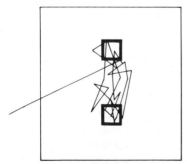

Two months of age

FIGURE 16-8   **Eye movements typical of 1- and 2-month-old infants.**

age spend most of their time dwelling on the internal details of a figure, with only an occasional eye movement beyond the contour boundary. The 4- or 5-year-old child begins to make eye-movement excursions toward the surrounding contour. At 6 and 7 years of age, there is a systematic scan of the outer portions of the stimulus with occasional eye movements into the interior. This development is shown in Figure 16-9 (Zaporozhets, 1965).

Eye-movement patterns have important consequences for certain perceptual discrimination tasks. Vurpillot (1968) monitored the eye movements of children between the ages of 2 and 9 years. They were presented with pictures of houses with different kinds of windows and were asked to indicate whether or not the houses appeared to be the same, a task that required systematic comparison of the windows. She found that the youngest children did not conduct a systematic search. Rather, they often continued searching through the houses even after looking at a pair of windows that were quite different. This lack of systematic viewing was accompanied by a low degree of accuracy in the discrimination judgments of the younger children. Older children, with more regular and systematic viewing patterns, were much more accurate. Similarly, Cohen (1981) found in a figure-matching task that 5- and 8-year-old children take longer to decide where to move their eyes than adults do in the same task. In addition, they make more eye movements and are less likely than adults to look directly at the matching target in their first eye movements. It is likely that these differences reflect differences in strategies of attention and information pickup, rather than differences in visual capacity, since eye movements seem to be strongly affected by task demands, meaning, context, and expectations (Antes & Penland, 1981; Findlay, 1981; Stark & Ellis, 1981).

Such differences in observing strategy may explain why as a child becomes older there is a gradual change in the way it comes to view patterns and the elements that make them up (Elkind, 1978). For instance, consider Figure 16-10. It con-

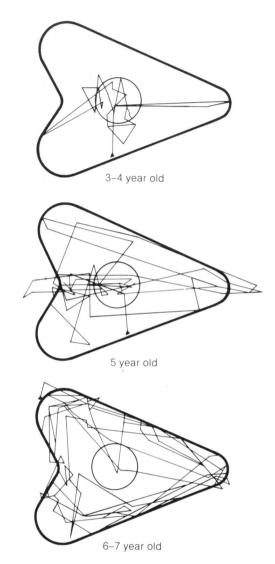

3–4 year old

5 year old

6–7 year old

FIGURE 16-9   Changes in eye movements from ages 3 to 6. (From Zaporozhets, 1965. Copyright The Society for Research in Child Development, Inc.)

sists of a number of objects (fruits and vegetables) that are organized into a larger figure (a bird). Children 4 and 5 years old report seeing only the parts ("carrots and a pear and an orange"). By the age of 7, children report seeing both the parts and the global organization ("fruits and carrots

FIGURE 16-10   A vegetable-fruit-bird figure used to measure part-versus-whole perception in children.

and a bird''). By 8 or 9 years, the majority of children respond in terms of both the parts and the global organization (''a bird made of fruits and vegetables'').

Filtering

Attention involves more than simply searching for targets and scanning the environment. Several of these other aspects have been shown to change systematically with age (Enns & Cameron, 1987). For instance, selective attention involves the component we call **filtering.** This refers to the ability to ignore irrelevant stimuli in the environment while more task-relevant stimuli are being processed. A number of studies have shown that children are more easily distracted by irrelevant stimuli (i.e., Day & Stone, 1980). Thus, in a card-sorting task, both children and adults show poorer performance if there are irrelevant as well as relevant features present; however, children show a much greater reduction in efficiency than do adults (Well, Lorch & Anderson, 1980).

There is an interesting set of phenomena that may show age changes in stimulus filtering more graphically. These are responses to **visual-geometric illusions,** which are simple line drawings in which the actual size, shape, or direction of some elements differs from the perceived size, shape, or direction (see Coren & Girgus, 1978). We have already encountered some of these illusions in Chapters 1 and 14; two of them are shown in Figure 16-11. Figure 16-11A shows the **Mueller-Lyer illusion,** in which the line marked x appears to be longer than the line marked y. Figure 16-11B shows the **Ponzo illusion,** in which the line marked w appears to be longer than the line marked z. This is the case in spite of the fact that x and y are physically equal in length, and w and z are also physically equal to each other.

One explanation for certain visual-geometric illusions is that the lines that induce the illusion become confused with the test lines, thus causing the distortion (Coren & Girgus, 1978). For instance, in the Mueller-Lyer illusion (16-11A), the upper figure *is* actually longer if you measure from wing tip to wing tip. Thus, confusing the wings with the horizontal line might add to the distortion. This idea is supported by the fact that focusing attention on the lines, and ignoring the wings, reduces the strength of the illusion (Coren & Girgus, 1972b), whereas directing attention to parts of a figure can produce stronger illusions (Coren & Porac, 1983a). If we accept this explanation, and if children are poorer at filtering out extraneous stimuli, then we should expect that children will show stronger visual illusions than adults. In general, we do find that visual illusions are larger for children and decrease with age, suggesting that children are less able to ignore the inducing lines when making their judgments (Coren & Girgus, 1978; Enns & Girgus, 1985; Pick & Pick, 1970). In one study, illusion magnitude (the degree to which individuals are susceptible to the perceived differences in line length) was found to decrease until about the age of 25 years (Porac & Coren, 1981).

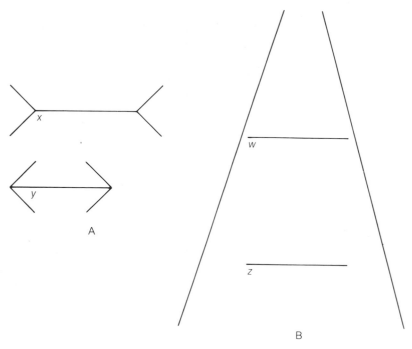

FIGURE 16-11   Two illusions that show age-related differences in their perception: (A) the Mueller-Lyer; (B) the Ponzo.

Encoding and Memory

Another factor that can affect perceptual development is the change in **encoding** ability. For a child to integrate and compare stimuli, he or she must have the ability to encode them and to remember other instances of a stimulus or the schemata associated with a particular class of stimuli. Thus, it is not surprising that a number of studies have shown that the ability to discriminate between visual patterns improves with age (Cratty, 1979).

An interesting example of the improvement of pattern recognition with age, which is probably dependent on improvements in encoding ability, involves the recognition of human faces. The very impressive achievements we noted above for 5- to 7-month-old infants in discriminating face from nonface stimuli should not be interpreted to mean that these infants have adultlike abilities in this area. The development of the ability to encode and

recognize faces continues for many years (Carey, 1981; Flin, 1980). Thus, we find that a rapid increase in the ability of children to recognize unfamiliar faces occurs between the ages of 6 and 10. To estimate the magnitude of this change we might note that under conditions where a 6-year-old will only recognize a little more than half of the faces previously shown her (60%), a 10-year-old will recognize nearly all of them (95%). Furthermore, improvement in ability can be observed even through adolescence to the age of 16 (Carey, Diamond & Woods, 1980).

There is one form of pattern discrimination error that seems to be characteristic of young children. This involves mirror reversals. Children confuse lateral mirror-image pairs (such as *p* and *q,* or *b* and *d*) more frequently than up-down mirror-image pairs (such as *p* or *b,* or *q* and *d*) (Springer & Deutsch, 1985). These confusions are quite common in young children (around 3 years old) and gradually decrease until about the age of 10 or 11 (Gaddes, 1980; Serpell, 1971). Some of the improvement seems to be associated with educational processes, since between the ages of 5 1/2 and 6 1/2 there is a sudden improvement in the ability to make these discriminations. It is likely that the improvement is caused by the formal instruction in reading and writing that usually begins at about that age. With appropriate training, kindergarten-aged children can learn the left-right discrimination quite well, although it still seems to be more difficult than the up-down discrimination (Clark & Whitehurst, 1974). Enns (1987) has demonstrated that the ability to make discriminations based on symmetries in patterns depends on the development of memory encoding ability, rather than simply on visual function.

When a child continues to have left-right confusions, he can experience problems later with reading. The specific term used for such reading disability (when it is not associated with other disturbances such as mental retardation, sensory impairment, or emotional problems) is **dyslexia.** Estimates of the incidence of dyslexia vary widely, but it seems that the problem affects no less than 2 percent of all children in Western countries, with the incidence perhaps being as high as 10 percent (Bannatyne, 1971; Gaddes, 1976; Spreen, 1976). This is a problem that seems to have a perceptual rather than an intellectual basis. The dyslexic individual may be highly talented in all other respects, except for the reading problem. There are many case histories of exceptional people who have been dyslexic, among them the inventor Thomas A. Edison, the surgeon Harvey Gushing, the sculptor Auguste Rodin, United States president Woodrow Wilson, and the author Hans Christian Anderson. One characteristic of all children who have been diagnosed as dyslexic is that they show confusions between the left-right mirror images of targets, although they have no problem with the up-down mirror images (Gaddes, 1980; Newland, 1972; Sidman & Kirk, 1974).

Children's inability to discriminate letter reversals suggests that they are relatively insensitive to the orientation of a stimulus. There is an interesting quirk associated with this issue. Consider a stimulus, such as a human face, that has a familiar orientation. When a face is inverted it seems to lose much of its facelike quality, and even very familiar individuals are difficult to identify when their photographs are turned upside down (Rock, 1974). Thus, it is not surprising to find that adult observers, who have had thousands of exposures to upright faces, show greater accuracy of identification when faces are upright than when they are inverted (Yin, 1970). However, the ability of 6-year-olds to identify faces is the same regardless of whether the face is presented in a normal or in an inverted position. By the age of 10 years, children's facial identification responses begin to look like those of adults; in other words, identification ability is disrupted when the faces are inverted (Carey & Diamond, 1977; Carey, Diamond & Woods, 1980). It seems that the adults' sensitivity to orientation differences makes it more difficult for them to identify inverted familiar faces than for 5- and 10-year-olds tested on the same task. You can explore the adult sensitivity to orientation in yourself by trying Demonstration Box 16-4.

PERCEPTUAL CHANGE IN ADULTS

Perceptual and sensory functions continue to change throughout the life span, although the rate of change is usually slower in adults than during infancy and childhood. Also, the earlier changes are toward increasing efficiency in perceptual processing, whereas the later changes, beginning around age 40, are toward decreased functioning, as sensory receptors age and neural efficiency drops (Corso, 1981).

Visual Function and Aging

A number of structural and neural changes occur in the aging individual that might be expected to reduce visual sensitivity. For instance, the aging eye generally shows a smaller pupil size, hence less

---

DEMONSTRATION BOX 16-4.   Orientation and Stimulus Recognition

Adults are more rigid in their reliance on normal orientations than are children. Look at the two figures here and you will probably find them quite difficult to identify, but if you invert the page you will see them suddenly become identifiable. This effect is especially striking for faces and for handwritten script.

A

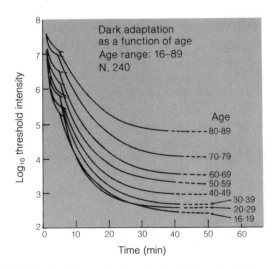

B

---

light enters the eye (Corso, 1981; Weale, 1982). The optics of the eye become less efficient since the crystalline lens continues to become yellower and darker (Coren & Girgus, 1972a), and even the cornea yellows somewhat (Lerman, 1984). Both of these factors also limit the amount of light reaching the retina. Of course, in the presence of reduced effective light input due to such factors, we would expect a decrease in sensitivity. Between 20 and 70 years of age, we find a consistent decrease in threshold sensitivities for the detection of spots of light (Fozard, Wolf, Bell, McFarland & Podolsky, 1977). This is particularly evident in dark adaptation. Although the time to reach minimum threshold remains the same, the maximum sensitivity eventually achieved decreases with age. This is shown in Figure 16-12 (McFarland, Domey, Warren, & Ward, 1960).

Some deterioration in vision may be due to loss of receptors with age, which may account for the gradual deterioration in color vision. It seems that sensitivity to the shorter wavelengths of light

FIGURE 16-12   Age changes in dark adaptation.
(From McFarland, et al., 1960)

(those that appear bluish) continually diminishes from early childhood until death (Bornstein, 1977; Lakowski, 1962). Also, some reduced function may be due to an age-related loss of neurons in the visual cortex. This neuron loss is quite extensive. Consider, for instance, the area of the cortex receiving foveal projections. In a 20-year-old this area contains about 46 million neurons per gram of tissue, whereas in an 80-year-old the neuronal density is reduced by nearly one-half, to only 24 million neurons per gram of tissue (Devaney & Johnson, 1980).

Although the number of remaining neurons is adequate for most visual tasks, we might expect this reduction in the number of responding units to show up as a reduction in visual acuity as well as in reduced sensitivity (Weale, 1986). Many studies have shown that visual acuity decreases with age; at age 40 nearly 94 percent of individuals have 20/20 visual acuity or better, whereas by age 80 only 6 percent of the population will have this level of acuity (Richards, 1977; Woo & Bader, 1978). The relationship between age and visual acuity can be seen in Figure 16-13.

The actual pattern of the acuity loss with age is quite interesting. Older observers are still able to resolve visual details, however the light level necessary for them to do so is greatly increased. In terms of our discussion in Chapter 4, we would say

that the contrast threshold is higher for these older observers (Leibowitz, Post & Ginsburg, 1980). Furthermore, it appears that the neural system that responds to transient stimulation (remember the Y cells discussed in Chapter 3) shows the greatest loss of sensitivity (Sekuler & Hutman, 1980). These findings suggest that in tasks such as night driving, where good acuity and response to relatively fast moving stimuli are required yet illumination levels are low, older individuals might be quite inefficient, and may even be at risk.

Age Effects on the Other Senses

There is much evidence, from the clinic as well as the laboratory, indicating that hearing ability declines with age. Generally speaking, hearing impairments will begin to appear during middle age and increase rapidly after age 60. About 15 percent of all people over 65 could be classified legally as deaf, and as many as 75 percent of all 70-year-olds have some hearing problems (Schaie & Geiwitz, 1982). The loss of hearing ability is much more marked for high-frequency stimuli (Corso, 1981). As can be seen from Figure 16-14, at age 70 there is still very little loss of threshold sensitivity for a 1000-Hz tone, but an 8000-Hz tone will show a reduction in threshold sensitivity of nearly 50 db.

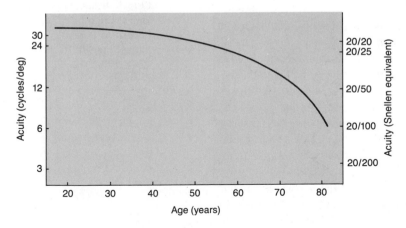

FIGURE 16-13   Age-related decrease in visual acuity.

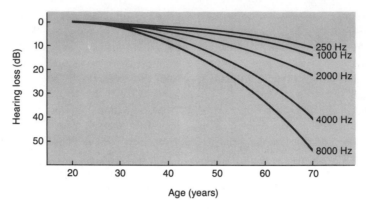

FIGURE 16-14   The age-related decrease in auditory sensitivity is particularly noticeable for the higher frequencies.

The sensitivity in a number of other modalities also decreases with advancing age. The pattern of change, however, is not always consistent. Thus, although older observers show a reduced sensitivity to touch (Thornbury & Mistretta, 1981), they do not show any decrease in their sensitivity to pain (Harkins & Chapman, 1977).

Some of the most noticeable changes with age occur in the realm of taste and smell. Odor sensitivity is greatly diminished, although the reduction is not uniform across all stimuli. For instance, elderly subjects seem best able to discriminate among fruity odors, as compared to other classes of scents (Schiffman & Pasternak, 1979). There is also a diminished sensitivity to the primary tastes. For instance, thresholds rise measurably, although not dramatically, for both salt and sugar (Grzegorczyk, Jones & Mistretta, 1979; Moore, Nielson & Mistretta, 1982). The combination of diminishing sensitivity to odor and taste in the elderly greatly reduces their ability to identify foods, especially when blended or pureed so that they are not recognizable by sight (Schiffman, 1977). Just how large a deficit results can be seen by comparing the performance of a group of 20-year-olds to a group of elderly subjects (average age of 73), and seeing how poorly the older do at recognizing foods by taste and smell alone. As can be seen in Table 16-2, in most instances the younger individuals do

twice as well, although on some common items, such as coffee, performance is about the same for both age groups.

Global Changes in Perceptual Performance

Several types of change seem to affect all the sensory modalities. The most important of these is a general slowing of neural responses, accompanied by an increasing persistence of the stimulus (ac-

Table 16-2.   The Percentage of 20-Year-Olds versus the Percentage of Elderly Individuals (Mean Age of 73 Years) Correctly Identifying Some Common Foods in Pureed Form (Based on Schiffman, 1977)

Food	20-Year-Olds	Elderly
Apple	81	55
Lemon	52	24
Strawberry	78	33
Broccoli	30	0
Carrot	63	7
Corn	67	38
Beef	41	28
Coffee	89	70
Sugar	63	57

tually slower recovery or clearing time). This means that older individuals have more trouble with briefly presented stimuli (Hoyer & Plude, 1980), show slower reaction times to stimulus onsets (Stern, Oster & Newport, 1980), and cannot readily identify stimuli arriving in a rapid sequence (Birren, Woods & Williams, 1980). This slowing of perceptual processing of the elderly individual becomes most apparent when the perceptual tasks are complex (Cerella, Poon & Williams, 1980; Cunningham, 1980).

Another general change that accompanies aging involves the distribution of attention to perceptual tasks (Botwinick, 1984). Much of this can be traced to the idea that a fixed amount of attentional resources can be divided among various tasks (see Chapter 15 and Kahneman, 1973). Older individuals seem to have more difficulty dividing their attention between various stimuli or input channels (Craik & Simon, 1980). In addition, they seem to have more difficulty filtering or extracting relevant from irrelevant targets in search or recognition tasks (Rabbitt, 1977; Wright & Elias, 1979). The more similar the irrelevant stimuli are to the target stimuli, the greater the difficulty all observers have in detecting targets in a search task. However, elderly observers have their performance disrupted at levels of difficulty that do not seem to affect younger observers (Farkas & Hoyer, 1980). Fortunately, when a task does not demand searching irrelevant stimuli to find a relevant stimulus, the deficits in attention in the aged do not appear (Kausler, 1982).

GLOSSARY

The following definitions are specific to this book.

Developmental approach   An approach to perception that presumes that chronological age is the best predictor of perceptual ability.

Dyslexia   A form of impaired reading ability characterized by confusion of letters that are left-right mirror images.

Encoding   Entering perceptual information into some form of short-term memory storage to allow recognition or other processing.

Filtering   Part of selective attention that involves screening out irrelevant stimuli while attending to relevant stimuli.

Forced-choice preferential looking   An experimental method in which observers watch infants and attempt to determine on the basis of their responses on which side of the visual field a stimulus was presented.

Habituation   The process by which an observer ceases to respond to a repeated stimulus.

Integration   The process by which an observer attempts to build an internal model of objects or relationships based on incoming stimulation and knowledge from previous interactions.

Mueller-Lyer illusion   An illusion of size in which the apparent length of a line is affected by the direction of its contextual wings.

Optokinetic nystagmus   An eye-movement sequence in which there is a smooth movement and a quick return in the presence of a moving pattern.

Perceptual learning approach   An approach to perception that maintains that the primary determinant of our perceptual abilities is our previous experience with certain environmental stimuli.

Ponzo illusion   An illusion of size in which the length of a line is perceptually affected by its place in the context of surrounding converging lines.

Preferential looking   A behavioral measure of infant discrimination in which target fixation time is assumed to be positively related to stimulus preference.

Rooting response   An infant reflex consisting of head turning in the direction of a touch to the face.

Saccadic eye movements   Sharp, jerky eye movements that place the images of objects that observers are attending to on the fovea.

Schemata   Internal models or hypotheses about the external world.

Search   Part of selective attention that involves scanning the visual field for a specific target stimulus.

Smooth-pursuit eye movement   Nonjerky movements used to track a smoothly moving target, as opposed to saccadic eye movements.

VEP   *See* Visually evoked potential.

Visual-geometric illusions   Simple line drawings in which the actual physical characteristics of certain elements differ from the perceived characteristics of those elements.

Visually evoked potential (VEP)   The change in the electrical activity of the brain produced in response to a visual stimulus.

CHAPTER
17

Learning and Experience

An article in the *New York Times* spoke of a tea expert who was called in to determine the components of a blend of tea that an American company was about to market. A small cup of it was poured for him. He sniffed it gently, sipped a bit, swished it around in his mouth a little, then looked up.

"I detect," he said crisply, "a rather good Assam, a run-of-the-mill Darjeeling, a mediocre Ceylon, and, of course, the tea bag" (Root, 1974).

Although we might be amazed at performances such as these, or similar ones of expert wine tasters, we must realize that this degree of perceptual discrimination has come about through years of training and experience. In other words, this expert had to *learn* to taste and identify these flavors.

In some of the previous chapters we have mentioned some ways in which our past history, experience, knowledge, and hypotheses affect our perception. Most people are willing to admit that some aspects of perception may be susceptible to the influences of experience, but they are often unaware of the magnitude of these effects. In fact, our past can even influence whether we perceive anything at all in certain circumstances. For example, suppose we briefly flash a visual stimulus (such as a word) in front of you. If we have chosen the duration and intensity of the stimulus carefully, you may be unaware of any aspect of the stimulus. If we flash the same stimulus again, we would expect that, again, you would see nothing. However, with repeated presentations something about its appearance will begin to change. Soon you will be able to make out fragments of this stimulus, and after a while these fragments will become more complex. Eventually the entire stimulus pattern will be identified on every trial (i.e., you can read the word), even though the luminance and exposure durations are the same as for the very first trials when you saw and identified nothing (Uhlarik & Johnson, 1978)! Your prior experience with this stimulus has changed your perceptual abilities in

some manner, and now you can see what was formerly invisible. In other words, during the course of the experiment you have learned to see this pattern.

EXPERIENCE AND DEVELOPMENT

As an organism develops, its nervous system matures, and over the years many changes in physiology and perceptual ability also come about simply because of physiological maturation. Of course, as the months and years roll by, the organism is also accumulating new experiences with the environment, and is encountering many chances to learn new perceptual coordinations. It is important for us to understand how the natural course of development interacts with an individual's life history to shape that individual's perception of the world.

Experience can affect the development of the individual's perceptual processes in several different ways. We have outlined these in Figure 17-1 (see Aslin, 1985; Gottlieb, 1981).

The strongest form of interaction between experience and development is **induction.** Here, the presence of some sort of relevant experience actually determines both the presence and final level of the ability (Figure 17-1A). The weakest form of effect we will call **maturation.** This actually represents no effect at all, and the ability might be expected to develop regardless of the individual's experience or lack of it (17-1B). Another possible interaction is **enhancement.** Here the final level of an ability, which is already present or developing, is improved because of experiential factors (17-1C). **Facilitation** increases the rate at which an ability develops, but not its final level, providing earlier acquisition of the skill but not greater proficiency (17-1D). Finally, **maintenance** serves to stabilize, or to keep, an ability that is already present (17-1E). Of course, different mechanisms might be expected to produce each of these patterns of interaction between development and experience.

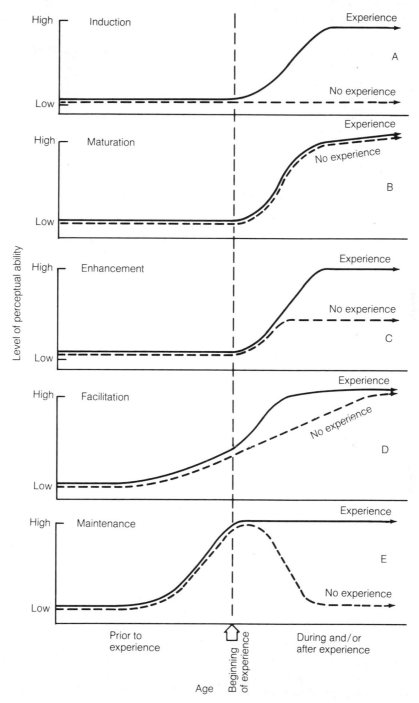

FIGURE 17-1 Various ways in which experience can interact with the development of perceptual abilities.

Restricted and Selective Rearing

The most direct method for assessing the relationship between development and experience is to deprive the observer of the opportunity to use a particular sensory modality from the moment of birth. After the individual has fully matured, we test the perceptual capacities in the deprived modality. If they have developed poorly, we would have demonstrated the need for experience in the development of normal functions. This technique is called **restricted rearing.** (We previously encountered this procedure in Chapter 10 when we discussed the development of depth perception.) A somewhat more elegant technique involves deliberately altering the pattern of experience that the developing organism is exposed to from birth. For example, an animal may be exposed to only diffuse light, vertical stripes, the color red, and so forth. Such a procedure should selectively bias, rather than eliminate, certain perceptual abilities, if experience plays a role in their development. This procedure is known as **selective rearing.**

Neurophysiological Effects

Recent research indicates that experience may play a role in the development of sensory physiological structures themselves. For instance, as discussed in Chapter 16, the visual pathways and visual cortex of the newborn differ from those of the adult; there are fewer responsive cells and these show lesser degrees of directional and orientational sensitivity (see also Hickey & Peduzzi, 1987; Norton, 1981a). Visual experience, in addition to the growth and maturation of the nervous system, seems to be necessary for the development of normal visual functioning. This has been demonstrated though restricted-rearing studies.

Let us consider what happens if we completely deprive an animal of any visual input by rearing it in the dark from birth. This animal will have a visual cortex that shows reduced overall responsiveness, when tested using the electrode implantation techniques discussed in Chapter 3. Furthermore, those cells that are found will not show the usual degree of orientation and movement selectivity (Blakemore, 1978; Leventhal & Hirsch, 1980). The visual cortex of such animals appears to be very immature, because of the absence of the usual history of visual experience.

Such neurophysiological disruption caused by the absence of visual experience can be found all along the visual pathways. Some effects are as peripheral as the retina, but they appear as well at other places such as the superior colliculus, the lateral geniculate nucleus, and the visual cortex (Movshon & van Sluyters, 1981; Riesen & Zilbert, 1975). Different aspects of the visual pathways seem to be more or less susceptible to such damage. Thus, we find that X and W cells are relatively unaffected by dark rearing, whereas Y cells are readily lost if no visual experience is available (Hoffmann & Sherman, 1975; Rothblat & Schwartz, 1978). These effects are not irreversible, since even animals who have been raised for a year following birth in total darkness show some recovery after several months of exposure to illuminated surroundings, although recovery is never complete (Cynader, Berman & Hein, 1976).

Much subtler neurophysiological changes come about through selective-rearing practices. For instance, in Chapter 3 we stated that cells in the visual cortex tend to show ocular dominance. This means that although most cells in the cortex can be activated by stimulation of either eye, they tend to respond more vigorously to one eye than to the other. The fact that most cells respond somewhat to each eye's input probably has to do with the depth cue of binocular disparity (see Chapter 10). Suppose that we rear an animal from birth so that it only views the world through one eye. Later we test separately the ability of the two eyes to produce a response in the visual cortex. We would probably find that the majority of the cells are activated by the experienced eye, and often less than 10 percent of the cells can be driven by the deprived eye (LeVay, Wiesel & Hubel, 1980).

The degree of disruption of normal functioning seems to depend on when the period of deprivation begins. If the animal is deprived of binocular viewing during the period of 3 weeks to 3 months after birth, large disruptions of the normal pattern of binocular response occur. However, if the monocular viewing period is instituted after 3 months of age, even for periods of up to a year, virtually no effect is found (Cynader, Timney & Mitchell, 1980; Held, 1985; Pettigrew, 1978b). This means that there is a particular time period during which the visual experience is most required and most effective. Such an interval is called a **critical period,** and it characterizes many aspects of the interaction between experience and development (Mitchell, 1981). Critical periods may correspond to periods of maximal growth and development in the nervous system (Aslin, 1985; Hickey, 1977). Any disruption of normal visual experience during the critical period, even for periods as short as 3 days, produces measurable changes in the responses of cells in the visual system (Freeman, Mallach & Hartley, 1981).

Perhaps the most subtle form of selective visual rearing involves limiting an animal to a world containing only contours oriented in one direction. Thus, an animal might be exposed to only vertically oriented lines from birth. This is accomplished by either affixing to the animal goggles that only contain lines of one orientation, or giving the animal experience for a few hours each day in an apparatus similar to that shown in Figure 17-2. This is simply a large cylinder containing nothing but vertical stripes and a clear plastic floor on which the animal stands. Notice that the animal is wearing a special collar that prevents it from seeing its own limbs.

What happens in the nervous system after exposure to this kind of selective rearing and stimulation might be called *environmental surgery*. Such surgery drastically alters the response characteristics of neurons in the visual cortex. Normally, when we insert an electrode into the visual cortex in order to map receptive fields, we find large numbers of cells that respond most strongly to lines in

FIGURE 17-2   An apparatus for selectively rearing a kitten so that its only visual experience will be with vertical lines.

a particular orientation, as we saw in Chapter 3, and the particular preferred orientations are rather evenly distributed. The left side of Figure 17-3 depicts this distribution as a set of lines each of which represents a neuron responding best to that orientation. However, recording from an animal that has

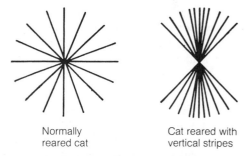

Normally
reared cat

Cat reared with
vertical stripes

FIGURE 17-3   Distribution of the preferred orientation of cortical receptive fields in a normally reared cat versus that for a cat reared with selective exposure to vertical lines. Each line indicates the preferred orientation of 1 cell.

never seen horizontal stripes produces quite a different result. In this animal, virtually no cells are responsive to horizontally oriented lines, resulting in a distribution of preferred stimulus orientations much like that shown on the right in Figure 17-3 (Hirsch & Spinelli, 1970; Movshon & van Sluyters, 1981). It is as if the absence of horizontally oriented stimuli in the environment has served as a (figurative) scalpel that has systematically cut off any responding to stimuli other than the vertical stimuli to which the animal was exposed. Again, there is a critical period between 3 weeks and 3 months, during which this sort of selective stimulation seems to be most effective (Mitchell, 1981; Rothblat & Schwartz, 1978).

Blake (1981) has summarized the evidence from such selective rearing studies saying, ''In effect, the neurophysiologists have compiled a set of recipes for creating animals with specific kinds of neural deficits at sites along the visual pathways'' (p. 97). The ingredients that go into these recipes are particular experiences, or the lack of certain normal experiences, with visual stimuli.

Perceptual Effects

How do all these unusual environmental experiences affect what the organism perceives? There is a slight divergence between the physiological and the behavioral data when we answer this question. Consider a kitten reared in total darkness until the age of 6 months. When we remove this kitten from darkness, it at first appears to be completely blind; however, within about 48 hours of exposure to illuminated surroundings the kitten begins to show some visual responsiveness. Various forms of sensory motor coordination begin to appear in a piecemeal fashion, and after a 6-week period of normal experience a great deal of recovery has occurred. Direct measures of visual acuity show a gradual improvement. If the animal had been dark-reared for only about 4 months, the acuity gradually would return to that of a normally reared cat; however, visual acuity never reaches normal levels for

animals that have been dark-reared for longer periods (Timney, Mitchel & Griffin, 1978). Although many of the physiological changes appear to be permanent, there seems to be enough plasticity in the animal to allow for considerable behavioral recovery of function after the initial period of deprivation. Still, there will be measurable deficits in many visual tasks, including obstacle avoidance, tracking, jumping under visual guidance, and eye blinks to oncoming objects, even after 2 years of normal experience (Mitchell, 1978; Rothblat & Schwartz, 1978).

Since selective rearing is a more subtle procedure than restricted rearing, it should not be surprising to find that its behavioral effects are often somewhat indirect and elusive. For instance, the most dramatic behavioral effects of rearing animals with one eye occluded is a reduction in the visual acuity of the deprived eye (Mitchell, 1981). However, there are a number of interesting visual field effects as well. **Visual field** refers to the region of the outside world to which an eye will respond, measured in degrees around the head. For instance, the top view of Figure 17-4 shows the visual fields for the right and left eyes of a cat. There is a rather large region of overlap between the two eyes in the frontal part of the field. This is the region of binocular vision, where either or both eyes of the cat should be able to see an object. Generally, if an interesting stimulus appears in the visual field of a cat, it will immediately turn its eyes and head toward it, displaying an orienting response (see Chapter 15). We can use this response to measure the effectiveness of stimuli in the visual field of the cat, and if we cover one eye at a time we can measure each visual field separately.

Let us first consider an animal that has been completely dark-reared. This animal shows a severe loss of response in the region of binocular overlap. Each eye seems to respond only to objects on its side of the head, as shown in the middle view of Figure 17-4. An animal reared with one eye occluded also does not show a binocularly responsive region of the visual field. The eye that had

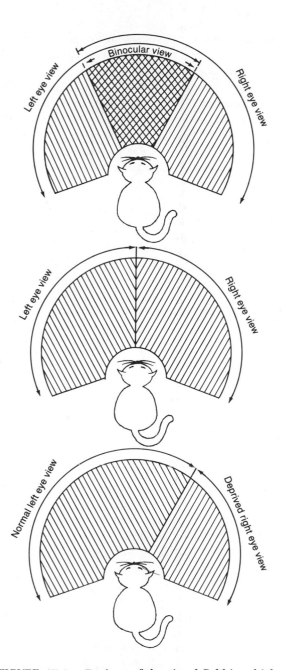

FIGURE 17-4 Regions of the visual field in which a cat will respond to visual stimuli presented to the right or left eye are altered by depriving one or both eyes of visual experience from birth. (Based on Sherman, 1973).

normal visual experience shows a normal visual field, overlapping well to the opposite side. However, the eye that did not receive visual experience acts as if it only responds to targets that are far to the side of the head, and excludes all of the visual field that the normal eye covers, as shown in the bottom view of Figure 17-4 (Sherman, 1973). A similar effect was reported for a young man who was born with a cataract that prevented any patterned vision in his left eye (his visual experience was similar to the monocularly reared animals we have been discussing). When this cataract was removed at age 19, the normal eye had its usual visual field size, but the patient simply could not detect any stimuli in a large portion of the region where the two eyes' views overlapped (the binocular region) with the deprived (cataract) eye. Although there was some recovery over the next 10 months, the visual field of the deprived eye never became as large as that of the normal eye (Moran & Gordon, 1982).

The other form of selective rearing, where an animal is reared under conditions of exposure to horizontal or vertical stripes alone, also produces a behavioral deficit in addition to the change in the distribution of cells in the cortex with a specific set of preferred orientations. Here the results are not as dramatic as we might expect. Animals who have been reared only with vertical stripes are not blind to horizontal stripes, rather they have measurably lower visual acuity for stripes in an orientation never seen during their rearing (Blasdel, Mitchell, Muir & Pettigrew, 1977; Hirsch, 1972).

Human Studies

Restricted-rearing studies cannot be conducted with human observers because of the possibility of producing long-lasting perceptual deficits. However, some clinical conditions reproduce the circumstances needed to study the effects of experience on perception. For example, Senden (1960) collected case reports of individuals who had suffered from lifelong blindness due to the presence of cataracts;

these individuals later had vision restored through a surgical procedure. After the removal of the cataracts, these adults were unable to identify familiar objects by sight, although they were capable of identifying them if they were allowed to touch the objects. For instance, when asked to discriminate between a square and a triangle, these individuals had to undertake the painstaking procedure of seeking out and counting the corners of the figure before the forms could be distinguished from each other.

These newly sighted observers seemed able to detect the presence or absence of an object in the visual field, but this seemed to be the extent of their abilities. For example, one patient was shown a watch and was asked whether it was round or square. When he seemed unable to answer, he was asked whether or not he knew the shape of a square or a circle. He was able to position his hands to form both a square and a circular shape, but he could not visually identify the shape of the watch. When the watch was placed in his hands, he immediately recognized it as being round. It appears that his sense of touch, although not more sensitive than that of a sighted person, had come through long experience to be a more reliable source of information about the world than his untrained sense of vision (see Warren, 1984).

There is an interesting naturally occurring analogy to selective rearing of the type used with cats in which they see only contours in a single orientation. This analogy arises from a common visual problem known as **astigmatism.** Astigmatism usually occurs if the cornea of the eye is not perfectly spherical, perhaps being flatter in some places and more curved in others. This deviation from perfect sphericity brings contours of some orientations into sharper focus than those in other orientations. Thus, with a vertical astigmatism, horizontal lines will be clear and vertical lines will be blurry, and so forth. The fact that this condition can mimic selective-rearing effects was shown by Freeman and Pettigrew (1973), who reared cats wearing cylindrical lenses that artificially created

an astigmatism. They were able to show that such selective rearing can also alter the distribution of preferred orientations of visual cortical neurons, causing a reduction of the number of cells preferring the blurred orientation. Severe astigmatism at an early age in humans results in a permanent loss of visual acuity in the direction of the astigmatism. This is an acuity loss due to neural changes, because it remains even after correcting for any optical errors, and is probably the result of selective restriction of exposure to contours in the astigmatic direction (Mitchell, 1980).

A variation of this same selective-rearing effect is caused by living in an urbanized environment. The nature of our carpentered cities means that we have frequent exposure to vertical lines (defining walls, corners, furniture legs, and so forth) and to horizontal lines (defining floors, ceilings, table edges, and so forth). Proportionally we have much less exposure to oblique lines. Therefore, as inhabitants of such a selectively stimulating environment, it might be expected that we would show reduced acuity for diagonal lines relative to horizontal and vertical lines. In fact, the human visual system is *anisotropic,* meaning that it often reacts differently to stimuli depending on their orientation. In general, the normal visual system shows a slight, but well-defined, preference for horizontal or vertical stimuli over diagonal stimuli. This is demonstrated in a number of acuity-related tasks, where resolution acuity and vernier acuity seem to be poorer for stimuli oriented diagonally (Bowker & Mandler, 1981; Corwin, Moskowitz-Cook & Green, 1977; Jenkins, 1985; Vogels & Orban, 1986). This phenomenon is known as the **oblique effect,** and can easily be demonstrated using Demonstration Box 17-1.

Some investigators feel that at least part of the oblique effect is caused by genetic factors (Leehey, Moskowitz-Cook, Brill & Held, 1975; Timney & Muir, 1976), but Annis and Frost (1973) provided some interesting data that are compatible with selective environmental effects. They compared the variations in acuity as a function of the orientation

DEMONSTRATION BOX 17-1.   The Oblique Effect

To demonstrate that visual acuity is better for horizontal or vertical stimuli than for obliquely oriented stimuli, prop this book up on a table so that you can see the three stimulus patterns. Now slowly walk backward from the book until you can no longer resolve clearly the oblique lines in the center circle.

It will appear uniform gray at this point, as your resolution acuity fails. Notice, however, that at this distance you still can see that the left circle contains vertical lines, and the right contains horizontal lines, thus indicating your greater visual acuity for these orientations.

of lines in a group of students from Queens University in Kingston, Ontario, with that observed in a group of Cree Indians from James Bay, Quebec. The students had all grown up in typical North American buildings. The Cree Indians, however, were among the last to be raised in traditional housing consisting of a cook tent (or *meechwop*) in summer, and a winter lodge (or *matoocan*) during the rest of the year. Both the insides and outsides of these structures consist of a rich array of contours, with no obvious preponderance of verticals and horizontals. In addition, the natural environment of the Cree shows no excesses of verticals and horizontals, in contrast to the urbanized environment of the students. In line with the selective-exposure hypothesis, the students showed the expected reduction in acuity for obliquely oriented contours, whereas the Cree, without this selective exposure, did not.

Although we have emphasized the visual modality in our discussions thus far, it is important to recognize that selective and restricted rearing in other senses also has measurable effects in humans and animals. In hearing, for example, it has been found that individuals who are deaf in one ear, or who are congenitally deaf, tend to have different brain organizations than do normal-hearing subjects (Neville, 1985; Neville, Schmidt & Kutas, 1983). Parts of the brain normally reserved for auditory processing now appear to be available for visual functions.

SENSORY-MOTOR LEARNING

One variable that seems to be essential for the development of normal visual functioning involves not only the eyes but also the entire body. It seems that normal perceptual development depends on active bodily movement under visual guidance. Holst and Mittelsteadt (1950) offered a distinction between stimulus input that simply acts on a passive observer, which they called **exafference,** and stimulation that changes as a result of an individual's own movements, called **reafference.**

Reafference has been suggested as being necessary for the development of accurate visually guided spatial behavior (Hein, 1980). An experiment by Held and Hein (1963) elegantly demonstrates this notion. They reared kittens in the dark until they were 8–12 weeks of age. From that age on, the kittens received 3 hours of patterned visual exposure in a "carousel" apparatus, shown in Figure 17-5. As you can see from the figure, one of the animals is active and can walk around freely. The other animal is passive and is carried around in a gondola that moves in exactly the same direction and at exactly the same speed as the movements of the active animal. Thus, the moving animal experiences changing visual stimuli as a result of its own movements (reafference); the passive animal experiences the same stimulation, but it is not the result of self-generated movements (exafference).

The animals were later tested on a series of behaviors involving depth perception. These included dodging or blinking when presented with a rapidly approaching object and the avoidance of the deep side of the visual cliff (see Chapter 10). They were also tested for the visual placing response, a

paw extension (as if to avoid collision) when the animal is moved quickly toward a surface. In all three measures, the active animals performed like normal kittens and the passive animals showed little evidence of depth perception.

An interesting extension of this work, which shows the specificity of experiential effects, was done by Hein, Held, and Gower (1970). They repeated the carousel experiment; however, each animal received both active and passive exposure. One eye was used when the visual exposure was active, and the other eye was used when the visual exposure was passive. They reported that when the kittens were tested on the actively exposed eye they seemed to have normal depth perception, whereas when tested on the passively exposed eye they acted as if they did not.

How much of the development of our visually guided behavior requires practice and exposure? Consider the simple tasks of reaching out and pick-

FIGURE 17-5   **Kitten carousel for active or passive exposure to visual stimulation.** (From R. Held, & A. Hein, 1963, *Journal of Comparative and Physiological Psychology*, 56. Copyright 1963 by the American Psychological Association. Reprinted by permission.)

ing up an object with one hand. This involves not only the accurate assessment of the distance and the size of the object, but the ability to guide your limb on the basis of the perceptual information. Hein and Held (1967) reared kittens in the dark until they were 4 weeks old. After this period, they were allowed 6 hours of free movement each day in a lighted and patterned environment. However, during the time when the cats received their exposure to patterned stimuli, they wore lightweight opaque collars that prevented them from seeing their bodies or paws while they moved about (see Figure 17-6). The remainder of the time, the kittens were placed in a dark room. After 12 days of such exposure, these animals showed normal depth perception, but their ability to accurately place their paws by visually directing them toward targets was quite poor. Nonetheless, after 18 hours of free movement in a lighted environment, with their paws visible, all directional confusions seemed to have disappeared.

Hein and Diamond (1971) conducted a similar experiment in which each of the cat's front paws was placed in a separate cone, rather than using a collar. One cone was opaque, and the other one was transparent so that the animal could see its limb. When tested using the limb they could see,

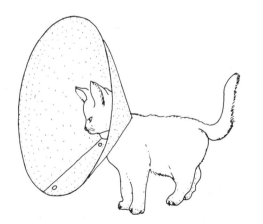

FIGURE 17-6   **Kitten in collar that prevents view of paws.** (From A. Hein, & R. Held, 1967, *Science*, 158, 390–92. Copyright 1967 by the American Association for the Advancement of Science.)

cats accurately placed their paws, but the unseen limb could not be accurately directed toward the targets. In another experiment, Held and Bauer (1967) reared a monkey for 34 days without sight of its limbs. When the animal was first able to see its arm, it acted startled and spent much time looking at its hand. The animal's behavior was awkward and inaccurate at first but improved rapidly with practice. When the other hand (which had not been previously exposed) was tested, it also showed inaccurate reaching until some experience had been gained.

There are reports of behaviors in human infants that seem similar to the responses of the deprived monkey. White (1971) reports that after the first month of life (during which infants are alert about 5% of the time), infants spend many hours watching their hands. Their reaching is quite inaccurate at first, but improves steadily. Actually, practice can speed up this process of perceptual development. If conditions are arranged so that there are many objects to reach for and to play with, infants develop accurate reaching behavior several weeks earlier than children who have not received this type of enriched experience. Experience with the sight of actively moving parts of the body seems to be a necessary condition for the successful development of visually guided behavior (Hein, 1980).

Perceptual Rearrangement

In 1896, George Stratton reasoned that if some aspects of the perception of space and direction were learned then it ought to be possible to learn a new set of spatial percepts. To test this, Stratton used a technique that altered spatial relations in the visual world (Stratton, 1897a,b). His technique involved wearing a set of goggles that optically rotated the field of view by 180 deg, so that everything appeared to be upside down. Such a procedure is called optical **rearrangement** (Welch, 1978).

More recently, Kohler (1962, 1964) elaborated on this procedure. Kohler's observers often wore optically distorting devices for several weeks. Observers reported that at first the world seemed very unstable, the visual field appearing to swing as the head was turned. During this stage of the experiment observers often had difficulty walking and needed help to perform very simple tasks. However, after about 3 days one observer was able to ride a bicycle, and after only a few weeks he was able to ski. The observers reported that they sporadically experienced the world as being upright. If they observed common events that have definite directional components, such as smoke rising from a cigarette or water pouring from a pitcher, they reported that the world appeared to be upright. This suggests that their ability to adapt to the optically rearranged visual input was facilitated by the notion of gravitational direction along with interaction with familiar events and objects. Kohler suggested that a real perceptual change had taken place, because when the inverting lenses were removed observers experienced a sense of discomfort. The world suddenly appeared to be inverted again, and they had difficulty moving about. However, the readaptation to the normal upright world was accomplished within a period of about 1 hour. Demonstration Box 17-2 shows how you can experience this inverted visual stimulation.

Most rearrangement studies involve a less dramatic change of optical input. A common technique is to use a wedge prism, which is a wedge-shaped piece of glass that bends, or refracts, light. The locations of objects viewed through the prism seem to be shifted in the direction of the apex (the pointed edge of the wedge). If an observer viewed the world through goggles containing such prisms and reached for an object, she would find herself missing it. After only a few minutes of practice, however, the observer's reaching would become

---

DEMONSTRATION BOX 17-2.   Optical Inversion

You can experience some of the effects associated with inverted optical stimulation by holding a mirror as shown in the accompanying figure. Walk around and view the world by looking up at the mirror. Notice that the world seems inverted, and also notice how the world swings as you turn. Now pour some water from a glass. Does the water pour up or down? Are you sure?

Pocket mirror

quite accurate. We would say that she has adapted to the prismatic distortion; in other words, she has compensated for the optical distortion. If the observer is consciously correcting for the distortion (for instance, saying to herself, "I must reach 10 deg to the right of where the object appears"), when the goggles were removed she would, of course, know that the distortion is no longer present. Being rational, she should then drop this conscious correction and reach for seen stimuli with her usual accuracy. However, suppose that some perceptual change has occurred. In this case we would expect that when the distorting prism is removed the visual world would appear to be shifted several degrees to one side. When reaching for an object the observer should err in the direction opposite to that of the initial distortion. This is what actually does occur. These errors are called **aftereffects.** The occurrence of aftereffects in prism adaptation is evidence that some perceptual rearrangement has occurred (Harris, 1980). This process is outlined in Figure 17-7.

A number of investigators have attempted to specify what conditions are necessary for adaptation to rearranged stimulation (Welch, 1978). Held and Hein (1958) have argued that adaptation depends on active movements, as does the development of visually guided behavior discussed earlier.

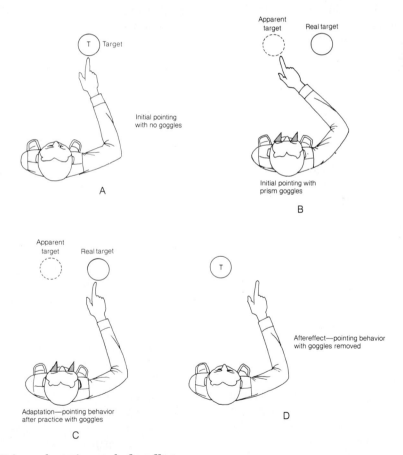

FIGURE 17-7   **Prism adaptation and aftereffect.**

They tested this notion by having an observer view his hand through a prism under one of three conditions. One was a no-movement condition, in which the observer viewed only his stationary hand. The second was a passive-movement condition, in which the observer's arm was swung back and forth by the experimenter. The third was an active-movement condition, in which the observer saw his hand through the prism while he actively moved it from side to side. There was considerable adaptation to the distortion produced by the prism under the active-movement condition, whereas in the other conditions there was not. These results have been verified several times (Pick & Hay, 1965).

Another series of experiments used conditions similar to the kitten carousel discussed earlier. Observers wearing displacing prism goggles either walked around for about 1 hour (active exposure) or were wheeled around in a wheelchair over the same path for about 1 hour (passive exposure). They were then measured to see if any perceptual change had taken place. Adaptation to the prismatic distortion occurred in the active condition but not during the passive exposure condition (Held & Bossom, 1961; Mikaelian & Held, 1964).

One important aspect of active movement under the optically distorted conditions seems to be that it provides observers with some sort of error feedback, which informs them of the direction and the extent of the distortion. This information provides a basis for learning a new correlation between the incoming stimuli and the conscious percept. The more information we give observers about the nature of their errors, the greater is the adaptation to the distortion (Coren, 1966; Welch, 1969, 1971).

Some investigators have suggested that error information in the absence of active movement is sufficient to produce prism adaptation. Howard, Craske, and Templeton (1965) had observers watch a rotating rod through an optical system that displaced it to one side. For some observers the rod appeared to be displaced to the side, and they merely watched it rotate. For another group the rod appeared displaced to the same degree; however, as the rod swung about it brushed each observer across the lips, indicating that it was directly in front of the observer rather than off to the side as it appeared. Although both groups were passive, the groups receiving the information that their percept was erroneous (being touched by a stimulus that looked like it would pass them by) showed perceptual adaptation, whereas the other group did not. Thus, information indicating how our percepts are in error may be sufficient to produce adaptation (Howard, Anstis & Lucia, 1974).

What actually changes during the adaptation process? This issue is still being debated. Some researchers believe that adaptation simply alters the felt position of various parts of the body (Harris, 1980). This is based on the observation that after prism adaptation, when observers are asked to point to a straight-ahead position (by feel alone), they tend to point off to the side. This indicates some proprioceptive or "felt" component in the aftereffect (Harris, 1980). Other data indicate that this may be only part of the process (Mikaelian, 1974; Redding & Wallace, 1976). For example, animals can still adapt to the visual displacement when the nerves that provide information about the position of the arm are severed (Bossom & Ommaya, 1968; Taub & Berman, 1968). The consensus is that a change is taking place in both proprioceptive and visual perception, which is the result of recalibration of the higher brain centers used to interpret perceptual input (Howard, 1982; Welch, 1978). Some direct evidence for this perceptual recalibration comes from an interesting experiment by Foley (1970, 1974). She placed wedge prisms in front of the eyes of observers so that the direction of displacement was different for each eye. Either one eye saw an upward displacement and the other a downward displacement, or one eye saw a displacement to the right and the other to the left. After several hours of exposure the two eyes were tested separately. The results indicated that each eye had adapted to its own particular distortion. This implies a perceptual recalibration. It seems likely that adaptation to optically rearranged stimuli involves a form of perceptual learning that alters the appearance of visual space, which, like many other forms of learning, is sensitive to what the observer is paying attention to (Redding, Clark & Wallace, 1985). However, whether learning to deal with rearranged spatial stimuli involves the same mechanisms that may have gone into the original development of our perception of space is not clear.

Illusion Decrement

There is another form of perceptual learning that is similar to rearrangement in that it involves learning to compensate for a perceptual error. It differs from the situations we have been discussing in that the error is not optical in nature, and the observer usually is not conscious either of the erroneous perception or of any perceptual change. This situation involves visual geometric illusions, which are simple line drawings that evoke percepts differing in size or shape from those expected on the basis of physical measurements of the stimuli. We have encountered several of these already, in Chapters 1, 11, 14, and 16, including the Mueller-Lyer illusion (see Figure 17-8), in which the horizontal line with the outward-turned wings appears longer than the line with the inward-turned wings, despite the fact that they are physically equal in length. Suppose we present the Mueller-Lyer figure to an observer and measure her susceptibility to the line-length distortion. Next we instruct her to begin moving her eyes across the figure, scanning from one end of the horizontal line to the other on both portions of the figure. We ask her to be as accurate as possible with her eye movements. At 1-minute intervals we stop the scanning process and take measurements of illusion magnitude until a total of 5 min of viewing time has elapsed. This simple process of inspection leads to a 40-percent reduction in the original illusion magnitude (Coren & Porac, 1984). This decrease, known as **illusion**

decrement, has been demonstrated many times (see Coren & Girgus, 1978; Porac & Coren, 1985).

What is happening in this situation? How does the observer know that the percept is wrong in the first place, and why does the size of the illusory effect decrease? The answer seems to lie in the pattern of the observer's eye movements (see Coren, 1986). If we measure the actual pattern of eye movements an observer makes over an illusion figure, we find that the eyes are directed to move as if the distorted percept were actually correct. In other words, if the eyes were resting on the end of the line in the perceptually elongated portion of the Mueller-Lyer figure (Figure 17-8A), an attempt to look at the far end of the line would produce an eye movement that is too long. This eye-movement error is in agreement with the percept, which tends to overestimate the length of the line. A corrective adjustment in the eye movement must be made if the fovea is to come to rest on the exact end of the line. The opposite happens for the underestimated portion of the Mueller-Lyer figure (Figure 17-8B). Here the eye movements are too short (again in agreement with the perceptual underestimation of the line length), and a corrective adjustment must be made. The eye movement patterns over the two portions of the figure are shown in Figure 17-8C.

In Chapters 15 and 16 we saw instances where patterns of eye movements could be used to tell us something about the information-processing abilities of an observer. The same reasoning can be applied to the study of eye-movement patterns across illusion configurations. As the observer views the illusory array, eye movements and eye-movement errors provide information about the existence (as well as the direction and the strength) of the illusory distortion. This error information can be used by the observer to correct the percept. This point of view is supported by the fact that an illusion decrement does not occur unless the observer is allowed to scan the figure (Coren, Girgus & Schiano, 1986; Coren & Hoenig, 1972; Festinger, White & Allyn, 1968).

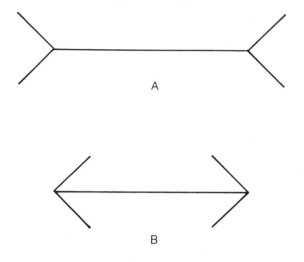

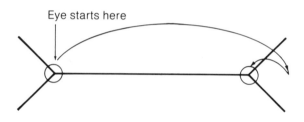

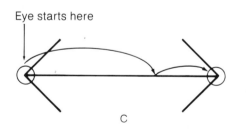

FIGURE 17-8   **The overestimated (A) and underestimated (B) portions of the Mueller-Lyer illusion, and (C) typical eye movements obtained when viewing them.**

The phenomenon of illusion decrement implies that perceptual learning is taking place. The information obtained from the eye movements is being used to reduce a perceptual error, and the direction of this change (from greater to lesser illusion susceptibility) mimics that associated with perceptual rearrangement studies. The most interesting aspect of this form of perceptual adjustment, however, is the fact that nothing about it appears to be available to consciousness. Unless provided with a ruler or a direct explanation, the observer does not consciously know that the original perception is in error, nor does she know that illusory error has been reduced as a result of her active interactions with the illusion figure! The percept simply becomes more accurate with no change in the observer's own awareness.

CONTEXT AND MEANING

Basically, all percepts are ambiguous. Consider a target that casts a square image on the retinal surface. The object the image represents could actually be one of an infinite number of different shapes at any distance or inclination relative to the observer, as shown in Figure 17-9. Since any retinal image can be caused by a variety of different physical targets in the world, it is surprising that our normal perceptual experiences are generally so unambiguous. Actually, what we perceive is the result of a decision-making process in which we deduce, on the basis of all available information, what the stimulus object is. This **transactional viewpoint** maintains that any current perceptual experience consists of a complex evaluation of the significance of stimuli reaching our receptors. Through our life experience we learn that certain objects or conditions have a high probability of being related to one another. On this basis we derive our "best bet" as to what we are viewing. In a sense, the world we are experiencing is more the result of perceptual processing than the cause of the perception (Coren, 1983; Ittelson, 1962). The transactional approach implies that if our expectations change, or our analysis of the situation

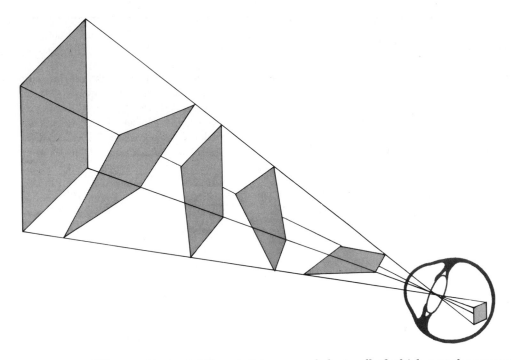

FIGURE 17-9 **Many different objects at different distances and slants, all of which cast the same square retinal image.** (From Coren & Girgus, 1978)

changes, then our perceptual experience will also change (Ames, 1951; Brunswick, 1955). A simple example of the effect of context and expectations can be seen in Demonstration Box 17-3.

Most of our percepts are constructed from incomplete stimuli. Look at Figure 17-10A. It is clear that this represents a dog, yet it should also be clear that there is no dog present. The figure is completely constructed in the mind's eye of the observer. The elephant in Figure 17-10B will probably be somewhat more difficult to identify. The less familiar the object, the more difficult is the identification. Furthermore, you must begin with the initial hypothesis that there is some object there in the first place, otherwise you may never see any pattern at all (Reynolds, 1985). However, once having seen (or "constructed") the figure, the meaningful organization will be apparent immediately when you look at it again. Our ability to perceive these stimuli as objects depends on our prior experience. This was shown by Steinfield (1967), who found that when observers were told a story about an ocean cruise they identified Figure 17-10C as a steamship in less than 5 sec. Observers who were told an irrelevant story took six times longer to identify the figure.

Some of the experiences that affect perception may take place outside of conscious awareness. For instance, much earlier in the chapter we spoke of an experiment in which researchers presented a word for so brief a time period that it could not be identified. They found that if the word was presented several times, even though the length of time of each presentation was not increased, the word was eventually identified (Haber & Hershenson, 1965; Uhlarik & Johnson, 1978). If the word was not identified on the first presentation, why should an observer be able to identify it after repeated exposures? Dodwell (1971) has suggested that very fast presentations of stimuli do not give the brain sufficient time to do the necessary computations required for identification. The partially processed stimulus is held in memory, and as the information extraction continues, hypotheses are formed and checked until the stimulus appears to make sense. At this point, the conscious identifi-

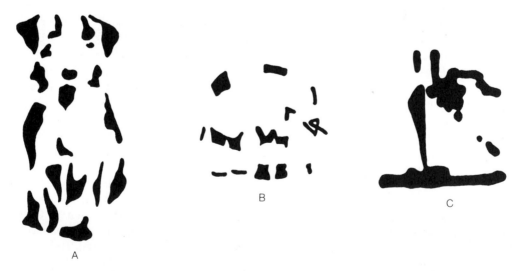

A   B   C

FIGURE 17-10   **Some degraded stimuli that may be seen as objects. (Based on Street, 1931)**

cation response takes place (Doherty & Keeley, 1972).

The same perceptual hypotheses, allowing us to eventually formulate a percept from minimal or degraded input, can also modify our perception so that it no longer accurately represents the stimulus. For example, Ross and Schilder (1934) presented observers with a series of briefly flashed line drawings. Some of the drawings were incomplete or distorted, such as three-armed people and faces with a mouth missing. A look at some of their observers' comments is informative. When presented with the side view of a dog with the left hind leg missing, the subject reported: "It's a dog, a wolf, two ears stand upright, a round mouth, a long tail." The experimenter then instructed the observer: "Look at his legs." Observer: "He has five toes on each leg." Experimenter: "Look at the hind legs." Observer: "I saw two; the tail goes up."

Despite continued pressure from the experimenter, the observer continued to correct the percept, filling in the missing leg on the hypothesis that dogs have four legs.

These researchers also used a drawing of a woman's head facing forward. She had two large eyes as well as a large third eye on her forehead. One observer described the picture as "a woman with long hair, black, two eyes, one nose, one mouth, two ears." The stimulus was presented again briefly, and the observer was asked if the forehead was in order, to which he replied, "Yes." After several other stimuli were presented again, the observer now reported: "The same woman I saw before. She is funny—big eyes, a big nose, and a big mouth." Experimenter: "Look at the forehead." Observer: "She has a small curl in the middle."

Even with more brief presentations, this observer still insisted that all that appeared on the forehead was a curl of hair. Third eyes do not occur normally, so we apparently correct our percept on the basis of our expectations—we see extra hair, not extra eyes. You may see how expectations alter our perception in Demonstration Box 17-4.

Language as well as expectations may modify percepts. This view was advanced by Whorf (1956) and Sapir (1939), who suggested that specific language labels for certain types of stimuli increase the accuracy of perceptual processing. They maintained, for example, that the Eskimo, whose language has a wide variety of different names for different kinds of snow, may be able to make better discrimination among types of snow than those of us who speak English and have only the single label *snow*.

An example of how language can affect perception is seen in a classic experiment conducted by Gottschaldt (1926, 1929), who gave observers from 3 to 520 presentations of a simple target. He then asked them to find this target in a more complex figure. Such a target is shown in Figure 17-11, where Figure A is embedded in Figure B. He reported that prolonged experience with the simple figure did not make it any easier to find when it was hidden in the more complex stimulus. Djang (1937) repeated this experiment. However, her

---

DEMONSTRATION BOX 17-4.   An Expectancy Effect on Perception

Turn to Color Plate 9 and *quickly* count the number of aces of spades that you see. Then return to this demonstration box. Although you probably only saw three aces of spades, there are actually five. Two of the aces of spades are printed in red ink, rather than black. Since you "expect" spades to be black, your recognition process for incongruent or unexpected stimuli is impaired.

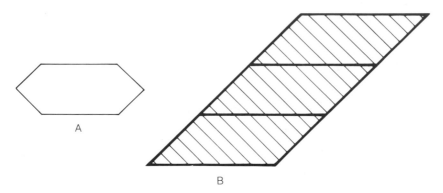

FIGURE 17-11   Figure A may be found embedded in Figure B.

servers did not just look at the simple stimulus; they were required to draw it. She reports that when such active practice is combined with exposure, there was an improvement in later identification of the simple component embedded in the more complex figure. Schwartz (1961) then added a language component. He had observers learn distinctive verbal labels to attach to each of the simple figures. This modification of the experiment resulted in an improved ability to find and identify the named stimuli.

However, verbal labeling can either help or hinder recognition. Ellis and Muller (1964) trained subjects using either a narrow labeling system (1 label for each shape) or a wide labeling system (1 label for 4 shapes). In later tests of recognition for these forms, the group using the narrow labeling approach performed better than a group that simply observed the shapes without labeling; the group who used the wide labeling system had the fewest correct recognitions. Thus, the wide labeling seemed to emphasize the learning of similarities between the stimuli, which later resulted in poorer discrimination and recognition.

Eyewitness Testimony

Language and expectation can also serve to modify our reports of what we have seen. Carmichael, Hogan, and Walter (1932) presented observers with simple line drawings and associated each with a label. Observers were then asked to reproduce these drawings. In general, their reproductions were biased in the direction of the verbal label. When presented with Figure 17-12A and told that it was a broom, observers tended to reproduce patterns similar to Figure 17-12B. When told that it was a rifle, observers tended to reproduce patterns similar to Figure 17-12C. In this experiment the reproductions occurred only a few moments after the stimulus was taken away. Such distortions in our recollections of what we have seen may have important consequences for many behaviors, including such things as scientific observation and eyewitness testimony (Wells & Loftus, 1984). For example, eyewitness reports of events that occurred during a crime tend to be remarkably unreliable, even when obtained immediately after the event. Observers have a tendency to include details that they could not have seen. Such details are often provided on the basis of the observer's expectations or biases (Buckhout, 1976; Loftus, 1979; Yarmey, 1979).

Loftus (1974) demonstrated how words used to question observers about a filmed auto accident could cause them to distort their perceptual memory. When witnesses were asked about what happened when one car ''smashed into another'' as opposed to using a more neutral phrase, such as ''made contact with the other,'' they were more

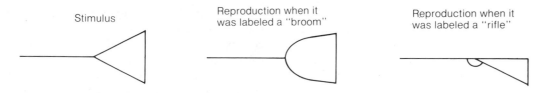

FIGURE 17-12   The effects of labels on later perceptual recall.

likely to report having seen broken glass flying about, even though there was none. We might argue that such distortion is a distortion in memory, rather than in perception. Unfortunately, whenever an observer reports what he has seen, he is always dealing with events that occurred in the past. For instance, the description of a picture flashed on a screen in front of an observer for a fraction of a second is really taken from his memory, since the image is no longer present by the time the observer begins his report. Thus, any perceptual report must have some memory component.

Increasing the time interval between the perception and the report increases the amount of deviation from what was actually observed. For instance, in another experiment Loftus (1974) showed observers a brief videotape of an automobile accident and then asked them questions about what they had just observed. For one group of observers one of the questions was, "How fast was the white sports car going while traveling along the country road?" For the other group the question was, "How fast was the white sports car going when it passed the barn while traveling along the country road?" In fact, there was no barn present. Yet when questioned about the incident a week later, more than 17 percent of the group exposed to the false suggestion about a barn answered the question "Did you see a barn?" by saying "Yes," as opposed to only 3 percent of the group that did not get such a suggestion.

When we have clearly perceived something the perceptual memory resists any later change. Thus, in one experiment subjects viewed a series of slides showing the theft of a large, bright red wallet. Virtually none of the observers could be in-duced later to recall the color of the wallet as brown (Loftus, 1979). In fact, recent evidence seems to indicate that the suggestions of false context that are provided after the actual perceptual event has occurred act only to fill in gaps in the perception, much as the observer's expectation that dogs have four legs caused the missing leg to be added perceptually in the experiment discussed earlier (Yuille, 1984). Structuring the questioning to fit the actual sequence of events may help to prevent such eyewitness errors, perhaps by restoring the original context that was present during the actual viewing of the event (Geiselman, Fisher, MacKinnon & Holland, 1986; Morris & Morris, 1985).

ENVIRONMENTAL AND LIFE HISTORY DIFFERENCES

We have seen earlier what effect the availability, or nonavailability, of particular environmental stimuli can have on the development of sensory systems, and hence on the observer's later perceptual abilities. There also are aspects of our environment and culture that may teach us different perceptual strategies, and may alter the expectations and analyses that we bring to each new perceptual situation. Thus, if we live in the desert or on the pampas or the plains, we are exposed to broad vistas of open space that are never experienced by a forest dweller. If we live in a technologically advanced country, we are exposed to visual stimuli (such as photographs and television) that are usually not available to someone dwelling in the African bush or the Australian outback. Such differences, especially when experienced over an entire lifetime, may have dramatic consequences for perceptual processes.

Picture Perception

In our civilized, urbanized, and media-intensive culture, we are inundated with images. Not just the images of our immediate environment, but images representing environments or objects that are not present. Some of these latter images are in the form of changing patterns of color or black and white shown on televisions and in cinemas. There are also photographs in magazines and newspapers, where we might "see" a baby elephant peaceably grazing a few feet in front of its gigantic mother, all in a 5-cm-square smudge of black ink on a perfectly flat surface. If you have some artistic talent, you may be able to represent such a scene with a few strokes of a pen on a sheet of paper, and thus be able to let your friends "see for themselves" what you have seen. This seems like a perfectly natural fact of life.

Pictures, of the sort that we encounter daily, are often viewed as simply "windows" through which we see other worlds (Haber, 1980). Certainly these images must follow all the same optical laws as the real world. Certainly every observer must follow these laws to interpret such stimuli in the same way that we do. Unfortunately, neither statement is completely "certain." Pictures do contain much information that mimics the optical patterns encountered in natural viewing (Gibson, 1979; Sedgwick, 1980), but there are many discrepancies between the pictured and real image. For instance, the actual sizes of the pictured images are usually too large or too small, which in turn ruins the geometrical correspondence between the image and the actual scene (Lumsden, 1980). Furthermore, even if we could make the geometry of perspective perfect, it would only be correct for one single viewing angle, and viewing any pictured image from a vantage point other than the viewpoint adopted by the camera or artist who produced

the picture ought to lead to distorted percepts (Kennedy & Ostry, 1976). However, such distortions do not appear (Rosinski & Farber, 1980). We could enlarge indefinitely this list of discrepancies between a real scene and a picture of it. For instance, the picture is flat, whereas the real world is three-dimensional; the picture is interpreted correctly even if its colors are all wrong, or even if there are no colors at all; and so forth. Such considerations have led some theorists to conclude that pictures may be statements in a sort of visual language that are created and interpreted according to the agreed-upon set of conventions in any given culture. Thus, they are not simply representations of reality at all (Gombrich, 1972; Goodman, 1968). At the very least, they must be interpreted as hypotheses shared among individuals growing up with a common heritage (Gregory, 1971). By either of these two theories, however, the perception of pictures must be learned in some manner.

Before we investigate whether we must learn to interpret pictures, it is important for us to specify that we are really talking about two separate skills. The first is the ability to identify objects depicted in a picture, and the second is the ability to interpret the three-dimensional arrangement implied in the flat image.

Hochberg and Brooks (1962) conducted a heroic experiment, using one of their children as the subject. The child was reared to the age of 19 months carefully shielded from any sort of pictorial representation. This meant that the television was never used in the child's presence, nor were there magazines or picture books. Even the labels on cans and boxes of food were removed or covered. When the child was tested after this restricted rearing, he had no difficulty identifying pictures of common items. This implies that we need not learn to interpret patterns or drawings as representations of real world objects.

The unlearned nature of picture identification seems to be supported by the fact that color photos are interpreted readily when shown to individuals who have lived in cultures where they have never experienced pictures (Hagen & Jones, 1978). How-ever, when black-and-white photos or drawings are used, individuals reared in isolated cultures some-times have difficulties that are strange to those who have been reared with the continuous company of graphic images. Deregowski (1980) has collected a number of such reports, including one from a Scot-tish missionary working in Malawi (a country in southwestern Africa between northern Rhodesia and Mozambique) nearly 75 years ago:

> Take a picture in black and white, and the natives cannot see it. You may tell the natives: 'This is a picture of an ox and a dog'; and the people will look at it and look at you, and that look says that they consider you a liar. Perhaps you say again, 'Yes, this is a picture of an ox and dog. Look at the horn of the ox, and there is his tail!' And the boy will say, 'Oh, yes and there is the dog's nose and eyes and ears!' Then the old people will look again and clap their hands and say, 'Oh yes, it is a dog.'

Clearly, such a report indicates that the indi-viduals involved did not respond to the photo with the immediate spontaneous object identification characteristic of our viewing of pictures. Still, when their attention was directed to the relevant aspects of the pattern they did have an ''Aha!'' ex-perience, indicating that the ability to identify the pattern was there, although they lacked training to direct their attention appropriately.

Although there may be a general ability to identify objects depicted in pictures, interpreting the implied spatial relationships seems to be more subject to cultural and educational influences. Iden-tifying depth in a flat image requires a certain amount of selection among the perceptual cues available. For instance, the photograph might in-clude such cues for depth as *linear perspective, interposition,* and *texture gradients,* among others mentioned in Chapter 10. However, there are also cues indicating that the picture is flat; there is no *binocular disparity* between items in the picture, and all the elements in the photo require the same degree of *accommodation* and *convergence* (see

Chapter 10). Thus, to see a drawing or a photo-graph as representing an arrangement of objects in three dimensions, rather than as a flat surface with different shadings of dark and light, you must at-tend to some depth cues and ignore others (Pick, 1987). An observer's particular perceptual strategy may depend on her life history and the relative fre-quency with which certain cues are encountered in the immediate environment.

Hudson (1960, 1962) attempted to separate cultural factors associated with the use of pictorial depth information. His technique consisted of using a series of pictures that depicted certain combina-tions of pictorial depth cues. Figure 17-13 shows one picture similar to those used by Hudson; as you can see, it depicts a hunting scene containing two pictorial depth cues. The first is **interposition,** in which objects closer to the observer block the view of portions of more distant objects. Since the hun-ter and the antelope are covering portions of the rocks, they appear closer to the observer than the rocks.

The second pictorial depth cue contained in this drawing is **familiar size.** We know the relative sizes of familiar objects; therefore, if an object is depicted as relatively small or large, we will judge its distance from us in a way consistent with our expectations based on its known size. For example, an elephant is a very large animal. However, in Figure 17-13 the elephant is one of the smaller items in the picture. If we are responding to the cue of familiar size, we would tend to see the elephant as being the most distant object in this hunting scene. When something as large as an elephant casts a smaller image than an antelope, the elephant must be farther away, since we know it is physi-cally larger than the antelope.

Hudson used these stimuli because they are uniquely constructed to allow for both **two-dimen-sional** (no use of pictorial depth) and **three-dimensional** (full use of pictorial depth) types of responses. Suppose we asked an observer to de-scribe what she saw in this picture. First we would expect her to identify correctly all the component

FIGURE 17-13   A figure used to test ability to respond to pictorial depth cues. (Based on Hudson, 1962)

objects in the picture. However, suppose we also asked her to describe the actions taking place. A correct three-dimensional response would indicate that the hunter was attempting to spear the antelope (which is, of course, nearer to him than the elephant if you are perceiving pictorial depth). A two-dimensional response would state that the hunter is attempting to spear the elephant, which is actually physically closer to the tip of the spear in the picture. Such a response would indicate that the observer had not responded to either the interposition or the familiar size cues that place the elephant at a greater perceptual distance from the hunter than the antelope.

Stimuli similar to these have been used in a number of studies conducted throughout Africa, to test observers from a number of tribal and linguistic groups (Deregowski, 1980). The results indicate that relatively isolated and uneducated African observers have difficulty seeing pictorial depth within these pictures, relative to more urbanized Western observers, a fact that has been verified using other types of pictures (Jahoda & McGurk, 1974). The ability to perceive three-dimensionality in pictures seems to be improved if more depth cues are added (Hagen & Jones, 1978; Killbride & Leibowitz, 1975), or if formal education, involving the use of picture books, drawings, and so forth, has been experienced (Killbride & Robbins, 1968; Leibowitz

& Pick, 1972; Pick, 1987). You can explore your own tendencies to use certain depth cues but not others by trying Demonstration Box 17-5.

Culturally determined conventions associated with the interpretation of pictures can be shown best in situations where the flat, stationary picture is supposed to depict not only three-dimensionality but also motion. For instance, Figure 17-14 depicts a scene in which there are three different forms of motion. From left to right, we see a speeding car, a boy rapidly whipping his head around, and a dog with a wagging tail. Of course, there is no actual motion, yet we "read" such motion into the picture. Within Western cultures, such interpretation of motion in pictorial arrays may appear as early as 4 years of age (Friedman & Stevenson, 1975). Non-Western cultures, without pictorial experience, however, virtually never "see" movement in such representations. The likelihood that movement will be seen in such an array increases with education, urbanization, and exposure to pictorial materials (Duncan, Gourlay & Hudson, 1973; Friedman & Stevenson, 1980).

Illusion and Constancy

There are certain facets of the environment that make us more or less responsive to certain patterns of depth cues appearing in pictures. For instance,

---

DEMONSTRATION BOX 17-5.   Cross-Cultural Differences in Perception

The figure accompanying this box is sometimes called the "Devil's tuning fork." Look at the figure for about 30 seconds or so; then close the book and try to draw it from memory. Return to this box when you have done this.

Most of you probably found this task to be quite difficult. The source of your difficulty comes from the fact that your cultural experience with graphic representations has caused you to interpret this two-dimensional stimulus as a three-dimensional object. Unfortunately, such an interpretation leads to problems since the depth cues implied in this figure are ambiguous. It is interesting to note that Africans who have not received formal education have no difficulty reproducing the figure. Since they do not interpret the figure as three-dimensional, they merely see a pattern of flat lines, which is easy to reproduce.

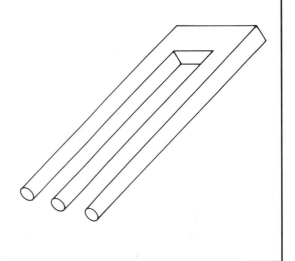

---

the **carpentered world hypothesis** begins with the observation that in the urbanized Western world, rooms and buildings are usually rectangular, many objects in the environment have right-angled corners, city streets have straight sides, and so forth. Surrounded by such an environment, we may learn to depend more heavily on depth cues based on linear perspective than would people who live in more primitive rural environments (Coren & Girgus, 1978; Gregory, 1966; Segall, Campbell & Herskovits, 1966). For example, rural, isolated Zulus have been described as surrounded by a circular culture. They live in round huts with round doors. They do not plough their land in straight lines but

tend to use curved furrows. Individuals living in such a world would not be expected to rely on linear perspective as heavily as those of us living in a more linear environment.

In a classic study Segall, Campbell, and Herskovits (1966) compared the responsiveness of individuals in carpentered versus noncarpentered environments to certain types of depth cues. However, instead of using Hudsonlike pictures as stimulus materials they chose a more subtle class of patterns, namely the visual-geometric illusions. Some of these configurations have already been discussed in Chapter 14, where we pointed out how susceptibility to size distortions in some figures,

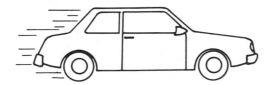

FIGURE 17-14   Scenes conventionally recognized as depicting motion by Western observers, but not necessarily by non-Western observers.

such as the Mueller-Lyer illusion, may be dependent on a three-dimensional interpretation of the pattern (to refresh your memory refer back to Figure 14-6). As we discussed then, the apparently longer portion of the Mueller-Lyer figure may be interpreted as a corner of a room receding in depth because the wings of the illusion act as linear perspective cues. The inappropriate application of size constancy based on this interpretation of the wings of the figure as perspective cues results in our overestimation of the size of this segment of the figure relative to the segment with the inward-turned wings. Since pictorial depth information is thought to play a role in the formation of these illusory percepts, these types of configurations are well-suited to an exploration of the carpentered world hypothesis.

Segall et al. (1966) gathered data from throughout Africa and also from several groups of people living in Evanston, Illinois. Although there are variations within the noncarpentered samples, the average Mueller-Lyer illusion was greater for the more urban groups. Similar results have been reported for other perspective-related illusions (Coren & Girgus, 1978; Deregowski, 1980; Killbride & Leibowitz, 1975).

Although the observed differences in illusion susceptibility for different cultural groups may be partially caused by factors other than experience with a carpentered world (Berry, 1971; Coren & Porac, 1978; Pollack & Silvar, 1967), there is ample evidence that the absence of experience with certain types of depth cues impairs certain other perceptual functions (such as size constancy) dependent on depth perception. One of the most striking examples of this was provided by the anthropologist Turnbull (1961). He observed the behavior of the Bambuti Pygmies, who live in the Ituri Forest in the Congo. Since they live in the dense rain forest, their vision is generally limited to short distances, with vistas that only extend for, at most 30 m. Therefore their life history seems to lack the visual experience needed to learn to use the depth cues responsible for the maintenance of size constancy at greater viewing distances. Turnbull noted one instance when he had taken his Bambuti guide, Kenge, out of the forest for the first time in his life. They were crossing over a broad plain and happened to spot a herd of buffalo:

> Kenge looked over the plains and down to where a herd of about a hundred buffalo were grazing some miles away. He asked me what kind of insects they were, and I told him they were buffalo, twice as big as the forest buffalo known to him. He laughed loudly and told me not to tell such stupid stories. . . . We got into the car and drove down to where the animals were grazing. He watched them getting larger and larger, and though he was as courageous as any Pygmy, he moved over and sat close to me and muttered that it was witchcraft. . . . Finally, when he realized that they were real buffalo he was no longer afraid, but what puzzled him still was why they had been so small, and whether they really had been small and suddenly grown larger, or whether it had been some kind of trickery. (From C. Turnbull, *American Journal of Psychology,* 74. Copyright 1961, The University of Illinois Press.)

Turnbull's description of Kenge's perceptual impressions suggests that our experience with particular stimuli prevalent in our immediate environment can result in differences in how we perceive new stimuli and situations. It seems that we learn to utilize stimulus information that we encounter frequently, but fail to learn to utilize stimulus information that is rare. This holds for the auditory as well as the visual environment.

Speech

The most dominant feature in our auditory environment is the constant flow of language sounds that surrounds us. As discussed in Chapter 12, each language uses a small set of word-differentiating *phonemes,* which are the functionally characteristic sounds of that language. Since different languages use different subsets and combinations of these phonemes, experiments on people reared in different linguistic settings offer a unique opportunity to observe the effects of specific kinds of experience on perception (see Kuhl, 1987). Because some sounds may be treated as distinctively different in some languages, and not in others—for instance, the sounds "r" as in *rope* and "l" as in *lope* are different phonemes in English, but not in Japanese—we would expect a bias in the auditory experience of individuals brought up surrounded by one or the other of these two languages. Numerous studies have shown that adults who have grown up with exposure to only one language often have difficulty discriminating certain linguistic contrasts characteristic of other languages (Strange & Jenkins, 1978; Werker & Tees, 1984). This type of difficulty may persist even if the adult has learned the other language and appears to be fluent in it. For example, Goto (1971) recorded pairs of words that contrasted the "r" and "l" sounds (such as *lead* vs. *read,* or *play* vs. *pray*). Several native Japanese speakers, who were bilingual in Japanese and English, could produce these sounds so that native English-speaking listeners could differentiate them without error. However, this seems to be a learned ability to *produce* rather than to perceive the phonemic difference, since, when asked to listen to recordings of pairs of words that contrasted these phonemes, the native Japanese speakers could not do so, even when listening to their own speech productions!

The mechanism responsible for our ability to discriminate some speech sounds but not others is still somewhat mysterious. Surprisingly, infants seem to be born with the ability to discriminate certain sound pairs not used in their native tongue, and appear to lose this ability as adults (Trehub, 1976; Werker & Tees, 1984). A striking example was provided by Werker, Gilbert, Humphrey, and Tees (1981), who presented English-speaking and Hindi-speaking adults with pairs of sounds that are differentiated as different phonemes in Hindi, but not in English. As we might expect, the adult Hindi speakers could make the discrimination, but the adult English speakers could not. The interesting result, however, is that 6-month-old infants could

make the discrimination. It seems that at some time during the first year of exposure to the language, infants begin to selectively respond to certain aspects of their linguistic environment and to selectively lose their ability to respond to phonemic distinctions not used in their native language (Werker & Tees, 1984).

This is not to say that individuals cannot learn to make certain phonemic distinctions. Evidence suggests that learning through exposure and experience plays a role in the ability to discriminate between various linguistic sounds, and some linguistic discriminations seem to be learned during the childhood years (Eilers, Wilson & Moore, 1979). However, this appears to be limited to certain dimensions of the sound. Tees & Werker (1984) showed that short-term intensive training improved the ability of native English speakers to make certain non-native (Hindi) speech discriminations, although after 5 years of language study the ability to make these discriminations was already apparent. An interesting additional finding pertained to individuals who spent their early years in a setting where Hindi was spoken (perhaps by a live-in relative). Even though these individuals had never studied the language, and as adults were unable to speak, understand, or write more than a few words of Hindi, it was found that they could make the phonemic discriminations that non-natives found impossible. Thus, their early experience seems to have "tuned" their speech-sound decoding capacity for certain dimensions even though they were not actually speaking the language.

In terms of our earlier discussion about the relationship between experience and development, these results suggest that different aspects of the perception of speechlike sounds follow different courses. Although some auditory discriminations are facilitated through contact with particular sounds in the linguistic environment, others are lost through their absence or rarity, thus showing that experience is necessary for their maintenance (cf. Walley, Pisoni & Aslin, 1981). Overall, this confirms that much of what we perceive and many of the perceptual distinctions we make are strongly influenced by the culture and environment in which we were reared.

Effects of Occupation

Even within a given culture there is selective exposure to different sets of environmental stimuli. You are exposed to your occupational setting for about one-half of your adult working life, and specific sets of occupational experiences can affect your perceptual abilities both at the physiological and at higher cognitive levels. One aspect of an occupation that may have physiological effects on a sensory system is the magnitude of sound, light, or chemical stimulation to which you are exposed.

Consider, for example, the amount of auditory input that bombards you in your occupational setting. Some work environments are relatively quiet (such as offices and small stores); others are associated with continuous, high-intensity noise (for example, factories and mills). Figure 17-15 illustrates the effects of noise on hearing for different occupations. The horizontal axis represents the frequencies at which hearing was tested in a sample

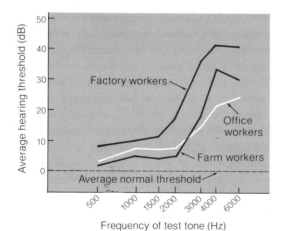

FIGURE 17-15   The effect of occupation on hearing. (Based on Glorig, Wheeler, Quigle, Grings & Summerfield, 1970)

of male office, farm, and factory workers. The 0-decibel point on the vertical axis represents the average minimum threshold for an auditory experience. The three curves on the graph plot the average threshold sound intensity at each of the frequencies used in the test. As you can see, the group of factory workers has a lowered sensitivity (higher average thresholds). Fortunately, many factory workers have begun to wear earphones while working; these help protect them from the destructive effects of continual noise exposure.

According to Kryter (1985), factory workers are not the only group that should be concerned about exposure to very loud sounds. For instance, soldiers exposed to the sound of gunfire and airline pilots exposed to engine noises have been shown to have hearing deficits. The loss tends to be greatest in the higher frequency ranges and seems to increase in severity as the length of the exposure increases. Thus, airline pilots who had 1,000–2,000 hr flying time in the noisy planes of the 1960s had an average audibility threshold of approximately 0 dB at a sound frequency of 4000 Hz, whereas more experienced pilots, with 10,000–16,000 hr flying time, had an average audibility threshold of 10 dB at that sound frequency.

Rice, Ayley, Bartlett, Bedford, Gregory, and Hallum (1968) have shown that performers of rock music may also suffer hearing losses. In Figure 17-16 average audibility thresholds are again plotted for various test frequencies. The lowest curve represents the thresholds of the control group of nonperformers. Notice that relative to nonperformers of the same age, the rock performers have elevated audibility thresholds (lower sensitivity). At 4000 Hz there is an approximately 20-dB difference between the thresholds of the performers and the controls. To give you a reference point, a 20-dB difference would be roughly equivalent to being able to hear a normal conversational tone as opposed to a shout. Figure 17-16 also shows the immediate effects of prolonged exposure to very loud sounds. The dotted curve on this graph plots the measured thresholds immediately after 85 min of

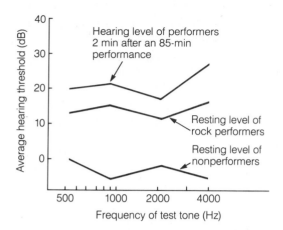

FIGURE 17-16   A comparison of the hearing of rock musicians to that of nonperformers. (Based on Rice et al., 1968)

exposure to very loud music; as you can see, the threshold at 4000 Hz has risen to 25 dB.

In a similar vein, there are occupations that expose the eyes to high-intensity lights (such as welding arcs and furnace blazes). In the same manner that exposure to prolonged high-intensity sound can impair hearing, exposure to prolonged high-intensity light can permanently impair vision (Noell, 1980).

Some occupations involve specific experiences or training programs that attempt to alter perceptual abilities. Pilots, especially those in the military, are often given training to improve the basic visual capacities associated with binocular depth perception, visual acuity, and so forth. There is a strong conviction among students who participate in such programs that such visual training is quite effective; however, actual optometric measures do not show any beneficial changes (Goodson & Rahe, 1981). Similarly, the police believe that because of their training and practical experiences they tend to develop a superior ability to observe details. Actually, much evidence indicates that this is not the case (see Loftus, 1979; Yarmey, 1979), although some recently developed training programs may improve this ability (Yuille, 1984).

Perceptual Set

Experiences we have in an occupational or other setting may bias our perception and interpretation of various stimuli. This seems to be because specific past experiences produce a sensitization or predisposition to ''see'' a situation in a certain way, especially when several alternative perceptual experiences are possible (as when the stimulus is ambiguous or degraded because of poor viewing conditions). Technically this is known as a **perceptual set,** and it refers specifically to the expectancies or predispositions an observer brings to the perceptual situation (Coren, 1984b). In many respects, set can be thought of as another example of

---

DEMONSTRATION BOX 17-6.   Set

Something of the flavor of perceptual set can be experienced by simply reading the set of words below out loud:

MACBETH MACARTHUR MACWILLIAMS
MACNAMARA MACDILLON MACDONALD
MACMASTER MACDOWELL MACHINES
MACKENZIE

Now look back at the next to the last word. Did you pronounce it as if it were organized as the name *Mac Hines,* or did you pronounce it as if it were organized as the more familiar and natural form that makes the common word *machines?* If you pronounced it as the name, organizing the prefix *Mac* into a separate unit, you were demonstrating the effects of perceptual set.

selective attention (as we discussed in Chapter 15), in which the observer is set to process some but not all incoming information, or to organize it in a specific manner. To get a better feeling as to how set operates, you might try Demonstration Box 17-6.

As an example, let us consider police as observers and eyewitnesses, since this is an occupation in which observation is an important part of the job. Some findings suggest that perceptual set may influence the observations of police in certain situations. In one study, police officers and civilians were shown films of a street scene over a period of several hours. Their task was to watch for various wanted people (whose photos were on display below the screen) and for certain types of actions (normal exchanges of goods vs. theft, and so forth). The police tended to report more alleged thefts than the nonpolice, but there was no significant difference between the police and civilians in their actual detection of people and actions (Clifford & Bull, 1978).

A more subtle demonstration of this effect of set was provided by Toch and Schulte (1961), who studied perception of violence and crime in ambiguous visual scenes. They simultaneously presented different pictures to each eye in a stereoscope (see Chapter 10). One eye was shown a violent scene and the other a nonviolent one, as in the pair of stimuli in Figure 17-17. If these two views are seen simultaneously by the two eyes, perceptual confusion should result. Observers tend to resolve this ambiguous situation in favor of one scene or the other; that scene then dominates the percept. Toch

and Schulte were interested in exploring the notion that police students would be predisposed to interpret this particular ambiguous situation in terms of the violent as opposed to the nonviolent scene. They compared the performance of advanced police administration students with two control groups: beginning police students and university students. In general they found that the advanced police students interpreted the stereograms as depicting violence approximately twice as many times as the other two groups. Thus, their data provide some

A

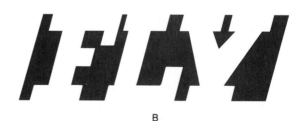

B

FIGURE 17-18   Although A may appear to be a relatively random collection of black shapes, perhaps depicting some sort of boot, it is actually similar to B in that it contains the word *FLY* depicted in the white areas, only in A the word is in Chinese calligraphy.

FIGURE 17-17   **A stereogram used to test for occupational influences on the perception of violence.** (From H. H. Toch, & R. Schulte, 1961, British Journal of Psychology, 52, 389–393)

evidence that certain occupations, especially those requiring intensive training, may set an individual to interpret ambiguous stimulation in a particular way.

We are not singling out the police for particular scrutiny. Perceptual set associated with occupational training and experience and education can affect all groups of individuals. An example of how our educational background can bias our perception can be seen by looking at Figure 17-18A. Most Western observers will see a complex pattern of black shapes, which, by some stretching of the imagination, might appear to cohere into some sort of a boot. Conversely, Figure 17-18B is quite different. Here the white spaces clearly shape the word *FLY* while the black spaces serve as the background. Our familiarity with the English language helps to focus our attention on this region of the figure, and we supply the missing contours, subjectively, to complete the percept (see Chapter 11). Actually, if you were an educated native Chinese, you might be more captured by Figure 17-18A, since it outlines in the white spaces between the black shapes the calligraphic character for the Chinese word *FLY,* and Figure 17-18B might appear to be merely five meaningless black shapes (see Coren, Porac & Theodor, 1987). Thus, much of what you see is determined by what your experience, culture, and education set you to see.

GLOSSARY

The following definitions are specific to this book.

Aftereffects   Errors in hand-eye coordination that follow adaptation to wedge-prism distortion.

Astigmatism   A selective visual bias caused by physical distortion of the cornea.

Carpentered world hypothesis   States that individuals living in urban environments characterized by straight lines and angles will tend to depend more on depth cues based on linear perspective than would people living in more primitive rural environments characterized by curved lines.

Critical period   An interval during which sensory experience is essential if perceptual development is to proceed normally.

Enhancement   An improvement in the final level of an existing ability caused by relevant experience.

Exafference   Stimulus input that acts on a passive observer.

Facilitation   An increase in the rate at which an ability develops, but not in its final level.

Familiar size   A cue to depth based on the known or remembered size of objects.

Illusion decrement   The decrease in the strength of a visual illusion with prolonged viewing.

Induction   A process in development whereby experience determines the presence and final level of an ability.

Interposition   The depth cue based on the blocking of an object or part of an object from view by another closer object.

Maintenance   Preservation of a developed ability by relevant experience.

Maturation   Development of an ability independent of experience.

Oblique effect   The phenomenon whereby acuity for diagonally oriented stimuli is poorer than for horizontally or vertically oriented stimuli.

Perceptual set   The expectancies or predispositions that an observer brings to a perceptual situation.

Reafference   Stimulus input that results from an observer's own movements.

Rearrangement   An experimental technique that alters spatial relations in the visual world.

Restricted rearing   An experimental technique in which an animal is reared without exposure to a particular class of sensory inputs.

Selective rearing   An experimental technique in which an animal is reared under conditions that bias the stimulus input it receives toward a particular class of stimuli (e.g., it sees only vertical stripes).

Set   *See* Perceptual set.

Three-dimensional   Possessing pictorial depth.

Transactional view point   Maintains that any perceptual experience consists of a complex evaluation of the significance of available stimuli based on expectations and experience.

Two-dimensional   Lacking pictorial depth.

Visual field   The portion of the visual environment to which an eye will respond, measured in degrees around the head.

Individual Differences

How often have you heard people arguing over whether a color is green or blue, whether the room was too hot or cold, or whether the coffee is too weak or strong? Such arguments may represent real differences in the perceptions of the individuals involved. Remember that perception is not simply a process by which the qualities of the world get transferred from ''out there'' to ''in here.'' Rather, your final conscious experience of a stimulus involves many levels of processing. Not only must the peripheral sensory receptors be stimulated but stimuli must be interpreted and encoded. As one ancient philosopher said, ''The eyes are blind; only the mind sees.'' If this premise is true, it is quite probable that individuals can differ in the way they perceive their worlds, since it is certainly true that no two minds seem to work in exactly the same way.

There are many factors that can cause individuals to have different perceptions even when encountering identical stimuli. For instance, consider Figure 18-1, which shows a common visual distortion called the **Poggendorff illusion.** For most people it appears that if you extend the line marked *A* it will pass below the line marked *B* by several mil-

limeters. Actually, *A* and *B* are directly in line with each other. The magnitude of this illusion differs among individuals depending on their age, their education, whether they are male or female, and even how well they do on spatial skills tests, like those that form part of many intelligence scales (Coren & Girgus, 1978; Coren & Porac, 1987; Girgus & Coren, 1987). Some of these factors are probably not surprising to you, since we have already discussed how age and past experience can affect perception (in Chapters 16 and 17). However, there are many other variables that operate to make each person's perceptual experiences somewhat unique. These include physiological factors, such as changes in the sensory receptors themselves or the neural apparatus that decodes the sensory information. There is also a contribution from an individual's cognitive, or perceptual, style, which is actually a reflection of personality differences and different approaches to gathering information from the environment. Even an individual's gender seems to cause differences in the way sensory information is processed. All these factors lead to individual differences in perception. One of the most interesting aspects of perception is the consideration of why the world you perceive may not necessarily be the same as the world perceived by others.

PHYSIOLOGICAL DIFFERENCES

Each of us can be seen as a complex physiological machine, and we certainly have seen how factors that alter the structure and function of our sensory apparatus will alter what we perceive. For example, nonfunctional retinal cones will cause color vision deficits. Calcium deposits on the bones of the inner ear will lessen the intensity of sounds from the environment while making your own voice seem very loud to you. In addition to such very specific factors, there are other physiological factors that affect the body generally and also affect perception as a side effect.

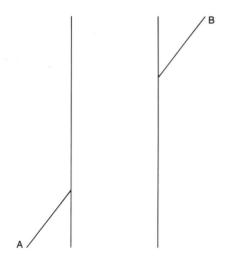

FIGURE 18-1 The Poggendorff illusion, in which line *A* appears as if it would pass below line *B* if extended, even though both are exactly aligned.

The Effects of Drugs

A number of drugs can cause marked changes in sensory capacities. For instance, smokers are continually ingesting a number of active chemicals. The most important of these is the poison nicotine; next in importance is the gas carbon monoxide. Since these chemicals enter the body predominantly via the mouth, it is not surprising that the major sensory effects of smoking tobacco are on the sense of taste. Absolute taste thresholds are higher for smokers than for nonsmokers, with smokers being especially insensitive to bitter tastes such as quinine (Kaplan & Glanville, 1964; Sinnot & Rauth, 1937). However, you may be surprised to find that smoking also affects vision. Most of these effects are probably due to the inhalation of carbon monoxide, a substance that has been shown to produce alterations in some visual tasks, particularly those involving sustained visual attention (Gliner, Horvath & Mihevic, 1983). In addition, smoking tends to reduce the ability to make light-intensity discriminations, especially under scotopic illumination conditions (Rhee, Kim & Kim, 1965). This might explain why smokers tend to have more nighttime driving accidents than nonsmokers. There is also evidence that ingestion of nicotine slows the rate of recovery from certain visual aftereffects (such as the afterimages associated with viewing bright targets, or the fatigue effects of prolonged staring at certain types of patterns, as we discussed in Chapters 4 and 5). It has been hypothesized that nicotine slows recovery from aftereffects because it increases neural inhibition within the visual system (Amure, 1978).

One general theme that characterizes the data describing the effects of drugs on perception is that drugs that depress neural activity—such as sedatives, barbiturates, tranquilizers, or alcohol—also decrease sensory acuity. For example, Helekant (1965) measured the effect of alcohol on taste sensitivity by recording directly from the chorda tympani nerve of a cat. This nerve conveys taste information from most of the tongue. Alcohol reduced responsiveness to sweet (sucrose), acid (acetic acid), salt (sodium chloride), and bitter (quinine) stimuli. The strongest reduction of taste response was for the bitter stimuli. Alcohol may also effect other sensory systems, and recent studies suggest that these effects may be cumulative. One study tested the auditory system and found that chronic alcoholics show delays in the neural response to auditory signals when compared to nonalcoholics (Begleiter, Porjesz & Chou, 1981). Studies of the effect of alcohol on visual abilities have produced similar findings. Research with chronic alcoholics has demonstrated differences in color vision, with alcoholics displaying a higher incidence of color vision deficiencies that nonalcoholic observers (Granger & Ikeda, 1968; Reynolds, 1979).

You do not have to be an alcoholic or a habitual drinker to show the effects of alcohol on visual perception. In some studies of nonalcoholic observers there are indications that higher doses of alcohol decrease an individual's ability to follow a moving target with the eyes (Flom, Brown, Adams & Jones, 1976; Levy, Lipton & Holzman, 1981) and also decrease the ability of the eye to accommodate or change the focus of the lens (Miller, Pigion & Martin, 1985). However, even small amounts of alcohol can decrease an observer's ability to detect the onset of a moving stimulus (MacArthur and Sekuler, 1982).

The overall sensitivity of the visual and auditory systems is also affected by many depressant drugs. A popular technique for measuring visual responsiveness is the **critical flicker fusion frequency** task (usually abbreviated CFF). This task requires an observer to view a flickering light. As the flicker rate is increased the observer will eventually no longer see the successive on-and-off cycles, but rather will see them fused into a steady, continuous light. The flicker speed that results in the perceptual shift from an apparently flickering to an apparently steady light is the CFF. The more sensitive the eye is to changes in illumination level, the faster the rate that the light must be cycled on and off to cause the perception of flicker to disappear. There is a similar task used in hearing called the **auditory flutter fusion (AFF)** task. In measuring the AFF a tone, rather than a light, is switched on and off repeatedly. The AFF is the rate that the tone must be cycled on and off for the listener to hear the signal as a continuous sound. Depressant drugs, such as alcohol and tranquilizers, tend to lower both the CFF and AFF, thus indicating that the visual and auditory systems are acting sluggishly and with less sensitivity under the influence of such drugs (Besser, 1966; Holland, 1960).

Drugs that increase the arousal level of the observer, such as stimulants like caffeine or amphetamines (and even some of the B vitamins), may in some instances improve the sensitivity of the observer. These effects, however, do not seem to be as widespread or as reproducible as those obtained with depressant drugs. We do find that amphetamines and caffeine tend to increase the responsiveness of both the visual and auditory systems when sensitivity is measured using CFF and AFF. Such drugs seem also to increase the sensitivity of the olfactory system (Turner, 1968).

Another technique used to monitor drug effects involves reversible figures, such as the one shown as Figure 18-2. When you look steadily at this figure (which is called the **Necker cube**) you will notice that it tends to reverse its apparent ori-

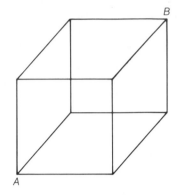

FIGURE 18-2   The Necker cube, in which the face with corner *A* sometimes appears nearer than the face with corner *B,* and sometimes reverses so that the face with corner *B* appears nearer.

entation from time to time. Sometimes the face with the corner labeled *A* seems closer than the face with the corner labeled *B,* and at other times *B* seems closer. Most people have a fairly constant rate of reversal for this figure. Many factors can affect the reversal rate, such as the way you attend to it (Reisberg & O'Shaughnessy, 1984; Wallace & Priebe, 1985). Depressive drugs, such as some tranquilizers, tend to slow the reversal rate (Phillipson & Harris, 1984). Demonstration Box 18-1 pro-

---

DEMONSTRATION BOX 18-1.   The Effects of Stimulants on Figure Reversals

For this demonstration you will need a friend and a watch. Have your friend monitor you while you look at Figure 18-2 for 1 minute. Call out each time the figure reverses its orientation and have your friend keep count. Next, drink a cup of coffee. Don't use decaffeinated coffee since we want you to receive a dose of caffeine. Since caffeine is a stimulant it should increase your visual responsiveness (as well as

keeping you awake for the rest of the chapter). The effects take about 15 minutes to appear; after this interval repeat the viewing process. Look at Figure 18-2 again for 1 minute while your friend records the number of reversals. You should find that the stimulant has increased the number of perceptual shifts that you experience.

vides a procedure for testing the effects of a stimulant on this phenomenon.

The hallucinogenic and psychoactive drugs—including LSD, mescaline, psilocybin, and marijuana—are often reported to have profound perceptual effects. For instance, Aldous Huxley (1963) described his visual experiences after taking mescaline saying: "First and most important is the experience of light. . . . All colors are intensified to a pitch far beyond anything seen in the normal state, and at the same time the mind's capacity for recognizing fine distinctions of tone and hue is notably heightened." Unfortunately, although some aspects of the subjective experience seem to be heightened, actual measurements do not always indicate increased sensory sensitivity. For instance, Hartman and Hollister (1963) found that LSD, mescaline, and psilocybin all reduced the accuracy of color discriminations. Carlson (1958) showed that LSD reduced visual sensitivity in a threshold task, and there are reports of blurred vision (Hoffer & Osmond, 1967) and slower than normal dark adaptation for observers under the influence of LSD (Ostfeld, 1961). Susceptibility to at least one visual geometric illusion, the Mueller-Lyer, increases under the influence of LSD (Edwards & Cohen, 1961). However, LSD does seem to improve auditory acuity and seems to enhance the CFF (Hoffer & Osmond, 1967; Williams, 1979).

Similarly, when observers are asked to describe their experiences after ingesting moderate doses of marijuana (cannabis), they often report improved visual clarity and acuity. Unfortunately, the experimental results indicate that as with LSD the actual perceptual effects involve losses in sensitivity. For instance, in a vigilance task where observers were asked to fixate a target and report stimuli appearing in the periphery of vision, those who had smoked marijuana produced fewer accurate reports. Such an effect could be due to a narrowing of attention induced by the drug, or it might occur because the observers could not be bothered to press the switch. This second explanation probably does not account for the results, since on those trials when the stimuli were reported, the reaction times were as quick as when observers were not under the influence of the drug (Moskowitz, Sharma & McGlothlin, 1972). Intake of marijuana has also been shown to increase the interstimulus interval at which visual masking occurs (visual masking is discussed in Chapter 11), indicating that it acts somewhat like a sedative and decreases the speed of visual information processing (Braff, Silverton, Saccuzzo & Janowsky, 1981). As with alcohol, prolonged use of marijuana seems to have a cumulative effect. This shows up particularly in color discrimination, which has been shown to be poorer in habitual marijuana users. These effects are particularly marked in the blue region (Adams, Brown, Haegerstrom-Portnoy & Flom, 1976).

There are also some more complex sensory effects that have been reported after the smoking of cannabis. Some observers experience changes in depth perception and distortions in the perception of size (Tart, 1971). In addition, there is a report that the autokinetic effect, which is the illusory movement of a stationary light viewed in total darkness (illustrated in Demonstration Box 13-8), may become exaggerated. This last observation has led one group of experimenters to caution against night driving while under the influence of marijuana (Sharma & Moskowitz, 1972). Yet marijuana, even at relatively high intake levels, does not seem to impair eye-movement facility, since neither saccadic eye movements nor the ability to pursue a moving visual stimulus with the eyes is affected by its ingestion (Flom, Brown, Adams & Jones, 1976).

Although contact with hallucinogenic drugs involves a departure from everyday behavior for most people, many of the stimulants (such as caffeine) and depressants (such as tobacco and alcohol) that alter perception are used commonly. Everyday drugs, including antihistamines and aspirin, can cause the perceptual responses of individuals to differ. For instance, aspirin may cause dimness of vision or ringing in the ears (Goodman & Gilman, 1965). Thus, an individual who has just had a cup of coffee or a martini, or who has tried to alleviate a headache, may differ from other individuals in perceptual responses because of the actions of the ingested drugs.

The Effects of Physical Pathology

There are many pathological conditions that affect perception. The most obvious of these are maladies that directly damage a particular receptor organ. Glaucoma, which causes a pressure increase inside the eye, can produce blindness if left untreated, and otosclerosis, which causes the bones of the middle ear to become immobile, will impair hearing. There are, however, some pathological conditions that cause disturbances in very special and complex aspects of perception, rather than simply causing a loss of sensitivity to a given stimulus dimension. Such effects are often caused by severe toxic conditions, such as carbon monoxide poisoning, as well as diseases or injuries that damage or reduce the functioning in some parts of the brain (Critchley, 1964; Davidoff, 1975; Luria, 1973). These can affect such complex functions as the ability to identify objects or to place them in space, and they may also affect the ability to distribute attention. In general, such a problem is called an **agnosia,** from the

Greek *a* meaning "not" and *gnosis* meaning "intuitive knowledge." People suffering from agnosias seem to perceive but are not capable of understanding the information presented to them.

Freud (1953) noticed a form of perceptual disturbance that he called **visual object agnosia.** Some of his patients were unable to identify familiar objects, although there seemed to be no psychopathological disturbance or readily detectable elementary damage to the visual apparatus. More recent work (Luria, 1973) has suggested that agnosias might arise from lesions in the secondary visual areas of the cortex. These lesions do not cause blindness nor do they seem to diminish visual acuity. Rather, they make it difficult for a person to combine parts of an object so as to identify it. For example, Luria describes a patient who was given a picture of a pair of eyeglasses. The patient examined the picture carefully in a manner indicating that he was confused and did not know exactly what it represented. He then started to guess. "There is a circle . . . and another circle . . . a crossbar . . . why, it must be a bicycle?"

Such patients also have problems in separating the parts of the figure from the overall context. Thus, if the patient is shown a drawing of a clock, such as is shown in Figure 18-3A, he can usually identify it correctly. However, if the clock is simply crossed out with a couple of lines, as in Figure

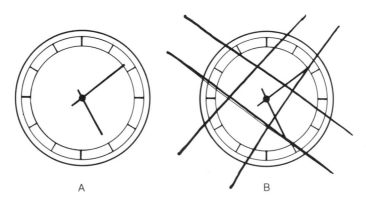

A   B

FIGURE 18-3   (A) A figure identified as a clock. (B) A figure no longer identifiable to a visual agnosic.

18-3B, the patient can no longer identify what the picture represents. Such a patient may identify a telephone, with a dial, as a clock, or perceive a sofa, upholstered in brown fabric, as a trunk. Such difficulties seem to be even more pronounced when the stimuli are presented for less than 500 msec.

What sort of underlying mechanisms are involved in these perceptual disturbances? As long ago as 1909, the Hungarian neurologist Balint made some observations that suggest an attentional mechanism. He found that his patients had a definite decrease in attention span, being able to see only one object at a time, regardless of its size. For instance, such a person could not place a dot in the center of a circle since this would require paying attention to both the circle and the dot simultaneously. This type of patient is said to be suffering from **simultagnosia.** Thus, if the patient were shown a series of overlapping objects, such as those in Figure 18-4, she might report a single object, for example, the hammer, and deny that she can see any of the others (Williams, 1970). If such individuals are asked to copy a simple drawing, such as the one shown as the specimen in Figure 18-5, they depict only its individual parts. Essen-

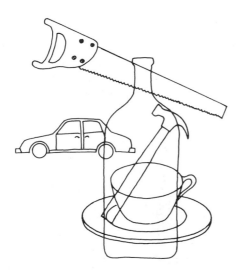

FIGURE 18-4   A test figure for simultagnosia.

tially, they give a visual list of most of the details, as opposed to an overall integration of the parts into a whole figure. A drawing typical of such a patient is shown as the copy in Figure 18-5.

Evidence from several physiological experiments implies that this defect is caused by disturbances in the temporal region of the cortex. It also seems to be specific to the way in which attention is distributed to the visual targets (Butters, Barton & Brody, 1970; Gerbrandt, Spinelli & Pribram, 1970). Luria (1973) claimed that injections of caffeine (to stimulate the appropriate region of the cortex) can reduce some of the symptoms, thus allowing the patient to be able to attend to two or three objects in the visual field simultaneously. Unfortunately, this improvement lasts only as long as the drug is active.

Some of the agnosias are quite general in scope and may involve more than one sensory modality. Patients with diseases of the parietal lobe of the brain may show a **spatial agnosia.** They have difficulty negotiating their way through the world. They make wrong turns even in familiar surroundings, do not easily recognize landmarks, and can become lost in their own homes. This problem does not appear to be caused by a defect in a single sensory modality. These patients seem to be just as impaired using their tactile or kinesthetic senses as their visual (Heaton, 1968; Weinstein, Cole, Mitchell & Lyerly, 1964). Such patients often show a unilateral neglect of space. For example, if asked to draw symmetrical objects, they will usually produce some sort of imperfection on one side. Thus, an individual with left-sided spatial agnosia would reproduce the specimen in Figure 18-6 as the copy shown.

Although some of these perceptual effects are quite general, others are very specific. For instance, there is a rare disorder called **prosopagnosia.** In this type of agnosia the patient has difficulty perceiving and identifying human faces. In extreme cases the patient may not even know his or her own face in a mirror. Prosopagnosia is of interest because the human face is a very important stimulus.

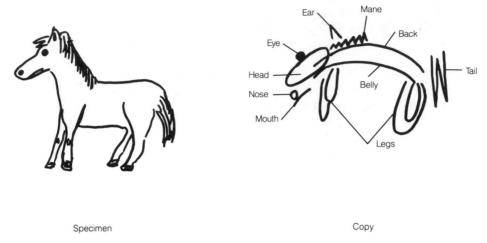

Specimen   Copy

FIGURE 18-5   **A target figure to be copied, and a reproduction typical of a person suffering from visual object agnosia.**

Your mother's face was probably one of the first visual forms to which you attended as an infant. When children draw, the face is usually the first part of the body to be depicted. So we find that facial perception is one of the aspects of form perception that is lost only in cases of serious brain injury, usually involving the right temporal lobe, and often returns much earlier than other cognitive functions when recovery from brain damage occurs (Heaton, 1968).

A related disorder is call **autotopagnosia,** which is the distorted perception of body image and body parts. For example, one patient, when asked to point to her ear, looked around for it and replied that she must have lost it (Pick, 1922). Finger agnosias and finger-naming difficulties are the most widely known forms of specific autotopagnosias, and these are thought to be associated with lesions in the left parietal portion of the brain (Pizorrolo, 1978).

Specimen   Copy

FIGURE 18-6   **A target figure to be copied, and a reproduction typical of a person with unilateral spatial agnosia.**

Although we have concentrated on the visual sense in this discussion, similar difficulties are found in speech and sound perception. These are usually grouped under the overall heading of **aphasia** (from *a* meaning ''not'' and *phasis* meaning ''utterance''). Aphasia sufferers have an inability to name common objects and often fail to recall the meanings of words designating common objects (Luria, 1972; Tsvetkova, 1972). In addition, there are specific auditory agnosias, resulting from damage to the auditory pathways, that lead to the selective loss of the perception of words, called *pure word deafness,* the perception of nonlinguistic sounds, called *sound agnosia,* and the perception of music, called *sensory amusia* (Pizorrolo, 1978). Thus, it should be clear that there are a large number of different forms of agnosia, or higher perceptual disruption. A number of these are listed and named in Table 18-1.

Most agnosias seem to have been caused by physiological damage, usually of the higher brain centers involved in the interpretation of stimuli. Thus, when we find agnosias, we tend often to find damage of particular brain sites. However, these are usually not the primary receiving areas of the cortex for that particular sensory modality. Visual agnosias often are associated with damage to the more forward portions of the occipital cortex, generally Areas 18 and 19, which are the secondary visual areas, and to the temporal lobes, which are tertiary visual processing areas and seem to be associated with complex visual analysis, as we saw in Chapter 3. Similarly for the other sensory modalities, the various forms of agnosia are associated with secondary and tertiary areas of the cortex rather than the primary receiving areas. A map of areas typically found to be damaged when an individual demonstrates various agnosias is shown as Figure 18-7.

Specifiable physiological differences are not the only source of individual differences in perception, however. In the next sections, we will

Table 18-1.   Some of the More Common Forms of Agnosia That Manifest Themselves as Complex Perceptual Deficits

Type of Agnosia	Sensory Modality	Perceptual Deficit
Object agnosia	Visual	Inability to name, recognize, or use objects
Color agnosia	Visual	Inability to associate colors with objects
Drawing agnosia	Visual	Inability to recognize drawn stimuli
Spatial agnosia	Visual	Deficits in stereoscopic vision and ability to relate objects in space
Simultagnosia	Visual	Inability to attend to more than one visual object at a time
Prosopagnosia	Visual	Inability to recognize faces
Unilateral neglect	Visual	Apparent deficit in processing stimuli on one side
Amusia	Auditory	Inability to recognize melodies, often accompanied by inability to reproduce rhythm or tempo
Sound agnosia	Auditory	Inability to identify the meaning of nonverbal sounds (i.e., bells, dog bark)
Sensory aphasia (Wernicke's aphasia)	Auditory	Inability to comprehend speech, although verbal production unimpaired (as opposed to motor or Broca's aphasia, which affects production but not comprehension)
Astereagnosia	Somatosensory	Inability to recognize objects by touch
Autotopagnosia	Somatosensory	Inability to name or localize body parts
Asomatagnosia	Somatosensory	Inability to recognize bodily states
Asymbolia for pain	Somatosensory	Inability to localize or properly react to pain

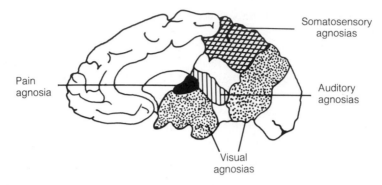

Pain
agnosia

Somatosensory
agnosias

Auditory
agnosias

Visual
agnosias

FIGURE 18-7   **Damage to particular portions of the brain is often associated with the indicated agnosias.**

sider factors affecting perception that may or may not have a physiological basis, or that may be the result of a combination of physiological and experiential processes. Unlike drug and specific sensory damage, the causes of gender and personality differences are harder to specify, although both appear to exist.

GENDER DIFFERENCES

The gender of an individual (whether a person is male or female) may partially determine what is perceived in any given stimulus situation. Gender, of course, carries with it many physiological implications. One of the most important of these is the massive chemical differences between the bodies of men and women due to the presence of specific male or female hormones. Hormones are carried in the blood, which infuses and supplies all our sensory receptors, and are found in many parts of the brain. Thus, it would not be surprising to find that men and women might differ in certain sensory and perceptual capacities.

Examples of gender differences in perception are found in both taste and olfaction. For instance, women, on average, have more acute senses of smell than men (Money, 1965). This difference seems to be directly attributable to hormonal influences since the acuity of a female's sense of smell

varies over the course of the menstrual cycle, reaching its peak at midcycle when estrogen (one of the major female hormones) levels are at their highest (Mair, Bouffard, Engen & Morton, 1978; Parlee, 1983). Women whose ovaries are less active than normal have impaired smell sensitivity, but this defect can be remedied by the administration of estrogen. Conversely, doses of androgen (such as the male hormone testosterone) make the sense of smell less sensitive (Schneider, Costiloe, Howard & Wolf, 1958).

Some hormonal effects on perception are quite subtle. For example, there is a gender difference in taste preference rather than in taste sensitivity; females prefer the sweet taste more than males do, and this preference varies with the menstrual cycle (Aaron, 1975). This is true for rats as well as humans. When the ovaries of female rats are removed, their preference for the sweet taste diminishes; therapeutic doses of estrogen restore the preference (Zucker, Wade & Ziegler, 1972). This may also help us to understand why women using contraceptive pills (which contain estrogen as a component) often complain that they have a tendency to overeat sweets and gain weight.

Male-female differences in sensory sensitivity are found in other modalities as well (McGuiness, 1976a). For example, women usually show greater touch sensitivity than men (Ippolitov, 1973; Weinstein & Sersen, 1961). They also show superior hearing sensitivity, especially at higher frequencies and in older people (Corso, 1959; McGuinness, 1972; Royster, Royster & Thomas, 1980). Women generally are more sensitive than men to pain produced by electric shock, and women's pain thresholds also seem to vary over the menstrual cycle (Goolkasian, 1980; Tedford, Warren & Flynn, 1977).

Gender differences in vision seem to be more complex. Males generally appear to have much better visual acuity under photopic conditions (Burg, 1966; Roberts, 1964), whereas females have lower absolute thresholds under scotopic conditions (McGuinness & Lewis, 1976). This difference seems to be present from childhood (see Brabyn & McGuinness, 1979). There is also some evidence that the visual acuity of women varies with their menstrual cycle (Parlee, 1983; Scher, Pionk & Purcell, 1981), being poorest just prior to and during menstruation. The hormone progesterone (another predominately female hormone) is often prescribed for women who suffer from severe anxiety or depression during menstruation. Progesterone relieves these symptoms and also restores visual acuity to its normal level in most patients (Dalton, 1964). When acuity is measured at different spatial frequencies (measurements of contrast sensitivity, see Chapter 4), females show greater sensitivity in the low spatial frequency ranges and males are more sensitive at the high spatial frequencies (Brabyn & McGuinness, 1979). Also, there is some suggestion that females dark-adapt more rapidly than males do (McGuinness, 1976b).

Visual-Spatial Abilities

An interesting and complex gender difference concerns visual-spatial abilities. These are tasks that involve nonverbal cognitive manipulations of objects, and may include the ability to visualize how objects will appear when they are rotated, to detect the orientations of and relationships between different stimuli, and to correctly perceive complex visual patterns (McGee, 1979). Such tasks seem to

produce consistent sex differences favoring males (Halpern, 1986). One of these involves **disembedding,** or the ability to disentangle a target object from a surrounding, and often confusing, context. For example, in Figure 18-8A, you see a figure marked *Target* that is hidden, or embedded, in the more complex figure beside it. The observer's task is to find the simple shape as quickly as possible. Such tasks are usually called the **embedded figures test** or the **hidden figures test.** A different spatial task involves the ability to recognize targets when they have been rotated. An example of this **mental rotation task** is shown in Figure 18-8B. The observer has to recognize the shape marked *Target* from among the three figures next to it. It is often difficult to recognize which shape is exactly the same as the target, since the correct shape has been rotated into a different spatial orientation.

Both disembedding and mental rotation tasks produce performance differences that favor males (Halpern, 1986; Wilson, DeFries, McClearn, Vandenberg, Johnson & Rashad, 1975). These differences are often quite sizable, amounting to 16 percent or more, depending on the tests involved (Sanders, Soares & D'Aquila, 1982). Males either are more accurate in their responses or show greater speed when completing such tasks (Blough & Slavin, 1987; Harris, 1981; Lohman, 1986). In addition, McGlone (1981) has shown that females approach these tasks differently than males. Females appear to make more rotational hand movements while completing cognitive rotations; in other words, they more frequently need concrete aids or verbal strategies to successfully complete the task (Clarkson-Smith & Halpern, 1983). Demonstration Box 18-2 provides an opportunity for you to test this sex-related difference in spatial ability for yourself.

Physiological Factors

Disembedding a figure, or recognizing it when it has been rotated in space, is a complex task that would seem to involve many learned skills, and

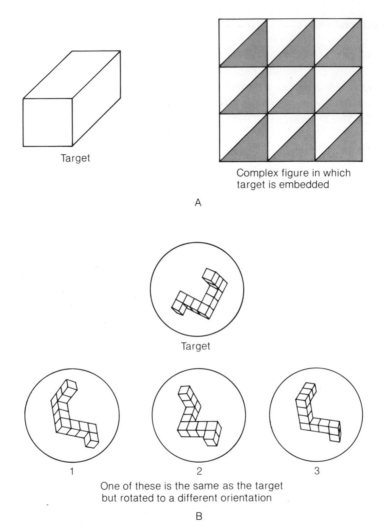

Target

Complex figure in which
target is embedded

A

Target

1   2   3

One of these is the same as the target
but rotated to a different orientation

B

FIGURE 18-8   (A) An embedded figures test in which the target is found in the more complex array. (B) A mental rotation test in which the target is found as one of the three test figures, but in a different orientation.

would seem to be affected by a familiarity with such things as maps and blueprints, which might involve the use of similar skills. So it is somewhat surprising to find that there is evidence suggesting that some of the same physiological factors distinguishing males from females might be partially re-

sponsible for these effects. Dawson (1967) used a series of these tests on a number of West African males who suffered from a disease that results in estrogen levels higher than those usually found in males. When tested on a series of spatial tasks, these males showed reduced spatial ability relative

DEMONSTRATION BOX 18-2.   Gender Differences in Mental Rotation

For this demonstration you will need a stopwatch or a wristwatch that allows you to read seconds (either with a sweep hand or digitally). You will also need a couple of male and female friends. Test them one at a time. First show them what is meant by a mental rotation task by using Figure 18-8B. If they have difficulty, point out that only Stimulus 3 can be rotated to be identical to the target, whereas the other 2 are differently shaped figures. Next, tell your observers that they will see another target figure and a set of 12 test figures. Five of the test figures are identical in shape to the target figures, and their task is to pick out those 5 as quickly as possible. Start your watch, show them the figure, and time how long it takes for them to find the 5 correct ones. If they get any wrong, tell them, but keep the time going until all 5 are found. The correct answers are on the bottom of page 528.

You should notice that, on average, females will take longer at this task than males. Another interesting observation should be that females are more likely to perceive the task as being difficult, as indicated by comments like "I can never do this sort of thing" or "I'm terrible at this," and so forth.

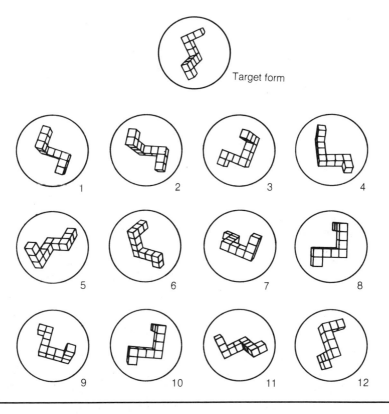

Target form

to a sample of nonaffected males. Similar effects were found in certain South American tribes, where the males habitually chew the leaves of the coca shrub, thus releasing cocaine, which when ingested decreases the secretion of the male hormone testosterone. Such males tend to show typical signs of feminization (including enlarged breasts, widened hips, softened skin texture, and the like), and also show reduced spatial abilities, similar to those of females. Male hormones influence these spatial abilities in the opposite way. Thus, males who produce little or are insensitive to androgen (e.g., testosterone) also show reduced spatial abilities, whereas females with high androgen (e.g., androstenedione) levels show greater spatial abilities (Hier & Crowley, 1982; Masica, Money, Ehrhardt & Lewis, 1969; Peterson, 1976). Hormonal effects in these complex spatial abilities have also been implicated by the finding that the spatial abilities of pregnant women (who have higher than usual levels of estrogen) differ from those who are not pregnant (Woodfield, 1984).

There are other factors consistent with physiological determination of spatial ability. For instance, the rate at which individuals mature seems to predict spatial performance. In this case, "maturing" means showing their secondary sexual characteristics. Typically, late maturing individuals are better on such spatial tasks than early maturing individuals (Petersen & Crockett, 1985; Waber, 1976, 1977). This is consistent with the usually observed gender differences since males tend to mature later than females.

Psychosocial Factors

We have been dealing with some of the physiological variables that seem to produce different patterns of perceptual abilities in males and females. Of course, there will be many factors relating to experience, life history, and cultural influences that will also affect perceptual behaviors. This is be-cause many aspects of perception are subject to learning influences, as we discussed in Chapter 17. Research has shown that even at an early age males and females may differ in the types of tasks and activities they engage in, and also in the tools, implements, or utensils they use in their everyday activities (see Harris, 1981). These factors can also influence some aspects of perception. Demonstration Box 18-3 provides an object-identification task that occasionally produces different responses from males and females. The task shows differences that are most likely to have an experiential basis rather than the kind of physiological basis we discussed above.

Perhaps the strongest data in favor of psychosocial factors contributing to gender differences in spatial skills comes from studies in which specific training was given to boys and girls using toys and games that have a spatial component and that are typically preferred by boys (such as blocks, tinker toys, or paper cut in geometric shapes). Individuals who received such training tended to do better on spatial skills tests, such as the embedded figures task, suggesting that there is a learned component for spatial ability (Smith, Frazier, Ward & Webb, 1983; Sprafkin, Serbin, Denier & Conner, 1983). However, improvement does not occur with training for all of the spatial skills that usually show gender differences (Thomas, Jamison & Hammel, 1973).

It seems likely that differences in spatial skills are due to the interaction between biological and psychosocial factors (Halpern, 1986). Such interactions may explain why identification behavior differs for individuals who are more strongly sex-typed, that is, who identify themselves to be "a typical male or female," versus those who are "androgynous," showing a mixture of typical male and female behaviors (Bem, 1981). They may also help to explain why male homosexuals resemble heterosexual females more than they resemble heterosexual males in terms of their performance on spatial tasks (Sanders & Ross-Field, 1986).

DEMONSTRATION BOX 18-3.   Sex Differences and Object Identification

Look at the three accompanying figures and decide what each looks like. Do this before reading any further.

Responses to patterns similar to these show differences depending on the sex of the observer. Most males view the top figure as a brush or a centipede, whereas females tend to view it as a comb or teeth. Most men view the middle figure as a target, whereas women tend to view it as a dinner plate (but both respond equally with "ring" and "tire"). Most men see the bottom figure as a head, whereas women tend to view it as a cup.

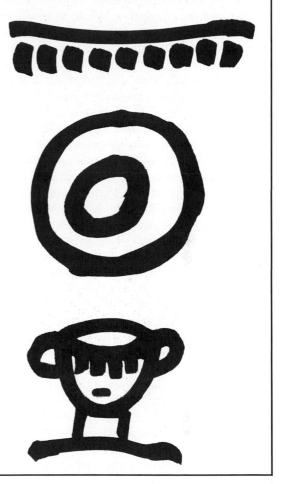

PERSONALITY AND COGNITIVE STYLE DIFFERENCES

There are myriad nonperceptual ways in which individuals differ from one another. Some are outgoing and sociable; others are withdrawn and prefer to be alone. Some are careful and methodical in everything; others are haphazard and unsystematic. The total of all these behavior traits composes the individual's personality. People with different personalities tend to behave differently in many social situations and tend to respond differently to information of various sorts. Do they also perceive the world differently?

There have been many attempts to link individual differences in personality to individual differences in perception. Often the perceptual responses themselves are used to classify individuals as belonging to one personality type or another. There is a lot of evidence that individuals differ in their ability to disembed figures from one another in tasks such as the one we discussed above and illustrated in Figure 18-8A (e.g., T. B. Ward, 1985). Some investigators have suggested that these tests not only separate individuals according to their spatial abilities but also separate individuals according to underlying personality type. Observers who have difficulty with this task are called **field dependent.** They have been classified by personality tests as being socially dependent, eager to make a good impression, conforming, and sensitive to their social surroundings (Konstadt & Forman, 1965; Linton & Graham, 1959; Ruble & Nakamura, 1972). Individuals who have little difficulty with such perceptual disembedding tasks are called **field independent** people. They have been characterized by the same tests as being self-reliant, inner-directed, and individualistic (Alexander & Gudeman, 1965; Crutchfield, Woodworth & Albrecht, 1958; Klein, 1970).

Witkin has been one of the major proponents of this approach. He and his associates look upon both the personality and perceptual effects as examples of an individual's **cognitive style** (Witkin & Berry, 1975). They maintain that perceptual, cognitive, personality, and social interactions all are affected by the same set of processes that determine how a person approaches the world. In effect, cognitive style is part of what we call in everyday language "life-style," affecting not only our habitual interpersonal and task-oriented behaviors but also the way we process information, and in effect, the way we perceive the world. Thus, by measuring how you normally respond in complex perceptual situations, we can predict to some extent how you will approach many other, nonperceptual aspects of your life.

Some investigators use perception as the starting point and move from there into predictions about personality; others have attempted to go in the opposite direction, predicting individual differences in perception from prior considerations of

personality theory. Characteristic of this approach is the work of Eysenck (1967). He divided individuals into two groups on the basis of whether they were outgoing and sociable **(extrovert)** or more withdrawn and self-contained **(introvert).** Eysenck found that he could classify individuals along this dimension on the basis of a simple questionnaire, and he speculated on some physiological differences that might account for the differences in personality traits. He suggested that extroverts have a neural system that is slower to respond and more weakly aroused by stimuli than that of introverts. In addition, they generate neural inhibition more quickly. If this physiological speculation is correct, then introverts should be more perceptually sensitive than extroverts.

Several studies have investigated the effect of introversion-extroversion on perception. Introverts do seem to have more sensitive perceptual systems as predicted by the theory. They show lower average thresholds for vision (Siddle, Morish, White & Mangen, 1969), hearing (Stelmack & Campbell, 1974), touch (Coles, Gale & Kline, 1971), and pain (Halsam, 1967). In addition, introverts are better at tasks requiring sustained attention or vigilance (Harkins & Green, 1975).

When studying the effects of personality factors on perception, it is important to be sure that we are measuring perceptual sensitivity rather than simply detecting differences in how observers respond. It could be the case that introverts simply say "Yes, I detected the stimulus" more often than extroverts. Signal detection theory (discussed in Chapter 2) allows us to separate these possibilities. When Stelmack and Campbell (1974) analyzed their data from this viewpoint, they found that introverts have more sensitive hearing than extroverts, even though extroverts are more biased toward saying yes.

Another way to ascertain sensitivity independent of the observer's response bias is to use direct physiological measurements. One technique is called **evoked response** recording. An electrode is placed on an observer's head over the region of the cortex receiving the primary sensory information for the sense modality being tested. Another electrode, elsewhere on the body, serves as a reference electrode. Any changes in the electrical activity of this brain region can be picked up by sensitive recording devices, and such activity presumably means that the sensory information has, at least, been registered in the brain. In this way, Stelmack, Achorn, and Michaud (1977) demonstrated that introverts seem to have greater auditory sensitivity than extroverts. Unfortunately, not all researchers have been able to verify these findings (Campbell, Baribeau-Braun & Braun, 1981). This may mean that nonsensory factors, such as motivation or distribution of attention, or even the sort of cognitive style we discussed above, rather than direct neurological differences, may account for the differences between introverts and extroverts on sensory tasks.

It is surprising nonetheless, that the answers to a few questions about how a person interacts with other individuals can be used to predict how one person's perceptual responses may differ from those of another. Demonstration Box 18-4 allows you to estimate your own degree of introversion and extroversion, and to test a typical perceptual preference for yourself.

Since personality factors that differ among those in the general population are related to differences in processing of sensory information, it is not surprising that there are dramatic perceptual effects associated with certain severe personality disorders. The perceptual responses that differentiate schizophrenic from nonschizophrenic observers is one area that has received a large amount of research attention. **Schizophrenia** (from the Greek for ''split mind'') is the most frequent diagnosis of a severe or psychotic personality disorder. It is usually characterized by a withdrawal (or ''splitting off'') from the environment, reduced levels of emotional response, a reduction in abstract thinking, and a general diminishing of daily activity. In other words, schizophrenia is a disorder that affects all aspects of the sufferer's social and cognitive life. Studies of the perceptual responses of schizophrenics have shown that they differ from control groups in their performance on time estimation (Wahl & Sieg, 1980), attentional tasks (Cegalis & Deptula, 1981), and even on the perception of visual aftereffects (Tress & Kugler, 1979). Several studies have shown also that schizophrenics display eye-movement patterns that differ from those of control groups; they perform poorly when they are asked to track a moving target with their eyes (Iacono, Peloquin, Lumry, Valentine & Tuason, 1982; Levin, Lipton & Holzman, 1981). Since poor eye-tracking behavior is also found in the

---

DEMONSTRATION BOX 18-4.   Introversion-Extroversion and Taste Perception

It is easy to determine your own standing on introversion versus extroversion by answering the following questions with a ''Yes'' or a ''No.''

Do you often wish for more excitement in life?
Do you often say things without stopping to think?
Do you like going out a lot?
Do other people think of you as being lively?
Do you like interacting with people?

If you answered all the questions ''Yes,'' you are rather extroverted; if you answered them all ''No,'' you are rather introverted.

Have some friends and/or relatives answer these questions, but add one additional item to the list.

Do you like spicy foods?

What answer do you expect extroverts versus introverts to give? What *sensory data* would lead you to expect that answer?

close relatives of schizophrenics (who are not affected with the disorder), it has been suggested that eye-movement behavior may be a genetic marker for the disorder (Iacono et al., 1982). This suggests that perceptual behavior can be used as an indicator of the presence of underlying processes that could promote personality disorders.

Overall, who you are, the kind of person you are, and the life history you have had all affect what you perceive in any stimulus situation. Since you differ along many dimensions from those around you, your perception of the world has a unique flavor. What you perceive in any situation is not necessarily the same as what is perceived by the person next to you.

GLOSSARY

The following definitions are specific to this book.

Agnosia   A pathological condition in which an individual can no longer attach meaning to a sensory impression.

Aphasia   A disorder characterized by difficulties involving speech and sound perception.

Auditory flutter fusion (AFF)   The rate of interruption of a continuous tone at which an observer first hears the tone as continuous.

Autotopagnosia   The distorted perception of body image and body parts.

Cognitive style   The overall personality and perceptual predispositions that are characteristics of a particular individual.

Critical flicker fusion frequency (CFF)   The minimum rate of a flickering light at which the light is perceived as continuous.

Disembedding   The ability to disentangle a target object from a surrounding, and often confusing, context.

Embedded figures test   A task used to determine spatial abilities, in which a subject is asked to find a simple shape hidden in a more complex figure.

Evoked response   Overall electrical response of the brain to presentation of a stimulus.

Extrovert   An outgoing and sociable person.

Field dependent   Descriptive of individuals exhibiting difficulty with embedded-figures tasks.

Field independent   Descriptive of individuals exhibiting little difficulty with embedded-figures tasks.

Hidden figures test   *See* Embedded figures test.

Introvert   A withdrawn and self-contained person.

Mental rotation task   A task in which observers are asked to recognize a visual target in different spatial orientations (rotations).

Necker cube   The drawing in Figure 18-2, in which the three-dimensional interpretation alternates between two equally compelling possibilities.

Poggendorff illusion   An illusion of direction that shows both age and gender differences.

Prosopagnosia   A perceptual disorder in which an individual cannot identify human faces.

Schizophrenia   A psychotic disorder characterized by withdrawal from the environment, reduced levels of emotional response, a reduction in abstract thinking, and a general diminishing of daily activity.

Simultagnosia   An attentional disorder in which an individual cannot pay attention to more than one stimulus at a time.

Spatial agnosia   A perceptual disorder in which individuals cannot accurately localize objects for themselves.

Visual object agnosia   An inability to identify familiar objects in the absence of psychopathology or organic damage to the visual apparatus.

Answers to Demonstration Box 18-2: 3, 6, 7, 9, 11.

APPENDIX

Primer of Neurophysiology

NEURONS AND THE NERVOUS
   SYSTEM
THE NATURE OF NEURAL ACTIVITY
TECHNIQUES TO MEASURE NEURAL
   FUNCTION

There are several places in the book where our discussions assume that you know some neurophysiology. You need to know some terminology for parts of the nervous system, how a neuron functions, and how we investigate neural activity in sensory systems. This appendix provides you with that information in a fairly condensed form. More details are available from any of several basic texts in biopsychology (e.g., Carlson, 1988; Kalat, 1984).

NEURONS AND THE NERVOUS SYSTEM

The human nervous system contains approximately 10 to 14 billion neurons. Figure A-1 shows some aspects of several types of neurons. A **sensory neuron** conducts information from sensory receptors (sometimes part of the sensory neuron itself) toward the brain, an **interneuron** conducts information between other neurons, and a **motor neuron** conducts nerve impulses outward to the muscles. Each of these neurons is a separate cell, generally composed of three distinct parts: a **cell body,** an **axon,** and **dendrites.** The cell body contains the nucleus (which contains the genetic material) and a large variety of other molecules that govern the functioning of the neuron. The dendrites are branching structures that make contact with incoming nerve fibers from other neurons, and the axons are usually long fibers that conduct nerve impulses toward other neurons (or muscle fibers). Axons typically terminate near dendrites of other neurons. Many, but not all, neurons have axons that are covered by protective and nutritive cells called **glial cells.** Some glial cells (including a variety called **Schwann cells**) form the **myelin sheath** around the axon, which, as you will see below, helps to increase the speed at which an ac-

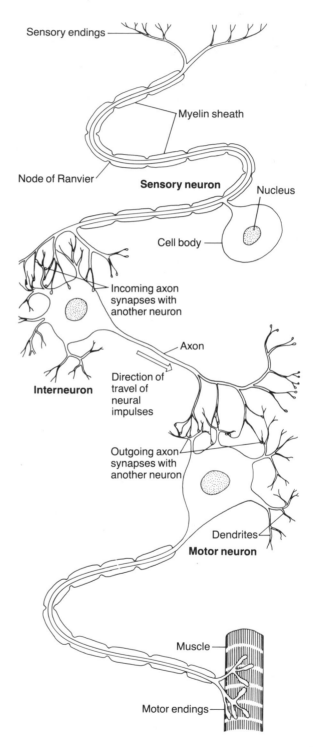

FIGURE A-1   Neurons of various types and their important parts and connections with each other.

tion potential travels along a neuron. The myelin sheath is interrupted about every millimeter by **nodes of Ranvier,** which are the gaps between successive glial cells. Most sensory and motor nerves are myelinated (have a myelin sheath); a notable exception are the small C neurons that terminate in the skin and respond best to noxious stimulation (see Chapter 9).

When many axons gather together into a pathway to carry information from one part of the body to the other, that pathway is called a **nerve.** Sensory information usually is carried by nerves to the **central nervous system (CNS),** which consists of the brain and the spinal cord. In the central nervous system, a pathway is no longer called a nerve but rather a **tract,** although the terms *fasciculus* or *peduncle* are used sometimes for certain pathways. A bundle of nerve fibers ascending the spinal cord is quite often referred to as a **lemniscus.** In addition to pathways in the central nervous system *(white matter)*, there are distinct regions containing *gray matter* (the cell bodies of many neurons grouped together). The islands of gray matter are referred to as **nuclei.** Much of the sensory information processing, and complex channeling of information, takes place in nuclei of the brain and spinal cord.

THE NATURE OF NEURAL ACTIVITY

Information is passed along neurons, and from one to another, by electrochemical changes in the neuron. When unstimulated, the inside of a neuron is electrically negative with respect to the outside, with a **resting potential** of about -70 millivolts (mV). This charge is due to the action of millions of *ions* (atoms that have gained or lost an electron, and hence are electrically charged). The most common ions involved in neural action are sodium (Na^+), potassium (K^+), chloride (Cl^-), and bicarbonate (HCO_3^-). The negative electrical charge of the neuron is the result of a dynamic chemical equilibrium involving the flow of various ions across the cell membrane, plus the existence of negatively charged proteins that are bound to the inside of the cell. The ions are not distributed equally on both sides of the membrane. Of the negative ions, chloride and bicarbonate are many times more common outside. Of the positive ions, sodium is 14 times more common outside, and potassium 28 times more common inside, mainly because of the **sodium-potassium pump,** a biochemical process that ejects 3 sodium ions for every 2 potassium ions it allows in. Also, potassium passes more easily through the membrane than does sodium.

When a neuron is stimulated, either by a physical stimulus or another neuron, the difference in electrical potential across the cell membrane either becomes less negative by moving toward 0 mV **(depolarization)** or more negative by moving farther away from 0 mV **(hyperpolarization).** This happens because the stimulation causes changes in the permeability of the cell membrane to various ions. Typically, when sodium is blocked from its usual (slow) flow across the membrane the negative charge inside the neuron increases (hyperpolarization). Conversely, if sodium ions are allowed to flow more rapidly into the cell the negative charge decreases (depolarization).

There are several different ways such stimulation occurs. Different sensory cells use different methods to change the environmental stimulation into a depolarization or a hyperpolarization. We discuss some of these processes in the chapters devoted to particular sensory systems, since they are rather specialized. For neurons stimulated by other neurons, however, the changes in permeability are fairly standard. They are caused by release of a **transmitter substance** across the **synapse** separating the two cells. Figure A-2 shows the most important parts of the synapse. The transmitter substance is stored in the **synaptic vesicle** located in the **synaptic knob** near the **presynaptic membrane,** and is released across the **synaptic cleft** in amounts determined by the amount of activity in the incoming neuron. Transmitter substance comes in two forms, **excitatory transmitter,** which

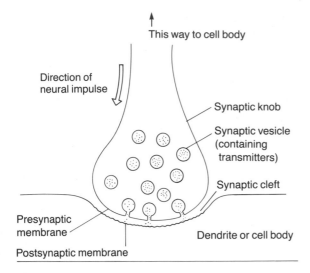

FIGURE A-2   A typical synapse. Transmitter substances are stored in the synaptic vesicles and released across the synaptic cleft.

depolarizes the **postsynaptic membrane,** and **inhibitory transmitter,** which hyperpolarizes the postsynaptic membrane. Both forms are found in numerous places in the central nervous system and there are several different varieties of each type. Transmitter substances are active only a short time after release, being quickly neutralized by enzymes that are always present in the synaptic cleft.

Usually, the stronger the excitatory stimulus to a neuron is, the greater the change in potential difference it causes. Such changes are called **graded potentials.** The neural responses in several sensory systems, such as the parts of the retina that respond first (namely photoreceptors, bipolars, horizontal cells), involve only a continuous graded change in electrical potential. For retinal amacrine and ganglion cells, however, and for virtually all nonsensory neurons, this is not the case. Instead, if a depolarization reaches some critical level, a more dramatic and rapid change in the electrical state of the neuron follows that is referred to as the **action potential** or **spike potential.** In the spike potential,

the initial small depolarization is suddenly followed by a much larger and more rapid depolarization when sodium ions flow into the axon. This rapid depolarization occurs within about 1 msec and is quickly reversed and followed by a period of hyperpolarization as potassium ions are pumped out. After this sudden swing in electrical charge, the potential returns to the resting level of −70 mV. During the time of hyperpolarization following a spike, called the **refractory period,** the neuron is much more difficult to excite.

These changes in electrical potentials in the axon can be recorded by various electrical recording devices, and one such recording is shown as Figure A-3. Increased stimulation does not change the size of the spike, but rather increases the number of responses per unit time. You might imagine that each neural response is a bark from a dog and the excitement of the dog is measured by the speed at which he is barking. Thus, the frequency of responses shows the level of stimulation. Because of the refractory period, the maximum rate at which spikes can occur is about 1,000 spikes per second. Most of the information carried to the central ner-

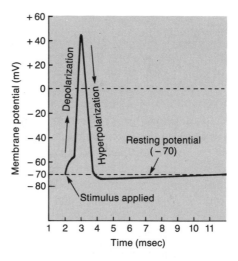

FIGURE A-3   A typical spike, or action potential.

vous system is in the form of a series of nerve spikes.

The change in ion flow causes the spike potential to move along the axon of the neuron until it stimulates the release of transmitter substance where the neuron makes synapses with dendrites or cell bodies of other neurons. The spike moves more quickly in thicker axons than in thin ones, with a maximum speed of about 10 m/sec. However, even the thickest axons require help in getting conduction speeds up to levels where they are useful for quick sensing and muscular action. This help is provided by the myelin sheath worn by many neurons (see Figure A-1). In such neurons, spikes jump electrically from one node of Ranvier to the next at the speed of electrical conduction, which is about 300 million m/sec, whereas the slower biochemical processes occur only in the dendrites, over the cell body, and in the nodes themselves. This allows net conduction speeds of up to 120 m/sec in myelinated cells. Remarkably, these conduction speeds measured with modern methods agree very well with those estimated by Helmholtz in 1850 using reaction-time techniques.

TECHNIQUES TO MEASURE NEURAL FUNCTION

Neural responses (mainly spikes) are measured using microelectrodes, which consist of tiny glass tubes (the tip might be .01 mm in size, or smaller) filled with salt water. The electrode is inserted into the cell body or the axon, and the potential difference between that electrode and another reference electrode outside the cell is amplified and then recorded by a computer, which converts the continuous voltages to digital numbers. The continuous signal is also usually displayed on an **oscilloscope,** which is a sensitive voltmeter that displays voltage changes over time. Typical spike responses are shown in Figure A-4, which shows two neurons responding at different rates.

The use of microelectrode techniques to record the activity of single neurons has produced some of the most exciting data in the field of sensory physiology. Generally, the procedure involves the application of a muscle relaxant combined with local anesthetics to reduce the discomfort from the restraining device used to hold the animal. A

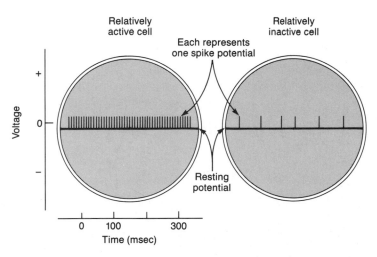

FIGURE A-4   **Oscilloscope records of spikes generated by two neurons penetrated by recording microelectrodes.**

stereotaxic instrument is used to allow the researcher to accurately place electrodes in the brain. Figure A-5 shows a cat with its head in a stereotaxic instrument. Note that the cat is viewing a screen on which visual stimuli may be presented. The electrode is attached through a set of amplifiers to the computer, the oscilloscope, and also often to a speaker. The loudspeaker transforms the amplified neural response into a series of pops or clicks, each click caused by a single spike. Researchers can then listen to the neural response, keeping their eyes free to tend to other matters. An increase in the rate of clicking means an increase in the frequency of cell firing, and a decrease means a reduction. An increase in firing rate when a stimulus is applied means that the neuron is being excited by the stimulus or whatever other neurons it is connected to that are responding to the stimulus. A decrease in firing rate indicates that the stimulus or other neurons are inhibiting the neuron from which recordings are being made. Typically, the records of neural activity along with the conditions under which they occurred are analyzed by the computer for patterns that indicate their functional significance.

GLOSSARY

The following definitions are specific to this book.

Action potential   The large depolarization of a neuron, 1 msec in duration, that occurs when a graded depolarization exceeds a certain threshold.

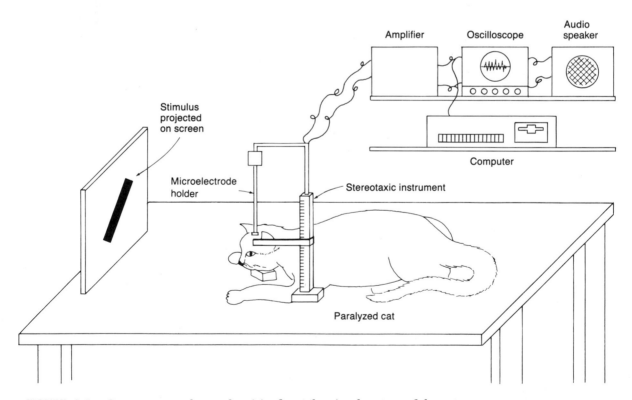

FIGURE A-5   Setup to record neural activity from the visual system of the cat.

Axon   The long, slender part of a neuron that conducts membrane potential changes away from the cell body and makes synapses with other neurons' dendrites or with muscle fibers.

Cell body   The part of a neuron that contains the nucleus.

Central nervous system (CNS)   The brain and the spinal cord.

Dendrites   The branching part of a neuron that makes synapses with other neurons' axons or with sensory receptors.

Depolarization   A change in electrical potential across the cell membrane of a neuron in the direction of lesser negativity.

Excitatory transmitter   A substance released across a synapse that causes the postsynaptic membrane to depolarize.

Glial cells   Cells that protect and feed neurons; some types form the myelin sheath as well.

Graded potential   A change in electrical potential across the cell membrane of a neuron that changes in magnitude as the stimulating event changes in magnitude.

Hyperpolarization   A change in electrical potential across the cell membrane of a neuron in the direction of greater negativity.

Inhibitory transmitter   A substance released across a synapse that causes the postsynaptic membrane to hyperpolarize.

Interneuron   A neuron that conducts information from one neuron to another.

Lemniscus   A bundle of nerve fibers ascending the spinal cord.

Motor neuron   A neuron that conducts spikes outward from the central nervous system to the muscles.

Myelin sheath   A covering of glial cells over the axon of a neuron that allows electrical conduction between nodes of Ranvier, and provides an overall increase in the speed of information transmission.

Nerve   A bundle of axons that carries neural information from one part of the body to another.

Nodes of Ranvier   Interruptions approximately every millimeter in the myelin sheath covering an axon.

Nuclei   Groups of cell bodies of neurons found in the spinal cord and brain.

Oscilloscope   A sensitive voltmeter that displays voltage changes over time.

Postsynaptic membrane   The cell membrane of a dendrite that is *receiving* transmitter substance across a synapse.

Presynaptic membrane   The cell membrane of a synaptic knob of a neuron that is *sending* transmitter substance across a synapse.

Refractory period   A period of time shortly after a spike during which a neuron is hyperpolarized and difficult to depolarize above threshold to generate another spike.

Resting potential   The usual electrical state of a neuron, typically with the inside about -70 mV with respect to the outside.

Schwann cells   One type of glial cells that form the myelin sheath around axons.

Sensory neuron   A neuron that carries information from a sensory receptor (often the neuron itself) toward the brain or spinal cord.

Sodium-potassium pump   A mechanism that ejects 3 sodium ions from inside the neuron for every 2 potassium ions it lets in; helps maintain the resting potential at -70 mV.

Spike potential   *See* Action potential.

Stereotaxic instrument   A device to allow electrodes to be placed precisely in neurons of experimental animals.

Synapse   The place where two neurons almost touch and across which one releases transmitter substance to stimulate the other.

Synaptic cleft   A small space separating a synaptic knob of an axon of one neuron, or sensory receptor, from the cell membrane of a dendrite of another neuron, or a muscle fiber; transmitter substances travel across the synaptic cleft.

Synaptic knob   One of the knoblike endings of an axon; there may be many thousands at the end of each axon.

Synaptic vesicle   A small reservoir in a synaptic knob that contains transmitter substance and releases the transmitter across the synaptic cleft when stimulated by a potential change in the cell membrane, usually a spike.

Tract   The most common name for a nerve in the central nervous system.

Transmitter substance   A substance released across the synaptic cleft when a neuron experiences a change in electrical potential, most usually a spike.

References

Aantaa, E. (1970). Light-induced and spontaneous variations in the amplitude of the electro-oculogram. *Acta Otolaryngologica*, (Suppl. 267).

Aaron, M. (1975). Effect of the menstrual cycle on subjective ratings of sweetness. *Perceptual and Motor Skills, 40*, 974.

Abbs, J. H., & Sussman, H. M. (1971). Neurophysiological feature detectors and speech perception: Discussion of theoretical implications. *Journal of Speech and Hearing Research, 14*, 23–36.

Abramov, I., Gordon, J., Henderson, A., Hainline, L., Dobson, V., & La Brossiere, E. (1982). The retina of the newborn human infant. *Science, 217*, 265–267.

Adam, N., Rosner, B. S., Hosick, E. C., & Clark, D. L. (1971). Effect of anesthetic drugs on time production and alpha rhythm. *Perception & Psychophysics, 10*, 133–136.

Adams, A. S., Brown, B., Haegerstrom-Portnoy, G., & Flom, M. C. (1976). Evidence for acute effects of alcohol and marijuana on color discrimination. *Perception & Psychophysics, 20*, 119–124.

Adams, J. A. (1977). Feedback theory of how joint receptors regulate the timing and positioning of a limb. *Psychological Review, 84*, 503–523.

Adams, R. D. (1977). Intervening stimulus effects on category judgments of duration. *Perception & Psychophysics, 21*, 527–534.

Akil, H., & Watson, S. J. (1980). The role of endogenous opiates in pain control. In H. W. Kosterlitz & L. Y. Terenius (Eds.), *Pain and Society* (pp. 201–222). Weinheim: Verlag Chemie.

Alexander, J. B., & Gudeman, H. E. (1965). Personal and interpersonal measures of field dependence. *Perceptual and Motor Skills, 20*, 70–86.

Alexander, K. R., & Shansky, M. S. (1976). Influence of hue, value, and chroma on the perceived heaviness of colours. *Perception & Psychophysics, 19*, 72–74.

Algom, D., Raphaeli, N., & Cohen-Raz, L. (1986). Integration of noxious stimulation across separate somatosensory communications systems: A functional theory of pain. *Journal of Experimental Psychology: Human Perception and Performance, 12*, 92–102.

Allison, A. C. (1953). The structure of the olfactory bulb and its relation to the olfactory pathways in the rabbit and the rat. *Journal of Comparative Neurology, 98*, 309–348.

Allman, J., Miezin, F., & McGuinness, E. (1985). Direction- and velocity-specific responses from beyond the classical receptive field in the middle temporal visual area (MT). *Perception, 14*, 105–126.

Allport, D. A., Antonis, B., & Reynolds, P. (1972). On the division of attention: A disproof of the single channel hypothesis. *Quarterly Journal of Psychology, 24*, 225–235.

Ames, A., Jr. (1951). Visual perception and the rotating trapezoid window. *Psychological Monographs, 65*, (14, Whole No. 324).

Ames, A., Jr. (1955). *The nature of our perception, apprehensions and behavior*. Princeton, NJ: Princeton University Press.

Amoore, J. E. (1969). A plan to identify most of the primary odors. In C. Pfaffman (Ed.), *Olfaction and taste III* (pp. 158–171). New York: Rockefeller University Press.

Amoore, J. E. (1970). *Molecular basis of odor*. Springfield, IL: Thomas.

Amoore, J. E. (1975). Four primary odor modalities of man: Experimental evidence and possible significance. In D. A. Denton & J. P. Coghlan (Eds.), *Olfaction and taste V* (pp. 283–289). New York: Academic Press.

Amoore, J. E., Pelosi, P., & Forrester, L. J. (1977). Specific anosmias to 5α-androst-16 en-3 one and w-pentadecaloctone: The urinous and musky odors. *Chemical Senses and Flavor, 5*, 401–425.

Amure, B. O. (1978). Nicotine and decay of the McCullough effect. *Vision Research, 18*, 1449–1451.

Andersen, G. J. (1986). Perception of self-motion: Psychophysical and computational approaches. *Psychological Bulletin, 99*, 52–65.

Andersen, G. J., & Braunstein, M. L. (1985). Induced self-motion in central vision. *Journal of Experimental Psychology: Human Perception and Performance, 11*, 122–132.

Anderson, N. H. (1970). Functional measurement and psychophysical judgment. *Psychological Review, 77*, 153–170.

Anderson, N. H. (1975). On the role of context effects in psychophysical judgment. *Psychological Review, 82*, 462–482.

Anderson, N. S., & Fitts, P. M. (1958). Amount of information gained during brief exposures of numerals and colors. *Journal of Experimental Psychology, 56*, 362–369.

Andrews, B. W., & Pollen, D. A. (1979). Relationship between spatial frequency selectivity and receptive field profile of simple cells. *Journal of Physiology, 287*, 163–176.

Annis, R. C., & Frost, B. (1973). Human visual ecology and orientation anisotropies in acuity. *Science, 182*, 729–731.

Anstis, S. M. (1978). Apparent movement. In R. Held, H. W. Leibowitz, & H. L. Teuber (Eds.), *Handbook of sensory physiology* (pp. 655–673). New York: Springer-Verlag.

Anstis, S. M., & Mather, G. (1985). Effects of luminance and contrast on direction of ambiguous motion. *Perception, 14*, 167–179.

Anstis, S. M., Rogers, B., & Henry, J. (1978). Interactions between simultaneous contrast and colored afterimages. *Vision Research, 18*, 899–911.

Antes, J. R. (1974). The time course of picture viewing. *Journal of Experimental Psychology, 103*, 62–70.

Antes, J. R., & Penland, J. (1981). Picture context effects on eye movement patterns. In D. Fisher, R. Monty, & J. Senders (Eds.), *Eye movements: Cognition and visual perception* (pp. 157–170). New Jersey: Lawrence Erlbaum.

Arend, L. E., & Goldstein, R. (1987). Lightness models, gradient illusions, and curl. *Perception & Psychophysics, 42,* 65–80.

Arlin, M. (1986). The effects of quantity, complexity, and attentional demand on children's time perception. *Perception & Psychophysics, 40,* 177–182.

Arvidson, K., & Friberg, U. (1980). Human taste response and taste bud number in fungiform papillae. *Science, 209,* 807–808.

Aschoff, J. (1979). Circadian rhythms: General features and endocrinological aspects. In D. T. Krieger (Ed.), *Endocrine rhythms.* New York: Raven.

Aschoff, J. (1981). *Handbook of behavioral neurobiology* (Vol. 4). New York: Plenum.

Aschoff, J. (1984). Circadian timing. *Annals of the New York Academy of Sciences, 423,* 442–468.

Ashby, F. G., & Perrin, N. A. (1988). Toward a unified theory of similarity and recognition. *Psychological Review, 95,* 124–150.

Aslin, R. N. (1981a). Development of smooth pursuit in human infants. In D. Fisher, R. Monty, & J. Senders (Eds.), *Eye movements: Cognition and visual perception.* New Jersey: Lawrence Erlbaum.

Aslin, R. N. (1981b). Experiential influences and sensitive periods in perceptual development: A unified model. In R. N. Aslin, J. R. Albers, & M. R. Petersen (Eds.), *Development of perception* (pp. 45–93). New York: Academic Press.

Aslin, R. N. (1985). Effects of experience on sensory and perceptual development: Implications for infant cognition. In J. Mehler & R. Fox (Eds.), *Neonate cognition: Beyond the blooming buzzing confusion* (pp. 157–184). Hillsdale, NJ: Lawrence Erlbaum.

Aslin, R. N. (1987). Motor aspects of visual development in infancy. In P. Salapatek & L. Cohen (Eds.), *Handbook of infant perception: Vol. 1. From sensation to perception* (pp. 43–113). Orlando, FL: Academic Press.

Aslin, R. N., & Dumais, S. (1980). Binocular vision in infants: A review and a theoretical framework. In H. Reese & L. Lipsett (Eds.), *Advances in child development and behavior:* (Vol. 15, pp. 54–95). New York: Academic Press.

Aslin, R. N., & Smith, L. B. (1988). Perceptual development. *Annual Review of Psychology, 39,* 435–473.

Atkinson, J. (1979). Development of optokinetic nystagmus in the human infant and monkey infant: An analogue to development in kittens. In R. D. Freeman (Ed.), *Developmental neurobiology of vision* (pp. 277–288). New York: Plenum.

Atkinson, J., & Braddick, O. (1981). Acuity, contrast sensitivity, and accommodation in infancy. In R. Aslin, J. Alberts, & M. Petersen (Eds.), *Development of perception: Psychobiological perspectives: Vol. 2. The visual system* (pp. 243–278). New York: Academic Press.

Atkinson, J., Braddick, O., & French, J. (1979). Contrast sensitivity of the human neonate measured by the visual evoked potential. *Investigative Ophthalmology and Visual Sciences, 18,* 210–213.

Attneave, F. (1954). Some informational aspects of visual perception. *Psychological Review, 61,* 183–193.

Attneave, F. (1955). Symmetry, information, and memory for patterns. *American Journal of Psychology, 68,* 209–222.

Aubert, H. (1886). Die bewegungsempfindung. *Archiv fuer die Gesamte Physiologie des Menschen and der Tiere, 39,* 347–370.

Augenstine, L. G. (1962). A model of how humans process information. *Biometrics, 18,* 420–421.

Avant, L. L. (1965). Vision in the ganzfeld. *Psychological Bulletin, 64,* 246–258.

Avant, L. L., & Lyman, P. J. (1975). Stimulus familiarity modifies perceived duration in prerecognition visual processing. *Journal of Experimental Psychology: Human Perception and Performance, 1,* 205–213.

Avant, L. L., Lyman, P. J., & Antes, J. R. (1975). Effects of stimulus familiarity upon judged visual duration. *Perception & Psychophysics, 17,* 253–262.

Baddeley, A. D. (1966). Time estimation at reduced body temperature. *American Journal of Psychology, 79,* 475–479.

Baird, J. C. (1975). Psychophysical study of numbers. IV. Generalized preferred state theory. *Psychological Research, 38,* 175–187.

Baird, J. C., Green, D. M., & Luce, R. D. (1980). Variability and sequential effect in cross modality matching of area and loudness. *Journal of Experimental Psychology: Human Perception & Psychophysics, 6,* 277–289.

Baird, J. C., Lewis, C., & Romer, D. (1970). Relative frequencies of numerical responses in ratio estimation. *Perception & Psychophysics, 8,* 358–362.

Baird, J. C., & Noma, E. (1978). *Fundamentals of scaling and psychophysics.* New York: Wiley.

Baker, C. L., & Braddick, O. J. (1985). Temporal properties of the short-range process in apparent motion. *Perception, 14,* 181–192.

Balint, R. (1909). Seelenlahmung des "Schauens," optische Ataxie, raumliche Störung der Aufmerksamkeit. *Monatsschr. Psychiatr. Neurol. 25,* 51–81.

Ball, W., & Vurpillot, E. (1976). La perception du mouvement en profondur chez le nourrisson. *L'Annee Psychologique, 67,* 393–400.

Balogh, R. D., & Porter, R. H. (1986). Olfactory preferences resulting from mere exposure in human neonates. *Infant Behavior and Development, 9,* 395–401.

Banks, M. S., & Dannemiller, J. L. (1987). Infant visual psychophysics. In P. Salapatek & L. Cohen (Eds.), *Handbook of infant perception: Vol. 1. From sensation to perception* (pp. 115–184). Orlando, FL: Academic Press.

Banks, M. S., & Salapatek, P. (1983). Infant visual perception. In M. M. Haith & J. J. Campos (Eds.), *Handbook of child psychology.* New York: Wiley.

Bannatyne, A. (1971). *Language, reading, and learning disabilities.* Springfield, IL: Thomas.

Barbeito, R. (1981). Sighting dominance: An explanation based on the processing of visual direction in tests of sighting dominance. *Vision Research, 21,* 855–860.

Barclay, C. D., Cutting, J. E., & Kozlowski, L. T. (1978).

Temporal and spatial factors in gait perception that influence gender recognition. *Perception & Psychophysics, 23,* 145–152.

Barlow, H. B. (1985). The role of single neurons in the psychology of perception. *Quarterly Journal of Experimental Psychology, 37A,* 121–145.

Bartleson, C. J. (1960). Memory colors of familiar objects. *Journal of the Optical Society of America, 50,* 73–77.

Bartoshuk, L. M. (1974). Taste illusions: Some demonstrations. *Annals of the New York Academy of Sciences, 237,* 279–285.

Bartoshuk, L. M. (1978). Gustatory system. In R. B. Masterton (Ed.), *Handbook of behavioral neurobiology: Vol. I. Sensory integration* (pp. 503–567). New York: Plenum.

Bartoshuk, L. M. (1979). Bitter taste of saccharine related to the genetic ability to taste the bitter substance 6-n-propythiouracil. *Science, 205,* 934–935.

Bashford, J. A. & Warren, R. M. (1987). Multiple phonemic restorations follow the rules for auditory induction. *Perception & Psychophysics, 42,* 114–121.

Batteau, D. W. (1967). The role of the pinna in human localization. *Proceedings of the Royal Society of London, Series B, 168,* 158–180.

Beauchamp, G. K., & Cowart, B. J. (1985). Congenital and experiential factors in the development of human flavor preferences. *Appetite, 6,* 357–372.

Beck, J. (1965). Apparent spatial position and the perception of lightness. *Journal of Experimental Psychology, 69,* 170–179.

Beck, J. (1966). Effects of orientation and of shape similarity on perceptual grouping. *Perception & Psychophysics, 1,* 300–302.

Beck, J. (1982). Textural segmentation. In J. Beck (Ed.), *Organization and Representation in Perception* (pp. 285–318). Hillsdale, NJ: Lawrence Erlbaum.

Beck, J., & Schwartz, T. (1979). Verner acuity with dot test objects. *Vision Research, 19,* 313–319.

Beck, N. C., & Siegel, L. J. (1980). Preparation for childbirth and contemporary research on pain, anxiety, and stress reduction: A review and critique. *Psychosomatic Medicine, 42,* 429–447.

Begleiter, H., Porjesz, B., Chou, C. L. (1981). Auditory brainstem potentials in chronic alcoholics. *Science, 211,* 1064–1066.

Beidler, L. M., & Smallman, R. L. (1965). Renewal of cells within taste buds. *Journal of Cell Biology, 27,* 263–272.

Bekesy, G. von. (1947). A new audiometer. *Acta Oto-laryngologica, 35,* 411–422.

Bekesy, G. von. (1959). Synchronism of neural discharges and their demultiplication in pitch perception on the skin and in learning. *Journal of the Acoustical Society of America, 31,* 338–349.

Bekesy, G. von. (1960). *Experiments in hearing.* New York: McGraw-Hill.

Bekesy, G. von. (1967). *Sensory inhibition.* Princeton, NJ: Princeton University Press.

Bem, S. L. (1981). Gender schema theory: A cognitive account of sex typing. *Psychological Review, 88,* 354–364.

Benedetti, F. (1985). Processing of tactile spatial information with crossed fingers. *Journal of Experimental Psychology: Human Perception and Performance, 11,* 517–525.

Bentham, J. van. (1985). Semantics of time. In J. A. Michon & J. L. Jackson (Eds.), *In time, mind, and behavior* (pp. 266–278). Berlin: Springer-Verlag.

Berbaum, K., Bever, T., & Chung, C. S. (1983). Light source position in the perception of object shape. *Perception, 12,* 411–416.

Berbaum, K., Bever, T., & Chung, C. S. (1984). Extending the perception of shape from known to unknown shading. *Perception, 13,* 479–488.

Berbaum, K., & Lenel, J. C. (1983). Objects in the path of apparent motion. *American Journal of Psychology, 96,* 491–501.

Berbaum, K., Tharp, D., & Mroczek, K. (1983). Depth perception of surfaces in pictures: Looking for conventions of depiction in Pandora's box. *Perception, 12,* 5–20.

Berg, K. M., & Smith, M. C. (1983). Behavioral thresholds for tones during infancy. *Journal of Experimental Child Psychology, 35,* 409–425.

Bergeijk, W. A. van. (1967). The evolution of vertebrate hearing. In W. D. Neff (Ed.), *Contributions to sensory physiology* (Vol. 2, pp. 1–49). New York: Academic Press.

Berger, G. O. (1896). Uber den Einfluss der Reizstarke auf die Dauer einfacher psychischer Vorgange mit besonderer Rucksicht auf Lichtreize. *Philosophische Studien, (Wundt), 3,* 38–93.

Berkley, M. A. (1982). Neural substrates of the visual perception of movement. In A. H. Wertheim, W. A. Wagenaar, & H. W. Leibowitz (Eds.), *Tutorials on motion perception* (pp. 201–229). New York: Plenum.

Berlin, B., & Kay, P. (1969). *Basic color terms.* Berkeley: University of California Press.

Bernstein, L. R., & Green, D. M. (1987). Detection of simple and complex changes of spectral shape. *Journal of the Acoustical Society of America, 82,* 1587–1592.

Berry, J. W. (1971). Mueller-Lyer susceptibility: culture, ecology, race? *International Journal of Psychology, 7,* 193–196.

Besser, G. (1966). Centrally acting drugs and auditory flutter. In A. Herxheimer (Ed.), *Proceedings of the Symposium on Drugs and Sensory Functions* (pp. 199–200). London: Churchill.

Bhatia, B. (1975). Minimum separable as function of speed of a moving object. *Vision Research, 15,* 23–33.

Biederman, I. (1987). Recognition-by-components: A theory of human image understanding. *Psychological Review, 94,* 115–147.

Biederman, I., Glass, A. L., & Stacey, E. W., Jr. (1973). Searching for objects in real-world scenes. *Journal of Experimental Psychology, 97,* 22–27.

Billings, B. L., & Stokinger, T. E. (1977). Investigation of several aspects of low-frequency (200 Hz) central masking. *Journal of the Acoustical Society of America, 61,* 1260–1263.

Birch, E. E., Shimojo, S., & Held, R. (1985). Preferential-looking assessment of fusion and stereopsis in infants aged

1–6 months. *Investigative Ophthalmology & Visual Science, 26,* 366–370.

Birren, J., Woods, A., & Williams, M. (1980). Behavioral slowing with age: Causes, organization, and consequences. In L. Poon (Ed.), *Aging in the 1980s* (pp. 293–308). Washington, D.C.: American Psychological Association.

Bishop, P. O. (1981). Binocular vision. In R. A. Moses (Ed.), *Adler's physiology of the eye: Clinical applications* (7th ed.). (pp. 575–649). St. Louis: Mosby.

Blake, R. (1981). Strategies for assessing visual deficits in animals with selective neural deficits. In R. N. Aslin, J. R. Alberts, & M. R. Petersen (Eds.), *Development of perception: Vol. 2. The visual system* (pp. 95–110). New York: Academic Press.

Blakemore, C. (1978). Maturation and modification in the developing visual system. In R. Held, M. W. Leibowitz, & H. L. Teuber (Eds.), *Handbook of sensory physiology: Vol. 8. Perception* (pp. 377–436). New York: Springer-Verlag.

Blakemore, C., & van Sluyters, R. C. (1975). Innate and environmental factors in the development of the kitten's visual cortex. *Journal of Physiology, 248,* 633–716.

Blakeslee, A. F., & Salmon, T. H. (1935). Genetics of sensory thresholds: Individual taste reactions for different substances. *Proceedings of the National Academy of Sciences of the U.S.A., 21,* 84–90.

Blamey, P. J., Dowell, R. C., Brown, A. M., Clark, G. M., & Seligman, P. M. (1987). Vowel and consonant recognition of cochlear implant patients using formant-estimating speech processors. *Journal of the Acoustical Society of America, 82,* 48–57.

Blasdel, G. G., Mitchell, D. E., Muir, D. W., & Pettigrew, J. D. (1977). A combined physiological and behavioral study of the effect of early visual experience with contours of a single orientation. *Journal of Physiology, 265,* 615–636.

Blazynski, C., & Ostroy, S. E. (1981). Dual pathways in the photolysis of rhodopsin: Studies using a direct chemical method. *Vision Research, 21,* 833–841.

Bliss, J. C., Katcher, M. H., Rogers, C. H., & Shepard, R. P. (1970). Optical-to-tactile image conversion for the blind. *IEEE Transactions on Man-Machine Systems, 11,* 58–65.

Block, R. A. (1974). Memory and the experience of duration in retrospect. *Memory and Cognition, 2,* 153–160.

Block, R. A. (1978). Remembered duration: Effects of event and sequence complexity. *Memory and Cognition, 6,* 320–326.

Block, R. A., George, E. J., & Reed, M. A. (1980). A watched pot sometimes boils: A study of duration experience. *Acta Psychologica, 46,* 81–94.

Blough, P. M., & Slavin, K. (1987). Reaction time assessments of gender differences in visual-spatial performance. *Perception & Psychophysics, 41,* 276–281.

Boer, L., & Keuss, P. (1982). Global precedence as a post perceptual effect: An analysis of speed accuracy trade off functions. *Perception & Psychophysics, 31,* 358–366.

Bolton, T. L. (1894). Rhythm. *American Journal of Psychology, 6,* 145–238.

Bonnet, C. (1984). Discrimination of velocities and mechanisms of motion perception. *Perception, 13,* 275–282.

Borg, G., Diamant, H., Oakley, B., Strom, L., & Zotterman, Y. (1967). A comparative study of neural and psychophysical responses to gustatory stimuli. In T. Hayashi (Ed.), *Olfaction and taste II.* (pp. 253–264). Oxford: Pergamon.

Bornstein, M. H. (1973). Color vision and color naming: A psychophysiological hypothesis of cultural difference. *Psychological Bulletin, 80,* 257–285.

Bornstein, M. H. (1975). The influence of visual perception on culture. *American Anthropologist, 77,* 774–798.

Bornstein, M. H. (1977). Developmental pseudocyanapsia: Ontogenetic change in human color vision. *American Journal of Optometry & Physiological Optics, 54,* 464–469.

Bornstein, M. H. (1981). Two kinds of perceptual organization near the beginning of life. In W. Collins (Ed.), *Aspects of the development of competence.* Hillsdale, NJ: Lawrence Erlbaum.

Bornstein, M. H. (1985). Infant into adult: Unity to diversity in the development of visual categorization. In J. Mehler & R. Fox (Eds.), *Neonate cognition: Beyond the blooming buzzing confusion* (pp. 115–138). Hillsdale, NJ: Lawrence Erlbaum.

Bornstein, M. H., Kessen, W., & Weiskopf, S. (1976). Color vision and hue categorization in young human infants. *Journal of Experimental Psychology: Human Perception and Performance,* 115–129.

Bornstein, M. H., & Monroe, M. D. (1978). Color-naming evidence for tritan vision in the fovea. *American Journal of Optometry & Physiological Optics, 55,* 627–630.

Bossom, J., & Ommaya, A. K. (1968). Visuo-motor adaptation (to prismatic transformation of the retinal image) in monkeys with bilateral dorsal rhizotomy. *Brain, 91,* 161–172.

Botte, M. C., Baruch, C., & Scharf, B. (1986). Loudness reduction and adaptation induced by a contralateral tone. *Journal of the Acoustical Society of America, 80,* 73–81.

Botte, M. C., Canavet, G., & Scharf, B. (1982). Loudness adaptation induced by an intermittent tone. *Journal of the Acoustical Society of America, 72,* 727–739.

Botwinick, J. (1984). *Aging and behavior: A comprehensive integration of research findings,* (3rd ed.). New York: Springer.

Bowen, R. W. (1981). Latencies for chromatic and achromatic visual mechanisms. *Vision Research, 2,* 1457–1466.

Bowker, D. O., & Mandler, M. B. (1981). Apparent contrast of suprathreshold gratings varies with stimulus orientation. *Perception & Psychophysics, 29,* 585–588.

Bowmaker, J. K., & Dartnall, H. J. A. (1980). Visual pigments of rods and cones in a human retina. *Journal of Physiology, 298,* 501–511.

Boyd, I. A., & Roberts, T. D. M. (1953). Proprioceptive discharges from the stretch receptors in the knee-joint of the cat. *Journal of Physiology (London), 122,* 38–58.

Boynton, R. M. (1971). Color vision. In J. W. King & L. A. Riggs (Eds.), *Woodworth and Schlossberg's experimental psychology* (3rd ed.). (pp. 315–368). New York: Holt, Rinehart & Winston.

Boynton, R. M. (1978). Ten years of research with the

minimally distinct border. In J. C. Armington, J. Krauskopf, & B. R. Wooten (Eds.), *Visual psychophysics and physiology: A volume dedicated to Lorrin Riggs* (pp. 193–207). New York: Academic Press.

Boynton, R. M. (1979). *Human color vision.* New York: Holt, Rinehart & Winston.

Boynton, R. M. (1988). Color vision. *Annual Review of Psychology, 39,* 69–100.

Boynton, R. M., & Gordon, J. (1965). Bezold-Brucke hue shift measured by color-naming technique. *Journal of the Optical Society of America, 55,* 78–86.

Braddick, O. J. (1980). Low-level and high-level processes in apparent motion. *Philosophical Transactions of the Royal Society of London, Series B, 290,* 137–151.

Braddick, O., & Atkinson, J. (1979). Accommodation and acuity in the human infant. In R. D. Freeman (Ed.), *Developmental neurobiology of vision* (pp. 289–300). New York: Plenum.

Braddick, O., Atkinson, J., Julesz, B., Kropfl, W., Bodis-Wollner, I., Raab, E. (1980). Cortical binocularity in infants. *Nature, 288,* 363–385.

Bradley, A., & Skottun, B. C. (1987). Effects of contrast and spatial frequency on vernier acuity. *Vision Research, 27,* 1817–1824.

Bradley, R. M., & Stern, I. B. (1967). The development of the human taste bud during the foetal period. *Journal of Anatomy, 101,* 743–752.

Braff, D. L., Silverton, L., Saccuzzo, D. P., & Janowsky, D. S. (1981). Impaired speed of visual information processing in marihuana intoxication. *American Journal of Psychiatry, 138 (5),* 613–617.

Braine, L. G., Plastow, E., & Greene, S. I. (1987). Judgments of shape orientation: A matter of contrasts. *Perception & Psychophysics, 41,* 335–344.

Brazelton, T., Scholl, M., & Robey, J. (1966). Visual responses in the newborn. *Pediatrics, 37,* 284–290.

Bregman, A. S. (1978). Auditory streaming: Competition among alternative organizations. *Perception & Psychophysics, 23,* 391–398.

Briand, K. A., & Klein, R. M. (1987). Is Posner's "beam" the same as Treisman's "glue"?: On the relation between visual orienting and feature integration theory. *Journal of Experimental Psychology: Human Perception and Performance, 13,* 228–241.

Bridges, C. D. B. (1986). Biochemistry of vision—A perspective. *Vision Research, 26,* 1317–1337.

Brillat-Savarin, J. A. (1971). *The physiology of taste: Or meditations on transcendental gastronomy.* (M. F. K. Fisher Trans.). New York: Knopf. (Original work published 1825)

Broadbent, D. (1958). *Perception and communication.* Oxford: Pergamon.

Broadbent, D. E., & Gregory, M. (1963). Vigilance considered as a statistical decision. *British Journal of Psychology, 54,* 309–323.

Broadbent, D. E., & Gregory, M. (1965). Effects of noise and of signal rate upon vigilance analyzed by means of decision theory. *Human Factors, 7,* 155–162.

Brodmann, K. (1914). Physiologie des gehirng. In F. Krause

(Ed.), *Allsemaie chirurgie der gehirnkrankheiten.* Stuttgart: F. Enke.

Brooks, R. A. (1981). Symbolic reasoning among 3-D models and 2-D images. *Artificial Intelligence, 17,* 205–244.

Brou, P., Sciancia, T. R., Linden, L., & Lettvin, J. Y. (1986). The colors of things. *Scientific American, 255 (3),* 84–91.

Brown, A. C., Beeler, W. J., Kloka, A. C., & Fields, R. W. (1985). Spatial summation of pre-pain and pain in human teeth. *Pain, 21,* 1–16.

Brown, B. (1972). Resolution thresholds for moving targets at the fovea and in the peripheral retina. *Vision Research, 12,* 293–304.

Brown, E. L., & Deffenbacher, K. (1979). *Perception and the senses.* New York: Oxford University Press.

Brown, P. E. (1972). Use of acupuncture in major surgery. *Lancet, 1,* 1328–1330.

Brown, P. K., & Wald, G. (1964). Visual pigments in single rods and cones of the human retina. *Science, 144,* 45–52.

Brown, R. E., & MacDonald, D. W. (Eds.). (1985a). *Social odours in mammals: Vol. 1.* Oxford: Clarendon.

Brown, R. E., & MacDonald, D. W. (Eds.). (1985b). *Social odours in mammals: Vol. 2.* Oxford: Clarendon.

Brown, S. W. (1985). Time perception and attention: The effects of prospective versus retrospective paradigms and task demands on perceived duration. *Perception & Psychophysics, 38,* 115–124.

Brown, T. S. (1975). General biology of sensory systems. In B. Scharf (Ed.), *Experimental sensory psychology* (pp. 69–111). Glenview. IL: Scott-Foresman.

Brown, W. (1910). The judgment of difference. *University of California, Berkeley, Publications in Psychology, 1,* 1–71.

Brownell, W. E., Bader, C. R., Bertrand, D., & de Ribaupierre, Y. (1985). Evoked mechanical responses of isolated cochlear outer hair cells. *Science, 227,* 194–196.

Bruce, C., Desimone, R., & Gross, C. G. (1981). Visual properties of neurons in a polysensory area in superior temporal sulcus of the macaque. *Journal of Neurophysiology, 46,* 369–384.

Bruner, J. S., Postman, L., & Rodrigues, J. (1951). Expectations and the perception of color. *American Journal of Psychology, 64,* 216–227.

Brunswick, E. (1952). The conceptual framework of psychology. *International Encyclopedia of Unified Science, 1, No. 10.*

Brunswick, E. (1955). Representative design and probabilistic theory in a functional psychology. *Psychological Review, 62,* 193–217.

Brunswick, E. (1956). *Perception as a representative design of psychological experiments.* Berkeley: University of California Press.

Brussell, E. M., & Festinger, L. (1973). The Gelb effect: Brightness contrast plus attention. *American Journal of Psychology, 86,* 225–235.

Bryden, M. P. (1982). *Laterality: Functional symmetry in the intact brain.* New York: Academic Press.

Buckhout, R. (1976). Eyewitness testimony. In R. Held & W. Richards (Eds.), *Recent progress in perception* (pp. 205–213). San Francisco: Freeman.

Bundesen, C., Larsen, A., & Farrell, J. E. (1983). Visual apparent movement: Transformations of size and orientation. *Perception, 12,* 549–568.

Burg, A. (1966). Visual acuity as measured by dynamic and static tests: A comparative evaluation. *Journal of Applied Psychology, 50,* 460–466.

Burns, E. M. (1981). Circularity in relative pitch judgments for inharmonic complex tones: The Shepard demonstration revisited, again. *Perception & Psychophysics, 30,* 467–472.

Butler, D. L., & Kring, A. M. (1987). Integration of features in depictions as a function of size. *Perception & Psychophysics, 41,* 159–164.

Butler, R. A. (1987). An analysis of the monaural displacement of sound in space. *Perception & Psychophysics, 41,* 1–7.

Butler, R. A., Levy, E. T., & Neff, W. D. (1980). Apparent distance of sounds recorded in echoic and anechoic chambers. *Journal of Experimental Psychology: Human Perception and Physiology, 6,* 745–750.

Butters, N., Barton, M., & Brody, B. A. (1970). Right parietal lobe and cross-model associations. *Cortex, 6,* 19–46.

Butterworth, G. (1981). The origins of auditory-visual perception and visual proprioception in human development. In R. D. Walk & H. L. Pick, Jr. (Eds.), *Intersensory perception and sensory integration* (pp. 37–70). New York: Plenum.

Cacace, A. T., & Margolis, R. H. (1985). On the loudness of complex stimuli and its relationship to cochlear excitation. *Journal of the Acoustical Society of America, 78,* 1568–1573.

Caelli, T. (1982). On discriminating visual textures and images. *Perception & Psychophysics, 31,* 149–159.

Caelli, T. (1984). On the specification of coding principles for visual image processing. In P. C. Dodwell & T. Caelli (Eds.), *Figural Synthesis* (pp. 153–184). Hillsdale, NJ: Lawrence Erlbaum.

Cagen, R. H., & Rhein, L. D. (1980). Biochemical basis of recognition of taste and olfactory stimuli. In H. van der Starre (Ed.), *Olfaction and taste VII* (pp. 35–44). London: IRL Press.

Cahoon, D., & Edmonds, E. M. (1980). The watched pot still won't boil: Expectancy as a variable in estimating the passage of time. *Bulletin of the Psychonomic Society, 16,* 115–116.

Cain, D. P., & Bindra, D. (1972). Response of amygdala single units to odors in the rat. *Experimental Neurology, 35,* 98–110.

Cain, W. S. (1969). Odor intensity: Differences in the exponent of the psychophysical function. *Perception & Psychophysics, 6,* 349–354.

Cain, W. S. (1977). Differential sensitivity for smell: "Noise" at the nose. *Science, 195,* 796–798.

Cain, W. S. (1979). To know with the nose: Keys to odor identification. *Science, 203,* 467–470.

Cain, W. S., & Engen, T. (1969). Olfactory adaptation and the scaling of odor intensity. In C. Pfaffman (Ed.), *Olfaction and taste III* (pp. 127–141). New York: Rockefeller University Press.

Cain, W. S., & Johnson, F., Jr. (1978). Lability of odor pleasantness: Influence of mere exposure. *Perception, 7,* 459–465.

Calis, G., & Leeuwenberg, E. (1981). Grounding the figure. *Journal of Experimental Psychology: Human Perception and Performance, 7,* 1386–1397.

Callaghan, T. C., Lasaga, M. L., & Garner, W. R. (1986). Visual texture segregation based on orientation and hue. *Perception & Psychophysics, 39,* 32–38.

Campbell, F. W., & Maffei, L. (1981). The influence of spatial frequency and contrast on the perception of moving patterns. *Vision Research, 21,* 713–721.

Campbell, F. W., & Robson, J. G. (1968). Application of Fourier analysis to the visibility of gratings. *Journal of Physiology, 197,* 551–566.

Campbell, K. B., Baribeau-Braun, J., & Braun, C. (1981). Neuroanatomical and physiological foundations of extraversion. *Psychophysiology, 18,* 263–267.

Canevet, G., Hellman, R., & Scharf, B. (1986). Group estimation of loudness in sound fields. *Acustica, 60,* 277–282.

Cannon, M. W., Jr. (1983). Contrast sensitivity: Psychophysical and evoked potential methods compared. *Vision Research, 23,* 87–95.

Carey, S. (1981). The development of face perception. In G. Davies, H. Ellis, & J. Shepherd (Eds.), *Perceiving and Remembering Faces* (pp. 9–38). London: Academic Press.

Carey, S., & Diamond, R. (1977). From piecemeal to configurational representation of faces. *Science, 195,* 312–314.

Carey, S., Diamond, R., & Woods, B. (1980). The development of face recognition: A maturational component. *Developmental Psychology, 16,* 257–269.

Carlson, C. R. (1983). A simple model for vernier acuity. *Investigations in Ophthalmology and Visual Science Supplement, 24,* 276.

Carlson, N. R. (1988). *Foundations of physiological psychology.* Boston: Allyn & Bacon.

Carlson, V. R. (1958). Effect of lysergic acid diethylamide (LSD-25) on the absolute visual threshold. *Journal of Comparative and Physiological Psychology, 51,* 528–531.

Carlson, V. R. (1977). Instructions and perceptual constancy judgments. In W. Epstein (Ed.), *Stability and constancy in visual perception: Mechanisms and processes* (pp. 217–254). New York: Wiley.

Carmichael, L., Hogan, H. P., & Walter, A. A. (1932). An experimental study of the effect of language on the reproduction of visually perceived forms. *Journal of Experimental Psychology, 15,* 73–86.

Caron, A., Caron, R., Caldwell, R., & Weiss, S. (1973). Infant perception of the structural properties of the face. *Developmental Psychology, 9,* 385–399.

Carpenter, D. L., & Dugan, M. P. (1983). Motion parallax information for direction of rotation in depth: Order and direction components. *Perception, 12,* 559–569.

Carson, C. R. (1983). A simple model for vernier acuity. *Investigative Ophthalmology and Visual Science, 276* (Suppl. 24).

Carter, R. R., & Hirsch, J. (1955). An experimental comparison of several psychological scales of weight. *American Journal of Psychology, 68,* 645–49.

Casey, K. L. (1978). Neural mechanisms of pain. In E. C. Carterette & M. P. Friedman (Eds.), *Handbook of perception: Vol. 6. Feeling and hurting* (pp. 183–230). New York: Academic Press.

Casey, K. L., & Morrow, T. J. (1983). Ventral posterior thalamic neurons differentially responsive to noxious stimulation of the awake monkey. *Science, 221,* 675–677.

Cattell, J. M. (1886). The influence of the intensity of the stimulus on the length of the reaction time. *Brain, 9,* 512–514.

Cavanaugh, P. (1984). Image transforms in the visual system. In P. C. Dodwell & T. Caelli (Eds.), *Figural Synthesis* (pp. 185–218). Hillsdale, NJ: Lawrence Erlbaum.

Cegalis, J. A., & Deptula, D. (1981). Attention in schizophrenia: Signal detection in the visual periphery. *Journal of Nervous and Mental Health Diseases, 169,* 751–760.

Cerella, J., Poon, L., & Williams, D. (1980). Age and the complexity hypothesis. In L. Poon (Ed.), *Aging in the 1980s* (pp. 332–345). Washington, D.C.: American Psychological Association.

Cernoch, J. M., & Porter, R. H. (1985). Recognition of maternal axillary odors by infants. *Child Development, 56,* 1593–1598.

Chapman, C. R. (1978). The hurtful world: Pathological pain and its control. In E. C. Carterette & M. P. Friedman (Eds.), *Handbook of perception: Vol. 6B. Feelings and hurting* (pp. 264–301). New York: Academic Press.

Chapman, C. R., Casey, K. L., Dubner, R., Foley, K. M., Gracely, R. H., & Reading, A. E. (1985). Pain measurement: An overview. *Pain, 22,* 1–31.

Cheeseman, J., & Merikle, P. M. (1984). Priming with and without awareness. *Perception & Psychophysics, 36,* 387–395.

Cheng, P. W. (1985). Restructuring versus automaticity: Alternative accounts of skill acquisition. *Psychological Review, 92,* 414–423.

Cheng, T. O. (1973). Acupuncture anesthesia. *Science, 179,* 521.

Cherry, E. C. (1953). Some experiments on the recognition of speech, with one and with two ears. *Journal of the Acoustical Society of America, 25,* 975–979.

Chevrier, J., & Delorme, A. (1983). Depth perception in Pandora's box and size illusion: Evolution with age. *Perception, 12,* 177–185.

Chocolle, R. (1940). Variations des temps de réaction auditifs en fonction de l'intensité à diverses fréquences. *Annee Psychologique, 41,* 65–124.

Chocolle, R. (1962). Les effets des interactions interaurales dans l'audition. *Journale de Psychologie, 3,* 255, 282.

Cholewiak, R. W., & Craig, J. C. (1984). Vibrotactile pattern recognition and discrimination at several body sites. *Perception & Psychophysics, 35,* 503–514.

Chomsky, N., & Miller, G. A. (1963). Introduction to the formal analysis of natural languages. In R. D. Luce, R. Bush, & E. Galanter (Eds.), *Handbook of mathematical psychology* (Vol. 2, pp. 269–321). New York: Wiley.

Choudhurt, B. P., & Crossey, A. D. (1981). Slow-movement sensitivity in the human field of vision. *Physiology and Behavior, 26,* 125–128.

Clark, H. H., & Clark, E. V. (1977). *Psychology and language: An introduction to psycholinguistics.* New York: Harcourt, Brace & Jovanovich.

Clark, J. C., & Whitehurst, G. S. (1974). Asymmetrical stimulus control and the mirror-image problem. *Journal of Experimental Child Psychology, 17,* 147–166.

Clark, W. C., & Yang, J. C. (1974). Acupunctural analgesia? Evaluation by signal detection theory. *Science, 184,* 1096–1098.

Clarkson-Smith, L., & Halpern, D. F. (1983). Can age-related deficits in spatial memory be attenuated through the use of verbal coding? *Experimental Aging Research, 9,* 179–184.

Clifford, B. R. & Bull, R. (1978). *The psychology of person identification.* London: Routledge & Kegan Paul.

Clifton, R. K., Morrongiello, B. A., & Dowd, J. M. (1984). A developmental look at an auditory illusion: The precedence effect. *Developmental Biology, 17,* 519–536.

Cogan, R., & Spinnato, J. A. (1986). Pain and discomfort thresholds in late pregnancy. *Pain, 27,* 63–68.

Cohen, K. (1981). The development of strategies of visual search. In D. Fisher, R. Monty, & J. Senders (Eds.), *Eye movements: Cognition and visual perception.* Hillsdale, NJ: Lawrence Erlbaum.

Cohen, W. (1958). Color perception in the chromatic Ganzfeld. *American Journal of Psychology, 71,* 390–394.

Cole, R. A., Rudnicky, A. I., Zue, V. W., & Reddy, D. R. (1980). Speech as patterns on paper. In R. A. Cole (Ed.), *Perception and production of fluent speech* (pp. 3–50). Hillsdale, NJ: Lawrence Erlbaum.

Coles, M. G., Gale, A., & Kline, P. (1971). Personality and habituation of the orienting reaction: Tonic and response measures of electrodermal activity. *Psychophysiology, 8,* 54–63.

Collings, V. B. (1974). Human taste response as a function of locus of stimulation on the tongue and soft palate. *Perception & Psychophysics, 16,* 169–174.

Comfort, A. (1971). Likelihood of human pheromones. *Nature, 230,* 432–433.

Condon, W. S., & Sander, L. W. (1974). Neonate movement is synchronized with adult speech: Interactional participation and language acquisition. *Science, 183,* 99–101.

Cooke, N. M., Breen, T. J., & Schvaneveldt, R. W. (1987). Is consistent mapping necessary for high-speed search? *Journal of Experimental Psychology: Learning, Memory, and Cognition, 13,* 223–229.

Cooper, B. Y., Vierck, C. J., Jr., & Yeomans, D. C. (1986). Selective reduction of second pain sensations by systemic morphine in humans. *Pain, 24,* 93–116.

Coren, S. (1966). Adaptation to prismatic displacement as a function of the amount of available information. *Psychonomic Science, 4,* 407–408.

Coren, S. (1969). Brightness contrast as a function of figure-ground relations. *Journal of Experimental Psychology, 80,* 517–524.

Coren, S. (1972). Subjective contours and apparent depth. *Psychological Review, 79,* 359–367.

Coren, S. (1983). Set. In R. J. Corsini (Ed.), *The encyclopedia of psychology.* New York: Wiley.

Coren, S. (1984a). Lens model (Brunswick). In R. J. Corsini (Ed.), *The encyclopedia of psychology* (Vol. 2, pp. 302–303). New York: Wiley.

Coren S. (1984b). Set. In R. J. Corsini (Ed.), *The encyclopedia of psychology* (Vol. 3, pp. 296–298). New York: Wiley.

Coren, S. (1986). An efferent component in the visual perception of direction and extent. *Psychological Review, 93,* 391–410.

Coren, S., Bradley, D. R., Hoenig, P., & Girgus, J. S. (1975). The effect of smooth tracking and saccadic eye movements on the perception of size: The shrinking circle illusion. *Vision Research, 15,* 49–55.

Coren, S. & Girgus, J. S. (1972a). Density of human lens pigmentation: In vivo measures over an extended age range. *Vision Research, 12,* 343–346.

Coren, S., & Girgus, J. S. (1972b). Differentiation and decrement in the Mueller-Lyer illusion. *Perception & Psychophysics, 12,* 466–470.

Coren, S., & Girgus, J. S. (1977). Illusions and constancies. In W. Epstein (Ed.), *Stability and constancy in visual perception: Mechanisms and processes* (pp. 255–284). New York: Wiley.

Coren, S., & Girgus, J. S. (1978). *Seeing is deceiving: The psychology of visual illusions.* Hillsdale, NJ: Lawrence Erlbaum.

Coren, S., & Girgus, J. S. (1980). Principles of perceptual organization and spatial distortion: The gestalt illusions. *Journal of Experimental Psychology: Human Perception & Performance, 6,* 404–412.

Coren, S., Girgus, J. S., & Schiano, D. (1986). Is adaptation of orientation-specific cortical cells a possible explanation of illusion decrement? *Bulletin of the Psychonomic Society, 24,* 207–210.

Coren, S., & Hakstian, A. R. (1987). Visual screening without the use of technical equipment: Preliminary development of a behaviorally validated questionnaire. *Applied Optics, 26,* 1468–1472.

Coren, S., & Hakstian, A. R. (1988). Color vision screening without the use of technical equipment: Scale development and cross-validation. *Perception & Psychophysics, 43,* 115–120.

Coren, S., & Hoenig, P. (1972). Eye movements and decrement in the Oppel-Kundt illusion. *Perception & Psychophysics, 12,* 224–225.

Coren, S., & Keith, B. (1970). Bezold-Brucke effect: Pigment or neural locus? *Journal of the Optical Society of America, 60,* 559–562.

Coren, S., & Komoda, M. K. (1973). Apparent lightness as a function of perceived direction of incident illumination. *American Journal of Psychology, 86,* 345–349.

Coren, S., & Porac, C. (1978). Iris pigmentation and visual-geometric illusions. *Perception, 7,* 473–478.

Coren, S., & Porac, C. (1983a). The creation and reversal of the Mueller-Lyer illusion through attentional manipulation. *Perception, 12,* 49–54.

Coren, S., & Porac, C. (1983b). Subjective contours and apparent depth: A direct test. *Perception & Psychophysics, 33,* 197–200.

Coren, S., & Porac, C. (1984). Structural and cognitive components in the Mueller-Lyer illusion assessed via cyclopean presentation. *Perception & Psychophysics, 35,* 313–318.

Coren, S., & Porac, C. (1987). Individual differences in visual-geometric illusions: Predictions from measures of spatial cognitive abilities. *Perception & Psychophysics, 41,* 211–219.

Coren, S., Porac, C., & Duncan, P. (1981). Lateral preference in pre-school children and young adults. *Child Development, 52,* 443–450.

Coren, S., Porac, C., & Theodor, L. H. (1987). Set and subjective contour. In S. Petry & G. E. Meyer (Eds.), *The perception of illusory contours* (pp. 237–245). New York: Springer-Verlag.

Cormack, R. H. (1984). Stereoscopic depth perception at far viewing distances. *Perception & Psychophysics, 35,* 423–428.

Cornsweet, T. N. (1956). Determination of the stimuli for involuntary drifts and saccadic eye movements. *Journal of the Optical Society of America, 46,* 987–993.

Cornsweet, T. N. (1970). *Visual Perception.* New York: Academic Press.

Cornsweet, T. N. (1985). Prentice Award Lecture: A simple retinal mechanism that has complex and profound effects on perception. *American Journal of Optometry and Physiological Optics, 62,* 427–438.

Correia, M. J., & Guedry, F. E. (1978). The vestibular system: Basic biophysical and physiological mechanisms. In R. B. Masterton (Ed.), *Handbook of sensory neurobiology: Vol. 1. Sensory integration.* New York: Plenum.

Corso, J. F. (1959). Age and sex differences in thresholds. *Journal of the Acoustical Society of America, 31,* 498–509.

Corso, J. F. (1981). *Aging sensory systems and perception.* New York: Praeger.

Corwin, T. R., Moskowitz-Cook, A., & Green, M. A. (1977). The oblique effect in a vernier acuity situation. *Perception and Psychophysics, 21,* 445–449.

Costanzo, R. M. & Gardner, E. P. (1981). Multiple-joint neurons in somatosensory cortex of awake monkeys. *Brain Research, 24,* 321–333.

Costanzo, R. M., & Graziadei, P. P. C. (1987). Development and plasticity of the olfactory system. In T. E. Finger & W. L. Silver (Eds.), *Neurobiology of taste and smell* (pp. 230–250). New York: Wiley.

Cowey, A. (1981). Why are there so many visual areas? In F. O. Schmitt, F. G. Worden, G. Adelman, & S. G. Dennis (Eds.), *The organization of the cerebral cortex.* (pp. 395–413). Cambridge, MA: MIT Press.

Cowley, J. J., Johnson, A. L., & Brooksbank, B. W. L. (1977). The effect of two odorous compounds on performance in an assessment-of-people test. *Psychoneuroendocrinology, 2,* 159–172.

Craig, J. C. (1977). Vibrotactile pattern perception: Extraordinary observers. *Science, 196,* 450–452.

Craig, J. C. (1978). Vibrotactile pattern recognition and masking. In G. Gordon (Ed.), *Active touch: The mechanism of recognition of objects by manipulation* (pp. 229–242). Oxford: Pergamon.

Craig, J. C. (1981). Tactile letter recognition: Pattern duration and modes of pattern generation. *Perception & Psychophysics, 30,* 540–546.

Craig, J. C. (1983a). The role of onset in the perception of sequentially presented vibrotactile patterns. *Perception & Psychophysics, 34,* 421–432.

Craig, J. C. (1983b). Some factors affecting tactile pattern recognition. *International Journal of Neuroscience, 19,* 47–58.

Craig, J. C., & Evans, P. M. (1987). Vibrotactile masking and the persistence of tactual features. *Perception & Psychophysics, 42,* 309–317.

Craig, K. D. (1978). Social modeling influences on pain. In R. A. Sternbach (Ed.), *The psychology of pain.* New York: Raven.

Craig, K. D., Best, H., & Ward, L. M. (1975). Social modelling influences on psychophysical judgments of electrical stimulation. *Journal of Abnormal Psychology, 84,* 366–373.

Craig, K. D., & Coren, S. (1975). Signal detection analysis of social modelling influences on pain expressions. *Journal of Psychosomatic Research, 19,* 105–112.

Craig, K. D., & Prkachin, K. M. (1978). Social modelling influences on sensory decision theory and psychophysiological indexes of pain. *Journal of Personality and Social Psychology, 36,* 805–815.

Craik, F., & Simon, E. (1980). The roles of attention and depth of processing in understanding age differences in memory. In L. Poon, J. Fozard, L. Cermak, & L. Thompson (Eds.), *New directions in memory and aging: Proceedings of the George A. Talland memorial conference* (pp. 95–112). Hillsdale NJ: Lawrence Erlbaum.

Crane, H. D. (1982). IHC-TM connect-disconnect in relation to sensitization and masking of a HF-tone burst by a LF tone. IV. *Journal of the Acoustical Society of America, 71,* 1183–1193.

Cratty, B. (1979). *Perceptual and motor development in infants and children.* Englewood Cliffs, NJ: Prentice-Hall.

Creed, R. S., Denny-Brown, D., Eccles, J. C., Liddell, E. G. T., & Sherrington, C. S. (1932). *Reflex activity of the spinal cord.* Reprint. London & New York: Oxford University Press, Clarendon, 1972.

Critchley, M. (1964). The problem of visual agnosia. *Journal of Neurological Science, 1,* 274.

Crook, C. (1987). Taste and olefaction. In P. Salapatek & L. Cohen. (Eds.), *Handbook of infant perception: Vol. 2. From perception to cognition* (pp. 237–264). Orlando, FL: Academic Press.

Crossman, E. R. F. W. (1953). Entropy and choice time: The effect of frequency unbalance on choice response. *Quarterly Journal of Experimental Psychology, 5,* 41–51.

Crutchfield, R. S, Woodworth, D. G., & Albrecht, R. E. (1958). *Perceptual performance and the effective person.* (WADC-TN-58-60). Lackland Air Force Base, TX: Wright Air Development Center. (NTIS No. AD-151-039).

Cuddy, L. L., Cohen, A. J., & Mewhort, D. J. K. (1981). Perception of structure in short melodic sequences. *Journal of Experimental Psychology: Human Perception and Performance, 7,* 869–883.

Cunningham, W. (1980). Speed, age and qualitative differences in cognitive functioning. In L. Poon (Ed.), *Aging in the 1980s* (pp. 327–331). Washington, D.C.: American Psychological Association.

Curcio, C. A., Sloan, K. R., Packer, O., Hendrickson, A. E., & Kalina, R. E. (1987). Distribution of cones in human and monkey retina: Individual variability and radial asymmetry. *Science, 236,* 579–582.

Cutler, W. B., Preti, G. Krieger, A., Huggins, G. R., Garcia, C. R., & Lawley, H. J. (1986). Human axillary secretions influence women's menstrual cycles: The role of donor extract from men. *Hormones and Behavior, 20,* 463–473.

Cutting, J. E. (1976). Auditory and linguistic processes in speech perception: Inferences from six fusions in dichotic listening. *Psychological Review, 83,* 114–140.

Cutting, J. E. (1978). Generation of synthetic male and female walkers through manipulation of a biomechanical invariant. *Perception, 7,* 393–405.

Cutting, J. E. (1986). *Perception with an eye for motion.* Cambridge, MA: MIT Press.

Cutting, J. E. (1987). Perception and information. *Annual Review of Psychology, 38,* 61–90.

Cutting, J. E., & Kozlowski, L. T. (1977). Recognizing friends by their walk: Gait perception without familiarity cues. *Bulletin of the Psychonomic Society, 9,* 353–356.

Cutting, J. E., & Proffitt, D. R. (1981). Gait perception as an example of how we may perceive events. In R. Walk & H. L. Pick, Jr. (Eds.), *Intersensory perception and sensory integration* (pp. 249–273). New York: Plenum.

Cutting, J. E., Proffitt, D. R., & Kozlowski, L. T. (1978). A biomechanical invariant for gait perception. *Journal of Experimental Psychology: Human Perception and Performance, 4,* 357–372.

Cynader, M., Berman, N., & Hein, A. (1976). Recovery of function in cat visual cortex following prolonged deprivation. *Experimental Brain Research, 25,* 139–156.

Cynader, M., Timney, B. N., & Mitchell, D. E. (1980). Period of susceptibility of kitten visual cortex to the effects of monocular deprivation extends beyond 6 months of age. *Brain Research, 191,* 545–550.

Daan, S., Beersma, D. G. M., & Borbely, A. A. (1984). Timing of human sleep: Recovery process gated by a circadian pacemaker. *American Journal of Physiology, 246,* 161–178.

Dacey, D. M. (1988). Dopamine-accumulating retinal neurons revealed by in vitro flourescence display a unique morphology. *Science, 240,* 1196–1198.

Dallenbach, K. M. (1927). The temperature spots and end-organs. *American Journal of Psychology, 39,* 402–427.

Dallenbach, K. M. (1939). Pain: History and present status. *American Journal of Psychology, 52,* 331–347.

Dallos, P. (1978). Biophysics of the cochlea. In E. C. Friedman & M. P. Carterette (Eds.), *Handbook of Perception: Vol. 4. Hearing* (pp. 125–162).

Dallos, P. (1981). Cochlear physiology. *Annual Review of Psychology, 32,* 153–190.

Dallos, P., Santos-Sacchi, J., & Flock, A. (1982). Intracellular recordings from cochlear outer hair cells. *Science, 18,* 582–584.

Dalton, K. (1964). *The premenstrual syndrome*. Springfield, IL: Thomas.

Dalziel, C. C., & Egan, D. J. (1982). Crystalline lens thickness changes as observed by pachometry. *American Journal of Optometry & Physiological Optics, 59,* 442–447.

Daniels, J. D., Pettigrew, J. D., & Norman, J. L. (1978). Development of single-neuron responses in kittens' lateral geniculate nucleus. *Journal of Neurophysiology, 41,* 1373–1393.

Darian-Smith, I., Sugitani, M., Heywood, J., Karita, K., & Goodwin, A. (1982). Touching textured surfaces: Cells in somatosensory cortex respond both to finger movement and to surface features. *Science, 218,* 906–909.

Dark, V., Johnston, W., Myles-Worsley, M., & Farah, M. (1985). Levels of selection and capacity limits. *Journal of Experimental Psychology: General, 114,* 472–497.

Dartnall, H. M. A. (1957). *The visual pigments*. London: Methuen.

Davidoff, J. B. (1975). *Differences in visual perception: The individual eye*. New York: Academic Press.

Dawson, J. L. (1967). Cultural and physiological influences upon spatial processes in West Africa. I. *International Journal of Psychology, 2,* 115–128.

Day, M. (1975). Developmental trends in visual scanning. In H. W. Reese (Ed.), *Advances in child development & behavior: Vol. 10* (pp. 154–193). New York: Academic Press.

Day, M. C., & Stone, C. A. (1980). Childrens' use of perceptual set. *Journal of Experimental Child Psychology, 29,* 428–445.

Day, R. H., Stuart, G. W., & Dickinson, R. G. (1980). Size constancy does not fail below half a degree. *Perception & Psychophysics, 28,* 263–265.

Day, R. S. (1968) *Fusion in dichotic listening*. Unpublished doctoral dissertation, Stanford University.

Day, R. S. (1970). Temporal order judgments in speech: Are individuals language-bound or stimulus-bound? *Haskins Laboratories Status Report, SR-21/22,* 71–87.

Delk, J. L., & Fillenbaum, S. (1965). Differences in perceived color as a function of characteristic color. *American Journal of Psychology, 78,* 290–293.

Delorme, A., & Martin, C. (1986). Roles of retinal periphery and depth periphery in linear vection and visual control of standing in humans. *Canadian Journal of Psychology, 40,* 176–187.

De Monasterio, F. M. (1978). Center and surround mechanisms of opponent-color X and Y ganglion cells of retina of macaques. *Journal of Neurophysiology, 41,* 1418–1434.

Deregowski, J. (1980). *Illusions, patterns and pictures: A cross-cultural perspective*. London: Academic Press.

Derrington, A. M., & Fuchs, A. F. (1981). The development of spatial-frequency selectivity in kitten striate cortex. *Journal of Physiology, 316,* 1–10.

Desimone, R., Albright, T. D., Gross, C. G., & Bruce, C. (1980). Responses of inferior temporal neurons to complex visual stimuli. *Society of Neurosciences: Abstracts, 6,* 581.

Desimone, R., & Gross, C. G. (1979). Visual areas in the temporal cortex of the macaque. *Brain Research, 178,* 363–380.

Deutsch, D. (1975). Two channel listening to musical scales. *Journal of the Acoustical Society of America, 57,* 1156–1160.

Deutsch, D. (1978). The psychology of music. In E. C. Carterette & M. P. Friedman (Eds.), *Handbook of perception: Vol. 10. Perceptual Ecology* (pp. 191–224). New York: Academic Press.

Deutsch, D. (Ed.). (1982). *The psychology of music*. New York: Academic Press.

Deutsch, D. (1986). A musical paradox. *Music Perception, 3,* 275–280.

Deutsch, D., & Feroe, J. (1981). The internal representation of pitch sequences in tonal music. *Psychological Review, 88,* 503–522.

Deutsch, J. A., & Deutsch, D. (1963). Attention: Some theoretical considerations. *Psychological Review, 70,* 80–90.

DeValois, R. L., Albrecht, D. G., & Thorell, L. G. (1982). Spatial frequency selectivity of cells in the macaque visual cortex. *Vision Research, 22,* 545–559.

DeValois, R. L., & DeValois, K. K. (1975). Neural coding of color. In E. C. Carterette & M. P. Friedman (Eds.), *Handbook of perception: Vol. V. Seeing* (pp. 117–168). New York: Academic Press.

DeValois, R. L., & DeValois, K. K. (1980). Spatial vision. *Annual Review of Psychology, 31,* 309–341.

DeValois, R. L., & DeValois, K. K. (1987). *Spatial vision*. New York: Oxford University Press.

DeValois, R. L., & Jacobs, G. H. (1984). Neural mechanisms of color vision. In I. Darian-Smith (Ed.), *Handbook of physiology: Vol. III. The nervous system* (pp. 425–465). Baltimore: Williams & Wilkins.

DeValois, R. L., Yund, E. W., & Hepler, N. (1982). The orientation and direction selectivity of cells in macaque visual cortex. *Visual Research, 22,* 531–544.

Devaney, K. O., & Johnson, H. A. (1980). Neuron loss in the aging visual cortex of man. *Journal of Gerontology, 35,* 836–841.

De Vries, H., & Stuiver, M. (1961). The absolute sensitivity of the human sense of smell. In W. A. Rosenblith (Ed.), *Communication processes* (pp. 159–167). New York: MIT Press.

De Vries, J. V. (1968). *Perspective*. New York: Dover. (Original work published 1604)

Diamant, H., Funakoshi, M., Strom, L., & Zotterman, Y. (1963). Electrophysiological studies on human taste nerves. In Y. Zotterman (Ed.), *Olfaction and taste* (pp. 191–203). Oxford: Pergamon.

Diamant, H., & Zotterman, Y. (1969). A comparative study on the neural and psychophysical response to taste stimuli. In C. Pfaffman (Ed.), *Olfaction and taste III* (pp. 428–435). New York: Rockefeller University Press.

Dichgans, J., & Brandt, T. (1978). Visual-vestibular interaction: Effects on self-motion perception and postural control. In R. Held, H. W. Leibowitz, & H. L. Teuber (Eds.), *Handbook of sensory physiology: Vol. 7. Perception* (pp. 755–804). New York: Springer-Verlag.

Dickhaus, H., Pauser, G., & Zimmerman, M. (1985). Tonic descending inhibition affects intensity coding of nociceptive responses of spinal dorsal horn neurons in the cat. *Pain, 23,* 145–158.

Diehl, R. L. (1981). Feature detectors for speech: A Critical reappraisal. *Psychological Bulletin, 89,* 1–18.

Dineen, I. T., & Meyer, W. J. (1980). Developmental changes in visual orienting behavior to featural versus structural information in the human infant. *Developmental Psychology, 13,* 123–130.

Ditchburn, R. W. (1973). *Eye movements and perception.* Oxford: Clarendon.

DiZio, P. A., & Lackner, J. R. (1986). Perceived orientation, motion, and configuration of the body during viewing of an off-vertical rotating surface. *Perception & Psychophysics, 39,* 39–46.

Djang, S. (1937). The role of past experience in the visual apprehension of masked forms. *Journal of Experimental Psychology, 20,* 29–59.

Dobson, V. (1976). Spectral sensitivity of the 2-month-old infant as measured by the visual evoked cortical potential. *Vision Research, 16,* 367–374.

Dobson, V., & Teller, D. Y. (1978). Visual acuity in human infants: A review and comparison of behavioral and electrophysiological studies. *Vision Research, 18,* 1469–1483.

Dodwell, P. C. (1971). On perceptual clarity. *Psychological Review, 78,* 275–279.

Dodwell, P. C., Humphrey, G. K., & Muir, D. W. (1987). Shape and pattern perception. In P. Salapatek & L. Cohen (Eds.), *Handbook of infant perception: Vol. 2. From perception to cognition* (pp. 1–80). Orlando, FL: Academic Press.

Doetsch, G. S., Ganchrow, J. J., Nelson, L. M., & Erickson, R. P. (1969). Information processing in the taste system of the rat. In C. Pfaffman (Ed.), *Olfaction and taste III* (pp. 492–511). New York: Rockefeller University Press.

Doherty, M. E., & Keeley, S. M. (1972). On the identification of repeatedly presented visual stimuli. *Psychological Bulletin, 78,* 142–154.

Donaldson, I. M. L., & Long, A. C. (1980). Interactions between extraocular proprioceptive and visual signals in the superior colliculus of the cat. *Journal of Physiology, 298,* 85–110.

Donchin, E. (1981). Surprise! . . . . Surprise? *Psychophysiology, 18,* 493–513.

Doner, J., Lappin, J. S. & Perfetto, G. (1984). Detection of three-dimensional structure in moving optical patterns. *Journal of Experimental Psychology: Human Perception and Performance, 10,* 1–11.

Doty, R. L. (1985). The primates III: Humans. In R. E. Brown & D. W. MacDonald (Eds.), *Social odours in mammals: Vol. 2.* (pp. 804–832). Oxford: Clarendon.

Doty, R. L., Applebaum, S., Zusho, H., & Settle, R. G. (1985). Sex differences in odor identification ability: A cross-cultural analysis. *Neuropsychologia, 23,* 667–672.

Doty, R. L., Green, P. A., Ram, C., & Yankell, S. L. (1982). Communication of gender from human breath odors: Relationship to perceived intensity and pleasantness. *Hormones and Behavior, 16,* 13–22.

Doty, R. L., Kligman, A., Leyden, J., & Orndorff, M. M.

(1978). Communication of gender from human axillary odors: Relationship to perceived intensity and hedonicity. *Behavioral Biology, 23,* 373–380.

Dowling, W. J., & Carterette, E. C. (Eds.). (1987). The understanding of melody and rhythm. *Special Issue of Perception & Psychophysics, 41,* 482–656.

Dowling, W. J., & Harwood, D. L. (1986). *Music cognition.* Orlando, FL: Academic Press.

Droscher, V. B. (1971). *The magic of the senses: New discoveries in animal perception.* New York: Harper.

Drum, B. (1980). Relation of brightness to threshold for light-adapted and dark-adapted rods and cones: Effects of retinal eccentricity and target size. *Perception, 9,* 633–650.

Drum, B. (1981). Brightness interactions between rods and cones. *Perception & Psychophysics, 29,* 505–510.

Duncan H. F., Gourlay, N., & Hudson, W. (1973). *A study of pictorial perception among the Bantu and white primary school children in South Africa.* Johannesberg: Witwatersrand University Press.

Duncker, K. (1929). Uber induzierte Bewegung (ein Beitrag zur Theorie optisch warigenommener Bewegung). *Psychologische Forschung, 2,* 180–259.

Durlach, N. I., & Braida, L. D. (1969). Intensity perception. I. Preliminary theory of intensity resolution. *Journal of the Acoustical Society of America, 46,* 372–383.

Easterbrook, J. A. (1959). The effect of emotion on cue utilization and the organization of behavior. *Psychological Review, 66,* 183–201.

Easton, R. D., & Basala, M. (1982). Perceptual dominance during lipreading. *Perception & Psychophysics, 32,* 562–570.

Edwards, A., & Cohen, S. (1961). Visual illusions, tactile sensibility and reaction time under LSD-25. *Psychopharmacologia, 2,* 297–303.

Efron, R. (1967). The duration of the present. *Annals of the New York Academy of Sciences, 138,* 713–729.

Efron, R. (1973). Conservation of temporal information by perceptual systems. *Perception & Psychophysics, 14,* 518–530.

Egan, J. P. (1975). *Signal detection theory and ROC-analysis.* New York: Academic Press.

Egeth, H. E., Virgi, R. A., & Garbart, H. (1984). Searching for conjunctively defined targets. *Journal of Experimental Psychology: Human Perception and Performance, 10,* 32–39.

Eichengreen, J. M., Coren, S., & Nachmias, J. (1966). Visual-cliff preference by infant rats: Effects of rearing and test conditions. *Science, 151,* 830–831.

Eijkman, E. G. J., Jongsma, H. J., & Vincent, J. (1981). Two dimensional filtering oriented line detectors and figural aspects as determinants of visual illusions. *Perception & Psychophysics, 29,* 352–358.

Eilers, R., Wilson, W., & Moore, T. (1979). Speech perception in the language innocent and the language wise: A study in the perception of voice onset time. *Journal of Child Language, 6,* 1–18.

Eimas, P. D., & Corbit, J. D. (1973). Selective adaptation of linguistic feature detectors. *Cognitive Psychology, 4,* 99–109.

Eimas, P. D., & Miller, J. D. (1980). Contextual effects in infant speech perception. *Science, 209,* 1140–1141.

Eimas, P. D., Siqueland, E. R., Jusczyk, P., & Vigorito, J. (1971). Speech perception in infants. *Science, 171,* 303–306.

Einstein, A., & Besso, M. (1972). *Correspondence 1903–1955.* Paris: Hermann.

Eland, J. M., & Anderson, J. E. (1977). The experience of pain in children. In A. Jacox (Ed.), *Pain: A sourcebook for nurses and other professionals.* Boston: Little, Brown.

Elkind, D. (1978). *The child's reality: Three developmental themes.* Hillsdale, NJ: Lawrence Erlbaum.

Ellingson, R. (1968). Clinical applications of evoked potential techniques in infants and children. *Electroencephalography and Clinical Neurophysiology, 24,* 293.

Ellingson, R., Lathrop, G., Nelson, G., & Donahy, T. (1972). Visual evoked potentials of infants. *Reveue d'Electrocence-phalographie et de Neurophysiologie Clinique, 2,* 395–400.

Ellis, H. (1905). *Sexual selection in man.* New York: Davis.

Ellis, H. C., & Muller, D. G. (1964). Transfer in perceptual learning following stimulus predifferentiation. *Journal of Experimental Psychology, 68,* 388–395.

Emmerson, P. G., & Ross, H. E. (1986). The effect of brightness on colour recognition under water. *Ergonomics, 29,* 1647–1658.

Emmerton, J. (1983). Pattern discrimination in the near-ultraviolet by pigeons. *Perception & Psychophysics, 34,* 555–559.

Engen, T. (1982). *Perception of odors.* New York: Academic Press.

Engen, T. (1987). Remembering odors and their names. *American Scientist, 75,* 497–503.

Engen, T., Lipsitt, L. P., & Kaye, H. (1963). Olfactory responses and adaptation in the human neonate. *Journal of Comparative and Physiological Psychology, 56,* 73–77.

Engen, T., & Tulunary, U. (1956). Some sources of error in half-heaviness judgments. *Journal of Experimental Psychology, 54,* 208–212.

Enns, J. T. (1986). Seeing textons in context. *Perception & Psychophysics, 39,* 143–147.

Enns, J. T. (1987). A developmental look at pattern symmetry in perception and memory. *Developmental Psychology, 23,* 839–850.

Enns, J. T., & Cameron, S. (1987). Selective attention in young children: The relations between visual search, filtering and priming. *Journal of Experimental Child Psychology, 44,* 38–63.

Enns, J. T., & Girgus, J. S. (1985). Perceptual grouping and spatial distortion: A developmental study. *Developmental Psychology, 21,* 241–246.

Epstein, W. (1973). The process of taking into account in visual perception. *Perception, 2,* 267–285.

Epstein, W., & Baratz, S. S. (1964). Relative size in isolation as a stimulus for relative perceived distance. *Journal of Experimental Psychology, 67,* 507–513.

Epstein, W., & Broota, K. D. (1986). Automatic and attentional components in perception of size-at-a-distance. *Perception & Psychophysics, 40,* 256–262.

Epstein, W., & Hanson, S. (1977). Discrimination of unique motion-path length. *Perception & Psychophysics, 22,* 152–158.

Epstein, W., Hatfield, G., & Muise, G. (1977). Perceived shape at a slant as a function of processing time and processing load. *Journal of Experimental Psychology: Human Perception and Performance, 3,* 473–483.

Epstein, W., & Lovitts, B. E., (1985). Automatic and attentional components in perception of shape-at-a-slant. *Journal of Experimental Psychology: Human Perception and Performance, 11,* 355–366.

Epstein, W., & Park, J. N. (1964). Shape constancy: Functional relationships and theoretical formulations. *Psychological Bulletin, 62,* 180–196.

Erickson, R. P. (1963). Sensory neural patterns and gustation. In Y. Zotterman (Ed.), *Olfaction and taste* (pp. 205–213). Oxford: Pergamon.

Erickson, R. P. (1985). Definitions: A matter of taste. In D. W. Pfaff (Ed.), *Taste, olfaction, and the central nervous system* (pp. 129–150). New York: Rockefeller University Press.

Erickson, R. P, & Covey, E. (1980). On the singularity of taste sensations: What is a taste primary? *Physiology & Behavior, 25,* 527–533.

Erickson, R. P., & Schiffman, S. S. (1975). The chemical senses: A systematic approach. In M. S. Gazzaniga & C. Blakemore (Eds.), *Handbook of psychobiology* (pp. 393–425). New York: Academic Press.

Eriksen, C. W., & Collins, J. F. (1968). Sensory traces versus the psychological movement in the temporal organization of form. *Journal of Experimental Psychology, 77,* 376–382.

Eriksen, C. W., & Hake, H. W. (1955). Absolute judgments as a function of stimulus range and number of stimulus and responses categories. *Journal of Experimental Psychology, 49,* 323–332.

Eriksen, C. W., & Hoffman, J. E. (1972). Some characteristics of selective attention in visual perception determined by vocal reaction time. *Perception & Psychophysics, 11,* 169–171.

Eriksen, C. W., & Murphy, T. D. (1987). Movement of attentional focus across the visual field: A critical look at the evidence. *Perception & Psychophysics, 42,* 299–305.

Eriksen, C. W., & St. James, J. D. (1986). Visual attention within and around the field of focal attention: A zoom lens model. *Perception & Psychophysics, 40,* 225–240.

Eriksen, C. W., & Yeh, Y. (1985). Allocation of attention in the visual field. *Journal of Experimental Psychology: Human Perception and Performance, 11,* 583–597.

Ernst, M., Lee, M. H. M., Dworkin, B., & Zaretsky, H. H. (1986). Pain perception decrement produced through repeated stimulation. *Pain, 26,* 221–231.

Erulkar, S. C. (1972). Comparative aspects of spatial localization of sound. *Physiological Review, 52,* 237–360.

Essen, D. C. van. (1979). Visual areas of the mammalian cerebral cortex. *Annual Review of Neurosciences, 2,* 227–263.

Essen, D. C. van. (1984). Functional organization of primate visual cortex. In A. Peters & E. G. Jones (Eds.), *Cerebral Cortex: Vol. 3* (pp. 259–329). New York: Plenum.

Evans, C. R., & Wells, A. M. (1967). Fragmentation phenomena associated with binocular stabilization. *British Journal of Physiological Optics, 24,* 45–50.

Evans, E. F. (1975). Cochlear nerve and cochlear nucleus. In W. D. Keidel & W. D. Neff (Eds.), *Handbook of sensory physiology: Vol. 2. Auditory system: Physiology (CNS). Behavioral Studies. Psychoacoustics* (pp. 1–108). New York: Springer-Verlag.

Evans, P. M. (1987). Vibrotactile masking: Temporal integration, persistence, and strengths of representation. *Perception & Psychophysics, 42,* 515–525.

Evans, P. M., & Craig, J. C. (1986). Temporal integration and vibrotactile backward masking. *Journal of Experimental Psychology: Human Perception and Performance, 12,* 160–168.

Eysenck, H. J. (1967). *The biological basis of personality.* Springfield, IL: Thomas.

Falk, J., & Bindra, D. (1954). Judgment of time as a function of serial position and stress. *Journal of Experimental Psychology, 47,* 279–282.

Falmagne, J. C. (1974). Foundations of Fechnerian psychophysics. In D. Krantz, R. C. Atkinson, R. D. Luce, & P. Suppes (Eds.), *Contemporary developments in mathematical psychology* (Vol. 2, pp. 121–159). San Francisco: Freeman.

Falmagne, J. C. (1985). *Elements of psychophysical theory.* New York: Oxford University Press.

Fant, G. (1967). Auditory patterns of speech. In W. Wathen-Dunn (Ed.), *Models for the perception of speech and visual form* (pp. 111–125). Cambridge, MA: MIT Press.

Fantz, R. L. (1961). The origin of form perception. *Scientific American, 204,* 66–72.

Fantz, R. L. (1965). Ontogeny of perception. In A. M. Schrier, H. F. Harlow, & F. Stollnitz (Eds.), *Behavior of nonhuman primates* (Vol. 2, pp. 365–403). New York: Academic Press.

Fantz, R. L., & Miranda, S. B. (1977). Visual processing in the newborn preterm, and mentally high-risk infant. In L. Gluck (Ed.), *Intrauterine asphyxia and the developing fetal brain* (pp. 453–471). Chicago: Year Book Medical Publishers.

Fantz, R. L., & Yeh, J. (1979). Configurational selectives: Critical for development of visual perception and attention. *Canadian Journal of Psychology, 33,* 277–287.

Farkas, M., & Hoyer, W. (1980). Processing consequences of perceptual grouping in selective attention. *Journal of Gerontology, 35,* 27–216.

Farrell, J. E. (1983). Visual transformations underlying apparent movement. *Perception & Psychophysics, 33,* 85–92.

Faurion, A., Saito, S., & MacLeod, P. (1980). Sweet taste involves several distinct receptor mechanisms. *Chemical Senses, 5,* 107–121.

Favreau, O. E., & Cavanagh, P. (1981). Color and luminance: Independent frequency shifts. *Science, 212,* 831–832.

Fechner, G. T. (1966). *Elements of psychophysics.* (H. E. Alder, Trans.). New York: Holt, Rinehart & Winston. (Original work published 1860)

Fender, D. H. (1971). Time delays in the human eye-tracking system. In P. Bach-y-Rita, C. C. Collins, & J. E. Hyde (Eds.), *The control of eye movements* (pp. 539–543). New York: Academic Press.

Festinger, L., Allyn, M. R., & White, C. W. (1971). The perception of color with achromatic stimulation. *Vision Research, 11,* 591–612.

Festinger, L., Coren, S., & Rivers, G. (1970). The effect of attention on brightness contrast and assimilation. *American Journal of Psychology, 83,* 189–207.

Festinger, L., & Easton, M. (1974). Inference about the efferent system based on a perceptual illusion produced by eye movements. *Psychological Review, 81,* 44–58.

Festinger, L., White, C. W., & Allyn, M. R. (1968). Eye movements and decrement in the Mueller-Lyer illusion. *Perception & Psychophysics, 3,* 376–382.

Filer, R., & Meals, D. (1949). The effect of motivating conditions on the estimation of time. *Journal of Experimental Psychology, 39,* 327–331.

Filsinger, E. E., & Fabes, R. A. (1985). Odor communication, pheromones, and human families. *Journal of Marriage and the Family, 47,* 349–360.

Findlay, J. (1981). Local and global influences on saccadic eye movements. In D. Fisher, R. Monty, & J. Senders (Eds.), *Eye movements: Cognition and visual perception* (pp. 171–179). Hillsdale, NJ: Lawrence Erlbaum.

Fisher, D. L., Duffy, S. A., Young, C., & Pollatsek, A. (1988). Understanding the central processing limit in consistent-mapping visual search tasks. *Journal of Experimental Psychology: Human Perception and Performance, 14,* 253–266.

Fisher, R. (1967). The biological fabric of time. In Interdisciplinary perspectives of time. *Annals of the New York Academy of Sciences, 138,* 451–465.

Fisk, A. D., & Schneider, W. (1981). Control and automatic processing during tasks requiring sustained attention: A new approach to vigilance. *Human Factors, 23,* 737–750.

Fitzpatrick, V., Pasnak, R., & Tyer, Z. E. (1982). The effect of familiar size at familiar distances. *Perception, 11,* 85–91.

Flandrin, J. M., & Jeannerod, M. (1981). Effects of unilateral superior colliculus ablation on oculomotor and vestibulo-ocular responses in the cat. *Experimental Brain Research, 42,* 73–80.

Flannery, R., & Butler, R. A. (1981). Spectral cues provided in the pinna for monaural localization in the horizontal plane. *Perception & Psychophysics, 29,* 438–444.

Flin, R. H. (1980). Age effects in children's memory for unfamiliar faces. *Developmental Psychology, 16,* 373–374.

Flock, H., & Freedberg, E. (1970). Perceived angle of incidence and achromatic surface color. *Perception & Psychophysics, 8,* 251–256.

Flock, H. R., & Nusinowitz, S. (1984). Visual structures for achromatic color perceptions. *Perception & Psychophysics, 36,* 111–130.

Flom, M. C., Brown, B. Adams, A. J., & Jones, R. T. (1976). Alcohol and marihuana effects on ocular tracking. *American*

Journal of Optometry and Physiological Optics, 53, 764–773.

Florentine, M. (1986). Level discrimination of tones as a function of duration. *Journal of the Acoustical Society of America, 79,* 792–798.

Fodor, J. (1983). *The modularity of mind.* Cambridge, MA: MIT Press.

Foley, J. E. (1970). Prism adaptation with opposed base orientation: The weighting of direction information from the two eyes. *Perception & Psychophysics, 8,* 23–25.

Foley, J. E. (1974). Factors governing interocular transfer of prism adaptation. *Psychological Review, 81,* 183–186.

Foulke, E., & Sticht, T. (1969). Review of research on the intelligibility and comprehension of accelerated speech. *Psychological Bulletin, 72,* 50–62.

Fox, R., Aslin, R. N., Shea, S. L., & Dumais, S. T. (1980). Stereopsis in infants. *Science, 207,* 323–324.

Fox, R., & McDaniel, C. (1982). The perception of biological motion by human infants. *Science,* 486–487.

Fozard, J., Wolf, E., Bell, B., McFarland, R., & Podolsky, S. (1977). Visual perception and communication. In J. Birren & K. Schaie (Eds.), *Handbook of the psychology of aging.* New York: Van Nostrand Reinhold.

Fraisse, P. (1963). *The psychology of time.* New York: Harper & Row.

Frank, M. (1975). Response patterns of rat glossopharyngeal taste neurons. In D. A. Denton & P. Coghlan (Eds.), *Olfaction and taste V* (pp. 59–64). New York: Academic Press.

Frank, M. E. (1985). On the neural code for sweet and salty taste. In D. W. Pfaff (Ed.), *Taste, olfaction, and the central nervous system* (pp. 107–128). New York: Rockefeller University Press.

Frankenhauser, M. (1959). *The estimation of time.* Stockholm: Almqvist & Wiksell.

Freeman, R., Mallach, R., & Hartley, S. (1981). Responsivity of normal kitten striate cortex deteriorates after brief binocular deprivation. *Journal of Neurophysiology, 45,* 1074–1084.

Freeman, R., & Pettigrew, J. (1973). Alteration of visual cortex from environmental asymmetries. *Nature, 246,* 359–360.

Fregnac, V., & Imbert, M. (1978). Early development of visual cortical cells in normal and dark reared kittens: Relationships between orientation selectivity and ocular dominance. *Journal of Physiology, 278,* 27–44.

Freud, S. (1953). *An aphasia.* London: Imago.

Frey, M. von., & Goldman, A. (1915). Der zeitliche Verlauf det Einstellung bei den Druckempfindungen. *Zeitschrift feur Biologie, 65,* 183–202.

Frey, M. von., & Kiesow, F. (1899). Uber die function der tastkorperchen. *Zeitschrift feur Psychologie, 20,* 126–163.

Freyd, J., & Tversky, B. (1984). Force of symmetry in form perception. *American Journal of Psychology, 97,* 109–126.

Friedman, A. (1979). Framing pictures: The role of knowledge in automatized encoding and memory for gist. *Journal of Experimental Psychology: General, 108,* 316–355.

Friedman, A., & Liebelt, L. (1981). On the time course of viewing pictures with a view towards remembering. In D.

Fisher, R. Monty, & J. Senders (Eds.), *Eye movements: Cognition and visual perception* (pp. 137–155). Hillsdale, NJ: Lawrence Erlbaum.

Friedman, R. B. (1980). Identity without form: Abstract representations of letters. *Perception & Psychophysics, 28,* 53–60.

Friedman, S. L., & Stevenson, M. (1975). Developmental changes in the understanding of implied motion in two-dimensional pictures. *Child Development, 46,* 773–778.

Friedman, S. L., & Stevenson, M. (1980). Perception of movements in pictures. In M. Hagen (Ed.), *Perception of pictures: Vol. 1. Alberti's Window: The projective model of pictorial information* (pp. 225–255). New York: Academic Press.

Frisby, J. P. (1980). *Seeing: Illusion, brain and mind.* Oxford: Oxford University Press.

Fuld, K., Wooten, B. R., & Whalen, J. J. (1981). The elemental hues of short-wave and extraspectral lights. *Perception & Psychophysics, 29,* 317–322.

Fuller, C. A., Lydic, R., Sulzman, F. M., Albers, H. E., Tepper, B., & Moore-Ede, M. C. (1981). Circadian rhythm of body temperature persists after suprachiamatic lesions in the squirrel monkey. *American Journal of Physiology, 241,* R385–R391.

Fulton, J. F., & Bailey, P. (1929). Tumors in the region of the third ventricle: Their diagnosis and relation to pathological sleep. *Journal of Nervous and Mental Disorders, 69,* 1–25, 145–164, 261–277.

Funakoshi, M., Kasahara, Y., Yamamoto, T., & Kawamura, Y. (1972). Taste coding and central perception. In D. Schneider (Ed.), *Olfaction and taste IV* (pp. 336–342). Stuttgart: Wissenshaftliche Verlagsgesellschaft MBH.

Funkenstein, H. H., Nelson, P. G., Winter, P. L., Wolberg, Z., & Newman, J. D. (1971). Unit responses in auditory cortex of awake squirrel monkeys to vocal stimulation. In M. B. Saschs (Ed.), *Physiology of the auditory system* (pp. 307–326). Baltimore: National Educational Consultants.

Gaddes, W. H. (1976). Prevalence estimates and the need for definition of learning disabilities. In R. M. Knights & D. J. Bakker (Eds.), *The neuropsychology of learning disorders.* Baltimore: University Park Press.

Gaddes, W. H. (1980). *Learning disabilities and brain function: A neurophysiological approach.* New York: Springer-Verlag.

Galanter, E. (1962). Contemporary psychophysics. In R. Brown, E. Galanter, E. Hess, & G. Mandler (Eds.), *New directions in psychology* (pp. 87–157). New York: Holt, Rinehart & Winston.

Ganchrow, J. R., Steiner, J. E., & Daher, M. (1983). Neonatal facial expressions in response to different qualities and intensities of gustatory stimuli. *Infant Behavior and Development, 6,* 189–200.

Gardner, E. B., & Costanzo, R. H. (1981). Properties of kinesthetic neurons in somatosensory cortex of awake monkeys. *Brain Research, 214,* 301–319.

Gardner, E. P. (1983). Cortical neuronal mechanisms underlying the perception of motion across the skin. In C. von Euler, O. Franzen, U. Lindblom, & D. Ottoson (Eds.), *Somatosensory mechanisms* (pp. 93–112). New York: Plenum.

Gardner, R. J. (1979). Lipophilicity and the perception of bitterness. *Chemical Senses and Flavor, 4,* 275–286.

Garner, W. R. (1953). An informational analysis of absolute judgments of loudness. *Journal of Experimental Psychology, 46,* 373–380.

Garner, W. R. (1962). *Uncertainty and structure as psychological concepts.* New York: Wiley.

Garner, W. R. (1974). *The processing of information and structure.* Potomac, MD: Lawrence Erlbaum.

Garner, W. R. (1978). Aspects of a stimulus: Features, dimensions and configurations. En E. H. Rosch & B. B. Lloyd (Eds.), *Cognition and categorization* (pp. 99–139). Hillsdale, NJ: Lawrence Erlbaum.

Garner, W. R., & Clement, D. E. (1963). Goodness of pattern and pattern uncertainty. *Journal of Verbal Learning and Verbal Behavior, 2,* 446–452.

Garner, W. R., & Hake, H. W. (1951). The amount of information in absolute judgments. *Psychological Review, 58,* 446–459.

Geiselman, R. E., Fisher, R. P., MacKinnon, D. P., & Holland, H. L. (1986). Enhancement of eyewitness memory with the cognitive interview. *American Journal of Psychology, 99,* 385–401.

Gelb, A. (1929). Die "Farbenkonstanz" der sehdinge. *Handbuch der normalen und pathologischen Physiologie, 12,* 549–678.

Geldard, F. A. (1972). *The human senses* (2nd ed.). New York: Wiley.

Gent, J. F. (1979). An exponential model for adaptation in taste. *Sensory Processes, 3,* 303–316.

Gerbrandt, L. K., Spinelli, D. N., & Pribram, K. H. (1970). Interaction of visual attention and temporal cortex stimulation on electrical activity evoked in striate cortex. *Electroencephalography and Clinical Neurology, 29,* 146.

Gescheider, G. A., & Verrillo, R. T. (1982). Contralateral enhancement and suppression of vibrotactile sensation. *Perception & Psychophysics, 32,* 69–74.

Gesteland, R. C. (1986). Speculations on receptor cells as analyzers and filters. *Experientia, 42,* 287–291.

Gesteland, R. C., Lettvin, J. Y., Pitts, W. H., & Rojas, A. (1963). Odor specificities of the frog's olfactory receptors. In Y. Zotterman (Ed.), *Olfaction and taste* (pp. 19–34). Oxford: Pergamon.

Getchell, T. V., & Getchell, M. L. (1987). Peripheral mechanisms of olfaction: Biochemistry and neurophysiology. In T. E. Finger & W. L. Silver (Eds.), *Neurobiology of taste and smell* (pp. 91–124). New York: Wiley.

Giachetti, I., & MacLeod, P. (1975). Cortical neuron responses to odours in the rat. In D. A. Denton & J. P. Coghlan (Eds.), *Olfaction and taste V* (pp. 303–307). New York: Academic Press.

Gibbons, B. (1986). The intimate sense of smell. *National Geographic, 170,* 324–361.

Gibson, J. J. (1950). *Perception of the visual world.* Boston: Houghton Mifflin.

Gibson, J. J. (1966). *The senses considered as perceptual systems.* Boston: Houghton Mifflin.

Gibson, J. J. (1979). *The ecological approach to visual perception.* Boston: Houghton Mifflin.

Gibson, R. H., & Tomko, D. L. (1972). The relation between category and magnitude estimates of tactile intensity. *Perception & Psychophysics, 12,* 135–138.

Gilbert, A. N., & Wysocki, C. J. (1987). The smell survey: Results. *National Geographic, 172,* 514–525.

Gilchrist, A. L. (1980). When does perceived lightness depend on perceived spatial arrangement? *Perception & Psychophysics, 28,* 527–538.

Gilchrist, A. L., Delman, S., & Jacobsen, A. (1983). The classification and integration of edges as critical to the perception of reflectance and illumination. *Perception & Psychophysics, 33,* 425–436.

Gilchrist, A. L., & Jacobsen, A. (1984). Perception of lightness and illumination in a world of one reflectance. *Perception, 13,* 5–19.

Gilinsky, A. S. (1955). The effect of attitude upon the perception of size. *American Journal of Psychology, 68,* 173–192.

Gillam, B. (1980). Geometrical illusions. *Scientific American, 242,* 102–111.

Gintzler, A. R. (1980). Endorphin-mediated increases in pain threshold during pregnancy. *Science, 210,* 193–195.

Girgus, J. S., & Coren, S. (1987). The interaction between stimulus variations and age trends in the Poggendorff illusion. *Perception & Psychophysics. 41,* 60–66.

Glass, A. L., & Holyoak, K. J. (1986). *Cognition.* New York: Random House.

Gliner, J. A., Horvath, S. M., & Mihevic, P. M. (1983). Carbon monoxide and human performance in a single and dual task methodology. *Aviation, Space and Environmental Medicine, 54,* 714–717.

Glorig, A., Wheeler, D., Quigle, R., Grings, W., & Summerfield, A. (1970). 1954 Wisconsin State Fair hearing survey: Statistical treatment of clinical and audiometric data. Cited in D. D. Kryter, *The effects of noise on man* (p. 116). New York: Academic Press.

Glucksberg, S., & Cowen, G. N., Jr. (1970). Memory for nonattended auditory material. *Cognitive Psychology, 1,* 149–156.

Gogel, W. C., & DaSilva, J. A. (1987a). A two-process theory of the response to size and distance. *Perception & Psychophysics, 41,* 220–238.

Gogel, W. C., & DaSilva, J. A. (1987b). Familiar size and the theory of off-sized perceptions. *Perception & Psychophysics, 41,* 318–328.

Gogel, W. C., Gregg, J. M., & Wainwright, A. (1961). *Convergence as a cue to absolute distance.* (Report No. 467, pp. 1–16). Fort Knox, KY: U.S. Army Medical Research Laboratory.

Gogel, W. C., & Koslow, M. (1972). The adjacency principle and induced movement. *Perception & Psychophysics, 11,* 309–324.

Goldfoot, D. A. (1981). Olfaction, sexual behavior and the pheromone hypothesis in the rhesus monkey: A critique. *American Zoologist, 21*, 153–164.

Goldfoot, D. A., Essock-Vitale, S. M., Asa, C. S., Thornton, J. E., & Leshner, A. I. (1978). Anosmia in male rhesus monkeys does not alter copulatory activity with cycling females. *Science, 199*, 1095–1096.

Goldfoot, D. A., Kravetz, M. A., Goy, R. W., & Freeman, S. K. (1976). Lack of effect of vaginal lavages and aliphatic acids on ejaculatory responses in Rhesus monkeys: Behavioral and chemical analysis. *Hormones and Behavior, 7*, 1–27.

Goldstein, E. B. (1980). *Sensation and Perception*. Belmont, CA: Wadsworth.

Goldstein, J. L. (1973). An optimum processor theory for the central formation of the pitch of complex tones. *Journal of the Acoustical Society of America, 54*, 1496–1516.

Goldstone, S., Boardman, W. K., & Lhamon, W. T. (1958). Effect of quinal barbitone dextro-amphetamine, and placebo on apparent time. *British Journal of Psychology, 49*, 324–328.

Gombrich, E. H. (1972). The mask and the face: The perception of physiognomic likeness in life and in art. In E. H. Gombrich, J. Hochberg, & M. Black (Eds.), *Art, perception and reality* (pp. 1–46). Baltimore: Johns Hopkins Press.

Goodman, L., & Gilman, A. (Eds.), (1965). *The pharmacological basis of therapeutics*. New York: Macmillan.

Goodman, N. (1968). *Languages of art*. New York: Bobbs-Merrill.

Goodson, R., & Rahe, A. (1981). Visual training effects on normal vision. *American Journal of Optometry and Physiological Optics, 58*, 787–791.

Goodwin, M., Gooding, K. M., & Regnier, F. (1979). Sex pheromone in the dog. *Science, 203*, 559–561.

Goolkasian, P. (1980). Cyclic changes in pain perception: A ROC analysis. *Perception & Psychophysics, 27*, 499–504.

Goto, H. (1971). Auditory perception by normal Japanese adults of the sounds "L" or "R". *Neuropsychologia, 9*, 317–323.

Gottlieb, G. (1981). Roles of early experience in species-specific perceptual development. In R. Aslin, J. Alberts, & M. Petersen (Eds.), *Development of perception: Psychobiological perspectives: Vol. 1. Audition, somatic perception and the chemcial senses* (pp. 5–44). New York: Academic Press.

Gottlieb, M. D., Kietzman, M. I., & Bernhaus, I. J. (1985). Two-pulse measures of temporal integration in the fovea and peripheral retina. *Perception & Psychophysics, 37*, 135–138.

Gottschaldt, K. (1926). Uber den Einfluss der Erfahrung auf die Wahrnehmung von Figuren. I. *Psychologische Forschung, 8*, 261–317.

Gottschaldt, K. (1929). Uber den Einfluss der Erfahrung auf die Wahrnehmung von Figuren. II. *Psychologische Forschung, 12*, 1–87.

Gottschaldt, K. M., & Vahle-Hinz, C. (1981). Merkle cell receptors: Structure and transducer function. *Science, 214*, 183–185.

Gouras, P., & Zrenner, E. (1981). Color coding in primate retina. *Vision Research, 21*, 1591–1598.

Graham, C. H. (1965). Visual space perception. In C. H. Graham (Ed.), *Vision and visual perception* (pp. 504–547). New York: Wiley.

Graham, C. H., & Hsia, Y. (1958). Color defect and color theory. *Science, 127*, 657–682.

Graham, N. (1980). Spatial-frequency channels in human vision: Detecting edges without edge detectors. In C. S. Harris (Ed.), *Visual coding and adaptability* (pp. 215–262). New York: Lawrence Erlbaum.

Graham, N. (1981). Psychophysics of spatial-frequency channels. In M. Kubovy & J. Pomerantz (Eds.), *Perceptual organization* (pp. 1–26). Hillsdale, NJ: Lawrence Erlbaum.

Granger, G. W., & Ikeda, H. (1968). Drugs and visual thresholds. In A. Herxheimer (Ed.), *Drugs and sensory functions* (pp. 299–344). London: Churchill.

Granrud, C. E. (1986). Binocular vision and spatial perception in 4- and 5-month-old infants. *Journal of Experimental Psychology: Human Perception and Performance, 12*, 36–49.

Granrud, C. E., Haake, R. J., & Yonas, A. (1985). Infants' sensitivity to familiar size: The effect of memory on spatial perception. *Perception & Psychophysics, 37*, 459–466.

Granrud, C. E., Yonas, A., & Pettersen, L. (1984). A comparison of monocular and binocular depth perception in 5- and 7-month-old infants. *Journal of Experimental Child Psychology, 38*, 19–32.

Gravetter, F., & Lockhead, G. R., (1973). Criterial range as a frame of reference for stimulus judgment. *Psychological Review, 80*, 203–216.

Green, B. G. (1984). Thermal perception on lingual and labial skin. *Perception & Psychophysics, 36*, 209–220.

Green, B. G. (1985). Heat pain thresholds in the oral-facial region. *Perception & Psychophysics, 38*, 110–114.

Green, B. G.(1986). Oral perception of the temperature of liquids. *Perception & Psychophysics, 39*, 19–24.

Green, B. G. (1987). The effect of cooling on the vibrotactile sensitivity of the tongue. *Perception & Psychophysics, 42*, 423–430.

Green, D. G., & Powers, M. K. (1982). Mechanisms of light adaptation in rat retina. *Vision Research, 22*, 209–216.

Green, D. M. (1976). *An introduction to hearing*. New York: Academic Press.

Green, D. M. (1987). *Profile analysis: Auditory intensity discrimination*. New York: Oxford University Press.

Green, D. M., Nachmias, J., Kearny, J. K., & Jeffress, L. A. (1979). Intensity discrimination with gated and continuous sinusoids. *Journal of the Acoustical Society of America, 66*, 1051–1056.

Green, D. M., & Swets, J. A. (1966). *Signal detection theory and psychophysics*. Reprint. New York: Krieger, 1974.

Green, D. W., Hammond, E. J., and Supramaniam, S. (1983). Letters and shapes: Developmental changes in search strategies. *British Journal of Psychology, 74*, 11–16.

Greenberg, M. J. (1981). The dependence of odor intensity on the hydrophobic properties of molecules. In H. R. Moskowitz & C. B. Warren (Eds.), *Odor quality and chemical struc-*

ture (pp. 177–194). Washington, D.C.: American Chemical Society.

Greene, H. A., & Madden, D. J. (1987). Adult age differences in visual acuity, stereopsis, and contrast sensitivity. *American Journal of Optometry and Physiological Optics, 64,* 749–753.

Gregory, R. L. (1966). *Eye and brain.* New York: World University Library.

Gregory, R. L. (1971). *Concepts and mechanisms of perception.* London: Duckworth.

Gregory, R. L. (1978). *Eye and brain.* (3rd ed.). New York: McGraw-Hill.

Grice, G. R., Nullmeyer, R., & Schnizlein, J. M. (1979). Variable criterion analysis of brightness effects in simple reaction time. *Journal of Experimental Psychology: Human Performance and Perception, 5,* 303–314.

Groos, G., & Daan, S. (1985). The use of the biological clocks in time perception. In J. A. Michon & J. L. Jackson (Eds.), *Time, mind and behavior* (pp. 65–74). Berlin: Springer-Verlag.

Groos, G., & Meijer, J. H. (1985). The effects of illumination on suprachiasmatic nucleous electrical discharge. *Annals of the New York Academy of Sciences.*

Gross, C. G., Rocha-Miranda, E. C., & Bender, D. B. (1972). Visual properties of neurons in inferotemporal cortex of the macaque. *Journal of Neurophysiology, 35,* 96–111.

Grossberg, J. M., & Grant, B. F. (1978). Clinical psychophysics. *Psychological Bulletin, 85,* 1154–1176.

Grossberg, S. (1987). Cortical dynamics of three-dimensional form, color, and brightness perception: I. Monocular theory. *Perception & Psychophysics, 41,* 87–116.

Grunau, R. V. E., & Craig, K. D. (1987). Pain expression in neonates: Facial action and cry. *Pain, 28,* 395–410.

Grzegorczyk, P. B., Jones, S. W., & Mistretta, C. M. (1979). Age-related differences in salt taste acuity. *Journal of Gerontology, 34,* 834–940.

Guitton, D., Crommelink, M., & Roucoux, A. (1980). Stimulation of the superior colliculus in the alert cat: Eye movement and neck EMG activity evoked when the head is restrained. *Experimental Brain Research, 39,* 63–74.

Gulick, W. L. (1971). *Hearing: Physiology and psychophysics.* London & New York: Oxford University Press.

Gurnsey, R., & Browse, R. A. (1987). Micropattern properties and presentation conditions influencing visual texture discrimination. *Perception & Psychophysics, 41,* 239–252.

Guzman, A. (1971). Analysis of curved line drawings using context and global information. *Machine Intelligence, 6,* 325–375. Edinburgh: Edinburgh University Press.

Gwiazda, J., Brill, S., Mohindra, I., & Held, R. (1980). Preferential looking acuity in infants from 2 to 58 weeks of age. *American Journal of Optometry and Physiological Optics, 57,* 428–432.

Haaf, R. (1977). Visual responses to complex facelike patterns by 15 and 20 week old infants. *Developmental Psychology, 38,* 893–899.

Haber, R. N. (1980). Perceiving space from pictures: A theoretical analysis. In M. Hagen (Ed.), *Perception of Pictures: Vol. 1. Alberti's Window: The projective model of pictorial information* (pp. 3–31). New York: Academic Press.

Haber, R. N., & Hershenson, M. (1965). The effects of repeated brief exposures on the growth of a percept. *Journal of Experimental Psychology, 69,* 40–46.

Hagen, M., & Jones, R. (1978). Cultural effects on pictorial perception: How many words is one picture really worth? In R. Walk & H. Pick (Eds.), *Perception and Experience* (pp. 171–212). New York: Plenum.

Hahn, H. (1934). Die Adaptation des Geschmackssinnes. *Zeitschraft fuer Sinnesphysiologie, 65,* 105–145.

Hainline, L. (1978). Developmental changes in the scanning of face and nonface patterns by infants. *Journal of Experimental Child Psychology, 25,* 90–115.

Haith, M. M., Bergman, T., & Moore, M. J. (1977). Eye contact and face scanning in early infancy. *Science, 198,* 853–855.

Hall, J. W. III, & Peters, R. W. (1982). Change in the pitch of a complex tone following its association with a second complex tone. *Journal of the Acoustical Society of America, 71,* 142–146.

Hall, M. J., Bartoshuk, L. M., Cain, W. S., & Stevens, J. C. (1975). PTC taste blindness and the taste of caffeine. *Nature (London), 253,* 442–443.

Hall, W. G., & Oppenheim, R. W. (1987). Developmental psychobiology: Prenatal, perinatal and early postnatal aspects of behavioral development. *Annual Review of Psychology, 38,* 91–128.

Halpern, B. P., & Meiselman, H. L. (1980). Taste psychophysics based on a simulation of human drinking. *Chemical Senses, 5,* 279–294.

Halpern, D. F. (1981). The determinants of illusory-contour perception. *Perception, 10,* 191–213.

Halpern, D. F. (1986). *Sex differences in cognitive abilities.* Hillsdale, NJ: Lawrence Erlbaum.

Halpern, D. L., Blake, R., & Hillenbrand, J. (1986). Psychoacoustics of a chilling sound. *Perception & Psychophysics, 39,* 77–80.

Halsam, D. (1967). Individual differences in pain threshold and level of arousal. *British Journal of Psychology, 58,* 139–142.

Hamalainen, H., & Jarvilehto, T. (1981). Peripheral neural basis of tactile sensations in man: I. Effect of frequency and probe area on sensations elicited by single mechanical pulses on hairy and glabrous skin of the hand. *Brain Research, 219,* 1–12.

Hamasaki, D. J., & Sutija, V. G. (1979). Development of X- and Y-cells in kittens. *Experimental Brain Research, 35,* 9–23.

Handel, S., & Garner, W. R. (1965). The structure of visual pattern associates and pattern goodness. *Perception & Psychophysics, 1,* 33–38.

Handel, S., & Oshinsky, J. S. (1981). The meter of syncopated auditory polyrhythms. *Perception & Psychophysics, 30,* 1–9.

Hanna, T. E., von Gierke, S. M., & Green, D. M. (1986). Detection and intensity discrimination of a sinusoid. *Journal of the Acoustical Society of America, 80,* 1335–1340.

Hardie, R. C., & Kirschfeld, K. (1983). Ultraviolet sensitivity of fly photoreceptors R7 and R8: Evidence for a sensitizing function. *Biophysics of Structure and Mechanism, 9,* 171–180.

Hardy, J. D., Wolff, H. G., & Goodell, H. (1943). The pain threshold in man. *Research Publications Association for Research in Nervous and Mental Disease, 23,* 1–15.

Hardy, J. D., Wolff, H. G., & Goodell, H. (1947). Studies on pain: Discrimination of differences in intensity of a pain stimulus as a basis of a scale of pain intensity. *Journal of Clinical Investigation, 26,* 1152–1158.

Hardy, J. D., Stolwijk, J. A. J., & Hoffman, D. (1968). Pain following step increase in skin temperature. In D. R. Kenshalo (Ed.), *The skin senses* (pp. 444–457). Springfield, IL: Thomas.

Harkins, S., & Green, R. G. (1975). Discriminability and criterion differences between extraverts and introverts during vigilance. *Journal of Research in Personality, 9,* 335–340.

Harkins, S. W., & Chapman, C. R. (1977). The perception of induced dental pain in young and elderly women. *Journal of Gerontology, 32,* 428–435.

Harmon, L. D. (1973). The recognition of faces. *Scientific American, 229,* 70–82.

Harmon, L. D., & Julesz, B. (1973). Masking in visual recognition: Effects of two dimensional filtered noise. *Science, 180,* 1194–1197.

Harper, R. S. (1953). The perceptual modification of coloured figures. *American Journal of Psychology, 66,* 86–89.

Harris, C. S. (1980). Insight or out of sight?: Two examples of perceptual plasticity in the human adult. In C. S. Harris (Ed.), *Visual coding and adaptability* (pp. 95–149). Hillsdale, NJ: Lawrence Erlbaum.

Harris, L. J. (1981). Sex related variations in spatial skill. In L. S. Liben, A. H. Patterson, & N. Newcombe (Eds.), *Spatial representation and behavior across the lifespan: Theory and application* (pp. 83–128). New York: Academic Press.

Harris, P., & MacFarlane, A. (1974). The growth of the effective visual field from birth to seven weeks. *Journal of Experimental Child Psychology, 18,* 340–348.

Harter, M., & Suitt, C. (1970). Visually-evoked cortical responses and pattern vision in the infant: A longitudinal study. *Psychonomic Science, 18,* 235–237.

Hartline, H. K. (1940). The receptive fields of optic nerve fibers. *American Journal of Physiology, 130,* 690–699.

Hartline, H. K., & Ratliff, F. (1957). Inhibitory interaction of receptor units in the eye of Limulus. *Journal of General Physiology, 40,* 357–376.

Hartman, A., & Hollister, L. (1963). Effect of mescaline, lysergic acid diethylamide and psilocybin on color perception. *Psychopharmacologia, 4,* 441–451.

Harvey, L. O., Jr., & Leibowitz, H. (1967). Effects of exposure duration, cue reduction, and temporary monocularity on size matching at short distances. *Journal of the Optical Society of America, 57,* 249–253.

Hatfield, G., & Epstein, W. (1985). The status of the minimum principle in the theoretical analysis of visual perception. *Psychological Bulletin, 97,* 155–186.

He, L. (1987). Involvement of endogenous opioid peptides in acupuncture analgesia. *Pain, 31,* 99–122.

He, L., Lu, R., Zhuang, S., Zhang, X., Pan, X. (1985). Possible involvement of opioid peptides of caudate nucleus in acupuncture analgesia. *Pain, 23,* 83–93.

Head, H. (1920). *Studies in neurology.* London & New York: Oxford University Press.

Heaton, J. M. (1968). *The eye: Phenomenology and psychology of function and disorder.* London: Tavistock.

Hecht, S., & Mandelbaum, M. (1938). Rod-cone dark adaptation and vitamin A. *Science, 88,* 219–221.

Hecht, S., Shlaer, S., & Pirenne, M. H. (1942). Energy quanta and vision. *Journal of General Physiology, 25,* 819–840.

Heckenmueller, E. G. (1965). Stabilization of the retinal image: A review of method, effects, and theory. *Psychological Bulletin, 63,* 157–169.

Heggelund, P. (1981a). Receptive field organization of simple cells in cat striate cortex. *Experimental Brain Research, 42,* 89–98.

Heggelund, P. (1981b). Receptive field organization of complex cells in cat striate cortex. *Experimental Brain Research, 42,* 99–107.

Hein, A. (1980). The development of visually guided behavior. In C. Harris (Ed.), *Visual coding and adaptability* (pp. 51–68). Hillsdale, NJ: Lawrence Erlbaum.

Hein, A., & Held, R. (1967). Dissociation of the visual placing response into elicited and guided components. *Science, 158,* 390–392.

Hein, A., Held, R., & Gower, E. C. (1970). Development and segmentation of visually controlled movement by selective exposure during rearing. *Journal of Comparative and Physiological Psychology, 73,* 181–187.

Hein, A., & Diamond, R. M. (1971). Contrasting development of visually triggered and guided movements in kittens with respect to interocular and interline equivalence. *Journal of Comparative and Physiological Psychology, 76,* 219–224.

Held, R. (1985). Binocular vision—behavioral and neuronal development. In J. Mehler & R. Fox (Eds.), *Neonate cognition: Beyond the blooming buzzing confusion* (pp. 37–44). Hillsdale, NJ: Lawrence Erlbaum.

Held, R., & Bauer, J. A. (1967). Visually guided reaching in infant monkeys after restricted rearing. *Science, 155,* 718–720.

Held, R., & Bossom, J. (1961). Neonatal deprivation and adult rearrangement: Complementary techniques for analyzing plastic sensory-motor coordinations. *Journal of Comparative and Physiological Psychology, 54,* 33–37.

Held, R., Dichgans, J., & Bauer, J. (1975). Characteristics of moving visual senses influencing spatial orientation. *Vision Research, 15,* 357–365.

Held, R., & Hein, A. (1958). Adaptation of disarranged hand-eye coordination contingent upon re-afferent stimulation. *Perceptual and Motor Skills, 8,* 87–90.

Held, R., & Hein, A. (1963). Movement-produced stimulation

in the development of visually guided behavior. *Journal of Comparative and Physiological Psychology, 56,* 872–876.

Held, R., & Hein, A. (1967). On the modifiability of form perception. In W. Wathen-Dunn (Ed.), *Models for the perception of speech and visual form* (pp. 296–304). Cambridge, MA: MIT Press.

Hellekant, G. (1965). Electrophysiological investigation of the gustatory effect of ethyl alcohol: The summated response of the chorda tympani in the cat, dog and rat. *Acta Physiologica Scandinavica, 64,* 392–397.

Hellstrom, A. (1979). Time errors and differential sensation weighting. *Journal of Experimental Psychology: Human Perception and Performance, 5,* 460–477.

Hellstrom, A. (1985). The time-order error and its relatives: Mirrors of cognitive processes in comparing. *Psychological Bulletin, 97,* 35–61.

Helmholtz, H. E. F. von. (1930). *The sensations of tone* (A. J. Ellis, Trans.). New York: Longmans, Green. (Original work published 1863)

Helmholtz, H. E. F. von. (1962). *Treatise on physiological optics.* (J. P. C. Southall, Ed. and Trans.). New York: Dover. (Original work published 1909)

Helson, H. (1959). Adaptation level theory. In S. Koch (Ed.), *Psychology: A study of a science* (Vol. 1, pp. 565–621). New York: McGraw-Hill.

Helson, H. (1964). *Adaptation level theory: An experimental and systematic approach to behavior.* New York: Harper.

Henmon, V. A. C. (1906). The time of perception as a measure of differences in sensations. *Archives of Philosophy, Psychology and Scientific Methods, No. 8.*

Henn, V., Cohen, B., & Young, L. (1980). Visual-vestibular interaction in motion perception and the generation of nystagmus. *Neurosciences Research Program Bulletin, 18,* 459–651.

Henn, V., Young, L. R., & Finley, C. (1974). Vestibular nucleus units in alert monkeys are also influenced by moving visual field. *Brain Research, 71,* 144–149.

Henning, H. (1915). Der Geruch. I. *Zietschrift fur Psychologie, 73,* 161–257.

Henning, H. (1916). Die Qualitatenreihe des Geschmaks. *Zeitschrift fur Psychologie, 74,* 203–219.

Hensel, H. (1981). *Thermoreception and temperature regulation.* New York: Academic Press.

Hering, E. (1964). Outlines of a theory of the light sense. (L. M. Hurvich & D. Jameson, Trans.). Cambridge, MA: Harvard University Press. (Original work published 1878)

Hernandez-Peon, R. (1964). Psychiatric implications of neurophysiological research. *Bulletin of the Meninger Clinic, 28,* 165–185.

Hershberger, W. (1987). Saccadic eye movements and the perception of visual direction. *Perception & Psychophysics, 41,* 35–44.

Hershenson, M. (1982). Moon illusion and spiral aftereffect: Illusions due to the loom-zoom system? *Journal of Experimental Psychology: General, 111,* 423–440.

Hess, E. H. (1950). Development of the chick's response to light and shade cues of depth. *Journal of Comparative and Physiological Psychology, 43,* 112–122.

Hick, W. E. (1952). On the rate of gain of information. *Quarterly Journal of Experimental Psychology, 4,* 11–26.

Hickey, T. L. (1977). Postnatal development of the human lateral geniculate nucleus: Relationship to a critical period for the visual system. *Science, 198,* 836–838.

Hickey, T. L., & Peduzzi, J. E. (1987). Structure and development of the visual system. In P. Salapatek & L. Cohen (Eds.), *Handbook of infant perception: Vol. 1. From sensation to perception* (pp. 1–43). Orlando, FL: Academic Press.

Hicks, R. E., Miller, G. W., Gaes, G., & Bierman, K. (1977). Concurrent processing demands and the experience of time in passing. *American Journal of Psychology, 90,* 431–446.

Hicks, R. E., Miller, G. W., & Kinsbourne, M. (1976). Prospective and retrospective judgments of time as a function of amount of information processed. *American Journal of Psychology, 89,* 719–730.

Hier, D. B., & Crowley, W. F., Jr. (1982). Spatial ability in androgen-deficient men. *New England Journal of Medicine, 306,* 1202–1205.

Higashiyama, A. (1985). The effects of familiar size on judgments of size and distance; an interaction of viewing attitude with spatial cues. *Perception & Psychophysics, 35,* 305–312.

Hirsch, H. V. (1972). Visual perception in cats after environmental surgery. *Experimental Brain Research, 15,* 409–423.

Hirsch, H. V., & Spinelli, D. N. (1970). Visual experience modifies distribution of horizontally and vertically oriented receptive fields in cats. *Science, 168,* 869–871.

Hirsh, I. J. (1948). The influence of interaural phase on interaural summation and inhibition. *Journal of the Acoustical Society of America, 20,* 536–544.

Hoagland, H. (1933). The physiological control of judgment of duration: Evidence for a chemical clock. *Journal of General Psychology, 9,* 267–287.

Hochberg, J. (1971). Perception. II. Space and movement. In J. W. Kling & L. A. Riggs (Eds.), *Woodworth and Schlossberg's experimental psychology.* (3rd ed.). (pp. 475–550). New York: Holt, Rinehart & Winston.

Hochberg, J. (1972). Nativism and empiricism in perception. In L. Postman (Ed.), *Psychology in the making* (pp. 255–330). New York: Knopf.

Hochberg, J. (1974). Higher-order stimuli and interresponse coupling in the perception of the visual world. In R. B. Macleod & H. L. Pick (Eds.), *Perception: Essays in honor of James J. Gibson* (pp. 17–39). Ithaca: Cornell University Press.

Hochberg, J. (1981). On cognition in perception: Perceptual coupling and unconscious inference. *Cognition, 10,* 127–134.

Hochberg, J. (1982). How big is a stimulus? In J. Beck (Ed.), *Organization and representation in perception* (pp. 191–218). Hillsdale, NJ: Lawrence Erlbaum.

Hochberg, J., & Beck, J. (1954). Apparent spatial arrangement and perceived brightness. *Journal of Experimental Psychology, 47,* 263–266.

Hochberg, J., & Brooks, V. (1960). The psychophysics of form: Reversible-perspective drawings of spatial objects. *American Journal of Psychology, 73,* 337–354.

Hochberg, J., & Brooks, V. (1962). Pictorial recognition as an unlearned ability. A study of one child's performance. *American Journal of Psychology, 75,* 624–628.

Hockey, G. R. (1970). Effect of loud noise on attentional selectivity. *Quarterly Journal of Experimental Psychology, 22,* 28–36.

Hoffer, A., & Osmond, H. (1967). *The hallucinogens.* New York: Academic Press.

Hoffman, J. E. (1980). Interaction between global and local levels of form. *Journal of Experimental Psychology: Human Perception and Performance, 6,* 222–234.

Hoffman, J. E., Nelson, B., & Houck, M. R. (1983). The role of attentional resources in automatic detection. *Cognitive Psychology, 51,* 379–410.

Hoffmann, K. P. (1979). Optokinetic nystagmus and single cell responses in the nucleus tractus opticus after early monocular deprivation in the cat. In R. D. Freeman (Ed.), *Developmental neurobiology of vision* (pp. 63–72). New York: Plenum.

Hoffman, K. P., & Sherman, S. (1975). Effects of early binocular deprivation on visual input to cat superior colliculus. *Journal of Neurophysiology, 38,* 1049–1059.

Holender, D. (1986). Semantic activation without conscious identification in dichotic listening, parafoveal vision, and visual masking: A survey and appraisal. *The Behavioral and Brain Sciences, 9,* 1–23.

Holland, H. (1960). Drugs and personality. XII. A comparison of several drugs by the flicker-fusion method. *Journal of Mental Science, 106,* 858–861.

Holst, E. von, & Mittelstadt, H. (1950). Das Reafferenzprincip (wechselwirkungen zeischen zentral Nervensystem und Peripherie). *Naturwissenschaften, 37,* 464–476.

Holway, A. F., & Boring, E. G. (1941). Determinants of apparent visual size with distance variant. *American Journal of Psychology, 54,* 21–37.

Honda, H. (1984). Functional between-hand differences and outflow eye position information. *Quarterly Journal of Experimental Psychology, 36A,* 75–88.

Houtsma, A. J. M., & Goldstein, J. L. (1972). The central origin of the pitch of complex tones: Evidence from musical interval recognition. *Journal of the Acoustical Society of America, 51,* 520–529.

Howard, I. P. (1982). *Human visual orientation.* Chichester: Wiley.

Howard, I. P., Anstis, T., & Lucia, H. C. (1974). The relative lability of mobile and stationary components in a visual-motor adaptation task. *Quarterly Journal of Experimental Psychology, 26,* 293–300.

Howard, I. P., Craske, B., & Templeton, W. B. (1965). Visuomotor adaptation to discordant exafferent stimulation. *Journal of Experimental Psychology, 70,* 189–191.

Howard, J. H., O'Toole, A. J., Parasuraman, R., & Bennett, K. B. (1984). Pattern-directed attention in uncertain frequency detection. *Perception & Psychophysics, 35,* 256–264.

Howell, P., Cross, I., & West, R. (Eds.), (1985). *Musical structure and cognition.* London: Academic Press.

Hoyer, W., & Plude, D. (1980). Attentional and perceptual processes in the study of cognitive aging. In L. Poon (Ed.), *Aging in the 1980s* (pp. 227–238). Washington, D.C.: American Psychological Association.

Hubbell, W. L., & Bownds, M. D. (1979). Visual transduction in vertebrate photoreceptors. *Annual Review of Neurosciences, 2,* 17–34.

Hubel, D. H., & Wiesel, T. N. (1962). Receptive fields, binocular interaction and functional architecture in the cat's visual cortex. *Journal of Physiology (London), 160,* 106–154.

Hubel, D. H., & Wiesel, T. N. (1968). Receptive fields and functional architecture of monkey striate cortex. *Journal of Physiology (London), 195,* 215–243.

Hubel, D. H., & Wiesel, T. N. (1979). Brain mechanisms of vision. *Scientific American, 82,* 84–97.

Hudson, W. (1960). Pictorial depth perception in subcultural groups in Africa. *Journal of Social Psychology, 52,* 183–208.

Hudson, W. (1962). Pictorial perception and educational adaptation in Africa. *Psychologia, Africana, 9,* 226–239.

Hudspeth, A. J. (1985). The cellular basis of hearing: The biophysics of hair cells. *Science, 230,* 745–752.

Hughes, H. C. (1986). Asymmetric interference between components of suprathreshold compound gratings. *Perception & Psychophysics, 40,* 241–250.

Hughes, H. C., Layton, W. M., Baird, J. C., & Lester, L. S. (1984). Global precedence in visual pattern recognition. *Perception & Psychophysics, 35,* 361–371.

Hughes, H. C., & Zimba, L. D. (1985). Spatial maps of directed visual attention. *Journal of Experimental Psychology: Human Perception and Performance, 11,* 409–430.

Humphrey, G. K., Humphrey, D. E., Muir, D. W., & Dodwell, P. C. (1986). Pattern perception in infants: Effects of structure and transformation. *Journal of Experimental Child Psychology, 41,* 128–148.

Humphreys, G. W. (1983). Reference frames and shape perception. *Cognitive Psychology, 15,* 151–196.

Humphreys, G. W. (1984). Shape constancy: The effects of changing shape orientation and the effects of changing the position of focal features. *Perception & Psychophysics, 36,* 50–64.

Hunzelmann, N., & Spillman, L. (1984). Movement adaptation in the peripheral retina. *Vision Research, 24,* 1765–1769.

Hurlbert, A. C., & Poggio, T. A. (1988). Synthesizing a color algorithm from examples. *Science, 239,* 482–485.

Hurvich, L. M. (1981). *Color vision.* Sunderland, MA: Sinauer Associates.

Hurvich, L. M., & Jameson, D. (1974). Opponent processes as a model of neural organization. *American Psychologist, 29,* 88–102.

Hutz, C. S., & Bechtoldt, H. P. (1980). The development of binocular discrimination in infants. *Bulletin of the Psychonomic Society, 16,* 83–86.

Huxley, A. (1963). *The doors of perception and heaven and hell*. New York: Harper.

Hyman, A., Mentyer, T., & Calderone, L. (1979). The contribution of olfaction to taste discrimination. *Bulletin of the Psychonomic Society, 13*, 359–362.

Iacono, W. G., Peloguin, L. J., Lumry, A. E., Valentine, R. H., & Tuason, V. B. (1982). Eye tracking in patients with unipolar and bipolar affective disorders in remission. *Journal of Abnormal Psychology, 91*, 35–44.

Imbert, M. (1985). Physiological underpinnings of perceptual development. In J. Mehler & R. Fox (Eds.), *Neonate cognition: Beyond the blooming buzzing confusion* (pp. 69–88). Hillsdale, NJ: Lawrence Erlbaum.

Ingram, R. M. & Barr, A. (1979). Changes in refraction between the ages of 1 and 3½ years. *British Journal of Ophthalmology, 63*, 39–342.

Intraub, H. (1985). Visual dissociation: An illusory conjunction of pictures and forms. *Journal of Experimental Psychology: Human Perception and Performance, 11*, 431–442.

Ippolitov, F. W. (1973). Interanalyser differences in the sensitivity-strength parameter for vision, hearing and cutaneous modalities. In V. D. Nebylitsyn & J. A. Gray (Eds.), *Biological bases of individual behavior* (pp. 43–61). New York: Academic Press.

Ittelson, W. H. (1951). Size as a cue to distance: Static localization. *American Journal of Psychology, 64*, 54–67.

Ittelson, W. H. (1960). *Visual space perception*. Berlin & New York: Springer-Verlag.

Ittelson, W. H. (1962). Perception and transactional psychology. In S. Koch (Ed.), *Psychology: A study of a science* (Vol. 4, pp. 660–704). New York: McGraw-Hill.

Jacobs, G. H. (1976). Color vision. *Annual Review of Psychology, 27*, 63–89.

Jacobs, G. H. (1986). Cones and opponency. *Vision Research, 26*, 1533–1541.

Jahoda, G., & McGurk, H. (1974). Pictorial depth perception: A developmental study. *British Journal of Psychology, 65*, 141–149.

James, W. (1890). *The principles of psychology*. New York: Holt, Rinehart & Winston.

Jameson, D., & Hurvich, L. M. (1959). Note on factors influencing the relation between stereoscopic acuity and observation distance. *Journal of the Optical Society of America, 49*, 639.

Jameson, D., & Hurvich, L. M. (1964). Theory of brightness and color contrast in human vision. *Vision Research, 4*, 135–154.

Jarvis, J. R. (1977). On Fechner-Benham subjective colour. *Vision Research, 17*, 445–451.

Javel, E. (1981). Suppression of auditory nerve responses I: Temporal analysis, intensity effects and suppression contours. *Journal of the Acoustical Society of America, 69*, 1735–1745.

Jen, D. H., & Steele, C. R. (1987). Electrokinetic model of cochlear hair cell motility. *Journal of the Acoustical Society of America, 82*, 1667–1678.

Jenkins, B. (1985). Orientational anisotropy in the human visual system. *Perception & Psychophysics, 37*, 125–134.

Jennings, J. A. M., & Charman, W. N. (1981). Off-axis image quality in the human eye. *Vision Research, 21*, 445–455.

Jensen, D., & Engel, R. (1971). Statistical procedures for relating dichotomous responses to maturation and EEG measurements. *Electroencephalography and Clinical Neurophysiology, 30*, 437–443.

Jesteadt, W. (1980). An adaptive procedure for subjective judgments. *Perception & Psychophysics, 28*, 85–88.

Jesteadt, W., Bacon, S. P., & Lehman, J. R. (1982). Forward masking as a function of frequency, masker level, and signal delay. *Journal of the Acoustical Society of America, 71*, 950–962.

Jesteadt, W., & Wier, C. C. (1977). Comparison of monaural and binaural discrimination of intensity and frequency. *Journal of the Acoustical Society of America, 61*, 1599–1603.

Jesteadt, W., Wier, C. C., & Green, D. M. (1977). Intensity discrimination as a function of frequency and sensation level. *Journal of the Acoustical Society of America, 61*, 169–177.

Johansson, G. (1976a). Visual motion perception. In R. Held & W. Richards (Eds.), *Recent progress in perception: Readings from Scientific American* (pp. 67–75). San Francisco: Freeman.

Johansson, G. (1976b). Spatio-temporal differentiation and integration in visual motion perception. *Psychological Research, 38*, 379–393.

Johansson, G., von Hofsten, C., & Jansson, G. (1980). Event perception. *Annual Review of Psychology, 31*, 27–63.

Johnson, C. H., & Hastings, J. W. (1986). The elusive mechanism of the circadian clock. *American Scientist, 74*(1), 29–36.

Johnson, D. H. (1980). The relationship between spike rate and synchrony in responses of auditory-nerve fibers to single tones. *Journal of the Acoustical Society of America, 68*, 1115–1122.

Johnson, M. A. (1986). Color vision in the peripheral retina. *American Journal of Optometry & Physiological Optics, 63*, 97–103.

Jones, L. A. (1986). Perception of force and weight: Theory and research. *Psychological Bulletin, 100*, 29–42.

Jonides, J. (1980). Towards a model of the mind's eye's movements. *Canadian Journal of Psychology, 34*, 103–112.

Jonides, J., & Mack, R. (1984). On the cost and benefit of cost and benefit. *Psychological Bulletin, 96*, 29–44.

Jonides, J., & Yantis, S. (1988). Uniqueness of abrupt visual onset in capturing attention. *Perception & Psychophysics, 43*, 346–355.

Julesz, B. (1971). *Foundations of cyclopean perception*. Chicago: University of Chicago Press.

Julesz, B. (1978). Perceptual limits of texture discrimination and their implications to figure-ground separation. In E. Leeuwenberg & H. Buffart (Eds.), *Formal Theories of Perception* (pp. 205–216). New York: Wiley.

Julesz, B. (1980). Spatial nonlinearities in the instantaneous perception of textures with identical power spectra. In C. Longuet-Higgins & N. S. Sutherland (Eds.), *The psychology of vision. Philosophical transactions of the Royal Society, London, 290,* 83–94.

Julesz, B. (1981). Textons, the elements of texture perception and their interactions. *Nature, 290,* 91–97.

Julesz, B., & Bergen, J. R. (1983). Textons, the fundamental elements in preattentive vision and perception of textures. *The Bell System Technical Journal, 62,* 1619–1645.

Julesz, B., & Schumer, R. A. (1981). Early visual perception. *Annual Review of Psychology, 32,* 575–627.

Jusczyk, P. W. (1986). Toward a model of the development of speech perception. In J. S. Perkell & D. H. Klatt (Eds.), *Invariance and Variability in Speech Processes* (pp. 1–19). Hillsdale, NJ: Lawrence Erlbaum.

Kaas, J. H. (1983). The organization of somatosensory cortex in primates and other mammals. In C. von Euler, O. Franzen, U. Lindblom, & D. Ottoson (Eds.), *Somatosensory mechanisms* (pp. 51–60). New York: Plenum.

Kaess, D. W. (1980). Instructions and decision times of size-constancy responses. *Perception & Psychophysics, 27,* 477–482.

Kahneman, D. (1966). Time-intensity reciprocity in acuity as a function of luminance and figure-ground contrast. *Vision Research, 6,* 207–215.

Kahneman, D. (1968). Method, findings, and theory in studies of visual masking. *Psychological Bulletin, 70,* 404–425.

Kahneman, D. (1973). *Attention and effort.* Englewood Cliffs, NJ: Prentice-Hall.

Kahneman, D., Norman, J., & Kubovy, M. (1967). Critical duration for the resolution of form: Centrally or peripherally determined? *Journal of Experimental Psychology, 73,* 323–327.

Kahneman, D., & Treisman, A. (1984). Changing views of attention and automaticity. In R. Parasuraman & D. R. Davies (Eds.), *Varieties of attention.* (pp. 29–61). Orlando, FL: Academic Press.

Kaiser, P. K., & Boynton, R. M. (1985). Role of the blue mechanism in wavelength discrimination. *Vision Research, 25,* 523–529.

Kalat, J. W. (1984). *Biological psychology.* (2nd ed.). Belmont, CA: Wadsworth.

Kaneko, A., Nishimura, Y., Tachibana, M., Tauchi, M., & Shimai, K. (1981). Physiological and morphological studies of signal pathways in the carp retina. *Vision Research, 21,* 1519–1526.

Kaplan, A., & Glanville, E. (1964). Taste thresholds for bitterness and cigarette smoking. *Nature (London), 202,* 1366.

Karmel, B. Z., & Maisel, E. B. (1975). A neuronal activity model for infant visual attention. In L. B. Cohen & P. Salapatek (Eds.), *Infant perception: From sensation to cognition: Vol. 1. Basic visual processes* (pp. 78–133). New York: Academic Press.

Kasamatsu, T. (1976). Visual cortical neurons influenced by the oculomotor input: Characterization of their receptive field properties. *Brain Research, 113,* 271–292.

Kauer, J. S. (1980). Some spatial characteristics of central information processing in the vertebrate olfactory pathway. In H. van der Starre (Ed.)., *Olfaction and taste VII* (pp. 227–236). London: IRL Press.

Kauer, J. S. (1987). Coding in the olfactory system. In T. E. Finger & W. L. Silver (Eds.), *Neurobiology of taste and smell* (pp. 205–232). New York: Wiley.

Kaufman, L. (1974). *Sight and mind: An introduction to visual perception.* London & New York: Oxford University Press.

Kaufman, L., & Rock, I. (1962). The moon illusion. *Scientific American, 207,* 120–130.

Kaufmann, R., Maland, J., & Yonas, A. (1981). Sensitivity of 5- and 7-month-old infants to pictorial depth information. *Journal of Experimental Child Psychology, 32,* 162–168.

Kausler, D. H. (1982). *Experimental psychology and human aging.* New York: Wiley.

Kawabata, N. (1986). Attention and depth perception. *Perception, 15,* 563–572.

Kaye, M., Mitchell, D. E., & Cynader, M. (1982). Depth perception, eye dominance and cortical binocularity of dark-reared cats. *Developmental Brain Research, 2,* 37–53.

Keithley, E. M., & Schreiber, R. C. (1987). Frequency map of the spiral ganglion in the cat. *Journal of the Acoustical Society of America, 81,* 1036–1042.

Keller, H. (1931). *The story of my life.* New York: Doubleday.

Kellman, P. J. (1984). Perception of three-dimensional form by human infants. *Perception & Psychophysics, 36,* 353–358.

Kellman, P. J., & Spelke, E. S. (1983). Perception of partly occluded objects in infancy. *Cognitive Psychology, 15,* 483–524.

Kendrick, K. M., & Baldwin, B. A. (1987). Cells in the temporal cortex of conscious sheep can respond preferentially to the sight of faces. *Science, 236,* 448–450.

Kennedy, J., & Ostry, D. (1976). Approaches to picture perception: Perceptual experience and ecological optics. *Canadian Journal of Psychology, 30,* 90–98.

Kennedy, J. M., & Domander, R. (1985). Shape and contour: The points of maximum change are least useful for recognition. *Perception, 14,* 367–370.

Kenshalo, D. R., & Isensee, O. (1983). Responses of primate SI cortical neurons to noxious stimuli. *Journal of Neurophysiology, 50,* 1479–1496.

Kenshalo, D. R., Nafe, J. P., & Brooks, B. (1961). Variations in thermal sensitivity. *Science, 134,* 104–105.

Kenshalo, D. R., & Scott, H. A., Jr. (1966). Temporal course of thermal adaptation. *Science, 151,* 1095–1096.

Keren, G., & Baggen, S. (1981). Recognition models of alphanumeric characters. *Perception & Psychophysics, 29,* 234–245.

Kessen, W., Salapatek, P., & Haith, M. M. (1972). The visual response of the human newborn to linear contour. *Journal of Experimental Child Psychology, 13,* 9–20.

Keverne, E. B. (1978). Olfactory cues in mammalian behavior. In J. E. Hutchinson (Ed.), *Biological determinants of sexual behavior* (pp. 727–763). Chichester: Wiley.

Khanna, S. N., & Leonard, D. G. B. (1982). Basilar membrane tuning in the cat cochlea. *Science, 215,* 305–306.

Kiang, K. Y. S., Rho, J. M., Northrop, C. C., Liberman, M. C., & Ryugo, D. K. (1982). Hair-cell innervation by spiral ganglion cells in adult cats. *Science, 217,* 175–177.

Kilbride, P. E., Hutman, L. P., Fishman, M., & Read, J. S. (1986). Foveal cone pigment density difference in the aging human eye. *Vision Research, 26,* 321–325.

Killbride, P. L., & Leibowitz, H. W. (1975). Factors affecting the magnitude of the Ponzo illusion among the Baganda. *Perception & Psychophysics, 17,* 543–548.

Killbride, P. L., & Robbins, M. (1968). Linear perspective pictorial depth perception and education among the Baganda. *Perception and Motor Skills, 27,* 601–602.

Kimura, K., & Beidler, L. M. (1961). Microelectrode study of taste receptors of rat and hamster. *Journal of Cellular and Comparative Physiology, 58,* 131–140.

Kinchla, R. A., Solis-Macias, V., & Hoffman, J. E. (1983). Attending to different levels of structure in a visual image. *Perception & Psychophysics, 33,* 1–10.

Kinchla, R. A., & Wolfe, J. (1979). The order of visual processing: "Top-down", "bottom-up", or "middle-out." *Perception & Psychophysics, 25,* 225–231.

Kirk-Smith, M. D., & Booth, D. A. (1980). Effects of androstenone on choice of location in other's presence. In H. van der Starre (Ed.), *Olfaction and taste VII* (pp. 397–400). London: IRL Press.

Kirk-Smith, M. D., Booth, D. A., Caroll, D., & Davies, P. (1978). Human social attitudes affected by androstenol. *Research communications in psychology, psychiatry and behavior, 3,* 379–384.

Kitzes, L. M., Gibson, M. M., Rose, J. E., & Hind, J. E. (1978). Initial discharge latency and threshold considerations for some neurons in cochlear nucleus complex of the cat. *Journal of Neurophysiology, 41,* 1165–1182.

Klatt, D. H. (1980). Speech perception: A model of acoustic-phonetic analysis and lexical access. In R. Cole (Ed.), *Perception and production of fluent speech* (pp. 243–288). Hillsdale, NJ: Lawrence Erlbaum.

Klatzky, R. L., Lederman, S. J., & Metzger, V. A. (1985). Identifying objects by touch: An "expert system." *Perception & Psychophysics, 37,* 299–302.

Klatzky, R. L., Lederman, S. J., & Reed, C. (1987). There's more to touch than meets the eye: The salience of object attributes for haptics with and without vision. *Journal of Experimental Psychology: General, 116,* 356–369.

Klein, G. S. (1970). *Perception, motives and personality.* New York: Knopf.

Klein, S. A., & Levi, D. M. (1985). Hyperacuity threshold of 1.0 second: Theoretical predictions and empirical validation. *Journal of the Optical Society of America, A2,* 1170–1190.

Kluender, K. R., Diehl, R. L., & Killeen, P. R. (1987). Japanese quail can learn phonetic categories. *Science, 237,* 1195–1197.

Kluver, H., & Bucy, P. C. (1937). "Psychic blindness" and other symptoms following bilateral temporal lobectomy in Rhesus monkeys. *American Journal of Physiology, 119,* 352–353.

Klymenko, V., & Weisstein, N. (1986). Spatial frequency differences can determine figure-ground organization. *Journal of Experimental Psychology: Human Perception and Performance, 12,* 324–330.

Knudsen, E. I., & Konishi, M. (1978a). A neural map of auditory space in the owl. *Science, 200,* 795–797.

Knudsen, E. I., & Konishi, M. (1978b). Center-surround organization of auditory receptive fields in the owl. *Science, 202,* 778–780.

Kobler, J. B., Isbey, S. F., & Casseday, J. H. (1987). Auditory pathways to the frontal cortex of the mustache bat, Pteronotus parnelli. *Science, 236.* 824–826.

Kohler, I. (1962). Experiments with goggles. *Scientific American, 206,* 62–86.

Kohler, I. (1964). The formation and transformation of the perceptual world. *Psychological Issues, 3* (Whole No. 4).

Kohler, W. (1923). Zur Theories des Sukzessivvergleichs und der Zeitfehler. *Psychologische Forschung, 4,* 115–175.

Kolb, B., & Whishaw, I. O. (1985). *Fundamentals of human neuropsychology* (2nd ed.). New York: Freeman.

Kolb, H., Nelson, R., & Mariani, A. (1981). Amacrine cells, bipolar cells and ganglion cells of the cat retina: A Golgi study. *Vision Research, 21,* 1081–1114.

Kolers, P. A., & Brewster, J. M. (1985). Rhythms and responses. *Journal of Experimental Psychology: Human Perception and Performance, 11,* 150–167.

Kolers, P. A., & Green, M. (1984). Color logic of apparent motion. *Perception, 13,* 249–254.

Kolers, P. A., & von Grunau, M. (1976). Shape and color in apparent motion. *Vision Research, 16,* 329–335.

Komoda, M. K., Festinger, L., Phillips, L. J., Duckman, R. H., & Young, R. A. (1973). Some observations concerning saccadic eye movement. *Vision Research, 13,* 1009–1020.

Konstadt, N., & Forman, E. (1965). Field dependence and external directedness. *Journal of Personality and Social Psychology, 1,* 490–493.

Kornbrot, D. E. (1984). Mechanisms for categorization: Decision criteria and the form of the psychophysical function. *British Journal of Mathematical and Statistical Psychology, 37,* 184–198.

Kosterlitz, H. W., & McKnight, A. T. (1981). Opioid peptides and sensory function. In D. Ottoson (Ed.), *Progress in sensory physiology* (Vol. 1., pp. 31–95). Heidelberg: Springer-Verlag.

Kozlowski, L. T., & Cutting, J. E. (1977). Recognizing the sex of a walker from a dynamic point-light display. *Perception & Psychophysics, 21,* 575–580.

Krauskopf, J., & Reeves, A. (1980). Measurement of the effect of photon noise on detection. *Vision Research, 20,* 193–196.

Kremenitzer, J. P., Vaughan, H. G., Kurtzberg, D., & Dowling, K. (1979). Smooth-pursuit eye movements in the newborn infant. *Child Development, 50,* 442–448.

Kries, J. von. (1895). Uber die Natur gewisser mit den psychischen Vorgangen verknupfter Ghirnzustande. *Zeitschrift fur Psychologie, 8,* 1–33.

Krueger, L. E. (1982). A word superiority effect with print and braille characters. *Perception & Psychophysics, 31,* 345–352.

Kruger, J. (1981). The difference between x- and y-type responses in ganglion cells of the cat's retina. *Vision Research, 21,* 1685–1687.

Kruger, J., & Gouras, P. (1980). Spectral selectivity of cells and its dependence on slit length in monkeys' visual cortex. *Journal of Neurophysiology, 43,* 1055–1069.

Krumhansl, C. L., Bharucha, J. J., & Kessler, E. J. (1982). Perceived harmonic structure of chords in three related musical keys. *Journal of Experimental Psychology: Human*

Perception and Performance, 8, 24–36.

Krumhansl, C. L., & Kessler, E. J. (1982). Tracing the dynamic changes in perceived tonal organization in a spatial representation of musical keys. *Psychological Review, 89,* 334–368.

Krumhansl, C. L., & Shepard, R. N. (1979). Quantification of the hierarchy of tonal functions within a diatonic context. *Journal of Experimental Psychology: Human Perception & Performance, 5,* 579–594.

Kryter, K. D. (1970). *The effects of noise on man.* New York: Academic Press.

Kryter, K. D. (1985). *The effects of noise on man.* (2nd ed.). Orlando, FL: Academic Press.

Kuffler, S. W. (1953). Discharge patterns and functional organization of mammalian retina. *Journal of Neurophysiology, 16,* 37–68.

Kuhl, P. K. (1987). Perception of speech and sound in early infancy. In P. Salapatek & L. Cohen (Eds.), *Handbook of infant perception: Vol. 2. From perception to cognition* (pp. 275–382). Orlando, FL: Academic Press.

Kuhl, P. K., & Meltzoff, A. N. (1982). The bimodal perception of speech in infancy. *Science, 218,* 1138–1141.

Kuhl, P. K., & Padden, D. M. (1983). Enhanced discriminability at the phonetic boundaries for the place feature in macaques. *Journal of the Acoustical Society of America, 73,* 1003–1010.

Kupchella, C. (1976). *Sights and sounds.* Indianapolis: Bobbs-Merrill.

Kurtz, D., & Butter, C. M. (1980). Impairments in visual discrimination performance and gaze shifts in monkeys with superior colliculus lesions. *Brain Research, 196,* 109–124.

Kuyk, T., Veres, J. G., III, Lahey, M. A., & Clark, D. J. (1986). The ability of protan color defectives to perform color-dependent air traffic control tasks. *American Journal of Optometry & Physiological Optics, 63,* 582–586.

LaBerge, D. (1983). Spatial extent of attention to letters and words. *Journal of Experimental Psychology: Human Perception and Performance, 9,* 371–379.

Ladefoged, P. (1975). *A course in phonetics.* New York: Harcourt Brace Jovanovich.

Lakowski, R. (1962). Is the deterioration of colour discrimination with age due to lens or retinal changes? *Farbe, 11,* 69–86.

Lakowski, R., Aspinall, P. A., & Kinnear, P. R. (1972). Association between colour vision losses and diabetes mellitus. *Ophthalmic Research, 4,* 145–159.

Lakowski, R., & Drance, S. M. (1979). Acquired dyschromatopsias: The earliest functional losses in glaucoma. *Documenta Ophthalmologica, Proceedings Series 19,* 159–165.

Lakowski, R., & Morton, B. A. (1977). The effect of oral contraceptives on colour vision in diabetic women. *Canadian Journal of Ophthalmology, 12,* 89–97.

Laming, D. (1986). *Sensory Analysis.* Orlando, FL: Academic Press.

Lamour, Y., Willer, J. C., & Guilbaud, G. (1983). Rat somatosensory (SmI) cortex. I. Characteristics of neuronal responses to noxious stimulation and comparison with responses to non-noxious stimulation. *Experimental Brain Research, 49,* 35–45.

Land, E. H. (1977). The retinex theory of color vision. *Scientific American, 237*(6), 108–128.

Landolt, E. (1889). Tableua d'optotypes pour la determination de l'acuite visuelle. *Societe Francais d'Ophthalmologie, 1,* 385ff.

Lappin, J. S., & Preble, L. D. (1975). A demonstration of shape constancy. *Perception & Psychophysics, 17,* 439–444.

Lauter, J. L., Herscovitch, P., Formby, C., & Raichle, M. E. (1985). Tonotopic organization in human auditory cortex revealed by positron emission tomography. *Hearing Research, 20,* 199–205.

Lawless, H. T., & Stevens, D. A. (1988). Responses by humans to oral chemical irritants as a function of locus of stimulation. *Perception & Psychophysics, 43,* 72–78.

Lea, S. E. G. (1984). *Instinct, environment, and behavior.* London: Methuen.

Leehey, S. C., Moskowitz-Cook, A., Brill, S., & Held, R. (1975). Orientational anisotropy in infant vision. *Science, 190,* 900–902.

Lefton, L. A. (1973). Metacontrast: A review. *Perception & Psychophysics, 13,* 161–171.

Lehmkuhle, S., & Fox, R. (1980). Effect of depth separation of metacontrast masking. *Journal of Experimental Psychology: Human Perception & Performance, 6,* 605–621.

Lehmkuhle, S., Kratz, K. E., Mangel. S. C., & Sherman, S. M. (1980). Spatial and temporal sensitivity of x- and y-cells in dorsal lateral geniculate nucleus of the cat. *Journal of Neurophysiology, 43,* 520–541.

Lehmkuhle, S., Kratz, K. E., & Sherman, S. M. (1982). Spatial and temporal sensitivity of normal and amblyopic cats. *Journal of Neurophysiology, 48,* 372–387.

Leibowitz, H. W., & Bourne, L. E. (1956). Time and intensity as determiners of perceived shape. *Journal of Experimental Psychology, 51,* 277–281.

Leibowitz, H. W., & Harvey, L. O., Jr. (1969). Effect of instructions, environment, and type of test object on matched size. *Journal of Experimental Psychology, 81,* 36–43.

Leibowitz, H. W., & Moore, D. (1966). Role of changes in accommodation and convergence in the perception of size. *Journal of the Optical Society of America, 56,* 1120–1123.

Leibowitz, H. W., & Owens, D. A. (1977). Nighttime accidents and selective visual degradation. *Science, 197,* 422–423.

Leibowitz, H. W., & Pick, H. (1972). Cross-cultural and educational aspects of the Ponzo perspective illusion. *Perception & Psychophysics, 12,* 430–432.

Leibowitz, H. W., Post, R. B., Brandt, T., & Dichgans, J. (1982). Implications of recent developments in dynamic spatial orientation and visual resolution for vehicle guidance. In A. H. Wertheim, W. A. Wagenaar, & H. W. Leibowitz (Eds.), *Tutorials on motion perception* (pp. 231–260). New York: Plenum.

Leibowitz, H. W., Post, R. B., & Ginsburg, A. (1980). The role of fine detail in visually controlled behavior. *Investigative Ophthalmology and Visual Science, 19,* 846–848.

Leibowitz, H. W., Shupert, C. L., Post, R. B., & Dichgans, J. (1983). Autokinetic drifts and gaze deviation. *Perception & Psychophysics, 33,* 455–459.

Leibowitz, H. W., Wilcox, S. B., & Post, R. B. (1978). The effect of refractive error on size constancy and shape constancy. *Perception, 7,* 557–562.

Leinonen, L. (1983). Integration of somatosensory events in the posterior parietal cortex of the monkey. In C. von Euler, O. Franzen, U. Lindblom, & D. Ottoson (Eds.), *Somatosensory mechanisms* (pp. 113–124). New York: Plenum.

Lennie, P. (1980). Parallel visual pathways: A review. *Vision Research, 20,* 561–594.

LePage, E. L. (1987a). Frequency-dependent self-induced bias of the basilar membrane and its potential for controlling sensitivity and tuning in the mammalian cochlea. *Journal of the Acoustical Society of America, 82,* 139–154.

LePage, E. L. (1987b). A spatial template for the shape of tuning curves in the mammalian cochlea. *Journal of the Acoustical Society of America, 82,* 155–164.

Lerman, S. (1984). Biophysical aspects of corneal and lenticular transparency. *Current Eye Research, 3,* 3–14.

LeVay, S., Wiesel, T. N., & Hubel, D. H. (1980). The development of ocular dominance columns in normal and visually deprived monkeys. *Journal of Comparative Neurology, 191,* 1–51.

Leventhal, A., & Hirsch, H. (1980). Receptive-field properties of different classes of neurons in visual cortex of normal and dark-reared cats. *Journal of Neurophysiology, 43,* 1111–1132.

Levin, S., Lipton, R. B., & Holtzman, P. S. (1981). Pursuit eye movements in psychopathology: Effects of target characteristics. *Biological Psychiatry, 16,* 255–267.

Levine, M. W., & Shefner, J. M. (1981). *Fundamentals of sensation and perception.* Reading, MA: Addison-Wesley.

Levy, D. L., Lipton, R. B., & Holzman, P. S. (1981). Smooth pursuit eye movements: Effects of alcohol and chloral hydrate. *Journal of Psychiatric Research, 16,* 1–11.

Lewis, J. W., Terman, G. W., Shavit, Y., Nelson, L. R., & Liebeskind, J. C. (1984). Neural, neurochemical, and hormonal bases of stress-induced analgesia. In L. Kruger & J. C. Liebeskind (Eds.), *Neural mechanisms of pain* (pp. 277–288). New York: Raven.

Liberman, A. M., (1982). On finding that speech is special. *American Psychologist, 37,* 148–167.

Liberman, A. M., Cooper, F. S., Shankweiler, D. P., & Studdert-Kennedy, M. (1967). Perception of the speech code. *Psychological Review, 74,* 431–461.

Liberman, A. M., Harris, K. S., Hoffman, H. A., & Griffith, B. C. (1957). The discrimination of sounds within and across phoneme boundaries. *Journal of Experimental Psychology, 54,* 358–368.

Liberman, A. M., & Mattingly, I. G. (1985). The motor theory of speech perception revised. *Cognition, 21,* 1–36.

Liberman, M. C. (1982). Single-neuron labeling in the cat auditory nerve. *Science, 216,* 1239–1241.

Lichte, W. H., & Borresen, C. R. (1967). Influence of instructions on degree of shape constancy. *Journal of Experimental Psychology, 74,* 538–542.

Lichtenstein, M. (1963). Spatio-temporal factors in cessation of smooth apparent motion. *Journal of the Optical Society of America, 53,* 302–306.

Lie, I. (1980). Visual detection and resolution as a function of retinal locus. *Vision Research, 20,* 967–974.

Liebeskind, J. C., & Melzack, R. (1987). The International Pain Foundation: Meeting a need for education in pain management. *Pain, 30,* 1.

Lim, D. J. (1980). Cochlear anatomy related to cochlear micromechanics: A review. *Journal of the Acoustical Society of America, 67,* 1686–1695.

Lindsay, P. H., & Norman, D. A. (1977). *Human information processing* (2nd ed.). New York: Academic Press.

Linton, H., & Graham, E. (1959). Personality correlates of persuasibility. In I. Janis (Eds.), *Personality and persuasibility.* New Haven, CT: Yale University Press.

Lipsett, L. P. (1977). Taste in human neonates: Its effect on sucking and heart rate. In J. M. Weiffenbach (Ed.), *Taste and development: The ontogeny of sweet preference* (pp. 125–140). Washington, D.C.: U. S. Government Printing Office.

Lisker, L., & Abramson, A. (1970). The voicing dimension: Some experiments in comparative phonetics. *Proceedings of the 6th International Congress of Phonetic Sciences,* 563–567.

Livingstone, M., & Hubel, D. (1988). Segregation of form, color, movement, and depth: Anatomy, physiology, and perception. *Science, 240,* 740–749.

Lockhead, G. R. (1966). Effects of dimensional redundancy on visual discrimination. *Journal of Experimental Psychology, 72,* 95–104.

Lockhead, G. R. (1970). Identification and the form of multidimensional discrimination space. *Journal of Experimental Psychology, 85,* 1–10.

Lockhead, G. R. (1972). Processing dimensional stimuli: A note. *Psychological Review, 79,* 410–419.

Lockhead, G. R. (1979). Holistic versus analytic process models: A reply. *Journal of Experimental Psychology: Human Perception & Performance, 5,* 746–755.

Lockhead, G. R., & Byrd, R. (1981). Practically perfect pitch. *Journal of the Acoustical Society of America, 70,* 387–389.

Lockhead, G. R., & King, M. C. (1977). Classifying integral stimuli. *Journal of Experimental Psychology: Human Perception and Performance, 3,* 436–443.

Loewenstein, W. R. (1960). Biological transducers. *Scientific American, 203,* 98–108.

Loftus, E. (1974). Reconstructing memory: The incredible eye witness. *Psychology Today, 8,* 116–119.

Loftus, E. (1979). *Eyewitness testimony.* Cambridge, MA: Harvard University Press.

Loftus, G., & Mackworth, N. (1978). Cognitive determinants of fixation location during picture viewing. *Journal of Experimental Psychology: Human Perception and Performance, 4,* 565–572.

Lohman, D. F. (1986). The effect of speed-accuracy tradeoff on sex differences in mental rotation. *Perception & Psychophysics, 39,* 427–436.

Long, G. R., & Cullen, J. K., Jr. (1985). Intensity difference limens at high frequencies. *Journal of the Acoustical Society of America, 78,* 507–513.

Loomis, J. M. (1981) Tactile pattern perception. *Perception, 10,* 5–27.

Loop, M. S. (1984). Effect of duration on detection by the chromatic and achromatic systems. *Perception & Psychophysics, 36,* 65–67.

Lowenstein, O., & Sand, A. (1940). The mechanism of the semicircular canal: A study of the responses of single-fiber preparations to angular accelerations and to rotation at constant speed. *Proceedings of the Royal Society of London, Series B, 129,* 256–275.

Luce, R. D., Green, D. M., & Weber, D. L. (1976). Attention bands in absolute identification. *Perception & Psychophysics, 20,* 49–54.

Luce, R. D., & Narens, L. (1987). Measurement scales on the continuum. *Science, 236,* 1527–1532.

Lumsden, E. (1980). Problems of magnification and minification: An explanation of the distortions of distance, slant, shape, and velocity. In M. Hagen (Ed.), *Perception of pictures: Vol. 1. Alberti's window: The projective model of pictorial information* (pp. 91–135). New York: Academic Press.

Luria, A. R. (1972). Memory disturbances in local brain lesions. *Neuropsychologia, 9,* 367–375.

Luria, A. R. (1973). *The working brain.* London: Penguin.

Lynn, P. A., & Sayers, B. M. A. (1970). Cochlear innervation, signal processing, and their relation to auditory time–intensity effects. *Journal of the Acoustical Society of America, 47,* 523–533.

MacArthur, R. O., & Sekuler, R. (1982). Alcohol and motion perception. *Perception & Psychophysics, 31,* 502–505.

MacDonald, D. W., & Brown, R. E. (1985). Introduction: The pheromone concept in mammalian chemical communication. In R. E. Brown & D. W. MacDonald (Eds.), *Social odours in mammals* (Vol. 1, pp. 1–18). Oxford: Clarendon Press.

MacFarlane, A. (1975). Olfaction in the development of social preferences in the human neonate. In Ciba Foundation Symposium 33: *The human neonate in parent-infant interaction* (pp. 103–177). Amsterdam: Elsevier.

Mach, E. (1959). *The analysis of sensations and the relation of the physical to the psychical.* New York: Dover. (Originally published 1886)

Mack, A., & Herman, E. (1972). A new illusion: The underestimation of a distance during pursuit eye movements. *Perception & Psychophysics, 12,* 471–473.

Mack, A., Heuer, F., Fendrich, R., Vilardi, K., & Chambers, D. (1985). Induced motion and oculomotor capture. *Journal of Experimental Psychology: Human Perception and Performance, 11,* 329–345.

MacKain, K., Studdert-Kennedy, M., Spieker, S., & Stern, D. (1983). Infant intermodal speech perception is a left hemisphere function. *Science, 219,* 1347–1349.

Mackworth, N. H. (1948). The breakdown of vigilance during prolonged visual search. *Quarterly Journal of Experimental Psychology, 1,* 6–21.

Mackworth, N. H., & Bruner, J. S. (1970). How adults and children search and recognize pictures. *Human Development, 13,* 149–177.

MacLeod, D. I. (1978). Visual sensitivity. *Annual Review of Psychology, 29,* 613–645.

MacLeod, P. (1971). An experimental approach to the peripheral mechanisms of olfactory discrimination. In G. Ohloff & A. F. Thomas (Eds.), *Gustation and olfaction* (pp. 28–44). New York: Academic Press.

MacLeod, R. (1947). The effects of "artificial penumbra" on the brightness of included areas. In A. Michotte (Ed.), *Miscellanea psychologica* (pp. 1–22). Paris: Librairie Philosophique.

MacNichol, E. F., Jr. (1986). A unifying presentation of photopigment spectra. *Vision Research, 29,* 543–546.

Madden, T. M., & Burt, G. S. (1981). Inappropriate constancy scaling theory and the Mueller-Lyer illusion. *Perceptual and Motor Skills, 52,* 211–218.

Mair, R. G., Bouffard, J. A., Engen, T., & Morton, T. (1978). Olfactory sensitivity during the menstrual cycle. *Sensory Process, 2,* 90–98.

Mandler, G. (1980). Recognizing: The judgment of previous occurrence. *Psychological Review, 87,* 252–271.

Manning, K. A., Riggs, L. A., & Komenda, J. K. (1983). Reflex eyeblinks and visual suppression. *Perception & Psychophysics, 34,* 250–256.

Marks, L. E. (1968). Stimulus range, number of categories, and form of the category scale. *American Journal of Psychology, 81,* 467–479.

Marks, L. E. (1974). On scales of sensation: Prolegomena to any future psychophysics that will be able to come forth as science. *Perception & Psychophysics, 16,* 358–376.

Marks, L. E. (1979a). Summation of vibrotactile intensity: An analogy to auditory critical bands? *Sensory Processes, 3,* 188–203.

Marks, L. E. (1979b). A theory of loudness and loudness judgments. *Psychological Review, 86,* 256–285.

Marks, L. E., Szczesiul, R., & Ohlott, P. (1986). On the cross-modal perception of intensity. *Journal of Experimental Psychology: Human Perception and Performance, 12,* 517–534.

Marks, W. B., Dobelle, W. H., & MacNichol, E. F. (1964). Visual pigments of single primate cones. *Science, 143,* 1181–1183.

Marley, A. A. J., & Cook, V. T. (1984). A fixed rehearsal capacity interpretation of limits on absolute identification performance. *British Journal of Mathematical and Statistical Psychology, 37,* 136–151.

Marr, D. (1974). The computation of lightness by the primate retina. *Vision Research, 14,* 1377–1388.

Marr, D. (1982). *Vision.* San Francisco: Freeman.

Marr, D., & Poggio, T. (1979). A computational theory of human stero vision. *Proceedings of the Royal Society (London) Series B(204),* 301–328.

Marshall, D. A., & Moulton, D. G. (1981). Olfactory sensitivity to α-ionine in humans and dogs. *Chemical Senses, 6,* 53–61.

Marslen-Wilson, W. D. (1980). Speech understanding as a psychological process. In J. C. Simon (Ed.), *Spoken language generation and understanding* (pp. 39–67). Dordrecht: Reidel.

Martin, D. K., & Holden, B. A. (1982). A new method for

measuring the diameter of the in vivo human cornea. *American Journal of Optometry and Physiological Optics, 59,* 436–441.

Martin, M. (1979). Local and global processing: The role of sparsity. *Memory and Cognition, 7,* 476–484.

Masica, D. N., Money, J., Ehrhardt, A. A., & Lewis, V. G. (1969). IQ, fetal sex hormones and cognitive patterns: Studies in testicular feminizing syndrome of androgen insensitivity. *Johns Hopkins Medical Journal, 124,* 34.

Masland, R. H. (1986). The functional architecture of the retina. *Scientific American, 255,* 102–111.

Massaro, D. W. (1987). *Speech perception by ear and eye: A paradigm for psychological inquiry.* Hillsdale, NJ: Lawrence Erlbaum.

Mather, J. A., & Fisk, J. D. (1985). Orienting to targets by looking and pointing: Parallels and interactions in ocular and manual performance. *Quarterly Journal of Experimental Psychology, 37A,* 315–338.

Matin, L. (1982). Visual localization and eye movements. In A. H. Wertheim, W. A. Wagenaar, & H. W. Leibowitz (Eds.), *Tutorials on motion perception* (pp. 101–156). New York: Plenum.

Matin, L., & MacKinnon, G. E. (1964). Autokinetic movement: Selective manipulation of directional components by image stabilization. *Science, 143,* 147–148.

Matthews, B. H. C. (1933). Nerve endings in mammalian muscle. *Journal of Physiology (London), 78,* 1–53.

Maunsell, J. H. R., & van Essen, D. C. (1983). Functional properties of neurons in middle temporal visual area of the macaque monkey. I. Selectivity for stimulus direction, speed, and orientation. *Journal of Neurophysiology, 49,* 1127–1147.

Maurer, D. (1975). Infant visual perception: Methods of study. In L. B. Cohen & P. Salapatek (Eds.), *Infant perception: From sensation to cognition, basic visual processes* (Vol. 1, pp. 1–77). New York: Academic Press.

Maurer, D., & Barrera, M. (1981). Infant's perception of natural and distorted arrangements of a schematic face. *Child Development, 52,* 196–202.

Maurer, D., & Lewis, T. L. (1979). A physiological explanation of infants' early visual development. *Canadian Journal of Psychology, 33,* 232–251.

Maurer, D., & Martello, M. (1980). The discrimination of orientation by young infants. *Vision Research, 20,* 201–204.

Maurer, D., & Salapatek, P. (1976). Development changes in the scanning of faces by young infants. *Child Development, 47,* 523–527.

Maxwell, J. C. (1873). *Treatise on electricity and magnetism.* Oxford: Clarendon Press.

Mayer, D. J., & Watkins, L. R. (1984). Multiple endogenous opiate and nonopiate analgesia systems. In L. Kruger & J. C. Liebeskind (Eds.), *Neural mechanisms of pain* (pp. 253–276). New York: Raven.

Mayhew, J. E. W., & Frisby, J. P. (1980). The computation of binocular edges. *Perception, 9,* 69–86.

McBurney, D. H. (1969). Effects of adaptation on human taste function. In C. Pfaffman (Ed.), *Olfaction and taste III* (pp. 407–419). New York: Rockefeller University Press.

McBurney, D. H., & Bartoshuk, L. M. (1972). Water taste in mammals. In D. Schneider (Ed.), *Olfaction and taste IV* (pp. 329–335). Wissenshafliche Verlagsgesellschaft MBH.

McBurney, D. H., & Gent, J. F. (1979). On the nature of taste qualities. *Psychological Bulletin, 86,* 151–167.

McBurney, D. H., Levine, J. M., & Cavanaugh, P. H. (1977). Psychophysical and social ratings of human body odor. *Personality and Social Psychology Bulletin, 3,* 135–138.

McCall, R. B. (1979). Individual differences in the pattern of habituation at five and ten months of age. *Developmental Psychology, 15,* 559–569.

McClain, L. (1983). Interval estimation: Effect of processing demands on prospective and retrospective reports. *Perception & Psychophysics, 34,* 185–189.

McClelland, J. L., & Elman, J. L. (1986). The TRACE model of speech perception. *Cognitive Psychology, 18,* 1–86.

McClintock, M. K. (1971). Menstrual synchrony and suppression. *Nature (London), 229,* 244–245.

McColgin, F. H. (1960). Movement threshold in peripheral vision. *Journal of the Optical Society of America, 50,* 774–779.

McCollough, C. (1965). Color adaptation of edge detectors in the human visual system. *Science, 149,* 1115–1116.

McCready, D. (1986). Moon illusions redescribed. *Perception & Psychophysics, 39,* 64–72.

McFarland, R. A., Domey, R. G., Warren, A. B., & Ward, D. C. (1960). Dark-adaptation as a function of age. I. A. statistical analysis. *Journal of Gerontology, 15,* 149–154.

McGee, M. G. (1979). Human spatial abilities: Psychometric studies and environmental, genetic, hormonal, and neurological influences. *Psychological Bulletin, 86,* 889–918.

McGlone, J. (1981). Sexual variations in behavior during spatial and verbal tasks. *Canadian Journal of Psychology, 35,* 277–282.

McGuinness, D. (1972). Hearing: Individual differences in perceiving. *Perception, 1,* 465–473.

McGuinness, D. (1976a). Away from a unisex psychology: Individual differences in visual sensory and perceptual processes. *Perception, 5,* 279–294.

McGuinness, D. (1976b). Sex differences in the organization of perception and cognition. In B. Lloyd & U. Archer (Eds.), *Exploring sex differences* (pp. 123–156). New York: Academic Press.

McGuinness, D., & Lewis, I. (1976). Sex differences in visual persistence: Experiments on the Ganzfeld and the after-image. *Perception, 5,* 295–301.

McGurk, H., & MacDonald, J. (1976). Hearing lips and seeing voices. *Nature, 264,* 746–748.

Meer, H. C. van der. (1979). Interrelation of the effects of binocular disparity and perspective cues on judgments of depth and height. *Perception & Psychophysics, 26,* 481–488.

Meiselman, H. L., Bose, H. E., & Nykvist, W. F. (1972). Magnitude production and magnitude estimation of taste intensity. *Perception & Psychophysics, 12,* 249–252.

Melzack, R., & Casey, K. L. (1968). Sensory, motivational, and central control determinants of pain. In D. R. Kenshalo (Ed.), *The skin senses* (pp. 423–443). Springfield, IL: Thomas.

Melzack, R., & Wall, P. D. (1965). Pain mechanisms: A new theory. *Science, 150,* 971–979.

Melzack, R., & Wall, P. D. (1982). *The challenge of pain.* Harmondsworth: Penguin.

Melzack, R., Wall, P. D., & Ty, T. C. (1982). Acute pain in an emergency clinic: Latency of onset and descriptor patterns related to different injuries. *Pain, 14,* 33–43.

Mergner, R., Anastasopoulos, D., Becker, W., & Deecke, L. (1981). Discrimination between trunk and head rotation: A study comparing neuronal data from the cat with human psychophysics. *Acta Psychologica, 48,* 291–302.

Merkel, J. (1885). Die zeitlichen Verhaltnisse der Willenstatigkeit. *Philosophische Studien (Wundt), 2,* 73–127.

Mershon, D. H., & Bowers, J. N. (1979). Absolute and relative cues for the auditory perception of egocentric distance. *Perception, 8,* 311–322.

Mershon, D. H., Desaulniers, D. H., & Amerson, T. L., Jr. (1980). Visual capture in auditory distance perception: Proximity image effect reconsidered. *Journal of Auditory Research, 20,* 129–136.

Mershon, D. H., Desaulniers, D. H., Kiefer, S. A., & Amerson, T. L., Jr. (1981). Perceived loudness and visually determined auditory distance. *Perception, 10,* 531–543.

Mershon, D. H., & Gogel, W. C. (1970). Effect of stereoscopic cues on perceived whiteness. *American Journal of Psychology, 83,* 55–67.

Mershon, D. H., & King, L. E. (1975). Intensity and reverberation as factors in the auditory perception of egocentric distance. *Perception & Psychophysics, 18,* 409–415.

Metzler, D. E., & Harris, C. M. (1978). Shapes of spectral bands of visual pigments. *Vision Research, 18,* 1417–1420.

Michael, C. R. (1981). Columnar organization of color cells in monkey's striate cortex. *Journal of Neurophysiology, 46,* 587–604.

Michael, C. R. (1985). Laminar segregation of color cells in the monkey's striate cortex. *Vision Research, 25,* 415–423.

Michael, R. P., & Keverne, E. B. (1968). Pheromones in the communication of sexual status in primates. *Nature, 218,* 746–749.

Michael, R. P., Keverne, E. B., & Bonsall, R. W. (1971). Pheromones: Isolation of male sex attractants from a female primate. *Science, 172,* 964–966.

Michael, S., & Sherrick, M. F. (1986). Perception of induced visual motion: Effects of relative position, shape and size of the surround. *Canadian Journal of Psychology, 40,* 122–125.

Michaels, C. F., & Carello, C. (1981). *Direct perception.* Englewood Cliffs, NJ: Prentice-Hall.

Michell, J. (1986). Measurement scales and statistics: A clash of paradigms. *Psychological Bulletin, 100,* 398–407.

Michon, J. (1985). The compleat time experiencer. In J. A. Michon & J. L. Jackson (Eds.), *Time, mind and behavior* (pp. 20–52). Berlin: Springer-Verlag.

Mikaelian, H. (1974). Adaptation to displaced hearing: A nonproprioceptive change. *Journal of Experimental Psychology, 103,* 326–330.

Mikaelian, H., & Held, R. (1964). Two types of adaptation to an optically-rotated visual field. *American Journal of Psychology, 77,* 257–263.

Miles, F. A., & Fuller, J. E. (1975). Visual tracking and the primate flocculus. *Science, 189,* 1000–1002.

Milewski, A. E. (1976). Infant's discrimination of internal and external pattern elements. *Journal of Experimental Child Psychology, 22,* 229–246.

Mill, J. (1829). *Analysis of the phenomena of the human mind.* London.

Millan, M. J. (1986). Multiple opioid systems and pain. *Pain, 27,* 303–347.

Millar, J. M., & Whitaker, H. A. (1983). The right hemisphere's contribution to language: A review of the evidence from brain-damaged subjects. In S. Sagalowitz (Ed.), *Language function and brain organization* (pp. 87–114). New York: Academic Press.

Miller, D. L., Moore, R. K., & Wooten, B. R. (1984). When push comes to pull: Impressions of visual direction. *Perception & Psychophysics, 36,* 396–397.

Miller, G. A. (1947). Sensitivity to changes in the intensity of white noise and its relation to masking and loudness. *Journal of the Acoustical Society of America, 19,* 609–619.

Miller, G. A. (1956). The magical number seven, plus or minus two: Some limits on our capacity for processing information. *Psychological Review, 63,* 81–97.

Miller, G. W., Hicks, R. E., & Willette, M. (1978). Effects of concurrent verbal rehearsal and temporal set upon judgments of temporal duration. *Acta Psychologica, 42,* 173–179.

Miller, J. (1982). Divided attention: Evidence for coactivation with redundant signals. *Cognitive Psychology, 14,* 247–279.

Miller, J. L., & Liberman, A. M. (1979). Some effects of later-occurring information on the perception of stop consonants and semivowel. *Perception & Psychophysics, 25,* 457–465.

Miller, N. D. (1965). Visual recovery from brief exposures to high luminance. *Journal of the Optical Society of America, 55,* 1661–1669.

Miller, R. J., Pigion, R. G., & Martin, K. D. (1985). The effects of ingested alcohol on accommodation. *Perception & Psychophysics, 37,* 407–414.

Mills, A. W. (1958). On the minimum audible angle. *Journal of the Acoustical Society of America, 30,* 127–246.

Mills, A. W. (1960). Lateralization of high-frequency tones. *Journal of the Acoustical Society of America, 32,* 132–134.

Milne, J. & Milne, M. (1967). *The senses of animals and men.* New York: Atheneum.

Mitchell, D. (1978). Effect of early visual experience on the development of certain perceptual abilities in animals and man. In R. Walk & H. Pick (Eds.), *Perception and experience,* New York: Plenum.

Mitchell, D. (1980). The influence of early visual experience on visual perception. In C. Harris (Ed.), *Visual coding and adaptability* (pp. 1–50). Hillsdale, NJ: Lawrence Erlbaum.

Mitchell, D. (1981). Sensitive periods in visual development. In R. Aslin, J. Alberts, & M. Petersen (Eds.), *Development of perception* (pp. 1–43). New York: Academic Press.

Monahan, J. S., & Lockhead, G. R. (1977). Identification of integral stimuli. *Journal of Experimental Psychology: General, 106,* 94–110.

Moncrieff, R. W. (1956). Olfactory adaptation and colour likeness. *Journal of Physiology (London), 133*, 301–316.

Money, J. (1965). Psychosexual differentiation. In J. Money (Ed.), *Sex research: New developments* (pp. 3–23). New York: Holt.

Montellese, S., Sharpe, L. T., & Brown, J. L. (1979). Changes in critical duration during dark-adaptation. *Vision Research, 19*, 1147–1153.

Montgomery, J. C., & MacDonald, J. A. (1987). Sensory tuning of lateral line receptors in Antarctic fish to the movements of planktonic prey. *Science, 235*, 195–196.

Mooney, R. D., Dubin, M. W., & Russoff, A. C. (1979). Interneuron circuits in the lateral geniculate nucleus of monocularly deprived cats. *Journal of Comparative Neurology, 187(3)*, 533–544.

Moore, B. (1977). *Introduction to the psychology of hearing.* Baltimore: University Park Press.

Moore, L. M., Nielson, C. R., & Mistretta, C. M. (1982). Sucrose taste thresholds: Age-related differences. *Journal of Gerontology, 37*, 64–69.

Moran, J., & Gordon, B. (1982). Long term visual deprivation in a human. *Vision Research, 22*, 27–36.

Moray, N. (1959). Attention in dichotic listening: Affective cues and the influence of instructions. *Quarterly Journal of Experimental Psychology, 11*, 56–60.

Moray, N. (1969). *Attention: Selective processes in vision and hearing.* London: Hutchinson Educational Ltd.

Morris, V., & Morris, P. E. (1985). The influence of question order on eyewitness accuracy. *British Journal of Psychology, 76*, 365–371.

Morrison, J. D., & Whiteside, T. C. D. (1984). Binocular cues in the perception of distance of a point source of light. *Perception, 13*, 555–566.

Moskowitz, H., Sharma, S., & McGlothlin, W. (1972). Effect of marijuana upon peripheral vision as a function of the information processing demands in central vision. *Perceptual and Motor Skills, 35*, 875.

Moskowitz-Cook, A. (1979). The development of photopic spectral sensitivity in human infants. *Vision Research, 9*, 113–114.

Mountcastle, V. B., Poggio, G. F., & Werner, G. (1963). The relation of thalamic cell response to peripheral stimuli varied over an intensive continuum. *Journal of Neurophysiology, 26*, 807–834.

Mountcastle, V. B., & Powell, T. P. S. (1959). Central nervous mechanisms subserving position sense and kinesthesis. *Bulletin of the Johns Hopkins Hospital, 105*, 173–200.

Movshon, J. A., & van Sluyters, R. C. (1981). Visual neural development. *Annual Review of Psychology, 32*, 477–522.

Mozel, M. M., Smith, B., Smith, P., Sullivan, R., & Swender, P. (1969). Nasal chemoreception in flavor identification. *Archives of Otolaryngology, 90*, 367–373.

Muir, D., & Field, J. (1979). Newborn infants orient to sounds. *Child Development, 50*, 431–436.

Mulligan, R. M., & Schiffman, H. R. (1979). Temporal experience as a function of organization in memory. *Bulletin of the Psychonomic Society, 14*, 417–420.

Munsell, A. H. (1915). *Atlas of the Munsell color system.* Maldin, MA: Wadsworth, Howland.

Murphy, C., & Cain, W. S. (1980). Taste and olfaction: Independence vs. interaction. *Physiology and Behavior, 24*, 601–605.

Murphy, T. D., & Eriksen, C. W. (1987). Temporal changes in the distribution of attention in the visual field in response to precues. *Perception & Psychophysics, 42*, 576–586.

Mustillo, P. (1985). Binocular mechanisms mediating crossed and uncrossed stereopsis. *Psychological Bulletin, 97*, 187–201.

Myers, A. K. (1982). Psychophysical scaling and scales of physical stimulus measurement. *Psychological Bulletin, 92*, 203–214.

Nagy, A. L. (1980). Short-flash Bezold-Brucke hue shifts. *Vision Research, 20*, 361–368.

Naka, Ken-Ichi (1982). The cells horizontal cells talk to. *Vision Research, 22*, 653–660.

Narens, L., & Luce, R. D. (1986). Measurement: The theory of numerical assignments. *Psychological Bulletin, 99*, 166–180.

Nathans, J., Piantanida, T. P., Eddy, R. L., Shows, T. B., & Hogness, D. S. (1986). Molecular genetics of inherited variation in human color vision. *Science, 232*, 203–210.

Navon, D. (1977). Forest before trees: The precedence of global features in visual perception. *Cognitive Psychology, 9*, 353–383.

Navon, D., & Gopher, D. (1979). On the economy of the human-processing system. *Psychological Review, 86*, 214–255.

Neff, D. L., & Green, D. M. (1987). Masking produced by spectral uncertainty with multicomponent maskers. *Perception & Psychophysics, 41*, 409–415.

Neisser, U. (1967). *Cognitive psychology.* New York: Appleton.

Neisser, U. (1976). *Cognition and reality: Principles and implications of cognitive psychology.* San Francisco: Freeman.

Neisser, U., & Becklin, R. (1975). Selective looking: Attending to visually specified events. *Cognitive Psychology, 7*, 480–494.

Nelson, R., Kolb, H., Robinson, M. M., & Mariani, A. P. (1981). Neural circuity of the cat retina: Cone pathways to ganglion cells. *Vision Research, 21*, 1527–1537.

Neuweiler, G., Bruns, V., & Schuller, G. (1980). Ears adapted for the detection of motion; or how echolocating bats have exploited the capacities of the mammalian auditory system. *Journal of the Acoustical Society of America, 68*, 741–753.

Neville, H. J. (1985). Effects of early sensory and language experience on the development of the human brain. In J. Mehler & R. Fox (Eds.), *Neonate cognition: Beyond the blooming buzzing confusion* (pp. 349–364). Hillsdale, NJ: Lawrence Erlbaum.

Neville, H. J., Schmidt, A., & Kutas, M. (1983). Altered visual evoked potentials in congenitally deaf adults. *Brain Research, 266*, 127–132.

Newhall, S. M., Burnham, R. W., & Clark, J. R. (1957). Comparison of successive with simultaneous color matching. *Journal of the Optical Society of America, 47*, 43–56.

Newhall, S. M., Nickerson, D., & Judd, D. B. (1943). Final

report of the O.S.A. subcommittee on spacing of the Munsell colors. *Journal of the Optical Society of America, 33,* 385–418.

Newland, J. (1972). Children's knowledge of left and right. Unpublished master's thesis, University of Auckland. Cited in M. C. Corballis & J. L. Beale (1976). *The psychology of left and right* (p. 167). Hillsdale, NJ: Lawrence Erlbaum.

Noble, W., & Gates, A. (1985). Accuracy, latency, and listener-search behavior in localization in the horizontal and vertical planes. *Journal of the Acoustical Society of America, 78,* 2005–2012.

Noda, H., Freeman, R. B., & Creutzfeldt, O. D. (1972). Neuronal correlates of eye movements in the cat visual cortex. *Science, 175,* 661–664.

Noell, W. (1980). Possible mechanisms of photoreceptor damage by light in mammalian eyes. *Vision Research, 20,* 1163–1172.

Norman, D. A. (1968). Toward a theory of memory and attention. *Psychological Review, 75,* 522–536.

Norman, D. A. (1969). Memory while shadowing. *Quarterly Journal of Experimental Psychology, 21,* 85–93.

Norman, D. A. (1976). *Memory and attention.* (2nd ed.). New York: Wiley.

Norman, D. A., Rumelhart, D. E., and the LNR Research Group. (1975). *Explorations in Cognition.* San Francisco: Freeman.

Norton, T. T. (1981a). Development of the visual system and visually guided behavior. In R. Aslin, J. Alberts, & M. Petersen (Eds.), *Development of perception: Psychobiological perspectives: Vol. 2. The visual system* (pp. 113–156). New York: Academic Press.

Norton, T. T. (1981b). Geniculate and extrageniculate visual systems in the tree shrew. In A. R. Morrison & P. L. Strick (Eds.), *Changing concepts of the nervous system* (pp. 377–410). New York: Academic Press.

Norwich, K. H. (1981). The magical number seven: Making a "bit" of "sense". *Perception & Psychophysics, 29,* 409–422.

Norwich, K. H. (1983). To perceive is to doubt: The relativity of perception. *Journal of Theoretical Biology, 102,* 175–190.

Norwich, K. H. (1984). The psychophysics of taste from the entropy of the stimulus. *Perception & Psychophysics, 35,* 269–278.

Norwich, K. H. (1987). On the theory of Weber fractions. *Perception & Psychophysics, 42,* 286–298.

Nusbaum, H. C., & Schwab, E. C. (1986). The role of attention and active processing in speech perception. In E. C. Schwab & H. C. Nusbaum (Eds.), *Pattern recognition by humans and machines: Vol. 1. Speech Perception* (pp. 113–157). Orlando, FL: Academic Press.

Oakley, B. (1985). Taste responses of human chorda tympani nerve. *Chemical Senses, 10,* 469–481.

O'Connell, R. J., & Mozell, M. M. (1969). Quantitative stimulation of frog olfactory receptors. *Journal of Neurophysiology, 32,* 51–63.

Ogasawara, K., McHaftie, J. G., & Stein, B. E. (1984). Two visual corticotectal systems in the cat. *Journal of Neurophysiology, 52,* 1226–1245.

Ohala, J. J. (1986). Phonological evidence for top-down processing in speech perception. In J. S. Perkell & D. H. Klatt (Eds.), *Invariance and variability in speech processes* (pp. 386–397). Hillsdale, NJ: Lawrence Erlbaum.

Oldfield, S. R., & Parker, S. P. A. (1984). Acuity of sound localisation: A topography of auditory space. II. Pinna cues absent. *Perception, 13,* 601–617.

Oldfield, S. R., & Parker, S. P. A. (1986). Acuity of sound localisation: A topography of auditory space. III. Monaural hearing conditions. *Perception, 15,* 67–81.

Olsho, L. W. (1984). Infant frequency discrimination. *Infant Behavior and Development, 7,* 27–35.

Olson, R., & Attneave, F. (1970). What variables produce similarity grouping? *American Journal of Psychology, 83,* 1–21.

Olzak, L. (1986). Widely separated spatial frequencies: Mechanism interactions. *Vision Research, 26,* 1143–1154.

O'Mahony, M. (1979). Salt taste adaptation: The psychophysical effects of adapting solutions and residual stimuli from prior tastings on the taste of sodium chloride. *Perception, 8,* 441–476.

O'Mahony, M., & Heintz, C. (1981). Direct magnitude estimation of salt taste intensity with continuous correction for salivary adaptation. *Chemical Senses, 6,* 101–112.

Ono, H. (1969). Apparent distance as a function of familiar size. *Journal of Experimental Psychology, 79,* 109–115.

Ono, H., & Comerford, T. (1977). Stereoscopic depth constancy. In W. Epstein (Ed.), *Stability and constancy in visual perception: Mechanisms and processes.* New York: Wiley.

Ono, H., & Weber, E. U. (1981). Nonveridical visual direction produced by monocular viewing. *Journal of Experimental Psychology: Human Perception & Performance, 7,* 937–947.

Ono, M. E., Rivest, J., & Ono, H. (1986). Depth perception as a function of motion parallax and absolute-distance information. *Journal of Experimental Psychology: Human Perception and Performance, 12,* 331–337.

Orban, G. A. (1984). *Neuronal operations in the visual cortex.* Berlin: Springer-Verlag.

Orban, G. A., Kennedy, H., & Maes, H. (1981a). Response to movement of neurons in areas 17 and 18 of the cat: Velocity sensitivity. *Journal of Neurophysiology, 45,* 1043–1058.

Orban, G. A., Kennedy, H., & Maes, H. (1981b). Response to movement of neurons in areas 17 and 18 of the cat: Direction sensitivity. *Journal of Neurophysiology, 45,* 1059–1073.

Ornstein, R. E. (1969). *On the experience of time.* London: Penguin.

Osaka, N. (1981). Brightness exponent as a function of flash duration and retinal eccentricity. *Perception & Psychophysics, 30,* 144–148.

Osterberg, G. (1935). Topography of the layer of rods and cones in the human retina. *Acta Ophthalmologica,* 6(Suppl.).

Ostfeld, A. (1961). Effects of LSD-25 and JB318 on tests of

visual and perceptual functions in man. *Federation Proceedings, Federation of American Societies for Experimental Biology, 20,* 876–883.

Ottoson, D. (1956). Analysis of the electrical activity of the olfactory epithelium. *Acta Physiologica Scandinavica, 35*(Suppl. 122), 1–83.

Owens, M. E. (1984). Pain in infancy: Conceptual and methodological issues. *Pain, 20,* 213–220.

Owsley, C. (1983). The role of motion in infants' perception of solid shape. *Perception, 12,* 707–717.

Oyama, T. (1968). A behavioristic analysis of Steven's magnitude estimation method. *Perception & Psychophysics, 3,* 317–320.

Oyama, T. (1986). The effect of stimulus organization on numerosity discrimination. *Japanese Psychological Research, 28,* 77–86.

Palmer, A. R., Winter, I. M., & Darwin, C. J. (1986). The representation of steady-state vowel sounds in the temporal discharge pattern of the guinea pig cochlear nerve and primarylike cochlear nucleus neurons. *Journal of the Acoustical Society of America, 79,* 100–113.

Palmer, C., & Krumhansl, C. L. (1987). Independent temporal and pitch structures in determination of musical phrases. *Journal of Experimental Psychology: Human Perception and Performance, 13,* 116–126.

Palmer, J. (1986). Mechanisms of displacement discrimination with and without perceived movement. *Journal of Experimental Psychology: Human Perception and Performance, 12,* 411–421.

Palmer, S. E. (1975a). The effects of contextual scenes on the identification of objects. *Memory and Cognition, 3,* 519–526.

Palmer, S. E. (1975b). Visual perception and world knowledge: notes on a model of sensory-cognitive interaction. In D. A. Norman & D. E. Rumelhart (Eds.), *Explorations in cognition* (pp. 297–307). San Francisco: Freeman.

Paquet, L., & Merikle, P. M. (1984). Global precedence: The effect of exposure duration. *Canadian Journal of Psychology, 38,* 45–53.

Parasuraman, R. (1984). Sustained attention in detection and discrimination. In R. Parasuraman & D. R. Davies (Eds.), *Varieties of attention.* (pp. 243–271). Orlando, FL: Academic Press.

Parasuraman, R., & Mouloua, M. (1987). Interaction of signal discriminability and task type in vigilance decrement. *Perception & Psychophysics, 41,* 17–22.

Parducci, A. (1965). Category judgment: A range-frequency model. *Psychological Review, 72,* 407–418.

Parker, D. E. (1980). The vestibular apparatus. *Scientific American, 243,* 118–135.

Parks, T. E. (1965). Post-retinal visual storage. *American Journal of Psychology, 78,* 145–147.

Parlee, M. B. (1983). Menstrual rhythms in sensory processes: A review of fluctuations in vision, olfaction, audition, taste and touch. *Psychological Bulletin, 93,* 539–548.

Pashler, H. (1984). Evidence against late selection: Stimulus

quality effects in previewed displays. *Journal of Experimental Psychology: Human Perception and Performance, 10,* 429–448.

Pashler, H. (1987). Detecting conjunctions of color and form: Reassessing the serial search hypothesis. *Perception & Psychophysics, 41,* 191–201.

Pasnak, R., Tyer, Z. A., & Allen, J. A. (1985). Effect of distance instructions on size judgments. *American Journal of Psychology, 98,* 297–304.

Pastore, R. E., Schmeckler, M. A., Rosenblum, L., & Szczesiul, R. (1983). Duplex perception with musical stimuli. *Perception & Psychophysics, 33,* 469–474.

Patterson, R. D. (1969). Noise masking of a change in residue pitch. *Journal of the Acoustical Society of America, 45,* 1520–1524.

Paulus, K., & Haas, E. M. (1980). The influence of solvent viscosity on the threshold values of primary tastes. *Chemical Senses, 5,* 23–32.

Paulus, K., & Reisch, A. M. (1980). The influence of temperature on the threshold values of primary tastes. *Chemical Senses, 5,* 11–21.

Peeples, D. R., & Teller, D. Y. (1978). White-adapted photopic spectral sensitivity in human infants. *Vision Research, 18,* 39–53.

Peichl, L., & Wassle, H. (1979). Size, scatter and coverage of ganglion-cell receptive-field centers in the cat retina. *Journal of Physiology (London), 291,* 117.

Pelosi, P., & Pisanelli, A. M. (1981). Specific anosmia to 1,8-cineole: The camphor primary odor. *Chemical Senses, 6,* 87–93.

Penfield, W., & Rasmussen, T. (1950). *The cerebral cortex of man.* New York: Macmillan.

Perkell, J. S., & Klatt, D. H. (Eds.). (1986). *Invariance and variability in speech processes.* Hillsdale, NJ: Lawrence Erlbaum.

Perl, E. R. (1984). Characterization of nociceptors and their activation of neurons in the superficial dorsal horn: First steps for the sensation of pain. In L. Kruger & J. C. Liebeskind (Eds.), *Neural mechanisms of pain* (pp. 23–52). New York: Raven.

Peterson, A. C. (1976). Physical androgyny and cognitive functioning in adolescence. *Developmental Psychology, 12,* 524–533.

Peterson, A. C., & Crockett, L. (1985, August). Factors influencing sex differences in spatial ability during adolescence. In S. L. Willis (Chair.), *Sex differences in spatial ability across the lifespan.* Symposium conducted at the Ninety-third Annual Convention of the American Psychological Association, Los Angeles.

Petrig, B., Julesz, B., Kropfl, W., Baumgartner, G., & Anliker, M. (1981). Development of stereopsis and cortical binocularity in human infants: Electrophysiological evidence. *Science, 213,* 1402–2405.

Petry, S., & Meyer, G. E. (1987). *The perception of illusory contours.* New York: Springer-Verlag.

Pettigrew, J. (1978a). Stereoscopic visual processing. *Nature, 273,* 9–11.

Pettigrew, J. (1978b). The paradox of the critical period for striate cortex. In C. W. Cotman (Ed.), *Neuronal plasticity* (pp. 311–330). New York: Raven.

Pfaff, D. (1968). Effects of temperature and time of day on judgment. *Journal of Experimental Psychology, 76,* 419–422.

Pfaffman, C. (1955). Gustatory nerve impulses in rat, cat, and rabbit. *Journal of Neurophysiology, 18,* 429–440.

Pfaffman, C. (1974). Specificity of the sweet receptors of the squirrel monkey. *Chemical Senses and Flavor, 1,* 61–67.

Pfaffman, C., Bartoshuk, L., & McBurney, D. H. (1971). Taste psychophysics. *Handbook of Sensory Physiology, 1,* 75–101.

Pfaffman, C., Frank, M., & Norgren, R. (1979). Neural mechanisms and behavioral aspects of taste. *Annual Review of Psychology, 30,* 283–325.

Pfeiffer, R. R. (1966). Classification of response patterns of spike discharges for units in the cochlear nucleus: Toneburst stimulation. *Experimental Brain Research, 1,* 220–235.

Phillips, C. G., Zeki, S., & Barlow, H. B. (1984). Localization of function in the cerebral cortex. *Brain, 107,* 328–360.

Phillips, D. P., & Brugge, J. F. (1985). Progress in neurophysiology of sound localization. *Annual Review of Psychology, 36,* 245–274.

Phillipson, O. T., & Harris, J. P. (1984). Effects of chloropromazine and promazine on the perception of some multistable visual figures. *Quarterly Journal of Experimental Psychology, 36A,* 291–308.

Piaget, J. (1969). *The mechanisms of perception.* (G. N. Seagrine, Trans.). New York: Oxford University Press.

Pick, H. L. (1987). Information and the effects of early perceptual experience. In N. Eisenberg (Ed.), *Contemporary topics in developmental psychology* (pp. 59–76). New York: Wiley.

Pick, H. L., Jr., & Hay, J. C. (1965). A passive test of the Held reafference hypothesis. *Perceptual and Motor Skills, 20,* 1070–1072.

Pick, H. L., Jr., & Pick, A. D. (1970). Sensory and perceptual development. In P. H. Mussen (Ed.), *Carmichael's manual of child development* (pp. 773–848). New York: Wiley.

Pierce, J. R. (1983). *The science of musical sound.* New York: Scientific American Books.

Piggins, D. J., Kingham, J. R., & Holmes, S. M. (1972). Colour, colour saturation and pattern induced by intermittent illumination: An initial study. *British Journal of Physiological Optics, 27,* 120–125.

Pinkers, A., & Marre, M. (1983). Basic phenomena in acquired colour vision deficiency. *Documenta Ophthalmologica, 55,* 251–271.

Pisoni, D. B. (1973). Auditory and phonetic codes in the discrimination of consonants and vowels. *Perception & Psychophysics, 13,* 253–260.

Pisoni, D. B., & Luce, P. A. (1986). Speech perception: Research, theory, and the principal issues. In E. C. Schwab & H. C. Nusbaum (Eds.), *Pattern recognition by humans and machines: Vol. 1. Speech perception* (pp. 1–50). Orlando, FL: Academic Press.

Pisoni, D. B., Nusbaum, H. C., Luce, P. A., & Slowiaczek,

L. M. (1985). Speech perception, word recognition and the structure of the lexicon. *Speech Communication, 4,* 75–95.

Pizorrolo, F. J. (1978). *The neuropsychology of developmental reading disorders.* New York: Praeger.

Plateau, M. H. (1872). Sur la mesure des sensations physiques, et sur la loi qui lie l'intensite de la cause excitante. *Bulletin de l'Academie Royale de Belgique, 33,* 376–388.

Podgorny, P., & Shepard, R. N. (1983). Distribution of visual attention over space. *Journal of Experimental Psychology: Human Perception and Performance, 9,* 380–393.

Poggio, G. F., & Mountcastle, V. B. (1960). A study of the functional contributions of the lemniscal and spinothalamic systems to somatic sensibility: Central nervous mechanisms in pain. *Bulletin of the Johns Hopkins Hospital, 106,* 266–316.

Pokorny, J., & Smith, V. C. (1986). Eye disease and color defects. *Vision Research, 26,* 1573–1584.

Pollack, I. (1952). The information of elementary auditory displays. *Journal of the Acoustical Society of America, 24,* 745–749.

Pollack, I. (1953). The information of elementary auditory displays. II. *Journal of the Acoustical Society of America, 25,* 765–769.

Pollack, I. (1978). Decoupling of auditory pitch and stimulus frequency: The Shepard demonstration revisited. *Journal of the Acoustical Society of America, 63,* 202–206.

Pollack, I., & Pickett, J. M. (1964). Intelligibility of excerpts from fluent speech: Auditory vs. structural context. *Journal of Verbal Learning and Verbal Behavior, 3,* 79–84.

Pollack, R. H., & Silvar, S. D. (1967). Magnitude of the Mueller-Lyer illusion in children as a function of pigmentation of fundus oculi. *Psychonomic Science, 8,* 83–84.

Pollen, D. A., Lee, J. R., & Taylor J. H. (1971). How does the visual cortex begin the reconstruction of the visual world? *Science, 173,* 74–77.

Poltrock, S. E., Lansman, M., & Hunt, E. (1982). Automatic and controlled attention processes in auditory target detection. *Journal of Experimental Psychology: Human Perception and Performance, 8,* 37–45.

Pomerantz, J. R. (1983). Global and local precedence: Selective attention in form and motion perception. *Journal of Experimental Psychology: General, 112,* 511–535.

Pomerantz, J. R. (1986). Visual form perception: An overview. In E. C. Schwab & H. C. Nusbaum (Eds.), *Pattern recognition by humans and machines: Vol. 2. Visual Perception* (pp. 1–30). Orlando, FL: Academic Press.

Pomerantz, J., Goldberg, D., Golder, P., & Tetewsky, S. (1981). Subjective contours can facilitate performance in a reaction-time task. *Perception & Psychophysics, 29,* 605–611.

Pomerantz, J. R., Sager, L. C., & Stoever, R. J. (1977). Perception of wholes and of their component parts: Some configural superiority effects. *Journal of Experimental Psychology: Human Perception and Performance, 1,* 422–435.

Pons, T. P., Garraghty P. E., Friedman, D. P., & Mishkin, M. (1987). Physiological evidence for serial processing in somatosensory cortex. *Science, 237,* 417–420.

Poppel, E. (1978). Time perception. In R. Held, H. W. Leibowitz, & H. L. Teuber (Eds.), *Handbook of Sensory Physiology: Vol. VIII. Perception* (pp. 713–729). New York: Springer-Verlag.

Popper, R., Parker, S., & Galanter, E. (1986). Dual loudness scales in individual subjects. *Journal of Experimental Psychology: Human Perception and Performance, 12,* 61–69.

Porac, C., & Coren, S. (1976). The dominant eye. *Psychological Bulletin, 83,* 880–897.

Porac, C., & Coren, S. (1981). Life-span age trends in the perception of the Mueller-Lyer: An additional evidence for the existence of two illusions. *Canadian Journal of Psychology, 35,* 58–62.

Porac, C., & Coren, S. (1985). Transfer of illusion decrement: The effects of global versus local figural variations. *Perception & Psychophysics, 37,* 515–522.

Porac, C., & Coren. S., (1986). Sighting dominance and egocentric localization. *Vision Research, 26,* 1709–1713.

Porter, R. H., Balogh, R. D., Cernoch, J. M., & Franchi, C. (1986). Recognition of kin through characteristic body odors. *Chemical Senses, 11,* 389–395.

Porter, R. H., & Moore, J. D. (1981). Human kin recognition by olfactory cues. *Physiology & Behavior, 27,* 493–495.

Posner, M. I. (1978). *Chronometric exploration of mind.* Hillsdale, NJ: Lawrence Erlbaum.

Posner, M. I. (1980). Orienting of attention. *Quarterly Journal of Experimental Psychology, 32,* 3–25.

Post, B., & Leibowitz, H. W. (1985). A revised analysis of the role of efference in motion perception. *Perception, 14,* 631–643.

Postman, L., & Egan, J. P. (1949). *Experimental psychology.* New York: Harper & Row.

Poulton, E. C. (1979). Models for biases in judging sensory magnitudes. *Psychological Bulletin, 86,* 777–803.

Poulton, E. C., Edwards, R. S., & Fowler, T. J. (1980). Eliminating subjective biases in judging the loudness of a 1-KHz tone. *Perception & Psychophysics, 27,* 93–103.

Powers, M. K., Schneck, M., & Teller, D. Y. (1981). Spectral sensitivity of human infants at absolute visual threshold. *Vision Research, 21,* 1005–1016.

Poynter, W. D., & Holma, D. (1985). Duration judgment and the experience of change. *Perception and Psychophysics, 33,* 548–560.

Preti, G., Cutler, W. B., Garcia, C. R., Huggins, G. R., & Lawley, H. J. (1986). Human axillary secretions influence women's menstrual cycles: The role of donor extract of females. *Hormones and Behavior, 20,* 474–482.

Price, J. L. (1987). The central and accessory olfactory systems. In T. E. Finger & W. L. Silver (Eds.), *Neurobiology of taste and smell* (pp. 179–204). New York: Wiley.

Prinzmetal, W. (1981). Principles of feature integration in visual perception. *Perception & Psychophysics, 30,* 330–340.

Prinzmetal, W., & Millis-Wright, M. (1984). Cognitive and linguistic factors affect visual feature integration. *Cognitive Psychology, 16,* 305–340.

Pritchard, R. M., Heron, W., & Hebb, D. O. (1960). Visual perception approached by the method of stabilized images. *Canadian Journal of Psychology, 14,* 67–77.

Puckett, J. deW., & Steinman, R. M. (1969). Tracking eye movements with and without saccadic correction. *Vision Research, 9,* 295–303.

Quinn, P. C., Wooten, B. R., & Ludman, E. J. (1985). Achromatic color categories. *Perception & Psychophysics, 37,* 198–204.

Rabbitt, P. (1977). Changes in problem solving ability in old age. In J. Birren & K. Schaie (Eds.), *Handbook of the psychology of aging.* New York: Van Nostrand Reinhold.

Rabbitt, P. (1984). The control of attention in visual search. In R. Parasuraman & D. R. Davies (Eds.), *Varieties of attention* (pp. 273–291). Orlando, FL: Academic Press.

Rabin, M. D., & Cain, W. S. (1984). Odor recognition: Familiarity, identifiability, and encoding consistency. *Journal of Experimental Psychology: Learning, Memory, and Cognition, 10,* 316–325.

Rabin, M. D., & Cain, W. S. (1986). Determinants of measured olfactory sensitivity. *Perception & Psychophysics, 39,* 281–286.

Rakerd, B., & Hartmann, W. M. (1985). Localization of sound in rooms, II: The effects of a single reflecting surface. *Journal of the Acoustical Society of America, 78,* 524–533.

Ramachandran, V. S. (1986). Capture of stereopsis and apparent motion by illusory contours. *Perception & Psychophysics, 39,* 361–373.

Ramachandran, V. S. (1988). Perceiving shape from shading. *Scientific American, 259,* 76–83.

Rand, T. C. (1974). Dichotic release from masking for speech. *Journal of the Acoustical Society of America, 55,* 678–680.

Randsom-Hogg, A., & Spillman, L. (1980). Perceptive field size in fovea of the light and dark adapted. *Vision Research, 20,* 221–228.

Ratliff, F. (1965). *Mach bands: Quantitative studies on neural networks in the retina.* San Francisco: Holden-Day.

Rayleigh, Lord (1907). On our perception of sound direction. *Philosophical Magazine, 13*(6), 214–232.

Raymond, J. E., Shapiro, K. L. & Rose, D. J. (1984). Optokinetic backgrounds affect perceived velocity during ocular tracking. *Perception & Psychophysics, 36,* 221–224.

Reason, J. (1984). Lapses of attention in everyday life. In R. Parasuraman & D. R. Davies (Eds.), *Varieties of attention* (pp. 515–549). Orlando, FL: Academic Press.

Redding, G. M., Clark, S. E., & Wallace, B. (1985). Attention and prism adaptation. *Cognitive Psychology, 17,* 1–25.

Redding, G. M., & Wallace, B. (1976). Components of displacement adaptation in acquisition and decay as a function of hand and hall exposure. *Perception & Psychophysics, 20,* 453–459.

Reddy, D. R. (1976). Speech recognition by machine: A review. *Proceedings of the IEEE, 64,* 501–531.

Reed, C. F. (1984). Terrestrial passage theory of moon illusion. *Journal of Experimental Psychology: General, 113,* 489–500.

Regan, D. M., & Beverly, K. I. (1982). How do we avoid confounding the direction we are looking and the direction we are moving? *Science, 215,* 194–196.

Rehn, T. (1978). Perceived odor intensity as a function of airflow through the nose. *Sensory Processes, 2,* 198–205.

Reisberg, D., & O'Shaughnessy, M. (1984). Diverting subjects' concentration slows figural reversals. *Perception, 13,* 461–468.

Remez, R. E., Rubin, P. E., Pisoni, D. B., & Carrell, T. D. (1981). Speech perception without traditional speech cues. *Science, 212,* 947–950.

Remington, R., & Pierce, L. (1984). Moving attention: Evidence for time-invariant shifts of visual selective attention. *Perception & Psychophysics, 35,* 393–399.

Repp, B. H. (1987). The sound of two hands clapping: An exploratory study. *Journal of the Acoustical Society of America, 81,* 1100–1109.

Restle, F. (1971). Visual illusions. In M. H. Appley (Ed.), *Adaptation-level theory* (pp. 55–69). New York: Academic Press.

Restle, F. (1978). Assimilation predicted by adaptation level theory with variable weights. In J. S. Castellan & F. Restle (Eds.), *Cognitive theory: Vol. 3* (pp. 75–92). Hillsdale, NJ: Lawrence Erlbaum.

Reynolds, D. C. (1979). A visual profile of the alcoholic driver. *American Journal of Optometry and Physiological Optics, 56,* 241–251.

Reynolds. R. I. (1985). The role of object-hypotheses in the organization of fragmented figures. *Perception, 14,* 49–52.

Rhee, K., Kim, D., & Kim, Y. (1965). The effects of smoking on night vision. *14th Pacific Medical Conference* (Professional papers).

Rhodes, G. (1987). Auditory attention and the representation of spatial information. *Perception & Psychophysics, 42,* 1–14.

Rice, C. G., Ayley, J. B., Bartlett, B., Bedford, W., Gregory, W., & Hallum, G. (1968). A pilot study on the effects of pop group music on hearing. Cited in K. D. Kryter (1970). *The effects of noise on man* (p. 203). New York: Academic Press.

Richards, W. (1977). Lessons in constancy from neurophysiology. In W. W. Epstein (Ed.), *Stability and constancy in visual perception: Mechanisms and processes* (pp. 421–436.), New York: Wiley.

Riesen, A., & Zilbert, D. (1975). Behavioral consequences of variations in early sensory environments. In A. Riesen (Ed.), *The developmental neuropsychology of sensory deprivation* (pp. 211–252). New York: Academic Press.

Rieser, J., Yonas, A., & Wikner, K. (1976). Radial localization of odors by human newborns. *Child Development, 47,* 856–859.

Riesz, R. R. (1928). Differential intensity sensitivity of the ear for pure tones. *Physical Review, 31,* 867–875.

Riggs, L. A., Ratliff, F., Cornsweet, J. C., & Cornsweet, T. N. (1953). The disappearance of steadily fixated visual test objects. *Journal of the Optical Society of America, 43,* 495–501.

Rijnsdorp, A., Daan, S., & Dijkstra, C. (1981). Hunting in the kestrel (Falco tinnunculus) and the adaptive significance of daily habits. *Oecologia, 50,* 391–406.

Roberts, J. (1964). *Binocular visual acuity of adults.* Washington, D.C.: U.S. Department of Health, Education and Welfare.

Roberts, M. & Summerfield, A. Q. (1981). Audio-visual adaptation in speech perception. *Perception & Psychophysics, 30,* 309–314.

Robertson, P. W. (1967). Color words and colour vision. *Biology and Human Affairs, 33,* 28–33.

Robinson, D. W., & Dadson, R. S. (1956). A redetermination of the equal-loudness relations for pure tones. *British Journal of Applied Physics, 7,* 166–181.

Robson, J. G. (1980). Neural images: The physiological basis of spatial vision. In C. S. Harris (Ed.), *Visual coding and adaptability* (pp. 177–214.). Hillsdale, NJ: Lawrence Erlbaum.

Rock, I. (1973). *Orientation and form.* New York: Academic Press.

Rock, I. (1975). *An introduction to perception.* New York: Macmillan.

Rock, I. (1983). *The logic of perception.* Cambridge, MA: MIT Press.

Rock, I., & Guttman, D. (1981). The effect of inattention on form perception. *Journal of Experimental Psychology: Human Perception and Performance, 7,* 275–285.

Rock, I., & Halper, F. (1969). Form perception without a retinal image. *American Journal of Psychology, 82,* 425–440.

Rockland, K. S., & Pandya, P. N. (1981). Cortical connections of the occipital lobe in the rhesus monkey: Interconnections between areas 17, 18, 19 and the superior temporal sulcus. *Brain Research, 212,* 249–270.

Rodieck, R. W. (1973). *The vertebrate retina: Principles of structure and function.* San Francisco: Freeman.

Rodieck, R. W. (1979). Visual pathways. *Annual Review of Neurosciences, 2,* 193–225,

Roelofs, C. O. (1935). Optische lokalisation. *Archiv fur Augenheilkunde 109,* 395–415.

Rogel, M. J. (1978). A critical evaluation of the possibility of higher primate reproductive and sexual pheromones. *Psychological Bulletin, 85,* 810–830.

Rohrbaugh, J. W. (1984). The orienting reflex: Performance and central nervous system manifestations. In R. Parasuraman & D. R. Davies (Eds.), *Varieties of attention.* (pp. 323–373). Orlando, FL: Academic Press.

Rollman, G. B., & Harris, G. (1987). The detectability, discriminability, and perceived magnitude of painful electric shock. *Perception & Psychophysics, 42,* 257–268.

Romani, G. L., Williamson, S. J., & Kaufman, L. (1982). Tonotopic organization of the human auditory cortex. *Science, 216,* 1339–1340.

Romano, P. E., Romano, J. A., & Puklin, J. E. (1975). Stereoactivity development in children with normal single vision. *American Journal of Ophthalmology, 79,* 966–971.

Root, W. (1974, December 22). Of wine and noses. *New York Times Magazine,* p. 14 et seq.

Rose, J. E., Brugge, J. F., Anderson, D. J., & Hind, J. E. (1967). Phase-locked response to low frequency tones in single auditory nerve fibers of the squirrel monkey. *Journal of Neurophysiology, 30,* 769–793.

Rose, J. E., Galambos, R., & Hughes, J. (1959). Microelectrode studies of the cochlear nuclei of the cat. *Johns Hopkins Hospital Bulletin, 14,* 211–251.

Rose, J. E., Galambos, R., & Hughes, J. (1960). Organization of frequency sensitive neurons in the cochlear nuclear complex of the cat. In G. L. Rasmussen & W. F. Windle (Eds.), *Neural mechanisms of the auditory and vestibular systems* (pp. 116–136). Springfield, IL: Thomas.

Rosinski, R., & Farber, J. (1980). Compensation for viewing point in the perception of pictured space. In M. Hagen (Ed.), *Perception of pictures: Vol. 1. Alberti's Window: The projective model of pictorial information.* New York: Academic Press.

Ross, H. (1975, June 19). Mist, murk and visual perception. *New Scientist,* 658–660.

Ross, H. E., Brodie, E., & Benson, A. (1984). Mass discrimination during prolonged weightlessness. *Science, 225,* 219–221.

Ross, H. E., & Reschke, M. F. (1982). Mass estimation and discrimination during brief periods of zero gravity. *Perception & Psychophysics, 31,* 429–436.

Ross, N., & Schilder, P. (1934). Tachistoscopic experiments on the perception of the human figure. *Journal of General Psychology, 10,* 152–172.

Rothblat, L., & Schwartz, M. (1978). Altered early environment: Effects on the brain and visual behavior. In R. Walk & H. Pick (Eds.), *Perception and experience* (pp. 7–36). New York: Plenum.

Royster, L. H., Royster, J. D., & Thomas, W. G. (1980). Representative hearing levels by race and sex in North Carolina industry. *Journal of Acoustical Society of America, 68,* 551–566.

Rozin, P. (1978). The use of characteristic flavorings in human culinary practice. In C. M. Apt (Ed.), *Flavor: Its Chemical, Behavioral, and Commercial Aspects* (pp. 101–127). Boulder, CO: Westview Press.

Rozin, P. (1982). "Taste-smell confusions" and the duality of the olfactory sense. *Perception & Psychophysics, 31,* 397–401.

Rozin, P., Ebert, L., & Schull, J. (1982). Some like it hot: A temporal analysis of hedonic responses to chili pepper. *Appetite, 3,* 13–22.

Rubin, E. (1915). *Synoplevede figuren.* Copenhagen: Glydendalske.

Rubin, E. (1921). *Visuell wahrgenommene figuren.* Copenhagen: Glydendalske.

Ruble, D. N., & Nakamura, C. Y. (1972). Task orientation versus social orientation in young children and their attention to relevant social cues. *Child Development, 43,* 471–480.

Ruggieri, V., Cei, A., Ceridono, D., & Bergerone, C. (1980). Dimensional approach to the study of sighting dominance. *Perceptual and Motor Skills, 51,* 247–251.

Runeson, S., & Frykholm, G. (1983). Kinematic specifications of dynamics as an informational basis for person-and-action perception: Expectation, gender recognition, and deceptive intention. *Journal of Experimental Psychology: General, 112,* 585–615.

Rusak, B., & Groos, G. (1982). Suprachiasmatic stimulation phase shifts rodent circadian rhythms. *Science, 215,* 1407–1409.

Rusak, B., & Zucker, I. (1979). Neural regulation of circadian rhythms. *Physiological Review, 59,* 449–526.

Rushton, W. A. H. (1962). Visual pigments in man. *Scientific American, 205,* 120–132.

Rushton, W. A. H. (1965). Cone pigment dynamics in the deuteranope. *Journal of Physiology (London), 176,* 38–45.

Russell, M.. J. (1976). Human olfactory communication. *Nature (London), 260,* 520–522.

Russoff, A. C. (1979). Development of ganglion cells in the retina of the cat. In R. D. Freeman (Ed.), *Developmental neurobiology of vision* (pp. 19–30). New York: Plenum.

Russoff, A. C., & Dubin, M. W. (1977). Development of receptive-field properties of retinal ganglion cells in kittens. *Journal of Neurophysiology, 40,* 1188–1198.

Sachs, M. B., & Kiang, N. Y. S. (1968). Two-tone inhibition in auditory nerve fibers. *Journal of the Acoustical Society of America, 43,* 1120–1128.

Salapatek, P. (1975). Pattern perception in early infancy. In L. B. Cohen & P. Salapatek (Eds.), *Infant perception: From sensation to cognition* (Vol. 1, pp. 133–248). New York: Academic Press.

Salapatek, P., & Kessen, W. (1973). Prolonged investigation of a plane geometric triangle by the human newborn. *Journal of Experimental Child Psychology, 15,* 22–29.

Samuel, A. G. (1981). Phonemic restoration: Insights from a new methodology. *Journal of Experimental Psychology: General, 110,* 474–494.

Samuel, A. G. (1986). Red herring detectors and speech perception: In defense of selective adaptation. *Cognitive Psychology, 18,* 452–499.

Sanders, B., Soares, M. P., & D'Aquila, J. M. (1982). Sex difference on one test of spatial visualization: A nontrivial difference. *Child Development, 53,* 1106–1110.

Sanders, G., & Ross-Field, L. (1986). Sexual orientation and visuo-spatial ability. *Brain and Cognition, 5,* 280–290.

Sanocki, T. (1987). Visual knowledge underlying letter perception: Font-specific, schematic tuning. *Journal of Experimental Psychology: Human Perception and Performance, 13,* 267–278.

Sapir, E. (1939). *Language.* New York: Harcourt, Brace & World.

Sawusch, J. R. (1986). Auditory and phonetic coding of speech. In E. C. Schwab & H. C. Nusbaum (Eds.), *Pattern recognition by humans and machines: Vol. 1. Speech Perception* (pp. 51–88). Orlando, FL: Academic Press.

Schaie, K. W., & Geiwitz, J. (1982). *Adult development and aging.* Boston: Little, Brown.

Scharf, B. (1964). Partial masking. *Acustica, 14,* 16–23.

Scharf, B. (1975). Audition. In B. Scharf (Ed.), *Experimental sensory psychology* (pp. 112–149.) Glenview, IL: Scott, Foresman.

Scharf, B. (1978). Loudness. In E. C. Carterette & M. P. Friedman (Eds.), *Handbook of Perception: Vol. IV. Hearing.* New York: Academic Press.

Scharf, B., Quigley, S., Aoki, C., Peachey, N., & Reeves, A. (1987). Focused auditory attention and frequency selectivity. *Perception & Psychophysics, 42,* 215–223.

Schenkel, K. D. (1967). Die beidohrigen Mithorschoellen von Impulsen. *Acustica, 18,* 38–46.

Scher, D., Pionk, M., & Purcell, D. G. (1981). Visual sensitivity fluctuations during the menstrual cycle under dark and light adaptation. *Bulletin of the Psychonomic Society, 18,* 159–160.

Schiffman, S. S. (1974). Physiochemical correlates of olfactory quality. *Science, 185,* 112–117.

Schiffman, S. S. (1977). Food recognition by the elderly. *Journal of Gerontology, 32,* 586–592.

Schiffman, S. S., & Dackis, C. (1975). Taste of nutrients: Amino acids, vitamins, and fatty acids. *Perception & Psychophysics, 17,* 140–146.

Schiffman, S. S., & Erickson, R. P. (1971). A theoretical review: A psychophysical model for gustatory quality. *Physiology & Behavior, 1,* 617–633.

Schiffman, S. S., McElroy, A. E., & Erickson, R. F. (1980). The range of taste quality of sodium salts. *Physiology & Behavior, 24,* 217–224.

Schiffman, S. S., & Pasternak, M. (1979). Decreased discrimination of food odors in the elderly. *Journal of Gerontology, 84,* 73–79.

Schiffman, S. S., Reilly, D. A., & Clark, T. B., III. (1979). Qualitative differences among sweeteners. *Physiology & Behavior, 23,* 1–9.

Schiller, P. H. (1986). The central visual system. *Vision Research, 26,* 1351–1386.

Schindler, R. A., & Merzenich, M. M. (Eds.), (1985). *Cochlear Implants.* New York: Raven.

Schleidt, M., Hold, B., & Attili, G. (1981). A cross-cultural study on the attitude towards personal odors. *Journal of Chemical Ecology, 7,* 19–31.

Schmiedt, R. A., Zwislocki, J. J., & Hamernik, R. P. (1980). Effects of hair cell lesions on responses of cochlear nerve fibers. I. Lesions, tuning curves, two-tone inhibition, and responses to trapezoidal-wave patterns. *Journal of Neurophysiology, 43,* 1367–1389.

Schnapf, J. L., & Baylor, D. A. (1987). How photoreceptor cells respond to light. *Scientific American, 256,* 40–47.

Schneider, B. A., & Bissett, R. J. (1981). The dimensions of tonal experience: A nonmetric scaling approach. *Perception & Psychophysics, 30,* 39–48.

Schneider, B. A., & Parker, S. (1987). Can we measure sensory intensity? In M. Teghtsoonian & R. Teghtsoonian (Eds.), *Fechner day 87* (pp. 29–33). Durham, NH: International Society for Psychophysics.

Schneider, D. (1969). Insect olfaction: Deciphering system for chemical messages. *Science, 163,* 1031–1037.

Schneider, G. E. (1969). Two visual systems. *Science, 163,* 895–902.

Schneider, R., Costiloe, J., Howard, R., & Wolf, S. (1958). Olfactory perception thresholds in hypogonadal women: Changes accompanying administration of androgen and estrogen. *Journal of Clinical Endocrinology, 18,* 379–390.

Schneider, S. L., Hughes, B., Epstein, W., & Bach-y-Rita, P. (1986). The detection of length and orientation changes in dynamic vibrotactile patterns. *Perception & Psychophysics, 40,* 290–300.

Schneider, W., Dumais, S. T., & Shiffrin, R. M. (1984). Automatic and control processing and attention. In R. Parasuraman & D. R. Davies (Eds.), *Varieties of attention.* (pp. 1–27). Orlando, FL: Academic Press.

Schneider, W., & Shiffrin, R. M. (1977). Controlled and automatic human information processing. I. Detection, search and attention. *Psychological Review, 84,* 1–66.

Schouten, M. E. H. (1980). The case against a speech mode of perception. *Acta Psychologica, 44,* 71–98.

Schubert, E. D. (1978). History of research on hearing. In E. C. Carterette & M. P. Friedman (Eds.), *Handbook of perception: Vol. IV. Hearing* (pp. 41–80). New York: Academic Press.

Schull, J., Kaplan, H., & O'Brien, C. P. (1981). Naloxone can alter experimental pain and mood in humans. *Physiological Psychology, 9,* 245–250.

Schulman, P. H. (1979). Eye movements do not cause induced motion. *Perception & Psychophysics, 26,* 381–383.

Schwartz, C. B. (1961). *Visual discrimination of camouflaged figures.* Unpublished doctoral dissertation, University of California at Berkeley.

Schwartz, S. H., & Loop, M. S. (1984). Effect of duration on detection by the chromatic and achromatic systems. *Perception & Psychophysics, 36,* 65–67.

Scott, T. R. (1987). Coding in the gustatory system. In T. E. Finger & W. L. Silver (Eds.), *Neurobiology of taste and smell* (pp. 355–378). New York: Wiley.

Scott, T. R., & Erickson, R. P. (1971). Synaptic processing of taste-quality information in the thalamus of the rat. *Journal of Neurophysiology, 34,* 868–884.

Sedgwick, H. (1980). The geometry of spatial layout in pictorial representation. In M. Hagen (Ed.), *Perception of pictures: Vol. 1. Alberti's window: The projective model of pictorial information* (pp. 33–90). New York: Academic Press.

Segall, M. H., Campbell, D. T., & Herskovits, M. J. (1966). *The influence of culture on visual perception.* Indianapolis: Bobbs-Merrill.

Sekuler, R. (1975). Visual motion perception. In E. C. Carterette & M. P. Friedman (Eds.), *Handbook of perception: Vol. 5* (pp. 387–433). New York: Academic Press.

Sekuler, R., Ball, K., Tynan, P., & Machmer, J. (1982). Psychophysics of motion perception. In A. H. Wertheim, W. A. Wagenaar, & H. W. Leibowitz (Eds.), *Tutorials on motion perception* (pp. 81–100). New York: Plenum.

Sekuler, R., & Blake, R. (1985). *Perception.* New York: Knopf.

Sekuler, R., & Ganz, L. (1963). A new aftereffect of seen movement with a stabilized retinal image. *Science, 139,* 419–420.

Sekuler, R., & Hutman, L. P. (1980). Spatial vision and aging: I. Contrast sensitivity. *Journal of Gerontology, 35,* 692–699.

Selfridge, O. G. (1959). Pandemonium: A paradigm for learning. In D. V. Blake & A. M. Uttley (Eds.), *Proceedings of the symposium on the mechanization of thought processes* (pp. 511–529). London: HM Stationery Office.

Semple, M. N., & Kitzes, L. M. (1987). Binaural processing of sound pressure level in the inferior colliculus. *Journal of Neurophysiology, 57,* 1130–1147.

Senden, M. von. (1960). *Space and sight: The perception of* space and shape in congenitally blind patients before and after operation. London: Methuen.

Serpell, R. (1971). Discrimination of orientation by Zambian children. *Journal of Comparative Physiology, 75,* 312.

Shaffer, H. L. (1975). Multiple attention in continuous verbal tasks. In P. M. A. Rabbitt & S. Dornic (Eds.), *Attention and Performance V.* London: Academic Press.

Shaffer, L. H. (1985). Timing in action. In J. A. Michon & J. L. Jackson (Eds.), *Time, mind and behavior* (pp. 226–242). Berlin: Springer-Verlag.

Shallice, T., & Vickers, D. (1964). Theories and experiments on discrimination times. *Ergonomics, 7,* 37–49.

Shannon, C. E., & Weaver, W. (1949). *The mathematical theory of communication.* Urbana: University of Illinois Press.

Shapley, R., & Enroth-Cugell, C. (1984). Visual adaptation and retinal gain controls. *Progress in Retinal Research, 3,* 263–346.

Shapley, R., & Reid, R. C. (1985). Contrast and assimilation in the perception of brightness. *Proceedings of the National Academy of Sciences of the U.S.A., 82,* 5983–5986.

Sharma, S., & Moskowitz, H. (1972). Effect of marijuana on the visual autokinetic phenomenon. *Perceptual and Motor Skills, 35,* 891.

Shea, S. L., Fox, R., Aslin, R. N., & Dumais, S. T. (1980). Assessment of stereopsis in human infants. *Investigative Ophthalmology, 19,* 1400–1404.

Shebilske, W. (1977). Visuomotor coordination in visual direction and position constancies. In W. Epstein (Ed.), *Stability and constancy in visual perception: Mechanisms and processes* (pp. 23–70). New York: Wiley.

Shebilske, W. L. (1976). Extraretinal information in corrective saccades and inflow vs. outflow theories of visual direction constancy. *Vision Research, 16,* 621–628.

Sheedy, J. E., Bailey, I. L., Buri, M., & Bass, E. (1986). Binocular vs. monocular task performance. *American Journal of Optometry & Physiological Optics, 63,* 839–846.

Shepard, R. N. (1964). Circularity in judgments of relative pitch. *Journal of the Acoustical Society of America, 36,* 2346–2353.

Shepard, R. N. (1982). Geometrical approximations to the structure of musical pitch. *Psychological Review, 89,* 305–333.

Shepard, R. N., & Zare, S. L. (1983). Path-guided apparent motion. *Science, 220,* 632–634.

Sherman, S. (1973). Visual field defects in monocularly and binocularly deprived cats. *Brain Research, 49,* 25–45.

Sherman, S. M. (1985). Parallel W-, X- and Y-cell pathways in the cat: A model for visual function. In D. Rose & V. G. Dobson (Eds.), *Models of the visual cortex* (pp. 71–84). Chichester: Wiley.

Sherrington, C. S. (1906). *Integrative action of the nervous system.* New Haven, CT: Yale University Press.

Shiffrin, R. M., & Schneider, W. (1977). Controlled and automatic human information processing. II. Perceptual learning, automatic attending and a general theory. *Psychological Review, 84,* 127–190.

Shimojo, S., & Held, R. (1987). Vernier acuity is less than grating acuity in 2- and 3-month olds. *Vision Research, 27,* 77–86.

Shimojo, S., & Richards, W. (1986). "Seeing" shapes that are almost totally occluded: A new look at Park's camel. *Perception & Psychophysics, 39,* 418–426.

Shockey, L., & Reddy, R. (1974, August). Quantitative analysis of speech perception: Results from transcription of connected speech from unfamiliar languages. *Paper presented at the Speech Communications Seminar.* Stockholm.

Shower, E. G., & Biddulph, R. (1931). Differential pitch sensitivity of the ear. *Journal of the Acoustical Society of America, 3,* 275–287.

Shulman, G. L., Remington, R. W., & McLean, J. P. (1979). Moving attention through visual space. *Journal of Experimental Psychology: Human Perception and Performance, 5,* 522–526.

Shulman, G. L., Sheehy, J. B., & Wilson, J. (1986). Gradients of spatial attention. *Acta Psychologica, 61,* 167–181.

Shulman, G. L., Wilson, J., & Sheehy, J. B. (1985). Spatial determinants of the distribution of attention. *Perception & Psychophysics, 37,* 59–65.

Siddle, D. A., Morish, R. B., White, K. D., & Mangen, G. L. (1969). Relation of visual sensitivity to extraversion. *Journal of Experimental Research in Personality, 3,* 264–267.

Sidman, M., & Kirk, B. (1974). Letter reversals in naming, writing, and matching to sample. *Child Development, 45,* 616–625.

Silver, W. L. (1987). The common chemical sense. In T. E. Finger & W. L. Silver (Eds.), *Neurobiology of Taste and Smell* (pp. 65–87). New York: Wiley.

Simmons, F. B., Epley, J. M., Lummis, R. C., Guttman, N., Frishkopf, L. S., Harmon, L. D., & Zwicker, E. (1965). Auditory nerve: Electrical stimulation in man. *Science, 148,* 104–106.

Sinclair, D. C., & Stokes, B. A. R. (1964). The production and characteristics of "second pain." *Brain, 87,* 609–618.

Sinnot, J., & Rauth, J. (1937). Effect of smoking on taste thresholds. *Journal of General Psychology, 17,* 155–162.

Sivian, L. S., & White, S. D. (1933). On minimum audible sound fields. *Journal of the Acoustical Society of America, 4,* 288–321.

Skowbo, D. (1984). Are McCollough effects conditioned responses? *Psychological Bulletin, 96,* 215–226.

Sloboda, J. A. (1985). *The musical mind: The cognitive psychology of music.* Oxford: Oxford University Press.

Small, L. H., & Bond, Z. S. (1986). Distortions and deletions: Word-initial consonant specificity in fluent speech. *Perception & Psychophysics, 40,* 20–26.

Smith, A., & Over, R. (1979). Motor aftereffect with subjective contours. *Perception & Psychophysics, 25,* 95–98.

Smith, D. V. (1985). Brainstem processing of gustatory information. In D. W. Pfaff (Ed.), *Taste, olfaction, and the central nervous system* (pp. 151–177). New York: Rockefeller University Press.

Smith, J., Hausfeld, S., Power, R. P., & Gorta, A. (1982). Ambiguous musical figures and auditory streaming. *Perception & Psychophysics, 32,* 454–464.

Smith, W. S., Frazier, N. I., Ward, S., & Webb, F. (1983). Early adolescent girls' and boys' learning of a spatial visualization skill-replications. *Journal of Education, 67,* 239–243.

Snellen, H. (1862). *Probebuchstaben zur bestimmung der sehscharfe.* Utrecht: Weijer.

Snyder, S. H. (1977). Opiate receptors and internal opiates. *Scientific American, 236,* 44–56.

So, Y. T., & Shapley, R. (1981). Spatial tuning of cells in and around lateral geniculate nucleus of the cat: X and y cells and perigeniculate interneurons. *Journal of Neurophysiology, 45,* 107–120.

Sokolov, E. N. (1975). The neuronal mechanisms of the orienting reflex. In E. N. Sokolov & O. S. Vinogradova (Eds.), *Neuronal mechanisms of the orienting reflex* (pp. 217–238). New York: Wiley.

Southwick, E., & Schiffman, S. S. (1980). Odor quality of pyridyl ketones. *Chemical Senses, 5,* 343–357.

Sperling, H. G. (1986). Spectral sensitivity, intense spectral light studies and the color receptor mosaic of primates. *Vision Research, 26,* 1557–1571.

Sperry, R. W. (1943). Effect of 180 degree rotation of the retinal field on visuomotor coordination. *Journal of Experimental Zoology, 92,* 263–277.

Spoendlin, H. H. (1978). The afferent innervation of the cochlea. In R. F. Naunton & C. Fernandey (Eds.), *Evoked electrical activity in the auditory nervous system* (pp. 21–42). New York: Academic Press.

Sprafkin, C., Serbin, L. A., Denier, C., & Conner, J. M. (1983). Sex-differentiated play: Cognitive consequences and early interventions. In M. B. Liss (Ed.), *Social and cognitive skills* (pp. 167–192). New York: Academic Press.

Spreen, O. (1976). Neuropsychology of learning disorders: Post conference review. In R. M. Knights & D. J. Bakker (Eds.), *The neuropsychology of learning disorders* (pp. 445–467). Baltimore: University Park Press.

Springer, S. P., & Deutsch, G. (1985). *Left brain, right brain* (rev. ed.). San Francisco: Freeman.

Srulovicz, P., & Goldstein, J. L. (1983). A central spectrum model: A synthesis of auditory-nerve timing and place cues in monaural communication of frequency spectrum. *Journal of the Acoustical Society of America, 73,* 1266–1276.

Stark, L., & Bridgeman, B. (1983). Role of corollary discharge in space constancy. *Perception & Psychophysics, 34,* 371–380.

Stark, L., & Ellis, S. (1981). Scanpaths revisited: Cognitive models direct active looking. In D. Fisher, R. Monty, & I. Senders (Eds.), *Eye movements: Cognition and visual perception* (pp. 193–226). Hillsdale, NJ: Lawrence Erlbaum.

Stebbins, W. C. (1980). The evolution of hearing in the mammals. In A. N. Popper & R. R. Fay (Eds.), *Comparative studies of hearing in vertebrates* (pp. 421–436). New York: Springer-Verlag.

Steinberg, A. (1955). Changes in time perception induced by an anaesthetic drug. *British Journal of Psychology, 46,* 273–279.

Steinfield, G. J. (1967). Concepts of set and availability and their relation to the reorganization of ambiguous pictorial stimuli. *Psychological Review, 74,* 505–525.

Stelmack, R. M., Achorn, E., & Michaud, A. (1977). Extravision and individual differences in auditory evoked response. *Psychophysiology, 14,* 368–374.

Stelmack, R. M., & Campbell, K. B. (1974). Extraversion and auditory sensitivity to high and low frequency. *Perceptual and Motor Skills, 38,* 875–879.

Stephan, F. K., & Nunez, A. A. (1977). Elimination of circadian rhythms in drinking activity, sleep, and temperature by isolation of suprachiasmatic nuclei. *Behavioral Biology, 20,* 1–16.

Stephens, P. R., & Young, J. Z. (1982). The stacocyst of the squid Loligo. *Journal of Zoology, (London), 197,* 241–266.

Stern, J. A., Oster, P. J., & Newport, K. (1980). Reaction time measures, hemispheric specialization, and age. In L. Poon (Ed.), *Aging in the 1980's* (pp. 309–326). Washington, D.C.: American Psychological Association.

Sternbach, R. A. (1963). Congenital insensitivity to pain: A review. *Psychological Bulletin, 60,* 252–264.

Sternbach, R. A., & Tursky, B. (1964). On the psychophysical power function in electric shock. *Psychonomic Science, 1,* 247–248.

Sternberg, S. (1975). Memory scanning: New findings and current controversies. *Quarterly Journal of Experimental Psychology, 27,* 1–32.

Stevens, D. A., & Lawless, H. T. (1986). Putting out the fire: Effects of tastants on oral chemical irritation. *Perception & Psychophysics, 39,* 346–350.

Stevens, J. C. (1979). Variation of cold sensitivity over the body surface. *Sensory Processes, 3,* 317–326.

Stevens, J. C., & Cain, W. S. (1986). Smelling via the mouth: Effects of aging. *Perception & Psychophysics, 40,* 142–146.

Stevens, J. C., & Marks, L. E. (1980). Cross-modality matching functions generated by magnitude estimation. *Perception & Psychophysics, 27,* 379–389.

Stevens, J. C., & Stevens, S. S. (1960). Warmth and cold: Dynamics of sensory intensity. *Journal of Experimental Psychology, 60,* 183–192.

Stevens, K. N., & House, A. S. (1972). Speech perception. In J. V. Tobias (Ed.), *Foundations of modern auditory theory* (Vol. 2, pp. 3–62). New York: Academic Press.

Stevens, S. S. (1935). The relation of pitch to intensity. *Journal of the Acoustical Society of America, 6,* 150–154.

Stevens, S. S. (1946). On the theory of scales of measurement. *Science, 103,* 677–680.

Stevens, S. S. (1956). The direct estimation of sensory magnitudes—loudness. *American Journal of Psychology, 69,* 1–25.

Stevens, S. S. (1959). Tactile vibration: Dynamics of sensory intensity. *Journal of Experimental Psychology, 57,* 210–218.

Stevens, S. S. (1961). The psychophysics of sensory function. In W. A. Rosenblith (Ed.), *Sensory communication* (pp. 1–33). Cambridge, MA: MIT Press.

Stevens, S. S. (1975). *Psychophysics: Introduction to its perceptual, neural, and social prospects.* New York: Wiley.

Stevens, S. S., & Galanter, E. (1957). Ratio scales and category scales for a dozen perceptual continua. *Journal of Experimental Psychology, 54,* 377–411.

Stevens, S. S., & Newman, E. B. (1934). The localization of

pure tones. *Proceedings of the National Academy of Sciences of the U.S.A., 20,* 593–596.

Stevens, S. S., Volkman, J., & Newman, E. B. (1937). A scale for the measurement of the psychological magnitude of pitch. *Journal of the Acoustical Society of America, 8,* 185–190.

Stevens, S. S., & Warshovsky, F. (1965). *Sound and hearing.* New York: Time-Life Books.

Stoffregen, T. A. (1985). Flow structure versus retinal location in the optical control of stance. *Journal of Experimental Psychology: Human Perception and Performance, 11,* 554–565.

Stone, L. S. (1960). Polarization of the retina and development of vision. *Journal of Experimental Zoology, 145,* 85–93.

Strange, W., & Jenkins, J. (1978). Role of linguistic experience in the perception of speech. In R. Walk & H. Pick (Eds.), *Perception and experience* (pp. 125–169). New York: Plenum.

Stratton, G. M. (1896). Some preliminary experiments on vision without inversion of the retinal image. *Psychological Review, 3,* 611–617.

Stratton, G. M. (1897a). Upright vision and the retinal image. *Psychological Review, 4,* 182–187.

Stratton, G. M. (1897b). Vision without inversion of the retinal image. *Psychological Review, 4,* 341–360.

Street, R. F. (1931). A gestalt completion test: A study of a cross section of intellect. New York: Bureau of Publication, Columbia University.

Streitfeld, B., & Wilson, M. (1986). The ABCs of categorical perception. *Cognitive Psychology, 18,* 432–451.

Stromeyer, C. F., III. (1978). Form-color aftereffects in human vision. In R. Held, H. Leibowitz, & H. L. Teuber (Eds.), *Handbook of sensory physiology* (Vol. 8, pp. 97–142). New York: Springer-Verlag.

Stroop, J. (1935). Studies of interference in serial verbal reactions. *Journal of Experimental Psychology, 18,* 624–643.

Stroud, J. M. (1955). The fine structure of psychological time. In H. Quastler (Ed.), *Information theory in psychology: Problems and methods* (pp. 174–207). Glencoe, IL: Free Press.

Stryer, L. (1987). The molecules of visual excitation. *Scientific American, 257,* 42–50.

Suedfeld, P. (1980). *Restricted environmental stimulation: Research and clinical applications.* New York: Wiley.

Supra, M., Cotzin, M. E., & Dallenbach, K. M. (1944). "Facial vision:" The perception of obstacles by the blind. *American Journal of Psychology, 57,* 133–183.

Svaetichin, G. (1956). Spectral response curves of single cones. *Acta Physiologica Scandinavica, 1,* 93–101.

Svaetichin, G., & MacNichol, E. F., Jr. (1958). Retinal mechanisms for achromatic vision. *Annals of the New York Academy of Sciences, 74,* 385–404.

Swarbrick, L., & Whitfield, I. C. (1972). Auditory cortical units selectively responsive to stimulus "shape." *Journal of Physiology (London), 224,* 68–69.

Swensson, R. G. (1980). A two-stage detection model applied to skilled visual search by radiologists. *Perception & Psychophysics, 27,* 11–16.

Swets, J. A. (1963). Central factors in auditory frequency selectivity. *Psychological Bulletin, 60,* 429–441.

Szentagothai, J. (1950). The elementary vestibulo-ocular reflex arc. *Journal of Neurophysiology, 13,* 395–407.

Tart, C. (1971). *On being stoned.* Palo Alto: Science & Behavior Books.

Taub, E., & Berman, A. J. (1968). Movement and learning in the absence of sensory feedback. In S. J. Freedman (Ed.), *The neuropsychology of spatially oriented behavior* (pp. 173–192). Homewood, IL: Dorsey.

Tedford, W. H., Warren, D. E., & Flynn, W. E. (1977). Alternation of shock aversion thresholds during menstrual cycle. *Perception & Psychophysics, 21(2),* 193–196.

Tees, R. C. (1974). Effect of visual deprivation on development of depth perception in the rat. *Journal of Comparative and Physiological Psychology, 86,* 300–308.

Tees, R. C., & Midgley, G. (1978). Extent of recovery of function after early sensory deprivation in the rat. *Journal of Comparative and Physiological Psychology, 92,* 768–777.

Tees, R. C., & Werker, J. F. (1984). Perceptual flexibility: Maintenance or recovery of the ability to discriminate nonnative speech sounds. *Canadian Journal of Psychology, 38,* 579–590.

Teeter, J. H., & Brand, J. G. (1987). Peripheral mechanisms of gustation: Physiology and biochemistry. In T. E. Finger & W. L. Silver (Eds.), *Neurobiology of taste and smell* (pp. 299–330). New York: Wiley.

Teghtsoonian, M. (1987). The structure of an experiment. In M. Teghtsoonian & R. Teghtsoonian (Eds.), *Fechner Day '87* (pp. 49–52). Northampton, MA: International Society for Psychophysics.

Teghtsoonian, R. (1971). On the exponents in Stevens' Law and the constant in Ekman's Law. *Psychological Review, 78,* 71–80.

Teghtsoonian, R. (1975). Review of psychophysics by S. S. Stevens. *American Journal of Psychology, 88,* 677–684.

Teghtsoonian, R., Teghtsoonian, M., Berglund, B., & Berglund, U. (1978). Invariance of odor strength with sniff vigor: An olfactory analogue to size constancy. *Journal of Experimental Psychology: Human Perception and Performance, 4,* 144–152.

Teller, D. Y. (1981). Color vision in infants. In R. Aslin, J. Alberts, & M. Petersen (Eds.), *Development of Perception, Physiological Perspectives: Vol. 2* (pp. 298–312). New York: Academic Press.

Teller, D. Y., & Bornstein, M. H. (1987). Infant color vision and color perception. In P. Salapatek & L. Cohen (Eds.), *Handbook of infant perception: Vol. 1. From sensation to perception* (pp. 185–237). Orlando, FL: Academic Press.

Teller, D. Y., & Movshon, J. A. (1986). Visual development. *Vision Research, 26,* 1483–1506.

Terenius, L., & Wahlstrom, A. (1975). Morphine-like ligand for opiate receptors in human CSF. *Life Sciences, 16,* 1759–1764.

Terheardt, E. (1974). Pitch, consonance and harmony. *Journal of the Acoustical Society of America, 55,* 1061–1069.

Thomas, E. A. C., & Weaver, W. B. (1975). Cognitive

processing and time perception. *Perception & Psychophysics, 17,* 363–367.

Thomas, H. (1983). Parameter estimation in simple psychophysical models. *Psychological Bulletin, 93,* 396–403.

Thomas, H., Jamison, W., & Hammel, D. D. (1973). Observation is insufficient for discovering that the surface of still water is invariently horizontal. *Science, 181,* 173–174.

Thornbury, J. M., & Mistretta, C. M. (1981). Tactile sensitivity as a function of age. *Journal of Gerontology, 36,* 34–39.

Timney, B. (1985). Visual experience and the development of depth perception. In D. J. Ingle, M. Jeannerod, & D. N. Lee (Eds.), *Brain mechanisms and spatial vision* (pp. 147–174). Dordrecht: Martinus Nijhoff.

Timney, B., Mitchel, D. E., & Griffin, F. (1978). The development of vision in cats after extended periods of dark rearing. *Experimental Brain Research, 31,* 547–560.

Timney, B., & Muir, D. W. (1976). Orientation anisotropy: Incidence and magnitude in Caucasian & Chinese subjects. *Science, 193,* 699–700.

Toch, H. H., & Schulte, R. (1961). Readiness to perceive violence as a result of police training. *British Journal of Psychology, 52,* 389–393.

Todd, J. T. (1983). Perception of gait. *Journal of Experimental Psychology: Human Perception and Performance, 9,* 31–42.

Todd, J. T., & Akerstrom, R. A. (1987). Perception of three-dimensional form from patterns of optical texture. *Journal of Experimental Psychology: Human Perception and Performance, 13,* 242–255.

Tomita, T. (1986). Retrospective review of retinal circuitry. *Vision Research, 26,* 1339–1350.

Torebjork, H. E., & Hallin, R. G. (1973). Perceptual changes accompanying controlled, preferential blocking of A and C fibre responses in intact human skin nerves. *Experimental Brain Research, 16,* 321–332.

Torebjork, H. E., Ochoa, J. L., & Schady, W. J. L. (1983). Role of single mechanoreceptor units in tactile sensation. In C. von Euler, O. Franzen, U. Lindblom, & D. Ottoson (Eds.), *Somatosensory mechanisms* (pp. 173–184). New York: Plenum.

Torgerson, W. S. (1961). Distances and ratios in psychophysical scaling. *Acta Psychologica, 19,* 201–205.

Townshend, B., Cotter, N., Van Compernolle, D., & White, R. L. (1987). Pitch perception of cochlear implant subjects. *Journal of the Acoustical Society of America, 82,* 106–115.

Townsend, J., & Ashby, F. G. (1982). Experimental test of contemporary mathematical models of visual letter recognition. *Journal of Experimental Psychology: Human Perception and Performance, 8,* 834–864.

Trehub, S. (1976). The discrimination of foreign speech contrasts by infants and adults. *Child Development, 47,* 466–472.

Trehub, S. E., & Schneider, B. A. (1987). Problems and promises of developmental psychophysics: Throw out the bath water but keep the baby. In M. Teghtsoonian & R. Teghtsoonian (Eds.), *Fechner Day '87* (pp. 43–47). Northampton, MA: International Society of Psychophysics.

Trehub, S. E., Schneider, B. A., & Endman, M. (1980). Developmental changes in infants' sensitivity to octave-band noises. *Journal of Experimental Child Psychology, 29,* 282–293.

Treisman, A. M. (1982). Perceptual groupings and attention in visual search for features and for objects. *Journal of Experimental Psychology: Human Perception and Performance, 8,* 194–214.

Treisman, A. M. (1986a). Features and objects in visual processing. *Scientific American, 255,* 114B–125.

Treisman, A. M. (1986b). Properties, parts, and objects. In K. R. Boff, L. Kaufman, & J. P. Thomas (Eds.), *Handbook of perception and human performance* (pp. 35–1 to 35–70). New York: Wiley.

Treisman, A. M., & Davies, A. (1972). Divided attention to ear and eye. In S. Kornblum (Ed.), *Attention and performance IV* (pp. 101–118). New York: Academic Press.

Treisman, A. M., & Gelade, G. (1980). A feature-integration theory of attention. *Cognitive Psychology, 12,* 97–136.

Treisman, A. M., & Gormican, S. (1988). Feature analysis in early vision: Evidence from search asymmetries. *Psychological Review, 95,* 15–48.

Treisman, A. M. & Schmidt, H. (1982). Illusory conjunctions in the perception of objects. *Cognitive Psychology, 14,* 107–141.

Treisman, M. (1963). Temporal discrimination and the indifference interval: Implications for the model of an internal clock. *Psychological Monographs, 77,* 1–31 (Whole No. 576).

Treisman, M. (1976). On the use and misuse of psychophysical terms. *Psychological Review, 83,* 246–256.

Treisman, M., & Watts, T. R. (1966). Relation between signal detectability theory and the traditional procedures for measuring sensory thresholds: Estimating d' from results given by the method of constant stimuli. *Psychological Bulletin, 66,* 438–454.

Treisman, M., & Williams, T. C. (1984). A theory of criterion setting with an application to sequential dependencies. *Psychological Review, 91,* 68–111.

Tress, K. H., & Kugler, B. T. (1979). Interocular transfer of movement aftereffects in schizophrenia. *British Journal of Psychology, 70,* 389–392.

Troland, L. T. (1921). The enigma of color vision. *American Journal of Physiological Optics, 2,* 23–48.

Tronick, E. (1972). Stimulus control and the growth of the infant's effective visual field. *Perception & Psychophysics, 11,* 373–376.

Tsal, Y. (1983). Movements of attention across the visual field. *Journal of Experimental Psychology: Human Perception and Performance, 9,* 523–530.

Tsvetkova, L. S. (1972). *Rehabilitative training in local brain lesions.* Moscow: Pedagogika Publishing House.

Turnbull, C. (1961). Some observations regarding the experiences and behavior of the Bambuti pygmies. *American Journal of Psychology, 74,* 304–308.

Turner, P. (1968). Amphetamines and smell threshold in man. In A. Herxheimer (Ed.), *Drugs and sensory functions* (pp. 91–100). Boston: Little, Brown.

Uhlarik, J., & Johnson, R. (1978). Development of form perception in repeated brief exposures to visual stimuli. In R. Walk & L. Pick, Jr., (Eds.), *Perception and Experience*. New York: Plenum.

Ullman, S. (1986). Visual routines: Where bottom-up and top-down processing meet. In E. C. Schwab & H. C. Nusbaum (Eds.), *Pattern recognition by humans and machines: Vol. 2. Visual perception* (pp. 159–218). Orlando, FL: Academic Press.

Umezaki, H. & Morrell, F. (1970). Developmental study of photic evoked responses in premature infants. *Electroencephalography and Clinical Neurophysiology, 28*, 55–63.

Ungerleider, L. G., & Mishkin, M. (1982). Two cortical visual systems. In D. J. Ingle, M. A. Goodale, & R. J. W. Mansfield (Eds.), *Analysis of visual behavior* (pp. 549–586). Cambridge, MA: MIT Press.

Uttal, W. (1981). *A taxonomy of visual processes*. Hillsdale, NJ: Lawrence Erlbaum.

Vallbo, A. (1981). Sensations evoked from the glabrous skin of the human hand by electrical stimulation of unitary mechano-sensitive afferents. *British Research, 215*, 359–363.

Vallbo, A. (1983). Tactile sensation related to activity in primary afferents with special reference to detection problems. In C. von Euler, O. Franzen, U. Lindblom, & D. Ottoson (Eds.), *Somatosensory mechanisms* (pp. 163–172). New York: Plenum.

van der Heijden, A. H. C., Wolters, G., Groep, J. C., & Hagenaar, R. (1987). Single-letter recognition accuracy benefits from advance cuing of location. *Perception & Psychophysics, 42*, 503–509.

Varner, D., Cook, J. E., Schneck, M. E., McDonald, M., & Teller, D. (1985). Tritan discriminations by 1- and 2-month-old human infants. *Vision Research, 6*, 821–831.

Vautin, R. G., & Berkley, M. A. (1977). Responses of single cells in cat visual cortex to stimulus movement: Neural correlates of visual after-effects. *Journal of Neurophysiology, 40*, 1051–1065.

Verriest, G. (1974). Recent advances in the study of the acquired deficiencies of color vision. *Fondazione "Gorgio Ranchi," 24*, 1–80.

Verrillo, R. T. (1975). Cutaneous sensation. In B. Scharf (Ed.), *Experimental sensory psychology* (pp. 150–184). Glenview, IL: Scott, Foresman.

Verrillo, R. T., & Bolanowski, S. J., Jr. (1986). The effects of skin temperature on the psychophysical responses to vibration on glabrous and hairy skin. *Journal of the Acoustical Society of America, 80*, 528–532.

Verrillo, T. R., Fraioli, A. J., & Smith, R. L. (1969). Sensation magnitude of vibrotactile stimuli. *Perception & Psychophysics, 6*, 366–372.

Vierck, C. (1978). Somatosensory system. In R. B. Masterston (Ed.), *Handbook of sensory neurobiology: Vol. 1. Sensory integration* (pp. 249–310). New York: Plenum.

Vimal, R. L. P., Pokorny, J., & Smith, V. C. (1987). Appearance of steadily viewed lights. *Vision Research, 27*, 1309–1318.

Vogels, R., & Orban, G. A. (1986). Decision factors affecting line orientation judgments in the method of single stimuli. *Perception & Psychophysics, 40*, 74–84.

Volkmann, F. C., Riggs, L. A., Aimee, G., & Moore, R. K. (1982). Measurements of visual suppression during opening, closing and blinking of the eyes. *Vision Research, 22*, 991–996.

Vurpillot, E. (1968). The development of scanning strategies and their relation to visual differentiation. *Journal of Experimental Child Psychology, 6*, 632–650.

Waber, D. P. (1976). Sex differences in cognition: A function of maturation rate? *Science, 192*, 572–574.

Waber, D. P. (1977). Sex differences in mental abilities, hemispheric lateralization and rate of physical growth at adolescence. *Developmental Psychology, 13*, 29–38.

Wade, N. J. (1984). *Brewster & Wheatstone on vision*. New York: Academic Press.

Waespe, W., & Henn, V. (1977). Neuronal activity in the vestibular nuclei of the alert monkey during vestibular and optokinetic stimulation. *Experimental Brain Research, 27*, 523–538.

Wahl, O. F., & Sieg, D. (1980). Time estimation among schizophrenics. *Perceptual and Motor Skills, 50*, 535–541.

Wald, G. (1968). The molecular basis of visual excitation. *Nature (London), 219*, 800–807.

Walk, R. D., & Gibson, E. J. (1961). A comparative and analytic study of visual depth perception. *Psychological Monographs, 75*, 1–44.

Wall, P. D. (1979). On the relation of injury to pain. *Pain, 6*, 253–264.

Wallace, B., & Priebe, F. A. (1985). Hypnotic susceptibility, interference and alternation frequency to the Necker cube illusion. *Journal of General Psychology, 112*, 271–277.

Wallace, P. (1977). Individual discrimination of humans by odor. *Physiology and Behavior, 19*, 577–579.

Wallach, H. (1939). On sound localization. *Journal of the Acoustical Society of America, 10*, 270–274.

Wallach, H. (1948). Brightness constancy and the nature of achromatic colors. *Journal of Experimental Psychology, 38*, 310–324.

Wallach, H. (1972). The perception of neutral colors. In R. Held & W. Richards (Eds.), *Perception: Mechanisms and models: Readings from Scientific American* (pp. 278–285). San Francisco: Freeman. (Original work published in Scientific American, 1963)

Wallach, H. (1987). Perceiving a stable environment when one moves. *Annual Review of Psychology, 38*, 1–27.

Wallach, H., & Becklen, R. (1983). An effect of speed on induced motion. *Perception & Psychophysics, 34*, 237–242.

Wallach, H., Becklen, R., & Nitzberg, D. (1985). Vector analysis and process combination in motion perception. *Journal of Experimental Psychology: Human Perception and Performance, 11*, 93–102.

Wallach, H., Newman, E. B., & Rosenzweig, M. R. (1949). The precedence effect in sound localization. *American Journal of Psychology, 62*, 315–336.

Walley, A., Pisoni, D., & Aslin, R. (1981). The role of early experience in the development of speech perception. In R. Aslin, J. Alberts, & M. Petersen (Eds.), *Development of perception: Psychobiological perspectives: Vol. 1. Audition, somatic perceptions, and the chemical senses* (pp. 219–256). New York: Academic Press.

Walls, G. L. (1951). A theory of ocular dominance. *AMA Archives of Ophthalmology, 45,* 387–412.

Ward, L. M. (1971). *Some psychophysical properties of category judgments and magnitude estimations.* Unpublished doctoral dissertation, Duke University, N.C.

Ward, L. M. (1972). Category judgments of loudness in the absence of an experimenter-induced identification function: Sequential effects and power function fit. *Journal of Experimental Psychology, 94,* 179–184.

Ward, L. M. (1973). Repeated magnitude estimations with a variable standard: Sequential effects and other properties. *Perception & Psychophysics, 13,* 193–200.

Ward, L. M. (1974). Power functions for category judgments of duration and line length. *Perceptual and Motor Skills, 38,* 1182.

Ward, L. M. (1975). Sequential dependencies and response range in cross-modality matches of duration to loudness. *Perception & Psychophysics, 18,* 217–223.

Ward, L. M. (1979). Stimulus information and sequential dependencies in magnitude estimation and cross-modality matching. *Journal of Experimental Psychology: Human Perception and Performance, 5,* 444–459.

Ward, L. M. (1982a). Mixed-modality psychophysical scaling: Sequential dependencies and other properties. *Perception & Psychophysics, 31,* 53–62.

Ward, L. M. (1982b). Determinants of attention to local and global features of visual forms. *Journal of Experimental Psychology: Human Perception and Performance, 8,* 562–581.

Ward, L. M. (1983). On processing dominance: Comment on Pomerantz. *Journal of Experimental Psychology: General, 112,* 541–546.

Ward, L. M. (1985). Covert focussing of the attentional gaze. *Canadian Journal of Psychology, 39,* 546–563.

Ward, L. M. (1986). Mixed-modality psychophysical scaling: Double cross-modality matching for "difficult" continua. *Perception & Psychophysics, 39,* 407–417.

Ward, L. M. (1987). Remembrance of sounds past: Memory and psychophysical scaling. *Journal of Experimental Psychology: Human Perception and Performance, 13,* 216–227.

Ward, L. M., & Lockhead, G. R. (1970). Sequential effects and memory in category judgments. *Journal of Experimental Psychology, 854,* 27–34.

Ward, L. M., Porac, P., Coren, S., & Girgus, J. S. (1977). The case for misapplied constancy scaling: Depth associations elicited by illusion configurations. *American Journal of Psychology, 90,* 609–620.

Ward, T. B. (1985). Individual differences in processing stimulus dimensions: Relation to selective processing ability. *Perception & Psychophysics, 37,* 471–482.

Ward, W. D. (1970). Musical perception. In J. V. Tobias (Ed.), *Foundations of modern auditory theory: Vol. 1.* (pp. 407–447). New York: Academic Press.

Ware, C. (1981). Subjective contours independent of subjective brighteners. *Perception & Psychophysics, 29,* 500–504.

Ware, C., & Cowan, W. B. (1987). Chromatic Mach bands: Behavioral evidence for lateral inhibition in human color vision. *Perception & Psychophysics, 41,* 173–178.

Warm, J. S., & McCray, R. E. (1969). Influence of word frequency and length on the apparent duration of tachistoscopic presentations. *Journal of Experimental Psychology, 79,* 56–58.

Warren, D. H. (1984). *Blindness and early childhood development.* New York: American Foundation for the Blind.

Warren, R. M. (1970). Perceptual restoration of missing speech sounds. *Science, 167,* 392–393.

Warren, R. M., Obusek, C. J., Farmer, R. M., & Warren, R. P. (1969). Auditory sequence: Confusion of patterns other than speech or music. *Science, 164,* 586–587.

Watanabe, T., & Katsuki, Y. (1974). Response patterns of single auditory neurons of the cat to species-specific vocalization. *Japanese Journal of Physiology, 24,* 135–155.

Watkins, L. R., & Mayer, D. J. (1982). Organization of endogenous opiate and nonopiate pain control systems. *Science, 216,* 1185–1192.

Weale, R. A. (1979). Discoverers of Mach-bands. *Investigative Ophthalmology and Visual Sciences, 18,* 652–654.

Weale, R. A. (1982). *Focus on vision.* Cambridge, MA: Harvard University Press.

Weale, R. A. (1986). Aging and vision. *Vision Research, 26,* 1507–1512.

Weber, E. H. (1834). *De pulen, resorptione, auditu et tactu: Annotationes anatomicae et physiologicae.* Leipzig: Koehler.

Webster, W. R., & Atkin, L. M. (1975). Central auditory processing. In M. S. Gazzaniga & C. Blakemore (Eds.), *Handbook of sensory psychobiology* (pp. 325–364). New York: Academic Press.

Wegener, B. (Ed.). (1982). *Social attitudes and psychophysical measurement.* Hillsdale, NJ: Lawrence Erlbaum.

Weil, A. T., Zinberg, E., & Nelson, J. N. (1968). Clinical and psychological effects of marijuana in man. *Science, 162,* 1234–1242.

Weinstein, E. A., Cole, M., Mitchell, M. S., & Lyerly, O. G. (1964). Anosognosia and aphasia. *Archives of Neurology, 10,* 376–386.

Weinstein, S. (1968). Intensive and extensive aspects of tactile sensitivity as a function of body part, sex, and laterality. In D. R. Kenshalo (Ed.), *The skin senses* (pp. 195–218). Springfield, IL: Thomas.

Weinstein, S., & Sersen, E. A. (1961). Tactual sensitivity as a function of handedness and laterality. *Journal of Comparative & Physiological Psychology, 54,* 665–669.

Weisenberg, M. (1984). Cognitive aspects of pain. In P. D. Wall & R. Melzack (Eds.), *Textbook of pain* (pp. 162–172). Edinburgh: Churchill Livingstone.

Weisstein, N. (1968). Rashevsky-Landahl neural net: Simulation of metacontrast. *Psychological Review, 75,* 494–521.

Weisstein, N. (1980). Tutorial: The joy of Fourier analysis. In

C. S. Harris (Ed.), *Visual coding and adaptability* (pp. 365–380). Hillsdale, NJ: Lawrence Erlbaum.

Weisstein, N., Harris, C., Berbaum, K., Tangney, J., & Williams, A. (1977). Contrast reduction by small localized stimuli: Extensive spatial spread of above-threshold orientation-selective masking. *Vision Research, 17,* 341–350.

Weisstein, N., Matthews, M., & Berbaum, K. (1974, November). *Illusory contours can mask real contours.* Paper presented at the meetings of the Psychonomic Society, Boston.

Weisstein, N., Ozog, G., & Szoc, R. (1975). A comparison and elaboration of two models of metacontrast. *Psychological Review, 82,* 325–343.

Weisstein, N., & Wong, E. (1986). Figure-ground organization and the spatial and temporal responses of the visual system. In E. C. Schwab & H. C. Nusbaum (Eds.), *Pattern recognition by humans and machines: Vol. 2. Visual perception* (pp. 31–64). Orlando, FL: Academic Press.

Welch, R. B. (1969). Adaptation to prism-displaced vision: The importance of target pointing. *Perception & Psychophysics, 5,* 305–309.

Welch, R. B. (1971). Prism adaptation: The "target pointing effect" as a function of exposure trials. *Perception & Psychophysics, 5,* 102–104.

Welch, R. B. (1978). *Perceptual modification: Adapting to altered sensory environments.* New York: Academic Press.

Welford, A. T. (1980). *Reaction times.* London: Academic Press.

Well, A. D., Lorch, E. P., & Anderson, D. R. (1980). Developmental trends in distractability: Is absolute or proportional decrement the appropriate measure of interference? *Journal of Experimental Child Psychology, 30,* 109–124.

Wells, G. L., & Loftus, E. (1984). *Eyewitness testimony: Psychological perspectives.* Cambridge: Cambridge University Press.

Werker, J., Gilbert, J., Humphrey, K., & Tees, R. (1981). Developmental aspects of cross-language speech perception. *Child Development, 52,* 349–355.

Werker, J. F., & Logan, J. S. (1985). Cross-language evidence for three factors in speech perception. *Perception & Psychophysics, 37,* 35–44.

Werker, J. F., & Tees, R. C. (1984). Cross-language speech perception: Evidence for perceptual reorganization during the first year of life. *Infant Behavior and Development, 7,* 49–63.

Werner, H. (1935). Studies on contour. *American Journal of Psychology, 47,* 40–64.

Werner, J. S. (1979). Developmental change in scotopic sensitivity and the absorption spectrum of the human ocular media. Unpublished doctoral dissertation, Brown University, RI.

Werner, J. S., & Wooten, B. R. (1979). Human infant color vision and color perception. *Infant Behavior and Development, 2,* 241–274.

Wertheimer, M. (1912). Experimentelle Studien uber das Sehen von Bewegung. *Zeitschrift fur Psychologie, 61,* 161–265.

Wertheimer, M. (1923). Principles of perceptual organization. Abridged translation by M. Wertheimer. In D. S. Beardslee & M. Wertheimer (Eds.), *Readings in perception* (p. 115–137). Princeton, NJ: Van Nostrand-Reinhold. (Original work published 1923, *Psychologische Forschung, 41,* 301–350)

Wertheimer, M. (1961). Psychomotor coordination of auditory and visual space at birth. *Science, 134,* 1692.

Westheimer, G. (1979). Spatial sense of the eye. *Investigative Ophthalmology and Visual Science, 18,* 893–912.

Wever, E. G. (1970). *Theory of hearing.* New York: Wiley.

Wever, R. A. (1979). *The circadian system of man.* New York: Springer-Verlag.

Whalen, D. H., & Liberman, A. M. (1987). Speech perception takes precedence over nonspeech perception. *Science, 237,* 169–171.

White, B. L. (1971). *Human infants.* Englewood Cliffs, NJ: Prentice-Hall.

White, B. W., Saunders, F. A., Scadden, L., Bach-y-Rita, P., & Collins, C. C. (1970). Seeing with the skin. *Perception & Psychophysics, 7,* 23–27.

White, C. (1963). Temporal numerosity and the psychological unit of duration. *Psychological Monographs, 77,* 1–37. (Whole No. 575)

White, C. W., Lockhead, G. R., & Evans, N. J. (1977). Multidimensional scaling of subjective color-blind observers. *Perception & Psychophysics, 21,* 522–526.

White, C. W., & Montgomery, D. A. (1976). Memory colours in afterimages: A bicentennial demonstration. *Perception & Psychophysics, 19,* 371–374.

White, K. D., & Odom, J. V. (1985). Temporal integration in global stereopsis. *Perception & Psychophysics, 37,* 139–144.

Whitfield, I. C. (1967). *The auditory pathway.* London: Arnold.

Whitfield, I. C. (1978). The neural code. In E. C. Carterette & M. P. Friedman (Eds.), *Handbook of perception: Vol. 4. Hearing* (pp. 163–183). New York: Academic Press.

Whitfield, I. C. (1980). Auditory cortex and the pitch of complex tones. *Journal of the Acoustical Society of America, 67,* 644–647.

Whitfield, I. C., & Evans, E. F. (1965). Responses of auditory cortical neurons to stimuli of changing frequency. *Journal of Neurophysiology, 28,* 655–672.

Whitsel, B. L., Dreyer, D. A., Hollins, M., & Young, M. G. (1979). The coding of direction of tactile stimulus movement: Correlative psychophysical and electrophysiological data. In D. R. Kenshalo (Ed.), *Sensory functions of the skin of humans* (pp. 79–108). New York: Plenum.

Whorf, B. L. (1956). Science and linguistics. In J. B. Carroll (Ed.), *Language, thought and reality: Selected writings of Benjamin Lee Whorf* (pp. 207–219). Cambridge, MA: MIT Press.

Whytt, R. (1751). *An essay on the vital and other involuntary motions of animals.* Edinburgh: Balfour & Neill.

Wickens, C. D. (1984). Processing resources in attention. In R. Parasuraman & D. R. Davies (Eds.), *Varieties of attention.* (pp. 63–101). Orlando, FL: Academic Press.

Wiener, N. (1961). *Cybernetics* (2nd ed.). Cambridge, MA: MIT Press.

Wier, C. C., Jestead: W., & Green, D. M. (1977). Frequency discrimination as a function of frequency and sensation level. *Journal of the Acoustical Society of America, 61,* 178–184.

Willer, J. C., Dehen, H., & Cambier, J. (1981). Stress-induced analgesia in humans: Endogeneuous opioids and naloxone-reversible depression of pain reflexes. *Science, 212,* 689–690.

Williams, D. R., MacLeod, D. I. A., Hayhoe, M. M. (1981). Foveal tritanopia. *Vision Research, 21,* 1341–1356.

Williams, J. M. (1979). Distortions of vision and pain: Two functional facets of D-Lysergic diethylamide. *Perceptual & Motor Skills, 49,* 499–528.

Williams, M. (1970). *Brain damage and the mind.* London: Penguin.

Willis, W. D. (1983). Descending control of nociceptive transmission by primate spinothalamic neurons. In C. von Euler, O. Franzen, U. Lindblom, & D. Ottoson (Eds.), *Somatosensory mechanisms* (pp. 296–308). New York: Plenum.

Willis, W. D. (1985). *The pain system. The neural basis of nococeptive transmission in the mammalian nervous system.* Basel: Karger.

Wilson, E. O. (1971). *The insect societies.* Cambridge, MA: Harvard University Press.

Wilson, H. R. (1986). Responses of spatial mechanisms can explain hyperacuity. *Vision Research, 26,* 453–469.

Wilson, J. R., DeFries, J. C., McClearn, G. C., Vandenberg, S. G., Johnson, R. C., & Rashad, M. N. (1975). Cognitive abilities: Use of family data as a control to assess sex and age differences in two ethnic groups. *International Journal of Aging and Human Development, 6,* 261–275.

Wilson, M. (1957). Effects of circumscribed cortical lesions upon somesthetic and visual discrimination in the monkey. *Journal of Comparative and Physiological Psychology, 50,* 630–635.

Witkin, H. A., & Berry, J. W. (1975). Psychological differentiation in cross-cultural perspective. *Journal of Cross-Cultural Psychology, 6,* 4–87.

Wolff, H. G., & Goodell, B. S. (1943). The relation of attitude and suggestion to the perception of and reaction to pain. *Research Publications, Associaton for Research in Nervous and Mental Disease, 23,* 434–448.

Wong, C., & Weisstein, N. (1982). A new perceptual context-superiority effect: Line segments are more visible against a figure than against a ground. *Science, 218,* 587–589.

Wong, E., & Weisstein, N. (1987). The effects of flicker on the perception of figure and ground. *Perception & Psychophysics, 41,* 440–448.

Woo, G., & Bader, D. (1978). Age and its effect on vision. *Canadian Journal of Optometry, 40,* 29–34.

Wood, R. W. (1985). The "haunted swing" illusion. *Psychological Review, 2,* 277–278.

Woodfield, R. L. (1984). Embedded figures test performance before and after childbirth. *British Journal of Psychology, 75,* 81–88.

Woodrow, H. (1951). Time perception. In S. S. Stevens (Ed.), *Handbook of experimental psychology* (pp. 1224–1236). New York: Wiley.

Woolard, H. H., Weddell, G., & Harpman, J. A. (1940). Observations of the neuro-historical basis of cutaneous pain. *Journal of Anatomy, 74,* 413–440.

Worchel, P., & Dallenbach, K. M. (1947). "Facial vision:" Perception of obstacles by the deaf-blind. *American Journal of Psychology, 60,* 502–553.

Wright, L. L., & Elias, J. W. (1979). Age differences in the effects of perceptual noise. *Journal of Gerontology, 34,* 704–708.

Wright, M. J., & Johnston, A. (1985). Invarient tuning of motion aftereffect. *Vision Research, 25,* 1947–1955.

Wright, N. H. (1964). Temporal summation and backward masking. *Journal of the Acoustical Society of America, 36,* 927–932.

Wright, R. H. (1977). Odor and molecular vibration: Neural coding of olfactory information. *Journal of Theoretical Biology, 64,* 473–502.

Wright, R. H. (1978a). Specific anosmia: A clue to the olfactory code or to something much more important? *Chemical Senses and Flavor, 3,* 235–239.

Wright, R. H. (1978b). The perception of odor intensity: Physics or psychophysics? *Chemical Senses and Flavor, 3,* 73–79.

Wright, R. H. (1978c). The perception of odor intensity: Physics or psychophysics II. *Chemical Senses and Flavor, 3,* 241–245.

Wright, R. H. (1982). *The sense of smell.* Boca Raton, FL: CRC Press.

Wright, W. D. (1929). A re-determination of the trichromatic mixture data. *Medical Research Council (Great Britain), Special Report Series, SRS-139,* 1–38.

Wright, W. D. (1952). The characteristics of tritanopia. *Journal of the Optical Society of America, 42,* 509–521.

Wurtz, R. H., & Goldberg, M. E. (1971). Superior colliculus cell responses related to eye movements in awake monkeys. *Science, 171,* 82–84.

Wyburn, G. M., Pickford, R. W., & Hurst, R. J. (1964). *Human senses and perception.* Toronto: University of Toronto Press.

Wyszecki, G., & Stiles, W. S. (1967). *Color science: Concepts and methods, quantitative data and formulas.* New York: Wiley.

Yaksh, T. L. (1984). Multiple spinal opiate receptor systems in analgesia. In L. Kruger & J. C. Liebeskind (Eds.), *Neural mechanisms of pain* (pp. 197–216). New York: Raven.

Yamamoto, T., Yayama, N., & Kawamura, Y. (1981). Central processing of taste perception. In Y. Katsuki, R. Norgren, & M. Sato (Eds.), *Brain mechanisms of sensation* (pp. 197–208). New York: Wiley.

Yantis, S., & Jonides, J. (1984). Abrupt onsets and selective attention: Evidence from visual search. *Journal of Experimental Psychology: Human Perception and Performance, 10,* 601–621.

Yarbus, A. L. (1967). *Eye movements and vision.* New York: Plenum.

Yarmey, A. (1979). *The psychology of eyewitness testimony.* New York: Free Press.

Yen, W. (1975). Sex-linked major gene influence on selected types of spatial performance. *Behavior Genetics, 5,* 281–298.

Yerkes, R. M., & Dodson, J. D. (1908). The relation of strength of stimulus to rapidity of habit formation. *Journal of Comparative Neurology and Psychology, 18,* 459–482.

Yin, R. K. (1970). Face recognition by brain injured patients—a dissociable ability. *Neuropsychologia, 8,* 395.

Yodogawa, E. (1982). Symmetropy, an entropy-like measure of visual symmetry. *Perception & Psychophysics, 32,* 230–240.

Yonas, A. (1981). Infants' response to optical information for collision. In R. N. Aslin, J. R. Alberts, & M. R. Petersen (Eds.), *Development of perception* (pp. 313–334). New York: Academic Press.

Yonas, A., Cleaves, W., & Pettersen, L. (1978). Development of sensitivity to pictorial depth. *Science, 200,* 77–79.

Yonas, A., Goldsmith, L. T., & Hallstrom, J. (1978). Development of sensitivity to information provided by cast shadows in pictures. *Perception, 7,* 333–341.

Yonas, A., & Granrud, C. E. (1985a). Development of visual space perception in young infants. In J. Mehler & R. Fox (Eds.), *Neonate cognition: Beyond the blooming buzzing confusion* (pp. 45–68). Hillsdale, NJ: Lawrence Erlbaum.

Yonas, A., & Granrud, C. E. (1985b). The development of sensitivity to kinetic, binocular and pictorial depth information in human infants. In D. Ingle, D. Lee, & M. Jeannerod (Eds.), *Brain mechanisms and spatial vision* (pp. 113–145). Dordrecht, Netherlands: Nijoff.

Yoneshige, Y., & Elliott, L. L. (1981). Pure-tone sensitivity and ear canal pressure at threshold in children and adults. *Journal of the Acoustical Society of America, 70,* 1272–1276.

Young, L. R. (1971). Pursuit eye tracking movements. In P. Bach-y-Rita, C. C. Collins, & J. E. Hyde. (Eds.), *The control of eye movements* (pp. 429–443). New York: Academic Press.

Young, R. A. (1977). Some observations on temporal coding of color vision: Psychophysical results. *Vision Research, 17,* 957–965.

Yuille, J. (1984). Research and teaching with police: A Canadian example. *International Review of Applied Psychology, 33,* 5–23.

Yund, E. W., Morgan, H., & Efron, R. (1983). The micropattern effect and visible persistence. *Perception & Psychophysics, 34,* 209–213.

Zakay, D., Nitzan, D., & Glicksohn, J. (1983). The influence of task difficulty and external tempo on subjective time estimation. *Perception & Psychophysics, 34,* 451–456.

Zaporozhets, A. V. (1965). The development of perception in the preschool child. *Monographs of the Society for Research in Child Development, 30,* 82–101.

Zeigler, H. P., & Leibowitz, H. (1957). Apparent visual size as a function of distance for children and adults. *American Journal of Psychology, 70,* 106–109.

Zigler, M. J. (1932). Pressure adaptation time: A function of intensity and extensity. *American Journal of Psychology, 44,* 709–720.

Zihl, J., von Cramon, D., & Mai, N. (1983). Selective disturbance of movement vision after bilateral brain damage. *Brain, 106,* 313–340.

Zimmerman, M. (1983). Centrifugal control of somatosensory inflow into the spinal cord. In C. von Euler, O. Franzen, U. Lindblom, & D. Ottoson (Eds.), *Somatosensory mechanisms* (pp. 285–296). New York: Plenum.

Zotterman, Y. (1959). Thermal sensations. In J. Fields, H. W. Magoun, & V. E. Hall (Eds.), *Handbook of physiology: Section 1. Neurophysiology, 1,* 431–458.

Zucker, I., Wade, G., & Ziegler, R. O. (1972). Sexual and hormonal influences on eating, taste preferences, and body weight of hamsters. *Physiology and Behavior, 8,* 101–111.

Zuidema, P., Gresnight, A. M., Bouman, M. A., & Koenderink, J. J. (1978). A quanta coincidence model for absolute threshold vision incorporating deviations from Ricco's Law. *Vision Research, 18,* 1685–1689.

Zurek, P. M. (1980). The precedence effect and its possible role in the avoidance of interaural ambiguities. *Journal of the Acoustical Society of America, 67,* 952–964.

Zwicker, E. (1958). Uber psychologische und methodische Grundlagen der Lautheit. *Acustica, 8,* 237–258.

Zwicker, E. (1986). A hardware cochlear nonlinear preprocessing model with active feedback. *Journal of the Acoustical Society of America, 80,* 146–153.

Zwislocki, J. J. (1978). Masking: Experimental and theoretical aspects of simultaneous, forward, backward, and central masking. In E. C. Carterette & M. P. Friedman (Eds.), *Handbook of perception: Vol. 4. Hearing* (pp. 283–336). New York: Academic Press.

Zwislocki, J. J., Damianopoulos, E. N., Buining, E., & Glantz, J. (1967). Central masking: Some steady-state and transient effects. *Perception & Psychophysics, 2,* 59–64.

Author Index

Subject Index